IRAN'S NUCLEAR OPTION

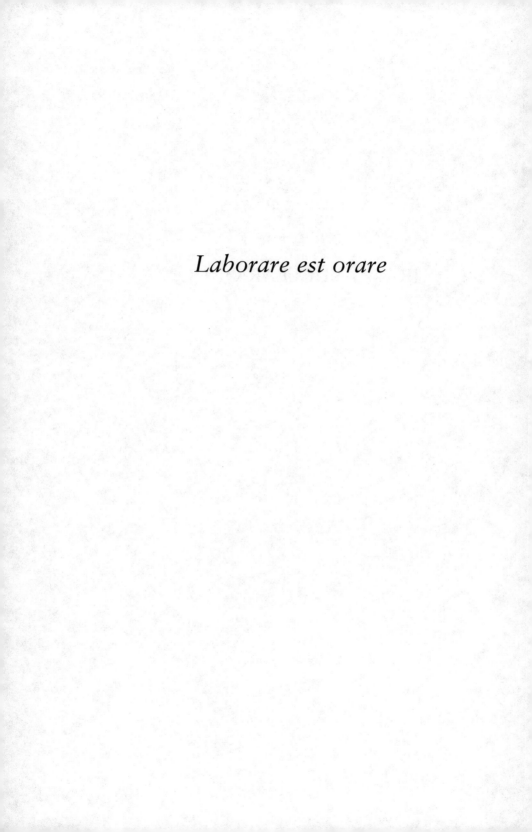

Laborare est orare

IRAN'S NUCLEAR OPTION

Tehran's Quest for the Atom Bomb

By
AL J. VENTER

CASEMATE
Philadelphia

Published by
CASEMATE

© 2005 by Al J. Venter

ISBN 1-932033-33-5

Distributed in the United Kingdom by
Greenhill Books/Lionel Leventhal Ltd.
Park House, 1 Russell Gardens,
London, NW11 9NN

Cataloging-in-Publication Data is available from the
Library of Congress.

First edition, first printing.

PRINTED AND BOUND IN THE UNITED STATES OF AMERICA.

CONTENTS

Preface   vii
Foreword *by Stephen Tanner*   xiii
Introduction   1

PART I: THE ISLAMIC REPUBLIC OF IRAN
1   Iran: Its People and Government   27
2   The Iran-Iraq War, 1980–1988   45
3   Iran's Shi'ites: Provocative and Driven   67

PART II: IRAN'S NUCLEAR PURSUITS
4   How Close is Iran to Building an A-Bomb?   85
5   Doomsday Scenario   109
6   Iran's Multi-Stemmed Centrifuge Program: An Overview   131
       by David Albright and Corey Hinderstein
7   Nuclear Link-up: South Africa and Iran   151
8   Case Study: South Africa's Atom Bomb   175

PART III: IRAN'S TROUBLED ROLE IN WORLD AFFAIRS
9   Building Guided Missiles to Hit Israel   195
10   Iran's History of Terror   213
11   Iran's Unconventional Weapons   237
12   Pasdaran: The Islamic Revolutionary Guard Corps   253
13   What's Next?   271

Appendix A   The Russia-Iran Nuclear Connection   299
Appendix B   IAEA Implementation of the NPT Safeguards
               Agreement in the Islamic Republic of Iran   315
Appendix C   Iran's Economy and Oil and Gas Resources   325
Appendix D   How Saddam Hussein Almost Built His Bomb   341
Appendix E   Close-Quarter Observations: The South African
               Nuclear Weapons Program   359
Appendix F   Iran's Missiles: Devils in the Detail
               by Charles P. Vick   373
Appendix G   Pasdaran's Protegé: Hizbollah   383

Acronyms, Technical, Arabic, and Persian Words and Phrases   403
Acknowledgments   413
Notes   423
Index   439

BY THE SAME AUTHOR

The Iraqi War Debrief: Why Saddam Hussein Was Toppled
(Casemate, 2003)
The Chopper Boys: Helicopter Warfare in Africa
(Stackpole Book, US, and Greenhill Books, UK, 1994)
War in Angola (Concord Publications, 1992)
Where to Dive: In Southern Africa and Off the Islands
(Ashanti Publishing, 1991)
Challenge: South Africa in the African Revolutionary Context
(Ed., Ashanti Publishing, 1988)
South African Handbook for Divers (Ashanti Publishing, 1987)
Africa Today (Macmillan, 1977)
The Black Leaders of South Africa (Siesta, 1976)
Africa At War (Devain Adair, 1974)
Under the Indian Ocean (Harrap, 1973)
Portugal's Guerrilla War (Munger Africana Library,
California Institute of Technology, 1973)
Underwater Africa (Purnell, 1971)
The Terror Fighters (Purnell, 1969)

PREFACE

In a work such as this there is a compelling issue that needs to be addressed, since in today's world, unfortunately, it increasingly clouds the ramifications of Islamic/Judaic/Western commentary. This is especially acute when a Westerner addresses matters that are religiously, culturally or even racially sensitive.

Anybody opposed to the barbarism of such mindless atrocities as suicide bombings or, for that matter, depictions on Al Jazeera of ten- and twelve-year-olds prancing over the bodies of mutilated Americans, is customarily deemed by the majority of Middle Easterners to be either Jewish or, more likely, a Zionist fellow-traveler.

This might be expected in a society where many regard any kind of association with an infidel—or any non-believer, for that matter— as akin to a social aberration. Consequently, in the minds of some of these faithful, it is simply impossible to countenance detached objectivity, nor can it be allowed to happen. By the same token, Jewish readers go quickly onto the defensive about anything negative concerning Israel. To some, such utterances are reflective of anti-Jewish sentiments. This places the reporter in an invidious situation, if only because pure facts are very rarely of his or her making.

I have many friends who are Muslim. I have seen conflict alongside and shared intimacies with a few of them. Having spent much time in the Arab world, I am not only accustomed to the inevitable clash of cultures but rather, I have always enjoyed my spells in places like Cairo, Beirut and Damascus. These are cities that can be at the same time both lethargic and utterly cacophonically disjointed. Similarly, I relish most forms of Arab cuisine. So too with Arab music, or at least some of it. But because I have also spent time covering hostilities from the Israeli side, this renders me suspect. It is a case of being damned no matter what, be you not of the right creed.

The same with my Jewish friends. I grew up in the distinctly Yiddish environment of Yeoville in Johannesburg, which, in its day, had a schul on just about every other suburban block. In a sense, though not Jewish myself (even if I seem to have been weaned on gefilte fish and gehakte herring) the Harry Lipschtzs' Norman Levys, Dianne Ginsburgs and others of that ilk were, and still are, my people. My mother's best friend was Dolly Sachs, husband of the late Bennie Sachs, the author and former aunt of Judge Albie Sachs in today's vibrant "New" South Africa. I didn't realize until years later, that with Dolly's sister, Violet Weinberg, both women were prominent members of the Central Committee of the South African Communist Party.

This did not prevent me from being labeled a Jew-baiter whenever I pronounced something out of kilter in the Jewish homeland. For one, the Israelis never forgave me for predicting in an issue of *Jane's Defence Weekly* not long after I returned to London from Lebanon— exactly a year before the event actually took place—that the IDF's effort against Hizbollah was kaput. Indeed, I had the temerity to suggest that the Israeli Army would soon leave its exclusion zone in southern Lebanon and retreat behind its own fences in northern Galilee. The fact is, I reported the situation as I saw it and in the eyes of some of my Jewish friends it labeled me as biased, even anti-Semitic.

Then I compounded things by favorably reviewing *Ha'aretz* correspondent Amira Hass' brilliant exposition of Palestinian travails under an IDF occupation force in her book "Drinking the Sea at Gaza." Though the work was eventually nominated for the Robert F. Kennedy Award, the perception was that I had taken sides. In point of fact, I had not, but in the convoluted politics of the Near East— whether you are Arab or Jew—such actions can, and often are, construed as flagitious.

I am reminded here of Roy Fuller, a fellow countryman, complaining in the London of the 1930s that a *Tribune* reviewer had alleged that he was anti-Semitic. He was later reassured by one of his contemporaries that it was impossible to mention the Jews in print "either favorably or unfavorably" without getting into trouble. Thus, taking any kind of side in Iran is likely to produce the same kind of hypothesis, invariably disjointed and one-sided.

At the same time, it is pointless to maintain that had Israel not existed (or had been eradicated from the contemporary lexicon by Arab force), that Iran would never have contemplated building the bomb. The cold reality is that politics in Tehran are so tortuous and idiosyncratic that there is nobody on earth who could predict what path these single-minded fundamentalists might follow.

In such things, the religion of a man or, for that matter, of a nation (except if it is Islam, and then still qualified according to Sunni, Sufi or Shi'ite precepts) matters not a whit.

Writing this book was not without its moments. In fact, with its focus on Iran's weapons of mass destruction programs, there had been a modicum of intrigue all along, compounded by my need to return to South Africa to examine the subject from another source.

I was still in South Africa in May 2004 when Geraldine Fraser-Moleketi, that country's Public Service and Administration Minister, gave notice that Iranian civil servants were to be recruited to bolster the country's administration. This was an odd decision since the two states have little in common, whether in culture, language, religion, historical tradition or even politics. Iran is a fundamentalist Islamic theocracy while South Africa is very much a democracy, though, with a two-thirds ruling majority in Parliament, it remains to be seen whether it stays one. In a sense, the Iranian/South African connection was almost like New Zealand recruiting Bangladeshis to help them run their country.

There were other reasons for concern, not least a new found coziness between Iran and South Africa in matters of defense, and the fact that South Africa had helped develop Iran's missile program. There was evidence too, that I was being watched and I felt that I needed to go about my work very carefully while still in that country.

Shortly afterward my house was broken into, but few things of value were taken. One of the items pilfered was my laptop, and to my consternation, the "robbers" had further incriminated themselves by leaving my desktop on. After that I had a hard time getting into my e-mails, indicating that it had been tampered with. This has since been confirmed by an IT specialist.

The question that really bugged me was whether the Iranians—and in particular the Pasdaran—were involved. Significantly, prior to my return to South Africa to complete research for this book, I had been repeatedly warned by American friends that I was crazy to go back, even for a week. At the same time, circumstances surrounding the robbery are interesting, if only because such an event might just indicate the shape of things to come in a future South Africa.

The robbery itself was disorientating. For more than a week my wife and I watched our home being cased by a most organized band of thugs, every one of them dressed in identical blue "workshop" coveralls that, curiously, were spotlessly clean. That was our first indication that something was amiss, especially in a society where most vagabonds hanging around in the street outside can barely feed themselves, never mind afford new clothes.

They struck while we were out, the thieves targeting only a few specific items apart from the laptop. Just about everything else of value was left behind, including TVs, several beautiful sets of hunting knives, cameras, cassette recorders and a host of CDs and tapes—many of them current and popular—as well as almost all of my wife's jewelry. Though they took one expensive item, much of what remained intact was of gold and silver, including a beautiful Ashanti bangle inlaid with pure gold an inch-and-a-half across. The "robbers" didn't touch it. From that oversight one can only infer that they were after something else.

It was surreal. We'd been robbed and then in another sense, we hadn't. Over several weeks that followed before I left the country, we knew we were being carefully observed. For instance, I would take my dog out after dinner and heads would duck behind the bushes above our house. But not before Lady, our alert Border Collie had warned me of the presence of intruders. This was especially disconcerting when you consider that South Africa today has the highest murder rate in the world and that the going rate for a "hit" in the townships is less than a thousand rand ($130). Frankly, it was tough on the nerves while it lasted.

What was most worrying was that all this activity was clearly linked to some of my writings which, by then, centered on both Iraq and Iran. Further, Tehran's Islamic Revolutionary Guards Corps (IRGC) has been shown to have been responsible for the killings of "Iran's enemies" across the globe (Chapter 13). Its tentacles spread everywhere that the mullahs have an interest, South Africa included, where the IRGC is responsible for Iran's diplomatic security.

Even the U.S. is not immune. When David Albright and Corey Hinderstein planned a conference involving an Iranian dissident who had fled to America, some ISIS staff were at the receiving end of anonymous death threats. The conference was called off—and that was in Washington, DC.

More to the point, Tehran's mullahs would have prevented this book from seeing the light of day were they able to do so.

What was really sad is that it is exactly this kind of clandestine activity that South Africa's new "Rainbow Government" swore ten years earlier to eschew. To me, it was a reversion to a time when

Apartheid ruled and security police swarmed everywhere you looked. Having been "politically" robbed was just one more manifestation of the new order.

There were some unusual anomalies that came with the heist. For instance, they took my Mini-Ruger carbine—complete with folding stock, thirty-round mags and aim-point sights. It wasn't locked in a safe and the police who were called in to investigate the break-in afterward were furious to learn it had been stolen. Irrespective of the fact that the robbers had kicked in the front door—it was standing open when we arrived—they warned that I would be the one criminally charged, and that a heavy fine would be levied. But I never was, which, in a country that has become almost obsessively gun-conscious, was peculiar.

That the intruders left behind my desktop computer (usually one of the first things grabbed in burglaries because of good resale value, especially in South Africa) is also strange. There must have been somebody sitting at my desk going through my files, however, because they were tidily moved around, though this is something only I would have noticed.

Apart from the smashed-in door, the place looked like it had actually been cleaned. Some of my drawers hadn't even been opened. There was a bunch of silver American dollars in one of the drawers and they weren't taken either. Clearly, it wasn't anything of value that the felons were after.

The crunch that the South African intelligence services were involved came when a member of the security services leaked the contents of a confidential letter that I had written to an American Embassy abroad, the contents of which could only have come from documents saved on the hard drive of my laptop. I was tipped off by several of my former Special Forces friends whose organizations, by then, had also been infiltrated by the country's National Intelligence Agency (NIA) and South Africa's Military Intelligence, largely because of the role these people were playing in illegal mercenary activities. South Africans are notorious for not being able to keep their traps shut, which, I suppose is just as well because it allowed me to know exactly who I was dealing with.

At the same time, things can hardly be rosy in a country that continues to maintain close ties with just about every government labeled "rogue" by the U.S. State Department. These include all of those dubbed "Axis of Evil" by American President Bush, about which, just then, I'd been writing a lot in several Jane's publications including *Jane's Islamic Affairs Analyst* and *Jane's Terrorism and Security Monitor*. For this reason I am not in a position to publicly thank any of my more discreet South African sources.

While all this was going on, the news emanating from Iran was rarely off Page One. First, Iranian President Mohammed Khatami, and then Tehran's energy minister went to great lengths to assure the West that Iran had no nuclear weapons ambitions. Meanwhile things inside the country moved ahead at a giddy pace. We had a London report, in late September 2004, that Iran had launched a Shahab-3 intermediate range missile with a nuclear warhead design.

Western intelligence sources said that the Iranian Defense Ministry had redesigned the original Shahab-3 warhead to accommodate nuclear weapons. It was also disclosed that the new warhead was more compact and designed as a "bottle-neck" in a throwback to U.S. and Soviet intercontinental ballistic missiles of the 1960s. In fact, the new warhead was seen on Iranian television during a report on the Shahab-3 the month before. Sources said the Shahab's nose had been changed from a conical design to that resembling a baby bottle. It was also suggested that the re-entry vehicle of the new Shahab-3 design resembled that of the original Soviet SS-9, a 1960s-era liquid-fuel intercontinental ballistic missile launched from a silo and which contained a nuclear warhead.

What is worrying here is that the third generation atom bomb—of the type that Korea is known to have set its aspirations on—precisely fits on to the nose of this Shahab-3 prototype.

That was followed by the Israeli government taking a powerful, uncompromising stance on the issue on September 29, 2004. Jerusalem declared that should Iran persist in going ahead with its nuclear weapons program, the Jewish state would react accordingly. The trouble here is that it would be impossible for the Israeli Air Force to knock out all of Tehran's weapons of mass destruction assets by conventional means. Or even be able to do so in a single strike, no matter how well co-coordinated.

And that, I fear, could mean only one thing . . .

FOREWORD

By Stephen Tanner

There's an irony in the fact that among the military challenges the United States faces today, none poses greater peril than the prospect of atomic weapons in the hands of our enemies. This may seem like an odd situation for the nation that won the Cold War, a conflict in which both sides bristled with so many thermonuclear warheads that the fate of humanity itself was believed to be at stake. But the post–Cold War era, which began in 1991 with the promise of a peace dividend, greater global prosperity, and the very real prospect of a Pax Americana, expired after a tragically short life. It was abruptly replaced by the post–9/11 era, an age that unveiled new threats to our security, more unpredictable, and perhaps more dangerous, than those that had come before.

This new conflict, termed the "War on Terror" by the White House, and perhaps more accurately a "clash of civilizations" by Harvard's Samuel Huntington, has required the United States to toss into the dustbin decades worth of carefully cultivated strategic thinking. Obsolete are such guiding principles as a "balance of power," "deterrence," and "mutual assured destruction," the latter a bedrock of Cold War thinking that also possessed its most fitting acronym, MAD. Given the new opponents we face in the post–9/11 era—driven by religious fanaticism more than geopolitical pragmatism, embracing mass death rather than seeking to avoid it—the rulebook has been thrown out the window.

In this book, Al J. Venter looks through the door opened by 9/11 to inform us of even more devastating potential arising from the world of Islam: the development of a nuclear weapons capability by Iran. An experienced war correspondent who has spent years covering conflicts from Angola, Somalia and Sierra Leone in Africa, through the Middle East to the Balkans, Central America and elsewhere, Venter calmly analyzes the nature of Iran's theocratic regime, its history of fomenting Islamic revolution through terrorism, and most importantly, its inexorable progress toward creating and deploying nuclear arms.

The author's perspective is all the more valuable for the insights he provides into the weapons program of his native South Africa. Whereas to most Americans the concept of nuclear proliferation tends to appear abstract, forever rumored and over the horizon in its practical affect, Venter has witnessed the successful development of atom bombs in his own country. He has also interviewed key participants and is able to warn us of the new diaspora of nuclear scientists who today crisscross national borders, motivated by money, politics, or simply by resentment at the demise of their previous regimes. While the U.S. government correctly eyes former Soviet scientists, and more recently the covert spread of Pakistani expertise, Venter informs us of the equally dangerous fount of knowledge that springs from Africa.

While reading this book it is impossible not to view Iran's nuclear program as the foremost gathering threat to the United States and its closest allies. North Korea, where a similar program has apparently reached fruition, is in the end a small fortress state, surrounded by larger, more prosperous powers that are active in providing an ameliorating influence. Pakistan's rogue program has been grudgingly accepted by the West due to the surety that its missiles need to be aimed east to offset its huge traditional antagonist, India. Iran is the most dangerous case of all, because it is larger than its neighbors and capable of dominating its region. It also possesses the heritage of a great civilization and former empires, and its current revolutionary regime is the world's most aggressive proponent of the manifest destiny of Shi'ite Islam.

There should also be no mistaking the fact that the possession of nuclear weapons by Iran would have a destabilizing effect far beyond its borders, rippling not only through the Middle East but causing shock waves throughout the world.

The country in most immediate danger would be Israel. After decades of vowing to destroy the Jewish state—albeit failing to do so with both conventional war and guerrilla tactics—the Islamic world would have the means to create a new Holocaust simply by pressing a few buttons. Israel, with five million people crammed into a slice of land the size of New Jersey, would be hard-pressed to withstand a first strike by Iran, which possesses over twelve times its population and thirty times its geographic area. Whereas during the Cold War the United States had a natural equivalency with its Communist opponents, Israel would be at a severe disadvantage the moment Iran went nuclear. It would be as if, during the Cold War, Britain alone had been forced to confront the Soviet Union.

Israel would feel an urgent need to wrest this Damocles Sword from the Iranian ayatollah's hands with every means at its disposal. On the model of its pre-emptive strike against Iraqi nuclear facilities at Osiraq in 1981, the IDF would come under pressure to destroy Iranian nuclear weapons resources before they became operational. But Iran is harder to reach than Iraq, and Tehran, too, learned a lesson from Osiraq, taking care to disperse and conceal its nuclear facilities in the years since. What if this time an Israeli pre-emptive strike failed, instead initiating the full-scale exchange of destructive power it had meant to forestall? How would the United States and the rest of the world respond if Iran did not initiate a war but only reacted to an Israeli first strike?

As for the U.S. "nuclear umbrella," which has traditionally been thought to cover Israel, the dilemma in Tel Aviv would be whether, if three hundred thousand Israelis were killed by an Iranian strike, a U.S. President would be willing to order the destruction of untold numbers of Iranian citizens in response, though they posed no threat to the U.S. homeland? In a country that still debates dropping the bomb on Hiroshima, America's capability of such ruthlessness is open to question. In Tel Aviv the verdict would be that the Israelis had better rely on their own resources, or initiative.

At the minimum, the result of a nuclear-armed Iran would be a revival of the Strangelovian scenarios that dominated strategic thinking on a larger scale during the Cold War. Premised by the fact that whoever struck first would have the advantage in an exchange, paranoia would reign foremost. Even if the Iranians intended their nuclear capability to serve a purely defensive purpose, the West, and most urgently Israel, could never be so sure. The slightest rustle in Iran—say the implementation of air-raid drills in Tehran—would rouse suspicion that the mullahs were about to initiate the dreaded conflict. The responding rustle on the Western side could cause the Iranians to believe they were about to suffer a pre-emptive attack. If Tel Aviv sensed that Tehran sensed a strike was on the way, it may indeed have to launch a strike to counter the misguided Iranian reaction. It would be like a showdown with both sides using a mirror to look into a mirror, with neither side able to risk being the second party to act.

The second danger posed by a Persian bomb would affect the United States directly. Though, unlike Israel, its very existence would not be at stake, its ability to project power at the center of the world's energy supply would be severely curtailed. Consider 2003's Operation Iraqi Freedom, which was justified by Bush administration officials with the phrase, "We don't want the smoking gun to be a mushroom cloud." If Iraq had already possessed a nuclear weapon, the United States would not have dared to forcibly overthrow Saddam Hussein's regime; neither, in 1991, would the U.S. and its allies have been able to roll back the Iraqi invasion of Kuwait. If the Islamic Republic of Iran were able to develop an atomic bomb, it would serve as a form of kryptonite against the superpower, providing a shield behind which Tehran could develop even more weapons and thence become a significant strategic threat.

The United States, of course, would always have the option to retire from the region, just as the British did after the Suez crisis of 1956. But while America draws far less a percentage of its oil imports from the Persian Gulf than does Europe and the Far East, it has long been the guarantor of the world's primary source of oil. To abdicate this responsibility would create a vacuum of power that other great nations would fill, causing America's status as the world's sole remaining superpower to evaporate. Though still possessing the world's greatest long-range destructive power, its ability to influence hearts and minds, encourage the spread of democracy, and guarantee the free flow of commerce would be lost.

The U.S. is better situated than other major powers to wean itself from Middle Eastern oil, but to allow those other powers to become stronger as a result would only create larger dilemmas in the future. It is not certain that an Iranian bomb would cancel U.S. conventional power in a confrontation, but the prospect that the sprawling U.S. airbase at Doha, for example, or a U.S. carrier task force in the Persian Gulf could go up in a blinding flash if the mullahs had their backs to the wall, would at least severely restrict our military options.

Aside from the dire danger to Israel and the curtailment of U.S. conventional flexibility, a nuclear-armed Iran would comprise an additional problem, the most unpredictable of them all: the possibility that the theocratic regime in Tehran would pass weapons to fanatic terrorists, who have no state of their own but possess an abiding determination to kill as many Americans as possible.

One should have no illusions about how such an event would transpire. The bomb would not come stamped with a return address in Tehran, accompanied by a proud message from the ayatollah. Picture instead the port of San Diego suddenly obliterated by an atomic blast with no prior warning. After a lengthy investigation, the delivery vehicle would be pinpointed as a Malaysian freighter under Panamanian registry, which had previously stopped off in half a dozen ports from Dubai to Hong Kong. After a year of false leads indicating North Korea or Pakistan, Iranian fingerprints would be found, while by then the world would have been embroiled in a new war. Another confusing factor would be the inevitable presence of millions of Westerners in the streets arguing for peace rather than for the retaliatory execution of millions of Islamic citizens.

Several factors mitigate against the usefulness of deterrence, or MAD, in any nuclear stand-off with Iran. In the case of Israel, even though it may possess a larger arsenal, it may simply be too small to survive an Iranian strike. The nation of Iran would be able to withstand an Israeli one, but its nuclear program, assuming the Israelis have correct targeting intelligence, would not. Thus the pressure on Israel to launch a pre-emptive attack, either through a massive use of conventional airpower or through tactical nuclear strikes, would become immense. Such a pre-emption would guarantee the survival of both states, while the Jewish state would find its very existence in jeopardy—in fact, hanging by a thread subject to the will of the Iranian ayatollah—if it failed to act first.

Second, as Al Venter describes in this book, radicals in the Islamic world have embraced martyrdom tactics, beginning most notably with the Shi'ite assaults on the U.S. Embassy and Marines in Lebanon. Since those 1983 attacks we have seen the martyrdom principle spread through the populations of Islam, culminating with the collective suicide of the 9/11 hijackers. During the Iran-Iraq War in the 1980s, Ayatollah Khomeini enlisted thousands of pubescent boys to lead human-wave assaults against Iraqi positions. He armed them primarily with little trinkets to hang around their necks, called "keys to heaven."

If Iran were to acquire nuclear weapons it is unclear how the concept of martyrdom—now glorified in the Islamic world—would come into play. According to Cold War logic, the fact that America could react to a hundred thousand of its own dead by inflicting ten million on the enemy served as a sufficient deterrent to the other side not to attack. But against a culture that glorifies death in "Holy War," the principle of deterrence dissolves. If millions of martyrs are created in order to eradicate the state of Israel, or severely damage the United

States, they might be honored for having made the supreme sacrifice.

A tenuous aspect of any nuclear confrontation with Iran would be the value that each side places on human life. For the West, the object would be not to lose any at all. On the other side, death on behalf of Allah is often considered desirable. Add to this the factor that a U.S. president would naturally feel constrained from ordering mass revenge killings of civilians, and a lack of logical balance can be perceived. A nuclear stand-off between a theocratic regime influenced by unknown depths of fanaticism and a stable democratic government would be inherently lopsided toward the less predictable party.

It's a grim paradox that were an Iranian leader to develop and use an atomic weapon, the vast majority of victims of the subsequent conflict would be innocent Iranians. But we have already seen one case in modern history where an absolute ruler decreed the destruction of his own people. In the Spring of 1945 Adolf Hitler decided that the German *Volk* had failed him, and he ordered a scorched earth policy in his own country to deny the Allies the fruits of victory. Calmer heads in the German chain of command ignored his orders. But what if Hitler had possessed nuclear weapons, with controls exclusively held in the hands of his most fanatic followers in the Nazi SS?

In Iran, the Pasdaran (Revolutionary Guards) have risen as an ideological alternative to the regular armed forces, not unlike the SS or the Soviet NKVD during World War II. Both more fanatic and fully funded than the regular forces, their command structure remains unclear to the West and the possibility exists that, as opposed to the series of structural safeguards that allowed the superpowers to navigate the Cold War, an Iranian nuclear capability could be controlled by a small group or even a single fanatic. There are some who still take comfort in the fact that even if the Islamic Republic of Iran developed an atom bomb, the threat to the United States, which possesses thousands of easily deliverable, state-of-the-art thermonuclear warheads, would be negligible. But then one must consider which is more dangerous to one's life and limb: a full division of heavily armed but well disciplined troops under firm command and control, or a single homicidal maniac with a loaded pistol?

To summarize the dangers that would be presented by nuclear weapons in the hands of the mullah regime of Iran:

Israel would find its very existence at stake, compelling it to strike first to eliminate the threat. If the IDF failed, the ancient Mideast could be thrust into the most destructive war in its history.

Second, the United States would find its strategic options for safeguarding the world's energy supply severely restricted. No longer able to rely on its overwhelming conventional power alone, it would either need to expand its doctrine by fielding frontline tactical nukes (holding its heavy thermonuclear weapons in reserve) or by letting its forces become increasingly impotent in the region.

Third, America, Israel, European nations, and others would find themselves far more vulnerable to a type of terrorist attack that would make 9/11 look like a pinprick. While it is unlikely that the Islamic regime in Tehran would provide nuclear weapons to terrorist organizations such as Al Qaeda or to its own protegé, Hizbollah, the risk—whether it be one percent or forty-nine—could not be tolerated.

This is not to cast aspersions on the people of Iran, who, as the author describes in the following pages, possess a long and often glorious history. It is rather to say that a state in which supreme power rests in the hands of Islamic clerics, in an evolving system barely a quarter-century old, is inherently untrustworthy with the most devastating weapons known to mankind. On October 31, 2004, the Iranian parliament voted unanimously in favor of continuing to reprocess uranium, despite entreaties from France, Germany and Britain, and the UN's watchdog agency to suspend the program. More worrisome was the chant that spontaneously went up in the parliament while the votes were being counted. It was "Death to America."

Since at this writing Iran has not yet developed a nuclear weapon, now is the time for responsible nations, in concert with the UN, to bring full effort to bear against its gaining the ability to do so. Ideally this can be achieved through diplomacy, supported by a broader effort to gain peace and stability throughout the region. The object should be to convince Tehran that not only shouldn't they destabilize the world by developing nuclear weapons, they won't need to in a world that proceeds under firm, humanitarian principles. If peaceful persuasion fails to work, all that can be suggested is that the West consider other options while it can.

To acknowledge the elephant in the room, America's 2003 invasion of Iran's neighbor, Iraq, has introduced new variables into the equation. Together with Israel's occupation of the West Bank and Gaza, the U.S. occupation of Iraq has done little to convince Tehran to cease efforts to increase its own strategic capability. On the other hand, an ironic result of Operation Iraqi Freedom may become the empowerment of the Shi'ites of Iraq for the first time in history, thus providing Iran a large natural ally, and a Shi'ite swath in southern Asia of great power proportions. Along with standing behind the concept of increasing Iran's immersion in the global economy, and providing security assurances that will preclude the mullahs' desire to gain atomic weapons, the U.S. must solve its current position in Iraq, which may be inadvertently increasing Iranian power and influence.

So far in this new millennium, American Intelligence has not covered itself in glory. From its failure to interdict Al Qaeda's operations on 9/11 and subsequent failure to capture its leadership, to the false assumptions that existed on either side of our military initiative in Iraq, we have not been well served by our essential front line in the conflict in which we are now engaged. In response to these failures, during the summer of 2004 the CIA saw a revolving door of three directors within three months, while the bi-partisan 9/11 Commission has recommended overhauling our entire system.

It is not pleasant but nevertheless essential to realize that the slow march of the Islamic Republic of Iran toward acquiring a nuclear weapons capability comprises an even larger danger than the ones we have seen so far in this decade. For this reason we owe thanks to Al J. Venter, and the numerous experts, operatives and scientists who have provided him assistance, for the ability to assess this new threat and deal with it prior to its reaching culmination. With his wealth of facts, analysis, and invaluable international perspective, Venter has given us a vital, insightful work. Most important, its publication means that when and if the next crisis occurs, the United States need no longer be surprised.

Military historian Stephen Tanner has written numerous books, most recently *The Wars of the Bushes: A Father and Son as Military Leaders, Afghanistan: A Military History from Alexander the Great to the Fall of the Taliban*, and (with Samuel A. Southworth) *U.S. Special Forces: A Guide to America's Special Operations Units*.

INTRODUCTION

The first question that needs to be answered by this book is how Iran managed, for almost two decades, to escape the attention of the West in its bid to acquire the wherewithal, skills and expertise needed to manufacture an atomic bomb. The mullahs are not yet there, but following some pretty intrusive detective work by the International Atomic Energy Agency (IAEA) in late 2003 and early 2004, everything points to Iran acquiring a nuclear capability within the next few years.

That revelation emerged in October 2003, when Tehran—by then almost a year in denial following ever more thorough inspections by Vienna—admitted that it had secretly been producing small quantities of weapons-grade uranium as well as plutonium. Indeed, that country's nuclear program is so advanced that on April 17, 2004, CNN ran a headline story titled "Iran Rushing to Build Nuke Bomb." This stated that Tehran would "complete its first nuclear bomb in between one and two years."

This is disturbing news. Certainly, it goes against the accepted wisdom that Iran is "some years" from testing a fissile device. Still more worrying is the report issued by the dissident National Council of Resistance of Iran (NCRI) which states that "the nuclear weapons effort by a special military unit functioning secretly outside the Iranian Atomic Energy Organization remains under the personal supervision of the Ayatollah Ali Khamene'i, Iran's supreme religious ruler."

What gives grist to this statement is that the NCRI is no fly-by-night, sensation-hungry group of publicists, even though the movement is on the U.S. State Department list of terror organizations. Also known as the People's Mujahedeen of Iran, the NCRI has been active for years and has lost many of its operators—some crack leaders included—to Iran's secret services. This is the same organization that originally tipped off the West about Iran's secret nuclear weapons research activities at Natanz and Arak. Until then neither Washington nor London had any idea of what was going on.

Something that emerged before that, and then only grudgingly

from official Tehran pronouncements, was that Iranian nuclear physicists were working in several nuclear facilities, some known to
Western intelligence agencies and others that were hidden. In at least
one of these establishments, an unknown number of centrifuge cascades used for uranium enrichment had been erected, some of
Pakistani origin, the rest possibly North Korean. There was some
speculation that there were Russian centrifuges involved in the program, though this has not been verified, or the IAEA is not telling.

This method of enriching uranium is an extremely complex discipline. It involves a process that separates gaseous isotopes by rotating
them rapidly in a spinning cylinder or tube. The core of the centrifuge,
the so-called rotor, runs at sixty thousand revs-per-minute or seven
times the speed of sound and is hardly the sort of thing you are likely
to find in your local Home Depot.

The engineering circumscriptions in developing this system are
formidable, if only because stresses incurred in such operations place
extraordinarily high demands on manufacturing. Here we're talking
about flow-forming maraging (alloy) steel as well as carbon fiber (or
similar composite materials) until very recently all of it First World
technology.

Centrifuges have become seminal to most Third World nuclear
programs. Pakistan uses them. So does North Korea, and South Africa
before that. We now know that Libya ordered a batch of several thousand.

Dr. David Kay, former Chief Weapons Inspector (Nuclear) with
UNSCOM in Iraq, told the U.S. Congress at a time when United
Nations weapons searches were still yielding results, that he was
astonished at the level of sophistication encountered in the Iraqi
nuclear program after Operation Desert Storm in 1991's Gulf War.
Though the UN was instrumental in destroying almost all that material shortly afterward, it is worth recalling his words, "I will never forget, on my second mission (to Iraq), arriving at a facility called Al
Ferat, which, had war not intervened, could have been the largest centrifuge facility in the entire European/Near Eastern theater. It was bigger than any in Western Europe," he declared, adding that only the
Soviet Union had larger centrifuge facilities.

Tehran, having learnt a thing or two over the years from its belligerent neighbor, did its level best to follow the same path taken by
Iraq to put weapons inspectors off the scent. While they initially cooperated to a remarkable extent after the Natanz and Arak disclosures,

that phase was comparatively short-lived. It ended with Tehran obfuscating just about every IAEA bid to assess the sophistication, extent or size of its nuclear-related projects.

It would go something like this: on Monday morning, a spokesman for the Iranian *Sazeman-e Energy Atomi* or more correctly, the Atomic Energy Organization of Iran (AEOI) would agree to nuclear inspections by the International Atomic Energy Agency. "Your people are welcome," ElBaradei would be told. "They can go wherever they please."

In follow-up meetings a day or two later, the Iranian representative at the IAEA would express doubts as to whether the exercise was feasible. Or perhaps the timing would not be quite right, he would suggest. All sorts of reasons would be proffered, like the scientist responsible for a certain facility not being available on a particular day, or somebody was ill or there had been a leak of a toxic substance at the factory which first had to be cleared. Finally by Friday or perhaps a week later, Tehran would come down hard with an explicit no.

It is worth observing that the former Iraqi dictator used similar tactics to try to dissuade United Nations weapons inspectors from going over his own suspect installations. At one stage they even "lost the keys" to a huge industrial estate.

Things started to gel in the wrong direction in Iran late March, 2004 when reports emerged that senior Iranian officials were overseeing efforts to conceal key elements of the country's nuclear program. One report, sourced to Western diplomats as well as an intelligence report carried in part by the *Los Angeles Times*[1] mentioned a committee having been set up late 2003 by the Islamic Republic to coordinate these efforts. That came after IAEA inspectors started to uncover evidence of this kind of activity, which is illegal, since Iran is a signatory to the Nuclear Nonproliferation Treaty.

The report goes on: "A diplomat, who spoke on the condition of anonymity, said the committee's most pressing tasks include trying to hide evidence at nearly three hundred locations throughout the country." With egg on the faces of many of those originally involved in the search for Saddam's hidden weapons of mass destruction, one needs to be circumspect each time such large numbers are given as fact, and for good reason. It would be difficult even for an acknowledged nuclear power like Britain to have three hundred nuclear sites. A more likely Iranian tally would be a score or two, but no more. So far, the IAEA is aware of about a dozen.

The committee is said to be composed of senior officials of the Atomic Energy Organization of Iran who are responsible only to the highest ranking government officials within the office of the Supreme Spiritual Guide. It is significant that neither President Khatami nor his sizeable presidential entourage is directly linked to this sensitive cartel at the head of the archetypal religious oligarchy.

"Iran has said that it will deny access to some suspect sites by international inspectors who are scheduled to continue their work today and cited a continuing New Year holiday as justification for barring the inspectors," said the report.

The article, by *Times* staff writers Douglas Frantz and Sonni Efron, added that "Washington would probably portray any Iranian cover-up as smoking gun evidence of a nuclear weapons program." They also made the point that the intelligence on which the report was based originated from outside the United States. In itself, this is significant because it indicates a greater international awareness of the problem now facing the West.

What is astonishing is that it took so long for the West to finally nail Iran. Nor is it something new. Dr. Nic von Wielligh, the South African scientist who was involved in numerous meetings of the Board of Governors and the general Conference of the IAEA between 1992 and 2002, reckoned that Tehran was invariably near the top of the list at annual Nuclear Suppliers Group (NSG) meetings. This was a week-long occasion when the various nuclear powers—by invitation only— would "compare notes" as to who was doing what, legal or otherwise in this abstruse milieu. Iran always featured prominently, which, he said, meant that they were obviously up to something.

What would emerge was that the Americans, Russians, British and the rest were very much aware of what Tehran was trying to do, to the extent that they even had names, addresses and telephone numbers of those involved. They would share information about who to watch for if that individual ventured abroad. Or possibly, news that there had been orders for dual-use material with nuclear application having reached a Paris or Frankfurt or Kuala Lumpur factory. Once a pattern had been established, it wasn't difficult to keep track, he explained, adding that while the NSG does not control the imports and exports of sensitive items that might or might not be linked to the proliferation of nuclear related material, the body does set common rules for those involved.

Obviously, the NSG has its detractors. Some Third World countries (like Egypt) have strong views that the group—originally known as the London Club—is an ultra-exclusive entity dedicated solely to prevent the spread of peaceful uses of nuclear technology. In a sense, Cairo is right. Certainly, von Wielligh concedes, the NSG is vigilant for those trying to dabble in such issues.

The South African nuclear program is included in this book because any nation intending to build a bomb of its own is likely to follow the same route. They would, from necessity, be using highly enriched uranium or, in the argot, HEU.

Let us then surmise that Iran is building the bomb. That being so, its likeliest option would be to follow the original South African pattern, which was abandoned not long before President Nelson Mandela's government took over in Pretoria. Both South Africa and Iran—while regional forces in their own backyards—are small fry compared to the big powers. But there is also the raw reality that if Pretoria could get it right then so could Tehran, though not, mark you, without outside help. It is only a question of time.

More important, while we know that the Iranians have been dabbling with plutonium, it seems almost certain that Tehran would opt for the tried-and-trusted gun-type device (Hiroshima) over the more complex implosion bomb (Nagasaki). While "simpler, quicker and cheaper," none of it is easy.

What worries America the most is that while the Iranian nuclear inspection issue launched by the IAEA in early 2003 started out well enough, things quickly went sour once Vienna began to make more explicit demands. Initially several nuclear-related facilities were made available. Granted, those concessions emerged only after the dissident Iranian group had blown the whistle, but it was a start. Then, as inspections became more intrusive, the Iranians took to their by now-familiar two-step routine.

Take one example: about nine months after the inspections had begun in 2003, Iran faced an October 31 IAEA deadline to allow nuclear inspectors "full and free" access to all its facilities. It then reneged a few weeks later with its representatives angrily walking out of an IAEA meeting where the authorities were trying to set new deadlines.

What is clear, said the *Washington Post*, is that the world now faces its own Iranian deadline, very much as it had to deal with numerous Iraqi deadlines while Saddam Hussein walked tall.

It went on: "If work at the extensive nuclear facilities uncovered around the country (during the past year) is not frozen, the fundamentalist Islamic regime will soon have the capacity to manufacture the key elements of nuclear weapons." For their part, Israeli officials say this "point of no return" could be reached sooner rather than later. Jerusalem has already hinted that if the West allows a similar situation to develop in Iran (as the international community faced in Iraq prior to Operation Iraqi Freedom) then it might act unilaterally, as one Knesset member phrased it, "to stop the rot." Time is running out for the Iranian program to be stopped by diplomatic or political means, he declared.

The Iranians perfectly understand this imbroglio, as evidenced by the manner in which they have stalled the IAEA. In all likelihood, they will continue to do so even if they formally agree to the agency's demands. This obfuscatory strategy, says the *New York Times*, "has a good chance of working unless the United States, Europe and Russia quickly start doing a better job of coordinating a common response."

What the Americans do concede is that transatlantic differences over Iran are not as great as those that frustrated just about everything that went on in Iraq. The United States and the European Union agree that the Iranian nuclear program is a serious threat. They also concur that Tehran's acquisition of a bomb should not be permitted to continue. So too with Russian President Vladimir Putin who seems to have grudgingly accepted the idea that recently disclosed Iranian activities are problematic.

Yet Moscow's atomic energy agency has insisted on continuing work on the large Bushehr nuclear power plant for generating electricity on the Gulf, a facility that would give Tehran a potential source of plutonium. And that despite the fact that the last thing Iran needs right now is more power. It is not only Washington that has pointed out that a much easier and cheaper way to go—if the real objective is to generate electric power—would be to harness Iran's gas resources: the country has the second largest natural gas deposits on the globe. In fact there is so much natural gas in Iran that much of it is going to waste since a good deal of it is either flared or vented. The oil industry has long said that it could be profitably diverted into a major source of energy; a large proportion could feasibly be exported to earn foreign exchange. Instead, Tehran has taken a nuclear direction and the rest of the world can only speculate why.

All the while, European governments persist in their failed policy of "critical dialogue" with a regime dominated by clerics. According to one report, the governments of Britain, France and Germany "recently dangled an offer of technological cooperation before Tehran in exchange for its acceptance of stepped-up inspections, ignoring objections from the White House," the *Times* concluded.

In Iran, things would have gone on in this vein indefinitely had a now-defunct subversive Iranian group The National Council of Resistance—an offshoot of the People's *Mujahadeen Khalk*—not disclosed the locations of the two secret nuclear weapons facilities in the desert.

The first of these was Natanz, initially depicted by Tehran's AEOI as "part of a desert eradication program." The other was a heavy water plant at Arak (for use in making weapons-grade plutonium) but ostensibly described by the authorities as either an energy company or a water purifying plant. The level of duplicity, in spite of manifest earlier cooperation, is regarded by many observers as culpable, and in some instances, flagrantly so.

Having established that things at both Natanz and Arak weren't kosher—by then some pretty graphic satellite photos had been taken of both sites[2]—the IAEA set about trying to unravel this mystery.

Initially, traces of HEU or ^{235}U were found at one of the locations. In a written riposte, the Iranians argued that since the equipment had come from Pakistan, it wasn't there as a result of their efforts. That line—ingenuous and misleading—altered slightly after a large centrifuge facility was found hidden behind a false wall made of boxes, and it has been that way throughout all these exchanges. Tehran would say one thing one day and do the opposite the next. As one observer succinctly phrased it: "The Iranians have been adept at changing the goal posts, remarkably so, in fact."

As for the HEU uncovered, it has yet to be determined whether the HEU is Iranian and therefore domestic, or whether it was something smuggled into the country from the former Soviet Union (FSU). It could easily have been among some of the tails of a consignment of weapons-related equipment delivered from Pakistan, though that is unlikely as nuclear material is never shipped without careful preparations beforehand, which includes a thorough cleaning (sanitization) process. Interestingly, similar HEU deposits were found on some of the centrifuges about to be delivered to Libya.

After some careful forensic work, the IAEA afterward belied the Iranian claim the HEU was "imported." It also questioned Tehran's insistence that the more advanced centrifuges uncovered were only for research. Not that either consequence was unexpected. At one stage, Tehran even prevented IAEA staff from setting up environmental monitoring units in some areas where the Atomic Energy Organization of Iran was active. They were particularly restrictive at some of their newly established uranium processing plants.[3]

What emerged too during the course of the year as a consequence of what has been taking place between Islamabad and Tehran, was the extraordinary amount of trafficking in illegal nuclear materials and personnel involving dozens of countries. Here Pakistan's clandestine role is manifest.

In the words of the *New York Times*, "The network is global, stretching from Germany to Dubai and from China to South Asia. It involves brokers and middlemen as well as suppliers. But what is striking about a string of recent disclosures, experts say, is how many roads appear to lead back to the Khan Research Laboratories in Kahuta, where Pakistan's own bomb was originally developed."

I quote: "In 2002 the United States was surprised to discover how North Korea had turned to the Khan laboratory for an alternative way to manufacture nuclear fuel, after the reactors and reprocessing facilities it had relied on for years were 'frozen' under a now shattered agreement with the Clinton administration."

Seymour Hersh cut to the core when he encapsulated these procedures in an article for *The New Yorker*[4] titled "The Deal." Focusing on the activities of Dr. Abdul Qadeer Khan, father of the Pakistani bomb, he suggested that Islamabad was not only supplying its neighbors with nuclear equipment and expertise, but had gone "wholesale."

Quoting Hussain Haqqani, a special assistant to three Pakistani prime ministers (before Musharraf came to power) and, at the time, a visiting scholar at the Carnegie Endowment for International Peace: "Once they had the bomb, they had a shopping list what to buy and where.

"A.Q. Khan can bring a plain piece of paper and show me how to get it done—the countries, people and telephone numbers. 'This is a guy in Russia who will get you small quantities of enriched uranium. You in Malaysia will manufacture the stuff. Here's who will miniaturize the warhead. And then go to North Korea and get the damn missile'."

Of Pakistan's role, he added, "This is not a few scientists pocketing money and getting rich. It's a state policy."

Exactly how advanced is the Iranian nuclear program? Nobody in the West is prepared to hazard a guess for no other reason than Iran is an unusually difficult country in which to poke about and ask questions, especially when issues relate to defense. Today, with almost two decades of research behind them, there can be little doubt that these protégés of the Supreme Leader Ali Hossein Khamene'i would have tried to overcome some of the intricate disciplines involved in making weapons grade uranium. No small task.

They might also have tried their hand at grappling other arcane issues such as the kind of explosive lenses needed to trigger a nuclear explosion and possibly, the extremely complex principles associated with spherical geography, linked to this kind of nuclear research.

More likely, Iran having been in a condition of intellectual decline following the rise of Ayatollah Khomeini's Islamic fundamentalism, there is every indication that they would have hired foreigners suitably qualified to do the work for them. Obviously the financial packages offered these expatriates would be way ahead of the emoluments received for similar work in the West. Pakistan too would have played a role, as it would have in any weaponization process that must logically follow if the Iranians try to build a bomb of their own. There are others involved.

As with Saddam Hussein's nuclear program, a number of foreigners—mostly Europeans—were hired by Tehran to help unravel some of the more intractable issues. Thus, it is essential to carefully examine the role of two Germans who were implicated in Iraq's nuclear weapons program, if only because their contribution was significant. Bruno Stemmler (who has since died) and Karl Heinz Schaab, both worked on developing a centrifuge separation process for enriching uranium for Baghdad.

For many years Schaab was employed as a specialist at MAN New Technology in Munich, a contract company that developed many components for the gas-ultracentrifuge, a sophisticated technique for the enrichment of uranium: it is also the source of energy in modern light-water reactors. But the exact same separation technology can be applied to the enrichment of weapons-grade uranium, which was why European governments have so strictly categorized it.

Schaab's aptitude was ultra-specific, focused as it was on the core of the centrifuge, the so-called rotor. He seemed to have little com-punction in handing over years of complex and secret European research to his newfound accomplices in Iraq. Up to that point, it had already cost the Munich company millions of dollars. At his trial, fol-lowing his voluntary return to Germany from Brazil (where he had fled) Schaab admitted that he sold classified MAN blueprints of a sub-critical centrifuge to the Iraqis for $40,000. Thirty-six carbon fiber rotors, equipment and technical assistance for about a million dollars followed soon afterward.

Another German involved in such things was Alfred Hempel, who supplied nuclear items to many countries, including Pakistan, India and South Africa. He sold hundreds of tons of heavy water, an item used in natural uranium-driven reactors as a moderator for triggering neutron-flow, thus gaining plutonium directly from the natural urani-um without the difficult process of enrichment. In correspondence found in subsequent investigations it was shown that Hempel declared his heavy water shipments as "Coca Cola." This German made a lot of money in the process, but died before he could spend his illicit gains. The true extent of foreign, and in particular, German involve-ment in the development of the Iraqi missile and nuclear program will probably never be known. As Ewen Buchanan, the UNSCOM spokesman put it to me when I visited his offices in New York, "While we know most of what went on, there are some serious gaps. Our job [in Iraq] was terminated prematurely and I fear that the West might eventually pay a serious price for this lapse."[5]

Then there is South Africa. Former President de Klerk had hardly vacated his plush office in the Union Buildings before the shenanigans started. A powerful pro-Islamic lobby within the cabinet of President Mandela immediately set to work to sell a variety of sophisticated weapons systems to, among others, Syria. Top of the range was a tank laser sighting device which had been developed (with considerable Israeli involvement, it should be noted) to the Syrian government. Had the deal gone through, Syrian armored divisions might have achieved some kind of battlefield advantage.

Enter Washington with a warning that was brief but explicit. If the systems were supplied to Damascus (there were several hundreds), in contravention of a UN arms embargo and to a country labeled "rogue" by the American State Department, the U.S. would invoke unspecified sanctions against Pretoria. Mandela backed down.

Among other military-related South African adventures in the region was the role of a group of mercenaries, all of them former Special Forces operatives, who spent several months in the late 1990s training a crack Libyan helicopter-borne counter-insurgency force. That contract included the sale of sophisticated electronic equipment including night vision goggles and unmanned aerial vehicles, all of it equipment banned by the U.S. arms embargo. Dealt with in more detail in Chapter 8, it is worth mentioning that all this happened with the cognizance and the blessings of both the South African Military Intelligence and the country's National Intelligence Agency (NIA).

Shortly thereafter, the same company was doing their thing in the Sudan where they put Sudanese Army commandos through their paces, again with the NIA in on the act (though this time, without the knowledge of SA Military Intelligence). The difference was that here was a crackerjack team of experienced white South African veterans training the soldiers of an Arab government in the intricacies of killing their fellow countrymen, all of them black dissidents waging a guerrilla campaign in the southern and western reaches of the Sudan. And though details of this operation have been published in the West, not a whisper of protest has emerged from the American Black Caucus, even though the killing of black African people by an Arab government has been labeled barbaric by the U.S. State Department.

On a lighter tack, there was also the South African-linked charade enacted after the fall of Jean-Bertrand Aristide, the deposed Haitian dictator. The rioters were still on the streets of Port-au-Prince when news arrived that a secret shipment of weapons was about to arrive on the troubled island aboard a South African Air Force jet. The guns, sent on instruction of President Thabo Mbeki, arrived too late to save Aristide's bacon, but the furor that followed was noteworthy for the intensity of debate that it generated in South Africa's Parliament.

In spite of strong protests from the Parliamentary opposition, the former Haitian president was granted political asylum in South Africa. But then that's the way the increasingly autocratic Mbeki does his business these days, at least when he is not traveling abroad.

In the same way questions are now being asked about the role of South African scientists in Iran.

According to Stuart Sterzel—a former Special Forces veteran and today, head of the country's Special Forces League who maintains close ties to the country's security apparatus—a delegation from Washington arrived in Pretoria in October 2002.

Their brief, according to Sterzel, was to make what he termed "financial offers to former South African nuclear scientists." This was in line with what had taken place a few years before in the former Soviet Union. There, Russian nuclear physicists were offered money to channel their efforts into something more productive than helping maverick governments develop weapons of mass destruction.

Trouble was, when the Americans made their offer in South Africa, there weren't any takers. Granted, there was a reason. Some members of the old South African nuclear establishment had accepted IAEA monitoring positions (at least four of them later went to Iraq under the auspices of the agency), others were, and still are, linked to South Africa's commercial nuclear facility at Koeberg, on the northern fringes of Cape Town. Still more had engaged in academic pursuits or gone into commerce and, word has it, some had done pretty well. Several had emigrated. But there were still a few gaps, which raises questions as to where they were. Why else would any one of them have rejected $80,000 to stay out of the illegal weapons business?

While we are still unsure about South Africa's former nuclear personnel, we have a pretty good idea what many of those involved in that country's intermediate ballistic rocket programs were doing. Of all the Islamic states involved in missile research, Iran followed close on the heels of Pakistan in being the most successful in launching long-range missiles. It comes as no surprise then that a number of South Africa's rocket scientists accepted offers to work for the Tehran government. But more of that later as well.

Instructive in this regard are comments made by the Israeli Mossad chief, Efrayim Halevi, at a closed session of the NATO Council in Brussels on June 26, 2002. The ambassadors of all nineteen NATO countries took part in the meeting and he had the following to say about Tehran's missile program:[6]

"In recent years, Iran has invested gigantic sums in the development of launch systems, mainly surface-to-surface missiles originally based on North Korean expertise. The Shahab-3, with a range of one-thousand-three-hundred miles has been tested successfully. Iranian Defense Minister Shamkhani publicly stated that Iran is trying to increase its range, carrying capability, and 'destructive capability.' Iran is also involved in the research and development of even longer-range missiles, which can reach Europe and in the distant future, even the United States.

"The Iranian defense minister denied this in public, but our view is different. This effort is being conducted under the cover of launching civilian satellites. I have to tell you that I see no reason for this entry into developing such long-range missiles. Who and what are the potential targets of these systems? I do not know."

Since then, in March 2004, the Iranian military tested their latest version of the Shahab-3 or "Shooting Star." Early reports indicated a touchdown more than a thousand miles distant, which brought all of Israel (as well as quite a few other countries in the region) within immediate strike range. The missile had apparently been strengthened to take a larger payload, and that this something might be nuclear, was not lost on any intelligence agency, Russia and China included.

Also significant, are comments made by the American Federation of Scientists. In referring to the Iranian missile program on its website on March 14, 2004, it made the interesting comment that "For many years, there has been a lack of understanding of the origination of Iran's strategic ballistic missile program. Equally absent from the public discussion about the Missile Technology Control Regime (MTRC) is the exchange of information between North Korean and Iranian launch vehicle strategic ballistic missile programs and the Chinese support of both."

Things tend to go haywire awfully quickly when issues related to terrorism go awry.

Take what happened in Spain in March 2004. Almost two hundred Spaniards were killed in bomb blasts on Madrid's domestic rail service early one weekday morning. The following Sunday, a popular, pro-American Spanish government was ousted in a hard-fought election by a Socialist majority whose first call was to "Bring back our boys from Iraq." Nobody had predicted that option: in fact it took just about everybody—the White House included—by surprise.

The same with the invasion of Afghanistan, which followed shortly after September 11. Only this time Washington wasted no time in preparing for war.

Then it was Libya's turn in the spotlight. This development had far reaching effects because several nations were spotlighted, Pakistan, Iran, some South East Asian countries, North Korea and South Africa among them.

What did emerge in early 2004 was the exposure of Colonel Muammar Gadhaffi as having been involved in the importation of a shipment of centrifuges to Libya. With huge oil resources, this largely rural Arab state not only aspired to nuclear parallelism, but also went some way toward trying to achieve that objective. That emerged after a ship carrying thousands of centrifuges was intercepted on its way to Tripoli last October.

The German freighter, en route from a Pakistani port via Dubai, was diverted under a NATO naval escort to Taranto in southern Italy shortly after it had passed through the Suez Canal. Intelligence agents boarded it and seized the centrifuges, the design of which—like much else in Pakistan's nuclear weapons program—were said to have been stolen from Urenco the European nuclear consortium.

It was this interception that ultimately forced the Libyan leader to "come clean" with his WMD programs.[7] He had no option, having been caught with his keffiya around his ankles.

How advanced was the Libyan nuclear program? According to the IAEA, Libya was years from producing a nuclear weapon (important pieces of equipment were dismantled and stored in boxes while plane-loads of documents were flown out of the country). Meanwhile, British and American officials who made secret visits to Libya's weapons laboratories countered that observation with one of their own. They declared that Colonel Gadhaffi was "well on his way" to making a nuclear bomb, though doubts have since been expressed as to the veracity of that statement.

What astounded everybody was the ease with which the complex bomb-making equipment was acquired by a country that had been repeatedly labeled maverick by the U.S. State Department. Said one of the inspectors afterward: "The scale and the sophistication of the networks supplying so-called rogue states seeking nuclear weapons are considerably more extensive than previously believed."

What is of most concern to the international community, is that if a country—oil industry resources notwithstanding—as relatively undeveloped as Libya, and with a largely non-contributing population composed of desert Bedouins, is able to acquire the kind of nuclear wherewithal that makes it a candidate for building atom bombs, then there is every likelihood that other nations might follow suit. This comment is obviously linked to al-Qaeda.

If this premise is right, said the *New York Times*, shortly after Gadhaffi had been exposed as a proliferator, then Libya obviously posed a far more serious threat than that detected by UN inspection teams.

"We saw uranium enrichment going ahead," said one senior diplomat with knowledge of the Anglo-American inspections. "We were satisfied that they were in the process of developing a weapon." He added: "Libya was third on our list of concern after North Korea and Iran."

Dr. ElBaradai conceded after the IAEA inspection that while there was no plutonium or HEU to speak of, nor had Libya achieved the sophistication to make any, there were quite a few surprises in store for his team in Libya.

"It was an eye opener to see how much material was being shifted from one country to the other," he declared after inspecting several sites, echoing some of the comments made earlier by Seymour Hersh. Dr. ElBaradai was also appalled at "the extent of the black market network."

What emerged, he explained, "was the existence of a shadowy network of middlemen involved in nuclear-related matters who tended to circumvent national export controls. These measures were supposed to control the movement of weapons of mass destruction. What I encountered in Libya proved that these controls are simply not working."

In truth, recent nuclear-related developments in Libya took the Western intelligence community very much by surprise.

While London and Washington were aware for some years that Gadhaffi was dabbling in chemical and biological weapons, nobody suspected that this defiant Arab nation had anything like the nuclear ambitions that were uncovered. Libya has always lacked any kind of home-grown technological ability, which is one of the reasons why almost the entire Libyan oil industry is run by expatriates.

What soon became clear to both the IAEA and to the West was that the centrifuges on their way to Libya originated in Pakistan. As one observer noted, such sales are usually strictly controlled in the majority of countries involved in such matters. But, he said, Pakistan has always played by its own rules.

The question that now begs is whether Pretoria might have had some kind of interest in Libya as well. Certainly the extent of Libya's nuclear research facilities that were shown in an extended exposé on NBC's 60 Minutes in March 2004, was way ahead of anything that Gadhaffi might have been able to develop on his own.

Nor is that the end of the story. According to the venerable Dr. Mohamed ElBaradai, there are "thirty five or forty countries believed to be capable in the long term of manufacturing nuclear weapons." Also, these perceptions have sinister connotations. Interviewed by the

French newspaper *Le Monde* at about the same time, he underscored the need for the international community to reinforce and update the Nuclear Non-Proliferation Treaty.

The treaty, which came into force in 1970, he declared, had been overtaken by a world "in which developing nuclear arms has become attractive not only to many countries, but also to terrorist groups."

Under current international law, said the IAEA chief, there was absolutely nothing illicit for a non-nuclear state to conduct uranium-enriching activities . . . or even to possess military-grade nuclear material. Should any country decide to break its commitment to the non-proliferation treaty, experts believe that it could produce a weapon in a comparatively short time.

"We are," he stated, "on the verge of just such a catastrophe."

Not long before the IAEA chief delivered that verdict, a related development emerged in the United States that alleged direct nuclear links with both Pakistan and South Africa.

Asher Karni, an orthodox Israeli living in Cape Town, was arrested by Federal authorities at Denver International Airport and charged with having orchestrated a deal to send two hundred electric components to Pakistan that could be used either as components for medical purposes or nuclear weapons. In this case, the items were triggered spark gaps, a range of sophisticated electrical switches that can be used to break up kidney stones and, at the same time, are ideal for use as nuclear detonators. The difference is that all of Pakistan's hospitals together would not have needed more than a half-a-dozen of the devices at any one time.

Reporting for the *Los Angeles Times*, Josh Meyer said that while friends and family maintained than Karni is a hard working electronics salesman, the FBI contends he is something more: "A veteran player in an underground network of traffickers in parts, technology and know-how for the clandestine nuclear weapons programs of foreign governments." As Meyer declared, "The Karni case offers a rare glimpse into what authorities say is an international bazaar teeming with entrepreneurs, transporters, scientists, manufacturers, government agents, organized-crime syndicates and, perhaps, terrorists . . . the case also provides a classic illustration of how illicit nuclear traffickers operate, readily skirting bans, disguising the real use for products, using middlemen to buy from legitimate manufacturers and routing shipments through several countries."

While Meyer does not offer a prognosis as to why Karni chose to set up shop in South Africa, it is no secret that in recent years, South Africa has emerged as a bolt-hole for international felons, including some on the run for major financial or political crimes as well as murderers. He makes the point that many of the shipments handled by Karni were routed through South Africa and then forwarded to the ultimate destination, often Pakistan. Whether any of these eventually landed in Iranian hands, we do not yet know.

Curiously, it was a South African tipster that ultimately got this Israeli entrepreneur nailed. He told authorities that Karni was using front companies, straw buyers and misleading shipping documents to sell restricted U.S. products to Pakistan and India.

Let us then look at some of the reasons for the international situation having been allowed to deteriorate the way it has. By late 2003, the United States Congress was provided with details of the Iranian nuclear program by the U.S. Central Intelligence Agency.[8] That was soon after Tehran allowed IAEA inspectors access to some of its enrichment facilities. In part, it reads as follows:

> The United States remains convinced that Tehran has been pursuing a clandestine nuclear weapons program, in violation of its obligations as a party to the Nuclear Nonproliferation Treaty (NPT). To bolster its efforts to establish domestic nuclear fuel-cycle capabilities, Iran sought technology that can support fissile material production for a nuclear weapons program.
>
> Iran tried to use its civilian nuclear energy program to justify its efforts to establish domestically or otherwise acquire assorted nuclear fuel-cycle capabilities.
>
> In August 2002, an Iranian opposition group disclosed that Iran was secretly building a heavy water production plant and a 'nuclear fuel' plant. Press reports later in the year confirmed these two facilities using commercial imagery and clarified that the "fuel" plant was most likely a large uranium centrifuge enrichment facility located at Natanz.
>
> Commercial imagery showed that Iran was burying the enrichment facility, presumably to hide it and harden it against military attack. Following the press disclosures, Iran announced at the International Atomic Energy Agency

September 2002 General Conference that it had 'ambitious' nuclear fuel cycle plans and intended to develop all aspects of the entire fuel cycle.

The question now is how much more of this kind of nuclear proliferation has been secreted by Tehran's mullahs. As one UN source told this writer: "Now that we've seen some of it . . . let's get to the rest. We know there is more."

A leading issue, assuming Iran eventually gets to develop the bomb, and possibly test it, is what Tehran might then do with such a lethal device.

The Israeli option is certainly the most obvious (and oft-declared) way for some of these zealots to go, though it would take a madman to try to drop an atom bomb on a city like Haifa or Tel Aviv. Israel would immediately retaliate and Tehran—together with a half-dozen other major Iranian cities—would end up as Hiroshima look-alikes, only far worse because the Jewish State would use thermonuclear bombs with yields hundreds of times greater.

Yet, one must also accept that those who strap bombs to their bodies for the purpose of taking as many of the enemy to kingdom come with them would probably not find it too difficult to use insanity as a plea if they were interrupted in pursuing such an objective.

One answer, indirectly provided by that most respected of American publications, *Scientific American*,[9] was the feasibility of an atomic attack on the global satellite system. Since the altitude at which such a device would be detonated would probably be between one and two hundred miles up (where most low earth orbit [LEO] satellites do their rounds), it would hardly need the most sophisticated of ballistic missiles to achieve that objective. A single Shahab-3 clone of the North Korean Scud/No-Dong MRBM would do the trick and, as we now know, Iran has lots of them.

Previous U.S. nuclear tests have already indicated the severe consequences of a single high altitude nuclear explosion (HANE). The results would be horrific. One such test with a yield of, say ten to twenty kilotons, as the Pentagon's Defense Threat Reduction Agency (DTRA) has suggested, would effectively wipe out all LEO satellites not specifically hardened (protected) to withstand the kind of radiation generated by such an explosion.

"K Dennis Papadopoulos, a plasma physicist at the University of

Maryland who studies the effects of HANEs for the U.S. Government, puts it slightly differently: 'A 10-kiloton nuclear device set off at the right height would lead to a loss of ninety per cent of all low-earth-orbit satellites within a month'."

The article is much more explicit and is worth taking in; especially since it also makes the point that any such explosion would bring society—as we know it today—almost to a halt. It also concludes that the side effects of a HANE blast could lead to more than $100 billion in replacement costs, "and this estimate does not even begin to account for the damage to the global economy from the loss of so many crucial space assets."

The magazine warns that despite this recent scrutiny, "The threat from HANEs has not been given 'anywhere near the attention it deserves'." That caution came from Representative Curt Weldon of Pennsylvania, a longtime advocate for missile and nuclear defense on the House Armed Services Committee.

THE PRESENT CRISIS

To fully understand the ramifications of Iran's nuclear weapons program—Tehran admitted in 2004 that it had been engaged in this kind of research and development for eighteen years—it is essential to comprehend the range of influences that have a bearing on such matters.

Iran concluded a Comprehensive Safeguards Agreement with the International Atomic Energy Agency (IAEA) as far back as December 1974, having been one of the first countries to sign the (nuclear) Non-Proliferation Treaty (NPT). Recent discoveries in that country are clearly a violation of the requirements of their Safeguards Agreement.

Further, the IAEA is often taken to task because it had not discovered these undeclared activities earlier. Not, it might be added, always rightly so.

A Comprehensive Safeguards Agreement has some important limitations built into it, due to the way in which it was negotiated decades ago (not by the IAEA but by its constituent member states). For example, IAEA inspectors cannot simply roam about and inspect what they wish. Similarly, there are strict limitations to access and information. It was only recently that new methods, for example so-called environmental analysis, have become available through which the analysis of swipe samples can yield important information on undeclared activities based on very small samples (lower limit 10–15 grams). Because there were no other checks in place, Saddam (and Iran) could run undeclared and undetected activities next to plants which were inspected for many years, but it was precisely through environmental sampling that undeclared activities were recently uncovered in Iran.

Thus, in terms of Comprehensive Safeguards, there is no obligation to report uranium mining operations. In fact, uranium comes under safeguards only when it has reached a certain purity as uranium hexafluoride (UF_6), or has been processed into a pure enough form as an oxide for use as fuel in heavy water reactors. In all fairness then, it is clear why Hans Blix (and others) visited Iran many times in the past without detecting any undeclared activities: they had no right to inspect or visit facilities not declared to them due to the way the Agreement was structured by member states, including the United States.

Due to these limitations, in view of WMD discoveries in Iraq after Operation Desert Storm, an agreement termed the Additional Protocol was negotiated. That now gives the IAEA access to substantially more information and also places to inspect, the latter, under certain circumstances, at very short notice. As a direct consequence, information on mining, the production of ore concentrates, fuel cycle-related R&D activities (even when no nuclear material is present), the manufacture of nuclear-related equipment and the import/export of Trigger List items and so on, must now be submitted. Thus, together with a comprehensive and focused analysis of all the information at its disposal (including satellite photos, information submitted by intelligence agencies and open source literature), the IAEA these days is in a much better position to detect undeclared material and activities.

Yet, let it never be understated, the Iranians can be distressingly—and, not to make too fine a point of it, conveniently—vague about what they might or might not be doing at any particular time, largely because it suits them. The same approach might apply to their assets. They know and the West is very much aware, that an inspection of this nature can be a rigorous and sometimes embarrassing affair.

That said, the actual construction of an atom bomb is fraught with huge technological and scientific demands, many of which cannot be embraced by countries without substantial industrial infrastructures which, of necessity, implies an extensive scientific subculture. And while the broader intricacies of bomb design are known by many—with, as we have seen, the actual blueprints suddenly surfacing in Libya—the problem with building a nuclear device has centered on the availability of fissile material for its core, unless of course, you have access to smuggled fissile material, possibly from the former Soviet Union (FSU).

For this and other reasons dealt with in this book, it is my belief that groups or states inclined towards massive-scale terrorist attacks are more likely to settle for a so-called "dirty bomb"—a conventional bomb spiked with radioactive material. This is a device that is comparatively simple to construct using conventional explosives available just about everywhere. It could be mixed with radioactive nuclear waste or other commercially available radioisotopes that are never as well guarded as highly enriched uranium or plutonium.

There is a lot of it around. A United Nations report[10] disclosed that there has been a huge rise in the illegal trafficking of radioactive material in recent years. There were fifty-one smuggling incidents involving radiological materials in 2003 compared to only eight in 1996. Since 1993, read the statement, there had been three hundred confirmed cases of trafficking, more than two thirds in the past five years alone. In addition, there were three hundred or more "unconfirmed" reports.

A recent article in the *International Herald Tribune*[11] told us that the United States "had been trying for years to retrieve nuclear materials that America and the former Soviet Union had sent around the world for research purposes." An audit announced in February 2004 found that only about half—or roughly eleven thousand pounds of the uranium that it sought—was ever likely to be recovered.

Quoting a speech made by U.S. energy secretary Spencer Abraham before the IAEA in Vienna, he said that efforts would be both expanded and accelerated to include used Soviet-era fuel from research reactors. The unused fuel, he declared, "typically contains large amounts of unused uranium of the type suitable for bombs which can be extracted and purified with chemical techniques that are sixty years old and are widely known."

In Western terms, the handling of radioactively "hot" material without the necessary sophisticated technical means would be a problem from a safety point of view. But, let it be stressed, this would not be the case for terrorists who are willing to give up their lives for this cause or that, invariably in the name of Allah.

Radioactive contamination spread by such a bomb, while not necessarily deadly, would, in all likelihood create great and lasting panic among a public terrified of radioactivity. Were such a device be detonated in Lower Manhattan, for instance, it could result in Wall Street being closed for decades and it is exactly this kind of dislocation that the modern-day zealot is aiming at.

Then there was the meeting between the IAEA's Mohamed ElBaradei and US President George W. Bush in March 2004. That this event didn't receive the attention that it deserved from the media is unusual, especially considering the ramifications. Truth is, their discussion had a good deal more to it than just Iran.

In an address before Washington's National Defense University a month before, Bush proposed seven measures to counter proliferation, some of which greatly alarmed the IAEA. The first was the Proliferation Security Initiative (PSI), a combined military/intelligence effort to take direct action against proliferators, thereby bypassing the IAEA. In effect, such action would emasculate the nuclear monitoring body. It would also make it look ineffective because it does not have the same powers to seize material, freeze assets and prosecute.

He further suggested a special committee ("governments in good standing with the IAEA") within the Board of the IAEA, something unheard of until then. The idea was that the committee would consist of states that, by then, would have joined the PSI. In turn, this would create an "inner cabinet" that would effectively run the IAEA's business. The conflict that would almost certainly emerge within the organization's membership from such a development would be appalling.

Bush suggested that "proliferators" should not serve on the Board and this created more dissension. For a start, it would be almost impossible for the Board to agree on who might be a proliferator, especially given the strong influence of the Group of 77 + China, mostly developing countries, many of them Arab-speaking and who deeply resent the overriding influence of the USA and its allies on the Board of the IAEA.

Another issue which surfaces from time to time is that in terms of safeguards obligations, there is absolutely nothing that prevents a country from building and running conversion, enrichment, fuel fabrication or, for that matter, even reprocessing plants. There are sufficiently well-developed safeguards approaches and methods to ensure that such plants are run for peaceful purposes only. Japan, it should be noted, is currently putting into operation one of the largest reprocessing plants in the world, without the international community being unduly concerned about the IAEA's implementation of safeguards and the possible misuse of plutonium obtained by Tokyo through the reprocessing of spent fuel.

Finally, a word on the nature and purpose of this book. It is difficult for some observers to understand why it is that Iran decided to keep its nuclear-related activities a secret. There are several reasons, one of which could be that this work is part of a nuclear weapons program. Or perhaps the level of obfuscation is aimed at keeping hidden the supplier(s) of the technology (which it did not possess before they arrived on the scene). Either way, the connotations are sinister. Yet this is a rather naïve approach in this age of freely available satellite imagery coupled to the kind of powerful analytic methods that were unthinkable even a decade ago. And let's face it, such things could never be kept hidden indefinitely.

On Iran's role within the confines of the international nuclear community, I had the good fortune to be guided in my pursuits by a former member of the IAEA Board who, at close quarters, was able to observe representatives from Iran at work during the 1995 and 2000 NPT Revcons, both of which he attended. In his own words: "I was struck by their very sharp and formidable negotiating skills . . . especially in 2000." It was then, he said, that Tehran's representatives, after lengthy deliberations managed to have their own wording inserted in the text of the Final Document. This was exactly what they had originally set out to get from the IAEA when these talks began.

As he declared: "They were relentless and focused, and by this I do not necessarily mean in a negative sense." What he really wanted to emphasize (and which some Westerners often overlook) was that the Iranian way of doing things is the age-old Middle East way of bargaining. Their recent stop-and-go tactic with the IAEA was an example of this.

"I do not think that we, accustomed to the more clinical Western approach, always appreciate this way of going about getting things done—especially the U.S., to which other cultures don't exist." Obviously, Iran had much to hide, and this was compounded by their traditional way of doing things.

His final word: "It was also interesting to me, while observing at meetings of the Board of Governors of the IAEA, how Iran at times complained because they felt themselves excluded by the Arab-speaking countries, in spite of their common religion (exacerbated, of course, by the variants thereof)."

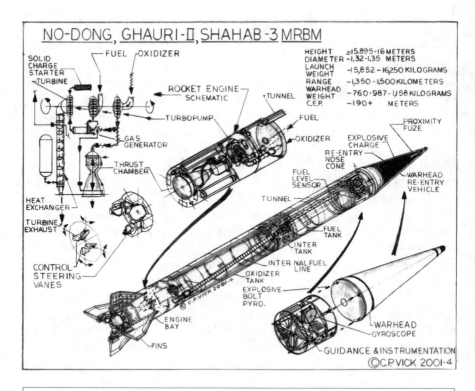

Cutaway diagram of the No-dong-A/Shahab-3 MRBM of Iran clearly shows its Soviet Scud-B design heritage along with the design differences associated with developments from North Korea, which stem from the Viktor P. Makeyev submarine-launched ballistic missile design bureau of the former Soviet Union. The schematic diagram and details are of the A.M. Isayev design bureau rocket engine and the strap-down guidance and warhead details.

PART I
THE ISLAMIC REPUBLIC OF IRAN

1

IRAN: ITS PEOPLE
AND GOVERNMENT

"The Iranian regime is not easy to understand. There is a gap
between its rhetoric and its actions; between its sense of grievance
and its inflammatory behavior; and between its ideological and
national interests. Nor are its actions consistent."
Paula deSutter: Center for Counterproliferation Research,
National Defense University, Washington DC

Iran is a country of contrasts. Influenced to some extent by Western
culture—and then only superficially—its rule by religious law is both
uncompromising and tenacious. While possessing seven percent of the
world's oil reserves, many of its people practice a lifestyle indistinguishable from that of their medieval forebears. This has resulted in
huge extremes between rich and poor, in spite of a reasonably healthy
economy. These contrasts might be easily discerned in pictures of a
shepherd boy and his flock of goats passing a modern oil rig, or in
headlines from December 2003 when news of Iran's nuclear program
vied with scenes from the destitute ancient city of Bam, whose mud-
brick structures had been collapsed by an earthquake.

Iran's almost seventy million people have a long history, during the
course of which a great Persian civilization evolved. Over millennia it
formed a number of empires that sometimes stretched well beyond its
borders. In this period, the country created sophisticated institutions,
many of which still continue to influence its Islamic regime today.
Despite the turmoil surrounding the establishment of its revolutionary
government, Iran's development has shown remarkable resilience.

Major trends affecting the Islamic Republic throughout much of
its history have been a tradition of monarchical government, represented in the latter part of the twentieth century by Mohammad Reza
Shah Pahlavi, the dominant role of the Shi'ites, Islamic clergy, personified by the Ayatollah Sayyid Ruhollah Musavi Khomeini and those

who succeeded him, and, since the late 19th century, pressure for Westernization or modernization.

Iran has been distinguished for having regimes that not only conquered neighboring areas but also devised ingenious institutions. The Achaemenids (550–330 B.C.) who ruled the first Iranian world empire—which stretched from the Aegean coast of Asia Minor to Afghanistan, as well as south to Egypt—created the magnificent structures at Persepolis, the remains of which still exist.

The Achaemenids also inaugurated a vast network of roads, a legal code, coinage, a comprehensive administrative system that allowed some local autonomy, and wide-ranging commerce. Iran influenced its conquerors too. Following its conquest of Iran, the Muslim Umayyad Empire (AD 661–750) adopted many Iranian institutions, such as Iran's administrative and monetary systems. The country was ravaged in the 13th century by the Mongol invasions, though the intruders from the northern steppe gradually became influenced by the more advanced civilization of their subjects. Tamerlane, the famous Mongol ruler (r. 1381–1405), made use of Iranian administrators in governing his far-flung territories.

Despite their primarily tribal origin for most of the country's history, the people of Iran have known only monarchical government, often of an absolutist type. For example, the Sassanids who ruled Iran for four centuries, beginning in AD 224, revived the Achaemenid term shahanshah (king of kings) for their ruler and considered him the "shadow of God on earth."

This concept was again revived in the late 18th century by the Qajar monarchy, which remained in power until Reza Khan, a military commander, had himself crowned as Reza Shah Pahlavi in 1926. Many considered Reza Shah's son, Mohammad Reza Shah, to be an absolutist ruler in his later days, especially because of his use of the internal security force SAVAK (*Sazman-e Ettelaat va Amniyat-e Keshvar*) to repress domestic opposition.

After the Muslim conquest, Iran was strongly influenced by Islam and, specifically, the political role exercised by the Shi'ite clergy. Such influence was established under the indigenous dynastic reign of the Safavids (1501–1722), who belonged to a Sufi religious order and made Shi'ite Islam the official religion of Iran, undertaking a major conversion campaign of Iranian Muslims. The precedent was revived in 1979 in a more thoroughgoing theocratic fashion by Ayatollah Khomeini.

In contrast to this traditional element in Iranian history has been the pressure toward Westernization that began in the late 19th century. Such pressures initially came from Britain, which sought to increase its commercial relations with Iran by promoting modernization of Iran's infrastructure and liberalization of its trade. British prodding had little effect, however, until Iranian domestic reaction to the growing corruption of the Qajar monarchy led to a constitutional revolution in 1905–1906. This revolution resulted in an elected parliament, or Majlis, a cabinet approved by the Majlis as well as a constitution guaranteeing certain personal freedoms of citizens.

Within less than twenty years, the program of Reza Shah stressed measures designed to reduce the powers of both tribal and religious leaders and to bring about economic development and legal and educational reforms along Western lines. Mohammad Reza Shah, like his father, promoted such Westernization and largely ignored the traditional role in Iranian society of conservative Shi'ite religious leaders.

He strengthened the military by considerably expanding its role in internal security matters to counteract the domestic opposition that arose after Mohammad Mossadeq's prime ministership. In addition, the Shah stressed defense against external enemies because he felt threatened by the Soviet Union, which had occupied Iranian territory during and after World War II.

To counter such a threat, the Shah sought American military assistance in the form of advisory personnel and sophisticated weaponry. He also harshly repressed the communist Tudeh Party and other dissident groups such as the Islamic extremist Mojahedin (*Mojahedin-e Khalq*, or People's Struggle) and Fadayan (*Cherikha-ye Fadayan-e Khalq*, or People's Guerrillas) organizations.

Meanwhile, the Shah promoted Iran's economic development by implementing a series of seven- and five-year economic plans, the first of which was launched in 1948. The programs emphasized the creation of the necessary infrastructure and the establishment of capital-intensive industry, initially making use of Iran's enormous oil revenues but seeking in the end to diversify the country's economy by expanding heavy industry. In the 1960s the Shah also paid attention to land reform, but the redistribution of land to peasants was slow, and in many instances the amount of land allocated to individual farmers was inadequate for economically viable agricultural production.

Moreover, Iran experienced high inflation as a result of the Shah's huge foreign arms purchases and his unduly rapid attempts at industrial modernization. Members of the bazaar, or small merchant class, benefited unevenly from these programs and gained less proportionately than the Shah's Westernizing elite. This lack of benefit from reforms was also true of the inhabitants of most small villages, who remained without electricity, running water, or paved roads.

Many factors contributed to the fall of the Shah. Observers most often cite such factors as concern over growing Western influences and secularization, the neglect of religious leaders, the repression of potential dissidents and of the Tudeh Party, and the failure of the bazaar class to achieve significant benefits from the Shah's economic development programs.

Following a brief secular provisional government after the Shah was overthrown in 1979, clerical forces loyal to Ayatollah Khomeini took control and launched a far-reaching Islamic revolution.

In Khomeini's revolutionary regime, the Ayatollah himself acted as policy guide and ultimate decision maker in his role as the pious jurist, or faqih, in accordance with the doctrine of *velayat-e faqih*, under which religious scholars guided the community of believers. Iran—officially renamed the Islamic Republic of Iran—became a theocratic state with its rulers representing God in governing a Muslim people, something not attempted previously even by the twelve Shi'ite Imams.

The constitution of 1979 designated Khomeini as the faqih for life. Other than appointing Khomeini faqih in perpetuity, the revolutionary constitution provided for political institutions to implement the legislative aspects of the government. An elected legislative assembly, the Majlis, charged with approving legislation devised by the executive, was dominated by Muslim religious leaders.

The constitution also created the Council of Guardians to ensure that laws passed by the Majlis conformed with Islam. In practice, the Council of Guardians has been conservative about economic legislation, blocking Majlis measures on land reform, for example.

To overcome this blocking of legislation, the Ayatollah Khomeini in January 1988 issued a ruling in which he claimed that the Islamic state had the same powers as the Prophet Mohammed, who was God's vice regent. Therefore, the state could set aside the *Qur'an* with regard to legislation if it were for the good of the community, he declared.

But conditions within society were still restrictive. As Whit Mason tells in his article[1] "Iran's Simmering Discontent," President Mohammed Khatami, from the start, felt compelled to make the expansion of women's rights a pillar of his program of liberalization. Mason grants that since his election in 1997, women have made considerable gains, far more than in other Mideastern Muslim countries, notably Saudi Arabia.

"Out of the two hundred and seventy-three members of Iran's Majlis, or parliament," Mason wrote, "eleven are female. Khatami has promoted several women to top positions in the government, and some sixty percent of places in universities go to females.

"But like much of the rest of his program, many of Khatami's efforts on behalf of women have been thwarted by hard-line conservatives. While women can get away with pushing their scarves farther back on their heads and can wear makeup and maybe even hold hands with their boyfriends in upscale neighborhoods without being harassed by the morals police, a woman's testimony in court still carries only half the weight of a man's. The 'blood money' paid to avoid the death penalty for causing the death of woman is only half that for the killing of a man; and family law accords all advantages in divorce and child custody to men. The Council of Guardians has blocked all efforts to reform the law in these instances."[2]

Other than through legislative institutions, political expression occurred in principle through political parties. However, the dominant political faction, the largely clergy-led Islamic Republican Party, established in early 1979, was dissolved in 1987 because it had become unmanageable. Subsequently, only one legally recognized political party, the Iran Freedom Movement (*Nehzat-e Azadi-yi Iran*), which had been established by former Prime Minister Mehdi Bazargan, operated in Iran.

Estimates of the number of persons opposed to the government or in prison varied. Officially, the latter number was given as nine thousand, but the anti-government Mojahedin maintained that a hundred and forty thousand was a more realistic figure. In 1988 opposition parties existed in exile, primarily in Western Europe, and included ethnic Kurdish movements and the Mojahedin Islamic extremists, as well as Marxists and monarchists. The Mojahedin also created the Iranian National Army of Liberation, which operated out of northern Iraq against the Khomeini regime.

After the Ayatollah's government came to power, it initially executed or imprisoned many members of the Shah's regime, including officers of the various armed services. But following the outbreak of the war with Iraq in 1980, substantial numbers of military men were released from prison to provide essential leadership on the battlefield or in the air war.

As early as June 1979, a counterforce to the regular military was created in the form of the Pasdaran (*Pasdaran-e Enghelab-e Islami*, or Islamic Revolutionary Guard Corps, or as commonly known in the West, Revolutionary Guards), an organization charged with safeguarding the Revolution. The Pasdaran became a significant military force in its own right and was overseen by a cabinet-level minister.

By 1988 the eight-year-old war with Iraq had evolved through various stages of strategy and tactics. Because Iran's population was approximately three times that of Iraq's, Iran's military manpower pool was vastly superior. Capitalizing on this advantage, in the early stages of the war, Iran engaged extensively in "human-wave" assaults against Iraqi positions, frequently using youths in their early teens.

This war strategy proved extremely costly to Iran in terms of human casualties; it was estimated that between three and four hundred thousand Iranians had been killed by 1987, and estimated loss of matériel was also large. The hostilities included a tanker war in the Persian Gulf and the mining of the Gulf by Iran, events that led to the involvement of the United States and other Western nations, which sought to protect their shipping and safeguard their strategic, economic, and political interests in the area. (See Chapter 2.)

Furthermore, a "war of the cities" was inaugurated in 1985, with each side bombarding the other's urban centers with missiles. Iran expended considerable effort in developing a domestic arms industry capable of manufacturing or modifying weapons and war matériel obtained from outside sources.

During this period Iran's principal arms supplier was China, from which it acquired Silkworm HY-2 surface-to-surface missiles, among other weapons systems. Iran also obtained missiles from the Soviet Union, which attempted to maintain amicable relations with both sides in the Iran-Iraq War. In addition, in the ground war, which initially had favored Iraq but then turned strongly in Iran's favor, in April 1988 Iraq succeeded in regaining the Faw Peninsula. Iraq thus recovered a significant part of the territory it had lost earlier to Iran.

The war severely strained Iran's economy by depleting its foreign exchange reserves and causing a balance of payments deficit. It also redirected manpower that would otherwise have been engaged in agriculture and industry.

By 1987 Iran's overall war costs were calculated at approximately US$350 billion. Moreover, wartime damage to urban centers in western Iran, such as Abadan, Ahvaz, Dezful, and Khorramshahr, caused refugees to flood into Tehran and other cities, further aggravating the housing shortage. The destruction of petroleum producing, processing, and shipping installations on the Persian Gulf reduced Iran's oil production and its export capability, thereby cutting revenues.

Sales of other domestic commodities, such as carpets, agricultural products, and caviar were unable to compensate for the lost oil revenue, which was further reduced by a world glut in crude. Thus, in 1988 the revolutionary regime faced a straitened economic future in which basic structural problems—such as the degree of state involvement in the economy and the successful implementation of agricultural reform—remained to be addressed. By the end of the war, Iraq, it should be noted, shared the same problems, resulting in Saddam Hussein's rash 1990 aggression against the rich sheikdom of Kuwait.

Iran's economic situation has influenced its foreign policy to a significant degree. Although ideological considerations based on revolutionary principles dominated in the early days of the Revolution, Iran's policies became more pragmatic as the war with Iraq progressed. For example, because of its need for weapons and other military matériel, the Khomeini regime was willing to purchase arms from Western nations and even from Israel. Initially, the revolutionary government had made a radical foreign policy change from the pro-Western stance of the Shah. The United States, because of its support of the Shah, was branded as the "Great Satan" and the Soviet Union as the "Lesser Satan."

Both capitalism and socialism were condemned as materialistic systems that sought to dominate the Third World. In practice, however, the United States was the major target, as evidenced most clearly by the seizure of the United States embassy in Tehran and the taking of American diplomats as hostages in November 1979.

Because of the Khomeini regime's desire to export revolution, regional monarchies with Western associations, such as Saudi Arabia, the Gulf states, and Jordan, were regarded with some hostility, particularly after these countries came to the support of Saddam Hussein during the Iran-Iraq War.

Iran's militant foreign policy in the region was manifestly reflected in the August 1, 1987 demonstrations during the Mecca pilgrimage.

As a result, over four hundred pilgrims were killed (the majority of them Iranian).

As a protest against Iranian actions in the Gulf, in late April 1988 Saudi Arabia severed diplomatic relations with Tehran. Another instance of Iran's militant policy was its funding and sponsorship of Islamic extremist organizations in Lebanon, particularly Islamic Amal and Hizbollah, which contributed to that country's civil war as well as to the ongoing conflict with Israel.

THE GOVERNMENT AND THE PEOPLE

Wilfried Buchta encapsulates the story of the Iranian revolution in the introduction to his book *Who Rules Iran*.[3] He reminds us that at the time Iran was celebrating the twentieth anniversary of its Islamic revolution in 1999, the country "once again refuted the gloomy predictions put forward by its critics." Essentially, he says, there had been those who, "since its beginnings predicted the revolution's rapid collapse." However, as Buchta describes, "Despite violent revolutionary upheavals (1971– 81), an eight-year war with Iraq (1980–88) and continuing internal power struggles to this day, the Islamic Republic has managed not only to survive, but to succeed in maintaining a considerable degree of political stability."

Moreover, the Shi'ite clergy has consolidated the monopoly of power first attained by Ayatollah Ruhollah Khomeini in 1979, allowing the ruling clerical elite to tolerate a limited degree of political pluralism as well as quadrennial presidential and parliamentary elections within the framework of the Islamic system.

Of course, as he points out, "Neither Khomeini nor his successor [Ayatollah Ali Hoseini Khamene'i] have been able to remedy the political, social and economic problems that led to the outbreak of revolution in 1979," as a consequence of which "Iran's perennial economic ills have become a nightmare for successive governments in Tehran."

Explaining the nature of the government, Buchta states that "Iran's power structure is the key to understanding the reasons for the clerical regime's stability as well as the tensions that have accompanied clerical rule."

Rather, he says, Iranian policy is determined by a multitude of often loosely connected and fiercely competitive power centers. Some of these are formal in nature and rooted in the constitution and codified regulations, and they manifest themselves in state institutions.

Other power centers, he explains, "are informal and are grouped either around religious-political associations of the Iranian leadership elite—which is split into various ideological wings—or around revolutionary foundations and security forces."

Looking at the broader picture, the Islamic Iranian revolution of 1979 resulted in the replacement of the monarchy by the Islamic Republic of Iran under Khomeini, who, as the self-proclaimed philosopher/king, first began formulating his concept of an Islamic government in the early 1970s. He did this while in exile in the Shi'ite learning and pilgrimage center of Najaf in Iraq.

Khomeini's principal objective was that government should be entrusted to Islamic clergy who had been appropriately trained in Islamic theology and jurisprudence. He referred to this ideal government as a *velayat-e faqih*, or the guardianship of the religious jurist. One of the more memorable pronouncements at the time was that the age of marriage for females was officially lowered from eighteen to nine.

Also established were groups who went under the nomenclature of "Party of God," or more commonly, morality squads who ensured that women did not wear make-up or display a single strand of hair if they ventured outdoors, together with the reinstitution of the medieval practice of stoning females to death for the crimes of adultery and prostitution. It became an era when every stray or obscure gesture by women could be regarded as "a disturbance of public safety." Sadly, little has changed in the interim, though clearly, these are not the kind of actions likely to endear a government to its population.

However, solipsist or not, Khomeini did not elaborate any concrete ideas about the institutions and functions of his ideal Islamic government. The translation of these concepts into a structure of inter-related governmental institutions was undertaken by the special Assembly of Experts, which drafted the Constitution of the Islamic Republic during the summer and fall of 1979.

For all the travails it experienced over the past few decades, Islamic Iran's political institutions have withstood serious challenges. These include the impeachment and removal from office of the first elected president and the assassination of the second; the assassination of a prime minister, several members of the cabinet, and deputies of the parliament or Majlis; an effort to overthrow the government by armed opposition; and a major foreign war. The constitutional government's demonstrated ability to survive these numerous crises inspired confidence among the political elite. None of it represents the epitome of any kind of political progress.

At the same time, a solid governmental infrastructure does exist. At the top is the faqih, the ultimate decision-maker. The constitution specifically named Khomeini (and those prominent individuals who were to succeed him) as faqih for life. It also provides a mechanism for choosing their successors. The role of the faqih—today, Iran's Supreme Guide Ali Khamene'i—has evolved into that of a policy wiseman and arbitrator among competitive views.

Below the faqih a distinct separation of powers exists between the executive and legislative branches. The executive branch includes an elected president and cabinet that must be approved by the elected legislative assembly, the Majlis. The judiciary is expected to be independent of both the executive and the Majlis but in practice, given the prevalence of clerics in the higher levels of government, it is not.

CONSTITUTIONAL FRAMEWORK

Five political entities control post-revolutionary Iran: the Supreme Islamic Jurisprudent or *velayat-e-faqih*; the Council of Guardians, a group of high level clerics who select the faqih; the President; the legislature or Majlis; and the Supreme Defense Council.

The most powerful is the Supreme (the word does tend to repeat itself in Iranian circles) Islamic Jurisprudent. As Paula deSutter tells us, "The position of faqih, as originally conceived, was to be held by a cleric who was a religious source of emulation (*marja taqlid*) eminently qualified as an Islamic jurist, and efficient administrator, and who enjoyed the confidence of the majority of the people." The first faqih, of course, was the Ayatollah Ruhollah Khomeini.

Essentially, the government is based upon the constitution that was approved in a national referendum in December 1979. (It was revised in 1989 in order eliminate the post of prime minister, thus increasing the responsibilities of the president.) This Republican Constitution replaced the 1906 constitution, which, with its provisions for a shah to reign as head of state, was the earliest constitution in the Middle East.

Soon after the Revolution, however, the provisional government of Mehdi Bazargan asked all Iranians sixteen years of age and older to vote in a national referendum on the question of whether they approved of abolishing the monarchy and replacing it with an Islamic republic. Subsequently, the government announced that a ninety-eight percent majority favored abrogating the old constitution and establishing such a republic. On the basis of this popular mandate, the provisional government prepared a draft constitution drawing upon some of the articles of the abolished 1906 constitution and the French constitution written under Charles de Gaulle in 1958.

Ironically, the government draft did not allot any special political role to the clergy or even mention the concept of *velayat-e faqih*.

Although the provisional government had initially advocated a popularly elected assembly to complete the constitution, Khomeini indicated that this task should be undertaken by experts. Accordingly the electorate was called upon to vote for an Assembly of Experts from a list of names approved by the government. The draft constitution was submitted to this seventy-three-member assembly, which was dominated by Shi'ite clergy.

The Assembly of Experts convened in August 1979 to write the constitution in final form for approval by popular referendum. The clerical majority was generally dissatisfied with the essentially secular draft constitution and was determined to revise it to make it more Islamic. Produced after three months of deliberation, the final document, which was approved by a two-thirds majority of the Assembly of Experts, differed completely from the original draft. For example, it contained provisions for institutionalizing the office of supreme religious jurist, or faqih, and for establishing a theocratic government.

The first presidential elections took place in January 1980, and elections for the first Majlis, or parliament, were held shortly thereafter. The Council of Guardians, a body that reviews all legislation to ensure that laws are in conformity with Islamic principles, was appointed during the summer of 1980.

Essentially, the constitution stipulates that the government of the Republic derives its legitimacy from both God and the people. It is a theocracy in the sense that the rulers claim that they govern the Muslim people of Iran as representatives of the divine being and the saintly Twelve Shi'ite Imams. The people have the right to choose their own leaders, however, from among those who have demonstrated both religious expertise and moral rectitude.

At the national level this is accomplished through parliamentary and presidential elections scheduled at four-year intervals. All citizens, beginning at age sixteen, are eligible to vote in these elections. There are also local elections for a variety of urban and rural positions.

The Faqih
The preamble to the Republican Constitution vests supreme authority
in the faqih. According to Article 5, the faqih is the just and pious
jurist who is recognized by the majority of the people at any period as
best qualified to lead the nation. In both the preamble and Article 107
of the constitution, Khomeini is recognized as the first faqih. Articles
108 to 112 specify the qualifications and duties of the faqih.

Duties include appointing the jurists to the Council of Guardians;
the chief judges of the judicial branch; the chief of staff of the armed
forces; the commander of the Pasdaran (or Islamic Revolutionary
Guards Corps); the personal representatives of the faqih to the
Supreme Defense Council; and the commanders of the army, air force
and navy, following their nomination by the Supreme Defense
Council.

The faqih is also authorized to approve candidates for presidential
elections. In addition, he is empowered to dismiss a president who has
been impeached by the Majlis or found by the Supreme Court to be
negligent in his duties.

Articles 5 and 107 of the constitution provide procedures for succession to the position of faqih. After Khomeini, it was stipulated that
the office be passed to an equally qualified jurist. It is also declared
that if a single religious leader with appropriate qualifications could
not be recognized consensually, religious experts elected by the people
were to choose from among themselves three to five equally distinguished jurists who would then constitute a collective faqih, or
Leadership Council.

The Presidency
The constitution stipulates that the president is "the holder of the
highest official power *next* to the office of faqih." In effect, the president is the head of state of the Islamic Republic, while the faqih
remains its most powerful figure.

Articles 113 to 132 pertain to the qualifications, powers, and
responsibilities of the president. The president is elected for a four-
year term on the basis of an absolute majority vote of the national
electorate and may be reelected for one additional term.

The president must be a Shi'ite Muslim and a man "of political
and religious distinction." He is empowered to approve the nomina-
tions of ministers, sign laws into force, and veto decrees issued by the
Council of Ministers, or cabinet.

Elected in January 1980, Abolhasan Bani Sadr was Iran's first president under the Constitution of 1979. His tenure of office was marked by intense rivalry with the IRP-dominated Majlis. Within a year of his election, relations between the president and his opponents in the Majlis had deteriorated so severely that the Majlis initiated impeachment proceedings against Bani Sadr. In June 1981, a majority of Majlis deputies voted that Bani Sadr had been negligent in his duties and requested that Khomeini dismiss him from office as specified under the Constitution.

Iran's second president, Mohammad Ali Rajai, was elected in July 1981 but was assassinated in a bombing at the prime minister's office the following August 30. He was replaced by Hojjatoleslam Ali Khamene'i in a special election held in October 1981. The current Iranian president, Mohammed Khatami, was elected in August 1997, reelected in 2001, and his second term is due to end in August 2005.

The Majlis

Articles 62 through 90 of the 1979 constitution invest legislative power in the Islamic Consultative Assembly, the parliament, or Majlis. Deputies are elected by direct, secret ballot once every four years.

Each deputy represents a geographic constituency, and every person sixteen years of age and older from a given constituency votes for one representative.

The Majlis cannot be dissolved: according to Article 63, "Elections of each session should be held before the expiration of the previous session, so that the country may never remain without an assembly." Article 64 established the number of representatives at two-hundred-and-seventy, but it also provides for adding one more deputy, at ten-year intervals, for each constituency population increase of one-hundred-and fifty thousand people. Five seats are reserved for the non-Muslim religious minorities: one each for Assyrian Christians, Jews, and Zoroastrians, and two for Armenian Christians.

The constitution permits the Majlis to draft its own regulations pertaining to the election of a speaker and other officers, the formation of committees, and the holding of hearings. When the first Majlis convened in the summer of 1980, the deputies voted to have annual elections for the position of speaker.

Rafsanjani was elected as speaker of the first Majlis and was reelected many times afterwards. The speaker is assisted by deputy speakers and the chairmen of various committees. The Majlis not only has the responsibility of approving cabinet members but also has the right to question any individual minister or anyone from the government as a whole about policies.

Articles 88 and 89 require ministers to appear before the Majlis within ten days to respond to a request for interpellation. If the deputies are dissatisfied with the information obtained during such questioning, they may request the Majlis to schedule a confidence vote on the performance of a minister or the government.

Article 69 stipulates that Majlis sessions be open to the public, that regular deliberations may be broadcast over radio and television, and that minutes of all meetings be published.

Since 1980 sessions of the Majlis have been broadcast regularly. The public airing of Majlis meetings has demonstrated that the assembly has been characterized by raucous debate. Economic policies, with the notable exception of oil policy, have been the most vigorously debated issues.

There are serious problems in the way that the system operates, however, according to Whit Mason who provided us with a valuable insight to modern Iran in his article "Iran's Simmering Discontent."[4]

Iranians, he tells us, are increasingly resentful of the mullahs for overriding the decisions of the democratically elected parliament and President Khatami. "The Council of Guardians, which is composed of twelve mullahs (six appointed by the supreme leader, and another six nominated by the judiciary and approved by Parliament)—roughly speaking, the Islamic Republic's equivalent of the Soviet Politburo—reviews all laws passed by parliament. This ensures that they conform to their reading of Islamic law. Among bills passed by parliament but rejected by the council were acts raising the legal age of marriage for women from nine to fifteen, facilitating the start-up of newspapers, and guaranteeing criminal defendants the right to have an attorney present during trial."[5]

Like the Council of Guardians, the entire judiciary is ultimately accountable to no one but the supreme leader, the *velayat-e-faqih*, or supreme jurist—Ayatollah Khamein'i.

The Judiciary

Article 156 of the constitution provides for an independent judiciary. According to Articles 157 and 158, the highest judicial office is the High Council of Justice, which consists of five members who serve five-year, renewable terms.

The High Council of Justice consists of the chief justice of the Supreme Court and the attorney general (also seen as State Prosecutor General), both of whom must be Shi'ite mujtahids (members of the clergy whose demonstrated erudition in religious law has earned them the privilege of interpreting laws), and three other clergy chosen by religious jurists.

The responsibilities of the High Council of Justice include establishing appropriate departments within the Ministry of Justice to deal with civil and criminal offenses, preparing draft bills related to the judiciary, and supervising the appointment of judges. Article 160 also stipulates that the minister of justice is to be chosen by the prime minister from among candidates who have been recommended by the High Council of Justice. The minister of justice is responsible for all courts throughout the country.

Article 161 provides for the Supreme Court, whose composition is based upon laws drafted by the High Council of Justice. The Supreme Court is an appellate court that reviews decisions of the lower courts to ensure their conformity with the laws of the country and to ensure uniformity in judicial policy. Article 162 stipulates that the chief justice of the Supreme Court must be a mujtahid with expertise in judicial matters. The faqih, in consultation with the justices of the Supreme Court, appoints the chief justice for a term of five years.

One of the most significant new codes was the Law of Qisas, which was submitted to and passed by the Majlis in 1982, one year after Beheshti's death in a bomb explosion. The Law of Qisas provided that in cases of victims of violent crime, families could demand retribution, up to and including death.

Other laws established penalties for various moral offenses, such as consumption of alcohol, failure to observe *hejab*, adultery, prostitution, and illicit sexual relations. Punishments prescribed in these laws included public floggings, amputations, and execution by stoning for adulterers. The entire judicial system of the country is supposed to have been de-secularized, but in practice—and in spite of the above, mullahs still tend to rule where important court decisions are made.

The attorney general, like the chief justice, must be a mujtahid and is appointed to office for a five-year term by the faqih (Article 162). The judges of all the courts must be knowledgeable in Shi'ite jurisprudence; they must meet other qualifications determined by rules established by the High Council of Justice.

Initially, there were insufficient numbers of qualified senior clergy to fill the judicial positions in the country, some former civil court judges who demonstrated their expertise in Islamic law and were willing to undergo religious training were permitted to retain their posts. In practice, however, the Islamization of the judiciary forced half of the former civil court judges out of their positions.

To emphasize the independence of judges from the government, Article 170 stipulates that they are "duty bound to refrain from executing governmental decisions that are contrary to Islamic laws."

Once again, Whit Mason has given us a fascinating insight into Iran's legal process under a section he titled "Injudicious Repression."

The hottest flashpoint in today's Iran, he tells us, is to be found in the country's courts. "Nowhere is the gulf between the mullahs and Iran's secular elite starker than in the judiciary, which, like the Council of Guardians, is answerable only to Khamene'i.

"Law students, lawyers, and subordinate judges are overwhelmingly progressive in their political orientation and study only the French and Belgian law that forms the basis of Iran's legal system. The presiding judge, on the other hand, is always a cleric with expertise in the Shi'ite version of Islamic law, or Sharia, with which the legal system has been sprinkled since (Ayatollah Khomeini's) revolution. The rulings of this judicial platypus would be comical if they did not have such a profound impact on peoples' lives."

Mason provides us with several judgments rendered in Iran's criminal courts that illustrate the mullahs' perspective and competence.

"A boy was sentenced to three months in prison for allegedly making flirtatious faces at a girl while she was walking along the street with her father. What was remarkable about the case is that he was across the street when he committed the offense, for which the court coined a special term, which translates as 'teleflirting'."

Various sections of Iran's statute books are color-coded, with the criminal statutes colored red. In one recent judgment, the clerical magistrate found a defendant guilty based not on any particular law, but on the "red pages." In another case, a convicted man was sentenced to imprisonment "until one week before the reappearance of the Mahdi," or in other words, "till Kingdom comes."

CITIES AND PEOPLE

Tehran, the capital, is the country's largest city and the second most populous city in the Middle East after Cairo.

A comparatively young metropolis by Middle Eastern standards, Tehran's origins date back about seven hundred years. The old part is a few miles to the northwest of ancient Rey, an important conurbation that was destroyed by the Mongol invasions of the 13th century.

Tehran was founded by refugees from Rey, but remained an insignificant small town until the end of the 18th century, when the founder of the Qajar dynasty chose it to be his capital. Tehran has been the capital of the country ever since.

The centralization of the government and the expansion of the bureaucracy under the Pahlavis, the last royal dynasty, were major factors in Tehran's rapid growth after 1925. The city's population doubled between 1926 and 1940 and tripled between 1940 and 1956, when it reached more than a million and a half. Tehran's population continued to grow rapidly, reaching almost three million by 1970. By 1986 it had grown to six million, and today it has reached nearly twelve million, the city's neighborhoods, designed on a grid system, expanding rapidly into what was formerly empty land.

Iran's second largest city is Mashhad in the east, with a population that more than doubled after 1976. Much of its growth was attributed to the large number of Afghan refugees during the 1980s. The historical origins of Mashhad are similar to those of Tehran inasmuch as the city essentially developed after the centuries-old city of Tus, near modern Mashhad, was destroyed by the Mongols. Mashhad has served as the principal commercial center of Khorasan since the 19th century, although its major growth has occurred only since the mid-1950s. It has also become an important manufacturing center and has numerous carpet, textile, and food-processing factories.

Iran's other major cities include Esfahan, Tabriz, and Shiraz, all of which have populations of over a million people.

A significant factor about Iran is the youth of its population, compared to the increasing percentage of older people in Europe, Russia, and the United States, whose population increasingly relies on immigration to maintain a younger demographic. According to the latest CIA study (September 2004), twenty-eight percent of Iran's population is fourteen years of age or younger, and the median age is twenty-three. The literacy rate among Iran's seventy million people is eighty percent (somewhat higher among males), and though the population's per capita income is not high by Western standards (some $7,000 a year) it compares favorably to its neighbors and many other countries in the Muslim world. Given Iran's vast oil and natural gas reserves, plus its relatively stable history of internal administration, it is possible to foresee the nation someday attaining First World status via its own human, natural, and industrial resources.

With such a youthful population steered toward literacy, the question arises whether a government guided by Islamic clerics can ultimately survive against future waves of native liberalism. Modern Iran's original revolutionary generation—that which came to the fore in 1979 on a tide of Islamic fervor—was badly bloodied throughout the 1980s in a fruitless war with Iraq. The new generation, growing up along with an acceleration in the development of computers and communications, may challenge the theological bent of its elders.

In February 2004 the world was astonished to see Iran's Guardian Council disqualify hundreds of candidates for election to the Majlis, or parliament, on the grounds that they did not possess proper Islamic credentials. Such an uproar rose from the Iranian public that the Supreme Guardian, Khameini himself, intervened to resinstate a number of the candidates. Of the now two hundred and ninety seats in parliament, nearly two hundred were claimed by conservatives, while reformers were elected to forty-eight and independents another thirty-nine. In the end it was a clear, if forceful, victory for the Islamic conservatives; but for a brief moment the world had gained a glimpse into the hybrid nature of today's Iran.

It is part theological regime harking back to the teachings of Mohammed, and part democracy influenced by Western concepts of individual rights. What remains to be seen is whether the next generation of Iranians will lean toward Western values, or adhere to Islam, nationalism, or perhaps even a resurrection of the once-great Persian Empire. Iran's geographic position has never allowed it to remain comfortable in self-defense. At the same time history tells us that it has always remained ambitious, capable of expanding its cultural influence or borders. In fact, during the 1980s, Iran waged the largest confrontational war the world has seen in half a century.

2

THE IRAN-IRAQ WAR, 1980–1988

Courtesy of the Federation of American Scientists

For many centuries, no single event has had quite as
severe effect on Iran and its people as the bitter eight-year war
that Tehran waged against Iraq. For the average Iranian it was a
social, political and military watershed. To have lost, would have
meant domination by an ancient foe. Consequently, with a
million or more casualties, very few families were left
untouched by its often senseless brutality.

The Iran-Iraq War permanently altered the course of Iranian history.
It strained every possible aspect of life in both countries like never
before, and led to severe dislocations.

Viewed from an historical perspective, the outbreak of hostilities
in 1980 was, in part, just another phase of the ancient Persian-Arab
conflict that had been fueled by 20th-century border disputes. Many
observers, however, believe that Saddam Hussein's decision to invade
Iran was a personal miscalculation based on ambition and a sense of
vulnerability.

Saddam Hussein, despite having made significant strides in forg-
ing an Iraqi nation-state, feared that Iran's new revolutionary leadership would threaten Iraq's delicate Sunni/Shi'ite balance and would
exploit Iraq's geostrategic vulnerabilities—Iraq's minimal access to the
Persian Gulf, for example. In this respect, Saddam Hussein's decision
to invade Iran has historical precedent; the ancient rulers of Meso-
potamia, fearing internal strife and foreign conquest, also engaged in
frequent battles with the peoples of the highlands.

The Iran-Iraq War was multifaceted and included religious
schisms, border disputes, and political differences. Conflicts contributing to the outbreak of hostilities ranged from centuries-old Sunni-
versus-Shi'ite and Arab-versus-Persian religious and ethnic disputes, to
a bitter personal animosity between Saddam Hussein and Ayatollah

Khomeini. Above all, Iraq launched the war in an effort to consolidate its rising power in the Arab world and to replace Iran as the dominant Persian Gulf state. Phebe Marr, a noted analyst of Iraqi affairs, stated that "The war was more immediately the result of poor political judgment and miscalculation on the part of Saddam Hussein," and "the decision to invade, taken at a moment of Iranian weakness, was Saddam's."

In reality, the war was nothing new. Iraq and Iran had engaged in border clashes for many years and had revived the dormant Shatt al Arab waterway dispute in 1979. Iraq claimed the hundred-and-thirty-mile channel up to the Iranian shore as its territory, while Iran insisted that the thalweg—a line running down the middle of the waterway—negotiated last in 1975, was the official border. The Iraqis, especially the Ba'ath leadership, regarded the 1975 treaty as merely a truce, not a definitive settlement.

The Iraqis also perceived revolutionary Iran's Islamic agenda as threatening to their pan-Arabism. Khomeini, bitter over his expulsion from Iraq in 1977 after fifteen years in An Najaf, vowed to avenge Shi'ite victims of Ba'athist repression. Baghdad became more confident, however, as it watched the once invincible Imperial Iranian Army disintegrate, as most of its highest ranking officers were arrested and many executed. In Khuzestan (Arabistan to the Iraqis), Iraqi intelligence officers incited riots over labor disputes, and in the Kurdish region, a new rebellion caused the Khomeini government severe troubles.

As the Ba'athists planned their military campaign, they had every reason to be confident. Not only did the Iranians lack cohesive leadership, but the Iranian armed forces, according to Iraqi intelligence estimates, also lacked spare parts for their American-made equipment.

Baghdad, on the other hand, possessed fully equipped and trained forces. Morale was running high. Against Iran's armed forces, including the Pasdaran (Revolutionary Guard) troops, led by religious mullahs with little or no military experience, the Iraqis could muster twelve complete mechanized divisions, equipped with the latest Soviet war matériel. With the Iraqi military buildup in the late 1970s, Saddam Hussein had assembled an army of a hundred-and-ninety-thousand men, augmented by twenty-two hundred tanks and four-hundred-and-fifty aircraft.

In addition, the area across the Shatt al Arab posed no major obstacles, particularly for an army equipped with Soviet river-crossing equipment. Iraqi commanders correctly assumed that crossing sites on the Khardeh and Karun rivers were lightly defended against their mechanized armor divisions; moreover, Iraqi intelligence sources reported that Iranian forces in Khuzestan, which had formerly included two divisions distributed among Ahvaz, Dezful, and Abadan, now consisted of only a number of ill-equipped battalion-sized formations.

Tehran was further disadvantaged because the area was controlled by the Regional 1st Corps headquartered at Bakhtaran (formerly Kermanshah), whereas operational control was directed from the capital. In the year following the Shah's overthrow, only a handful of company-sized tank units had been operative, and the rest of the armored equipment was poorly maintained.

For Iraqi planners, the only uncertainty was the fighting ability of the Iranian Air Force, equipped with some of the most sophisticated American-made aircraft. Despite the execution of key air force commanders and pilots, the Iranian Air Force had effectively displayed its might during local riots and demonstrations.

The air force was also active in the wake of the failed United States attempt to rescue American hostages in April 1980. This show of force impressed Iraqi decision makers to such an extent that they decided to launch a massive preemptive air strike on Iranian air bases in an effort similar to the one that Israel employed during the June 1967 Arab-Israeli War.

IRAQI OFFENSIVES, 1980–82

Despite the Iraqi government's concern, the eruption of the 1979 Islamic Revolution in Iran did not immediately destroy the Iraqi-Iranian rapprochement that had prevailed since the 1975 Algiers Agreement.

As a sign of Iraq's desire to maintain good relations with the new government in Tehran, President Bakr sent a personal message to the Ayatollah Khomeini offering "his best wishes for the friendly Iranian people on the occasion of the establishment of the Islamic Republic."

In addition, as late as the end of August 1979, Iraqi authorities extended an invitation to Mehdi Bazargan, the first president of the Islamic Republic of Iran, with the aim of improving bilateral relations. The fall of the moderate Bazargan government in late 1979, however, and the rise of Islamic militants preaching an expansionist foreign policy quickly soured relations.

The principal events that touched off this rapid deterioration occurred during the spring of 1980. In April, the Iranian-supported Ad Dawah attempted to assassinate Iraqi foreign minister Tariq Aziz.

Shortly after that failed grenade attack, Ad Dawah was suspected of attempting to assassinate another Iraqi leader, Minister of Culture and Information Latif Nayyif Jasim. In response, the Iraqis immediately rounded up members and supporters of Ad Dawah and deported to Iran thousands of Shi'ites of Iranian origin. In the summer of 1980, Saddam Hussein ordered the executions of presumed Ad Dawah leader Ayatollah Sayyid Muhammad Baqr as Sadr and his sister.

In September 1980, border skirmishes erupted in the central sector near Qasr-e Shirin, with an exchange of artillery fire by both sides. A few weeks later, Saddam Hussein officially abrogated the 1975 treaty between Iraq and Iran and announced that the Shatt al Arab was returning to Iraqi sovereignty. Iran rejected this action and hostilities escalated as the two sides exchanged bombing raids deep into each other's territory, beginning what was to be a protracted and extremely costly war.

Baghdad originally planned a quick victory over Tehran. Saddam expected the invasion of the Arabic-speaking, oil-rich area of Khuzistan to result in an Arab uprising against Khomeini's fundamentalist Islamic regime. This revolt did not materialize, and the Arab minority remained loyal to Tehran.

On September 22, 1980, formations of Iraqi MiG-23s and MiG-21s attacked Iran's air bases at Mehrabad and Doshen-Tappen (both near Tehran), as well as Tabriz, Bakhtaran, Ahvaz, Dezful, Urmia (sometimes cited as Urumiyeh), Hamadan, Sanandaj, and Abadan. Their aim was to destroy the Iranian Air Force on the ground—a lesson learned from the Israelis' Six-Day War.

They succeeded in destroying runways and fuel and ammunition depots, but much of Iran's aircraft inventory was left intact. Iranian defenses were caught by surprise, but the Iraqi raids failed because Iranian jets were protected in specially strengthened hangars and because bombs designed to destroy runways did not totally incapacitate Iran's very large airfields.

Within hours, Iranian F-4 Phantoms took off from the same bases, successfully attacked strategically important targets close to major Iraqi cities, and returned home with very few losses. Simultaneously, six Iraqi army divisions entered Iran on three fronts in an initially successful surprise attack, where they drove as far as five miles inland and occupied a huge swathe of Iranian territory.

As a diversionary move on the northern front, an Iraqi mechanized mountain infantry division overwhelmed the border garrison at Qasr-e Shirin, a border town in Bakhtaran (formerly known as Kermanshahan) Province, and occupied territory twenty miles eastward to the base of the Zagros Mountains. This area was strategically significant because the main Baghdad-Tehran highway traversed it.

On the central front, Iraqi forces captured Mehran, on the western plain of the Zagros Mountains in Ilam Province, and pushed eastward to the mountain base. Mehran occupied an important position on the major north-south road, close to the border on the Iranian side.

The main thrust of the attack was in the south, where five armored and mechanized divisions invaded Khuzestan on two axes, one crossing over the Shatt al Arab near Basra, which led to the siege and eventual occupation of Khorramshahr, and the second heading for Susangerd, which had Ahvaz, the major military base in Khuzestan, as its objective.

Iraqi armored units easily crossed the Shatt al Arab waterway and entered the Iranian province of Khuzestan. Dehloran and several other towns were targeted and were rapidly occupied to prevent reinforcement from Bakhtaran and Tehran. By mid-October, a full division advanced through Khuzestan headed for Khorramshahr and Abadan and the strategic oil fields nearby.

Other divisions headed toward Ahvaz, the provincial capital and site of an air base. Supported by heavy artillery fire, the troops made a rapid and significant advance—almost fifty miles in the first few days.

In the battle for Dezful in Khuzestan, where a major air base is located, the local Iranian army commander requested air support in order to avoid a defeat. President Bani Sadr, therefore, authorized the release from jail of many pilots, some of whom were suspected of still being loyal to the Shah. With the increased use of the Iranian Air Force, Iraqi progress was somewhat curtailed.

The last major Iraqi territorial gain took place in early November 1980. On November 3, Iraqi forces reached Abadan but were repulsed by an Islamic Revolutionary Guards Corps (Pasdaran) unit. Even though they surrounded Abadan on three sides and occupied a portion of the city, the Iraqis could not overcome the stiff resistance; sections of the city still under Iranian control were resupplied by boat at night.

On November 10, Iraq captured Khorramshahr after a bloody house-to-house fight. The price of this victory was high for both sides, approximately six thousand casualties for Iraq and even more for Iran.

Iraq's blitz-like assaults against scattered and demoralized Iranian forces led many observers to think that Baghdad would win the war within a matter of weeks. In fact, Iraqi troops did capture the Shatt al Arab and seize a thirty-mile wide strip of Iranian territory.

Iran may have prevented a quick Iraqi victory by a rapid mobilization of volunteers and deployment of loyal Pasdaran forces to the front. Besides enlisting the Iranian pilots, the new revolutionary regime also recalled veterans of the old imperial army, although many experienced officers, most of whom had been trained in the United States, had been purged.

Furthermore, the Pasdaran and Basij (what Khomeini called the "Army of Twenty Million" or People's Militia) recruited at least a hundred thousand volunteers. Approximately double that number of soldiers were sent to the front by the end of November 1980. They were ideologically committed troops (some members even carried their own shrouds to the front in the expectation of martyrdom) and fought bravely despite inadequate armor support.

For example, on November 7 commando units played a significant role, with the navy and air force, in an assault on Iraqi oil export terminals at Mina al Bakr and Al Faw. Iran hoped to diminish Iraq's financial resources by reducing its oil revenues. Tehran also attacked the northern pipeline in the early days of the war and persuaded Syria to close the Iraqi pipeline that crossed its territory.

Iran's resistance at the outset of the Iraqi invasion was unexpectedly strong, but it was neither well organized nor equally successful on all fronts. Iraq easily advanced in the northern and central sections and crushed the Pasdaran's scattered resistance there. Iraqi troops, however, faced untiring resistance in Khuzestan. President Saddam Hussein of Iraq may have thought that the approximately three million Arabs of Khuzestan would join the Iraqis against Tehran. Instead, many allied with Iran's regular and irregular armed forces and fought valiantly in the battles at Dezful, Khorramshahr, and Abadan.

Soon after capturing Khorramshahr, the Iraqi troops lost their initiative and began to dig in along their line of advance.

Tehran rejected a settlement offer and held the line against the militarily superior Iraqi force. It refused to accept defeat, and in January 1981 gradually began a series of counteroffensives. Both volunteers and regular armed forces were eager to fight, the latter seeing an opportunity to regain prestige lost because of their association with the Shah's regime.

Iran's first major counterattack failed, however, for political and military reasons. President Bani Sadr was engaged in a power struggle with key religious figures and eager to gain political support among the armed forces by direct involvement in military operations. Lacking military expertise, he initiated a premature attack by three regular armored regiments without the assistance of the Pasdaran units. He also failed to take into account that the ground near Susangerd, muddied by the preceding rainy season, would make resupply difficult.

As a result of his tactical decisions, the Iranian forces were surrounded on three sides. In a long exchange of fire, many Iranian armored vehicles were destroyed or had to be abandoned because they were either stuck in the mud or needed minor repairs. Fortunately for Iran, however, the Iraqi forces failed to follow up with another attack.

Iran also stopped Iraqi forces on the Karun River and, with limited military stocks, unveiled its "human wave" assaults, which used thousands of Basij (Popular Mobilization Army or People's Army) volunteers.

After Bani Sadr was ousted as president and commander-in-chief, Iran gained its first major victory, when, as a result of Khomeini's initiative, the army and the Pasdaran suppressed their rivalry and cooperated to force Baghdad to lift its long siege of Abadan in September 1981. Iranian forces also defeated Iraq in the Qasr-e Shirin area in December 1981 and January 1982. The Iraqi armed forces were hampered by their unwillingness to sustain a high casualty rate and therefore refused to initiate a new offensive.

Despite Iraqi success in causing major damage to exposed Iranian ammunition and fuel dumps in the early days of the war, the Iranian Air Force prevailed initially in the air war. One reason was that Iranian airplanes could carry two or three times more bombs or rockets than their Iraqi counterparts. Moreover, Iranian pilots demonstrated considerable expertise. For example, the Iranian Air Force attacked Baghdad and key Iraqi air bases as early as the first few weeks of the war, seeking to destroy supply and support systems. The attack on Iraq's oil field complex and air base at Al Walid, the operational base for T-22 and Il-28 bombers, was a well-coordinated assault. The targets were more than 500 miles from Iran's closest air base at Urumiyeh, so the F-4s had to refuel in midair for the mission.

Iran's Air Force relied on F-4s and F-5s for assaults and a few F-14s for reconnaissance. Although Iran used its Maverick missiles effectively against ground targets, lack of airplane spare parts forced Iran to substitute helicopters for close air support. These same helicopters served not only as gunships and troop carriers but also as emergency supply transports.

In the mountainous area near Mehran, helicopters proved advantageous in finding and destroying targets and maneuvering against antiaircraft guns or man-portable missiles.

During Operations Karbala Five and Karbala Six, the Iranians reportedly engaged in large-scale heli-borne operations on the southern and central fronts, respectively. Chinooks and smaller Bell helicopters, such as the Bell 214A, were escorted by Sea Cobra choppers.

In confronting the Iraqi air defense, Iran soon discovered that a low flying group of two, three, or four F-4s could hit targets almost anywhere in Iraq. Using American tactics developed in Vietnam, Iranian pilots overcame Iraqi/Soviet SA-2 and SA-3 antiaircraft missiles. They were less successful against Saddam's SA-6s.

Iran's Western-made air defense system seemed more effective than Iraq's Soviet-made counterpart. Nevertheless, Tehran experienced difficulty in operating and maintaining Hawk, Rapier, and Tigercat missiles, and instead used antiaircraft guns and man-portable missiles.

IRAQI RETREATS, 1982–84

The Iranian high command passed from regular military leaders to the clergy in mid-1982.

In March 1982, Tehran launched its Operation Undeniable Victory, which marked a major turning point as Iran penetrated Iraq's "impenetrable" lines, split Iraq's forces, and forced the Iraqis to retreat. Its forces broke the Iraqi line near Susangerd, separating Iraqi units in northern and southern Khuzestan.

Within a week, they succeeded in destroying a large part of three Iraqi divisions. This operation, another combined effort of the army, the Pasdaran, and Basij, was a turning point in the war because the strategic initiative shifted from Iraq to Iran.

In May 1982, Iranian units finally regained Khorramshahr, but with extremely high casualties. After this victory, the Iranians continued to maintain pressure on the remaining Iraqi forces, and President Saddam Hussein announced that the Iraqi units would withdraw from

Iranian territory. That was followed by his ordering a withdrawal to the original international borders, believing that Iran would agree to end the war.

Iran refused to accept this withdrawal as the end of the conflict, and continued with thrusts into Iraq. In late June 1982, Baghdad stated its willingness to negotiate a settlement of the war and to withdraw its forces from Iran. Again Iran refused.

In July 1982 Tehran launched Operation Ramadan on Iraqi territory, near Basra. Although Basra was within range of Iranian artillery, the clergy used "human-wave" attacks by the Pasdaran and Basij against the city's defenses, apparently waiting for a coup to topple the Iraqi leader. This was one of the biggest land battles since 1945.

Ranging in age from only nine to more than fifty, these eager but relatively untrained soldiers swept over minefields and fortifications to clear safe paths for the tanks. All such assaults faced Iraqi artillery fire and the casualties were horrendous. They did enable Iran to recover some territory before the Iraqis could repulse the bulk of the invading forces.

By the end of 1982, Iraq had been resupplied with new Soviet materiel, and the ground war entered a new phase. Iraq used newly acquired T-55 tanks and T-62 tanks, BM-21 Stalin Organ rocket launchers, and Mi-24 helicopter gunships in a bid to prepare a Soviet-type three-line defense, replete with obstacles, minefields, and fortified positions. Saddam's Combat Engineer Corps proved efficient in constructing bridges across water obstacles, in laying minefields, and in preparing new defense lines and fortifications.

Throughout 1983 both sides demonstrated their ability to absorb and to inflict severe losses. Iraq, in particular, proved adroit at constructing defensive strong points and flooding lowland areas to stymie the Iranian thrusts, hampering the advance of mechanized units. Both sides also experienced difficulties in effectively utilizing their armor. Rather than maneuver, they tended to dig in tanks and use them as artillery pieces. Furthermore, both sides failed to master tank gunsights and fire controls, making themselves vulnerable to anti-tank weapons.

In 1983 Iran launched three major, but unsuccessful, human wave offensives, again with huge losses. On February 6, Tehran, using two hundred thousand "last reserve" Pasdaran troops, attacked along a twenty-five-mile stretch near Al Amarah, a couple of hundred miles southeast of Baghdad.

Backed by air, armor, and artillery support, Iran's six-division thrust was strong enough to break through. In response, Baghdad countered with massive air attacks, involving more than two hundred sorties, many flown by attack helicopters. More than six thousand Iranians were killed that day, having achieved only minute gains.

Similarly, in April 1983, the Mandali-Baghdad north/central sector witnessed fierce fighting, as repeated Iranian attacks were stopped by Iraqi mechanized and infantry divisions.

Casualties throughout remained high, and by the end of 1983, an estimated hundred-and-twenty thousand Iranians and about half that number of Iraqis had been killed. Despite these losses, Iran by late 1983 held a distinct advantage in the attempt to wage and eventually win the war of attrition.

Beginning in 1984, Baghdad's military goal changed from controlling Iranian territory to denying Tehran any major gain inside Iraq. Furthermore, Iraq tried to force Iran to the negotiating table.

First, President Saddam Hussein sought to increase the war's manpower and economic cost to Iran. For this purpose, Iraq purchased new weapons, mainly from the Soviet Union and France. Iraq also completed the construction of what came to be known as "killing zones" (which consisted primarily of artificially flooded areas near Basra) to stop Iranian units. In addition, according to *Jane's Defence Weekly* and other sources, Baghdad used chemical weapons against Iranian troop concentrations and launched attacks on many economic centers.

Despite Iraqi determination to halt further Iranian progress, Iranian units, in March 1984, captured parts of the Majnun Islands, whose oil fields had economic as well as strategic value.

Second, Iraq turned to diplomatic and political means. In April 1984, Saddam Hussein proposed to meet Ayatollah Khomeini personally in a neutral location to discuss peace negotiations. But Tehran rejected this offer as well, and restated its refusal to negotiate with President Hussein.

Third, Iraq sought to involve the superpowers as a means of ending the conflict. The Iraqis believed this objective could be achieved by attacking Iranian shipping. Initially, Baghdad used borrowed French Super-Etendard aircraft armed with Exocet missiles.

In 1984 Iraq returned these airplanes to France and purchased approximately thirty Mirage F-1 fighters equipped with Exocets. Iraq launched a new series of attacks on shipping on February 1, 1984.

THE WAR OF ATTRITION, 1984–87

By 1984 it was reported that some three hundred thousand Iranian soldiers and at least a quarter million Iraqi troops had been killed or wounded.

Most foreign military analysts felt that neither the Iraqis nor the Iranians used their modern equipment efficiently. Frequently, sophisticated materiel was left unused, when a massive modern assault could have won the battle for either side. Tanks and armored vehicles were dug in and used as static artillery, instead of being maneuvered to lead or to support an assault.

William O. Staudenmaeir, a seasoned military analyst, reported that "the land-computing sights on the Iraqi tanks [were] seldom used. This lowered the accuracy of the T-62 tanks to World War II standards." In addition, both sides frequently abandoned heavy equipment in the battle zone because they lacked the skilled technical personnel needed to carry out minor repairs.

Analysts also assert that the two states' armies showed little coordination and that some units in the field have been left to fight largely on their own. In this protracted war of attrition, soldiers and officers alike failed to display initiative or professional expertise in combat.

Difficult decisions, which should have had immediate attention, were invariably referred by section commanders to the capitals for action. Except for predictable bursts on important anniversaries, by the mid-1980s the war was stalemated.

In early 1984, Iran had begun Operation Dawn V, which was meant to split the Iraqi 3rd Army Corps and 4th Army Corps near Basra. An estimated half million Pasdaran and Basij forces, using shallow boats or on foot, moved to within a few miles of the strategic Basra-Baghdad waterway.

Between February 29 and March 1, in one of the largest battles of the war, the two armies clashed and inflicted more than twenty-five-thousand fatalities on each other. Without armored and air support of their own, the Iranians faced Iraqi tanks, mortars, and helicopter gunships.

Within a few weeks, Tehran opened another front in the shallow lakes of the Hawizah Marshes, just east of Al Qurnah, in Iraq, adjacent to the confluence of the Tigris and Euphrates rivers. Iraqi forces, using Soviet- and French-made helicopter gunships, inflicted heavy casualties on five Iranian brigades (fifteen-thousand men) in this Battle of Majnun.

Lacking equipment to open secure passages through Iraqi mine-fields, and having too few tanks, the Iranian command again resorted to the suicidal human-wave tactic. In March 1984, an East European journalist claimed that he "saw tens of thousands of children, roped together in groups of about twenty (to prevent the faint-hearted from deserting), make such an attack."

The Iranians made little, if any, progress despite these sacrifices. Perhaps as a result of this performance, a few weeks later, Tehran, for the first time, used a regular army unit, the 92nd Armored Division, at the Battle of the Marshes. Within a four-week period between February and March 1984, the Iraqis reportedly killed forty-thousand Iranians and lost nine thousand of their own men, but even this was deemed an unacceptable ratio, and in February the Iraqi command ordered the use of chemical weapons.

Despite repeated Iraqi denials, between May 1981 and March 1984, Iran charged Iraq with forty uses of chemical weapons. The year 1984 closed with part of the Majnun Islands and a few pockets of Iraqi territory in Iranian hands. Casualties notwithstanding, Tehran had maintained its military posture, while Baghdad was reevaluating its overall strategy.

The major development in 1985 was the increased targeting of population centers and industrial facilities by both combatants. In May, Iraq began aircraft attacks, long-range artillery attacks, and sur-face-to-surface missile attacks on Tehran and other major Iranian cities.

Between August and November, Iraq raided Kharg Island forty-four times in a futile attempt to destroy its installations. Iran responded with its own air raids and missile attacks on Baghdad and other Iraqi towns. In addition, Tehran systematized its periodic stop-and-search operations, which were conducted to verify the cargo contents of ships in the Persian Gulf and to seize war materiel destined for Iraq.

The only major ground offensive, involving an estimated sixty-thousand Iranian troops, occurred in March 1985, near Basra; once again, the assault proved inconclusive except for heavy casualties.

In 1986, however, Iraq suffered a major loss in the southern region. On February 9, Iran launched a successful surprise amphibious assault across the Shatt al Arab and captured the abandoned Iraqi oil port of Al Faw.

The occupation of Al Faw, a logistical feat, involved thirty-thousand regular Iranian soldiers who rapidly entrenched themselves. Saddam Hussein vowed to eliminate the bridgehead "at all costs," and in April 1988 the Iraqis succeeded in regaining the Al Faw peninsula.

Late, in March 1986, the UN secretary general, Javier Perez de Cuellar, formally accused Iraq of using chemical weapons against Iran. Citing the report of four chemical warfare experts whom the UN had sent to Iran in February and March 1986, the secretary general called on Baghdad to end its violation of the 1925 Geneva Protocol on the use of chemical weapons.

The UN report concluded that "Iraqi forces have used chemical warfare against Iranian forces." The weapons used included both mustard gas and nerve gas.

The report further stated, "The use of chemical weapons appeared to be more extensive [in 1981] than in 1984." Iraq attempted to deny using chemicals, but the evidence, in the form of many badly burned casualties flown to European hospitals for treatment, was overwhelming. According to a British representative at the Conference on Disarmament in Geneva in July 1986, "Iraqi chemical warfare was responsible for about ten thousand casualties."

In March 1988, Iraq was again charged with a major use of chemical warfare while retaking Halabjah, a Kurdish town in northeastern Iraq, near the Iranian border.

The Iranian Foreign Minister at the time, Ali Akbar Velayati had a lot to say about the use of these weapons at the January 1989 Paris Conference on the Prohibition of Chemical Weapons. In another report titled "Emergency Treatment of Chemical Weapons Casualties—Field Experiences," published in the ASA Newsletter by Dr. Amir Saghafinia in June 1991,[1] there were at least ten thousand Iranian troops killed together with about five thousand civilians. Another fifty thousand were moderately or severely injured and a similar number suffered mild injuries.

Meanwhile, the war went on. Unable in 1986 to dislodge the Iranians from Al Faw, the Iraqis went on the offensive; they captured the city of Mehran in May, only to lose it in July 1986. The rest of 1986 witnessed small hit-and-run attacks by both sides, while the Iranians massed almost half-a-million troops for another promised "final offensive," which did not occur.

But in July the Iraqis, perhaps for the first time since the outbreak of hostilities, began a concerted air-strike campaign.

Heavy attacks on Kharg Island forced Iran to rely on makeshift installations farther south in the Gulf at Sirri Island and Larak Island. Thereupon, Iraqi jets, refueling in midair or using a Saudi military base, hit Sirri and Larak. The two belligerents also attacked a hundred-and-eleven neutral ships in the Gulf in 1986.

Meanwhile, to help defend itself, Iraq had built impressive fortifications along the eight-hundred-mile war front.

Iraq devoted particular attention to the southern city of Basra, where concrete-roofed bunkers, tank- and artillery-firing positions, minefields, and stretches of barbed wire, all shielded by an artificially flooded lake eighteen miles long and about a mile and a half wide were constructed. Most visitors to the area acknowledged Iraq's effective use of combat engineering to erect these barriers.

By late 1986, rumors of a final Iranian offensive against Basra proliferated. On January 9, 1987, Operation Karbala Five began, with Iranian units pushing westward between Fish Lake and the Shatt al Arab. This annual "final offensive" captured the town of Duayji and inflicted twenty thousand casualties on Iraq, but at the cost of three times as many Iranian casualties. In this intensive operation, Baghdad also lost forty-five airplanes.

Attempting to capture Basra, Tehran launched several attacks, some of them well-disguised diversion assaults such as Operation Karbala Six and Operation Karbala Seven.

Iran finally aborted Operation Karbala Five on February 26, 1987. Although the Iranian push came close to breaking Iraq's last line of defense east of Basra, Tehran was unable to score the decisive breakthrough required to win outright victory, or even to secure relative gains over Iraq.

In late May 1987, just when the war seemed to have reached a complete stalemate on the southern front, reports from Iran indicated that the conflict was intensifying on Iraq's northern front.

This assault, Operation Karbala Ten, was a joint effort by Iranian units and Iraqi Kurdish rebels. They surrounded the garrison at Mawat, endangering Iraq's oil fields near Kirkuk and the northern oil pipeline to Turkey.

Believing it could win the war merely by holding the line and inflicting unacceptable losses on the attacking Iranians, Iraq initially adopted a static defensive strategy. This was successful in repelling successive Iranian offensives until 1986 and 1987, when the Al-Faw peninsula was lost and Iranian troops reached the gates of Al-Basrah.

Embarrassed by the loss of the peninsula and concerned by the threat to his second largest city, Saddam ordered a change in strategy. From a defensive posture, in which the only offensive operations were counterattacks to relieve forces under pressure or to exploit failed Iranian assaults, the Iraqis adopted an offensive strategy. More decision-making authority was delegated to senior military commanders.

The change also indicated a maturing of Iraqi military capabilities and an improvement in the armed forces' effectiveness. The success of this new strategy, plus the attendant change in doctrine and procedures, virtually eliminated Iranian military capabilities.

As the war continued, Iran was increasingly short of spare parts for damaged airplanes and had lost a large number of airplanes in combat. As a result, by late 1987 Iran had become less able to mount an effective defense against the resupplied Iraqi air force, let alone stage aerial counterattacks.

THE TANKER WAR, 1984–87

Much of Iraq's export capability was lost during the Iran-Iraq War, either to war-related damage or due to political reasons. In 1982, for instance, Syria (allied with Iran at the time) closed the five-hundred-mile, 650,000-bbl/d-capacity Banias pipeline, which had been a vital Iraqi access route to the Mediterranean Sea and European oil markets.

By 1983, Iraq's export capabilities were only 700,000 bbl/d, or less than 30 per cent of operable field production capacity at that time.

Iran's revenue share fell after the 1978/79 Iranian Revolution, followed soon thereafter by the Iran-Iraq War for much of the 1980s.. All Iranian onshore crude oil production and output from the Forozan field (which is blended with crude streams from the Abuzar and Doroud fields) is exported from the Kharg Island terminal located in the northern Gulf. The terminal's original capacity of seven million bbl/d was nearly eliminated by more than nine thousand bombing raids during the Iran-Iraq War.

The tanker war seemed likely to precipitate a major international incident for two reasons. First, some seventy percent of Japanese, half of West European, and seven percent of American oil imports came from the Persian Gulf in the early 1980s. Second, the assault on tankers involved neutral shipping as well as ships of the belligerent states.

The tanker war had two phases. The relatively obscure first phase began in 1981, and the well-publicized second phase started in 1984.

As early as May 1981, Baghdad had unilaterally declared a war zone and had officially warned all ships heading to or returning from Iranian ports in the northern zone of the Gulf to stay away or, if they entered, to proceed at their own risk. The main targets in this phase were the ports of Bandar-e Khomeini and Bandar-e Mashur; very few ships were hit outside this zone. Despite the proximity of these ports to Iraq, the Iraqi navy did not play an important role in the operations.

Instead, Baghdad used Super Frelon helicopters equipped with Exocet missiles or Mirage F-1s and MiG-23s to hit its targets. Naval operations came to a halt, presumably because Iraq and Iran had lost many of their ships by early 1981; the lull in the fighting lasted for two years.

In March 1984, the tanker war entered its second phase when Iraq initiated sustained naval operations in its self-declared eight hundred-mile maritime exclusion zone, extending from the mouth of the Shatt al Arab to Iran's port of Bushehr. In 1981 Baghdad had attacked Iranian ports and oil complexes as well as neutral tankers and ships sailing to and from Iran.

In March 1984 an Iraqi Super Etendard fired an Exocet missile at a Greek tanker south of Kharg Island. Until the March assault, Iran had not intentionally attacked civilian ships in the Gulf. Neutral merchant ships became favorite targets, and the long-range Super-Etendards flew sorties farther south. Seventy-one merchant ships were attacked in 1984 alone, compared with forty-eight in the first three years of the war.

Iraq's motives in increasing the tempo included a desire to break the stalemate, presumably by cutting off Iran's oil exports and by thus forcing Tehran to the negotiating table. Repeated Iraqi strikes failed to put Iran's main oil exporting terminal at Kharg Island out of commission, however.

The new wave of Iraqi assaults, however, led Iran to reciprocate. In April 1984, Tehran launched its first attack against civilian commercial shipping by shelling an Indian freighter. Iran attacked a Kuwaiti oil tanker near Bahrain on May 13 and then a Saudi tanker in Saudi waters five days later, making it clear that if Iraq continued to interfere with Iran's shipping, no Gulf state would be safe.

Most observers considered that Iraqi attacks outnumbered Iranian assaults by three to one. Iran's retaliatory attacks were largely ineffective because a limited number of aircraft equipped with long-range anti-ship missiles and ships with long-range surface-to-surface missiles were deployed. Moreover, despite repeated Iranian threats to close the Strait of Hormuz, Iran itself depended on the sea-lanes for vital oil exports. These sustained attacks cut Iranian oil exports in half, reduced shipping in the Gulf by twenty-five percent, led Lloyd's of London to increase its insurance rates on tankers, and slowed Gulf oil supplies to the rest of the world; at the same time, the Saudi decision in 1984 to shoot down an Iranian Phantom jet intruding in Saudi territorial waters played an important role in ending both belligerents' attempts to internationalize the tanker war.

Iraq and Iran accepted a 1984 UN-sponsored moratorium on the shelling of civilian targets, and Tehran later proposed an extension of the moratorium to include Gulf shipping, a proposal the Iraqis rejected unless it were to include their own Gulf ports.

Iraq began ignoring the moratorium soon after it went into effect and stepped up its air raids on tankers serving Iran and Iranian oil-exporting facilities in 1986 and 1987, attacking even vessels that belonged to the conservative Arab states of the Persian Gulf. Iran responded by escalating its attacks on shipping serving Arab ports in the Gulf. As Kuwaiti vessels made up a large portion of the targets in these retaliatory raids, the Kuwaiti government sought protection from the international community in the fall of 1986.

The Soviet Union responded first, agreeing to charter several Soviet tankers to Kuwait in early 1987.

Washington, which had been approached first by Kuwait and which had postponed its decision, eventually followed Moscow's lead. United States involvement was sealed by the May 17, 1987, Iraqi missile attack on the USS *Stark*, in which thirty seven crew members were killed. Baghdad apologized and claimed that the attack was a mistake.

Ironically, Washington used the *Stark* incident to blame Iran for escalating the war and sent its own ships to the Gulf to escort eleven Kuwaiti tankers that were "reflagged" with the American flag and had American crews.

Iran refrained from attacking the United States naval force directly, but it used various forms of harassment, including mines, hit-and-run attacks by small patrol boats manned by Pasdaran crews, and periodic stop-and-search operations.

On several occasions, Tehran fired its Chinese-made Silkworm missiles on Kuwait from Al Faw Peninsula. When Iranian forces hit the reflagged tanker *Sea Isle City* in October 1987, Washington retaliated by destroying an oil platform in the Rostam field and by using US Navy SEAL commandos to blow up a second one nearby.

Within a few weeks of the *Stark* incident, Iraq resumed its raids on tankers but moved its attacks farther south, near the Strait of Hormuz. Washington played a central role in framing UN Security Council Resolution 598 on the Gulf war, passed unanimously on July 20; Western attempts to isolate Iran were frustrated, however, when Tehran rejected the resolution because it did not meet its requirement that Iraq should be punished for initiating the conflict.

In early 1988, the Gulf was a crowded theater of operations. At least ten Western navies and eight regional navies were patrolling the area, the site of weekly incidents in which merchant vessels were crippled. The Arab Ship Repair Yard in Bahrain and its counterpart in Dubayy, United Arab Emirates (UAE), were unable to keep up with the repairs needed by the ships damaged in these attacks.

SUPERPOWER INVOLVEMENT

Iranian military gains inside Iraq after 1984 were a major reason for increased superpower involvement in the war. In February 1986, Iranian units captured the port of Al Faw, which had oil facilities and was one of Iraq's major oil-exporting ports before the war.

In early 1987, both superpowers indicated their interest in the security of the region. Soviet deputy foreign minister Vladimir Petrovsky made a Middle East tour expressing his country's concern over the effects of the Iran-Iraq War.

In May 1987, United States assistant secretary of state Richard Murphy also toured the Gulf emphasizing to friendly Arab states the United States commitment in the region, a pledge which had become suspect as a result of Washington's transfer of arms to the Iranians, evidently as an incentive for them to assist in freeing American hostages held in Lebanon.

In another diplomatic effort, both superpowers supported the UN Security Council resolutions seeking an end to the war.

The war appeared to be entering a new phase in which the superpowers were becoming more involved. For instance, the Soviet Union, which had suspended military shipments to both Iran and Iraq in 1980, resumed large-scale arms shipments to Iraq in 1982 after Iran banned the (Communist) Tudeh and tried and executed most of its leaders.

Subsequently, despite its professed neutrality, the Soviet Union became the major supplier of sophisticated arms to Iraq. In 1985 the United States began clandestine direct and indirect negotiations with Iranian officials that resulted in several arms shipments to Iran.

By late spring of 1987, the superpowers became more directly involved because they feared that the fall of Basra might lead to a pro-Iranian Islamic republic in largely Shi'ite-populated southern Iraq. They were also concerned about the intensified tanker war.

SPECIAL WEAPONS

To avoid defeat, Iraq sought out every possible weapon. This included developing a self-sustaining capability to produce militarily significant quantities of chemical warfare agents. In defense, integrating chemical weapons offered a solution to the masses of lightly armed Basij and Pasdaran.

Chemical weapons were singularly effective when used on troop assembly areas and supporting artillery. Similarly, when conducting offensive operations, Iraq routinely supported the attacks with deep fires and integrated chemical fires on forward defenses, command posts, artillery positions, and logistical facilities.

During the Iran-Iraq War, Iraq developed the ability to produce, store, and use chemical weapons. These included H-series blister and G-series nerve agents. Iraq built these agents into various offensive munitions including rockets, artillery shells, aerial bombs, and warheads on the Al Hussein Scud missile variant. There is also good evidence that Iraqi fighter-attack aircraft dropped mustard and tabun-filled five hundred-pound bombs and half-ton bombs containing mustard gas on Iranian targets.

Other reports indicate that Iraq may have also installed spray tanks on an unknown number of helicopters or dropped fifty five-gallon drums filled with unknown agents (probably mustard) from low altitudes.

Iran launched an unsuccessful attack on the Iraqi Osiraq nuclear reactor on September 30, 1980.

For its part, almost a year later, on June 7, 1981, Israel initiated an air attack on the same Iraqi Osiraq reactor, destroying it. Iraq launched seven air attacks on the Iranian nuclear reactor at Bushehr between 1984 and 1988 during the Iran-Iraq War, ultimately destroying the facility.

In response to Iranian missile attacks against Baghdad, the Iraqis fired almost two hundred missiles over a six week period at Iranian cities in 1988. That was an intense period of conflict commonly referred to as the "War of the Cities."

The Iraqi missile attacks caused little destruction, but each warhead had a psychological and political impact—boosting Iraqi morale while causing almost a third of Tehran's population to flee the city. The threat of rocketing the Iranian capital with missiles capable of carrying chemical warheads is cited as a significant reason why Iran accepted a disadvantageous peace agreement.

WAR TERMINATION

Four major battles were fought from April to August 1988, in which the Iraqis routed or defeated the Iranians. In the first offensive, named Blessed Ramadan, Iraqi Revolutionary and regular Army units recaptured the Al-Faw peninsula.

The thirty-six-hour battle was conducted in a militarily sophisticated manner with two main thrusts, supported by heli-borne and amphibious landings, and low-level fixed-wing attack sorties.

In this battle, the Iraqis effectively used chemical weapons (CW), using nerve and blister agents against Iranian command and control facilities, artillery positions, and logistics points. Three subsequent operations followed much the same pattern, although they were somewhat less complex. After rehearsals, the Iraqis launched successful attacks on Iranian forces in the Fish Lake and Shalamjah areas near Basra and recaptured the oil-rich Majnun Islands.

Farther to the north, in the last major engagement before the August 1988 cease-fire, Iraqi armored and mechanized forces penetrated deep into Iran, defeating Iranian forces and capturing huge amounts of armor and artillery. In the fall of 1988, the Iraqis displayed in Baghdad captured Iranian weapons amounting to more than three-quarters of the Iranian armor inventory and almost half of its artillery pieces and armored personnel carriers.

The Iran-Iraq war lasted nearly eight years, from September of 1980 until August of 1988. It ended when Iran accepted United Nations Security Council Resolution 598, leading to an August 20, 1988 cease-fire.

Casualty figures are uncertain, though estimates suggest more than one and a half million war and war-related casualties—perhaps as many as a million people died, many more were wounded, and millions were made refugees. Iraq's victory was certainly not without cost. The Iraqis suffered an estimated three-hundred-and-seventy-five-thousand casualties, the equivalent of 5.6 million for a population the size of the United States. Another sixty thousand were taken prisoner by the Iranians. Iran's losses may have included more than a million people killed or maimed.

The war claimed at least three-hundred thousand Iranian lives and injured more than a half-a-million out of a total population, which by the war's end, was nearly sixty million.

Without diminishing the horror of either war, Iranian losses in the eight-year Iran-Iraq war appear modest compared with those of the European contestants in the four years of World War I, shedding some light on the limits of the Iranian tolerance for martyrdom.

During the Great War, German losses were over 1,700,000 killed and over four million wounded [out of a total population of over sixty-five million]. Germany's losses, relative to total national population, were at least five times higher than Iran. France suffered over 1,300,000 dead and more than four million wounded. The percentages of pre-war population killed or wounded were nine percent of Germany, eleven percent of France, and eight percent of Britain.

At the end, virtually none of the issues which are usually blamed for the war had been resolved. Although Iraq won the war militarily, and possessed a significant military advantage over Iran in 1989, the 1991 Persian Gulf War reduced Iraq's capabilities to a point where a rough equivalent existed between Iran and Iraq-conditions similar to those found in 1980.

The UN-arranged cease-fire merely put an end to the fighting, leaving two isolated states to pursue an arms race with each other, and with the other countries in the region. The Iraqi military machine—numbering more than a million men with an extensive arsenal of CW, extended range Scud missiles, a large air force and one of the world's larger armies—emerged as the premier armed force in the Persian Gulf region. In the Middle East, only the Israel Defense Force had superior capability.

Khomeini died on June 3, 1989. The Assembly of Experts—an elected body of senior Iranian clerics—chose the outgoing president of the republic, Ayatollah Ali Hoseini Khamene'i, to be his successor as the "Supreme" national religious leader in what proved to be a smooth transition. In this regard he was senior even to the elected president of the country, an anomaly seen only in the most repressive of states such as North Korea and, until recently, Libya.

In August 1989, Ali Akbar Hashemi Rafsanjani, the speaker of the National Assembly, was elected President by an overwhelming majority. The new clerical regime gave Iranian national interests primacy over Islamic doctrine.

A variety of unresolved humanitarian issues from the Iran-Iraq war include a failure to identify combatants killed in action and to exchange information on those killed or missing. Iran agreed to the release of more than five-thousand Iraqi POW's in April 1998, and news organizations reported intermittent meetings throughout the remainder of the year between Iranian and Iraqi government officials toward reaching a final agreement on the remaining POW's held by each side.

The Iranian government pledged to settle the remaining POW issues with Iraq in 1999. And joint Iran-Iraq search operations were initiated to identify remains of those missing in action.

3

IRAN'S SHI'ITES:
PROVOCATIVE AND DRIVEN

**The Shi'ites, with their doctrinal emphasis
on martyrdom and victimhood, thrive on
their own marginalization.**

The Shi'ites, unquestionably, are Iran. And Iran is almost overwhelmingly Shi'ite. It has been that way for more than a thousand years.

There was a time, not very long after the death of Mohammed the Prophet, Peace be unto Him, when Shi'ite dynasties ruled as far afield as Egypt, Tunisia and parts of the Eastern Mediterranean. Then came the religious schism in the early centuries of Islam that drove Sunnis and Shi'ites irrevocably apart, an event which the London *Economist* says "was blamed for blunting the new religion's expansion." Later, it states, the schism was responsible for weakening Moslems in general and opening the way to invasion by infidel hordes.[1]

"Yet for the last eight hundred years or so, sectarian divisions have lain mostly dormant. Shias tended to live mostly in isolation and on the margins—in the mountains of Lebanon and Yemen, on the hot, swampy shores of the Persian Gulf, in self-contained Indian trading communities. In Iran, where they formed a majority, Shi'ism overlapped with and reinforced an exclusive Iranian national identity."[2]

While I—an unbeliever in the eyes of the average Shi'ite faithful—could hardly do justice to the tapestry of rich and varied tenets of such a dedicated Islamic tradition, it would be remiss of me not to include a look at this great culture. Space constraints aside, it will be brief and insightful.

Most significant perhaps, I cherish the friendship of my Shi'ite friends and associates, and there are many, both in Lebanon and in West Africa. I have done business with some and gone to war with others. They, in turn, have made me aware of their astonishing depth of commitment, for it is not only east of Suez that the Shi'ite heritage —sometimes provocative, always driven—continues to make its mark.

67

In associating with these people, I tended to encounter a basic, honorable society. In going into combat in Sierra Leone with Hassan Delbani—he was one of our side gunners in the rickety old Mi-24 helicopter gunship that eventually drove Foday Sankoh's rebels from the gates of Freetown—I encountered a tough and resourceful combatant. He is also among the bravest men I know, having gone in under fire after the rebels had overrun parts of the city, and singlehandedly rescued hundreds of civilians from an uncertain fate. I'd have him at my back in a tight spot anytime.[3]

In characterizing Hassan in my book *War Dog: Fighting Other People's Wars* as the new face of Shi'ite Islam—AK in one hand, laptop in the other (together with requisite cell phone on his belt)—I sought to depict a remarkably versatile generation of fighters that has emerged from the ruins of Tyre, Sidon and Beirut's southern suburbs.

Exactly the same situation holds true now for Iran, where a heady confrontation between old and new will eventually lead to that country taking its rightful place within the community of nations. Even the Shi'ite hierarchy is aware that history does not stand still.

But the Shi'ites also have their enemies, most of them traditional. U.S. Intelligence sources speak of a recent letter purported to have been written by Abu Musab al Zarqawi, who is said to lead the al-Qaeda insurgency in Iraq. The Shi'ites, he declared, are a more pernicious enemy than the Americans and the best strategy for the poor, weak and sleepy Sunnis is to "strike their religious, military and other cadres"—in other words, to stoke *fitna*,[4] "so as to preclude the transfer of power to a Shi'ite dominated democracy."

On the morning of the 2004 Ashoura, a Shi'ite day of mourning and bloody self-flagellation that commemorates Shi'ite suffering at the hands of the Sunnis, a Kuwaiti, Sheikh Hamed al-Ali, posted on his website a letter condemning the rite as "the world's biggest display of heathens and idolatry." He accused Iraq's Shi'ites of "plotting to assassinate Sunni leaders, grab the Gulf's oil and form an evil axis linking Washington, Tel Aviv and the Shi'ite holy city of Najaf."

Something similar applies to Saudi Arabia's puritan revival known as Wahhabism. This fundamentalist sect has been particularly hostile towards Shi'ites in the Kingdom in a tradition that is both brutal and antagonistic and that goes back centuries.

Even today, *The Economist* tells us, the large Saudi Shi'ite minority is still denied many rights "and vilifies it in the Kingdom's school textbooks."

RELIGIOUS LIFE IN CONTEMPORARY IRAN

Washington's Library of Congress, Federal Research Division, Country Studies, provides a comprehensive overview on the subject on its website.[5] The overwhelming majority of Iranians—at least ninety percent of the total population—are Muslims who adhere to Shi'ite (or Shi'a) Islam, it states. In contrast, the majority of Muslims throughout the world follow Sunni Islam. Of the several Shi'ite sects, the Twelve Imam or Twelver (*ithna- ashari*), is dominant in Iran; most Shi'ites in Bahrain, Iraq, and Lebanon also follow this sect.

All Shi'ite sects originated among early Muslim dissenters in the first three centuries following the death of the Prophet Mohammed in AD 632.

The principal belief of Twelvers, but not of other Shi'ites, is that the spiritual and temporal leadership of the Muslim community passed from Mohammed to Ali and then sequentially to eleven of Ali's direct male descendants, a tenet rejected by Sunnis. Over the centuries various other theological differences have developed between Twelver Shi'ites and Sunnis.

Distinctive Beliefs

Although Shi'ites have lived in Iran since the earliest days of Islam, and there was one Shi'ite dynasty in part of Iran during the 10th and 11th centuries, it is believed that most Iranians were Sunnis until the 17th century.

The Safavid dynasty made Shi'ite Islam the official state religion in the 16th century and aggressively proselytized on its behalf. It is also believed that by the mid-17th century most people in what is now Iran had become Shi'ites, an affiliation that has continued.

All Shi'ite Muslims believe there are seven pillars of faith, which detail the acts necessary to demonstrate and reinforce faith.

The first five of these pillars are shared with Sunni Muslims. They are *shahada*, or the confession of faith; *namaz*, or ritualized prayer; *zakat*, or almsgiving; *sawm*, fasting and contemplation during daylight hours during the lunar month of Ramazan; and *hajj*, or pilgrimage to the holy cities of Mecca and Medina, once in a lifetime if financially feasible.

The other two pillars, which are not shared with Sunnis, are *jihad*—or crusade to protect Islamic lands, beliefs, and institutions, and the requirement to do good works and to avoid all evil thoughts, words, and deeds.

Twelver Shi'ite Muslims also believe in five basic principles of faith: there is one God, who is a unitary divine being, in contrast to the trinitarian being of Christians; the Prophet Mohammed is the last of a line of prophets beginning with Abraham and including Moses and Jesus, and he was chosen by God to present His message to mankind; there is a resurrection of the body and soul on the last or judgment day; divine justice will reward or punish believers based on actions undertaken through their own free will; and Twelve Imams were successors to Mohammed. The first three of these beliefs are also shared by non-Twelver Shi'ites and Sunni Muslims.

The distinctive dogma and institution of Shi'ite Islam is the Imamate, which includes the idea that the successor of Mohammed be more than merely a political leader.

The Imam must also be a spiritual leader, which means that he must have the ability to interpret the inner mysteries of the *Qur'an* and the *shariat*. The Twelver Shi'ites further believe that the Twelve Imams who succeeded the Prophet were sinless and free from error and had been chosen by God through Mohammed.

The Imamate began with Ali, who is also accepted by Sunni Muslims as the fourth of the "rightly guided caliphs" to succeed the Prophet.

Shi'ites revere Ali as the First Imam, and his descendants, beginning with his sons Hassan and Husayn (variously also seen as Hosein and Hussein), continue the line of the Imams until the Twelfth, who is believed to have ascended into a supernatural state to return to earth on judgment day.

Shi'ites point to the close lifetime association of Mohammed with Ali. When Ali was six years old, he was invited by the Prophet to live with him, and Shi'ites believe Ali was the first person to make the declaration of faith in Islam.

Ali also slept in Mohammed's bed on the night of the *hijra*, or migration from Mecca to Medina, when it was feared that the house would be attacked by unbelievers and the Prophet stabbed to death. He fought in all the battles Mohammed did except one, and the Prophet chose him to be the husband of his favorite daughter, Fatima.

In Sunni Islam an imam is the leader of congregational prayer. Among the Shi'ites of Iran the term imam traditionally has been used only for Ali and his eleven descendants.

None of the Twelve Imams, with the exception of Ali, ever ruled an Islamic government. During their lifetimes, their followers hoped that they would assume the rulership of the Islamic community, a rule that was believed to have been wrongfully usurped. Because the Sunni caliphs were cognizant of this hope, the Imams generally were persecuted during the Umayyad and Abbasid dynasties. Therefore, the Imams tried to be as unobtrusive as possible and to live as far as was reasonable from the successive capitals of the Islamic empire.

During the 9th century Caliph Al Mamun, son of Caliph Harun ar Rashid, was favorably disposed toward the descendants of Ali and their followers. He invited the Eighth Imam, Reza (765–816), to come from Medina to his court at Merv (Mary in Turkmenistan). While Reza was residing at Merv, Mamun designated him as his successor in an apparent effort to avoid conflict among Muslims.

Reza's sister Fatima journeyed from Medina to be with her brother but took ill and died at Qom. A shrine developed around her tomb, and over the centuries Qom has become a major Shi'ite pilgrimage and theology center.

Mamun took Reza on his military campaign to retake Baghdad from political rivals.

On this trip Reza died unexpectedly in Khorasan. Reza was the only Imam to reside or die in what is now Iran. A major shrine, and eventually the city of Mashhad, grew up around his tomb, which has become the most important pilgrimage center in Iran. Several important theological schools are located in Mashhad, associated with the shrine of the Eighth Imam.

Reza's sudden death was a shock to his followers, many of whom believed that Mamun, out of jealousy for Reza's increasing popularity, had him poisoned. Mamun's suspected treachery against Reza and his family tended to reinforce a feeling already prevalent among his followers that the Sunni rulers were untrustworthy.

The Twelfth Imam is believed to have been only five years old when the Imamate descended upon him in AD 874 at the death of his father. The Twelfth Imam is usually known by his titles of *Imam-e Asr* (the Imam of the Age) and *Sahib az Zaman* (the Lord of Time). Because his followers feared he might be assassinated, the Twelfth Imam was hidden from public view and was seen only by a few of his closest deputies. Sunnis claim that he never existed or that he died while still a child.

Shi'ites believe that the Twelfth Imam remained on earth, but hidden from the public, for about seventy years, a period they refer to as the lesser occultation (*gheybat-e sughra*).

Shi'ites also believe that the Twelfth Imam has never died, but disappeared from earth in about 939. Since that time the greater occultation (*gheybat-e kubra*) of the Twelfth Imam has been in force and will last until God commands the Twelfth Imam to manifest himself on earth again as the Mahdi, or Messiah.[7] Shi'ites believe that during the greater occultation of the Twelfth Imam he is spiritually present—some believe that he is materially present as well—and he is besought to reappear in various invocations and prayers. His name is mentioned in wedding invitations, and his birthday is one of the most jubilant of all Shi'ite religious observances.

The Shi'ite doctrine of the Imamate was not fully elaborated until the tenth century. Other dogmas were developed still later.

A characteristic of Shi'ite Islam is the continual exposition and reinterpretation of doctrine. The most recent example is Khomeini's expounding of the doctrine of *velayat-e faqih*, or the political guardianship of the community of believers by scholars trained in religious law. This has not been a traditional idea in Shi'ite Islam and is, in fact, an innovation. The basic idea is that the clergy, by virtue of their superior knowledge of the laws of God, are the best qualified to rule the society of believers who are preparing themselves on earth to live eternally in heaven.

The concept of *velayat-e faqih* thus provides the doctrinal basis for theocratic government, an experiment that Twelver Imam Shi'ites had not attempted prior to the Iranian Revolution in 1979.

Religious Obligations

In addition to the seven principal tenets of faith, there are also traditional religious practices that are intimately associated with Shi'ite Islam. These include the observance of the month of martyrdom, Moharram, and pilgrimages to the shrines of the Twelve Imams and their various descendants.

The Moharram observances commemorate the death of the Third Imam, Husayn (or Hussein), who was the son of Ali and Fatima and the grandson of Mohammed. He was killed near Karbala in Iraq in AD 680 during a battle with troops supporting the Umayyad caliph. Husayn's death is commemorated by Shi'ites with passion plays and is an intensely religious time.

Pilgrimage to the shrines of Imams is a specific Shi'ite custom. The most important shrines in Iran are those for the Eighth Imam in Mashhad and for his sister Fatima in Qom. There are also important secondary shrines for other relatives of the Eighth Iman in Rey, adjacent to south Tehran, and in Shiraz. In virtually all towns and in many villages there are numerous lesser shrines, known as *imamzadehs*, which commemorate descendants of the imams who are reputed to have led saintly lives. Shi'ite pilgrims visit these sites because they believe that the imams and their relatives have power to intercede with God on behalf of petitioners.

The shrines in Iraq at Karbala and An Najaf are also greatly revered by Shi'ites. It is a tenet of the Faith to go on pilgrimage to the Iraqi holy rites.

Religious Institutions and Organizations
(From a prayer meeting at the University of Tehran, courtesy of the United Nations [John Isaac])

Historically, the single most important religious institution in Iran has been the mosque. In towns, congregational prayers, as well as prayers and rites associated with religious observances and important phases in the lives of Muslims, took place in mosques. It is interesting that Iranian Shi'ites, before the Revolution, did not generally attach great significance to institutionalization, however, and there was little emphasis on mosque attendance, even for the Friday congregational prayers. Mosques were primarily an urban phenomenon, and in most of the thousands of small villages there were no mosques. Mosques in the larger cities began to assume more important social roles during the 1970s; during the Revolution they played a prominent role in organizing people for the large demonstrations that took place in 1978 and 1979. Since that time their role has continued to expand, so that today mosques play important political and social roles as well as religious ones.

Another religious institution of major significance was a special building known as a *hoseiniyeh*, which existed in urban areas and traditionally served as sites for recitals commemorating the martyrdom of Husayn, especially during the month of Moharram.

In the 1970s, some *hoseiniyehs*, such as the Hoseiniyeh Irshad in Tehran, became politicized as prominent clerical and lay preachers used the symbol of the deaths as martyrs of Husayn and the other Imams as thinly veiled criticism of Mohammad Reza Shah's regime, thus helping to lay the groundwork for the Revolution in 1979.

Institutions providing religious education include madrassahs and maktabs. Madrassahs, or seminaries, historically have been important for advanced training in Shi'ite theology and jurisprudence.

Madrassahs are generally associated with noted Shi'ite scholars who have attained the rank of ayatollah. There are also some older madrassahs, established initially through endowments, at which several scholars may teach. Students, known as *talabehs*, live on the grounds of the madrassahs and are provided stipends for the duration of their studies, usually a minimum of seven years, during which they prepare for the examinations that qualify a seminary student to be a low-level preacher, or mullah.

At the time of the Revolution, there were slightly more than eleven thousand *talabehs* in Iran; approximately sixty percent of these were studying at the madrassahs in the city of Qom, another twenty-five percent were enrolled in the important madrassahs of Mashhad and Esfahan, and the rest were at madrassahs in Tabriz, Yazd, Shiraz, Tehran, Zanjan, and other cities.

Maktabs, primary schools run by the clergy, were the only educational institutions prior to the end of the nineteenth century when the first secular schools were established, and declined in numbers and importance as the government developed a national public school system beginning in the 1930s. Nevertheless, maktabs continued to exist as private religious schools right up to the Revolution. Since 1979 the public education system has been desecularized and the maktabs and their essentially religious curricula merged with government schools.

Another major religious institution in Iran is the shrine. There are more than a thousand shrines that vary from crumbling sites associated with local saints to the imposing shrines of Imam Reza and his sister Fatima in Mashhad and Qom, respectively.

These more famous shrines are huge complexes that include the mausoleums of the venerated Eighth Imam and his sister, tombs of former shahs, mosques, madrassahs, and libraries.

Imam Reza's shrine is the largest and is considered to be the holiest. In addition to the usual shrine accouterments, Imam Reza's shrine contains hospitals, dispensaries, a museum, and several mosques located in a series of courtyards surrounding his tomb. Most of the present shrine dates from the early fourteenth century, except for the dome, which was rebuilt after being damaged in an earthquake in 1673. The shrine's endowments and gifts are the largest of all religious institutions in the country.

Traditionally, free meals for as many as a thousand people a day are provided at the shrine. Although there are no special times for visiting this or other shrines, it is customary for pilgrimage traffic to be heaviest during Shi'ite holy periods. It has been estimated that more than three million pilgrims visit the shrine annually.

Visitors to Imam Reza's shrine represent all socioeconomic levels. Whereas piety is a motivation for many, others come to seek the spiritual grace or general good fortune that a visit to the shrine is believed to ensure. Commonly a pilgrimage is undertaken to petition Imam Reza to act as an intermediary between the pilgrim and God.

Since the 19th century, it has been customary among the bazaar class and members of the lower classes to recognize those who have made a pilgrimage to Mashhad by prefixing their names with the title mashti.

The next most important shrine is that of Imam Reza's sister, Fatima, known as *Hazarat-e Masumeh* (the Pure Saint). The present shrine dates from the early sixteenth century, although some later additions, including the gilded tiles, were affixed in the early nineteenth century.

Other important shrines are those of Shah Abdol Azim, a relative of Imam Reza, who is entombed at Rey, near Tehran, and Shah Cheragh, a brother of Imam Reza, who is buried in Shiraz.

A leading shrine honoring a person not belonging to the family of Imams is that of the Sufi master Sayyid Nimatollah Vali near Kerman. Shi'ites make pilgrimages to these shrines and the hundreds of local imamzadehs to petition the saints to grant them special favors or to help them through a period of troubles.

Because Shi'ites believe that the holy Imams can intercede for the dead as well as for the living, cemeteries traditionally have been located adjacent to the most important shrines in both Iran and Iraq. Corpses were transported overland for burial in Karbala in southern Iraq until the practice was prohibited in the 1930s. Corpses are still shipped to Mashhad and Qom for burial in the shrine cemeteries of these cities.

The constant movement of pilgrims from all over Iran to Mashhad and Qom has helped bind together a linguistically heterogeneous population. Pilgrims serve as major sources of information about conditions in different parts of the country and thus help to mitigate the parochialism of the regions.

A traditional source of financial support for all religious institutions has been the *vaqf*, a religious endowment by which land and other income-producing property is given in perpetuity for the maintenance of a shrine, mosque, madrassah, or charitable institution such as a hospital, library, or orphanage.

A *mutavalli* administers a *vaqf* in accordance with the stipulations in the donor's bequest. In many *vaqfs* the position of *mutavalli* is hereditary. Under the Pahlavis, the government attempted to exercise control over the administration of *vaqfs*, especially those of the larger shrines. This was a source of conflict with the clergy, who perceived the government's efforts as lessening their influence and authority in traditional religious matters.

The former government's interference with the administration of *vaqfs* led to a sharp decline in the number of *vaqf* bequests. Instead, wealthy and pious Shi'ites chose to give financial contributions directly to the leading ayatollahs in the form of *zakat*, or obligatory alms.

The clergy, in turn, used the funds to administer their madrassahs and to institute various educational and charitable programs, which indirectly provided them with more influence in society. The access of the clergy to a steady and independent source of funding was an important factor in their ability to resist state controls and eventually helped them direct the opposition to the shah.

The Religious Hierarchy
From the time that Twelver Shi'ite Islam emerged as a distinct religious denomination in the early 9th century, its clergy, or ulama, have played a prominent role in the development of its scholarly and legal tradition; however, the development of a distinct hierarchy among the Shi'ite clergy dates back only to the early 19th century.

Since that time the highest religious authority has been vested in the mujtahids, scholars who by virtue of their erudition in the science of religion (the *Qur'an*, the traditions of Mohammed and the imams, jurisprudence, and theology) and their attested ability to decide points of religious conduct, act as leaders of their community in matters concerning the particulars of religious duties.

Lay Shi'ites and lesser members of the clergy who lack such proficiency are expected to follow mujtahids in all matters pertaining to religion, but each believer is free to follow any mujtahid he chooses. Since the mid-19th century it has been common for several mujtahids concurrently to attain prominence and to attract large followings. During the 20th century, such mujtahids have been accorded the title of ayatollah. Occasionally an ayatollah achieves almost universal authority among Shi'ites and is given the title of *ayatollah ol ozma*, or grand ayatollah. Such authority was attained by as many as seven mujtahids simultaneously, including Ayatollah Khomeini, in the late 1970s.

To become a mujtahid, it is necessary to complete a rigorous and lengthy course of religious studies in one of the prestigious madrassahs of Qom or Mashhad in Iran or An Najaf in Iraq and to receive an authorization from a qualified mujtahid.

Of equal importance is either the explicit or the tacit recognition of a cleric as a mujtahid by laymen and scholars in the Shi'ite community. There is no set time for studying a particular subject, but serious preparation to become a mujtahid normally requires fifteen years to master the religious subjects deemed essential.

It is uncommon for any student to attain the status of mujtahid before the age of thirty; more commonly students are between forty and fifty years old when they achieve this distinction.

Most seminary students do not complete the full curriculum of studies to become mujtahids. Those who leave the madrassahs after completing the primary level can serve as prayer leaders, village mullahs, local shrine administrators, and other religious functionaries. Those who leave after completing the second level become preachers in town and city mosques. Students in the third level of study are those preparing to become mujtahids. The advanced students at this level are generally accorded the title of hojjatoleslam when they have completed all their studies.

The Shi'ite clergy in Iran wear a white turban and an aba, a loose, sleeveless brown cloak, open in front. A sayyid, who is a clergyman descended from Mohammed, wears a black turban and a black aba.

Unorthodox Shi'ite Religious Movements
Shah Ismail, the founder of the Safavid dynasty, who established Twelver Shi'ite Islam as the official religion of Iran at the beginning of the 16th century, was revered by his followers as a Sufi master.

Sufism, or Islamic mysticism, has a long tradition in Iran. It developed there and in other areas of the Islamic empire during the 9th century among Muslims who believed that worldly pleasures distracted from true concern with the salvation of the soul.

Sufis generally renounced materialism, which they believed supported and perpetuated political tyranny. Their name is derived from the Arabic word for wool, *suf*, and was applied to the early Sufis because of their habit of wearing rough wool next to their skin as a symbol of their asceticism. Over time a great variety of Sufi brotherhoods was formed, including several that were militaristic, such as the Safavid order, of which Ismail was the leader.

Although Sufis were associated with the early spread of Shi'ite ideas in the country, once the Shi'ite clergy had consolidated their authority over religion by the early seventeenth century, they tended to regard Sufis as deviant. At various periods during the past three centuries some Shi'ite clergy have encouraged persecution of Sufis, but Sufi orders have continued to exist in Iran. During the Pahlavi period, some Sufi brotherhoods were revitalized. Some members of the secularized middle class were especially attracted to them, but the orders appear to have had little following among the lower classes.

The largest Sufi order was the Nimatollahi, which had khanehgahs, or teaching centers, in several cities and even established new centers in foreign countries. Other important orders were the Dhahabi and Kharksar brotherhoods. Sufi brotherhoods such as the Naqshbandi and the Qadiri also existed among Sunni Muslims in Kordestan. There is no evidence of persecution of Sufis under the Republic, but the brotherhoods are regarded suspiciously and generally have kept a low profile.

Iran also contains Shi'ite sects that many of the Twelver Shi'ite clergy regard as heretical. One of these is the Ismaili, a sect that has several thousand adherents living primarily in northeastern Iran. The Ismailis, of whom there were once several different sects, trace their origins to the son of Ismail who predeceased his father, the Sixth Imam. The Ismailis were very numerous and active in Iran from the 11th to the 13th century. They are known in history as the "Assassins" because of their practice of killing political opponents.

The Mongols destroyed their center at Alamut in the Alborz Mountains in 1256. Subsequently, their living imams went into hiding from non-Ismailis. In the 19th century, their leader emerged in public as the Agha Khan and fled to British-controlled India, where he supervised the revitalization of the sect. The majority of the several million Ismailis in the 1980s live outside Iran. Another Shi'ite sect is the Ahl-e Haqq. Its adherents are concentrated in Lorestan, but small communities also are found in Kordestan and Mazandaran.

The origins of the Ahl-e Haqq are believed to lie in one of the medieval politicized Sufi orders. The group has been persecuted sporadically by orthodox Shi'ites. After the Revolution, some of the sect's leaders were imprisoned on the ground of religious deviance.

Sunni Muslims

Sunni Muslims constitute approximately eight percent of the Iranian population. A majority of Kurds, virtually all Baluchis and Turkomans, and a minority of Arabs are Sunnis, as are small communities of Persians in southern Iran and Khorasan.

The main difference between Sunnis and Shi'ites is that the former do not accept the doctrine of the Imamate. Generally speaking, Iranian Shi'ites are inclined to recognize Sunnis as fellow Muslims, but as those whose religion is incomplete.

Shi'ite clergy tend to view missionary work among Sunnis to convert them to true Islam as a worthwhile religious endeavor. Since the Sunnis generally live in the border regions of the country, there has been no occasion for Shi'ite-Sunni conflict in most of Iran. In those towns with mixed populations in West Azerbaijan, the Persian Gulf region, and Baluchistan, tensions between Shi'ites and Sunnis existed both before and after the Revolution.

Religious tensions have been highest during major Shi'ite observances, especially Moharram.

Non-Muslim Minorities[6]

While members of these faiths are, according to the country's constitution, free to practice their religion and instruct their children, the government interferes with the administration of their schools. Some members of these faiths have been victims of harassment, persecution, and extra-judicial killing.

Baha'is—The largest non-Muslim minority in Iran is the Baha'i community. There was a community of several hundred thousand Baha'is in Iran in 1986, but with the ascendancy of the mullahs, these people have been increasingly persecuted by the Tehran Government.

The Baha'i faith is considered by those in charge in Tehran to be a heretical sect and has been brutally persecuted in an effort to eliminate it. Consequently, Baha'is are prohibited from teaching or practicing their faith or maintaining links to Baha'is abroad. Nor are Baha'i students allowed to attend universities. Their property has been confiscated, including cemeteries and holy sites. According to a 2001 State Department report, hundreds, perhaps thousands of Bahai's have been killed since the 1979 fundamentalist revolution.

Scattered in small communities throughout Iran with a heavy concentration in Tehran, most Baha'is are urban, but there are some Baha'i villages, especially in Fars and Mazandaran. The majority of Baha'is are Persians, but there is a significant minority of Azarbaijani Baha'is, and there are even a few among the Kurds.

Baha'ism is a religion that originated in Iran during the 19th century as a reformist movement within Shi'ite Islam. Initially it attracted a wide following among Shi'ite clergy and others dissatisfied with society.

The political and religious authorities joined to suppress the movement, and since that time the hostility of the Shi'ite clergy to Baha'ism has remained intense. In the latter half of the 19th century, the Baha'i leader fled to Ottoman Palestine—roughly present-day Israel—where he and his successors continued to elaborate Baha'i doctrines by incorporating beliefs from other world religions.

By the early 20th century, Baha'ism had evolved into a new religion that stressed the brotherhood of all peoples, equality of the sexes, and pacifism.

Christians—Iran's indigenous Christians include an estimated quarter million Armenians, some thirty-two thousand Assyrians, and a small number of Roman Catholic, Anglican, and Protestant Iranians converted by missionaries in the 19th and 20th centuries.

The Armenians are predominantly urban and are concentrated in Tehran and Esfahan; smaller communities exist in Tabriz, Arak, and other cities. A majority of the Assyrians are also urban, although there are still several Assyrian villages in the Lake Urmia region.

Armenians and Assyrians were recognized as official religious minorities under the old, 1906 constitution. Although these people have encountered individual prejudice, they have not been subjected to persecution. During the 20th century, Christians in general have participated in the economic and social life of Tehran. The Armenians, especially, achieved a relatively high standard of living and maintained a large number of parochial primary and secondary schools.

The Republican Constitution of 1979 also recognized the Armenians and Assyrians as official religious minorities. They are entitled to elect their own representatives to the Majlis and are permitted to follow their own religious laws in matters of marriage, divorce, and inheritance. Other Christians have not received any special recognition, and there have been a number of incidents of persecution of Iranian Anglicans.

All Christians are required to observe the new laws relating to attire, prohibition of alcohol, and segregation by sex at public gatherings. Christians have resented these laws because they have infringed on their traditional religious practices. In addition, the administration of the Armenian schools has been a source of tension between Christians and the government.

The Ministry of Education has insisted that the principals of such schools be Muslims, that all religion courses be taught in Persian, that any Armenian literature classes have government approval, and that all female students observe *hejab* inside the schools.

Iranian Jews—In 1986 there were an estimated fifty thousand Jews in Iran, a decline from about eighty-five thousand in 1978.

The Iranian Jewish community is one of the oldest in the world, being descended from Jews who remained in the region following the Babylonian captivity, when the Achaemenid rulers of the first Iranian empire permitted Jews to return to Jerusalem.

Over the centuries the Jews of Iran became physically, culturally, and linguistically indistinguishable from the non-Jewish population. The overwhelming majority of Jews speak Persian as their mother language, and a tiny minority Kurdish. The Jews are predominantly urban and by the 1970s were concentrated in Tehran, with smaller communities in other cities such as Shiraz, Esfahan, Hamadan, and Kashan. Until the 20th century the Jews were confined to their own quarters in the towns. In general the Jews were an impoverished minority, occupationally restricted to small-scale trading, money lending, and working with precious metals.

Since the 1920s, Jews have had greater opportunities for economic and social mobility. They have received assistance from a number of international Jewish organizations, including the American Joint Distribution Committee, which introduced electricity, piped water, and modern sanitation into Jewish neighborhoods.

The Jews gradually gained increased importance in the bazaars of Tehran and other cities, and after World War II some educated Jews entered the professions, particularly pharmacy, medicine, and dentistry. The Constitution of 1979 recognized Jews as an official religious minority and accorded them the right to elect a representative to the Majlis.

Like the Christians, the Jews have not been persecuted. Unlike the Christians, the Jews have been viewed with suspicion by the government, probably because of the government's intense hostility toward Israel. Iranian Jews generally have many relatives in Israel—some forty-five thousand Iranian Jews emigrated from Iran to Israel between 1948 and 1977—with whom they are in regular contact.

Since 1979 the government has cited mail and telephone communications as evidence of "spying" in the arrest, detention, and even execution of a few prominent Jews. Although these individual cases have not affected the status of the community as a whole, they have contributed to a pervasive feeling of insecurity among Jews regarding their future in Iran and have helped to precipitate large- scale emigration. Most Jews who have left since the Revolution have settled in the United States.

Zoroastrians—In 1986 there were more than thirty thousand Zoroastrians in Iran. They speak Persian and are concentrated in Tehran, Kerman, and Yazd.

Zoroastrianism initially developed in Iran during the 7th century BC. Later, it became the official religion of the Sassanid Empire, which ruled over Iran for approximately four centuries before being destroyed by the Arabs in the 7th century AD.

After Iran's incorporation into the Islamic empire, the majority of its population was gradually converted from Zoroastrianism to Islam, a process that was probably completed by the 10th century.

PART II
IRAN'S NUCLEAR PURSUITS

4

HOW CLOSE IS IRAN TO BUILDING AN A-BOMB?

"Iran has been developing a nuclear fuel cycle. Have
they taken the step from that into weaponization? We
have not seen that. But I am not yet excluding
that possibility."

Mohamed ElBaradei, head of the IAEA, to a
U.S. Congressional Subcommittee, March 17, 2004

All that is certain about Iran's program is that there is nobody in the West who has any idea how far Tehran has advanced in its bid to achieve a nuclear weapons capability.

Neither the British SIS nor the American CIA can say how far its programs have progressed. Even the Russians—Iran's principal supplier of conventional weapons and, more recently, of a nuclear reactor along the coast at Bushehr—won't say. To be fair, they probably don't know. Tehran is likely to keep everybody not closely linked to its nuclear weapons in the dark, at least until it has conducted its first nuclear test. Then, like Pakistan, having displayed its ability to detonate the bomb, Iran can sit back and watch the kerfuffle.

Once Tehran has proven its nuclear capability there is absolutely nothing that anybody—or any nation—will be able to do about it. It would be a *fait accompli*. Done! In a sense, an Iranian bomb is likely to be viewed by the people of Iran as the ultimate bequest from the grave of the late Ayatollah Khomeini.

Right now, there is a considerable amount of debate going on about the possibility of Tehran even being able to get as far as Pakistan in building such a weapon. By its own admission to the International Atomic Energy Agency (IAEA), no less, Iran has been going at it hard for almost two decades. We know too from these disclosures that the country has managed to overcome or possibly override, with foreign help, many of the elemental technical issues involved.

In fact, Iran's uranium enrichment program is more advanced than previously thought and, according to Marshall Breit of the Carnegie Endowment for International Peace, "Tehran may be only a few years away from being able to produce enough highly enriched uranium to make a nuclear weapon."

What he says is that in the broader context of nuclear physics, Iran seems to have pursued two different methods for enriching uranium: gas centrifuge enrichment and laser enrichment (though neither atomic vapor laser isotope separation [AVLIS] nor molecular laser [MLIS] have yet proven to be very successful and are currently not used commercially anywhere for uranium enrichment). It has also made significant gains towards the separation of plutonium, another fissile material. According to Breit, "Iran's plutonium program is less advanced than its uranium program but there are at least four known facilities currently planned or under construction that, when complete, would allow Iran to manufacture material for use in nuclear weapons."

Clearly, the mullahs have spent much time, money and effort to get this far, which some pundits suggest might even include a fundamental weaponization stage. For its part the IAEA says very little, though if you have to judge by some of its pronouncements, its frustration as an international nuclear monitoring body with regard to Iran is almost palpable. Iran's relationship with the International Atomic Energy Agency has always been problematic.

For much of the time that it has cooperated, the level of interplay between Tehran and the UN body has been punctuated by apparent goodwill one moment and the most resolute and intransigent stonewalling the next. That distinctly comes across in the IAEA's "restricted distribution" Board of Governors report titled "Implementation of the NPT Agreement in the Islamic Republic of Iran," dated February 24, 2004.

While the first report "welcomed Iran's offer of active cooperation and openness and its positive response to the demands of the Board in the resolution adopted" the previous September, the second "strongly deplored Iran's past failures and breaches of its obligations to comply with the provisions of the Safeguards Agreement as reported by the Director General." It went on to urge Tehran to adhere strictly to its obligations in both "letter and spirit." Part of the problem stemmed from what, in inspection parlance, is meant by "correct, complete and final pictures" of Iran's past and present nuclear programs. Herein lies the rub.

Issues are compounded still further by Westerners often forgetting when dealing with Iran and other Islamic countries that their way of doing business is not as clear-cut as it might be in Manchester or Atlanta. There is a very distinct Middle East way of bargaining that is all about saving face and one-upmanship. Thus, while their approach is often not as "clinical" as we in the West would like, issues are hardly facilitated by the fact that Tehran has been shown to have much to hide. The immediate consequence of this state of affairs is that Iran has been thoroughly duplicitous in its dealings with representatives of the IAEA.

On the other hand, there have been moments since Tehran decided to come clean on its nuclear programs in 2003, when things would proceed smoothly. Weapons inspectors would move in and look at various sites, make their observations, install monitors and so on. That would be followed by a demand not very long afterward that all such activity stop immediately.[1]

It hasn't been lost on any of these people that the sort of problems encountered by the IAEA, beginning in February 2003, are similar to those experienced in Iraq under Saddam Hussein. Like Iraq in the past, the mullahs would offer "full and final" reports. Then, once the inspectors began to detect anomalies or nondisclosures, a furious debate would follow, sometimes in private but more often in public with requisite press reports, some of them abrasive. To be fair, inspection impediments in   Iraq were much more flagrant than in Iran, though this could still change.

Obviously, obstructionism of this nature tends to inculcate bad feeling all round. That would be followed by another "full and final" report and the cycle of duplicity would be repeated. Most times, though, the Atomic Energy Organization of Iran (AEOI) would provide just enough information to keep the inspectors from raising objections and make it impossible to garner the kind of international consensus needed to take tougher action, for instance, in the Security Council. History, as we have seen so often before, has a peculiar way of repeating itself.

It's an endless, inconclusive business, said one observer, adding that in a way, it was a bit like the game of catch me if you can, with rather more serious consequences for the international community if, in the end, not everything comes to light. Language and innuendo of the sort we've seen emerge from exchanges between Tehran and the West often compound matters. Take one example:

Following the adoption by the UN nuclear organization of a

"compromise" solution to Iran's nuclear dossier in November 2003, Tehran promptly hailed the deal as a "victory for Iran and an obvious failure for America and Israel," even though the Jewish state had nothing to do with these negotiations.

While the IAEA statement "strongly deplored" Iran's eighteen years of covert nuclear activities (and having previously gone through the wringer when faced with a similar problem in Iraq) the head of the nuclear watchdog organization, Mohamed ElBaradei, made it known that he would not refer Tehran's deceptions to the UN Security Council for the imposition of possible sanctions. He, as well as every-body else who had watched the same sort of thing take place in Iraq with UNMOVIC (that UN body was only responsible for chemical, biological and missile inspections), and the IAEA not very long before, were acutely aware that even if he did so, a moribund UN would sit on its hands.

How else when three of its five permanent members—France, China, and especially Russia—were more than likely to veto anything that might affect their commercial interests with the recalcitrant state? They didn't rock the boat with Iraq: they are even less likely to do so with Iran. Also, as Marshall Breit observed, "Because of the current dismal state of Iraq, members of the Security Council are especially hesitant to push hard on another front."

Nevertheless, for several months, inspections did go well and the IAEA gradually uncovered a more complete picture of the Iranian nuclear program. Suddenly Tehran called off a nuclear inspection mis-sion scheduled for the second week of March 2004. Questioned about reasons why, the Iranian representative at the IAEA, Pirooz Husseini was quoted as saying something about the gesture not being political-ly motivated but rather due to "the approaching of the Iranian New Year." This delay came as Non-Aligned and Western diplomats were struggling to break a deadlock at the IAEA over a U.S. resolution that would condemn Tehran's leaders for hiding parts of its nuclear pro-gram, and send the matter to the Security Council.

That was followed by a statement by the Iranian foreign minister, Kamal Karrazi, that "It is our perfectly legitimate right to enrich ura-nium." To which one American official in Vienna ventured, "Why else would Iran be enriching uranium to weapons grade if it did not intend to build the bomb?"

At the same time, Karrazi's statement, up to a point, is correct. There is nothing that prevents a country from enriching uranium as long as it is done under safeguards. Enriching does not necessarily imply HEU. It could also be LEU for Bushehr reactor fuel, something that could be a problem for Iran to obtain internationally (as with South Africa and its Koeberg nuclear reactor program in the Apartheid days). Tehran, it should be mentioned, is perfectly aware of the kind of problems that emerge when there are real or imagined political constraints. As they point out to their critics, yesterday South Africa; tomorrow Iran.

Then came ElBaradei's high level talks with President Bush in Washington on March 17, 2004, after which he briefed a Congressional Committee about what his organization had uncovered in Iran. Though there was no comment on the issue, recent disclosures in Pakistan about A.Q. Khan and his associates providing rogue states (Iran included) with nuclear expertise must have featured prominently.

According to the *Wall Street Journal,* the Bush and ElBaradei meeting covered a wide range of topics, including IAEA verification of Iran's nuclear efforts, as well as ideas how to control what appeared to be burgeoning nuclear proliferation within the international community. They also dealt with an urgent need to restrict the number of countries that can enrich uranium and reprocess plutonium for use in nuclear fuel or bombs, thereby, as a result, making everybody else with civil nuclear reactors dependent on nations with these facilities.

On Tehran, the IAEA could not have been more explicit. While acknowledging that Iran had provided help, it was obvious that all was not well with the inspection program when ElBaradei declared, "My answer is that the jury is still out." Clearly there were some serious things going on in Iran that worried him. He told the President, "We would like to continue to work hard on inspecting Iran before we come to a conclusion. We expect full cooperation, full transparency if Iran wants to prove that its program is for peaceful purposes."

As was made clear earlier, the meeting between ElBaradei and Bush in March 2004 concerned a good deal more than Iran. The fact that Libya, only months before had suddenly revealed itself as a potential nuclear power, was a major topic as well.

At the same time, the thrust of President Bush's suggestions to ElBaradei had several unavoidable implications. What it boiled down to was that the future of nations, or, indeed vast regions of the globe, could not be entrusted to a United Nations body when other organizations within that same international body had shown themselves to be inefficient, lacking in both direction and responsible control and, more often than not, had shown themselves or their administrations to be thoroughly corrupt. The UN Oil-for-Food Program in Iraq is only one example, with many senior functionaries implicated in taking rake-offs worth many millions of dollars.

The American president was at pains to avoid painting the IAEA with the same brush. One got the impression he felt that while ElBaradei's group was doing sterling work, it was feasible that there might come a time when things could change.

All of which, begs the question: On what aspect of the Iranian nuclear program did the IAEA think Tehran was holding out? Is it unthinkable that Iran might have completed construction of its first fissile device and is now preparing for a test? Certainly, that would allow a measure of transparency, with the argument in Tehran running along the lines of "showing the West what it wants to see and letting us get on with real issues."

Breit made the point that there is some parallel with the so-called Libyan nuclear program. "While the scope and size of Gadhaffi's program pales in comparison with what we now know about that of Iran, Libya had attained a weapons design in Pakistan. It is surely within reason that Iran has also acquired a design," he suggests. At the same time, while the design details are not that important for a simple device, the availability of nuclear material is.

For ElBaradei to have been as forthright as he was after meeting the American president, there must be something substantial in the Iranian nuclear domain that he believed had not yet been disclosed. But neither he nor Washington were prepared to say what it was. Yet, if you had gone on to read details of the meeting in Tehran's English press, things couldn't have been better. Iran had complied with all the IAEA's demands and everybody was happy, said a report in *Iran News*.

Things changed rapidly after ElBaradei's Washington sojourn. A day later, a statement in *IranMania News* accused the IAEA chief of "playing the role of mediator between Tehran and arch-foe Washington" during his U.S. visit.[2]

"The Islamic Republic has not tasked Mr. Baradei with any message for the American leadership," said foreign ministry spokesman Hamid Reze Asefi, quoted by the student news agency ISNA.

Washington's reply was forthright, coming from State Department spokesman Adam Ereli: "The fact is that Iran knows what those issues of concern are (terrorism, nuclear program, support for terrorist groups). We haven't seen movement on any of those things."

That was followed by an impassioned outburst from Hassan Rowhani, the official in charge of Iran's nuclear program when he criticized Britain, France and Germany for not defending Tehran's views at recent talks on international inspections. The previous week, the IAEA had adopted a tough resolution that raised questions over Iran's failure to declare its possession of certain equipment and materials which could be used to make nuclear weapons.

"The IAEA resolution was not drafted in a fair way," said Rowhani, head of his country's Supreme National Security Council.

What then do we know about the Iranian nuclear program? The international community does have satellite images of the goings on at Natanz and Arak, two nondescript towns a couple of hundred miles south of Tehran. Thanks to a September 16, 2004 BBC report, we now also know about the Parchin base complex southeast of Tehran which could be used to test atom bomb components.

At Arak these show a heavy water plant similar to the nuclear-related heavy water facilities used in Pakistan's bomb program. Photos taken of the massive Natanz facility show something akin to a uranium enrichment plant coupled to a centrifuge facility.

David Albright confirmed that the work being conducted at Natanz and Arak might be related to the production of highly enriched uranium and heavy water which, he explained could be used for the production of nuclear weapons. Interestingly, the disclosures came in the wake of strong denials by Mohammed Javad Zarif, Iran's ambassador to the United Nations that his country is building something nuclear.

The anté was upped by the *New York Times* when Craig S. Smith wrote on March 11, 2004 that the "alarm had been raised over the quality of uranium found in Iraq."[3]

United Nations nuclear inspectors, he said, "had found traces of extremely highly enriched uranium in Iran, of a purity for use in a nuclear bomb." Some of this stuff, HEU in the lingo, had been enriched to 90 percent (though much of it was only 37 percent). He also suggested that while the Agency had previously admitted to finding "weapons grade" traces in a preliminary search in 2003, it had not revealed that some reached such a high degree of enrichment. So far nobody has had the temerity to pose the question: why not?

What was also disconcerting was that Iran's defense minister, Ali Shamkhani, disclosed for the first time on March 10, 2004 that the

Iranian military had produced centrifuges to enrich uranium. He added the rider that these were strictly for civilian users, the Associated Press reported from Tehran. A senior American official quoted afterward by Smith had his own view on the subject: "It's rather strange, don't you think, that the military gets involved in the electric power generating business, or that they forgot to mention this before when they were 'fully disclosing' all details of their program?"

That said, there are things going on in Iran that are worrying, more so following initial inspections in Iran by the IAEA when the Tehran Government blocked all further nuclear–related inspections.

Issues were further compounded in early March 2004 when Iran disclosed that it had conducted a successful test of its much-vaunted Shahab-3 missile, which, the Americans say, can carry a one-ton pay-load over a distance of thirteen hundred miles, or comfortably within the Israeli envelope. The timing of Iran's announcement about the Shahab-3 and the size of its payload suggested that the missile could be intended to carry a nuclear warhead.

It is not that the Americans—or, for that matter, Whitehall—don't know about such things. Earlier, in June 2003, John Bolton, U.S. Under Secretary of State for Arms Control and International Security, told a Congressional Committee that the United States had observed for some time that Iran was involved in a clandestine nuclear weapons program.[4] He revealed in closed session that Iran was developing "a uranium mine, a massive uranium enrichment facility designed to house tens of thousands of centrifuges as well as a heavy water pro-duction plant," adding that such facilities would support the produc-tion of highly enriched uranium and plutonium for nuclear weapons.

"While Iran claims that its nuclear program is peaceful and trans-parent, we are convinced it is otherwise," Bolton declared. "One unmistakable indicator of military intent is the secrecy and lack of transparency surrounding Iran's nuclear activities." [It should be men-tioned that a heavy water plant is still far away from weapons mater-ial. Fertile material must be irradiated in a specific type of reactor and then reprocessed in special features to separate the plutonium, which must then be converted into a metal of the correct metallurgical form.]

Looking back, there is no question that Saddam Hussein's often irra-tional and militaristic actions played a seminal role in causing Tehran to look toward a nuclear option.

The two countries fought an eight-year war that was bloody, bitter and acrimonious and left more than a million Iranians killed or maimed. Though official tallies are vague, the number of Iranian troops KIA is something on the order of three hundred thousand. Consequently, it came as no surprise when the CIA told Congress in the mid-1980s that there was every indication that Iran was driven to build nuclear weapons because it feared that its bellicose neighbor might be doing the same.

That need became especially urgent, a well-placed intelligence source in the American capital told *Jane's Terrorism and Security Monitor*, after UNSCOM was forced out of Iraq in 1998. It didn't help that there were endless debates in the UN Security Council about how its successor might be reconstituted, if at all.

It was David Albright's view at the time that the Iranians were being driven to produce the weapon for no better reason than to prevent being annihilated as a nation. "Tehran is alarmed at what they know is taking place just across the border. They don't want to be caught seriously short a second time," he told me prior to Gulf War II.

Strangely enough, Iran never used this as an argument as to why they developed their program. Dr. von Wielligh was informally given to understand while still on the Board of Governors at the IAEA that such an explanation could have made things a lot easier for Iran had they actually done so.

There are several pointers which indicate that a lot more might be taking place in Iran that most Western observers would like to believe.

For instance, Iranian attempts to buy highly enriched uranium and plutonium on the East European black market are well sourced and documented. In late September 2004, according to the BBC, two men with Iranian connections were arrested in Bishkek, capital of Kyrgyzstan, trying to sell a large amount of plutonium on the black market. The radioactive material was packed in sixty containers and was intercepted by agents working for the national security service.

Tehran has also been shopping for nuclear technical know-how. Moreover, the authorities are aware that the Iranians recruited foreign specialists for its WMD research and development programs, including a number of South African scientists who were formerly involved in their own country's now-defunct missile programs.

They weren't the only ones. Michael Eisenstadt of The Washington Institute for Near East Policy tells us in his monograph, *Iranian Military Power,* of an alleged German intelligence report cited by Izvestia on October 20, 1992, following the collapse of the Soviet Union, that fourteen Russian nuclear scientists found employment in Iran. Another fifty engineers and two hundred technicians also concluded contracts with Moscow. This need not be regarded as sinister—with the Bushehr reactors running, a nuclear infrastructure needs to be established and maintained, including safety, licensing and maintenance requirements.

That was followed by a *U.S. News & World Report* story on April 17, 1995 about Russian scientists working as paid consultants on ballistic missile design in Iran.

On the nuclear side, research has been taking place at various locations. The IAEA knows of some of them, including the Tehran Nuclear Research Center (TNRC) which includes hot cells located in the Jabr Ibn Hayan Laboratories, the Natanz site (much of it underground, raising an altogether different set of questions), Karaj, Lashkar Ab'ad, the pilot plant for laser enrichment, the heavy water facility at Arak as well as the Esfahan Nuclear Technology Center (ENTC). Until its nuclear assets were dismantled and moved, there was also the innocuously-named Kalaye Electric Company. Vienna accepts that there might be other nuclear assets that remain hidden.

On Natanz, while hot cells might indicate reprocessing, the fact that they are underground is not enough to hide it. Releases of fission products leave a tell-tale signature which can easily be picked up when using modern detection methods.

Noteworthy is Tehran's October 21, 2003 letter to the IAEA acknowledging that it had conducted laboratory and bench-scale conversion experiments in the Uranium Conversion Laboratory (UCL) at the ENTC as well as at the former Radiochemical Laboratories located at the TNRC and the Jabr Ibn Hayan Laboratories. For these purposes nuclear fuel imported in 1977, 1982 and 1991 had been used.[5] It also admitted having transferred "relevant dismantled equipment used in these process at the TNRC" to the Radioactive Waste Storage Facility at Karaj.

One of the problems facing the international community in trying to assess the WMD potential of Iran is the country's size. By any standards, Iran is immense, a good fifty thousand square miles bigger than Alaska. With those proportions, even with the most advanced satellite surveillance equipment, it is impossible to keep track of everything.

Some details are known. According to Iranian expatriate sources—including those with the anti-Iranian subversive group

Mojahedin-e-Khalq—there is a cadre of between three and four thousand personnel at work at various nuclear-related sites in Isfahan, south of the capital. A second, secret weapons design center is located at Moallam Kelaieh, near the Caspian Sea.

Two more nuclear research sites are at the nuclear power plant at Bushehr on the Gulf, where Russian crews are building Iran's only nuclear power station. (It was partially destroyed during the war with Iraq.) There is also Tehran's Sharif University, long suspected to be the cradle of Iran's fledgling nuclear program.

An Israeli diplomatic source in Washington indicated to this writer during one of his visits to the U.S. capital that because so much attention was given to this institution in the past, it was to be expected that the Iranians would fragment their nuclear activities and spread them around the country. He explained that following the Israeli Air Force attack on Iraq's materials test reactor Tammuz-1 at Osiraq in June, 1981, Tehran, as a direct consequence, "likes to spread its strategic assets about."

It is significant, perhaps, that any of these developments have taken place at all. Shortly after the death of the Ayatollah Ruhollah Khomeini, the country's leading mullahs—quoting excerpts from the Holy *Qur'an*—declared that harnessing nuclear energy whether for civil or military purposes, was contrary to the most basic precepts of Islam. That approach was reversed not long afterward, even though the public line remains clear: "Iran is not, nor will it ever be a nuclear power," it's diplomats proclaim.

Then, in 1989, former premier Ali Akbar Rafsanjani observed that "Iran simply cannot ignore the nuclear reality in the modern world." Nor was the possibility of Iran exploring chemical and biological warfare ruled out. In a speech to military officers, he stated. "Chemical and biological weapons are the poor man's atomic bombs and can easily be produced. We should at least consider them for our defense." He went on: "Although the use of such weapons is inhuman, the (Iran/Iraq) war taught us that international laws are only scraps of paper."

There has since been a lot of effort in Iran toward trying to acquire foreign WMD expertise and technology in all three NBC disciplines. Pakistan, for instance, was asked for uranium gas centrifuge technology and agreed to train Iranian scientists at its Institute for Nuclear Science and Technology near Islamabad. We now know that this association was far more extensive than anybody believed possible.

Pakistan's role was always seminal to Iran acquiring the level of advanced nuclear technology to make bombs. That came forcibly across in one of the biggest scandals to emerge in the new millennium, when Pakistan's chief nuclear scientist, Abdul Qadeer Khan, confessed to sharing his country's nuclear technology with Iran, Libya, and North Korea. Everything was detailed in a twelve-page document presented by Khan to President Pervez Musharraf. The basics of these disclosures remain confidential and only some of it has been shared with the West.

Earlier, Pakistan's covert nuclear program generated controversy when the IAEA, in November 2003 while probing Iran's nuclear program, found evidence that Pakistani scientists had aided their neighboring country. In separate deals, Western intelligence sources say Pakistani scientists also traded uranium enrichment with North Korea and Libya.

The international nuclear body provided the list of at least five scientists and officials associated with another nuclear body, the Kahuta Research Laboratories (KRL), a uranium enrichment plant headed by A.Q. Khan from 1976 to 2001. None of it was for free—the money involved resulted in millions of dollars being transferred into Pakistani bank accounts, prompting just about everybody who has been able to look into the scandal to suggest that it was simply impossible for Islamabad not to be aware of what was going on.[6]

The damage caused is severe. Says Michael Krepon, founding president of the Henry L. Stimson Center, "If half of this is true, it suggests a huge breakdown in [proliferation] oversight that must be repaired."[7]

Other countries are involved. Argentina was approached in the early days about acquiring nuclear expertise and equipment and, until U.S. pressure was brought to bear, responded favorably. So, too, with Cuba. Similarly, reactors were sought from China, Russia and India. Also contacted were Poland, Czechoslovakia and Italy. The results, as far as can be reckoned, have been mixed, since Washington managed to block only some of these efforts.

Meanwhile, Beijing entered the picture. American officials believe that China helped to construct a uranium hexafluoride (UF_6) plant under a secret nuclear cooperation agreement signed in 1991.[8] In such a plant, uranium ore concentrates are converted to gaseous uranium hexafluoride which could be fed into an enrichment plant for the production of HEU. The intelligence was coupled to reports circulating in the Russian media of a shipment of uranium hexafluoride gas going directly from China to Iran late in 1994. Of note, too, were March, 1995 reports[9] that "Iran is now capable of producing UF_6 gas in research installations run by the AEOI."

More recently, China inked a sales agreement with Iran to build two Quinshan-class 300 MW power reactors at Darkhovin. This is the site where Framatome, a French company initially planned to build four nuclear plants in the late 1970s. Though the status is uncertain, the Chinese installations were expected to cost about $1 billion. That was followed by a report in the American publication *NuclearFuel* that it had uncovered a joint U.S./German sting operation in which former Soviet nuclear warheads were offered to the Islamic Republic of Iran for $3 million apiece.[10]

A Hanover (Germany) businessman, who suggested the deal to an Iranian procurement officer in 1993, testified to German prosecutors shortly afterward. Specifics remain classified, but what emerged is that attempts to buy nuclear warheads—as well as a variety of other military items—appears to fall within the jurisdiction of Iran's Defense Industries Organization (DIO) which, claims German Intelligence, is a clandestine nuclear and military procurement agency.

There was the also the visit to South Africa shortly afterward by Reza Amrollahi, head of AEOI and at that stage, deputy president for Iran's atomic affairs. This incident continues to collect fallout. What we do know is that Minister Amrollahi approached Dr. Waldo Stumpf, chief executive of the South African Atomic Energy Corporation (AEC) with a "shopping list" of items required for the manufacture of atomic bombs.

A short while earlier, South Africa—under the auspices of Pretoria's Apartheid regime—had built six A-bombs, all in the twenty to twenty-four kiloton range. South Africa's nuclear arsenal was subsequently dismantled under the auspices of the IAEA and several Western monitoring agencies, including the Americans.

AEC's former chief executive Stumpf has since issued lengthy disclaimers (including one before Parliament in Cape Town). He denied any recollection of a meeting with Amrollahi, even though he told this writer that it had happened at his Pelindaba office near Pretoria in 1997. That much was subsequently confirmed by a former South African cabinet minister, Pik Botha. He told Mungo Sogget of the Johannesburg *Mail & Guardian* that the event had taken place. Moreover, said Botha, "I was there when it happened." (This issue is detailed further in Chapter 7).

While there have been some differences of opinion regarding the route that Tehran has chosen in order to develop its nuclear weapons programs, all indications are that it is focused on the trilogy of uranium enrichment (gas centrifuge), a laser isotope system that is somewhere between AVLIS and MLIS—neither of which have yet been developed into commercially viable plants—as well as a weapons-orientated means of delivery.

There has also been work on separating plutonium for use in an implosion-type weapon. However, unlike HEU, work on plutonium presents formidable technological and safety obstacles. Not only must the plutonium be separated from very radioactive fission products for which hot cells with remote handling equipment are required, but specially designed equipment and handling procedures to prevent accidental criticality are also of utmost importance, especially with plutonium in solution. Many criticality accidents have been reported in the past in the U.S. and Britain, usually involving material in solution.

A criticality accident results from the initiation of an unintended chain reaction, but does not result in a nuclear explosion. The radiation given off, however, is sufficiently strong to lead to the death of persons in the near vicinity, often immediately.

What Iraq's nuclear scientists quickly discovered was that whatever system they chose to build their bomb—AVLIS, MLIS or gas centrifuge—all three are fraught with the most complex disciplines. Certainly, none were suited to the budgets or doctrines of developing countries. Also, any such projects are a formidable drain on the economy. The Iranians are consequently stuck with the reality that they are neither technologically advanced nor scientifically adept enough to go it alone, even though there are many expatriate Iranians perfectly at home in advanced Western research establishments.

There is good reason for the mullahs making the choice they did. While the idea behind the centrifuge system[11] is complex, problems associated with creating a practical device to separate the lighter fissile Uranium 235 (^{235}U) isotope from the heavier ^{238}U, are formidable. Uranium hexafluoride gas introduced into a rotating centrifuge contains both isotopes. To separate them, the spinning cylinder or rotor must turn at such high speeds that centrifugal forces causes paint to fly off. The slightest instability—where the rotor spins thirteen hundred times a second—will cause bearings to fail and rotors to crash in an instant.

This becomes even more difficult where multiple-linked centrifuges (which can be scores, hundreds or, more likely, thousands) form what nuclear technicians refer to as a cascade, an essential adaptation if useful amounts of HEU are to be produced. Pakistan had been trying for years to master these intricacies until it got it right with its stolen blueprints and know-how obtained in URENCO plants, and then with additional foreign technical aid.

Also, judging by developments in Iran itself (and the kind of equipment that was acquired, clandestinely or otherwise) it would appear that their program is double-headed. Primary attention is being accorded to the two basic nuclear weapons, the implosion bomb and the simpler, gun-type weapons system.

In missile technology, which is coupled to the nuclear program because ultimately a means of delivery is essential, Iran has made good progress, largely, it is believed, because of South African involvement.

Iran also bought a variety of missile delivery systems from the Chinese, North Koreans and, it is believed, swapped information with Pakistan. The Russians continued to be helpful until fairly recently, though there is much that happens in the domain of the former Soviet Union (FSU) that the West knows nothing about.

In the confusion surrounding Iran's nuclear weapons programs, the West is aware that Tehran has been most active in trying to acquire weapons-usable nuclear materials, plutonium or HEU. This is not surprising. For years, there have been reports of Iranian agents having been busy in the newly independent states of the FSU trying to buy the stuff. One example will do.

In November 1994, the United States disclosed that it had completed an airlift of more than half a ton of weapons-grade uranium from Ust-Kamenogorsk in Kazakhstan to the United States. The shipment, packed in more than a thousand specially designed steel transport drums, was flown to Dover Air Force base in Delaware and finally moved by road to Oak Ridge, Tennessee. Ostensibly—after a protracted and complicated series of negotiations—the material was handed over in exchange for U.S. aid.

The uranium at the Ublinsky Metallurgical Plant had apparently been left behind in the confusion of the Soviet collapse largely as an oversight. In any event, the plant was believed to have been specializing in low enriched uranium (LEU) and exotic metals. Work on HEU in Kazakhstan (as elsewhere in the former Soviet Union) was a closely-guarded secret.

What concerned the Americans was that there had been reports of Iranian meddling even before Washington became aware that HEU was stored there. These indicated that groups of Iranians had been ferreting around the plant, which was not unusual since Iran maintains the second largest embassy in Kazakhstan. Even the Russians concede that Tehran's intelligence infrastructure throughout the region is focused, often using the talents of dissident Muslims and liberal dollar handouts to achieve their objectives. Throwing money about was (and still is) a useful ploy in a society where officials can go for months without being paid. There are also at least a dozen documented cases of Iranian agents trying to acquire fissile material in the FSU as well as in Europe, further evidence of Tehran's long-term objectives.

It is instructive that the U.S. initially asked the Kazakh government to block any possible Iranian transactions regarding the Ublinsky facility. As subsequent events have shown, there was clearly enough doubt in the minds of Washington's security chiefs that the authorities at Ulba were either unable or unwilling to resist Iranian offers. For that reason they took appropriate action.

What is of real concern today, though, is that until the Americans and most FSU states came to grips with the problem, Ulba was one of dozens of such nuclear storage depots behind the old Iron Curtain where security hardly rated serious consideration during the transitional period.

More worrisome have been reports out of the Commonwealth of Independent States (CIS, the free-market successor to the USSR) indicating serious Russian mafia activity. Operators linked to the Russian underworld are known to accept bids from all comers: and there is little regard for long-term political or security implications. How else in a society where, by March 1994, the Russian Federal Counterintelligence service (now the FSB) reported that there had been nine hundred thefts from military and nuclear plants?

There were also seven hundred items of secret technology stolen in the second half of 1993 alone, much of it insider activity.

All this has relevance to what is happening in Iran today. Following the 1989 disclosure by Reza Amrollahi, then head of Iran's nuclear effort, that uranium deposits had been discovered near Saghand in the east of the country, he said soon afterward that additional deposits had been found in ten other locations. Amrollahi announced that Iran would be opening a uranium processing plant to make the country self-sufficient in yellowcake (which is the source material for conversion to uranium hexafluoride and its subsequent enrichment to reactor-grade or weapons-grade material).

Enter the IAEA. After revelations that Iran might be developing an unsafeguarded supply of enriched uranium, the organization—under the auspices of the Nonproliferation Treaty—made a cursory visit to Saghand and five other suspect nuclear sites. But there were nine more uranium mines mentioned by Amrollahi that were given the all clear without inspections in loco.

To be correct, Iran was under no obligation to report uranium mines before it had signed the Additional Protocol. It is also an incorrect assumption that the NPT gave the IAEA the authority for inspections of the mines. All inspections, at whatever location or plant, are done under a Safeguards Agreement or the more-recently negotiated Additional Protocol.

That said, IAEA inspectors did not ask to be shown other locations near Saghand where a milling plant(s) might have been located. Yet two years before that, a report from the Iranian Majlis gave details of a "uranium bullion plant" that would employ eight hundred people that was to be established in the Saghand area. This was all published information.

Then, according to the American publication *Iran Brief*, Amrollahi told a Tehran radio interviewer that Iran would open three more yellowcake milling facilities in addition to the one at Saghand. Two of these sites were identified as Bandar Abbas and Bandar-e Langeh, both on the Gulf.

Taken together, this is an incredibly large supply of material that is distinctly nuclear related. Why else would Iran be devoting so much effort and to a process involved in the preparation of uranium dioxide? Although the Bushehr nuclear power station will use some of it, the amount coming out of the ground is far ahead of what might be needed for any domestic program.

As Britain and America keep saying, with Iran's massive oil reserves, the very idea of more nuclear power stations remains spurious.

Meanwhile—in spite of protests to the contrary—in building the billion dollar Bashehr reactor on the coast, with the prospect of contracts for two more such reactors in the offing, Moscow continues to play a significant role.

Adding to earlier fears that the Iranians were moving in this direction, was the signing of several classified protocols between Tehran and Moscow. Part of the deal involves training aspirant Iranian nuclear physicists (ten to twenty a year) at Russian universities and developing more uranium mines. There was also a commitment to negotiate additional contracts for research reactors and to build gas centrifuges for enriching uranium, but American pressure canceled that.

In regard to Bushehr, Moscow claims that any Russian-supplied reactor would be intensely safeguarded by the IAEA. Plutonium-laden spent fuel, it stipulates, would be returned to where it came from as per terms of the contract. For their part, the Americans are skeptical. They maintain that agreements that involve international security arrangements are often useless, especially in a country bent on achieving a nuclear objective. What is significant here is that Iran has already implied that it hopes to eventually produce fuel for the plant domestically, which, as Marshall Breit explains, would—barring an international arrangement—result in themselves controlling all spent fuel from the reactor/s.

At issue here is whether plutonium separated from spent civil reactor fuel can actually be used for making nuclear weapons. The Americans, interestingly enough, have always said that it can, and have apparently demonstrated such a weapon. Others are not so sure. The problem with civil reactor-grade plutonium is that it contains lots of undesirable ^{238}Pu which causes pre-ignition of the ^{239}Pu (the bomb material) and results in the bomb fizzling rather than detonating.

As David Albright points out (speaking from experience gained while serving in Iraq with IAEA Action Teams and his practical and scientific knowledge of the implications) a large power reactor, or reactors, would eventually discharge quantities of plutonium in spent fuel. This raises the possibility that some of this material could be diverted for weapons use if Iran chose to do so. Thus, if it believed that it faced threats to its security, as it did from Iraq in the past, Iran could easily abrogate its treaty obligations.

Albright goes on: "Russia has the largest uranium-enrichment centrifuge program in the world. Iran's attempt to buy such plants from Moscow has already alerted many Western governments of the possibility that Tehran might covertly seek out centrifuge assistance from Russian companies and experts. What we do know is that they didn't have to try too hard in the past, since there were many companies in the FSU that were desperate for business. There are recorded instances where some of them were willing to evade weakly-enforced national export control laws.

"Because Russian centrifuges are sub-critical models that are relatively unsophisticated (compared to the most modern European machines) they may be easier for Iran to develop and manufacture," he speculates. "In addition, Russia built millions of them. This further raises the possibility that Tehran could somehow acquire large numbers of surplus machines, perhaps 'under the counter'."

Western specialists stress that once Iran has acquired this expertise, there is nothing to stop it from passing classified material on to other interested parties such as Syria or North Korea. *The Wall Street Journal* originally pointed to the possibility of the "on-off-on" Syrian-Iraqi axis that might eventually, of necessity, include Iran as one of the consequences of frustration with what is going on elsewhere in the Middle East. And while the alliance might be moribund now, political allegiances change, it declared.[12]

There have been several more exposures in recent years, including those made by Dr. Fred Wehling, a Senior Research Associate at the Center for Nonproliferation Studies, Monterey Institute of International Studies. He told this writer that while Russian missile exports to Syria are also an issue, Moscow has been a leading exporter of nuclear and missile technology, as well as conventional weapons to Tehran.

The author of *Irresolute Princes: Kremlin Decision Making in Middle East Crises* (St Martin's Press, 1997), Dr. Wehling published his findings in *The Nonproliferation Revue* (Winter, 1999).[13] He stated that the Russian government's apparent support for, or its inability to prevent, transfers to Iran of technology related to nuclear weapons and ballistic missiles had raised serious concerns in the U.S., Israel and other countries.

Both Washington and Jerusalem protested vigorously once Russian involvement became known. The U.S., said Wehling, had applied economic sanctions on Russian firms and research institutes suspected of transferring sensitive technology to Tehran, and he cites the July 28, 1998 "Statement by the President Expanding the President's Executive Order on Weapons of Mass Destruction." Some of the entities mentioned were sanctioned for attempting to supply Iran with maraging steel, which, Wehling thinks, may have been intended for Pakistani-designed centrifuges for enriching uranium.

Yet, he says, "Russia's Ministry of Atomic Energy (Minatom) for some time afterward continued aggressively to promote exports of nuclear technology and materials to Iran." Likewise, Russian missile firms and research institutes, strapped for cash and short of orders while the country was mired in an economic crisis, looked to Tehran and other countries of proliferation concern for markets for their products and technology. Russia has reviewed its export policies under Putin, but obviously intends to complete construction and supply nuclear fuel under IAEA safeguards for the Bushehr reactor complex.

Russian environmentalist Aleksey Yablokov supports these views. He went on record as saying that the U.S. might very well have legitimate reasons to suspect Russian institutes of cooperating with Iran in "strategic areas," adding that initial Minatom plans for cooperation with Iran included a military component. It was notable that this was going on in spite of President Yeltsin's assurance in 1994 that this same military component would be removed. By the time it stopped—and under President Putin, there is no interchange of these technologies that the West is aware of— it was too late.

It was Yablokov's view that individual Russian defense organizations had become involved in supplying nuclear technology to Iran. He referred to the fact that an Iranian spy was arrested in Moscow at about that time for obtaining technical information on missiles and that one of the sanctioned facilities was known to be developing a chemical component of missile fuel for Iranian interests. Among nuclear exports listed by Dr. Wehling are the following:

- Moscow disclosed in 1999, that Minatom—which had already completed a large part of the first reactor facility—would go ahead with building the VVER-1000 reactor for the first Bushehr nuclear power plant. There were already more than a thousand Russians employed there. He confirmed that some Iranians were being trained at Russian establishments.
- Apart from the $800 million VVER-1000 light-water power reactor deal at Bushehr, the construction of five more nuclear were being negotiated. These include three additional power reactors of unspecified size, one 30–50 MWth research reactor and one 40 MWth heavy-water research reactor. There are also ongoing discussions regarding a nuclear APWS-40 desalinization plant. If signed, these contracts would ultimately be worth $2–$3 billion to Moscow.

News of the 40MWt heavy-water reactor first appeared when U.S. intelligence sources reported that Russia's Scientific Research and Design Institute of Power Technology (NIKIET) and another nuclear research institute (probably the Mandeleev University of Chemical Technology) were in the process of negotiating a nuclear reactor sale to Iran.

Months later, Washington imposed sanctions on both bodies as well as against the Moscow Aviation Institute. According to initial reports, negotiations over the sale had been ongoing for more than six months. While no equipment for this reactor was ever shipped, personnel and blueprints were known to have been exchanged. The reports raised specific concerns about the personal involvement of the then-Russian Minister of Atomic Energy, Adamov, in these transactions. This was the same man who had served as director of NIKIET until his ministerial appointment came through in 1998.

Wehling quotes U.S. nonproliferation expert Gary Milhollin as saying that "If Iran succeeds in importing a research reactor like this, it will open the way to making a bomb."

Also highlighted in the report, in the category of enrichment, mining and milling, is a uranium conversion facility. There had been nuclear materials transfers planned for LEU fuel rods for the VVER-1000 reactor, two-thousand tons of natural uranium as well as training for Iranian physicists and technicians at the Kurchatov Institute and the Novovoronezh Nuclear Power Plant.

It is interesting that Viktor Mikhailov, former First Deputy Minister of Atomic Energy, was quoted on a Kremlin International News Broadcast that Russia had helped Iran design a uranium mine. Work had already started in 1992 with preliminary studies for a facility that would, by now, have had an annual output of between a hundred and two hundred tons. Mikhailov also said that Iran was seeking Russian assistance in uranium and isotope enrichment.

There were further connections related to missile proliferation. Articles in the Western press reported that the scientific production associations Trud (located in Samara) and Energomash transferred technology related to the RD-214 rocket engine, which was being incorporated into Tehran's SS-4 medium-range rocket engine. Intelligence sources maintained that this was the result of well-placed Israeli "leak."

A report by ITAR-TASS and *Voprosy Besopasnosti* carried quick denials by both the Russian president and prime minister.

What is known from reliable sources is that the Russian firm Samara State Scientific and Production Enterprise-NK Engines (affiliated with NPO Trud) received engineering drawings for turbopump components from an Iranian concern and contracted to produce the requested parts. Soon afterward, NK Engines received additional technical information about the parts from their Iranian customers, and then realized that the parts were for a rocket engine, most likely the RD-214. An export license was applied for and the application rejected, with the FSB seizing all documents relating to the canceled transaction.

Proliferation Research and Assessment Program (PRAP) staff at the Monterey Institute disclosed this information in an interview with U.S. missile experts (whose names were withheld by request).

One of the more significant developments linked to these findings was the testimony before Congress by former CIA Director George Tenet. Though relations between Russia and America had improved markedly by then, he averred that there were some notable gaps. Despite sanctions, Russia was "backsliding" on its commitments to restrict the transfer of missile technology to Russia. While he accepted that there were positive signs in Moscow's performance on this issue, there was no sustained improvement. He disclosed that in the previous six months expertise and materials from Russia had assisted Iranian missile programs in training, testing and other areas.

That followed a statement by the then-First Deputy Prime Minister Yuriy Maslyukov. He declared that Russia was willing to tighten controls on exports of missile technology to Iran if the U.S. could offer proof of illicit transfers. Basically, the onus lay with Washington to prove wrongdoing, he added cryptically.

Shortly afterward, his colleague, the then-Russian Minister of Defense Igor Sergeyey, stated that control over nonproliferation of nuclear missile technologies did exist in Russia. Referring to the U.S. imposing sanctions on various Russian bodies, Sergeyey maintained that those institutes could not in any event "supply Iran with missile technologies they did not possess." Instead, he suggested that the sanctions issue was being used as a pretext for something that was not yet clear.

"While every country has the right to apply sanctions, what America has done is unethical," he is quoted in *V.Rossii yest kontrol za neraprostraneniyem raketno-yadernykh tekhnologii-Minoborony.*

Though much of this is history, it makes for a pertinent background on what Iran was looking for in the late 1990s. It also points toward specific objectives, some of which are regarded by military specialists as offensive. Among other Russian missile exports to Iran in that period were the following:[14]

- Twenty-one tons of maraging steel of unknown manufacture (but possibly Inor Production Association and exported by MOSO and Yevropalas 2000);
- Composite material used for ballistic warheads, manufactured by NII Grafit;
- Unspecified missile guidance components from the Polyrus Scientific Research Institute and more than half a ton of special alloys and foils from Inor Production Association and exported by Moscow's arms marketing organization, Rosvooruzheniye;
- The alleged exportation of wind tunnel and related facilities from the Russian Central Aerohydrodynamic Institute (TsAGI), exported by Rosvooruzheniye, the official marketing arm of the Russian Republic.

5

DOOMSDAY EQUATION

"A 10-kiloton bomb is smuggled into Manhattan
and explodes at Grand Central. Some half-a-million
people are killed and the U.S. suffers $1 trillion in
direct economic damage."

Scenario cited in a 2003 report from the John F. Kennedy
School of Government, Harvard University

In the wake of some of the most damning evidence of nuclear proliferation of our times, driven, as some say, solely by the avarice of a
handful of Pakistani scientists, the international community is only
now coming to grips with the damage done.

At the same time, there is much speculation that it was not only
greed that motivated A.Q. Khan and company but that the Pakistani
government obtained funds for their expensive weapons program by
selling this technology to whoever would pay the kind of money
demanded. It should be recalled that after Dr. Abdul-Quadeer Khan's
public apology, the Pakistani president decided not to act against him,
a peculiar approach for a scientist who marketed his country's most
precious secrets for money that ostensibly went into his own pocket.

The thread of Pakistani complicity unfolds across three continents.
Evidence continues to emerge—and will go on doing so—of other
nations who exploited the loophole of trust: China, Turkey, Russia,
several European and other former Soviet Union countries and, to the
surprise of all, even Libya, a nation better suited for tending camels
and collecting oil revenues from foreign companies exploiting their
reserves than the need to embark on a program of developing weapons
of mass destruction.

Interestingly, Israeli intelligence had warned several times early in
the new millennium that Moammar Gadhaffi was involved in developing a nuclear weapons program of his own. It was such a ludicrous
supposition that nobody took any notice, even though I did a report

at the time for *Jane's Islamic Affairs Analyst* which was spiked. There were those who scoffed at what they believed was an obvious Mossad effort at disinformation.

The truth is, nuclear links between Iran and Pakistan—and Libya for that matter—go way back. Within days of Pakistan's "final" atomic test, Iran's foreign minister, Kamal Kharazi, flew into Islamabad and hailed Pakistan's "Islamic bomb." He was met by his counterpart, Mr. Gohar Ayub Khan.[1]

"Muslims now feel more confident that Pakistan's nuclear capability will play a role of deterrence to Israel's nuclear capability," exclaimed Mr. Kharazi at a news conference. *News International Pakistan* said that talks between the two countries would "focus on peace in Afghanistan and on the nuclear crisis with India." Nothing was mentioned about previous Pakistani participation in Iran's covert nuclear weapons program, nor was anybody present bold enough to ask.

While Tehran continues to deny that it is building an atomic bomb, the West has assembled a substantial body of evidence suggesting that while Iran had signed the Nuclear Non-Proliferation Treaty (NPT)—as had Iraq—it was secretly pursuing a broad, organized effort to develop nuclear weapons. According to the American-based *The Bulletin of the Atomic Scientists*,[2] "Some implicate the (Iranian) defense ministry in illegal foreign procurement activities and possible nuclear weapons work at military sites."

For years now, Pakistan has been linked to Iran's nuclear program. *The Washington Post* recalled that Clinton told Boris Yeltsin at one of their first summits that America had evidence that Iran was pursuing a nuclear weapons acquisition blueprint. It had been drawn up at least four years earlier with the aid of Pakistani officials, Clinton revealed.[3]

As early as 1995, the *New York Times* disclosed that senior American and Israeli officials had said, "Iran might be able to build a bomb in five years." The consensus in Washington a decade later is that the mullahs are further ahead "in the race toward nuclear parity" than was Iraq when the UN Special Commission for Iraq (UNSCOM) abruptly halted Saddam's nuclear program after the 1991 Gulf War.

Other reports mentioned the recruitment to Iran's clandestine nuclear program of foreign scientists and technicians, including Russians and Pakistanis.[4] Since then, the going rate for someone with the required skills in that country had increased from $5,000 to somewhere around $10,000 a month, depending on experience. Now, it seems, there are also South African nuclear physicists involved. Rocket scientists from Pretoria's defunct missile program have been helping the Iranians hone these skills for years, so it would seem a natural progression to use those with the necessary skills available in other scientific disciplines, especially if they are unable to earn a living and feed their children on their own turf.

Pakistan's involvement with Iran involves more substantive issues, particularly with regard to some of the acknowledged alliances in the region. India's border dispute with China has obviously resulted in closer Pakistani-Chinese ties, and, by inference, a deepening friendship between Beijing and Tehran.

China, since the mid-1980s, has been a supplier of nuclear-related technologies to Iran. Beijing provided three sub-critical and zero-power reactors as well as an electromagnetic isotope separation (EMIS) machine for enriching uranium. A small 80-kilowat thermal research reactor followed. Washington acknowledges that while none of this hardware is capable of producing more than small quantities of nuclear weapons material, EMIS machines can (and have been) reverse-engineered.

Significantly, reckons David Albright, China also helped Iran create nuclear fuel facilities for uranium mining, fuel fabrication, uranium purification and zirconium tube production. (See Jane's *Pointer*, Feb. 1998.) Already in the pipeline almost a decade ago, despite strong American protests, were facilities to produce uranium metal and uranium hexafluoride (UH_6).

Saddam Hussein in his day received some Indian aid in developing weapons. It was a development that seriously displeased Tehran. For a while there was even speculation in intelligence circles about a "rogue alliance" between Iraq and Iran, though it made no sense because the two countries were deeply suspicious of each other. The continuing animosity stemmed as much from Saddam's persecution of his own Shi'ite majority as from the terrible damage and loss of life caused by the eight-year war between the two nations.

Looking back, it would seem that India's involvement with Saddam was more than a casual sharing of information, which might have been one of the reasons why the Iraqi dictator publicly supported India's nuclear tests. At the same time, a Baghdad weekly owned by one of his sons announced that India had agreed to enroll several groups of Iraqi engineers "in advanced technological courses." The training was unspecified, but American intelligence analysts were concerned at that time that Iraq might acquire illicit assistance in the nuclear or ballistic missile areas.[5]

Nuclear relations between Iraq and India date back as far as 1974 when Saddam Hussein flew to India, specifically to sign a nuclear cooperation treaty with Indira Gandhi, then Prime Minister. That this little-known treaty did not cause an international backlash at the time is surprising: it involved an exchange of nuclear scientists as well as training and technology. According to ISIS, "India taught Iraq many tricks, including how to acquire nuclear technology under the guise of peaceful nuclear energy."

One Iraqi intelligence agency document to emerge in the aftermath of the 2003 invasion of Iraq stated that in 1990 (a year before Operation Desert Storm), Dr. Abdul-Qadeer Khan, through an intermediary, offered to provide Saddam Hussein with key nuclear weapons assistance for a large sum of money. It is interesting, therefore, that American intelligence estimates of Iran's progress toward developing a bomb today puts Tehran farther ahead than Baghdad at the time that UNSCOM closed down the Iraqi nuclear program.

In a rare interview given to an American television network in May 1995, former Iranian President Rafsanjani told ABC that his country had neither nuclear weapons nor was it seeking to acquire or to develop them. "If [Washington] can prove a single case, then we will accept all other allegations," he declared to the camera.

Even today, a decade later, Rafsanjani's statement remains significant for several reasons, the first being that he was not telling the truth. By then the Iranian nuclear program was eight years old. More salient, it was one of those rare occasions when anyone in Iran—least of all the head of state—had allowed himself to be to be drawn out on such a controversial issue. In one of his comments afterward, former Secretary of State Warren Christopher said, "Based on a wide variety of data, we know that since the mid-1980s, Iran has had an organized structure dedicated to acquiring and developing nuclear weapons."

In organization, programs, procurement and covert activities, he went on, "Iran is pursuing the classic route to nuclear weapons which has been followed by almost all states that have recently sought a nuclear capability." He referred specifically to Iraq, where, because of a weak industrial infrastructure that could not support the demands of a nuclear effort, it needed to seek personnel, technology, equipment and materials for these weapons abroad.

At the heart of Iran's ongoing nuclear programs stands Russia. In defiance of American pressure, Russia declared in July 2002 that it would finish construction of the $840 million nuclear reactor in Bushehr, and as we have seen, confirmed earlier reports that it plans to build five more reactors over the next decade (another in Bushehr and four in Ahvaz, forty miles from Tehran), all for an additional $10 billion.[6]

U.S. concerns focus not on the mishandling of nuclear material from the 1,000-megawatt Bushehr light-water reactor—Russia promises to import it as waste fuel—but on the possibility that Russian know-how and expertise will create a core cadre of Iranian nuclear experts who could then apply their acquired knowledge to a weapons program. For its part, Moscow steadfastly refutes such an eventuality. It underscores its argument by pointing to having declined Iranian demands in 1990 to build a more powerful heavy-water reactor. The Russians also claim to have turned down Tehran's request for gas centrifuges[7] (though again, Moscow was under serious pressure from Washington to do so).

In a brilliant exposition on Russia's role in Iran and its long-term effect on the West, Dr. Victor Mizin, a former Russian diplomat specializing in arms control, nonproliferation and global security problems, offered some thoughts on the subject in a paper published by MERIA, the Middle East Review of International Affairs. Titled "The Russia-Iran Nuclear Connection and U.S. Policy options," Dr. Mizin, who at the time was the Diplomat-in-Residence and Senior Research Associate with the Center for Nonproliferation Studies of the Monterey Institute for Nonproliferation Studies in Monterey, California, tackled the issue head on. (See Appendix A)

Desperate for a practical solution, he suggested that it was not impossible that the United States might ultimately turn to the idea of a limited Osiraq-type airstrike or, possibly, larger-scale military operations to knock out the major Iranian nuclear facilities.[8]

On attempting to monitor Tehran's nuclear program, he declared, "As many experts concur, the current international arrangements-demonstrate their glaring inefficacy to halt attempts of the most dangerous, destabilizing and proliferation-prone regimes to obtain nuclear technologies, assets and know-how." The major drawback of the Non-Proliferation Treaty (NPT), a product of the Cold War era, he said, was that "it permits any state to accomplish its nuclear weapons program short of finally assembling a nuclear explosive device itself."

The NPT does not observe any distinction between well-behaved members of the international community such as, say Denmark, and aggressive or failed quasi-states like war-ridden Liberia, totalitarian North Korea or Saddam-era Iraq. Moreover, as he pointed out, these are the types of regimes that frequently dominate some UN-run agendas.

It is what Dr. Mizin has to say about Russia's consequent relations with the West and arms sales to Third World countries that are important:

> Though generally inclined to promoting good relations with the West—which is vital for its economic well-being and development—Russia has yet to shirk off its Soviet-era policy of external arms and technology transfers and aid to rogue states and countries of proliferation concern. This policy continues despite the fact that these traditional clients are declared enemies of the United States, a purported strategic partner.
>
> Russia's inability to secure larger investments from the West is influenced by the country's internal problems—rampant corruption, bureaucratic mismanagement, and crumbling socio-economic infrastructure—which lie behind the facade of steady growth. . . .
>
> The economic shortfall here then provides an additional incentive for Russians to argue that they need to sell sophisticated weaponry and dual-use items to states like China, India, Syria, and Iran as legitimate trade operations. There should be no problem in doing this, Moscow claims, as it pledges strict observance of nonproliferation and export control treaties. In any case, these weapons systems and technology find few eager or legal customers in the West or Western-aligned countries.

Dr. Mizin argues that the rationale for these connections is not solely economic. Moscow is promoting its own network of alliances, ostensibly to offset current U.S. unilateralism and strengthen its position as a leading global player. "Indeed, Russia has regained much ground, even if it still falls short of the international role it enjoyed during the existence of the USSR," he declares.

"In this pattern, Iran is emerging as the exemplar for Russia's global positioning in the 21st century, as well as in U.S.-Russian bilateral dialogue. This is especially true regarding the nuclear issue, an area where Moscow has historically tried to appear as the leading protagonist, though it has often bent existing international norms."

An insider to the politics of the Kremlin, Dr. Mizin allows us the luxury of a rare and penetrating glimpse into the Machiavellian maneuvering at which President Vladimir Putin has proven adept. In this respect, he plays all his cards simultaneously when dealing with the subtleties of the Russian-Iranian connection:

> Russia's relations with Iran are inconsistent and characterized by discord within Moscow's political and military circles. There is a compact pro-Western group, who think that cooperation with the major industrial states, primarily the United States, could benefit Moscow much more than murky dealings with questionable partners like China, Iran, Iraq, or Libya. The recent friction with Iran regarding regional problems in the Caspian Sea basin strengthened this position.
>
> There is also another powerful group consisting of the representatives of the floundering Russian Defense Industrial Complex (OPK) and the special services. This group promotes a different course of developing traditional strategic and economic ties with China and India or such former Moscow clients as Iran, Syria, and North Korea, while maintaining only conditional token cooperation with Washington in the global arena. It attempts to lobby its position through a "class-friendly" faction of KGB veterans in Putin's entourage.
>
> It seems that the members of this faction are driven not only by the desire to ensure purely economic benefits for the survival and expansion of the ailing Russian defense enterprises (and for their personal enrichment), but also by an inbred animosity toward America that goes back almost a century.
>
> This group sees the United States as Moscow's main adversary from the Cold War era and an alleged impediment to Russia's great power revival. The defense industry, secret services, and the disgruntled military's mistrust of the goals of current U.S. foreign and military policy—perceived as being ultimately anti-Russian—leads them to predictably conclude that Washington is attempting to impose arbitrary restraints on Russian exports of high technologies in order to stymie their country as a competitor for influence in the CIS.

Third, says Dr. Mizin, there is the usual midway faction represented mostly by OPK officials and managers who change their positions depending on the context:

> Today, by winning an occasional large-scale contract say, from Lockheed Martin, they can actively lobby for the expansion of Russian-American cooperation in space. But tomorrow—as money peters out—they would turn to buyers from rogue regimes or other suspicious clients. Thus, the particular instability of the Russian economy seems to provide the basic reason for the duality and inconsistency of Moscow's policy concerning the dangers of WMD-related technology transfers, specifically to Iran.

Proponents of special ties with preferred clients in the Third World have actively pushed for a continuation of arms deals with Iran, states Mizin.[9]

They were particularly resolute in advocating the annulment of the Chernomyrdin commitment—a deal made in June 1995 between former U.S. Vice President Al Gore and then-Russian Premier Viktor Chernomyrdin to stop military cooperation with Iran in 2000 after the completion of previous contracts. This faction finally prevailed in 2000 after the disclosure of the secret deal by the *New York Times* on October 13, 2000, which, according to the *Washington Times*, Gore had agreed not to make public to any third parties, including the U.S. Congress.

At the same time, persistent calls by Washington to terminate Russian exports to Iran were portrayed by these circles in Moscow as motivated by the desire of American corporations to save future opportunities in the Iranian market for themselves. To prove this, they cited the recent writings of such foreign policy heavyweights as Henry Kissinger, Zbigniew Brzezinski, and Brent Scowcroft that advocated closer ties with the putatively reformist Iranian political elite.[10]

Looking at the broader scenario, the idea of Moscow's leaders providing Tehran with the wherewithal to build its own nuclear device—with or without NPT safeguards, primitive or otherwise—makes about as much sense as it would for the Americans to equip Cuba with ICBMs.

There are several reasons. The first is that Iran borders on several FSU states, just about all of them with strong Islamic traditions. A half hour spent looking at news reports out of the region reveals that Moscow is today viewed with great suspicion and indeed, deep-rooted odium by almost all Islamic countries. This is the direct consequence of the manner in which the Kremlin has handled its ongoing Chechnyan conflict. This crisis—another bitter contest between Islam and forces that oppose the tenets of the *Qur'an*—is now more than a decade old and in its wake has left several hundred thousand people dead, wounded or dispossessed, most of them Chechnyans of Moslem faith. No wonder then that Chechnya has become a most prolific al-Qaeda recruiting ground.

Sentiments expressed on several Chechnyan and other Islamic websites are explicit that it is only Moslems who are targeted and that it is Russian troops doing the killing. Some are filled with horrifying images of human rights transgressions that make for a powerful impact. An impression that lingers is one of intransigence and a cold-hearted culpability on the part of the Kremlin, and as far as any Muslim is concerned—devout or otherwise—this war has become hugely personal. In the eyes of Allah, consequently, many feel that it is unconscionable. In a word, then, Chechnya is Russia's Intifada, where no quarter is expected or given.

An interesting sidelight is the public reaction of some Islamic countries. Pakistan's *Jamaat-e-Islami*, in a recent publication titled "Memorandum on the Situation in Chechnya,"[11] declared that the Russians were using chemical weapons against the civilian population. It made the point: what the one can do, so can the other. It would consequently be a supreme irony if one of the states that has received clandestine help from Moscow in developing weapons of mass destruction—we know about Iraq, Syria, Pakistan, Libya and others—was to supply those same assets to a group of anti-Moscow rebels in a preponderantly Islamic FSU state. Nor has it been lost on the Kremlin that should relations between Moscow and Tehran go sour, Iran might eventually be at the forefront of mullah ire.

Even Algiers has come into the picture. Though Moscow wasn't a direct participant, it certainly knew that "backward" Algeria had shown interest in getting its own atomic-bomb. Until February 1992, Algeria was secretly building a Chinese-supplied reactor at Ain Oussera, a remote site in the Atlas Mountains south of Algiers.[12] While that country's military leaders have since signed the NPT and abandoned this ridiculous quest, it caused a stir when details first emerged, courtesy of the Spanish secret service. (More about the program can be found on the ISIS websight at <isis-online.org>.)

Even Yeltsin, in his day, acknowledged to the Americans that ultimately, WMD might be turned on his own people. But as one former Soviet strategist declared at the time (in relation to supplying Iran with nuclear expertise), "It is better to assist these people, our neighbors, now, so we know what they are doing and where they are in the process, than to let them venture into uncharted terrain in the future." The thrust of the Russian argument rests on the fact that not only does Iran have the right under NPT provisions to possess a full range of safeguarded fuel-cycle facilities, but that the IAEA (with Russians in attendance) will, of necessity, do what it needs in order to ensure that the process is not abused.

Yet the premise is contradictory in the light of what had been taking place earlier in Iraq. In spite of some pretty blatant and public differences right now, that case history is eventually likely to be regarded as the ultimate Middle East catalogue of duplicity and deceit. As one UNSCOM observer noted, "The Iraqis lied with fluency from Day One." More important, dealings with Baghdad resulted in a lot of skepticism in some quarters as to whether the IAEA was really capable of doing the job for which it was intended.

The Washington Post put its case for this argument in April, 1995, when it reminded its readers that after the Gulf War ended in 1991, the UN went on to discover that Saddam Hussein had pursued a $10 billion secret nuclear weapons program under the very noses of IAEA inspectors. It noted that there were more than ten thousand people employed in the program. Dr. David Kay told Congress in one of his debriefs on Capital Hill that the true figure was probably closer to twenty thousand.

Based upon confidential interviews with returning inspectors, a 1993 study by the Pentagon's Defense Nuclear Agency concluded, "Iraq often successfully manipulated the inspections. The lesson here is mandatory: that any potential violator in the future may be able to out-wait the inspection process through delays and denials."

According to the Post, "Several Americans who had worked at the IAEA (in Iraq) publicly attacked its inspectors as weak-kneed, milquetoast UN types. Some U.S. nuclear weapons scientists returned from IAEA-supervised missions to Baghdad grumbling that Hans Blix (then head of the IAEA) wouldn't know a nuclear bomb if he tripped over one." (See Appendix D for an insight on the original Iraqi nuclear program.)

On a practical level, Iran's WMD program falls squarely within the orbit of Tehran's most secret security body, the Islamic Revolutionary Guard Corps (IRGC), better known in Iranian circles as the Pasdaran, an organization with which we will deal later in more detail.

Created in the early days of the revolution, the Pasdaran still takes the lead in the production and employment of nuclear, chemical and biological weapons. Paula A DeSutter, whose insightful thesis on the Iranian IRGC and its role in the country's nuclear establishment was published by the Center for Counterproliferation Research at Washington's National Defense University, details much of it.[13]

She tells us that the role of the Pasdaran extends far beyond the country's frontiers. It is the inspiration and main source of succor behind the anti-Israel Hezbollah movement in southern Lebanon. More recently, Pasdaran has been said to have links with al Qaeda.

For some years the Pasdaran was involved in a comprehensive training program involving the Sudan's security personnel. The Pasdaran negotiated the lease to the Sudan's two main Red Sea ports, Suakin and Port Sudan. Again, one might ask for what purpose, since Iran is hardly a regional power in the Indian Ocean.

Ms. DeSutter's assessment is comprehensive. She describes the IRGC as an effective post-revolutionary unit that "has not only survived, but thrived . . . with a structure reminiscent of the old Bolshevik Red Army."

As she observes, the IRGC would be the "focal point for Iranian efforts to 'export the revolution'." It says a lot that by the end of the Iran-Iraq war, the IRGC was directing thirty-seven secret weapons development projects and working closely with another revolutionary entity that acted as its "Corps of Engineers," the "Construction Jihad" or "Crusade for Reconstruction."

More bizarre is the fact that the IRGC is answerable to no one but the man who inherited the mantle of Supreme Spiritual Guide from the late Ayatollah Khomeini. The role of Iran's present-day Supremo, Sayyid Ali Khamene'i, within the administration, supersedes even that of President Khatami, head of the country's so-called "popular government."

In point of fact, Khatami's influence (or lack of it) has no bearing on what is taking place behind the shuttered world of Iranian security. Even its darker secrets, including the country's WMD potential, elude him because that is the way it works in a religious oligarchy. He would, for instance have no real knowledge of matters nuclear, though there is every likelihood—Tehran, in many respects having a village mentality in its upper echelons when it comes to state secrets—he would be aware of the consequences should the Israelis decide to do something about it.

The single biggest problem facing the West is attempting to penetrate Iran's formidable security mantle, including the ultra-fundamentalist and secretive Pasdaran. It starts and ends with the premise that if you are not Iranian and Shi'ite you are excluded from just about everything. Religion, race, ethnicity, and political orientation all play a role. There is also the need to speak Farsi—Arabic on its own won't do if you are to lift the veil.

Though things have eased fractionally in recent years, Westerners are only grudgingly welcome in the country. Visa applications can take a month to process, though anybody from a country enjoying favored-nation status, like South Africa, can get one in a week. An office attached to the Pasdaran vets all prospective applications from embassies abroad.

There is simply no ignoring the fact that the movement of all non-residents in the country, including diplomats, is monitored, often closely. While staying at any hotel, either in the capital or in the interior, your baggage is more than likely to be searched. To question something as sensitive as the country's nuclear weapons program would invite immediate attention.

There have been a few breaks. Iranian opposition groups tend to keep close tabs on developments inside the country and appear to be well funded by Langley. Also, the population at large, especially the younger set, are not nearly as anti-Western or anti-American as their parents might have been. The fact that there is a large community of Iranians living abroad—some put the figure in excess of a million—helps to foster this sentiment and encourage interest in just about everything foreign. Beyond the everyday image that most of us nurture of present-day Iran, linked as it is to a system of harsh political and religious control, Americans are a lot more popular than most foreigners expect.

Then there are Iran's expatriate politicians. Individuals such as former Iranian President Abol Hassan Bani Sadr (living in exile in Europe and still giving interviews) have created extensive underground contacts, including some within Khatami's own entourage.

These are people who, with time, have become thoroughly disillusioned with the country's politics, overwhelmed as it is by the kind of restrictive religiosity that prevents women from displaying a single strand of hair or open flesh, be it on their arms or necks. Most of these people abominate the ruling elite. One effect over the years has been more defections to the West than anybody in Tehran would like to admit.

Given the swirling brew of sentiment in the country, details occasionally emerge more by design than by accident. Much valuable data on Iranian nuclear developments was provided by Iranian General Sardar Shafagh, formerly a member of the IRGC and, in his day, a key player in Iran's uranium enrichment program. He disappeared in Moscow in mid-1995 while negotiating nuclear contracts with the Russian organization Minatom. According to Bani Sadr, he had with him a batch of important documents and, as he will ask with a smile, who knows where these are now?

With all these developments in mind, there are people on both sides of the Atlantic that ask the obvious question: What is really behind Iran's attempt to acquire nuclear weapons? More to the point, what is it that motivates those involved?

The immediate answer, among the majority of Iranians, is Israel. The Jewish state—you are likely to be told in Tehran—is both a nuclear power and an aggressor. To Iranians the conclusion is irrevocable. Any kind of debate to the contrary, even among opponents of the government, is out of the question.

With the strong American financial and military support that Jerusalem enjoys, the Islamic consensus is that the Jewish state simply cannot be trusted. They point not only to ongoing hostilities in Gaza and the West Bank but to Israel's invasion of Lebanon and its destruction of Iraq's reactor at Osiraq.

In addition to concerns about Israel, there is a subliminal suspicion that a new and revitalized Iraq might eventually come to harbor territorial designs, perhaps not this decade, but the next, or the one after that. This is a palpable fear among some Iranians and it is especially prevalent among those who lost family in the 1980s war. It happened before, Iranians will remonstrate, and they will also remind you that the two countries have been enemies for centuries. Conflict could occur again, they argue, if only because U.S. forces are not going to be around forever.

At the same time, everybody is aware that the Shi'ite community in Iraq constitutes about sixty percent of the population. All things being equal, there must eventually be a Shi'ite government installed in Baghdad. Thus, while some apologists continue to believe that Iran has reason for a deterrent, the prospect of Shi'ites taking power in Baghdad argues against its logic.

There is also the view propounded by David Albright that had the Iran-Iraq war gone on long enough, the Iranians would most certainly have been on the receiving end of the first of Saddam's primitive atom bombs. He almost certainly would have gained the capability had coalition forces not stepped in with Desert Storm.

There is another even more palpable fear in Tehran these days that the United States—its forces now ensconced in Iraq along the length of its western frontiers—might ultimately use some excuse to launch the same kind of military stratagem against the Iranians that crippled Iraq in the Spring of 2003. Though this scenario is unlikely considering America's present-day military obligations in Iraq, it has been the subject of endless debates in the Majlis. According to those who know the country, such discussions are commonplace in the streets and markets, whether in the capital, Isfahan or Qom. In one form or another, this issue is touched on just about every day in the Iranian press and on television, usually under the heading "America the Aggressor."

What cannot be ignored is that in official Iran today, there is a powerful wellspring of animosity toward the West that is bitter and deep-rooted. Whatever the reason, history has proven often enough in the past century that such attitudes do not bode well for the future

The Islamic equation is still another issue. With the end of the Cold War, there is evidence that Iran sees itself on the cutting edge of a more forceful international role. Though not Arab itself, this could involve the country dominating a good part of the Arab-Moslem world, as well as the western half of the Indian Ocean. While Iran has not yet challenged the hegemony of New Delhi, it has made some notable gains.

One of the biggest surprises to emerge in the wake of the invasion of Iraq was that Tehran finally decided to cooperate with the IAEA to allow for formal inspections of its nuclear weapons program. Though the results have not been altogether satisfactory, America and Europe now know much more about what has been going on nuclearwise south of the Caspian Sea than before. On October 21, 2003, as part of a deal brokered by Britain, France, and Germany, Iran finally yielded to intense international pressure and agreed to sign the Additional Protocol to the Safeguards Agreement, which would allow the IAEA short-notice access to its nuclear facilities.

It should be observed that there is much more to the Additional Protocol than short-notice inspections. It requires more information, including on R&D, to be submitted, as well as access to locations and activities traditionally not required by Safeguards Agreements. Concurrently, Tehran did consent to provide an account of all its nuclear-related activities and to suspend its highly controversial uranium enrichment program.

However, an observation made by Professor Victor Mizin is that it remains to be seen whether this accord, finally signed after intense diplomatic pressure in December 2003, will actually result in Iran foregoing its drive for a nuclear fuel cycle program.

As he says, "To prevent the appearance of another nuclear weapon state, it is critically important that the international community seal the external channels that provide nuclear technologies which enhance Iran's capability to acquire nuclear weapons. This requires effective U.S. policies toward Tehran's most active suppliers. In dealing with the most prominent of these, Russia, the dialogue has so far been almost a fiasco for the American nonproliferation strategy."

First reports about the extent and nature of Iran's nuclear assets raised as many questions as answers, in part because it took the West so long to do something about the issue.

The National Council of Resistance of Iran, the opposition group that first reported the nuclear complex at Natanz (quoted at length by the *Washington Post*) said that Iran continued to receive assistance from China and North Korea, among other countries. Council spokesman Alireza Jafarzadeh said Iranian officials had visited both states over the past decade to seek technical help with uranium enrichment. More recently, two Chinese officials visited Iran to oversee mining of uranium ore near the town of Yaz, the group asserted. This report could not be independently verified.

It was Jafarzadeh's view that Western policies were partly to blame for the failure to detect Iran's secret programs in the first place, never mind deter or eliminate them. He said U.S. and European administrations should have adopted a more forceful posture rather than seeking rapprochement with more moderate Iranian leaders such as Khatami, whose leadership, incidentally, coincided with a dramatic acceleration of Iran's nuclear program.

"We warned repeatedly that if the international community would not take immediate and decisive measures, the regime could reach the point of no return with their nuclear weapons program," Jafarzadeh said. "They might well be very close to that."

But, says the *Post*, Rose Gottemoeller, a senior Energy Department official under former president Bill Clinton and now a senior associate at the Carnegie Endowment for International Peace, suggested that the emerging crisis over Iran was hardly due to U.S. inattention. The past three administrations were "hugely concerned" that Iran was secretly developing new capabilities, and had achieved major successes in blocking known attempts by Iran to acquire nuclear technology from Russia and China.

"The Clinton administration lobbied Russia for years to stop assisting Iran. Russia at one point suspended plans to sell laser separation technology to Iran following protests from Washington. U.S. officials feared that it would be used to help Iraq enrich uranium.

"Gottemoeller acknowledged that previous U.S. efforts 'focused too much on the Russian connection and not enough on our relations with Iran.' She added that the arguments for direct diplomacy are even more compelling now, if Iran is to be dissuaded from turning its new nuclear assets into weapons. She also pointed out that North Korea recently expelled the IAEA and is pushing toward the construction of a nuclear weapon." It was President Bush who referred to Iran, Iraq and North Korea as an "Axis of Evil."

"Our three 'axis of evil' designees seem to have decided to push hard to provide themselves with weapons if they're going to be in the constant attention of the United States," Gottemoeller said. "We need a more proactive, positive way of engaging them first and then trying to shut these things down."

Nor has this form of cooperation been easy. A UN resolution that originally gave Iran some months to disclose all its nuclear activities didn't work out as planned. The same with those that followed. After some initial disclosures in 2003, Tehran declared that it would now "go by the book and not do anything beyond its existing commitments." A radio broadcast from Tehran added that Iran would reduce its cooperation with the IAEA following the demand that it prove its nuclear aims are peaceful.

The original deadline was agreed on the basis of a report by IAEA director general Dr. Mohamed ElBaradei, which listed the discovery of weapons-grade uranium together with other evidence that signaled

Tehran's involvement in an atomic bomb program. Since then, there have been more revelations that Tehran has been working on trying to make weapons-grade uranium, including several facilities with centrifuge uranium separation equipment.

For their part, Iran's ayatollahs continue to maintain that their nuclear program is "designed to meet only the country's energy needs, and has absolutely no military use." Washington disputes this, having declared that Iran, with almost unlimited supplies of oil, is one country in the world that does not need nuclear power stations.

At a special CIA briefing before Congress recently, U.S. lawmakers were told in closed session that Iran was not only involved in a clandestine nuclear program, but that the country is on a fast track to producing the final end product. Iran could have its first prototype bombs ready for testing by late 2005, they were told.

An Israeli source quoted by the *Washington Post* went further. It stated that "the point of no return" could be reached by the middle of 2005. If work at extensive nuclear facilities uncovered around the country during the past year was not frozen, it went on, "the fundamentalist Islamic regime will soon have the capacity to manufacture the key elements of nuclear weapons." Worse, there is a considerable body of evidence that not all of Iran's nuclear assets—including more extensive gas centrifuge enrichment plants for making weapons-grade uranium—have been declared and that some secret sites remain hidden, implying clandestine nuclear weapons activity.

Dr. ElBaradei's report on Iran's nuclear program has caused consternation not only in Western intelligence circles but also in several Arab capitals fearful of an expanded Shi'ite regional power base.

Apart from releasing new information about that country's gas centrifuge program at Natanz (which is capable of producing between twenty and thirty-five pounds of weapons-grade uranium a year, or enough fissile material to arm one such bomb), other significant issues were raised. *The Bulletin of the Atomic Scientists* (September/October 2003) listed more findings attributed to the IAEA that Iran has failed to meet its nuclear obligations:

> *An undeclared uranium import.* In response to an IAEA request, Iran recently acknowledged that in 1991 it received from China a ton of natural uranium hexafluoride, about a thousand pounds of uranium tetrafluoride, and roughly the

same amount of uranium dioxide. This material was stored at the previously undeclared Jabr Ibn Hayam Multipurpose Laboratories (JHL), located at the Tehran Research Center. Iran provided none of this information until the IAEA asked for it. To make matters worse, China provided the IAEA with details about its export only after repeated inquiries, indicating a significant level of collusion between the two countries.

Undeclared uranium metal production. Iran stated that it converted almost all of the uranium tetrafluoride into uranium metal at JHL. The production of uranium metal is unusual and can indicate a nuclear weapons effort that uses metallic forms of natural uranium or highly enriched uranium.

Natural uranium target production. Iran said that it had used some of the uranium oxide to make "targets for irradiation" in the Tehran research reactor. These targets were then sent to another Tehran facility to separate iodine-131 in a lead-shielded cell. While legitimate, the question now posed is whether plutonium was also separated from these targets, or whether other undeclared "targets" were produced, irradiated, and processed to obtain separated plutonium. Such activities would allow Iran to learn to separate plutonium, a necessary step in diverting plutonium for use in nuclear weapons.

Missing uranium hexafluoride. Iran stated that it did not process any of its imported uranium hexafluoride, and specifically, that it did not use any in gas centrifuge testing. However, nearly two kgs are missing from the storage cylinders. Iran claimed that the material had leaked out of the cylinders more than a year earlier. The IAEA is still investigating this claim. A small centrifuge testing program would be expected to use about sixteen to twenty-five pounds of uranium hexafluoride, but it could get by on two or three. And the fact that Iran used much of its imported uranium dioxide and tetrafluoride, makes it difficult to accept the possibility that it did not use any of this hexafluoride.

A heavy-water reactor. In May 2002, Iran told the IAEA for the first time that it intended to build a 40-megawatt-thermal heavy-water reactor at Arak. This is the site of the clandestine heavy-water production facility whose existence was first revealed publicly by an Iranian opposition group in August 2002. Iran also announced that it intends to begin building a fuel-fabrication plant for the reactor at Esfahan later this year. The reactor at Arak would produce eight to ten kgs of pluto-nium annually, enough for about two nuclear weapons each year.

There are also unanswered questions about South African rocket sci-entists hired by Tehran to work on Iran's nuclear program. The unof-ficial word around Pretoria these days is that there are also South African nuclear physicists in Tehran's pay.

Though procedures may have changed since 2001, all movement of South African missile personnel was channeled through the admin-istrative offices of a parastatal former Armscor subsidiary Denel Aviation. That took place at their headquarters near Kempton Park on the outskirts of Johannesburg. (More of that later.)

North Korea too, is involved, with several reports from Langley of Pyongyang's scientists working in Iranian nuclear plants. More recent-ly, following disclosures from Seoul, the CIA highlighted North Korea having on at least six occasions transported containers believed to be carrying missiles to Iran by air. American intelligence satellite data showed Iranian Il-76 transport planes making direct flights with these weapons onboard from Pyongyang's Sunan Airport.

After analyzing information obtained through various channels, the Americans concluded that disassembled warheads and MRBM 1.3 liquid-fueled Nodong missiles (the same type of missile sold to Pakistan in 1998 and dubbed the Ghauri II) were onboard. It is worth noting that North Korea changed its export procedures following the interception of a North Korean vessel carrying missiles on its way to Yemen in December 2002.

Referred to as Shahab-3, this Iranian clone of a Russian scud can, in theory, carry a one-ton payload. Its size and range make it compat-ible with the concept of nuclear warhead delivery. In fact, Russian sources claim that the mere existence of the Shahab-3 missile program, with its relatively poor accuracy (Circle of Error Probable: one to three kms), implies that it is most likely meant to carry a strictly WMD payload.[14]

The latest news is that the Shahab-3 was successfully tested in

March 2004 over a range of thirteen hundred miles. Every Israeli city is now within range of Tehran's missiles.

The last word on the subject should rightly belong to Barry Rubin, editor of *The Middle East Review of International Affairs* (or more commonly, MERIA). An internationally recognized authority on Iran,[15] he has consistently warned that Tehran is involved in serious nuclear work. So, too have Andrew Koch and Jeanette Wolf in their article[16] "Iran's Nuclear Procurement Program: How Close to the Bomb?"

In a major contribution to the subject in the *Middle East Intelligence Bulletin*, Rubin recalled a statement delivered by Ayatollah Ali Akbar Hashemi Rafsanjani, then chairman of Iran's powerful Expediency Council at the University of Tehran in December 2001.[17] To a packed house of academics, scholars and government officials he declared: "If one day the Islamic World is also equipped with weapons like those that Israel possesses now, then the imperialists' strategy will reach a standstill because the use of even one nuclear bomb inside Israel will destroy everything." In the doctrine of the Islamic Republic, Rubin noted, "Nuclear weapons would be not just for their deterrent effect, but rather to pursue ideological goals." Looking at the scope and complexity of Tehran's nuclear programs, he might just be right.

More pertinently, Rafsanjani was not the first high-level Iranian official to advocate developing nuclear weapons, though he was the first to publicly propose going all the way. Both former defense minister Akbar Torkan and former deputy president and leading reformist Ayatollah Mohajerani (whom Khatami subsequently appointed his Minister of Islamic Guidance) have made impassioned pleas for Iran to join the nuclear club.

Rubin points out that apart from the nuclear reactor complex at Bushehr—open to inspection by the IAEA—there are many other nuclear-related sites scattered throughout the country that are not. Some of these include:

- Isfahan, which the Federation of American Scientists has identified as the primary location of Iran's nuclear weapons program. Also important is its Nuclear Technology/Research Center, the largest in the country with about three thousand scientists. Facilities include a 27 KWth (thermal) Miniaturized Neutron Source Reactor originally from China.

- The Tehran Nuclear Research Center, located in a suburb of Amirabad, contains an American five megawatt research reactor and a uranium yellowcake production facility. This is also home to the Atomic Energy Organization of Iran's Center for Theoretical Physics and Mathematics which conducts R&D relating to nuclear physics and plasma physics
- One of the most interesting sites—because it is controlled by Iran's Islamic Revolutionary Guard Corps—is at Darkhovin, south of Ahvaz. Any facility linked to the IRGC implies WMD development, and in this case, nuclear, because it was to have been the site of two 300 megawatt Qinshin reactors.
- Karaj is the site of Iran's Nuclear Research Center for Agriculture and Medicine and includes a Chinese calutron, a Belgian cyclotron as well as a radiochemistry and a dosimeter laboratories.
- Mu'allimn Kalayeh, in the mountains near Qasvin, which dissident intelligence sources have said includes facilities to house uranium enrichment gas centrifuges. IAEA inspections yielded nothing, but neither did similar inspections of similar sites in Iraq, which later proved to be linked to WMD.
- Some controversy surrounds Nekka near the Caspian Sea, which one group maintained was the site of an underground nuclear reactor facility. This report is unconfirmed, but then even the Israelis were successful in hiding underground nuclear assets at Divona from international inspection teams. The IAEA has an interest in developments here which is also the site of significant oil industry development.
- The Bonab Atomic Energy Research Center near Tabriz has long been of interest to Vienna's IAEA. Hans Blix toured the site in 1997 and though his inspection was cursory, he declared afterward that there was no evidence of clandestine nuclear activity. He said as much about some Iraqi nuclear sites that were later proved to be linked to WMD development.
- Saghand, as we have seen, is one of the likely sites of this kind of subterfuge since uranium deposits cover an area of almost a hundred square miles which, the *Middle East Intelligence Bulletin* maintains, has perhaps five thousand tons of uranium oxide (with ^{235}U content of about one per cent).[18]

One intelligence report that persistently surfaces—and has yet to be properly examined by the appropriate authority—is that Iran and

North Korea have close nuclear links. A while back, the *Washington Post*'s Joby Warrick reported on the subject in some detail.[19] He made the point that recent disclosures of secret nuclear facilities in Iran and North Korea, combined with the North's determination to resume plutonium production, "presented the U.S. with its most serious nuclear challenge since the early 1990s."

He went to suggest that Washington had long suspected the two countries "of quietly seeking uranium-based nuclear arms." More disturbing, he declared, was "how much they managed to achieve before anybody noticed."

Warrick stated: "For example, Iran's secret nuclear program was disguised for two years as a water irrigation project in the country's northern desert. Then satellite photos disclosed that construction near Natanz was never intended to pump water, but instead was for enriching uranium."

6

IRAN'S MULTI-STEMMED CENTRIFUGE PROGRAMS: AN OVERVIEW

By David Albright, President of the Institute for Science and International Security (ISIS) in Washington DC, and Corey Hinderstein, a Senior Analyst at ISIS[1]

"After Iran's first story of how it acquired uranium enrichment technology was rejected, evidence of a more complex procurement network began to emerge."

Iran has been secretly developing the capability to make nuclear weapons, and in particular, developing the wherewithal to produce separated plutonium and highly enriched uranium.

Since they first learned of Iran's secret activities in late 2002, officials of the International Atomic Energy Agency have been concerned that Iran has been violating the Nuclear Non-Proliferation Treaty, and have struggled to convince the country to make its nuclear activities more transparent. Citing Iran's failure to disclose various nuclear materials, facilities, and activities, on June 19 2003 a "Chairwoman's Statement" summing up the meeting of the IAEA Board of Governors criticized Iran for its failure to fulfill its safeguards obligations under the NPT.

Worries about Iranian nuclear activities were heightened shortly thereafter once Iran had conducted a successful test of the Shahab-3 missile, which can carry a one-ton payload almost a thousand miles. The timing of Iran's announcement about the Shahab-3 and the size of its payload suggested that the missile was intended to carry a nuclear warhead.

Although the IAEA acknowledged that Iran has taken some cooperative steps since its facilities at Natanz were first revealed, it called upon Iran to take additional steps, including answering more questions about alleged undeclared uranium enrichment activities, uranium conversion work, and programs involving heavy water.

Iran's reaction at the time was to reject the notion that it had a nuclear weapons program. It intended, Iranian officials said, to install some seven thousand megawatts of nuclear electrical generating capacity over the next twenty years, which would require a substantial investment in a wide range of peaceful nuclear activities. Iran described its level of transparency as typical, and reiterated that it had cooperated fully with the IAEA and would continue to do so. Iran also rejected the request to implement the additional protocol without a quid pro quo.

On June 29, 2003, Iranian Foreign Minister Kamal Kharrazi told the Associated Press, "When Iran signs the protocol, others should take positive steps," including providing nuclear assistance. Iranian officials wanted additional power reactors, or at least a U.S. commitment to stop its attempts to block Iran's acquisition of nuclear power reactors from Russia or elsewhere. Some Iranian officials implied that more reactors may not be enough, and that Iran wanted access to all peaceful technology, including sensitive fuel-cycle facilities like enrichment plants and plutonium separation facilities.

In late February 2003, Gholam Reza Aghazadeh, head of the Iranian Atomic Energy Organization (IAEO), told the *Boston Globe*'s Elizabeth Neuffer that Iran wanted Germany to fulfill its prior obligation to provide low-enriched uranium fuel, part of the original deal when Germany was building the Bushehr power reactor. Germany decided over a decade ago not to finish the reactor, but Aghazadeh complained that Iran now had to pay to get the fuel from Russia.

TRUTH AND CONSEQUENCES

Although the U.S. did not succeed in its attempt to convince other nations that Iran had violated the NPT sufficiently to warrant a harsh international response, the chair's statement represented a dramatic international rejection of Iran's demand to receive something in return for signing the protocol. Most of the nations involved initially resisted taking action based on the U.S. evidence, which they viewed as circumstantial. They were particularly hesitant given the widespread skepticism about U.S. intelligence information about Iraq's weapons of mass destruction. But the United States did manage to gain support for putting additional pressure on Iran to be fully transparent. Also included was a September 2003 deadline which, as it transpired, was not met.

Notably, Russia, Japan, and the European Union have historically rejected the U.S. policy of isolating Iran, choosing engagement instead. But by mid-2003, all were firm in demanding that Iran sign the protocol and fully answer questions being asked by the IAEA.

Before that crisis, the EU had a policy of engagement with Iran known as "conditional dialogue," which aimed at improving trade and cooperation, provided that Iran made improvements in the areas of nonproliferation, terrorism, and cooperation with the Middle East peace process. However, EU foreign ministers, in response, emphasized in a statement that Iran would be required to cooperate fully with the IAEA and "implement urgently and unconditionally." The additional protocol declared that trade talks and the nuclear issue were "interdependent." For his part, British Foreign Secretary Jack Straw traveled to Tehran with the message that unless Iran implemented the protocol unconditionally and quickly, "confidence will not be improved, and the international community will be profoundly reluctant to lift the sanctions."

Meantime, it was lost on none of the participants that Moscow has been Iran's main nuclear supplier, selling Iran the $800 million Bushehr reactor scheduled for completion in 2005. Russia was expected to start sending fuel for the first loading toward the end of 2004, after it had obtained an agreement from Iran to return spent fuel back to Russia, though at this writing the latter part of the agreement has not yet been formalized. Embarrassed by revelations of secret nuclear activities, the Kremlin has also urged Tehran to be more transparent.

Before that, President Vladimir Putin was reported to have told the United States and Britain that Russia would not provide fuel for Bushehr unless Iran implemented the safeguards protocol. Although subsequent communications from senior Russian officials appeared to contradict Putin's statement, the overall message from the Kremlin is that Iran needs to be significantly more transparent.

One Western official pointed out that Russia could hesitate to finalize its spent fuel agreement with Iran, and without it not send fuel for Bushehr. Or, he said, Russia could delay shipments, permitting it to exert pressure on Iran without formally conditioning the completion of Bushehr on Iran signing the protocol.

Since then Japan has also put pressure on Iran, and senior foreign ministry officials visited Tehran in 2003 to convey the message. Media reports did not indicate any significant breakthroughs and Japan has so far resisted U.S. pressure to link Iran's signing of the protocol with its current negotiations with Iran to develop the large Azadegan oil field in southwest Iran. Tokyo fears that if it makes such a linkage, Russia or China would end up winning the contract instead, undermining Japan's objective of securing long-term oil supplies. Still, lack of progress on transparency may lead the Japanese to slow down negotiations or take other actions.

Although U.S. efforts have so far not convinced its allies to cut off economic or nuclear assistance if Iran refuses to address the IAEA's concerns, a stage might be reached where the Security Council could decide to impose economic sanctions. If that happened, many states would feel compelled to reduce trade with Iran or halt joint energy projects.

SAFEGUARDS REPORT

At the heart of the current dispute is the IAEA's report on Iran's implementation of safeguards, issued publicly in June 2003. The IAEA described a series of developments and concerns that were the basis of the board's finding that Iran had failed to meet its obligations. This report also provided the most detailed publicly available information about Iran's extensive nuclear activities.

What is known is that Iran has built significant parts of its nuclear program in secret over the last decade. Aghazadeh even admitted that Iran had accelerated its uranium enrichment and heavy-water production programs in about 1998. That was followed by Iran revealing many other activities to the IAEA, though the Agency suspects that Tehran may have additional undeclared nuclear activities or facilities.

As a result, IAEA inspectors asked the Khatami government for considerably more information and access than they would normally have requested without a protocol in effect. But Tehran was not yet asked formally to comply with a "special inspection" at any site, as the Ageny has preferred to seek voluntary cooperation instead.

GAS CENTRIFUGES

The most important unresolved issue centers on Iran's gas centrifuge uranium enrichment program, which Mohamed AlBaradei, head of the IAEA, characterized as "sophisticated" when he visited Natanz in February 2003. Following that, the IAEA asked for details about the program.

What the IAEA has been trying for a while now is to understand the centrifuge program's history—experiments that Iran conducted to prove its centrifuges, together with the origins of its technology, including foreign procurement. Iran provided written information, permitted inspectors wide access at the Natanz facilities and allowed the IAEA to take environmental samples at Natanz and other centrifuge-related locations. These samples are critical to modern inspections because they can detect minute traces of enriched uranium and plutonium.

The media later reported that an environmental sample taken at Natanz in the winter or spring contained traces of enriched uranium, which, the Iranians said, was probably brought to the site inadvertently on equipment or tools from elsewhere, perhaps from an overseas supplier or from an undeclared Iranian facility. Other samples from Natanz were also found to contain enriched uranium. At that stage, results from other sites showed none of this.

In reaction, Iran told the IAEA that it had not enriched any uranium, despite having installed a large number of centrifuges in a cascade at the Natanz pilot plant. Normally, a program would operate single-centrifuge "test stands" that would enrich small amounts of uranium to test and optimize centrifuge designs. Iran declared that although it began research and development about six years before, it depended on extensive modeling and simulation, including tests of centrifuge rotors with and without inert gases.

These tests were conducted at several locations, including Amir Khabir University and the IAEO in Tehran, without using any nuclear material. Iran then said that it intended to start single-machine tests with uranium at the Natanz pilot plant in 2003.

Unquestionably, this approach is unusual, and the IAEA doubts that Iran could be so far along in the development process without having enriched any uranium. Absent considerably more detail—possibly including the extent of information and expertise gained from abroad—the IAEA had difficulty in accepting Iran's statement.

Part of the problem, as explained by ISIS senior analyst Corey Hinderstein, was Tehran's predilection not to open the door to full and free disclosures. She referred to it as what she likes to call "the discovery, denial, evidence, partial admission, inconsistency and more complete disclosure syndrome."

Basically, she explained, it goes something like this: "Disclosures would be made, either by outside sources or from within Iran's nuclear establishment. This would be followed shortly afterward by a denial. When more evidence was produced, the Iranians would partially admit, and then only to some of what had been going on. That was inevitably followed by further inconsistencies and eventually a more complete admission would follow." But that was still not all of it, she worried. It was a most unsatisfactory state of affairs, she declared, adding that it was very much in the pattern of what had taken place once Iraq's nuclear program was uncovered by UN weapons inspectors and IAEA inspectors after the 1991 Gulf War.

Based on open source information about possible enrichment activities at the Kalaye Electric Company in Tehran, the IAEA was at first rebuffed when it asked to visit the plant in 2003 in order to take environmental samples to determine if any enriched uranium had been produced at the site. Iran had initially responded that the facility was a watch factory, but that it also made certain centrifuge components. Initially it denied the inspectors' requests, claiming that it did not have to allow access until the protocol had been implemented. Iran subsequently reconsidered and allowed the IAEA limited access in March 2003 and full access two months later, but it refused to permit environmental sampling. Iran still refused to allow sampling during AlBaradei's visit in July 2003.

Previously the IAEA had been denied access to two rooms or workshops. A senior Western official interviewed at the time worried that Iran had denied access to allow time to clear out any evidence of uranium enrichment. He suspected that the rooms had held centrifuges, perhaps in a cascade, and had enriched uranium. According to U.S. media and experts quoting Bush administration officials, satellite images showed trucks going in and out of the site, implying that the rooms had been sanitized. The images, however, were inconclusive upon close scrutiny, according to a reporter who queried senior officials. Because of all the suspicions, environmental sampling may be requested as the only way to determine conclusively whether the site has enriched uranium.

Shortly afterward, the IAEA asked to visit additional sites, some of which were selected based on information provided by the National Council of Resistance of Iran, an opposition group. The group identified two sites west of Tehran that it said were related to small-scale gas centrifuge development work, which, when finished, could serve as alternative locations for cascades.

According to a senior Western official, two of the people listed by the opposition group as involved at these sites were known to have been involved in Iran's gas centrifuge program. Commercial satellite images showed that at least one of the sites had extensive physical security.

Iran told the IAEA that the sites were related to its nuclear organization, but were involved in agricultural and medical work—a description at odds with the high security that had been observed at the sites. Months later the inspectors had still not visited them or obtained sufficient information to make any judgments about their purpose.

Questions were also raised about the uranium conversion facility that Iran had been building at Esfahan. This plant is designed to make large quantities of uranium hexafluoride (UH_6) in addition to uranium dioxide and uranium tetrafluoride. Iran claimed not to have operated any laboratory or pilot facilities before building this major plant. Because learning to make uranium hexafluoride, the feedstock for a gas centrifuge plant, is not an easy task, there are some observers who now believe that Iran must have an undeclared pilot plant or have operated one in the past.

ADDITIONAL ISSUES

The safeguards report laid out other developments that contributed to the board's finding that Iran failed to meet its safeguards obligations. These include:

An undeclared uranium import. In response to an IAEA request, Iran recently acknowledged that in 1991 it received from China one thousand kilograms of natural uranium hexafluoride, four hundred kilograms of uranium tetrafluoride, and the same amount of uranium dioxide. This material was stored at the previously undeclared Jabr Ibn Hayam Multipurpose Laboratories (JHL) located at the Tehran Research Center.

Iran said it did not have to report the importation of a relatively small amount of natural uranium. However, the IAEA, declared that reporting was indeed required for the material and its subsequent processing, as well as the locations where it was received, processed, and stored. Iran provided none of this information until the IAEA asked for it. To make matters worse, China provided the IAEA with information about its export only after repeated inquiries.

Undeclared uranium metal production. Iran stated that it converted almost all of the uranium tetrafluoride into uranium metal at JHL. The production of uranium metal is unusual and can indicate a nuclear weapons effort that uses metallic forms of natural uranium or highly enriched uranium. The IAEA asked Iran about its planned use for the material and officials in Tehran stated that the purpose of the uranium metal was as shielding against radiation in containers that store irradiated fuel or materials. Such a use is suspect, however, because the uranium metal appears much too refined for shielding material.

Natural uranium target production. Iran said that it had used some of the uranium oxide to make targets for irradiation in the Tehran research reactor. The targets were then sent to another Tehran facility to separate iodine-131 in a lead-shielded cell. Such an activity is legitimate; iodine is useful in medical and civilian research applications, and the Iranians involved in this work have published their results in open technical reports.

The question is whether plutonium was also separated from these targets or whether other undeclared targets were produced, irradiated, and processed to obtain separated plutonium. Such activities would allow Iran to learn to separate plutonium, a necessary step in using plutonium in nuclear weapons.

Missing uranium hexafluoride. Iran stated that it did not process any of its imported uranium hexafluoride, and specifically, that it did not use any in gas centrifuge testing. However, nearly two kilograms are missing from the storage cylinders. Iran claimed that the material had leaked out of the cylinders more than a year before. The IAEA continues to investigate this claim.

A small centrifuge testing program would be expected to use about ten to fifteen kilograms of uranium hexafluoride, but it could get by on one to two kilograms. And the fact that Iran used much of its imported uranium dioxide and tetrafluoride makes it harder to accept the possibility that it did not use any of the hexafluoride.

A heavy-water reactor. In May 2003, Iran told the IAEA for the first time that it intended to build a 40-megawatt thermal heavy-water reactor at Arak. This is the site of the heavy-water production facility whose existence was first revealed publicly by an Iranian opposition group in August 2002.

According to a senior Western official, reactor construction was expected to start within a year or two. Iran also announced that it intended to begin building a fuel-fabrication plant for the reactor at Esfahan.

Iran said that this reactor was part of a long-term program to manufacture heavy-water power reactors. But long before any such plan might be realized, the reactor at Arak would produce eighteen to twenty-five pounds of plutonium annually, or enough for about two nuclear weapons each year.

Before it could use any of the plutonium in a nuclear weapon, however, it would first have to separate the plutonium from the irradiated fuel. Although Iran is not reported to have stated that it has conducted any plutonium separation activities, the irradiation and processing of natural uranium targets increases suspicion that Iran is researching plutonium separation.

THE NATANZ ENRICHMENT PLANT

The 2003 IAEA report included new information about Iran's gas centrifuge program at Natanz. This site houses a pilot gas centrifuge plant and a much larger, production-scale centrifuge facility.

The pilot plant was slated to hold about a thousand centrifuges by the end of 2003. The previous February it had about one hundred and sixty centrifuges operating without uranium. Despite the board's request, Iran introduced uranium into single test centrifuges soon after the board meeting. Initially, at least, Iran planned to use another safeguarded source of uranium hexafluoride in these early tests—a small stock that had been maintained under safeguards, acquired years ago from a European country. The imminent activation of this plant alarmed the board of governors and led to the request that Iran delay the processing of uranium, the reason being that the IAEA had not had sufficient time to implement a safeguards plan for this important facility.

According to senior Western officials, the current Iranian centrifuge has a separative capacity (ability to enrich uranium) of about two separative work units (swu) per year, per centrifuge. Media reports of significantly higher capacities are erroneous, according to these knowledgeable officials.

Because the centrifuge uses an aluminum rotor with a diameter of about four inches, this capacity would be consistent with a supercritical, optimized aluminum-rotor machine of the "G2-type." Gernot Zippe was involved in building this type of machine in Germany in the late 1960s and early '70s; it is composed of two almost twenty-inch-long aluminum rotor tubes connected by a bellows.

Media reports state that Iran received design assistance from Pakistan or from individual Pakistanis more than a decade ago. Iran's centrifuge design is similar to the type that Pakistan obtained secretly in the mid-1970s from Urenco facilities in the Netherlands. The G2 and its predecessor G1-type aluminum machines, developed by Zippe and his colleagues, were not very efficient. Zippe's G1-type machine had a capacity of about 0.6 swu per year, implying an output of 1.2 swu per year for the G2 design. Iran is believed to have optimized or otherwise increased capacity to about two swu per year.

Although the pilot plant is relatively small, it could produce as much as fifteen to twenty-five pounds of weapon-grade uranium a year, depending on the "tails assay" (the fraction of ^{235}U remaining in the waste) and the manner in which the centrifuges are organized into cascades. Because centrifuges are flexible, even if the cascades are arranged to produce only low-enriched uranium, weapon-grade uranium can be produced by "batch recycling" the end product back into the feed point of the cascade until the desired level of enrichment is reached. Thus, by the end of 2005, this plant could produce twenty-five to thirty-five pounds of weapon-grade uranium, enough for a nuclear weapon.

According to the IAEA safeguards report, Iran plans to start installing centrifuges in the main enrichment halls of the Natanz facility in 2005, after testing and confirming its centrifuge design in the pilot plant. Eventually, these cascade halls will hold fifty-thousand centrifuges, according to the report. No project completion date was provided, but indications are that it would take five to ten years to install this number of centrifuges.

Separative capacity of later centrifuges would probably increase, but Iran may not succeed in installing all fifty-thousand. In any case, based on the current plan, we project that the Natanz facility will eventually have a capacity of at least one hundred thousand swus per year. This is roughly the capacity to provide annual reloads of one

Bushehr reactor, but far short of the enriched uranium needed to provide fuel for all the nuclear power reactors Iran plans to build over the next twenty years.

The same capacity would be sufficient to produce about eight hundred pounds of weapon-grade uranium annually. At between twenty-four to thirty-two pounds per weapon, that would be enough for roughly twenty-five to thirty nuclear weapons per year.

If Iran operated Natanz to make low-enriched uranium fuel until it decided to make weapon-grade uranium, it would be able to rapidly enrich the low-enriched material to weapon-grade. For example, if Natanz was operating at full capacity and recycled low-enriched uranium (five percent ^{235}U) as "feed," the facility could produce enough weapon-grade uranium for a nuclear weapon in a few days.

WHAT SHOULD BE DONE

In the worst case, Iran could feasibly have a nuclear weapon by the end of 2005. There are some who argue even sooner. Under many scenarios, it could obtain and significantly expand its nuclear arsenal in the second half of the decade by producing both HEU and plutonium. Although some would argue that a solution to the Iranian nuclear problem could be delayed, it is axiomatic that the longer the wait for a solution, the more extensive Iran's program would become and the harder, politically, for Iran to reverse itself.

One of the consequences of all these developments is that while Iran has admitted to the IAEA that it made secret efforts to procure the wherewithal to make sophisticated gas centrifuges to enrich uranium, there are many gaps that exist. Indeed, there are few who believe that Tehran has told the whole story of its extensive foreign procurements. A year later, Iranian officials continue to insist that they obtained sensitive centrifuge drawings and components through "intermediaries," and that they did not know the original source of the items.

Recent Pakistani government investigations are undercutting that assertion. These magnify concerns that Iran made only a partial declaration to the IAEA. Senior Pakistani gas centrifuge experts and officials admitted to Pakistani government investigators that they provided centrifuge assistance to Iran, Libya, and North Korea. Initially, details were sketchy about exactly who or what was involved in these transfers, or, for that matter, when they occurred and how they were arranged. Although Islamabad has denied authorizing any of the transfers—characterizing them as the work of rogue scientists—existing evidence points elsewhere. There is a body of evidence indicating at least some measure of Pakistani government knowledge, if not outright collusion.

Nor is that the end of it. Iran had many other important suppliers. Individuals and companies in Europe and the Middle East also played a key role in supplying Iran's centrifuge program. In this regard, China has emerged as the most important supplier to Iran's program to produce uranium compounds, including uranium hexafluoride, the highly corrosive gas used in centrifuges.

Although Iran encountered many difficulties in making and operating centrifuges, postponing by many years the construction of a pilot centrifuge plant, it would appear to have secretly achieved self-sufficiency in centrifuge manufacturing by the mid-to late 1990s.

And while Western intelligence agencies detected many of Iran's sensitive procurements, they missed some key ones. Because it had only incomplete information, the United States had trouble convincing its allies until 2002 or 2003 that Iran's effort to build secret gas centrifuge facilities had reached an advanced state. Lacking actionable information or intrusive inspections, the IAEA was unable to determine until only fairly recently that Iran had significantly violated its obligations under the Nuclear Non-Proliferation Treaty.

THE PROGRAM'S TIMELINE

To fully understand what has been going on nuclearwise in Iran, it is necessary to examine the timeline of events as they took place.

Iran stated in its 2003 declarations to the IAEA that it began its gas centrifuge program in 1985 during its bloody war with Iraq. This decision is widely perceived as having been part of an effort to make highly enriched uranium for nuclear weapons.

Iran claimed that the only purpose of its centrifuge program was to make fuel for the German-supplied Bushehr power reactor—a claim that is highly dubious, given the fact that in 1985 Germany had suspended all work at the reactor, at least until the war ended. After the war, Germany never resumed construction. In early 1995, Russia signed a contract to finish the job, yet throughout the decade, when the fate of the reactor at Bushehr was uncertain, Iran accelerated its gas centrifuge program.

Little is available about Iran's initial efforts in 1985. What information did it already have about centrifuges, since modern designs are all classified? What design did the program first study? What were its initial plans? Had there, by then, been offers of assistance from Pakistanis or other individuals that encouraged the Iranians to start the program?

Iran quickly began procuring items. For example, in 1985 it acquired key "flow-forming" equipment from the German firm Leifeld. This material is useful in forming steel and aluminum centrifuge tubes. At least one Leifeld flow-forming machine is currently used in Iran's gas centrifuge manufacturing complex. There is also the issue that Leifeld personnel might have been knowledgeable about centrifuges when they sold the items to Iran. (What is known is that around 1987, Leifeld demonstrated its flow-forming equipment in Iraq, showing a video containing sensitive information about producing maraging steel rotors for a Urenco-type gas centrifuge.)

In 1987 Iran made a significant breakthrough, obtaining a complete set of centrifuge drawings and some centrifuge components. This specific procurement may have been part of a much larger package that helped Iran understand and build centrifuges. Unquestionably, acquiring the drawings and a few components must have been tremendously helpful. With detailed designs in hand, Iran could skip many of the more difficult research steps. It was unlikely to have had the technical experience to discover the intricacies of a modern centrifuge or master the complex disciplines involved in manufacturing of centrifuge components on its own. Pakistan and Iraq also needed to obtain detailed centrifuge designs and assistance for their centrifuge programs to advance beyond a rudimentary level.

Armed with component specifications and drawings, Iran would be able to design and implement a strategy to develop a reliable centrifuge and create a manufacturing infrastructure to make thousands of centrifuges. It would be able to find foreign companies to make specific components, often unwittingly. In parallel, it could locate companies that would sell the equipment Iran needed to make the components itself.

Iran acquired drawings of a modified variant of an early-generation Urenco centrifuge built by the Netherlands. Some experts familiar with these drawings have assessed that, based on the design's materials, dimensions, and tolerances, it is a modified precursor to the Dutch M4 centrifuge. This design has four aluminum rotor tubes connected by three maraging steel bellows. The rotor has a diameter of about four inches (100 mm) and the entire machine is about six feet tall.

However, inspectors noticed that someone modified the design in distinctive ways. In addition, the original drawings were shown to inspectors, and their labels are in English, not Dutch or German. According to intelligence information, the design resembles one built by Pakistan in the 1980s and early 1990s that is sometimes called the P1. In addition, the centrifuge components Iran bought match those bought by Pakistan.

There was other evidence that pointed to Pakistan as the source of the drawings and of at least some of the components. Much of the highly enriched uranium that the IAEA found in Iran by taking environmental samples may be consistent with material produced in Pakistan.

WHO PROVIDED THESE DRAWINGS?

The media have reported that senior Pakistani gas centrifuge officials, including Abdul Qadeer Khan, the father of Pakistan's centrifuge program, provided multiple centrifuge designs to Iran and other countries. As of late January, however, no charges had been filed against any of the officials.

Toward the end of 2003 Iran provided the IAEA with a list of five middlemen and company officials whom, it said, provided the drawings and other key items. Iran characterized these middlemen, who are European and Middle Eastern, as putting together orders—buying items from various companies and delivering them to Iran.

The exact role of some of these individuals is murky. Did they act as agents of their respective companies, or were they acting alone as consultants? They are also believed to have supplied or arranged shipments of items to Pakistan.

Of those named, three are Germans who were involved in selling a range of dual-use and other civilian and military items to Pakistan, many countries in the Middle East, and elsewhere. Iran's statement to the IAEA implied that one or more of the three Germans obtained a classified centrifuge design from Pakistan and sold it to Iran.

It is more likely that a Pakistani or group of Pakistanis provided the drawings to Iran along with the names of those Iran could approach for help in acquiring components and essential items. Any

Pakistanis involved in this scheme would likely have been from the Khan Research Laboratories, where the Pakistani centrifuge program is based.

The Pakistanis' main motivation would probably have been financial. In the mid-1980s, connections between Iran and Pakistan were growing in many areas. In addition, the Pakistani gas centrifuge program or its members may have needed money.

In any case, the drawings are unlikely to have been developed by the Iranians themselves. Based on proven and alleged cases involving Iraqi and Pakistani centrifuge experts, the sale of centrifuge drawings is often a "sweetener," or accompanied by offers for the sale of other, more profitable items, such as materials, components, or machine tools to make components. Thus, Iran's statement about its procurements of drawings and some components in 1987 and the naming of a handful of individuals is consistent with the start of significant assistance from knowledgeable Europeans, Middle Easterners, and Pakistanis.

IRAN'S PROCUREMENTS

In the 1980s, Iran created an extensive procurement system to acquire necessary items for its centrifuge program from around the world. It used front companies to order the equipment and falsely declare non-nuclear uses, and it established secret transportation routes.

These efforts were not always successful. Alert government or company officials stopped many orders. Some of Iran's purchases involved defective centrifuge components. Nonetheless, over many years, Iran succeeded in acquiring thousands of sensitive centrifuge components and all the equipment it needed to be self-sufficient in the manufacture of centrifuges in the future. In Iran's quest, foreigners played key roles in organizing the purchase and shipment of items.

In late 2003 Iran provided the IAEA with a long list of equipment suppliers, including when the equipment was purchased. Iran has also not removed or otherwise hidden nameplates that contain company names and serial numbers.

In the late 1980s and early '90s, many of the items Iran wanted were loosely controlled by national or international export controls. Many were acquired legally, at least in the sense that suppliers did not knowingly break the then-lax export control laws, and government bureaucracies did not scrutinize the exports for their actual purpose.

Iran acquired a long list of items, including high-strength aluminum, maraging steel, electron beam welders, balancing machines, vacuum pumps, computer-controlled machine tools, and flow-forming machines for both aluminum and maraging steel. Many of these items were obtained in Europe, especially from Germany and Switzerland. Suppliers trained Iranians in the use of critical equipment and taught them associated technologies needed in a centrifuge program.

The assistance of at least some of the named middlemen would have been important. They would have known which companies could provide desired items and which would be willing to do business with Iran. If any of these individuals had extensive knowledge about centrifuges and their manufacture, their help could have been invaluable in identifying the right suppliers of equipment, materials, and the necessary know-how.

During its initial procurement effort in the late 1980s and early '90s, Iran acquired only a limited number of centrifuge components. The number was consistent with a program that was then focusing on trying to build and operate single centrifuges for testing.

But then, as Iran has said, between 1993 and 1995, it received through middlemen enough components to build five hundred centrifuges. It is from centrifuges made from these imported components that traces of highly enriched uranium have been found by the IAEA, at both the site at Natanz and at Kalaye Electric in Tehran.

As of late January 2004, the manufacturer of these components has not been publicly identified, and Iran has yet to provide any documentation about this purchase. On the surface, Iran appears so far to be protecting the actual supplier of these components. Putting in such a large order would imply, however, that Iran had by now decided on a particular centrifuge design. It also indicates that by the mid-1990s Iran was ready to build a major cascade or pilot plant.

This order included large numbers of the most sensitive centrifuge components, including bellows, which raises troubling questions about the effectiveness of export controls at a time when they were being tightened throughout Europe—and after Pakistan had given the United States assurances it would not engage in such assistance.

There are several theories about the origin of these components, including:

European, Pakistani, or other companies made the components to specifications provided by middlemen, Iranian agents, or Iranians in the centrifuge program themselves; or Pakistan sold off surplus components that it made itself or purchased in Europe or in developing countries. Pakistan is known to have replaced its P1 centrifuge with a more advanced P2, or all-maraging steel rotor machine, starting in the mid-1980s. By about 1995, Pakistan had probably phased out most of its P1 machines and had extra, unused components left over.

Despite importing all these components, Iran said in its statements to the IAEA in 2003 that it had trouble getting the centrifuges to work. It has declared that it did not enrich any uranium until 1999, and then produced uranium enriched to no more than 1.2 percent ^{235}U. This statement, however, is very much at odds with the process of settling on a design. Typically, before building a large number of centrifuges, program leaders want to test the design with uranium hexafluoride.

Iran told the IAEA that in addition to problems with the quality of the imported components and the difficulty it encountered making components of sufficient quality for high-speed centrifuges, it also had problems assembling and running centrifuges. These factors led to delays. In addition, the need for increased secrecy and security led to a decision in 1995 to move out of the existing facility in Tehran, causing further delays.

Shutting down the sophisticated operations in Tehran may have also been motivated by increased international scrutiny, particularly in 1995. In any case, before the IAEA accepts Iran's declaration, the timing of the program needs to be better understood.

DECLARED FACILITIES AND ACTIVITIES

According to Iranian declarations in October and November 2003, until 1997 the centrifuge program was centered at Iran's Atomic Energy Organization facilities in Tehran, with laboratory work conducted at the Plasma Physics Laboratory of the Tehran Nuclear Research Center. The first head of the gas centrifuge program was a former head of Iran's plasma physics program.

Iran told the IAEA that in 1997 the majority of the program was relocated to Kalaye Electric in Tehran. This move, which was motivated partly by the need for additional security, was difficult and caused further delays in the program. Nonetheless, from 1997 to

2002, Iran operated single machines and small cascades of ten or twenty machines; achieved the ability to make all the components itself; and gained some success in testing centrifuges both with and without uranium hexafluoride. It also decided to construct enrichment facilities at Natanz.

In 2002, research, development, and assembly operations were moved to Natanz. This facility is now the primary site of the Iranian gas centrifuge program. It consists of centrifuge assembly areas and a pilot fuel-enrichment plant slated to hold a thousand centrifuges. A production-scale fuel-enrichment plant is under construction at Natanz, and is scheduled to hold about fifty-thousand centrifuges. Before it voluntarily suspended activity in November 2003, Iran was operating both single machine tests and small cascades with uranium hexafluoride at the pilot plant.

Before the suspension, Iran was assembling four-rotor machines similar to the P1 design. Each has a separative capacity of roughly three separative work units per year. Earlier, based on information that the capacity was about two swus per year, we had speculated that Iran had a centrifuge with two aluminum rotor tubes connected by a bellows, and the machine was properly optimized to produce enriched uranium. Based on more recent information, our current understanding is that the Iranian machine is as described above and that it is not optimized.

Although the pilot plant is relatively small, if finished it could produce about sixteen pounds of weapon-grade uranium a year, depending on the "tails assay" (the fraction of ^{235}U lost to waste) and the manner in which the centrifuges are organized into cascades. Because centrifuges are flexible, even if the cascades are arranged to produce only low-enriched uranium, weapon-grade uranium can be produced by "batch recycling"—sending the end product back into the feed point of the cascade over again until the desired level of enrichment is reached.

We project that the production plant could eventually have a capacity of at least one hundred and fifty thousand swus per year, which is enough capacity to provide annual reloads of the nearly completed power reactor at Bushehr, but far short of the enriched uranium it would need to provide fuel for all the civilian power plants Iran plans to build over the next twenty years.

Alternatively, the same capacity could be used to produce roughly five hundred kilograms of weapon-grade uranium annually. At twenty-four to thirty-two pounds per weapon, that would be enough for twenty-five to thirty nuclear weapons per year.

Natanz could be operated to make low-enriched uranium fuel until Iran decided it wanted to make weapon-grade material. It would not take long to enrich the low-enriched material to weapon grade. For example, if Natanz was operating at full capacity and recycled the end product—low-enriched uranium (five percent ^{235}U)—back into the feed point, the facility could produce enough weapon-grade uranium for a single weapon within days.

PLANNING FOR THE FUTURE

Iran's centrifuge procurement effort involved extensive secret procurement networks, both before and after the 1991 Persian Gulf War, when nations were tightening their export controls on sensitive items. Understanding just what Iran did, how it got help, and who helped, are critical in verifying Iran's declarations to the IAEA, and in identifying and fixing weaknesses in existing national and international export controls.

There is as yet only a sketchy answer to the question of who, exactly, provided sensitive centrifuge drawings and components to Iran. The footprints are being traced, however. Complete declarations from Iran, and honest investigations by Pakistan of its scientists' past activities are needed to fill out the picture of Iran's extensive centrifuge procurement activities, as well as Pakistani assistance to the secret nuclear programs of Iran and others.

7

NUCLEAR LINK-UP:
SOUTH AFRICA AND IRAN

"Iran has said that its nuclear program is purely for peaceful purposes, while the United States contends that it has secretly tried to produce nuclear weapons."

"Alarm Raised Over Quality of Uranium Found in Iran,"
Craig S. Smith, *New York Times*, March 11, 2004

Always opportunistic, Tehran's mullahs did not wait until 1993 for Nelson Mandela to move into Tuinhuis, the residence of the State President in Cape Town, before becoming active in the subcontinent. Numerous intelligence reports out of Pretoria from that period talk of Iranians arriving in batches in South Africa from the early 1990s onward. Almost overnight their madrassahs sprang up wherever there were enough receptive Muslims of the Shi'ite persuasion to provide a congregation.

Some came as individuals, traders or entrepreneurs eager to examine export and other possibilities. Others arrived in groups, quite a few headed by senior clerics who were unmistakable in their long robes and distinctive round turbans, some of them black, indicating that they were sayyid (directly descended from the prophet Mohamed) and others white. It was not the sort of thing you missed while traveling on the highway between Johannesburg and Durban.

There was much in South Africa to interest the Iranians. The country has large, ultra-modern cities with resplendent residential suburbs that occasionally eclipse what places like Sydney, Long Island, Geneva and Los Angeles have to offer. They also boast some of the biggest shopping malls in the world, offset by sprawling, suppurating slums which have become synonymous with Africa in the 21st century.

Anomalies apart, South Africa is also home to the biggest industrial infrastructure on the continent, a legacy of the former Apartheid regime. It has a most sophisticated road, rail and telecommunications grid—there are more miles of rail tracks laid in South Africa than the rest of the African continent together—and, most important to any-body from the Middle East, the country, until very recently, was the tenth biggest exporter in the world of weapons.

Having just emerged from a two-decade war in Angola and Namibia, the array of sophisticated military hardware produced was impressive, much of it of a kind that those Islamic countries out of favor with the West, until then, had only been able to view from a distance.

It was, and still is, war material of good quality and value, some quite advanced. A lot of it—laser tank sights (the same ones that Syria wanted and that were produced by Eloptro, a Denel subsidiary); a 155mm self-propelled artillery system capable of lobbing base-bleed projectiles almost thirty miles (and including the G6, a self-propelled version of the same weapon); third generation night vision goggles; an in-flight jet refueller; a stand-off guided bomb; an air-to-air missile family; a new-era torpedo; a new generation of tactical "frequency hopping" radios; unmanned aerial vehicles; a vast range of munitions; some of which is now being sold in Europe and guided missiles from Kentron—some of this stuff originally designed and built in conjunc-tion with Israeli engineers working alongside their South African counterparts in South African arms factories.

Even the British Army had a stake. In January 2003 the Minister of Defence in London placed a $10 million order with Denel for a hundred LH 40C hand-held laser rangefinders. This was hardly the kind of thing you were likely to encounter in some downtown Karachi or Cairo industrial estate.

Other exchanges of military technology in joint ventures report-edly included technical knowledge acquired from the canceled Israeli "Lavi" fighter program, some of which was applied to the South African Air Force Cheetah fighter (which is basically an upgraded French Mirage). For the Iranians, the joint Israeli-South African space program was a bonus.

Everybody was aware that there would an abrupt change of guard when the ANC took over from President de Klerk's almost lily white National Party. Over the years Mandela's cronies had fostered close ties with many countries, including some labeled "rogue" by Wash-ington, and among that batch was Iran. Links were also strong with states like Cuba, Syria, the Sudan and a handful of others who make no secret of the fact that they regard Israel as Enemy Number One.

With President Thabo Mbeki having taken over as Head of State from the venerable Mandela, the new South African political dispensation continues to hold this view, especially since the Pretoria leader tends to surround himself with people like Dr. Essop Pahad, who was appointed a cabinet minister after the 2004 general elections. Pahad, like his brother Aziz—a deputy minister of foreign affairs—is regarded as a powerful proponent of stronger South African ties with the Islamic world and is said by those who know him to have fostered Iranian, Iraqi (under Saddam) and Libyan associations for many years. Judging by recent public pronouncements, Pahad is certainly no friend of the Americans.

With Libya's peremptory about face and Gadhaffi having thrown open his books to Western intelligence agencies (which are likely to disclose heavy South African involvement in that country's chemical and biological weapons programs) it is not certain whether this situation will remain. Thus, while politically maverick states are still the flavor of the day, any kind of link, military or otherwise, between Pretoria's new political hierarchy and Jerusalem is not even a consideration.

Indeed, it has gone much further. Within a year of President Mandela taking over the government from the Apartheid powers, South Africa became a vocal exponent of radical opposition to Israel. His government quickly displayed strong sentiments critical of America's role in the Middle East. Even today, Mandela rarely has a good word to say about Washington, and he has always been vocal about the "innocence" of Saddam Hussein. It follows then that there are few non-Islamic countries quite as vituperative about Operation Iraqi Freedom as South Africa. As some commentators in Johannesburg said at the time, if you watched South African Broadcasting Corporation (SABC) television or e-TV, you would be forgiven for thinking that these were English-language versions of what went out on Iraqi television under the Ba'athists.

For Tehran, these developments were a gift. Overnight, with President de Klerk sent into the political wilderness (though he was still, with Mandela, to pick up a Nobel Peace Prize) the single biggest draw card to improve relations between the two countries must have been the fact that Pretoria had a history of building atom bombs. Even more appealing to the maladroit mullah mindset was the fact that this had been done in the relatively short space of seven years.

For decades, South Africa's nuclear program had been subject to much innuendo and conjecture. The average citizen was aware that something significant had taken place, but many of its secrets remained intact until the end. Pretoria was able to keep such a tight lid on developments that it was not until South Africa disclosed the whereabouts of Advena, a nuclear facility in Pretoria West (to develop and manufacture nuclear warheads), that the CIA was made aware of it. It was to Advena that a number of Atomic Energy Corporation engineers and scientists were transferred to complete final assembly of the six atom bombs and where they were stored in huge underground vaults.

In 1993 de Klerk addressed the South African nation and told them that a very substantial nuclear weapons program had existed, that atom bombs had been built and that the program had been subsequently abandoned. However, he had nothing to say about the fate of those who had worked there. That these weapons of mass destruction had been dismantled was irrelevant, in view of the fact that quite a few of the original scientists and technicians were now unemployed.

What also emerged at the time was that South Africa had undertaken the largest guided missile project in Africa, with much of the research and development—as well as production—having been accomplished in record time in conjunction with Israeli rocket scientists. Unlike the bomb program, work on missile projects was still ongoing in the early 1990s. But with de Klerk about to vacate the presidency, strong pressure from Washington caused those projects to also be shelved.

This resulted in some acrimony, the Americans being seen to have interfered in what many regarded as a perfectly legitimate scientific and commercial pursuit. There was even talk at one stage of developing—again with Israeli help—a South African satellite.

The turn of events caused more unemployment, this time among a select scientific group who had been responsible for building the country's biggest missile yet. This was the "Arniston" or RSA-2 rocket—a variation of the Israeli-built Jericho II—that was launched in the direction of Marion island in the south Indian Ocean. It successfully splashed down a thousand miles away on its first test flight.

Once the new black regime had been sworn in, it took no time at all for relations between South Africa and almost the entire Islamic international community to go from cordially friendly to most favored nation. While groups of Iranians sought permission from Pretoria to set up businesses in all the major commercial centers, there were strings of their countrymen touring South African weapons factories. There were also a lot of meetings behind closed doors.

South African-Israeli relations were meanwhile put on hold and security at Jerusalem's legation in Pretoria was upgraded to the highest level. Even trying to park a car in the street outside (as I did several times prior to going to the Middle East) drew an immediate response from the embassy's security guards. Things came to a head in May 2004 when there was talk in Pretoria of actually severing relations with Jerusalem.

By now, cooperation between South Africa and Iran had started to worry the U.S. State Department. Things weren't helped by a succession of earlier visits by President Mandela to Libya, then already fostering insurrection out of Liberia into Sierra Leone.

Not very long before that, a meeting between Mandela and then Iranian President Ali Akbar Rafsanjani also raised eybrows. Afterward, a furious Rafsanjani declared: "Iran and South Africa will not allow the United States to determine our fate and our destiny."

Already, according to a report headlined "Bending the Rules" by Milan Vesely in *Toward Freedom*, there were indications that Iran was recruiting South African nuclear scientists to work in their own nascent atomic energy program. Whatever the truth, Rafsanjani's remarks did not rest comfortably with some government departments in the West.

President Clinton's well publicized tour of Africa followed, during which he made an issue of South Africa's close relationship with Libya. The White House also made known that it was less than pleased with Mandela's resistance to U.S. sanctions against both Iraq and Cuba. Several foreign policy analysts speculated at the time that, caught as it was between the aspirations of a previously deprived population and a stringent recession, South Africa might opt to sell nuclear or other technology. That possibility may well have spurred Clinton's vehement opposition to the $2 billion deal made by South Africa to supply Syria with updated tank-cannon stabilizing equipment.

There is no question that Tehran was interested in South Africa's nuclear capability. By its own admission to the IAEA late 2003, by the mid-1990s, Iran by then was almost ten years into a fairly sophisticated nuclear weapons program and, by some accounts, was having a hard time of it.

Nobody is sure—or rather, nobody in South Africa is prepared to say—at what stage Tehran finally decided to grasp the nuclear nettle and put forward a case for some kind of cooperation between the two countries. Nor would it have been made in public.

Iran's own nuclear physicists, as with the Iraqis before them, had not taken long to be flummoxed both by the astronomical cost of these newfound disciplines, as well as by some of the intricacies that any nuclear enterprise entails. Issues would have been compounded had they started from scratch, as they were probably obliged to do.

Like their South African counterparts, they too would have had to get past some of the complex principles related to subjects like nuclear physics, uranium enrichment, stabilizing the HEO core in a gun-type atom bomb and, possibly, building molds for an implosion device had they decided to walk that road. They would also have to grapple with some of the issues associated with things as arcane as spherical geography. South Africa had already been through that mill and when you speak to some of their nuclear scientists today, they admit to having been many times perplexed by some of the skills that they needed to inculcate.

In spite of problems and setbacks—and there were many—the South Africans eventually mastered the complex technology of nuclear weapons construction, be it only enough to produce six atom bombs. The Iranians, we now know, wanted a share of it.

It was perhaps to be expected that with a new government in place in Pretoria—coupled to a political party that remains demonstrably anti-American—that some of this knowledge might be garnered by Tehran, if not by coercion, then "for services rendered," possibly as a trade-off for oil.

It was in late May 1997, quite by chance, that I asked for and was given an opportunity to meet the man who was then in charge of South Africa's nuclear program. From Johannesburg, while on a visit to South Africa from the United States, I called Dr. Waldo Stumpf's office for an appointment. I asked him for some advice regarding an article that I was doing for Jane's. It was nuclear related, I explained, something about Iraq. The half-dozen South African atom bombs that had been built in the 1970s and 1980s were history, but Dr. Stumpf, a quiet-spoken, round-faced scientist had been around in the industry for many years and if anybody could help, I was certain that it was he.

It was difficult, he said, because of timing. He was leaving the next day for Syria. "But come along anyway and let's see what we can do." The drive to Pelindaba, on the outskirts of Pretoria, should normally have taken me fifty minutes. I got there in less than half-an-hour.

After stringent security checks at the gate, I was ushered into the office of the man who was the chief executive officer of NECSA, The Nuclear Energy Corporation of South Africa, a position he held for the period 1990 to 2001 (when it was still called the Atomic Energy Corporation). Because of constraints, I had expected the meeting with the man who has worked in the nuclear industry for three decades to last perhaps ten minutes. It was an hour before I left Pelindaba.

Dr. Waldo Stumpf, a Fellow of the South African Academy of Engineering, has an impressive academic record. He holds a BSc Eng (Metallurgy) from the University of Pretoria and a PhD from Sheffield, apart from a string of other qualifications, most of them in engineering. After completing his studies at Sheffield in 1968 on microstructural aspects of ferritic chromium steels during hot working, he regularly taught a postgraduate course on phase transformations in solids within the department. Professionally, his particular area of interest lies in the optimization of physical properties of metals and alloys through microstructural optimization by the design of heat treatment or hot working processes or by alloy design. Quite a mouthful.

Having finished our business, Dr. Stumpf questioned me at length about my own activities as a correspondent—I had published more than a dozen books by then and he was familiar with my work. Had he not been, I probably wouldn't have got through the door. This was a very busy man.

He was also curious about my personal forays into some of the Arab countries. I had only recently returned from Damascus.

It was then that his mood turned conspiratorial. Almost offhand, he admitted that a few months earlier he'd played host to a group of Iranians at the Pelindaba nuclear establishment. Among them, he confided, was Iran's deputy minister of atomic affairs, Reza Amrollahi.

"I got a call from the President's office in Cape Town soon after getting into the office that morning—not President Mandela himself, but one of his aides. I was told that a high-level Iranian party, including Amrollahi, who I already knew from international meetings that we had both attended, was on its way to Pretoria. There were no ifs or buts: they would be here by noon," was the message.

What was immediately troubling, Stumpf confided, was the haste with which it had all been arranged. Nothing was according to form.

If there had been time, he would have liked to have had one of the international observers present, someone from the International Atomic Energy Agency. However, there was no time. In any event, the IAEA has a monitoring role in South Africa and does not have personnel permanently stationed at Pelindaba.

"But I knew that I had to have somebody else in the office while discussions took place. These were sensitive issues. It wouldn't be in either my or Pelindaba's interest to meet alone with an Iranian deputy minister, especially someone involved with matters nuclear. So I called Pik Botha, who until a short time before was my immediate superior"

Botha, a veteran South African politician last seen holding a post in the cabinet of his erstwhile ANC "enemy," had been South Africa's minister of Energy and Minerals Affairs until the post was taken over by Manuel Paduna. Fortunately he was in Pretoria that day. As Stumpf explained, Pelindaba had once fallen within Botha's bailiwick.

"I phoned him, told him what was taking place and asked that he be there. He would be with me within the hour, he replied."

The Iranian party arrived in good time, just as Cape Town had said they would, and, according to Stumpf, the encounter was formal but friendly. For a short while they talked about Minister Amrollahi's visit to South Africa, what he had seen and what he still had planned.

"Then the man handed me a file, and I knew exactly what was taking place. It wasn't a big pile of papers, just a few lists." The documents, he explained, contained a comprehensive catalogue of items needed for the manufacture of an atomic bomb. There were some very advanced things asked for, like blueprints, industrial, chemical and laboratory equipment, and other essentials required for this kind of weapon production. "Obviously we were stunned," Stumpf said.

The two South Africans rejected the request out of hand. Stumpf told the Iranian minister that in accordance with the provisions of the Non-Proliferation Treaty, there was no way that either he or members of his staff at Pelindaba could comply. He pointed out that not only had South Africa recently signed the NPT, but as everybody present in the room knew, the country had destroyed its entire nuclear weapons arsenal. Additionally, every document relating to the manufacture of atom bombs had been shredded in the presence of IAEA and American officials.

"I informed him that since Iran was a NPT signatory, the nature of the visit was, if anything, compromising. We South Africans were being asked to break international law."

Stumpf admitted to having been completely non-plussed by the Iranian's effrontery, embarrassed by the charade. What surprised him the most, he said, was that it was almost as if the man had been primed to expect him to comply with his request. It was a bad call whichever way it was viewed, he reckoned.

Stumpf used the opportunity to remind his guest of what had happened not very long before in Iraq following Operation Desert Storm. Once the names of German scientists recruited by Saddam Hussein to work in his nuclear weapons program had become known in the weapons' strip-search by the IAEA Action Team and UNSCOM, several warrants of arrest had been issued through Interpol. Two of those involved in the Iraqi effort had been charged with treason. One was still in jail, he added.

"With deference, I made it clear that it would simply not be possible for us to help. Besides, there were international safeguards in place at Pelindaba to prevent exactly that from happening."

Aware that he might have exceeded his brief in telling me all this, Waldo Stumpf insisted that everything was to remain off-record. For a month or two afterward, it stayed that way. At the same time, I was deeply troubled, specifically because of long-term international security implications. This was too potent a matter to let rest, I couldn't help feeling.

Back in London immediately afterward, I mentioned my meeting at the Pelindaba nuclear establishment to Clifford Beal, the American-born editor of Jane's *International Defense Review*. Now it was my turn for confidences. I was extremely worried by what I'd been told, I said. I suggested that if it were true that Iran was seriously interested in building nuclear weapons, the ramifications were incalculable. The lives of untold numbers of people could be at stake if this thing ever got to the fruition stage. Not only that, but the new South African government would have been complicit in helping an aberrant Islamic state develop a device that could inalterably tip the balance of power in a region half the size of Europe.

"The world has a right to know," I said, explaining the nature of my meeting with Dr. Stumpf.

On the last point, Clifford's view was that I should follow the dictates of my conscience. He knew my style, as well as the way I worked. By then I'd been contributing to IDR—first in Geneva, and afterwards in Coulsdon, Surrey—for almost a quarter century.

Looking back, I am aware now that though my actions might have been considered insidious by some members of the Fourth Estate, it was a long and difficult decision to expose this charade. Inchoate to begin with, the issue took time to harden into something tangible. At the same time, I was no agitator manque discreetly incubating something seditious. Rather, this was a matter that, in the interests of the international community, demanded action. Nor was there ignoring the reality that, in the longer term, there were real implications of nuclear war in the Near East. It was a situation impossible to ignore.

The article was published in the September, 1997 issue of Jane's *International Defense Review*, which came out in late August. Days later it was picked up by the London *Times* under the headline "Iran Sought Pretoria Nuclear Deal."

In the interests of veracity, and because I was aware that I'd betrayed a trust, I'd gone a step further. Just before IDR went to press, I contacted Phillip van Niekerk, an old friend from Sierra Leone's mercenary days—we had covered the activities of Executive Outcomes together while working in West Africa. At that stage Phillip ran South Africa's most politically outspoken weekly, *The Mail & Guardian*, then still partly owned by Britain's *Guardian* newspaper. His job as editor gradually evolved into something of a personal crusade, assuming a role as aggressive watchdog in covering polemical government activities.

I was in a desperate quandary about the matter and I told him so, taking the trouble to explain why. Up to that point my report of the Stumpf interview was based solely on the basis of "I said, he said." What I needed was help to back up my report.

Phillip agreed to look into the matter. If it added up, he said, he'd run the story a week after it appeared in London.

In retrospect, it was good that he did. Van Niekerk immediately tasked Mungo Sogget, the *Mail & Guardian*'s senior investigative journalist, to look into what had taken place. Sogget was a good choice as someone had once referred to him as having "the demeanor of a pit bull," though probably not to his face.

Consequently, when Pik Botha was asked by Sogget in a phone call to his home in Pretoria a day or two later whether Amrollahi's visit had in fact taken place and whether the learned Dr. Stumpf had been presented with a nuclear "shopping list," Mr Botha replied that he was not only aware of the event, but, he emphatically declared, "I was there when it happened."

Once the articles were out, the South African government reacted with vigor. Within days the issue was raised in Parliament in Cape Town and I was branded a liar. In answer to a Parliamentary question, Stumpf declared that "The entire story is fiction . . . Venter made it all up." The only time he had ever met with any Iranian official, he said, was at a dinner in the presence of a large number of people. Dr. Stumpf also denied that Deputy Minister Reza Amrollahi had ever visited South Africa. Clearly, he had been well primed.

Nor was Pik Botha ever so forthcoming again. Shortly after returning to America, I related the saga to another old friend, Dr. Jonathan Tucker, head of the Chemical and Biological Weapons Nonproliferation Program at the Monterey Institute of International Affairs in California. I also gave him Botha's personal phone number. Only later did I hear that the South African minister had slammed down the receiver as soon as Tucker raised the Amrollahi issue.

With that, Pretoria went into overdrive. The South African government issued a statement on September 11 stating that "The country's Atomic Energy Corporation (AEC) had never been involved in business transactions with Iran. Nor were any being considered at present," said Mineral and Energy Affairs Minister Penuell Maduna. In a written reply to National Party member Johan Marais, when he tabled the matter in Parliament, he declared that the Atomic Energy Corporation CEO, Dr. Waldo Stumpf "had never held a meeting with Iran's deputy minister of atomic affairs Reza Amrollahi, as claimed by local and foreign news media."

In turn, Stumpf swore that the only meeting that he, or any other AEC official, had ever had with any Iranian government official took place in March 1995 in a public restaurant in Cape Town with Iranian petroleum minister Gholam Reza Aghazadeh. "Stumpf had been asked to attend the courtesy dinner by former Mineral and Energy Affairs Minister Pik Botha during Aghzadeh's visit to South Africa in connection with a possible oil storage deal at Saldanha. Though Botha did not attend the dinner, Iranian petroleum officials and other South African officials were present," Maduna said.[1]

If all this were true, one needs to ask why Dr. Stumpf would choose to be evasive about such a sensitive issue, especially at a time when it must have been clear to him that Tehran was covertly committed to building the bomb? That things were exacerbated by Pik Botha—irrespective of what he told Mungo Sogget—coming out in strong support of his statement, could only have compounded the fraud. More pertinent, why did both men, respected professionals in their own spheres of influence, choose to lie about something so critical? This was an issue that could ultimately result in the course of history being irrevocably changed in the most volatile region in the world.

Both men must have known the answer to that one. So, I'm sure, did all the South African cabinet ministers involved.

There is no disputing that Reza Amrollahi had been in the country at the time in question and that the meeting took place, if only because the circumstances were verified, first by Stumpf himself (to me personally) and afterward by Pik Botha (to Mungo Sogget) who, though a colleague, is somebody that I've never met. Most salient of all is the fact that Tehran admitted in 2003 that it had been trying to build an atom bomb for almost two decades. That, alone, totally vindicates the argument.

Unquestionably, both Botha and Stumpf must have been put under severe pressure by the South African authorities to recant. One must ask why should they have been forced to do so?

It is also worth noting that though this writer was vilified in Parliament, the entire issue—thoroughly controversial as it is—was allowed to rest right there. For his part, Stumpf, who is highly regarded by his peers, had every opportunity to test my claims in court. He could have leveled defamation charges at me and claimed damages from both Jane's and *The Mail & Guardian*, as I would certainly have done were I were in his shoes and believed I'd been wronged. Instead, he has done nothing.

Nor did the South African government take further action, even though nuclear weapons issues in that country are still subject to restrictions. There is also the matter of something as disputatious as my making public information relating to WMD.[2] The Official Secrets Act is still in force in South Africa.

One can only speculate whether the reticence of both men might have had something to do with their state pensions being withheld if they refused to cooperate, or if the government used some other form of leverage. In any case, they are going to have to live with the truth of the matter.

Interestingly, the issue was taken up not long afterwards by Washington. On December 4, 1997, James Rubin, spokesman for the State Department issued a statement in his Daily Press Briefing that made mention of the original report. It had been erroneous, Rubin told those present, and I quote:

> We are aware of a variety of press reports, dating back several months, suggesting that Iranian officials have requested South African assistance in providing Iran with technology which could assist development of a nuclear weapons program.
>
> One report alleged that a meeting between South Africans and Iranian nuclear officials occurred in South Africa in 1996. In response to that report, South African officials publicly clarified many inaccuracies in the report.
>
> The United States has high confidence in South Africa's commitment to its obligations under the Non-Proliferation Treaty not to assist efforts of any other countries—including Iran—to acquire nuclear weapons. South Africa's solid nuclear nonproliferation credentials are well known to us. In addition to being a signatory to the NPT, it played a significant role in securing indefinite extension of the Non-Proliferation Treaty in 1995. It is a member of the nuclear suppliers' group, and voluntarily abandoned its own nuclear weapons program in 1992 . . .

The issue was clearly vital enough for somebody at the U.S. Embassy in Pretoria to have spoken to senior members of the South African government. It is not impossible that they addressed President Mandela himself. Well loved and respected by all, he told the Americans that no such thing had ever happened. Clearly, Washington accepted everything he said at face value. At the same time, one needs to recall that those were South Africa's "Rainbow" years when the country had just emerged from decades of isolation. It had rejoined the community of nations a short while before, so there was really no reason for anybody to dispute his assurances.

To my discredit, it might have been argued, the entire brouhaha had originally been kick-started by an old hack, then living in America. Yet nobody even lifted the phone to ask me what had happened, in spite of Mungo Sogget having obtained the corroboration of one of Nelson Mandela's own ministers.

Clearly, somebody at State needs to answer questions as to why an issue as important as supplying nuclear wherewithal to Iran was not only ignored but actually downplayed, and on a government platform before the international media. Already in 1997 there was a good body of evidence that Tehran was going nuclear. Yet, it took until 2003 for the Iranians to admit that their country had been developing a nuclear weapons program "for the past eighteen years."

Dr. Waldo Stumpf had given us a seven-year head-start. Certainly, the West would have gained a lot of ground if somebody had taken notice of what had transpired.

Comfortably ensconced as a visiting professor of international relations at the London School of Economics in 2004, nobody is better placed today than former assistant secretary of state James P. Rubin to do a bit of scratching of his own as to why a critical issue such as South Africa having been asked to give support to Iran on a vital nuclear issue, and then lying about it afterward, had taken place.

As they say, the event happened on his watch. But then so did a lot of other sensitive things during Clinton's tenure in the White House.

There were several nuclear-related matters that occurred at about the same time. Some of these involved Iran and should have rung bells.

- An attempt to export a zirconium tube factory from a South African Atomic Energy Corporation establishment to China, with the possibility of it being redirected to Iran (Jane's *Pointer*, February 1, 1998). Zirconium cladding is used for nuclear elements and would be needed for Iran's nuclear effort at the Bushehr (or other, planned) reactors. The plant was prepared for dispatch from Pelindaba without necessary end-user certificates and other clarifications having been completed by the South African government. Western intelligence sources were aware at the time that China had been contracted to build such a factory for the Tehran Government and fears were expressed in Washington that the South African shipment might ultimately be diverted to the Near East (*NuclearFuel*, December 29, 1997).

- The disappearance of drums of fissile waste material from Pelindaba which, despite winding down the atom bomb project, was still one of the most closely guarded establishments in Africa. This was a serious matter, according to Dr. Ben Sanders of the Program for Promoting Nuclear Nonproliferation. He was aware of waste from discarded medical radiation sources stolen from a facility in Brazil in the early Nineties. It was eventually found, dumped next to a slum and some children playing there were contaminated.

- Another issue to surface was conjecture as to whether secret atom bomb tests in the South Indian Ocean in September 1979 actually took place. Were South African or, possibly, Israeli nuclear weapons detonated? David Albright, president of Washington's Institute for Science and International Security said in the Nov./Dec. 1997 issue of *Bulletin of the Atomic Scientists* that "There are just too many unanswered questions that continue to bedevil this issue." He suggested that more transparency from the South African government was necessary. Dr. Nic von Wielligh dismisses the matter for several reasons. First, he says, South Africa's Y-plant produced its first HEU only towards the end of 1979. This was confirmed by the IAEA in their subsequent forensic analysis. Second, the heavy atom bombs produced by South Africa (exceeding one ton) were designed and built for underground demonstration tests. At the time there was simply no means available to deliver such a device for an atmospheric explosion over the South Indian Ocean.

- Then there are questions as to exactly how much weapons-grade uranium South Africa produced while the Pretoria regime was engaged in its atom bomb project. At issue is not so much whether the figures for the amount of highly enriched uranium provided by South Africa's Atomic Energy Corporation were accurate (all subjected to lengthy audits by Vienna's IAEA), but rather, why Pretoria never allowed unrestricted access to official records for analysis?

Until recently, the Atomic Energy Corporation of South Africa was the largest installation of its kind in the Southern Hemisphere. Originally called the Atomic Energy Board (established in 1961) it was renamed the Atomic Energy Corporation (AEC) after the amalgamation of nuclear activities on the Valindaba and Pelindaba sites in 1985.

During the 1970s and 1980s the AEC was involved in (but not solely responsible for) South Africa producing six fission bombs in the twenty to twenty-four kiloton (kT) range. By then Armscor had taken over the development and manufacture of nuclear weapons at a special facility at Advena in Pretoria West.

There were other factors. Nelson Mandela's cabinet contained an inordinate number of Asians, almost all of them of Islamic orientation.

This was (and still is) strange, considering that the country's Asian population makes up perhaps five per cent of the whole. In mid 1997, these included Dullah Omar (Justice and Intelligence Services), MV Moosa (Constitutional Development), Kadar Asmal (Water Affairs), Aziz Pahad (Deputy Minister of Foreign Affairs) and his brother Essop Pahad (who was Deputy Minister in the Office of the President).

All of these notables, closely bonded over years of opposing Apartheid, either in jail or in exile, advocated strong ties with their friends in the Islamic world, Iran included. Most were, and still are, demonstrably hostile toward the United States, Britain and other Western interests. Not for nothing were they referred to in local media parlance as "South Africa's Karachi Connection," though arguably their links may have been stronger with Tripoli and Tehran (and, of course, Havana) than Islamabad.

The same holds with Mandela's successor, President Thabo Mbeki. Some of his closest cabinet advisors are Islamic and include quite a few of the same people that served under Madiba: Dullah Omar, Aziz Pahad; Kadar Asmal, who, by now has gone on to become Chairman of the National Conventional Arms Control Committee, as well as Abdul Minty, whose brief included responsibility for Pelindaba and other South African nuclear assets. Indeed, with time, the clique moved into a number of positions that demonstrated powerful clout

According to Washington sources, some of these ministers, as is their right, traveled extensively, as does Mbeki today. (His critics jibe that he spends more time abroad than at home, which is not exactly true, but you get the message.) Countries often visited by some of his ministers include Iran, the Sudan, Syria, Cuba, Libya and, while Saddam Hussein still strode tall, Iraq. Minty is known to have maintained links with Iran's spiritual leader, Ali Khamene'i.

It says something that the sale of sensitive nuclear material intended for Tehran, using China as an intermediary (without first having followed the standard procedures prescribed by the Nuclear Suppliers Group), took place when Minty was in charge of such things.

The shipment of a zirconium tube factory to China some time during 1997 makes for an interesting case study in unconventional proliferation.

Zirconium is a grayish-white lustrous metal commonly used in an alloy form (i.e. zircalloy) to encase fuel rods in nuclear reactors, and here too there is a Tehran connection. With Iran striving vigorously for self-sufficiency in all aspects of its domestic nuclear program, it would, as a requirement, be in need of, if not now then some time in the future, a zirconium tube factory. However, Tehran is banned from acquiring such a facility under restrictions imposed by the international NSG.

The easy way for Iran to overcome this imbroglio might have been for it to have taken advantage of its close ties to Moscow and possibly buy such a plant there. Russia has a lot of it and in the past has proved extraordinarily eager to provide Iran with just about all its needs. Instead, what emerged in 1997, the same year that Dr. Waldo Stumpf recanted on his original story, was evidence that the Iranian government—in complicity with Beijing—had an interest in trying to acquire the product from South Africa.

What is known is that the dispatch of the South African zirconium plant had progressed almost to the point of it being shipped out of the country without mandatory end-users certificates. The publication *NuclearFuel* stated in its issue dated December 19, 1997, that Washington feared the plant might end up in Iran since China, a short while before, had contracted with Tehran to build a zirconium plant at one of its nuclear facilities.

The story finally emerged after a group of about forty Chinese technicians entered South Africa on "business" visas in August 1997. They spent several months at Pelindaba preparing the plant for shipment. It was already packed into reinforced cases, though nobody is prepared to say on whose authority. Only after details surfaced in a South African newspaper file did the police raid the place and arrest these foreigners for "working illegally in the country." Business visas, the police said, did not permit aliens to work in South Africa and certainly not a large number of mainland Chinese.

On ministerial authority, the Chinese were immediately released from custody, even though the Ministry of Home Affairs was explicit that the activity of the group had violated the terms of their stay.

Most notable, was the observation by some members of the diplomatic community that the Chinese had gained regular and routine access to an extremely high-security nuclear establishment without anyone officially questioning their presence. By the time the police arrived, they had been industriously working there for several months. One source claims that the group was putting in ten and twelve-hour shifts, six days a week. Somebody was in a hurry.

What was of concern to those familiar with the issue, was that while the original contract for the sale was concluded between South Africa and China in the summer of 1997, almost nothing was made public about the deal. It only became newsworthy when "illegals" were arrested. Had this event not caught the eye of an alert journalist, a source within the government told me, there might have been nothing to prevent the entire multi-million dollar plant from leaving the country. And that would have taken place even though South Africa is a signatory to the NSG.

According to David Albright, the Nuclear Suppliers Group provides clear dual-use guidelines for the export of such equipment.

"It would appear that these were not observed," he stated. This is pertinent because under SA Government regulations, the Council for Nonproliferation of Weapons of Mass Destruction of the Department of Trade and Industry—an interagency export control body headed by Mr. Abdul Minty—requires end-user certificates for the sale of any dual-use or nuclear related equipment. In effect, such sales are not permitted to take place without Government sanction.

At issue here, said *NuclearFuel*, is a plant that had been used until 1993 to make zirconium tubing for fuel loaded at the two Koeberg nuclear reactors just north of Cape Town.[3] Early 1997, the AEC requested tenders for the sale of this facility. Brokered in the Channel Islands by a firm calling itself Pacific Development Services, a deal was concluded with the China National Nonferrous Industry Corporation at Shaanzi in north-central China. The price, quoted by Dr. Stumpf was $4.6 million.

What is more strange is that subsequent attempts by the media to make contact either with the broker or his company failed. This raises another matter: If the deal between the governments of China and South Africa was legitimate, why would anyone have involved an obscure middleman who is not only untraceable, but has yet to come forward to clarify some of the more sensitive questions? Surely, there is something rotten here.

Since then, Stumpf has said in a public statement, "We will get an end-user statement from China before the plant leaves South Africa."

Originally the zirconium plant at Pelindaba had been part of a nuclear fuel production complex for Koeberg and cost $42 million to build. Since final qualification of the tube plant for nuclear-grade zirconium alloy cladding was achieved in 1988, it had produced seventy-five thousand of these tubes for the Cape reactors. The plant was shut down in 1993 after international sanctions against South Africa were lifted and cheaper tubes became available from France. The AEC has since stated that it had tried to convert the zirconium factory to non-nuclear use but failed because of "the very specialized nature of the installation."

According to a statement issued at the time by the South African Ministry of Foreign Affairs, "There are three pieces of equipment in the zirconium plant which require official authorization under the Nuclear Suppliers' Group dual-use guidelines." Stumpf described these as CNC machine tools used to make complex molds.

Washington's comments on the subject included a statement that, independent of a pledge provided by China to cease nuclear trade with Iran (in exchange for nonproliferation certification by the Americans), it was not impossible that Beijing could still go through with the export to Tehran. Questioned about the Iranian link, Stumpf said that the sale to China was limited only to equipment in the plant. "China won't get any transfer of technology," he added.

It is interesting that shortly afterward, a question, not entirely unrelated, was raised about denials within South Africa's Parliament of President Mandela's government having allowed a number of training camps for the pro-Iranian Hizbollah (Party of God) guerrilla organization to be established in South Africa. Hizbollah, we are aware, is involved in a protracted insurgency against Israel and, from time to time, still launches rockets into northern Galilee. When reports of the camps first appeared, they were vigorously denied by a cabinet spokesperson in Cape Town. Only after Inkatha—the mainly Zulu Parliamentary opposition party—provided accurate details of their location and the nature of the insurgency training that was being provided to Hezbollah cadres, was the minister responsible prepared to concede that this was in fact so. The camps would be closed, he said.

More disturbing was the fact that former members of the South African Special Forces were believed to have been involved in the training and there had apparently been a good deal of emphasis on tactics associated with landmine warfare which, in the interim, saw an escalation in southern Lebanon during the final stages of the Israeli presence there. From this writer's own observation, many mine warfare systems evolved by South African forces in Angola were used against the Israeli Army in the disputed Lebanese "security zone," until the IDF withdrew.

When this correspondent visited Beirut in August 1997, Ibrahim

Moussawi, spokesman for the Party of God, told him that South Africans had never been involved in Hizbollah training. Nor, said Moussawi, had any Hizbollah guerrillas ever gone to Africa. Subsequent Jane's disclosures have indicated the presence of Hizbollah training bases in the Sudan.[4] It is significant that all these activities are linked to the Pasdaran, the Islamic Revolutionary Guards Corps, which has been responsible for Hizbollah training and weapons supplies from about 1982 onward.

Following the appearance of the original article about the sale of the tube factory in *Pointer*, a Jane's publication ("Is Iran in RSA-China Zirconium Deal?"), South African cabinet minister Abdul Minty wrote a letter of protest to the Jane's Information Group in Britain.

Dated March 9, 1998, it states: ". . . the article is filled with half-truths and innuendo and the author's 'investigation' uses as a basis another inaccurate report appearing in *NuclearFuel*." Minty also maintained that South African relations with the United States in regard to nuclear matters were exemplary.

He went on to say that the thrust of the article was inaccurate: "It indicates, incorrectly, that the whole contract was done under cover of darkness and even with the hope that the zirconium tube plant could leave (the country) without anyone knowing that South Africa had not complied with all the requirements of the Nuclear Suppliers Group."

That is "clearly not part of this government's policy nor style," the minister wrote. So, one needs to ask, what exactly are the facts?

- Details of the contract came to light after police, acting on a tip-off, raided Pelindaba because a large group of Chinese had entered South Africa on business visas and were working there, illegally. On prima facie evidence, they had no right to be in the country for any other purpose, never mind have access and work at a high security nuclear-sensitive installation. As a result, a journalist with the Independent newspaper group broke the story.
- The application to export the equipment on the NSG dual-use equipment list was made five days after the paper first reported the account of the planned sale to China. This was confirmed in a letter from Stumpf, to the editor of *NuclearFuel* dated January 13, 1998.
- According to a subsequent report in *NuclearFuel* (March 9); only after the story appeared in the press was it disclosed that the

Chinese had been working at Pelindaba. This fact also appeared in Stumpf's letter. Following these events, according to *NuclearFuel,* "Western officials and experts raised concern that South Africa's export control regime was not functioning smoothly."

Immediately afterward there were conflicting exchanges among some of the South African officials involved in the fracas. Reliable sources in Washington indicate that there may have been serious differences between Stumpf and Minty, but not enough to have had Stumpf fired. Such an action might have opened even more cans of worms. In any event, Dr. Stumpf has since taken up an academic position at Pretoria University.

On March 4, 1998, Minty challenged Stumpf's account. He explained to Mark Hibbs, author of the original article in *NuclearFuel,* that following press reports, he had personally investigated the matter, and "determined that the AEC application had not been submitted to the Secretariat of the export control revue body last December" (as Stumpf said it had). Instead, said Minty, "It was delivered by hand courier on January 5 of this year."

Minty also confirmed that visas issued to the Chinese were perfectly in order. "They had been processed by the Department of Home Affairs and were valid." It will be recalled that in his letter to *Jane's Intelligence Review,* Minty rejected the concept that there had been unease in Washington about what was going on at Pelindaba.

In comment, *NuclearFuel* stated in a report (March 9, 1998) that "When press reports of a planned export to China were aired, officials at the Department of State said that America would raise the issue with South Africa, in part, because China, in an apparently separate transaction, had agreed to export a zirconium tube plant to Iran, a country that Washington believes aims to develop a nuclear weapons capability." It also stated that late the previous year, two U.S. non-proliferation officials had observed that, in their view, the record of the export-permitting process in South Africa indicated that most likely, some kind of procedural mistake had been made.

NuclearFuel highlighted another issue involving Armscor at the same time. The magazine observed that the organization that had previously been responsible for South Africa's clandestine nuclear weapons program, appeared to be involved in an ongoing political battle with South Africa's black leadership. The magazine stated that "The firm's role in nuclear arms control matters has been blunted."

Minty denied this: "It is simply not true that there is any friction with Armscor," he declared. But Minty's statement that March (according to Mark Hibbs, author of the original article) definitively spelt out that Armscor played almost no role in the nuclear export control process, even though Armscor personnel (all of them well qualified specialists in a country where such expertise is limited) would, under normal circumstances, be the best equipped to do so. After all, these were the same people who originally built South Africa's arsenal of atom bombs, Hibbs observed.

In addition—with regard to the exclusion of Armscor from NPC's subordinate Control Committee—the document declared: "Armscor has no direct role whatever in matters related to nuclear issues other than its collective role as a member of the NPC. There, its primary task is to provide an input in dual-use technologies and equipment that form part of conventional weapons systems."

It was not surprising that some South African politicians (none of them linked to the government) as well as some members of the media, questioned the possibility of the existence of a hidden agenda.

While all this was taking place, *The Bulletin of the Atomic Scientists*, one of the most influential magazines dealing with international nuclear issues, recommended that circumstances surrounding a purported nuclear test in the southern oceans in September, 1979 be examined afresh. It suggested that this should be done under the auspices of the then President Nelson Mandela. More visits by President Mandela (twice in one week) to Libya's President Gadhaffi caused further disquiet in the West during this period.

Libya, we now know, tried to buy South African chemical and biological weapons' technology, to the extent that the former head of the South African CB weapons program, Dr. Wouter Basson, had to be reinstated in the South African armed forces in his original rank of Brigadier-General after he had been fingered as head of South Africa's chembio programs during the Apartheid era. Ronnie Kasrils, then South Africa's deputy minister of defense and a member of the Communist Party (and today head of Intelligence in South Africa), said at the time that that was the only way that (the government) was able to keep tabs on the man.

Basson had already spent some months on an unspecified assignment in Libya. Questioned afterward about what he did there by Dr. Jonathan Tucker of the Monterey Institute of International Studies, Basson intimated that "it wouldn't be worth my life to answer that question." In an observation to this writer, Tucker noted that throughout his meeting, the two men were discreetly monitored by South African security agents as they sat talking in a café in Pretoria.

Then came a spate of clandestine political activities that directly involved some of the top echelons of the South African government and, in particular, its military component, since none of it could or would have taken place had Pretoria not been directly involved.

A report from this period, datelined London and published by *Africa Confidential*, stated that a group of South African mercenaries was operating in Libya under the name NFD Securities. Work there included training Libyan Special Forces in advanced counter-insurgency techniques and intelligence gathering. Some phases involved the use of Libyan Air Force Mi-24 helicopters fitted with infrared cameras obtained from a South African government arms manufacturer: training was in methods of countering rebel activity.

To this end, the South Africans sold the Libyans night vision equipment as well as unmanned aerial vehicles (UAVs) as well as a range of other hi-tech security equipment. This was a large-scale contract and there could be little doubt that the South African government was aware of it even though there was no paper trail (or any other kind of trail) linking Pretoria to Tripoli in these adventures.

What is interesting is that much of the stuff involved in these deals was on the restricted list. And because there are stringent laws in place in South Africa about such matters, the entire affair must have had Mbeki's blessing. The word in Pretoria is that the order to supply this stuff—as well as the soldier of fortune input—came from the top. This was followed by something even more bizarre because it involved an ongoing war where Arab soldiers were killing black civilians. The Libyan contract over, NFD was offered a similar deal in the Sudan.

The British paper said that some of the work involved former mercenary personnel training Sudanese Special Forces in anti-guerrilla operations, which, it suggested, was a serious matter. Islamic Sudan has been at war for decades against the mainly Christian southern Sudanese tribal people, in a conflict where more than two million have been killed. Basically, it was Arabs killing black people. The name NFD is interesting because it is composed of the names of the three principal members of the company, all of them former South African Special Forces personnel. Each of them contributed an initial.

There was former SADF Special Forces operative "Brigadier"

Nick van Den Bergh, who had spent a couple of years running an Executive Outcomes (EO) mercenary outfit in Angola. I spent a weekend at his home in Angola while doing a story there for Jane's *International Defense Review*. Second is Frederick Christoffel Grove, ex-deputy commander of South Africa's Parachute Battalion. Then came NFD's operations manager Duncan Rykaart, a former colonel in the SADF's crack Recce Commando. Rykaart was my escort officer in the mid-1990s when, under the auspices of the Executive Outcomes mercenary organization, I visited the old Cuban Air Force base at Cabo Ledo and Saurimo, capital of the Angolan diamond fields in the northeast of the country.

What became clear before NFD was disbanded was that the company was no run-of-the-mill privateer set-up. It had a substantial number of former South African Special Forces personnel in its employ and had direct access to state-of-the-art weapons systems then emerging from South African arms factories. It also had a lot of money. Sources have since confirmed that its directors ended up buying an expansive (and expensive) piece of property at 13 Gouws Street in Raslouw on the outskirts of Pretoria. This was the very same complex that had originally belonged to Executive Outcomes, for whom all of them had once worked.

After news of NFD operations in Libya and the Sudan emerged, Rykaart denied any knowledge of either the Libyan or Sudanese contracts, even though he had been fingered as having taken the lead role in negotiations with Khartoum. "Someone has been masquerading, misusing our company name to get work," Rykaart told *Africa Confidential*. He stressed that that had happened a lot in the old EO days. And while he insisted that his company had no foreign security contracts, the NFD website at the time boasted a client base in Egypt, the Congo (Brazza), Uganda, Sierra Leone, Angola and Bulgaria.

That these individuals were able to operate under the auspices of the South African military, selling restricted military items to states that had been blacklisted by the UN, indicated that they had powerful protection at the top. That tentacle stretches all the way back to the cabinet of South African president Thabo Mbkei.

A combination of these and other factors are affecting Washington's long-term relations with South Africa. Among some Americans, there is a growing skepticism about Pretoria's prevarication on issues now regarded as among the most sensitive of the age in which we live.

8

CASE STUDY:
SOUTH AFRICA'S ATOM BOMB

"The South African nuclear program was an extreme
response to its own 'identity crisis.' Nuclear weapons
became a means to achieving a long-term end of a closer
affiliation with the West. A South Africa yearning to be
identified as a Western nation—and receive guarantees
of its security—rationalized the need for
a nuclear deterrent.'

"Out of (South) Africa: Pretoria's Nuclear Weapons Experience,"
by USAF Lt. Colonel Roy E. Horton III: Occasional Paper No 27,
USAF Institute for National Security Studies, August 1999

For decades South Africa was the single most powerful state on the
continent of Africa. In terms of military prowess, sophisticated
weapons development (which continues), industrial output (enhanced
still further today) and an army and air force that proved adaptable
both to fighting insurgency as well as the ability to take on a huge
Soviet and Cuban backed armored strike force in southern Angola, as
it did in 1987, Pretoria's military record, depending on your perspective, was impressive. However dubious that distinction might be in
terms of lives taken and damage done, the South African Defence
Force achieved massive success from the late 1960s onward in a succession of low-intensity wars—and some pretty awesome conventional confrontations—throughout much of the sub-continent.

With the handing over of power to a black majority government
in the early 1990s, all that is now history. In point of fact, if South
Africa were to be invaded today by even a marginal force from
Zimbabwe, there are observers of the opinion that the SADF has been
so drained of its effectiveness and that it would be hard pressed to
react effectively.

Yet things were different within the living memory of many South
Africans of all races. With a white government in Pretoria, the old

175

regime entrenched race laws under a series of uncompromising and unscrupulous edicts that were cumulatively referred to as Apartheid. Simply put, it meant that if you were white, you were all right. But it was also a time when the Cold War had almost run its course, signaled by that ultimate of totems, the collapse of the Berlin Wall.

Almost overnight, with the release of Nelson Mandela from twenty-seven years of prison, much of it spent on Robben Island, parameters throughout the sub-continent suddenly changed. In the late 1980s, South Africa under President F.W. de Klerk began to abandon its racial priorities in favor of what was termed "a coming together of all the races." Within five years, political power in the country was accorded to the African National Congress (ANC), an extremely diverse political group—blacks, Asians, people of mixed blood (so-called Coloreds) and even a handful of whites whose collective leadership—Mandela and his fellow inmates apart—had spent almost all its years in exile.

Arguably, South Africa could be regarded as the first military power to have relinquished total political control to its opponent without having been defeated in battle, a circumstance that is viewed— right or wrong—by many South Africans today as suicidal.

That wasn't the only first. Shortly after the new black ANC government had moved into the offices vacated by de Klerk's National Party, first reports started to appear that Pretoria, under the guidance of both the Americans and the International Atomic Energy Agency, had scuppered its atom bomb program. It also abandoned the most advanced guided missile program in Africa, though that was forced on Pretoria under threats of extending trade sanctions.

Though details were sparse at first, it gradually emerged that the country had built six complete atom bombs, all in the twenty-kiloton range, together with enough nuclear material for a seventh. With that, hundreds of pounds of highly enriched uranium was placed under IAEA scrutiny. The nuclear parts of these devices were melted down and the casings physically destroyed, especially those of tungsten. Almost symbolically, metal from the non-nuclear parts were used to fashion miniature plows. South Africa's first president under the new order, Nelson Mandela, was the first to get one of these reminders of another, harsher age.

Another reality of that epoch is that in an age of unparalleled proliferation of weapons of mass destruction, South Africa is so far the only country in the world to have voluntarily abandoned a successful ongoing nuclear weapons program. In years past there had been a number of countries that had begun planning for building the bomb and then abandoned or froze the idea when horrific financial and logistical realities began to bite. Among these were Taiwan, Sweden, Argentina, Libya, South Korea, Australia, Brazil, Algeria, Spain, Egypt and a handful of others, some of whom initially thought it would be easy. Of recent relevance, of course, are Pakistan, Iraq, Iran and North Korea.

One of the first questions most often asked was why these people should have thought it necessary to build the bomb in the first place. The immediate answer, as with Israel today, could probably be encapsulated in a single word—survival. To which critics of South Africa's race dominated policies would probably have added "of the white race."

The fact is that by the time that de Klerk and his National Party cabinet made the decision to call a halt to racial discrimination, the nation had been engaged in two decades of military conflict.

Pretoria's most determined adversary was Angola. Its seasoned and well-blooded army, FAPLA (*Forcas Armadas Popular Libertacao de Angola*) was not only equipped and trained by the Soviet Bloc, but also bolstered by Soviet, North Korean, Yugloslav advisors and technicians as well as by fifty thousand Cuban troops.

Because of South Africa's Apartheid laws, the issue was further exacerbated by a United Nations-imposed arms embargo. Pretoria was prevented from acquiring most kinds of advanced foreign military hardware that it needed to contain the threat from the north. That included military aircraft.

While a lot of weapons that emerged from South African factories were well designed, tested and battle-honed, the outlay dug great holes into the country's budget. The range of goods coming out of hundreds of arms factories included the full panoply of infantry squad weapons and infantry fighting vehicles. These included the Ratel and Rooikat as well as the Buffel (buffalo) troop carrier together with a secondary range of mine-protected vehicles. Some of these (and their subsequent clones) were indispensable in the conflict then being waged by the "white south" against Moscow's surrogates in Angola and several have since seen good service with the UN and other bodies in places as diverse as Iraq, Kosovo, South Lebanon and Rwanda.

Also built locally were a variety of artillery pieces. The 155mm G-5 howitzer was good enough to have been exported to many countries in the Near East, including Iraq when that country was at war with

Iran. Add to this tally a complement of mortar and rocket systems, mines, claymores and the rest and the SADF was more than adequately equipped to deal with just about all the vagaries encountered in its ground war. In addition, the country produced enough third generation communications equipment coupled to an outstanding level of medical backup for South Africa to make for a formidable adversary, even by today's standards.

What Pretoria had no answer for was air power. Unable to build its own fighters and support aircraft, the South African Air Force could not counter the squadrons of MiG-29s and Sukhoi strike aircraft, as well as Mi-24 helicopter gunships, with which the Angolan Air Force had been equipped. As with Vietnam, Cuba, Egypt, and dozens of other countries transfixed by Moscow, these machines were flown by Cuban, East German and Soviet pilots.

Obviously, South Africa's Apartheid leaders had to look for another remedy if they were going to prevent their forces from being overwhelmed and it was for this reason that the bomb was first considered. Domestic needs also pointed South Africa in the direction of a nuclear option. As Dr. Waldo Stumpf declared, South Africa's political isolation was coupled to a growing nuclear isolation. "During the 1970s, some of the nuclear weapon states and in particular the U.S., increasingly started to apply unilateral restrictions on nuclear trade or exchange of information and technology with South Africa," he wrote.

"In 1976, the U.S. government unilaterally refused further exports under a long standing contract between the U.S. and Pretoria of fuel elements for the Safari research reactor which had been under safeguards of the IAEA since its commissioning in 1965. South Africa's pre-paid payment for the canceled consignment was also retained by the Carter Administration and its return was approved only after Reagan had taken office in 1981.

"In 1978 Congress enacted the Nuclear Non-Proliferation Act (NPA) which precluded the transfer of any kind of nuclear technology to countries not party to the NPT. This act was applied retroactively on all previous agreements and contracts and directly led to the refusal of export permits to South Africa for the shipment to France of its own uranium already enriched by US Department of Energy for the Koeberg Nuclear Power station."

Though the bombs eventually produced by Pretoria might have been regarded as an unwieldy effort to join the world's ultra-exclusive

Nuclear Club—they were clumsy, overly bulky and of a World War II gun-type vintage—the South Africans achieved their initial objective. It was only a question of time before Armscor scientists would be able to limit their size and weight, which would then have allowed them to be deployed in the country's burgeoning guided missile program.

It is interesting that, by then, a collaborative effort had been initiated with Israel on missile development. The Jewish state had already fielded its first ballistic missile, the Jericho-1, and was in the process of working on the longer-range Jericho-2 (which could carry a one-ton payload about a thousand miles). Some of the testing for these weapons took place along South Africa's South Cape coast at the Overberg Test Range, near Arniston, a bit more than a hundred miles from Cape Town, in part because Israel has no eastward-facing test range of its own.

Its scientists meanwhile, were involved in trying to perfect the bomb so that it could be delivered by one of four missile projects the country was working on. At that stage, Pretoria's first fissile devices were so bulky that, should the need have arisen, only obsolete British-built Buccaneer strike aircraft could have been used to deploy them.

Though it is significant that South Africa, like Israel, did not boast about the fact that it had nuclear capability, this was due in part to a policy of what is termed "deliberate uncertainty," which, in some political quarters, is often more effective in achieving objectives than telling. At the same time, both Washington and London were aware that Pretoria was fast approaching the point where it would have had the clout to militarily reshape things in its corner of the globe. Though hardly a match for any of the major powers, it wasn't lost on the strategists of either country that atom bombs dropped onto the heads of the inhabitants of several African capitals had implications that could severely affect events far beyond the frontiers of South Africa. This was before Mandela's release and at a time when the Cold War was real.

Indeed, by the late 1980s, Chester Crocker, U.S. Under Secretary of State for Africa, had started multiple negotiations that involved South Africa, Angola, Portugal, Cuba, the United States as well as the Soviet Union. The fact that Pretoria had the bomb and wasn't boasting about it was probably the single most powerful motive for peace.

South Africa's nuclear weapons program was minuscule compared to that of other states. On March 26, 1993, the London *Sunday Times* published an interview with a former South African nuclear scientist who was involved in the weapons program until the mid-1970s. He said that while he was at Pelindaba, there were about thirty scientists working on the bomb project.

Also, the country's deterrent strategy, described at the time of disclosures made by President De Klerk, was based on three phases (discussed by the government in August 1977 and approved in April 1978):

- *Phase one:* The first was the "strategic uncertainty" issue during which its nuclear capability would be neither acknowledged nor denied. (As Dr von Wielligh points out, no real offensive tactical application of nuclear weapons was then foreseen—as was later the case—which was why, initially, there was no deliberate effort to construct a smaller, lighter bomb).
- *Phase two:* Should its territory be threatened militarily, then the government would covertly acknowledge the existence of its nuclear weapons to leading Western governments, particularly the United States.
- *Phase three:* If this partial disclosure failed to lead to the required assistance in defusing the situation, the government would publicly acknowledge its capability or demonstrate it with an underground test.

Most notably, the strategy was calculated to bring Western governments to South Africa's aid in the event of an overwhelming attack by Soviet supported military forces in Southern Africa. However, it is the view of some that the prime objective in developing its limited nuclear capability was to force the West, particularly the United States, to provide a guarantee of sorts to offset the Soviet Union's capacity for "nuclear escalation dominance."

This could very well have happened had the country come under a full-scale conventional attack, not impossible if the Namibian war was expanded (with Soviet support) to include a second front in Caprivi. It could be said that the nuclear card was political bluff intended to blackmail the United States (and other Western powers) into coming to Pretoria's assistance should the country be on the verge of being overrun.[1]

Another reason for espousing such a doctrine was the desire to increase Western concerns about South Africa's nuclear intentions, which led to the establishment in 1977 of Vastrap, a potential nuclear testing site in the remote Kalahari Desert where Pretoria had hoped to conduct an underground nuclear test. The preparations being made at the time was for a dummy run (an "instrumented" test without an actual nuclear core). Preparations for this event were detected by Soviet satellite surveillance and subsequently abandoned, after, it has been suggested, Washington threatened to prohibit sales of commercial aircraft and parts, which would effectively have grounded South African Airways' mainly Boeing fleet.

Though the country never intentionally moved beyond phase one, some officials have said that they believed that once Western or Soviet intelligence discovered that Armscor had checked the condition of at least one of the shafts at Vastrap for a possible underground test during the mid-1980s, this exercise convinced them that the country was deadly serious about its nuclear capability. In turn, it resulted in them putting pressure on the Soviet Union and Cuba to withdraw from Angola. Whether the weapons and the strategy ever served this purpose has not been proved and is consequently impossible to determine.

According to an article carried by *The Risk Report*[2] titled "South Africa's Nuclear Autopsy," its nuclear program was run by the Atomic Energy Corporation in conjunction with Armscor, whose scientists routinely culled open-source literature, including U.S. Navy manuals on nuclear weapon systems, safety and design.

Essentially, Pretoria's quest for a bomb did not, as some pundits are quoted, begin in 1971. The initial reason for the building of a nuclear explosive (in the days of the old Atomic Energy Board) was from the point of view of a peaceful nuclear explosion in line with the objectives of the "Ploughshare Project" in the U.S. The Nuclear Non-Proliferation Treaty which entered into force in March, 1970, in fact, makes provision in Article V for peaceful nuclear explosions (though never applied in practice) which could potentially be used for the excavation of dams, in mining, in clearing navigational channels and so on. It is significant that the approval of the first R&D project to investigate the possibility of an explosive device was given by the Minister of Mining in 1971 and not by the Minister of Defence. Further, Armscor only took over in the actual construction of the nuclear devices after a change of emphasis from peaceful to military uses in 1978.

For its role, the newly renamed AEC was charged with its most difficult task, producing highly enriched uranium fuel.

Prior to 1985, the Uranium Enrichment Corporation (UCOR, established in 1970) and the Atomic Energy Board existed as two separate entities on the Valindaba and Pelindaba sites respectively, with contact only at the highest management levels. In 1982 UCOR and NUCOR (previously the Atomic Energy Board) were converted to companies and the Atomic Energy Corporation established as their controlling body. Three years later both were integrated under the AEC and ceased to exist as separate entities.

UCOR, as Dr. von Wielligh explained, was responsible for producing uranium hexafluoride from ore concentrates received from South African mines. It was then enriched to weapons-grade HEU in the Pilot Enrichment (Y) Plant or (later) for enriching up to the level required for the Koeberg Nuclear Plant (low enriched uranium or LEU) in a separate enrichment establishment, the Z plant.

HEU produced by UCOR was sent to the AEB on the Pelindaba site where uranium hexafluoride was converted to metal. This, in turn, was used to produce the nuclear cores for the weapons or for the manufacture of HEU for the SAFARI research reactor (due to the American boycott in exporting nuclear materials to the Apartheid regime).

Tasked to build the actual weapon in its nuclear program, was the mammoth state-owned organization known as Armscor that handled all such projects of military significance, the majority catering specifically for the needs of the country's ongoing wars within and beyond its frontiers.

Once the country had decided to "go nuclear," it took only seven years for its scientists to build an atomic bomb like the one the United States dropped on Hiroshima. The effort required about a thousand experts, but, according to Dr. Stumpf, the man who inherited South Africa's nuclear establishment, "Less than five or ten people had an oversight of the entire program." Top secret clearance was only granted to persons born in South Africa and with no other citizenship. For some tasks, says the report, more sophisticated equipment was needed, so Pretoria resorted to smuggling.

"I am not at liberty to divulge anything that we import . . . we do not identify our suppliers." This was all that Dr. Stumpf, CEO of South Africa's Atomic Energy Corporation, would say when he fielded questions during a 1993 meeting at the South African Embassy in Washington.

He declared categorically that South Africa "had no help from anybody on nuclear weapons technology. . . . We gave no help to any-body and we received no help. On other things, yes . . . [but] not on enrichment technology, not on nuclear weapons technology."

Stumpf admitted that South Africa imported nuclear materials over the years, including low-enriched uranium, but he would not say where it came from. As von Wielligh reminds us, the imported LEU was never part of the nuclear weapons program but intended for use in reactors.

Less secrecy accompanied South Africa's guided missile program.

According to *Risk Report*, Israel was South Africa's hands-down most important missile supplier. Pretoria got most of what it needed from Tel Aviv and for much of it, the course was a two-way street. Exchanges included the transfer of approximately fifty tons of South African yellowcake (uranium ore concentrate) in exchange for thirty grams of tritium, the heaviest hydrogen isotope customarily used to boost the explosive power of atom bombs.

Incorporated into the core of the bomb, a tritium plug can quite substantially raise the yield of, for instance, a 20 kT bomb by four or five times. Pakistan claims to have thermonuclear capability, but in the view of American nuclear physicist Dr Bogdan Maglich—at one stage one of the heads of CERN in Geneva, as well as involvement in the Indian nuclear program—"That's a clever bit of disinformation in a bid to counter Delhi's advances in this field." Islamabad, says Maglich, uses tritium to boost its fissile weapons and apparently does it well enough to produce some impressive results. Others are not so sure.

The tritium received from Israel never found a home in the South African nuclear weapons program. Instead, with a half-life of twelve years, much of it had deteriorated by the time a halt was called to weapons production. At one stage some tritium was commercially used to illuminate advertising billboards but nobody can tell whether it was successful or not.

The secrecy surrounding its A-bomb efforts often forced Pretoria to make do with low-tech equipment. "These guys were immensely proud of what they achieved under sanctions," said a U.S. State Department official once Pretoria had opened its door to IAEA and American inspection. "They came up with their own home-spun tech-nology," he added.

From the late 1970s through early 1990, South Africa produced

HEU at its pilot-scale enrichment plant at Pelindaba. The key technology, claimed an American-based report, was called "split-nozzle gaseous diffusion," which was rumored to have been supplied by West Germany in the early 1970s. But this is incorrect.

Dr von Wielligh reminds us that there is no enrichment process with that name. Rather, the different types of enrichment processes are:

- Gas centrifuge (the most common method today)
- Gaseous diffusion (originally used in the U.S. for the Manhattan Project)
- Aerodynamic methods (separation nozzles or vortex tubes)
- Chemical or ion exchange (not really used in practice)
- Laser-based enrichment (AVLIS or MLIS)

The German company STEAG became involved in an economic study of the vortex, or UCOR vortex tube method of uranium enrichment. This gave rise to the misconception that South Africa obtained its isotope separation technology from Germany, i.e. the so-called Becker process, an aerodynamic method of making use of separation nozzles. This, he stresses, is not the same as the South African process, though both methods are based on aerodynamic phenomena, but that is where any similarity stops.

Backing this development, Dr. Abraham Johannes Andries Roux, president of the South African Atomic Energy Board, maintained at the time that ninety per cent of the plant was manufactured in South Africa. The foreign content was purchased "through normal channels and was in no way crucial for the completion of the project," he declared.

Obviously, the need for secrecy made this kind of shopping difficult. According to the industry newsletter *NuclearFuel*, South Africa needed tungsten, which is useful for making neutron reflectors for bomb packages. As von Wielligh tells us, Tungsten serves to reflect escaping neutrons back into the core of the bomb, thereby reducing the quantity of nuclear material needed for criticality. But since the Nuclear Suppliers Group (NSG) had controlled tungsten for export since the late Seventies, Pretoria was forced to find secret sources in Rhodesia, Zambia and Zaire, according to a US analyst. At the same time, no one is willing to say exactly who sold what to whom.

Something that surprised IAEA inspectors who visited South

African nuclear plants once the country had decided to come clean, was that much of the equipment was low-tech. "They were very creative," a U.S. participant commented. He reported that South African scientists regularly adapted lower-tech equipment to complex tasks. For example, two-axis machine tools normally used for simple manufacturing were reportedly adapted to create complex three-dimensional shapes for South Africa's gun-type nuclear bomb. Among this IAEA group were nationals from the UK, France, Russia, Greece, Germany and of course, the United States.

By mid-1977, the AEC had completed its first bomb package, but the enrichment plant at Pelindaba, known as the "Y-Plant," did not begin producing the high-enriched uranium fuel until 1978. A second package was built in 1978, and by late 1979 the Y-plant had processed enough enriched uranium for a single bomb core. Pretoria built six nuclear devices between 1977 and 1989 and the design for each was essentially the same.

A fairly constant recurring (and controversial) theme while South Africa's nuclear weapons program progressed, was whether a full-fledged nuclear test ever took place. While Soviet satellites detected preparations for a test site in the Kalahari Desert in 1977. Washington and Moscow pressured Pretoria to shut it down. In September 1979, however, an American Vela satellite detected a distinctive double flash off the southern coast of Africa. This data offered strong evidence that the flash had been caused by a low-yield nuclear explosion.

In June 1980, the CIA reported to the National Security Council that the two-to-three kiloton nuclear test had probably involved Israel and South Africa. U.S. intelligence confirm that it had tracked frequent visits to South Africa by Israeli nuclear scientists, technicians and defense officials in the years preceding the incident and concluded that "clandestine arrangements between South Africa and Israel for joint nuclear testing operations might have been negotiable."

Such speculation was fueled in 1986 when Israeli nuclear technician Mordechai Vanunu was interviewed by the London *Sunday Times*. Vanunu said that it was common knowledge at Dimona that South African metallurgists, technicians, and scientists were there on joint technical exchange programs.

The truth is more compelling. First says Dr. von Wielligh, South Africa's Y-plant produced *enough* HEU for its first bomb only toward the end of 1979. This was confirmed by the IAEA in their subsequent study and forensic analysis of operating and production records of the

Y-plant. Second, the very heavy first devices (exceeding one ton) were designed and built for underground demonstration tests or such jet bombers as South Africa possessed. At the time there was simply no means available to deliver such a device for an atmospheric explosion over the South Indian Ocean.

Furthermore, he states, "In discussions on a personal level with high-level officials involved in the project (including Dr Wynand de Villiers, at one stage head of the South Africa's nuclear project) it was categorically denied that that SA had been involved in such a test for all the above reasons."

Due to circumstantial evidence (for example, the unexplained tardiness of the U.S. to do atmospheric tests after the alleged explosion) the theory was advanced that the test could have been some kind of cooperation between the U.S. and Israel on an Israeli test vehicle. In fact, Dr. de Villiers told von Wielligh that he was of the opinion that this is what might have happened and that to blame South African involvement afterwards was only a rather useful smoke screen to avoid implication.

As Dr. de Villiers apparently stated, "In the Apartheid era, who would have believed South Africa anyway?"

After Pretoria acceded to the Nuclear Non-Proliferation Treaty in 1991 and the Safeguards Agreement with the IAEA entered into force in the same year, inspectors from the IAEA started visiting South African nuclear plants not only to implement the agreement but also to verify that Pretoria had accounted for all its secret bomb material. One of the lead inspectors told *Risk Report*: "It was a tremendous experience . . . we enjoyed the highest level of cooperation that you could hope for . . . we were able to reconstruct the activity of the enrichment facility on a daily basis, and do forensic analysis of the records."

But no information whatsoever was provided on the suppliers. The Agency's mandate was only to assess the "correctness and completeness" of Pretoria's nuclear material reports. "We couldn't ask the source of the materials," said one of the inspectors. "If we had, they would have said: 'None of your business'."

At the same time, the South Africans were very discreet about where things had originally come from, the inspector disclosed. "There was nothing we saw to indicate Israeli fingerprints," he added. This was perhaps to be expected, since Israel never used HEU for the construction of a nuclear device. (Instead, Jerusalem chose to go the plutonium route.)

South African gun-type HEU bombs, it should be noted, differ radically from implosion-type plutonium devices, which the Jewish state manufactured, and, as von Wielligh suggests, is another reason why there could not have been cooperation between the two countries.

He does concede though that the thinking in Pretoria during this critical time did include the concept of investigating the construction of a plutonium-based implosion bomb. The matter was serious enough "for a decision to have been made to go ahead and built a plutonium plant at the mouth of the Gouritz River in the Cape. Land was even bought for that purpose but never used."

On South Africa's guided missiles, he said, "The IAEA, by virtue of its statute, was strictly limited to nuclear matters and had no mandate to investigate its missile program. Such authority can only be voted on by the UN Security Council, as was the case with UNSCOM in Iraq."

Not everything went according to plan. Two press reports, the first by Reuters on March 27 1994, headed "Scientists Willing To Disclose Arms Secrets—Paper," and another, "Atomic Scientists Close To Talking," which appeared in *Jane's Defence Weekly* a week later (April 2, 1994) suggested deep dissatisfaction with the ranks of South Africa's nuclear fraternity.

What it boiled down to, according to an abstract published by the Monterey Institute of International Studies, was that South African nuclear and rocket scientists threatened to expose classified details about the country's arms industry unless they were collectively paid more than four million rand (then about $1.5 million). The money was compensation for being laid off by Advena, the top secret Denel nuclear warhead manufacturing subsidiary, they maintained.

A spokesman claiming to represent sixteen scientists, said that their disclosures would "prove embarrassing both for the Armaments Corporation of South Africa (Armscor), Denel (an offshoot of Armscor), as well as President F.W. de Klerk's National Government." In 1993 when de Klerk announced the destruction of South Africa's nuclear weapons capability, he claimed that no foreign assistance was provided for the development of nuclear weapons, but made no mention of South Africa's missile capability. What is known is that Israel supplied rocket technology to South Africa as well as details on how to convert a space launch vehicle into a nuclear ballistic missile.

Pretoria wasted little time in taking action. Within weeks, the Transvaal Supreme Court issued an order gagging the group. They were prohibited from disclosing information to the media or unauthorized personnel regarding the "obtaining, marketing, importing, exporting, development, manufacture, maintenance or repair of armaments by Armscor or its subsidiaries." The decision followed a suit by Armscor claiming that disclosure of the information might harm South Africa's chances of admission to international bodies to which it wished to become a member.

The first test bomb was built at Pelindaba and completed toward the middle of 1977. At the time there was not yet any HEU available and in any event, the device was intended for the "instrumented" dummy run at the Vastrap facility in the Kalahari. The second bomb was also constructed at Pelindaba and was the first fitted with HEU (produced by the Y plant) in November 1979. Armscor only completed its first device at Advena's Circle Facility in 1982.

David Albright, a veteran in reporting the South African nuclear program has always provided a good insight to what went on at the southern tip of Africa. Writing in *The Bulletin of the Atomic Scientists* in June 1993, he disclosed that "Advena had extensive capabilities aimed at building a highly reliable gun-type nuclear weapon deliverable by aircraft." The device was designed to rigorous specifications in order to avoid the need for a full-scale nuclear test. Another long-time observer of the South African nuclear program said that it made sense that South African scientists and engineers would have designed the "best crude gun-type device." However, he added, "What does not make sense is that they would have stopped there."

"Erected during the 1980s," Albright continued, "Advena had manufacturing capabilities apparently sufficient to produce more sophisticated nuclear weapons if South Africa had decided to go that way. Although there is no evidence that it produced more weapons than it declared, Advena's competencies imply that South Africa was working on more sophisticated designs, including implosion-type weapons (about which the IAEA was fully informed: von Wielligh). If built, these weapons could have been deployed on advanced delivery systems, such as ballistic missiles, which South Africa was concurrently working on.

"After the government abandoned its nuclear weapons program in

1989, Advena was converted to a commercial facility offering high-tech products for the aerospace, mining, medical, and other industries. Effective, at least for a while, the company became an experiment in the conversion of nuclear weapons-related expertise to the commercial production of sophisticated metallurgical, explosive, electronic, and pyrotechnical products for domestic and export markets.

It is interesting to see how bomb work progressed. "In the fall of 1992," according to Albright, "*NuclearFuel* identified Building 5000 at Pelindaba as the site of early nuclear weapons manufacturing, and it is now believed that the first device was prepared there.

"On March 26, 1993, the London *Sunday Times* published an interview with a former South African nuclear scientist who was involved in the weapons program until the mid-1970s who said that the scientists worked in secret in Buildings A and D, which were in a high-security compound located well off a road leading to the recreation area at the facility."

Also disclosed was that by October 1978, says Albright, "The government decided to shift its emphasis from peaceful to military devices. Armscor was given the responsibility for manufacturing, with the AEC providing the uranium. Personnel were transferred to Armscor, although the AEC continued to provide theoretical and health physics support to the Armscor weapons operation.

"In 1981, Armscor completed two buildings at Kentron Circle, a main manufacturing building and an environmental test facility. The main building manufactured and stored nuclear devices. The environmental test facility was involved in testing the reliability of the device under real-world conditions. This capability was particularly important because the weapons were expected to be reliable without the benefit of full-scale nuclear testing.

"A completed nuclear device, made by the AEC and loaded with HEU in 1979, was transferred to Advena and placed in storage. According to Armscor, the AEC device was not considered a 'qualified' design, which meant that there was not an adequate degree of assurance that it would detonate as intended or that it would not detonate accidentally.

"Advena manufactured its first atom bomb in April 1982; the delay probably reflecting the problems at the Y-Plant. But even this second device was considered a 'pre-qualification' model. Design refinements and final qualification took another two to three years, after which the design was 'frozen' for production. When the program was canceled in November 1989, Advena had six of them in its security vaults.

"Because of the design's simplicity, because redundancy was built into the device whenever possible, and because Advena had an aggressive qualification program, Armscor was confident that the atom bomb would work without a full-scale nuclear test.

"It is somewhat difficult to understand why it took so long to 'qualify' a device based on simple gun-type principles. But, said Armscor, Advena had to 'develop everything in-house due to the security requirements of the program.' The device and subsystems were studied carefully to insure that they would be highly reliable and exceed safety requirements. With everything handled at Advena, and with stringent specifications, it could easily take several years to accomplish the task.

"Although a successful gun-type device is easier to build than an implosion-design weapon, it still presents demanding mechanical and metallurgical challenges. For example, the barrel must be able to withstand the firing of a high-density uranium plug, which is about ten times denser than a normal artillery shell and generates ten times as much pressure on the barrel breach. Even with specialized gun barrels supplied by the US Navy, America's Manhattan Project took a significant amount of time to solve this problem.

"Armscor stated that Advena had problems in the early years in achieving repeatability of projective velocity and repeatability of the symmetry requirements when the projectile is shot into the other subcritical mass; in determining the density of neutron reflectors and in attaining adequate reliability of the arming and safing devices.

"Advena was expanded in the mid-1980s. Additional offices and laboratories were built to accommodate more personnel. But Armscor says no nuclear material ever entered these new buildings. A company spokesman maintained that Advena not only made nuclear devices, but provided other products and services to other Armscor divisions.

"When the nuclear weapons program ended, Advena employed about three hundred people. Within a year, that number was reduced by about two-thirds. On April 1, 1992, Advena became a division of a new commercial group, Denel (Pty) Ltd., which took over more than twenty of Armscor's twenty-six subsidiaries and facility companies."

Albright also detailed South Africa's pilot enrichment facility,[3] which was centrifuge-based. In an interview with Albright in South Africa in

February 1994, Anthony Jackson, leader of the team responsible for the design and commissioning of the Y-Plant, said that the attainment of an industrial production level required years of trial and error. Because the plant was for a "strategic" purpose, funding to sort out all the engineering and chemical problems was never an issue.

Construction of the Y-Plant started in late 1970, the first stages of the lower end of the cascade went on-line by the end of 1974 and the full cascade, designed to produce weapons-grade uranium, started operation in March 1977. Because of the long equilibrium time of the plant, the first and relatively small withdrawal of HEU occurred in January 1978.[4]

He disclosed that according to South African AEC officials, the actual output of the plant was on average closer to ten-thousand separative work units (swu)[4] per year than the nominal output of twenty-thousand swu's. That meant that the plant could produce between one-hundred-and-thirty to two hundred pounds of enriched uranium a year. This quantity was more than enough for the designated one explosive a year of the type that South Africa's nuclear scientists built, which was a gun-type device containing about one-hundred-and-twenty pounds of HEU.

KEY EVENTS IN SOUTH AFRICA'S NUCLEAR WEAPONS PROGRAM[5]

Year	Activity
1950s and 1960s	Scientific work on the feasibility of peaceful nuclear explosives and support to nuclear power production efforts
1969	AEB forms group to evaluate technical and economic aspects of nuclear explosives
1970	AEB releases report identifying wide applications for nuclear explosives
1971	R&D for gun-type device approved for "peaceful use of nuclear explosives"
1973	AEB places research priority on gun-type design over implosion and boosted weapon designs
1974	PM Vorster authorizes funding for work on nuclear device and preparation of test site
1977	AEB completes assembly of nuclear device (less HEU core) for "cold test" in the Kalahari Desert

Soviet Union and the U.S. detect preparations for the nuclear test and pressure South Africa into abandoning the test
AEB instructed to miniaturize device; groundwork laid for ARMSCOR to take program lead

1978   Y-Plant uranium enrichment plant produces first batch of HEU
Three-phase strategic guidelines established for nuclear deterrent policy
Botha "Action Committee" recommends arsenal of seven nuclear weapons and ARMSCOR formally assumes control of program

1979   "Double-flash" event detected; first device with HEU core produced by AEB.

1982   First deliverable device produced by ARMSCOR; work continues to improve weapon safety and reliability

1985   ARMSCOR strategy review expands original three-phase strategy to include specific criteria to transition to next deterrent phase

1987   First production model produced; total of six weapons built with enough HEU for a seventh at program termination but which was never built. Armscor revisits Kalahari test site at Vastrap and erects a large steel hanger over test shafts and prepares for a possible nuclear test.

1988   Angola, Cuba, and South Africa formally agree on Namibia's independence and schedule for Cuban troops to withdraw from Angola

1989   F.W. de Klerk elected President and orders weapon production halted

1990   Y-Plant formally shut down and nuclear weapons dismantlement begins

1991   South Africa signs the NPT and enters into a comprehensive safeguard agreement

1993   President de Klerk publicly discloses details of the former South African nuclear deterrent program

The worrisome thing is that the world learned the full scope of Pretoria's nuclear weapons program only after it was successful. If Tehran is able to follow suit, there will be little chance that Iran, like South Africa, will voluntarily dismantle its arsenal.

PART III
IRAN'S TROUBLED ROLE IN WORLD AFFAIRS

9

BUILDING GUIDED MISSILES TO HIT ISRAEL

With technical assistance from Charles P. Vick,
Senior Fellow, Space Policy, GlobalSecurity.org

"[Iran's] reformists and conservatives agree on at least one thing:
weapons of mass destruction are a necessary component
of defense and a high priority."
CIA Director George Tenet, before the
Senate Armed Services Committee, February 2, 1999

Unbeknown to just about anybody outside Pretoria, the Iranians, for several years, have had South African rocket scientists in their employ to help enhance their missile arsenal. Indeed, their presence in Iran is one of the best kept secrets in the Middle East, except that the American CIA and DIA as well as Britain's SIS are aware of it.

Essentially, their presence could be one of the reasons—together with a number of Russian specialists on contract—why Iran has has made such remarkable progress in developing a variety of fairly advanced guided missiles. These strides, within an otherwise unsophisticated society (and without an industrial infrastructure of any real consequence), has surprised many observers, among them members of the Federation of American Scientists (FAS).

As far as South African participation is concerned, these are the same boffins who spent more than a decade hand-in-glove with a select group of Israeli specialists putting together and refining the "Arniston" [also referred to as the RSA-3], South Africa's first intermediate range ballistic missile. A variant of Israel's Jericho II, its first successful launch was from Overburg, at one time a strategic South African military site near Bredasdrop in South Africa's Southern Cape region.

Under the threat of trade sanctions from America, Pretoria ended its missile collaboration with Israel in 1992 and then halted all ballistic missile development the following year. The next step was for Pretoria to join the Missile Technology Control Regime (MTCR). As the price for membership, South Africa had to vow that it would give up long-range missile development and cancel its space launch effort. That was shortly before the newly-elected President Nelson Mandela accepted the chalice from his predecessor, ex-President F.W. de Klerk.

As a consequence, South African companies that had actually built the rockets, such as Kentron, Houwteq and Somchem, were forced to cut back massively and eliminate key technologies, something that had not been factored into the agreement and which caused a great deal of anguish within the country's scientific community. Houwteq, the main contractor for the space launcher, was obliged to dismantle its largest rockets and even retrieve blueprints and technical files from its many subcontractors.

Almost overnight, with a new political dispensation in South Africa in place, the missile program was obliterated. All the effort and outlay—the financial investment alone totaled many hundreds of millions of U.S. dollars—amounted to virtually nothing.[1]

That it was pushed through with unwarranted haste (certainly nobody in Washington had taken time to consider the long-term consequences) was a mistake. The disbanding of South Africa's quite remarkable little space age-industry left a sizeable body of professionals—hundreds of men and women—disaffected and out of work. And almost all were of one mind: the ugly Americans had not only interfered with their lives and careers, but had also caused great financial hardship. Indeed, the bitterness that resulted persists to this day.

Without question, these professionals had done some very good work. U.S. officials confirmed later (and they told Congress) that the CIA had evidence of a full-scale partnership between Israel and South Africa to develop, test and produce long-range missiles and rockets. In record time, these folks had achieved considerable success in two decades of building advanced missile systems under the auspices of several Armscor affiliates.

Test launches, of which there were many, took place at two principal South African missile sites: the first at the Missile Test Range adjacent to the St. Lucia area of present-day KwaZulu/Natal. That was eventually superseded by the bigger Overberg Test Range (OTR), mainly a launch and test facility for Low Earth Orbiting satellites in the old De Hoop nature reserve in the Cape.

In parallel with the OTR was an Air Force installation to facilitate

the use of the test range instrumentation for airborne flight tests located at the nearby town of Bredasdorp. This was known as the Test
Flight and Development Centre (TFDC).

In conjunction with these establishments, the Houwteq development and manufacturing facilities were set up at Houw Hoek (also
near Cape Town). This was for the development and systems-integrate
reconnaissance satellites and to integrate rockets then being built with
their payloads. Obviously, these could be either for reconnaissance or
a warhead. There was even a systems engineering facility established
at the nearby Stellenbosch University.

Another linked facility was at Somerset West. This was the
Somchem development and engineering facility for large rocket
motors—the same establishment, incidentally, where Armscor housed
one of its biggest explosives, propellants and rocket systems factories.
Also involved was Kentron (missiles and other guided systems) as well
as a facility at Irene, near Pretoria, for the development, manufacture
and systems integration of inertial components and platforms, essential for the guidance of the launching rocket and of the satellite, as well
as for its orientation in space. Finally, there was the nuclear warhead
manufacturing and assembly facility at Advena, in Pretoria West.

Concurrently, Armscor set up a facility for the development and
manufacture of a launch vehicle system at one of its plants at
Centurion, also on the outskirts of Pretoria. The authors of *Armament
and Disarmament*, the excellent little South African publication previously mentioned, tell us that what made this product different, was
that the huge vehicles produced there had all-terrain capability to
ensure survivability from a possible pre-emptive strike.

At Eloptro, near Kempton Park on the outskirts of Johannesburg
Armscor created a sophisticated development and production facility
for optical and electro-optical systems (including ground control seg-
ment components) for reconnaissance satellites. Still producing quality systems for export today, Eloptro's role was to facilitate production
of an electro-optical system that achieved a resolving power of something more than three-feet at ground level, arguably the first Third
World nation to have done so.

A U.S. government functionary whose job it was to track missile
proliferation told *Risk Report* that South Africa's space launcher, the
RSA-3, was built around the same solid motors that powered Israel's
Jericho-II missile and its "Shavit" space launcher.

What gradually became clear once more details of the program emerged for public scrutiny, was that with time—together with a good infusion of Israeli know how—this tiny band of scientists and engineers would have been able to provide the South African military with a good deal more than a simple answer to many of the surface-to-surface variants that its ground forces then faced in Angola.

Thus, it was not long before the majority of those that had been involved started looking about for other opportunities. They simply had no option if they were to survive. By some accounts, things stayed that way until Iran's mullahs started arriving at what was then still called Jan Smuts Airport in Johannesburg.

While all this was going on, not everything was quite as clear-cut as indicated here. For some years, South Africa had paid a heavy price for its decision to smuggle in parts from abroad, and faced American wrath in particular for its ballistic missile program.

In September 1990, U.S. Customs agents shut down a company in Florida called York Ltd for illegally shipping computerized guidance equipment for large ballistic missiles to South Africa. According to a Customs spokesperson, the company was selling isolators and circulators built to military specifications to South Africa's Telecom Industries.

Previously, in 1988, there had been an incident when U.S. Customs seized five South Africa-bound gyroscopes. According to an affidavit by an undercover agent, Armscor wanted a total of thirty-eight gyroscopes for anti-tank missiles. The government indicted two Americans and three South Africans in what turned out to be an elaborate series of scams to hide the real end-user. The scheme included shipping equipment to a front company in Israel.

The most flagrant transgressions were committed by a Pennsylvania-based company called International Signal and Control (ISC). From 1984 to 1988, ISC sent South Africa more than $30 million in military-related equipment, including telemetry tracking antennae to collect data from missiles in flight and gyroscopes for guidance systems, as well as photo-imaging film readers, all of which would form the "backbone" of a medium-range missile system. Some of this technology was reportedly transferred to Iraq. Then Fuchs International, a South African firm, was indicted in 1991 by a federal grand jury for providing Iraq with parts for ammunition fuses, used in artillery shells fired against allied troops during the Gulf War.

Armscor and ISC Chairman James Guerin were next. Guerin pled guilty and served time in prison. U.S. prosecutors hoped Armscor would help them convict Guerin's partner, Robert Clyde Ivy, a former Armscor employee.

Very few details of South Africa's missile program ever appeared in the country's press. The little that did showed only that the guided missile program had reached a fairly advanced stage by the time that research was abandoned.

Once Washington's demands started to crunch, there was a strong reaction from an unexpected source: a headline in the Johannesburg *Sunday Times*[2] read, "Nuclear Scientists Threaten To Reveal Secret Arms Programs: 'Blackmail' Admitted."

The spokesman for the group claimed that Israel had supplied rocket technology to South Africa as well as details on how to convert a space launch vehicle into a nuclear ballistic missile. The South African space program, it disclosed, was originally intended to deliver nuclear weapons, using a "clone" of the Israeli two-stage solid-propellant Jericho-II missile.

The report went on: "In 1988 and 1989, two mobile launchers were built and tested at the Armscor proving group at Advena, but were never used. The missile, code-named RSA3, only underwent static testing."[3] According to a spokesman for the dissident group, from 1989 to 1992 more than two hundred South Africans secretly visited Israel and worked on missile programs. Israel sold technology to South Africa that would make its missiles accurate to within about half a mile by using a system of explosives used to blow open ports called thrusts, that could stop missile burns at a specific point in flight, thus allowing it to fall onto the target area. In October 1989, Israel and South Africa issued a formal statement denying that they were cooperating on a medium-range nuclear missile.

Less than five years later—following the threat of telling all—an order was issued by the Transvaal Supreme Court that prevented those scientists involved in research programs from taking further action.

Earlier, in an article dealing primarily with South Africa's admission to possessing enriched uranium, the weekly *Mail & Guardian* made reference to the rocket tests in Arniston. It suggested strong South Africa's interest in a nuclear missile delivery capability, but by then the South African Defence Force (SADF) had shelved the lot. The motivation to develop such a system was probably related more to issues of status than military need, somebody in Pretoria commented.

Obviously there were others who read these reports, and, as Hitler demonstrated more than half-a-century before, dissident scientists, given the opportunity, tend to vote with their feet. Consequently, with some assistance from elements within Mandela's own inner sanctum, it could not have been too difficult for any interested Iranian—or Cuban, Libyan or Syrian for that matter—to make contact with those cognoscenti who had been disaffected in order to make them a few offers of their own.

That this had happened came home rather forcibly during the couple of months that I spent at Denel Aviation in Johannesburg in 2000. Denel, at that stage, was involved with the production of a local helicopter hybrid, the AH-2A Rooivalk, an excellent machine with a combat range of almost five hundred miles. Armed with a 20mm dual-feed, gas-operated cannon in the nose and supplemented by locally produced ZT-6 long-range anti-armor missiles, these helicopters are a formidable adversary in the kind of bush wars that periodically plague Africa. In some respects the Rooivalk and the U.S. Apache are look-alikes. Performance-wise, they are not dissimilar.

The trouble at that point, though, was that Denel Aviation, the Rooivalk's manufacturer, was faced with a huge credibility problem. It had a product that—while ideal for the purpose for which it was built—had not found a single foreign buyer, and not for want of trying. Denel had spent millions on marketing and the Rooivalk had been displayed at numerous air shows around the globe. As a result, the company had serious financial problems, not least a threat from the government to abandoned the project altogether.

It had already cost Denel Aviation a mint in research and development. That included a concomitant engineering component that ran into tens of millions of dollars, together with all the staff, tooling and machinery needed for such a venture. In addition, there had been the expense of building a squadron of these choppers for the South African Air Force. SAAF's 16 Squadron started taking them onboard in July 1999. In effect, the Denel Aviation helicopter enterprise had swallowed a not immodest portion of the South African budget.

Try as it might, the company could find nobody willing to take it, which was surprising because this rotor craft is an outstanding weapons platform and Denel Aviation had been successful in a variety of other aviation projects launched in partnership with corporations such as Sweden's SAAB, Italy's Agusta as well as British Aerospace.[4]

At one stage it was thought that Malaysia might bite. That was followed by promising noises from the Middle East, but nothing consequential developed there either.

By now, even the company had to question why nothing had turned out the way it had hoped. To any outsider, the answer was obvious. Rooivalk's problem was not the helicopter, or even its combat specifications, which are excellent, but rather, South Africa itself.

The argument among any potential buyer abroad would probably go something like this: why spend $19 million for a South African-built machine when you can get a brand new Apache straight out of the Boeing factory—together with a vastly superior back-up infrastructure—for a fraction more? Or, for perhaps a quarter of that amount, a refurbished Russian Mi-24 gunship: the same helicopter, incidentally (the Hind in NATO jargon), that had already given a good account of itself in numerous Third World wars.

There were also some unsettling political questions. With the highest murder rate in the world, how secure was South Africa in the long term? Then there was the corruption issue, very prominently displayed in the South African media whenever a new scandal arose and which, even today, remains intrusive at all levels of state. That most appointments to top positions in a government-owned body like Denel were political was also problematic. In short, nobody was prepared to point to the obvious because that would have meant playing the race card.

It was with some surprise, therefore, that I took at call at my home in Chinook, Washington from Rob Jonker, production manager for the Rooivalk project at Denel Aviation in the Fall of 1999. Would I come to South Africa and help with marketing the Rooivalk? A month, possibly two, was all that was needed, he suggested. It was to be an all-expenses paid jaunt with a commensurate fee. And a car for the duration.

He had seen my book, *The Chopper Boys: Helicopter Warfare in Africa*, published in Britain and the U.S. a few years before[5] and he reckoned that some of the pictures in that publication might help. I should bring with me everything that I had on file, he suggested. It was a good offer and I was met by Rob at Johannesburg Airport in the first week of January 2000 and taken to my hotel in Sandton which was to be my home for the next two months.

Apart from photographs, the kind of effort required of me was pretty basic. Company marketing staff went through my photos to see what could be used in compiling the kind of brochure that management thought might help with sales. Meanwhile, with Howard Thacker—a spirited figure within Denel Aviation who tended to dominate PR activity at the plant—I would help with copy.

During the time that I was there, I could come and go as I pleased. Access to Denel Aviation's huge facility—during the Apartheid era it had been the Atlas Aircraft Corporation and lay on the opposite side of the runway to the main terminal at Johannesburg Airport—was stringently controlled by an army of security personnel, some of them armed.

First stop therefore, was clearance: to get into the aircraft manufacturing facility that I needed to document and photograph. That done, I was issued with an electronic card that allowed me day and night access through a complex and efficient control system at the main gate. (Though the system was not secure enough to prevent thieves from stealing dozens of the company's design computers in a well coordinated night raid not long afterward.)

It was clear from the start that the company had a problem in getting its message across to the world. Seeing a gap, I took things a step further and suggested to a member of the board that a stronger approach might be for me to do a sequel to *The Chopper Boys*. I would include a chapter on the company's helicopter, singling out South Africa as the first-ever Third World country that had succeeded in building a sophisticated combat rotor craft.

I explained that with the Border War having forced the pace, South Africa had developed a considerable industry of servicing, upgrading, maintaining, revamping and now, building, helicopters. That argument was shot down by one of Denel's African directors. It was rubbish, he said. South Africa's twenty-year war in Angola and former South West Africa had nothing to do with it. The whites had been thoroughly thrashed by the Cubans, he declared, reflecting the official line in the cabinet. Of course, it was all nonsense: Black Apartheid in reverse, said one of the managers.

Undeterred, I went ahead anyway. With Thacker's help, I even produced a twenty-four page, color dummy. This, I suggested, would help those involved to see what I had in mind. Obviously South Africa's two-decade Border War came into it. How else, since helicopters were the rationale of Denel Aviation's existence?

While this was going on, there were some curious developments at the factory. It started with a heavy security curtain being drawn over the arrival, at an adjacent site, of several Algerian Mi-24 helicopter gunships. These were to be revamped by an associate company, but, Thacker told me, pictures were verboten. I was warned off even "thinking about doing something for Jane's," though in the end, I did.

There were also peculiar comings and goings at Denel Aviation, which was probably to be expected with a company eager to sell its wares to the devil if it had to, because its first commercial sale still had yet to happen.

Then, by chance—while waiting at the local travel company (where Sizwe Car Hire had offices) for something to replace my first car which ended up with mechanical problems—I discovered several people who were on their way to Tehran. What was interesting was that an affiliate travel company on the premises of Denel Aviation appeared to be responsible for the issuing of tickets. Some of those heading for Iran, I discovered, had formerly worked on South Africa's guided missile projects.

This movement of personnel between Johannesburg and Tehran had apparently been going on for some years, a member of the staff confided later. Much of it was coordinated in the main block known as A6, where Rob Jonker had his offices.

What were South Africans doing in Iran? Nobody with whom I came into contact knew, or perhaps they weren't prepared to say, except that some of these people were away for long periods. Similarly, no-one would say exactly where they were based, whether they lived in isolation in guarded security compounds in or around Tehran or elsewhere, or, for that matter, even whether their families accompanied them. It was intimated early on that I should not ask too many questions.

As with its nuclear program, prior to Tehran having to disclose to Vienna's International Atomic Energy Agency in 2003 that it had, indeed, launched programs to produce plutonium and enriched uranium, much of what has appeared in print about Iran's missile program has been based on conjecture. The fact that the country was able to successfully fire the occasional test missile over ever-longer distances helped fuel this debate.

A report by the Central Intelligence Agency on November 12, 2003 brought this issue into perspective:

> Ballistic missile-related cooperation from entities in the former Soviet Union, North Korea, and China over the years has

helped Iran move toward its goal of becoming self-sufficient in the production of ballistic missiles. Such assistance during the first half of 2003 continued to include equipment, technology, and expertise. Iran's ballistic missile inventory is among the largest in the Middle East and includes some eight-hundred-mile range Shahab-3 medium-range ballistic missiles (MRBMs) and a few hundred short-range ballistic missiles (SRBMs) - including the Shahab-1 (Scud-B), Shahab-2 (Scud C), and Tondar-69 (CSS-8) - as well as a variety of large un-guided rockets.

Already producing Scud SRBMs, Iran announced that it had begun production of the Shahab-3 MRBM and a new solid-propellant SRBM, the Fateh-110. [Iranian press report-ing, Tehran IRNA, 11 Sep 2002] In addition, Iran publicly acknowledged the development of follow-on versions of the Shahab-3. It originally said that another version, the Shahab-4, was a more capable ballistic missile than its predecessor, but later characterized it as solely a space launch vehicle with no military application. Iran is also pursuing longer-range ballis-tic missiles.

That situation has since been updated by another successful test-firing of a Shahab-related missile over a distance of thirteen hundred miles.

Coming closest to the nub of missile developments in Iran in recent years has possibly been Kenneth Katzman's instructive *Report for Congress: Iran—Arms and Weapons of Mass Destruction*, written for the Congressional Research Service, Library of Congress.[6] Up-dated in January 2003, Katzman—a specialist in Middle Eastern affairs—made the point that Iran's experiences in its war with Iraq "convinced the Iranian leadership to enhance (its) ability to develop and deliver weapons of mass destruction." While Iran did fire North Korean-supplied Scud missiles at Baghdad during the war, "Iraqi retal-iation demonstrated that Baghdad's missile technology capabilities far exceeded those of Iran during that conflict." Katzman observed that, since 1996, published reports and U.S. officials had been citing Russia as a primary source of Iran's ballistic missile programs.

"Press reports and U.S. official statements and reports since 1997 have indicated that Russian entities have provided Iran's missile pro-grams with training, testing equipment and components, including specialty steels and alloys, tungsten-coated graphite, gyroscopes and other guidance technology, rocket engine and fuel technology, laser equipment, machine tools and maintenance manuals.

"The Russian technology assistance to Iran frustrated the Clinton Administration and Congress. Through a combination of engagement and selected imposition of sanctions, [Washington] sought to enlist greater Russian cooperation in halting the technology flow, with mixed success," Katzman tells us.

Of note is his observation that critics in Congress took a different view, "arguing for broad and sustained application of sanctions on Russia and its entities on the grounds that the Russian government had been insincere in its pledges to crack down on technology exports to Iran."

That Iran has established a sophisticated guided missile program is no longer in any doubt. What the West does not know—because Iran offers the international community no information about its WMD programs (and neither the Americans nor the Israel are effusive about their own intelligence gathering activities)—is how many missiles Tehran intends to build. What the West is aware of is that there are five Shahab missile prototypes, with some of the more recent versions incorporating extensive Russian power sources as well as guidance/gyroscopic technology.

MISSILE DESIGNATION
Cross Country Comparison

USSR (heritage)	DPRK	Iran	Pakistan
SS-N-4/Scud-B	No-Dong-1	Shahab-3	Ghauri II
SS-N-4/Scud-B	Taep'o-dong-1/Paeutudan-1		Shahab-4 (Pending?)
SS-N-4/Scud-B	NKSL-1*	Shahab-4/Kosar?	
	Taep'o-dong-2	Shahab-5?	
NKSL-X-2**		Shahab-6/IRSL-X-4	

* IranSL-X-1, NKSL-1 is an unofficial designation created by Charles P. Vick. The NKSL-1 is a Taep'o-dong-1 missile with a third stage and satellite added.
** IranSL-X-2, NKSL-X-2 is an unofficial designation created by Charles P. Vick. The NKSL-X-2 is a Taep'o-dong-2 or 2a or 2b or 3 missile with a third stage and satellite added.
(Source: GlobalSecurity.org)

These illustrations detail what is believed to be the trend driven design heritage path taken by the Iranian ballistic missile program based on the Scud-B/Shahab-1, Scud-C/Shahab-2, and No-dong-A/Shahab-3, designs.

This provided the basis for the Taep'o-dong-1/Shabab-4 concept along with the Taep'o-dong-2/Shahab-5 and its Shahab-5/Taep'o-dong-2A or 2B satellite launch vehicle design concepts.

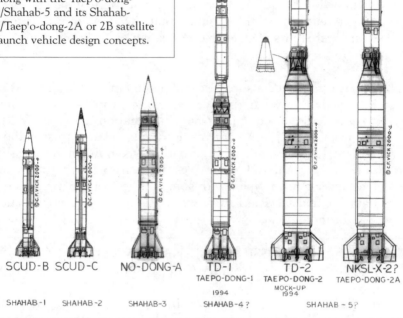

SCUD-B   SCUD-C   NO-DONG-A   TD-1   TD-2   NKSL-X-2?
                                        TAEPO-DONG-1   TAEPO-DONG-2   TAEPO-DONG-2A
                                            1994   MOCK-UP
                                                          1994
SHAHAB-1   SHAHAB-2   SHAHAB-3   SHAHAB-4?   SHAHAB-5?

The Iris sounding rocket design displayed by Iran some years ago is believed to constitute its contribution to the Shahab-5/Taep'o-dong-2a, or 2b upper stage design. There are indications that the Shahab-6/Taep'o-dong-3 of North Korea (not shown) is very advanced in development but whether Iran has benefited from North Korea's revised design approach and thus would drop the Shahab-4 and Shahab-5 in favor of the Shahab-6 is uncertain.

However, there are alternative approaches that Iran may have at some point considered, such as the Iraqi missile design method of clustering several Shahab-3's for a first stage and several Scud-C/D's as the second stage with a solid motor bus third stage to create a satellite launch vehicle. Possibly some combination of these may have utilized solid motor designs for the upper two stages, although this approach seems to have been abandoned in favor of the North Korean design approach illustrated.

There are those who believe that the Shahab-3—the same missile that was fired more than a thousand miles in early 2004—to be no more than an interim measure and that Tehran's focus will now be concentrated on the Shahab-4 with its longer range and larger payload capacity. Unlike its predecessor, the Shahab-4 is a product of exclusively Russian ballistic technology and, by all accounts, its development is expected to be completed within two or three years. It appears that Iran has shifted back from its original design for the Shahab-4 to a more North Korean-based design if they are developing it at all.

Western experts reckon that at this pace, Tehran will have developed the long-range Shahab-5 or Shahab-6 intercontinental ballistic missile (ICMB) capable of reaching the U.S. within five or six years, though some authorities doubt this level of competence without serious foreign technological input. Right now, the core of Iran's current missile force consists of between two to three hundred North Korean-supplied Scud-B and Scud-C missiles, with ranges of two and three hundred miles respectively. Katzman disclosed that Pyongyang also supplied ten to fifteen mobile launchers.

According to the *Middle East Intelligence Bulletin*, Iran's latest tests of its intermediate-range ballistic missile had brought the country a step closer to developing a viable strategic threat, not only to Israel but to several nations in the Middle East that lean toward Western interests. Turkey, a NATO member, would be bracketed among these.

A subsequent CIA report suggests that during the next five years Iran is more likely to develop intermediate-range ballistic missiles based on Russian technology before developing an ICBM, but that the same technology would be used. "Iran could test such an IRBM before the end of that period," it read. In the period 2006–2010, says the document, Western strategists believe that Iran will in all likelihood test an IRBM. "All assess that Iran could flight-test an ICBM that could deliver nuclear weapon-sized payloads to many parts of the United States in the latter half of the next decade, again, using Russian technology acquired over the years," says Langley. Some also think that Iran is likely to test an ICBM—possibly as an SLV without an RV impact downrange—before 2010.

At present, it is Iran's Shahab-3 that remains the focus of attention, largely because Tehran has acquired quite a few over the years.

Derived from North Korea's No Dong surface-to-surface missile, the Shahab-3 is a single-stage intermediate-range ballistic missile powered by liquid fuel. Measuring fifty-four feet, it can carry a warhead of almost a ton more than four thousand miles an hour.

Katzman's report states that China provided Tehran with its version of the Russian SA-2, but it was "past sales to Iran of anti-ship cruise missiles that caused the most significant concern." He makes issue of the fact that anti-ship missiles improve Iran's ability to strike at U.S. forces and installations or commercial shipping in the Gulf.

Also of interest is his report that China delivered to Iran fifteen Hudong fast attack craft, five of which went to the Pasdaran (IRGC).

Since most of the work handled by this organization is clandestine, and the corps is responsible solely to Iran's Supreme Spiritual Guide, Sayyid Ali Khamene'i, there has been speculation in intelligence circles as to what role these boats will play. Or even whether they might be intended for some other theater of insurgency, possibly abroad.

For years, declared Charles P. Vick, formerly of the Federation of American Scientists and now GlobalSecurity.org, there has been absent from public discussion about the Missile Technology Control Regime any kind of exchange of information between North Korean and Iranian launch vehicle strategic ballistic missile programs and the Chinese support of both. At the same time, the Federation stated on its website, there are several motivations for Iran's pursuit and officially acknowledged progress in developing an indigenous missile production industry.

First, says the FAS, it is possible that such disclosures might demonstrate that Iran is developing into something of a growing power, against Israel especially. Second, Iran may wish to intimidate other countries in the region from pursuing aggression as a strategy, and in so doing, draw on its experience of war with Iraq. Another possibility is to eliminate Tehran's reliance for its ballistic missiles and related technology on foreign entities. Here, the focus has been on the Russian Federation and, more recently, on the People's Republic of China. The Democratic People's Republic of Korea also comes to mind since ties between the two states has been cemented by close technological cooperation over several years.

But Tehran is also cautious of its ties with Pyongyang. One idea that has some currency is that "the unreliable economy of North Korea may necessitate it to cease its 'rogue state' behavior, which, in search of economic aid from Western countries, would include halting the support given to Iran."

MISSILE PROGRAMS DEVELOPMENT
By Charles P. Vick[7]

Iranian interest in ballistic missile acquisition is directly traceable to its war with Iraq in the mid-1980s.

During this conflict, Iraq's modified Scud missiles out-numbered and out-ranged those of Iran. Iran turned to North Korea to supply it with ballistic missiles. North Korea obliged, sending Iran Scud-Bs, seventy-seven of which were fired against targets in Iraq during the second "War of the Cities" in 1988. There was a certain irony in this transaction: the missiles provided by North Korea had been reverse-engineered from Scuds it had obtained from Egypt in the early Eighties. During that war, Egypt was a staunch supporter of Iraq and clearly shows that proliferation activity knows no loyalties.

By the early 1990s Iran had turned again to North Korea to acquire ballistic missiles. (Some analysts believe that Iran was involved in North Korea's No Dong program from its outset in the late 1980s and that it provided substantial funding.) By the mid-1990s Iran had as many as ten No Dongs—either in component form or as completed missiles—all of which evolved from Scud-based technology and are thought to provide the building blocks for North Korea's Taepo-dong missiles.

Over the same period Iran had begun to establish the infrastructure that would permit it to produce ballistic missiles within the country, ending its dependence on outside suppliers. By the early to mid-1990s, Iran had also secured considerable technical support from Russia and China for its Scud-based program, support that continues to this day.

The result of proliferation activity involving Iran is worth underscoring. In the comparatively short period of a decade—from the time it became involved in North Korea's No Dong program—Iran has arrived at the threshold of ICBM capability. Recall the judgment of the Rumsfeld Commission in 1998: "Iran now has the technical capability and resources to demonstrate an ICBM-range ballistic missile, similar to the [North Korean] TD-2 [itself based on scaled-up Scud technology], within five years of a decision to proceed—whether that decision has already been made or is yet to be made."

Press reports suggest that in November 1999 North Korea transferred a dozen No Dong engines to Iran. It is reported that those engines were tested in February 2000. Iran successfully flight-tested the Shahab-3, which is its version of the No Dong on July 15, 2000. In fact, in March 2000 the Iranian defense minister suggested the Shahab-3 was fully operational as of that February.

The Iranians have released some details—sparse, but interesting—concerning two programs beyond the Shahab-3 and these are also covered by the GlobalSecurity.org web sites.

Referred to as the Shahab-4 and Shahab-5, the characteristics of both programs—that is, whether they are Iranian versions of the Taepo-dong or single or multiple stage variants on the Soviet-era SS-4 and SS-5 or something else—are unknown. Those references to the SS-4 and SS-5 are, in fact, incorrect interpretations of what was merely referring to similar missile technologies in the actual Iranian missiles and not copies of Russian hardware. It is not impossible that their appellations cover a number of Iranian programs. Whatever names they carry, all evidence suggests that Iran, like every other ballistic missile power, is aiming at missiles that are bigger and of longer range.

The FAS also discloses that most of Iran's missile development industry is located in Karaj, outside Tehran. The country's missile infrastructure also includes a Chinese-built missile plant near Semnan, larger North Korean-built facilities at Isfahan and Sirjan which can produce liquid fuels and some structural components as well as missile test facilities at Shahroud and the Shahid Hemat Industrial Group research facility south of Tehran.

Historically, Iranian missile "production" consists primarily of assembling imported ballistic missile kits. In an effort to decrease this dependence on the overseas market, Iran is seeking to develop an indigenous missile and weapons production capability infrastructure and this is possibly where the South African connection comes in.

Iran's ballistic missile production facilities program is located in two underground tunnels between (Kuh-e-parbl) Bandar Abbas and Bushehr, which become a reality as early as 1996. However, the Scud-B/Shahab-1 system is now said to be in production using a significant portion of locally manufactured components.

Current Iranian missile inventories tend to be speculative, with lower stockpile estimates likely to be more credible than anything higher. Estimates of Iran's inventory of Scud-B/Shahab-1 ballistic missiles ranges from fifty to as many as three hundred, with a "guaranteed range" of about two hundred miles. The stockpile of Iranian Scud-Cs capable of hitting targets between three and four hundred miles away has been estimated at between fifty and as many as four hundred and fifty.

In addition to pursuing a domestic ballistic missile production program, Iran has been eager to acquire foreign missiles and technology.

For example, Iran targeted China's M-9 (three-hundred-and-fifty miles/half-ton and the M-11 (two-hundred miles/half-ton) single-stage, solid-propellant, road-mobile missiles, but American pressure on China so far, has prevented transfers from taking place.

Furthermore, the People's Republic of China may also be assisting Iran in extending the range of the operational HY-1 and the HY-2 Silkworm cruise missiles. Added range to these missiles could present a serious security threat to Persian Gulf shipping activities.[8]

In addition, according to Jane's, deployment of the Tondar-68, Iran-700 and the Fatch-110 (Victorious-110) NP-110 original designator tactical missile are largely dependent on continuing Chinese assistance. The company also disclosed that China supplied Iran with the CSS-8 missile system.

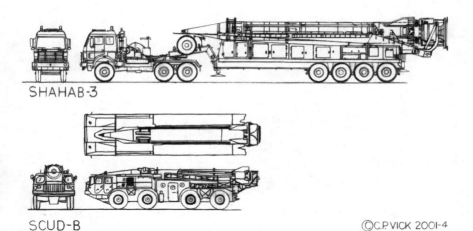

SHAHAB-3

SCUD-B   ©C.P.VICK 2001-4

These two illustrations show the Iranian Shahab-3 MRBM on its Transport Erector Launcher (TEL) along with the Soviet Scud-B/Shahab-1 on its TEL.

The Iranian TEL appears to be a home design. Shahab-3 in its deployed configuration requires a fleet of support vehicles including several propellant tanker trucks as well as several support personnel and command/control vehicles in addition to the officer's vehicle and troop carriers.

ASSESSMENT OF WHAT REALLY COUNTS

Both North Korea and Iran seem to be using the "building block approach" to develop what they describe as space boosters. However, says the Federation, these missiles, if the appropriate decision were made, could be revised and deployed as a "Limited Range ICBM" capable of carrying a weapon. Time estimates of this possibility are vague and range from five to ten years. In addition, further research and development utilizing the existing missile technology could eventually yield a Full Range ICBM in approximately ten to fifteen years.

10
IRAN'S HISTORY
OF TERROR

"Those who believe that they can moderate these people
with either technology or dialogue are fooling themselves.
They are risking this nation's security."
Mehdi Haeri Khorshidi, a leader of the opposition group,
Iranian National Conference, in a document published
in Washington, DC

The above comment is harsh. It came from someone who once thought that the Ayatollah Khomeini was Allah's gift to mankind. There was a time when Mehdi Haeri Khorshidi believed that the Iranian revolution would ultimately save the world. As a student and disciple of the sainted one, Khorshidi, a dissident politico who was once described by Tehran's media as "the rebel," thought that his mentor would one day become the new Mahatma. "Instead," he declared, "he turned out to be a Nero."

It may be significant that Khorshidi was a classmate of Mohammed Khatami, the Iranian president and, politically, a lightweight compared to some of the more committed mullahs. The two have known each other for more than a quarter century. First they studied, and afterward they worked together.

"I have heard so much in the United States about the great hope for him, largely because he was initially hailed in the West as a moderate, which was fair enough to begin with because he was elected largely on a protest vote." However, as Khorshidi points out, the Iranian presidency at this point is unalterably symbolic: the man is little more than an administrative figurehead. Any real clout in Iran is lodged firmly in the hands of the country's Supreme Spiritual Guide, Sayyid Ali Hoseini Khamene'i.

"Just don't wait for any Ayatollah Gorbachev to come riding in on a white stallion of reform. These are not the people with whom it is possible to conduct a rational dialogue," he concludes.

While there have been some positive gestures from the government of Prime Minister Khatami, a recent U.S. State Department report on Iran indicated that, since 1979, Tehran has been behind at least a thousand deaths of what are colloquially termed "Enemies of the State."

"Those are the ones that we know about," said a spokesman for the opposition. He suggested that there could be more.

Countries where Iranian secret agents have been active include almost all of Europe and much of North Africa, as well as several Asian states.[1] The number of Iranian dissidents liquidated in Europe is reckoned to be well into three figures. Some of those responsible for such killings were eventually brought to trial in Germany.

The newsletter *Iran Brief* reported that Iranian activity of a more nefarious nature had recently been expanded. It stated, "Senior Iranian intelligence operatives have been entering the U.S. clandestinely." One of its agents, the *Brief* disclosed, had conducted an assassination on American soil. The victim was Mr. Ali Tabatabai, a former diplomat at the Iranian Embassy in Washington DC and, for a while before he was murdered, an outspoken critic of the revolutionary regime. The killer was an American Black Muslim recruit, David Belfield, who subsequently fled to Iran.

Though Osama bin Laden's al-Qaeda movement has now superseded Iranian subversives as the main source of terror in the West, there has been a considerable level of Iranian input in attacks against American and Saudi interests in the Arabian Peninsula, including bomb attacks. But Iranian terror acts differ from those that take place in Turkey, or the kind formerly implemented by the IRA. In keeping with stringent Iranian security mandates, which go to extraordinary lengths to avoid implicating the country in any kind of clandestine activity, very few of the operators are known to have been local.

Basically, Tehran gets other nationals to do its dirty work, which is a trait sometimes shared by bin Laden's mob. Some have been of Palestinian or Saudi origin. Still more were Lebanese, Egyptian, Algerian, Sudanese or other nationalities. For this, and a raft of other reasons (including the security mantle that pervades all goings on inside Iran), it has always been difficult to pinpoint the extent of actual Iranian participation.

Tehran long ago became adroit in covering its tracks. The idea for doing so, according to one defector, was that it would make retaliation that much more difficult in the event of a major international terrorist strike—especially if some kind of low-key capability involving pathogens or chemical agents was involved.

A case in point during the Lebanese civil war was Beirut's Islamic Jihad, then (and still) controlled directly from Tehran through a multiplicity of intricate connections. For a long time Islamic Jihad had no visible leader. There was nobody physically "contactable" by the media or for that matter even by the diplomatic community. If the movement's leaders made any kind of approach at all, it was usually by way of a runner: a kid would be pulled off the street, handed a document together with some cash, and pointed in the right direction.

What frustrated everyone—the Americans, the British, the Israelis and even the Falanghist Lebanese Forces and others—was that the organization that was responsible for many violent acts had no address. Also, it had no office. Consequently, any kind of retribution was impossible. While some observers regarded Islamic Jihad as more of a "phantom" organization than a full-fledged insurgent movement, it left a chain of assassinations and bombs in its wake. There was certainly nothing phantom about its actions.

Eventually, through the kind of duplicitous grapevine that exists in just about every Arab society, it was finally established that the man responsible for much of the carnage was Imad Mugniyah, a notorious killer who, Arab author Hala Jaber tells us, had been a member of the PLO's so-called "elite" Force 17 run by a trusted Al Fatah lieutenant, Ali Hassan Salameh (also known as Abu Hassan). Essentially, he was Arafat's man.

Remember the name Mugniyah, if only because he has not yet finished his business. Early on, he and his cronies were referred to as "Khomeini's Fatah Islamites." All these people, we now know—and the CIA has confirmed—had Pasdaran, and, in turn, Hizbollah connections.

Read what Isabel Kershner had to say about the man in her report "The Changing Colors of Imad Mugniyah" in *Jerusalem Report*:[2]

Since the early 1980s Mugniyah, a Lebanese Shi'ite, has served as Hizbollah's "special operations" chief, in charge of the organization's bombing, hijacking, kidnapping and overseas terrorism campaigns. He is credited with responsibility for a long string of terrorist outrages costing hundreds of lives, including the U.S. Marines base and U.S. Embassy bombings in Beirut in 1983 as well as the destruction by explosives of the Israeli Embassy in Argentina in 1992.

Now there are indications that after years of hiding in Iran, Mugniyah is back in Lebanon, coordinating links between Hizbollah and Osama bin Laden's al-Qaeda network. He is also believed to be helping al-Qaeda rebuild its terrorist infrastructure in the Middle East and Africa, following the destruction of its base in Afghanistan.

A combination of the two international Islamic terror networks of Hizbollah and al-Qaeda would represent a nightmare for the counter-terrorist community.

Having dropped off the radar screen of foreign intelligence agencies for some time, Mugniyah reappeared on the FBI's list of twenty-two most wanted terrorists published in the aftermath of the World Trade Center and Pentagon attacks of September 11. A reward of $25 million was offered for information leading to his apprehension.

In January 2002 he was named by Israeli security officials as a key operator in the *Karine A* weapons ship affair, in which he served as liaison between the Palestinians and Iran. This was the ship with a load of weapons captured in the Red Sea by Israeli navy commandos in January 2002.

Officials in Jerusalem agree that Mugniyah is back in Lebanon. They suggest that he might be operating under different identities including that of Jawwad Nur al-Din, a previously unknown figure who was elected to Hizbollah's top decision-making Shura Council last summer.

A report in *Jane's Foreign Report* published on September 19, 2001 first raised the possibility that Mugniyah co-directed the Twin Towers attack together with Ayman al-Zawahiri, bin Laden's No. 2 in al-Qaeda, but neither the Israelis nor the Americans are so sure. And though Israeli security officials won't talk about Mugniyah or Hizbollah-al-Qaeda links, Israel's defense minister, Benjamin Ben-Eliezer, told journalists in February, 2002 in New York that "more and more information is coming that members of al-Qaeda are entering Lebanon and joining Hizbollah." He reportedly called Imad Mugniyah "worse than bin Laden."

Meanwhile, a report by German terrorism expert Rolf Tophoven gained the attention of officials in Jerusalem.

Writing in the daily *Die Welt* in February, Tophoven stated that one of bin Laden's top lieutenants, the Palestinian Abu Zubaydeh, was in the Ein El-Hilweh Palestinian refugee camp near the southern port of Sidon in Lebanon, working on establishing a new infrastructure for al-Qaeda with the assistance of Hizbollah.

Basing his information on CIA and Israeli military intelligence sources, Tophoven said that an important partner in this enterprise was the Islamic Revolutionary Guards Corps based in Lebanon's Syrian-controlled Be'qa Valley. This group of subversives are said to have helped hundreds of al-Qaeda operatives cross the border from Afghanistan to Iran and on to the Iranian island of Kish. The *Karine A*, with a cargo of weapons headed for Suez, also came from Kish. According to Tophoven, Abu Zubaydeh reached Lebanon on a similar kind of boat.

In a telephone interview with *The Jerusalem Report* from Germany, Tophoven went further, suggesting that Mugniyah might even be a possible heir to Osama bin Laden, along with Abu Zubaydeh and an al-Qaeda fugitive known as Adil, a former officer in the Egyptian army's counter-terror unit.

While Tophoven perceives only a loose connection between Mugniyah and the September 11 attacks, he did say that even before September 11, bin Laden started to reorganize his terrorist network to establish a "second front" that could continue regardless of his own fate. In that context, he suggested, Ayman Zawahiri was installed as commander of the Balkans area, where he says, thousands of al-Qaeda supporters operated under the guise of non-governmental organizations. Mugniyah, meanwhile, was appointed commander of the Middle East and Africa.

Imad Mugniyah seems to have had links with al-Qaeda for years. Ali Muhammad, an al-Qaeda operative tried in America for his part in the U.S. Embassy bombings in Tanzania and Kenya, revealed in testimony that he had helped arrange a meeting between Mugniyah and bin Laden in Sudan as early as 1993.

Magnus Ranstorp, an expert on Hizbollah and deputy director of the Centre for the Study of Terrorism and Political Violence at the University of St Andrews in Scotland, added that the suspects in the East Africa embassy bombings also mentioned individuals who had gone to Lebanon for explosives training with Hizbollah. "The military manuals of al-Qaeda showed innovation in the making of explosives including RDX and C4," he explained, "but there was an admission that some of its members had gone to Lebanon to get that expertise."

If the relationship between Hizbollah and al-Qaeda was previously confined to training and know-how, Tophoven suggested that it was now turning into one of much closer coordination. For his part, Ranstorp stressed that the relationship between Hizbollah and Iran was not "unidimensional, but was based on multiple linkages and points of contact between different power centers, clerics and foundations."

Hizbollah's secretary general Hassan Nasrallah, for example, is thought to be the personal representative in Lebanon of Iranian supreme leader Ayatollah Khamene'i. Other Hizbollah clerics have their own links within Iran's theocracy.

"The best description for Imad Mugniyah is that he stands with one foot in Iran and one in Hizbollah," said Ranstorp. "The weight he puts on each foot depends on the security and operational needs at any given time." According to well-placed sources, Mugniyah was asked to leave Iran and returned to Lebanon in the wake of the September 11 attacks.

Interestingly, one of the only two photos known to exist of Mugniyah is now on the FBI website, along with a notice of the $25 million reward. But with rumors rife that the terror mastermind has undergone several rounds of plastic surgery, it is assumed that he may by now be totally unrecognizable.

That terror is being used to coerce and intimidate the Iranian population is indisputable. This issue is underscored by a recent Amnesty International report headlined: "Iran Has Executed Tens of Thousands." According to Associated Press, Iran has also kept large numbers of political prisoners languishing in jail. Moreover, opposition activists have been targeted for attack and even Iranian dissidents who fled abroad are not safe, the London-based rights group said in a hefty multi-page report. Indicative of this is Tehran's steadfast refusal to allow human rights investigators into the country.

Dissidents living abroad have been increasingly targeted. The report said that over the past two decades, numerous opponents of religious rule in Iran who had been living outside the country were "assassinated in circumstances suggesting they may have been extra-judicially executed by government agents." It outlined several examples of this state-sponsored murder. It also cited cases of long-term political prisoners held without trial.

For example, four leaders of religious minority groups—three Christians and a Sunni Muslim—were found dead recently in suspicious circumstances, believed killed by Iranian government agents, the report said.

Not long before that, a Western judicial system held Iran's leaders directly responsible for international terrorism in April 1997 when a German court ruled that they had ordered the murders of three Iranian Kurdish opposition activists in Berlin. The court said that a Committee for Special Operations in Tehran had approved the September 1992 killings at a Greek restaurant in Berlin, and declared that the committee's members included both Iran's president as well as the country's paramount spiritual leader.

The man directly responsible for the killings was Kazem Darabi, an Iranian expatriate living in Germany. Further, the German prosecutor took the unusual step of accusing the Iranian head of state Ayatollah Khamene'i and then President Rafsanjani as being responsible for the murders. Iran immediately responded by threatening German diplomats in Tehran and the German judiciary, as well as Iran's political and economic ties with Germany (ergo: oil supplies). That was followed by German and Iranian ambassadors being abruptly recalled. The EU subsequently issued a statement inviting all its members to withdraw their ambassadors from the recalcitrant state.

In France, meanwhile, a Parisian prosecutor accused the Iranian chief of intelligence, Ali Fallahian, of ordering a killing, and in Germany a warrant was issued for Fallahian's arrest.

In addition, Tehran has never taken any action to repudiate the religious ruling (*fatwa*), or its related $2 million bounty, that called for the death of Salman Rushdie and anyone associated with publishing his book, *The Satanic Verses*.

Obviously, any kind of state controlled terror has its consequences, especially once mass media gets involved. This was graphically illustrated with the callous murder of American journalist Daniel Pearl by al-Qaeda activists in Karachi, Pakistan. In turn, public opinion is powerfully and negatively influenced. These days, even governments must accept the consequences of "shooting the messenger."

The events above plunged German and EU relations with Iran into a state of crisis and one needs to look back a little to understand the extent of human rights excesses perpetrated by the Iranians in recent times. For its part, the U.S. State Department issued what it termed the "Iran Report on Human Rights Practices for 1996," released by the Bureau of Democracy, Human Rights, and Labor, January 30, 1997.

The document recorded that "The Iranian government's human rights record remains poor and that there was no evidence of significant human rights improvement during the year. Systematic abuses include extrajudicial killings and summary executions; disappearances; widespread use of torture and other degrading treatment; harsh prison conditions; arbitrary arrest and detention; lack of fair trials; infringement on citizens' privacy rights and restriction of the freedoms of speech, press, assembly, association, religion, and movement.

"The Government represses political dissidents while the ruling clerics effectively control the electoral process, thereby denying citizens the right to change their government. Women face legal and social discrimination and the Government weighs heavily against minorities. It also restricts important worker rights. Freedom of expression remained firmly under government control and became more severely restricted in the wake of the parliamentary elections. The Government closed several newspapers, disqualified candidates, barred speakers, and intimidated opposition gatherings by encouraging Hizbollah attacks."

In a critical note, it stated that most executions in political trials "amounted to summary executions because basic procedural safeguards were lacking." The UN Special Rapporteur on Extrajudicial, Summary, or Arbitrary Executions noted "the persistent allegations of violations of the right to life in the Islamic Republic of Iran."

Although the Iranian domestic press long ago stopped reporting most executions as of 1992, these killings continue in substantial numbers. Amnesty International (AI) reported that more than a hundred people were executed in 1996, a substantial increase over the previous year's total of fifty executions. Because of draconian state control of media outlets, later statistics are muddied, except that reports of these excesses continue to reach the West, often through those permanently having escaped or possibly clandestine contact with outside sources.

▲

otestors in present day Iraq - Photograph: Mark Corcoran, Australian Broadcasting Corporation (ABC-TV), 2004

Parade involving a Shahab missile on its carrier. September 22, 1999 - Photograph: Mohsen Shandiz/CORBIS

▼

Satellite image of The Iranian Gas Centrifuge Uranium Enrichment Plant at Natanz, September 2002. Here one can see evidence of considerable construction activity - some of which (see center buildings) appears to be below ground level.

Image courtesy of ISIS/DigitalGlobe

The same facility photographed in February 2003. The site comprises three large underground structures, which will be the main uranium enrichment buildings and an above-ground area enclosed by a security fence that contains six large buildings. This area contains operating centrifuge assembly facilities and a centrifuge pilot plant. There is also a large building that is the main administrative building.

Another Satellite image, this time of a facility located near the town of Arak. This appears to be a heavy water plant under construction. Heavy water, which is ordinary water enriched in the hydrogen isotope deuterium, is used as a moderator in one type of nuclear reactor.

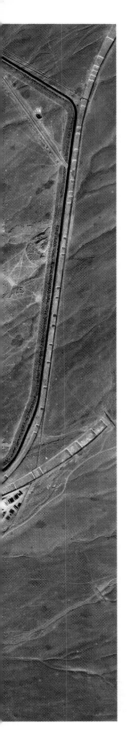

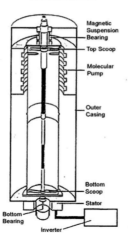

Magnetic
Suspension
Bearing

Top Scoop

Molecular
Pump

Outer
Casing

Bottom
Scoop

Stator

Bottom
Bearing

Inverter

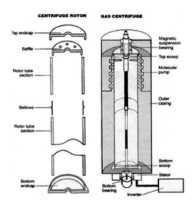

CENTRIFUGE ROTOR   GAS CENTRIFUGE

Top endcap

Baffle

Rotor tube
section

Bellows

Rotor tube
section

Bottom
endcap

Bottom
bearing

Magnetic
suspension
bearing

Top scoop

Molecular
pump

Outer
casing

Bottom
scoop

Stator

Inverter

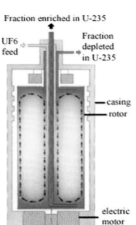

Fraction enriched in U-235

UF6
feed

Fraction
depleted
in U-235

casing
rotor

electric
motor

Three schematic diagrams showing the principal behind the gas centrifuge.

Top left, source: David Albright, drawing Janos Rothstein. Above, source: Albright, D. and Hibbs, M. 'Iraq's shop-till-you-drop nuclear program' *Bulletin of the Atomic Scientist* , vol 48, no. 3 (April 1992). Left:: courtesy of ISIS.

A 'cutaway' Iraqi SCUD missile (captured during Gulf War 1) after US scientists had finished exmaining it at Pacific Northwest National Labs, Hanford, Washington

Author photo

Significant former nuclear weapons related facilities at the Pelindaba / Valindaba complex near Pretoria, South Africa. December 1991

Advena central laboratories on the outskirts of Pretoria where South Africa's atom bombs were assembled and stored: (The building complex in the right half of the photograph)

Y-Plant for Uranium Enrichment

Building 5100

Building 5200

Building 5000

Denel Aviation in South Africa one part of South Africa's military industrial complex - the largest on the African continent (see Chapter 8).

The 'Rooivalk' combat helicopter was being built at the Denel factory on the outskirts of Johannesburg when the author recently worked at the complex for two months. As a technologically advanced country, South Africa is clearly a valuable asset to those countries who seek its expertise, especially with regard to advanced weapons systems, both legal and illegal.

t: Hizbollah flags are commonplace in Lebanon and parts of Iran; Centre: ten-foot high Hizbollah posters of the e Ayatollah Khomeini decorate the landscape in South Lebanon and right: UN soldier shows a plaster cast of a dside bomb (into which explosives are packed) alongside a similar-shaped rock.   Author photos

Israeli Navy unit on patrol against Hizbollah ltrators in the Eastern Mediterranean.   Author photo

▲   *Israeli Defense Force anti-mine patrol along the Lebanese frontier.*   Author photo

▶

nited Nations strong- oint in South Lebanon, region commonly ferred to those who now the region as Hizbollahland' because is Islamic guerrilla my has unrestricted ccess adjacent to the raeli frontier.

uthor photo

▲ Hizbollah's forward operational base for anti-Israeli activities is in the ancient city of Tyre, South Lebanon.
Author photo

▲ Cairo, unofficial capital of the Arab world has nuclear-related developments in Iran under close focu
Author photo

WE RESIST
ما ایستاده‌ایم
كلنا مقاومة

◄

The face of contem
rary Iranian oppos
to western and par
ularly Armerican p
cy in the Middle E

This photograph ar
the others in this pl
spread and on the l
cover of the book u
taken by Australia
Broadcasting
Corporation (ABC
journalist and repo
Marc Corcoran in
2004.

They offer a fascin
ing glimpse into wh
is essentially a close
society.

Photo: Mark Corcoran, 20

Inhuman punishments have become more commonplace, including two cases of stoning. Those executed included Mehrdad Kalany, who was executed on charges that included "meeting and talking" with Reynaldo Galindo Pohl, the former UN Special Representative, and the delegation that accompanied him.

Then Ahmed Bakhtiari—a member of the Iranian People's Fedaian Organization (Minority)—was executed on charges of participation in a terrorist group and terrorist operations, as well as other criminal charges. Rahman Radjabi Hamvand, a member of the Kurdish Democratic Party of Iran, was executed. The charges against him stemmed from a complaint by a private individual that was later withdrawn. AI reported that Hedayatollah Zendehdel and Abolghasem Majd-Abkahi were believed to have been hanged after seven years' detention without trial and conviction on mainly political charges.

Exiles and human rights monitors report that many of those executed for alleged criminal offenses, primarily narcotics charges, were actually political dissidents. In addition a November 1995 law criminalized dissent and applied the death penalty to offenses such as "attempts against the security of the State, outrage against high-ranking Iranian officials, and insults against the memory of Imam Khomeini, and against the Leader of the Islamic Republic."

Tehran continued its repression of the Sunni minority, both inside and outside Iran. A fifty-year-old Sunni cleric, Molawi Ahamed Sayyad, imprisoned by the government from 1990–95, disappeared at Bandar Abbas airport. His body was later found in a city suburb. Six members of the IRGC arrested him at the airport and he is believed to have died in their custody. Afterward, forty-six-year-old Molavi Abdul Malek, a Sunni cleric and Iranian Balouchi leader was reportedly murdered by Iranian intelligence operatives in Karachi. Also reported killed in a related incident were Iranian Sunni Molavi Abdulmalek, the son of a prominent Iranian Sunni cleric as well as Jamshid Zahi, another prominent Iranian Sunni figure.

The government has also continued to terminate political opponents abroad. Opposition leaders Zahrah Rajabi and Abdul Ali Moradi were murdered by Iranian agents in Istanbul. In Iraq, eight members of the Kurdish Democratic Party of Iran were killed by elements of the Islamic Revolutionary Guards. A former official from the Shah's regime, Reza Masluman died mysteriously in Paris. His murder (as it was afterward pronounced) is believed to have been ordered by the Tehran government.

Credible reports indicate that security forces continue to torture detainees and prisoners. Common methods include suspension for long periods in contorted positions, burning with cigarettes, and, most frequently, severe and repeated beatings with cables or other instruments on the back and on the soles of the feet. Concurrently, a new law was enacted that reinforces Islamic punishments such as flogging, stoning, amputations, and public executions.

So too with Iranian prison conditions which are inordinately harsh. Some prisoners are held in solitary confinement or denied adequate food or medical care in order to force confessions, sometimes for years. Female prisoners have reportedly been raped or otherwise tortured while in detention. In the past, prison guards have intimidated family members of detainees and have sometimes tortured them in their presence.

Clearly, the Iranian revolution, which began on such a promising note with the return of the Ayatollah Khomeini from exile, has purposely and systematically become an instrument of terror.

Former Iranian President Abol Hassan Bani Sadr—in exile in Europe for almost a quarter century—said as much when he addressed the media in Berlin not long ago. That followed a warrant being issued for the arrest of former Iranian Intelligence Minister, Ali Fallahian, after having been identified as the man responsible for the killings in what is now known as the Mykonos trial. Bani Sadr told the court that the murders had been sanctioned jointly by Supreme Leader Khamene'i and former President Hashemi Rafsanjani.

He also disclosed that there were almost twenty organizations in Tehran, each one of them located in a different government ministry, that were involved in some form of terrorist activity across the globe. It was Bani Sadr who gave the prosecutor in Berlin details about the networks, their functions and many of the names of those involved. He also told the court that within the framework of Iranian constitutional law, or vilayat fakih, that only the "Supreme Guide," Khamene'i, could sentence someone to death.

"It cannot be a political decision," he stated. "What they are doing right now is acknowledging that these murders are justified from a religious point of view."

"In 1987, former President Rafsanjani issued the order to create a special council for affairs which should remain absolutely secret and not subject to decisions or discussion by the Majlis (the Iranian parliament). These secret affairs included confidential contracts with foreign countries, arms purchases, and details about the country's nuclear, biological and chemical warfare programs as well as the manhunt of opponents, both domestic and foreign."

He went on: "The members of this council included Khamene'i, Rafsanjani, Ali Akbar Velayati (former Minister of Foreign Affairs), Ali Mohammed Besharati-Jahromi (former Interior Minister), Ali Fallahian (an erstwhile Intelligence Minister), Mohsen Rezai (Commander of the Islamic Revolutionary Guards Corps), Reyshari (a former secret services chief and head of Khamene'i's Special Bureau) as well as Hijazi (Director of Intelligence in the Khamene'i Bureau)."

Many of these people were replaced by Khatami, but quite a few continue to hold powerful sway, he added.

Bani Sadr said that even after all these years in exile, he was still able to keep close tabs on developments inside Iran. His contacts extended to sources within the government in Tehran and elsewhere. He suggested that there were many people in the country who were utterly disillusioned with the fundamentalist approach to social and political issues imposed on the country by Khamene'i and his followers. These were the same people who most times did his unquestioned bidding if changes brought about by Khatami's liberal administration were not in line with what they believed the Qur'an expounds, or possibly, should expound.

"Khatami and his people are eager for change, but their hands are tied," he told one expatriate source. Further, any kind of opposition to Khamene'i's long-term Islamic vision was quickly dealt with, often brutally. Obviously, in speaking to the Western media, Bani Sadr has himself become a target of Iranian hit squads.

While this has been going on, said one observer in the West who preferred not to be named because he still had family "inside," it is hard to understand how the administration of George W. Bush can let dialogue with Tehran advance to the point where the Iranians had the effrontery to believe they could get away with encouraging al-Qaeda to strike at American targets in Saudi Arabia.

"The Shi'ite Islamic regime of Iran, generally described as tottering, nonetheless has the brass to brandish four sticks over the Bush administration's head. One is al-Qaeda. Another is the Lebanese Hizbollah; the third is the Palestinian Jihad Islami terror group, which is funded from Tehran and used as a conduit to the fourth, Yasser Arafat, his al Aqsa Martyrs Brigades, and Hamas."

It is important to understand how this organized bedlam evolved. Much of it followed the success of the revolution when the ultra-sectarian Ayatollah Khomeini embarked on an agenda known as *Mashru al-Thawra al-Iranillah*, or what was colloquially referred to as the Project of the Iranian Revolution.

In simple terms, his program of "reconstitution" was aimed at furthering Islam by reviving the Islamic *Ummah*, the world-wide Islamic nation which, he envisioned, would be headquartered in Iran. Though he never said as much in any of his public pronouncements, it was always implied by those closest to him that this "green revolution" would be led by himself as the *Amir al-Muminum* (Commander of the Faithful). Already, it would seem, Iran had imperial interests in mind.

To further these ends, said Bani Sadr, he founded the IRGC, or Pasdaran, which gradually emerged as the most totalitarian instrument of power in the country. In the view of the late Ayatollah, Bani Sadr added, the revolution marked the second advent of what was viewed by Shi'ites everywhere as "the true Islam."

His declared goal was to spread its influence worldwide, in the words of Ayatollah Montazeri, the man who, at one stage, was one of his most devout disciples, "to capture the Islamic spirit and imagination of the faithful wherever they prostrate themselves before Allah."

Since it is impossible to track everything that takes place in a country "as xenophobic as an ingrown toenail," only some known terrorist bases (as well as nuclear and other WMD sites) have been pinpointed.

The first Iranian terrorist training camp to have been identified by Western agents was at Manzarieh Park (on the northern outskirts of Tehran). It now serves as a distribution and coordinating unit for foreigners recruited for the revolutionary cause—including a handful of Americans (mostly black). For a while there were dissident Irish nationals there as well. Manzarieh is estimated to have trained upwards of three to five thousand terrorists between 1981 and the early 1990s.

Other camps identified were at Hamadan, southwest of the capital; Qazvim, in the northeast, and, the biggest of all, Imam Ali, immediately east of Tehran where most foreign nationals were hosted. Since these names first appeared in print, some are believed to have been discontinued, though with present security restrictions in place, this has been impossible to verify. In any event, nobody goes about asking questions about such things in present-day Iran.

In the interim, these camps have played important roles in the ongoing war against those who oppose the authorities. The Iranian-trained hit-team captured by the Turks in October 1994 came from Imam Ali. Turkish Intelligence—to be sure, using some persuasion—was able to extract a remarkably accurate profile of the current Iranian intelligence system.

"Graduate" work (as well as preparations for suicide bombings) was Marvdasht's role, on the Persopolis plateau off the Esfahan road to the south of the capital. A defector to the West, Colonel Ali Vesseghi, reckoned that some instruction there included "road work." That involved condemned prisoners driving trucks filled with explosives at each other in an attempt to gauge the effect on specific targets. It was a prelude, he said, to more suicide bombings aimed at Western targets.

Bushehr on the Gulf coast—today the site of Iran's first nuclear reactor being built by the Russians—had a major facility on the outskirts of town that was involved in a totally different kind of terrorism. At the city's air base, trainees were taught to fly single-engined Pilatus Porters as a prelude to what some described as "suicide missions." After this activity became the subject of an American intelligence report, unconfirmed reports said that it had been shifted to Won Son in North Korea. The aircraft acquired by Iran for this purpose (said to be intended for destroying the homes of leaders in the Gulf and Near East regions) included Cessna Citations and Falcon Fanjets— and all this years before September 11.

Currently, underwater demotion, mining and offensive seaborne activity is taught by Pasdaran elements at Bandar Abbas, as are Lebanese Hizbollah recruits in miniature two-man submarines (all of which I saw detailed in threat-identification posters at one of the Israeli operational bases that I visited in northern Galilee in the late 1990s). Also, the intricacies of "high-end" explosives and booby traps are prominent among subjects on the agenda at several camps around Isfahan.

Recent reports out of Iran have indicated that aviation and airport terrorism is now handled in the remote northeast of the country. The entire Western-built airport on the outskirts of the religious city of Mashhad (not far from the Afghan border) is devoted to this purpose. After the downing of an Iran Air A300 Airbus by an American warship in the Gulf, a similar facility was established at Shiraz.

Thousands of Iranians together with numerous foreigners have graduated from these establishments. While a lot were killed in the war with Iraq, some are known to have been sent to the West, posing as bona fide refugees. While these "sleepers" might have been inactive for a decade (a rather distinct Cold War pattern) they can be activated at any time.

More than twenty years after the Ayatollah Ruhollah Khomeini returned in triumph to Iran to complete the revolution that would create the Islamic Republic, the country, if anything, is more isolationist than ever. While some tourists are allowed to visit, the anti-Western outlook is explicit. For instance, the slogan "Death to America" festoons parts of Tehran Airport. It is routinely chanted by all students before Friday prayers.

According to Khomeini's successor, these are "signals that must be preserved like a flag." Similarly, former deputy foreign minister Hossein Sheikholeslam echoed the views of many others when he said before the last elections, "Israel must be annihilated."

There is also evidence that indicates Tehran has entered a more aggressive "international" phase. The government appears to be prepared to back words with action, which is one of the reasons why, in Washington's view, Iran remains "the world's principal state sponsor of terrorism."

Among acts laid at Tehran's door have been the attempted assassination of Egypt's President Hosni Mubarak (using Sudanese agents in Addis Ababa, the Ethiopian capital); the downing of a Panamanian airliner on a route that was known to be used by many Jewish businessmen; the destruction of a Jewish cultural center in Argentina; a machine-gun attack on worshipers at a Turkish synagogue; and the sponsoring of suicide bombers in Israeli cities. Hizbollah, as I was told by Major General Yoram Yair, erstwhile Israeli military attaché in Washington, receives at least $100 million a year for its efforts in southern Lebanon.

According to former CIA director James Woolsey, the Party of God, prior to September 11, killed more Americans than any other terrorist group in the past half century. That tally does not include the nineteen American servicemen and women who died in the Khobar Towers bombing in Dhahran. Also, former FBI Director Louis Freeh testified on Capitol Hill that both Lebanese Hizbollah and the Palestinian group Hamas "have placed supporters inside the U.S. who could be used to support an act of terrorism here."[3]

Nor are conditions likely to change. It says something that the more liberal Khatami, when first elected, was one of only four candidates (out of a pool of more than two hundred hopefuls) who survived vetting by the Council of Guardians. In any event, under the country's constitution, the Iranian President remains subordinate to the supreme leader. This post will belong to Ayatollah Ali Khamene'i until he dies.

In certain critical respects, Khamene'i is now more potent politically than his late great mentor Khomeini, which is significant in a country that holds seven per cent of the world's proven oil reserves together with the second-largest natural-gas deposits.

To understand the machinations of Iranian-sponsored terrorism, it is essential to grasp the extent of the power wielded by Tehran's most secret security service, the Pasdaran, formally referred to as the Islamic Revolutionary Guard Corps (See Chapter 12).

Sources within several American government departments have warned that there are groups—both men and women—being trained for subversive work abroad by this organization. Until very recently, Pasdaran operatives were known by Western Intelligence to be active in the Sudan training a variety of subversives, including fundamentalist from Egypt, Algeria, Tunisia, Eritrea, Uganda and elsewhere. This sort of activity could not take place had it not been sanctioned by Khartoum. In South Africa there are Iranians working with the country's National Intelligence Agency or NIA, though you won't get anybody in Pretoria to acknowledge their presence.

It is significant that the IRGC's original role was supposed to have been largely cultural, described by one member of the Majlis as "safeguarding the achievements of the Islamic revolution." Militarily, the force is designated to support the regular army when required, which it did with some success during the Iran-Iraq war when its strength peaked at about three-quarters of a million,[4] mostly men but with a smattering of women. The current manpower of the Pasdaran is roughly about a quarter of that.

Pasdaran has its own independent chain of command. It is answerable, first, through its commander-in-chief, directly to Sayyid Ali Khamene'i, and there is a minister in the Iranian cabinet who deals with nothing else but the IRGC.

The Guards Corps, according to Arab writer Hala Jaber, was created to realize the dream of the Ayatollah Khomeini. Its original role was "to spread the word of the revolution and rescue the deprived of the world from the domination of the superpowers." Their task, Khomeini is quoted as saying, was to be carried out through flagrant military intervention (Lebanon) and through subtle political interference—whatever else that was intended to imply.

For some years after the 1991 Gulf War, Pasdaran was active throughout the Near East region and in countries which allied themselves with Iraq during the eight-year Iran-Iraq war. In Saudi Arabia, for instance, IRGC cadres were involved for a while in planning and instigating riots during the annual Hajj pilgrimage. For a long time Turkey remained high on the agenda and much effort and cash still goes toward trying to disrupt Ankara's alliance with Jerusalem.

IRGC agents are known to occupy positions at all Iranian embassies. They have been most prominent in small countries such as Cyprus, and things stayed that way for a long time until Nicosia— alarmed by burgeoning terror in the eastern Mediterranean and also a strong desire to join the EU—managed to put a stop to it. It wasn't all that long ago that Cyprus was a major conduit for Iranian operatives and assassins into Europe.

Under diplomatic cover, Pasdaran agents have recruited proxies and cells for operations in many countries. Much of the money used by cash-strapped Sudan to train and equip foreign insurgents, for example, came from Pasdaran. In turn, as we have seen, Khartoum granted the Iranian Navy a twenty-year tenure over two principle Sudanese naval bases on the Red Sea.

Elsewhere, since 1991, Pasdaran agents have given Hamas about $20 million a year to foster their version of the revolution within Israel. Islamic Jihad has an office in Tehran, as do almost all major fundamentalist Moslem organizations. These range from Algeria's Islamic Salvation Front to the Moro secessionists in the Philippines, as well as the radical South African Islamic group People Against Gangsterism and Drugs (PAGAD).

The Pasdaran's "Order of Battle" is worth looking at. Since the Gulf War, the organization has been divided into four categories: soldiers, fighters, officers and commandants. By 1993, after re-structuring, Pasdaran formations were as follows: eleven Regional HQ (fully manned); two Armored Divisions (on mobilization) and twenty-four Infantry Divisions (cadre strength). All are "official" activities. What is important as far as Western intelligence agencies are concerned is that Pasdaran fulfills various clandestine security roles, including intel-

ligence and the Iranian SAVAMA secret police. All subversive activities, whether domestic or foreign, fall within this brief.

Judith Miller, a former head of the *New York Times* Cairo bureau,
tells us that over the years a serious of tragic "accidents" have befall-
en leading government figures. Had any of these individuals needed to
be liquidated, she says, the job would have been left to the Pasdaran,
the body responsible for most "wet work" in the Islamic Republic.

In 1994, the head of intelligence in the Supreme Leader's office,
along with three senior aides, died in a car crash. A year later Mansour
Satari, chief of the air force, and seven of his senior officers were killed
when their military jet exploded on take-off at Isfahan military airport. A diplomat in Tehran who investigated the disaster told Miller
that the plane had been sabotaged. Shortly thereafter, Ahmed
Khomeini, the revered Imam's son, who had become increasingly critical of both Khamene'i and of Rafsanjani, suddenly and inexplicably
died. A poisoning was suspected.[5]

Iran's very comprehensive nuclear programs—the nuclear reactor
at Bushehr is public (Iran is a signatory to the Nuclear Non-
Proliferation Treaty) and the other covert—are the direct responsibility of the Pasdaran command structure, no matter what Tehran says to
the contrary.

Sardar Shafagh, one of the country's erstwhile nuclear leaders (he
defected to the West while on a visit to Minatom in Moscow in 1995)
was a Pasdaran general. Since then, Shafagh has apparently been the
source of much valuable intelligence, including the fact that Tehran is
doing what it can to build its own nuclear bomb. He is now in the
United States.

An interesting sidelight here, is that a prime mover in the Iranian
nuclear program is the prominent former Shi'ite-Iraqi dissident
Hussein al-Sharistani who, as a student, had worked with the leader
of the Iraqi nuclear program, Dr. Jafer D. Jafar at the Imperial College
in London. Early on, both were jailed by Saddam Hussein for reasons
linked to their politico-religious Shi'ite faith. Jafar soon recanted.
Sharistani never did because he felt that Saddam always took such a
brutal line on his people and he refused to be intimidated. He paid a
terrible price: in 1979. Sharistani was jailed and tortured into paraly-
sis for more than three weeks because of his suspected links to Iranian
Shi'ite clergy.

Give the mullahs their dues: Tehran never forgot the plight of their
"Son of the Faith." By the time coalition forces invaded Iraq during

Operation Desert Storm, Sharistani was being held in isolation at the top security military barracks at Abu Ghraib Prison, more recently the scene of dreadful American excesses against Iraqi prisoners. During an air raid over Tehran, a car arrived at the base with a letter signed personally by Saddam Hussein. It demanded that Sharistani be handed over to the bearer. No one questioned such authority in Iraq and the exchange took minutes.

Obviously, the letter was a forgery. Somehow, in spite of the war, Sharistani found himself free and in Tehran in three or four days. Nobody ever explained how his rescuers managed to ferret him through the front lines of a very active region of conflict. Once in Iran, it is said that he again involved himself in nuclear matters.

Sharistani's snatch was an operation that was both bold and opportunistic. It illustrates the lengths to which Tehran is prepared to go to achieve its objectives. No one is saying what happened to Sharistani's Iraqi jailers except that, to a man, they disappeared not long afterward.

Other nationals helping in the Iranian covert nuclear program include, among others, North Koreans, Pakistanis, renegade Russian scientists, and a handful of South Africans who had been out of work since their own nuclear weapons projects were shelved in 1991. There is also, it is said, a couple of Argentinians and an Australian, but that report has not been confirmed.

In spite of its pariah status, many countries have flouted American demands to curtail contact with the Khamene'i government.

Germany, in particular, continues to maintain an unusually high profile relationship with Tehran, much as it did with Saddam Hussein's Iraq until the American invasion in 2003. In 1992, at Bonn's initiative, the EU formally adopted its policy of "critical dialogue," the banner under which Europe cultivated ties with several countries of which the U.S. is critical. Germany and its partners reached out diplomatically toward Tehran as well, exchanging parliamentary and governmental delegations up to the ministerial level.

Then came a measure of intelligence cooperation between Bonn and Tehran that caught everybody off guard. Customarily, this is the sort of engagement entered into between friends, and details are invariably secret. Yet reports leaked to the press indicated at the time that German intelligence had given its Tehran counterpart computers, software and photographic equipment. Also, Iranian agents were receiving specialist training from German experts, not only in Iran but at German Intelligence HQ in Munich.

Ostensibly, the goal of these endeavors is said to be to cultivate closer ties with Tehran and, one imagines, maintain some sort of presence behind closed doors.

Peter Frisch, for a while President of the Office for the Protection of the Constitution in Germany (and that country's head of counterterrorism) made it clear while he was still in office that Bonn was very much aware of what he termed the Iranian (and Islamic) threat. Addressing a strategic studies conference in Jerusalem, he said that the kinds of extremes that were now being demonstrated by some Islamic nations were the greatest danger of the next century. He specifically singled out Iran.

Frisch touched on both nuclear and weaponization issues, stating that Iran had acquired missiles that could eventually hit Germany, almost two thousand miles away.

On nuclear weapons,[7] Frisch told the gathering, "While I don't think that (Iran) has the atomic bomb, they are trying very hard to get it."

With the end of the Cold War, strong evidence has emerged indicating that Iran sees itself at the cutting edge of a more forceful international role, not only in the Middle East but further afield as well. Though not an Arab nation itself, this could involve Iran dominating a good part of the Arab world, as well as the western half of the Indian Ocean. Both Indonesia and the Philippines are said to factor into this equation. And while not yet challenging India's hegemony, there have been some notable gains, one of which is the Sudan.

Agreements have also been signed with other nations in the region for the use of their ports for Iranian warships. Mozambique, and, for a while, Madagascar, are among them. The same has happened in South Africa, though Pretoria denies this, as it does with just about everything relating to closer links with radical countries, Iran and Robert Mugabe's Zimbabwe included.

There is also a different dimension to potential Iranian terror in the long term. Already we have seen a Pasdaran offshoot—Hizbollah—implicated in an attempt to shoot down an Israeli passenger airliner in the Kenyan port city of Mombasa using shoulder-fired surface-to-air missiles (SAMs, or in the jargon, Manpads).

Also, at least two ships, possibly three, carrying weapons (two of them had SAMs onboard) were intercepted in the Red Sea or the eastern Mediterranean (once they had passed through Suez) in the past two or three years. All had begun their journeys in Iranian waters. In this regard, it is the anti-aircraft missile systems that are of most interest to the West. And since the threat of their deployment is real, they—and their potential striking ability—are worth examining in some detail.

The frightening aspect is that there are few complex weapons systems that come with simpler instructions for their use. You point, lock-on and pull the trigger: the missile does the rest. The entire operation takes seconds.

Worse, there are currently about half a million Manpads out there, with some of the simpler systems on the illicit arms market available for as little as $1,000. According to a recent issue of *Jane's Intelligence Review*, there are one hundred and fifty thousand shoulder-fired missiles in unauthorized circulation around the world, with another three hundred and fifty thousand in defense stockpiles. Jane's estimates that almost thirty militia groups and terrorist organizations own shoulder-fired SAMs.

This kind of activity could escalate, especially if someone in Tehran decides to take drastic action.

America's *Time* magazine recently suggested that as governments bolstered their defenses against insurgencies, terrorists were likely to go after ever-softer targets: "When you cannot fight your foe on the battlefield, you will hit his embassies."

Time correspondent Mark Thompson went on to suggest that "If the terrorists were unable to board a U.S. airliner with box-cutters, they might be able to target it with a surface-to-air missile."[8]

What is worrying about this premise is that in 2003 alone there were five separate incidents involving Russian or Chinese-made hand-held missiles deployed against commercial airliners.

The first took place in November 2002 when three men with links to al-Qaeda tried to buy Stinger SAMs from FBI agents in Hong Kong. That same month, members of a Kenya-based terror cell (with links stretching all the way through Somalia to Hizbollah together with an al-Qaeda input) fired two Russian-designed SA-7s at an Israeli airliner departing Mombassa.

Six months later, the British government deployed half a battalion of troops at London's Heathrow international airport because intelligence reports indicated that al-Qaeda planned to fire portable missiles at civilian aircraft. That was followed by the interception not long afterward of a truckload of supersonic Manpads by Saudi authorities near Jeddah.

A late report out of Riyadh, the Saudi capital, indicated that the missiles were destined for militants linked to a bin Laden cell in the Kingdom. Not unexpectedly, the discovery led to the immediate suspension of British Airways flights to Saudi Arabia, a ban that remained in place for more than a month.

Then came the arrest by the FBI of British citizen Hemant Lakhani, together with Moinudden Ahmed Hameed of Malaysia, on charges of trying to smuggle a Russian SA-18 surface-to-air missile into the U.S., with plans to supply Arab dissidents already on American soil with fifty more. Though the FBI has always remained cagey about what really took place, one source suggested that Air Force One—the Boeing 747 regularly used by the President of the United States—might have been the objective.

While these events are a significant departure from previous terror attempts, the consignment of ground-to-air missiles captured in Saudi Arabia has serious implications for the West.

Dr. Saad al-Fagih of the London-based Movement for Islamic Reform said the Saudi incident was uncovered purely by chance, but that Special Security forces were then called to the scene. It was later concluded, he said, that the SAMs had been smuggled in overland from Yemen and that at least one of these missiles might already have been used in a bid to shoot down a U.S. Air Force transport jet near Riyadh. Its empty launcher tube had been discarded near the capital.

These revelations followed the discovery of moves by an extremist cell to put Riyadh airport under surveillance. Documents were found in a car revealing that members had mapped out the exact location of checkpoints and other security measures. This coincided with the testimony given by an al-Qaeda suspect that an attack that was being planned on British interests in Saudi Arabia.

Writing in *Asia Times*, American defense strategist David Isenberg pointed out that trying to shoot down civilian jets with missiles was nothing new. Two Rhodesian prop-driven Viscounts were downed by SA-7s in the late 1970s, and a Sudan Airways jet was shot down in 1986 with a combined loss of one hundred and sixty-seven lives. Rebels in Congo shot down a Congo Airlines Boeing 727 in 1998 with forty people killed.

Other countries that have experienced missile attacks on domestic airliners include Angola, the former Soviet Republic of Georgia, Bosnia, Costa Rica, Mozambique, Mauritania, Somalia and Armenia.

The FBI conservatively estimates that there have been about thirty instances in which shoulder-fired SAMs have hit civilian planes, causing more than five hundred deaths.

America's RAND Corporation makes a higher tally. Its analysis shows that as many as forty civilian airliners were shot down by these weapons between 1975 and 1992, causing up to almost eight hundred deaths. Many of these missiles, such as the French Mistral, the U.S. Stinger, British Blowpipe, Swiss Oerlikon and the full Russian range of SA-7, SA-14, SA-16 and SA-18 Manpads, are widely available and much sought after on the international arms black market centered in Eastern Europe.

Isenberg declares that it is easy to understand why: SAMs are relatively inexpensive and easy to conceal: the average hand-held ground-to-air missile is about six feet long, roughly two or three inches in diameter and might weigh anywhere between twelve and forty-something pounds. They are also simple to use, being fired very much like a rifle. The launcher tube rests on the operator's shoulder, who aims through a simple set of metallic sights and pulls a trigger.

He points at CIA estimates, when Afghan mujahadeen were still fighting the Soviets. Seventy percent of the time a Stinger missile was fired by the rebels, "an aircraft or a helicopter was hit." Manpads operate by targeting the heat of an aircraft engine and provide little warning to the pilot of their proximity prior to impact, thus complicating the use of even the most effective countermeasures.

The U.S. administration has acted swiftly to find a solution to the problem. Already some U.S. Air Force cargo planes have initiated the use of what are called Large Aircraft Infrared Countermeasures (LAIRCM) that render a missile's navigation inoperable. LAIRCM automatically detects, tracks and jams infrared missiles, sending a high-intensity laser beam into the missile's seeker, disrupting its guidance system. The crew requires no action. The pilot simply is informed that a threat missile was detected and jammed.

Though this system has proved one hundred percent effective in the test phase, the cost of designing new commercial aircraft and retrofitting older commercial aircraft with this system would exceed $25 billion.

"Inexpensive, yet lethal, surface-to-air missiles have proliferated around the globe and unfortunately are in the hands of our potential adversaries," says Arnold Welch, vice president for Infrared Counter-measures Programs at Northrop Grumman's Defensive Systems Division in Rolling Meadows, Illinois. "It is essential that our military pilots and air crews have this sophisticated type of protection in order to perform their missions and return safely."

Another source has indicated that the issue has achieved top priority status in America. Federal officials, increasingly concerned that terrorists will attack U.S. commercial aircraft with shoulder-fired missiles are developing plans to thwart such strikes with measures that range from sophisticated anti-missile technology to simple changes in takeoff schedules.

A U.S. interagency task force, led by the Transportation Security Administration (TSA) and including representatives of the Pentagon, the FBI and the State Department (a group that reports to the National Security Council in Washington) is now coordinating emergency inspections of every large U.S. airport to determine their vulnerability to the small, portable missiles, a senior U.S. government official said. The task force is also planning a public education campaign designed to teach police departments and citizens who live and work near airports to identify the missiles if they see them being assembled.

While acknowledging their alarm at the danger posed by portable missiles that may be fired at the approximately sixty-seven hundred commercial aircraft operating in the United States, administration officials stress that the highest echelons of the U.S. government are focused on the danger.

"We have drawn together the best thinkers in government and in the contracting world" to address the issue in recent months, said one senior U.S. government official. "We now grasp the threat, and we grasp our options."

Notably (and in character), the Israelis have come up with a solution of their own, which they have already fitted to all their own commercial passenger and military aircraft. The recent failed attempt to down one of their passenger jets with a shoulder-fired missile in Mombasa has focused attention on the "Britening," an Israeli-built missile warning system for commercial airlines. According to its developers, the system (still under close security wraps but commercially available to select nations) automatically senses missiles and sends a light beam to deflect them from the plane.

11

IRAN'S
UNCONVENTIONAL WEAPONS

**As the eponymous character in Dr. Strangelove
observes, "Isn't the whole point of a Doomsday
Machine . . . lost if you keep it a secret?"**
"Israel's Nukes," *The Economist*, April 24, 2004

One of the more disturbing revelations recently made by Kenneth
Katzman, a State Department specialist in Middle Eastern affairs, concerned evidence that Iran had recruited Russian scientists to work on
its biological warfare program.[1] Katzman went on to expand on the
issue by disclosing that recent U.S. proliferation reports mentioned
that Iran had sought chemical weapons technology and chemical pre-
cursors from Russia as well as China.

He also made the point that those official U.S. statements on
efforts to dissuade Russian WMD-related technology sales tend to
omit discussions of chem-bio technology. Outside assistance to Iran's
chemical and biological programs "is difficult to prevent, given the
dual-use nature of the materials, the equipment being sought, and the
many legitimate end-users of these items." In a sense it is like
UNSCOM's Iraqi WMD debate of the mid-1990s. Irrespective of the
fact that Iran is a signatory of the Chemical Weapons Convention
(CWC), it is unlikely to terminate its CW program any time soon.

The CIA's Nonproliferation Center had this to say on the subject:

> Iran has continued to upgrade and expand its chemical
> weapons production infrastructure and chemical munitions
> arsenal, despite signing the CWC in January 1993. Iran pro-
> duces a variety of chemical agents, including blister, blood,
> and choking agents. As part of this expansion, Iran is spend-
> ing large sums of money on long-term capital improvements to
> its chemical warfare program, suggesting that it intends to
> maintain a CW capability well into the future.

The same holds true for biological weapons. Iran is believed to have begun its BW programs while still at war with Iraq. This production, which was initiated by the Islamic Revolutionary Guards Corps, was already underway by 1986, as evidenced in an April 1986 announcement by the Minister of the IRGC. He stated: "The armament industries of the Corps have made notable progress in the missile, aircraft, biological, chemical, and nuclear fields . . ."

Official U.S. assessments of the Iranian biological weapons program indicate a fairly substantial BW production and weaponization program.

Paula deSutter tells us that the Iranian BW program is embedded within Iran's extensive biotechnology and pharmaceutical industries so as to obscure its activities. The Iranian military has used medical, education and scientific research organizations for many aspects of BW agent procurement, research, and production. Iran has failed to submit the data declarations called for in the CBMs.

Officially, "The United States Government reiterates its previous finding that Iran probably has produced biological warfare agents and apparently has weaponized a small quantity of those agents. Biological weapons can be delivered in the same munitions that deliver chemical weapons, including artillery shells, rockets, bombs, missile warheads, and covert devices."

Katzman's report is effusive about China's role. Since the early 1990s, he discloses, U.S. officials identified companies on the Chinese mainland as suppliers of Iran's chemical weapons programs, although some U.S. officials attributed this kind of assistance to Iran to a lack of export controls by the Chinese government.

On March 22, 1997, he states, Secretary of State Madeline Albright imposed U.S. sanctions under the Chemical and Biological Warfare Elimination Act of 1991 on two PRC firms. These were the Nanjing Chemical Industries Group and the Jiangsu Chemical Engineering and Technology Import/Export Corporation. Also affected were five PRC citizens, as well as Cheong Lee Ltd, a Hong Kong company for "knowingly and materially" aiding Iran's chemical weapons programs.

He goes on to say that the Clinton Administration said that there was no evidence that Beijing knew anything about the transfers, which, prime facie, is rubbish. China has one of the most oppressive, cephalopodan security systems in the world, and very little can hap-

pen there without the authorities being aware of it, especially something as critically sensitive as chemical or biological warfare proliferation.

In the words of one Washington political old-timer, that kind of
comment punctuated many excesses during Clinton's tenure. That
view was reinforced only two weeks later with the State Department
announcing the suspension of an Exim Bank loan for an American
firm's exports to the Nanjing firm mentioned above.

It is also Katzman's view that the Bush Administration takes a very
different line on such matters: "It clearly believes that there are entities in China assisting in Iran's chemical weapons program," he says
in his report.[2]

"In four separate determinations, the Bush Administration has
imposed sanctions on several chemical firms based in China . . . in the
first three, they were imposed pursuant to the Iran Nonproliferation
Act of 2000." One of these firms was the same one whose name
cropped up in 1997: the Jiangsu corporation.

John Pike's GlobalSecurity.org also deals with the subject. His website[3] states that "Iran is currently able to employ chemical weapons
and is progressing in its development of a large self-supporting CW
infrastructure." This activity, he points out, is taking place in spite of
Tehran having ratified the new Chemical Weapons Convention, under
which it is obligated to eliminate its chemical weapons assets over a
period of years.

"Nevertheless it continues to upgrade and expand its chemical
warfare production infrastructure and munitions arsenal. The magnitude of this effort suggests that the Iranian leadership intends to maintain a robust CW capability." He goes on to underscore Katzman's
contention that it was events in the Iran-Iraq War that are at the core
of this activity, when "Iran used chemical agents to respond to Iraqi
chemical attacks on several occasions during that conflict. Since the
early 1990s, (Tehran) has put a high priority on its CW program
because of its inability to respond in kind to Baghdad's chemical
attacks and the discovery of substantial Iraqi efforts with advanced
agents, such as the highly persistent nerve agent VX.[4]

Like the CIA, GlobalSecurity maintains that Iran manufactures
weapons for a variety of CW agents: "Iran's stockpile of chemical
weapons is believed to include nerve and blister agents. Iran is estimated to have an inventory of several thousand tons of various agents

including sulfur, mustard, phosgene and cyanide agents. . . . Along with shell and bomb delivery systems, Iran may also be producing CW warheads for its missile systems."

Listing production details, the website reckons production capacity to be as much as a thousand tons a year, with major facilities at Damghan, almost two hundred miles east of Tehran. Other facilities are located at Esfahan, Parchin and Qazvin.

Pike accepts that the Iranian CW infrastructure is rather poorly characterized in the open literature, "and given the reported scope of this program, it must be assumed that as many as a dozen other facilities have significant chemical weapons development, production, storage or training facilities."

In the aftermath of the Anglo-American invasion of Iraq in 2003, one controversy that continues to surround Saddam Hussein's weapons of mass destruction is whether they were the figment of some politicians' imaginations. In the same way, there are a lot of people who dismiss the possibility that more September 11s might be in the offing.

Ten backpack bombs on the Spanish rail system in and around Madrid put the damper on that notion, if only for a while because people tend to forget quickly. Before that there were dozens killed in Bali, followed by a similar spate of bombings in Turkey, Tunisia and Morocco. There will be more.

America meanwhile presses ahead with a security program that is nationwide. While the country is simply too big for the implementation of blanket protection for all its citizens, a lot is being done because both London and Washington continue to express fears of another major terrorist hit.

Indeed, in late March 2004, Britain barely avoided a major bomb attack when a combined swoop by seven hundred police pounced on a cell of radical Moslems who had been preparing to detonate half-ton fertilizer bombs at two of the country's airports, one of them Gatwick. These were the same kind of explosives used in the Bali and in subsequent Moroccan blasts.

What puts this attempt in a category of its own was that in uncovering this cache, British security experts discovered a large supply of osmium tetroxide, a highly toxic substance which, one of the plotters disclosed while under interrogation, was to be disseminated with the explosives. That way, he said, the blast would have a much more potent outcome. While osmium tetroxide is no great guns in the CW gambit—it attacks soft tissue—the chemical can, as one authority told London's *Daily Telegraph,* "lead to an asthma-like death within close confines."

People became so jumpy about terrorist attacks in Europe immediate afterward that some days later the BBC carried a report of a poison gas attack in Bulgaria. A chemical was thrown into the visitors' area of a Sofia traffic police office and forty people were affected, one of them critically, the story claimed. Authorities identified that substance as chloropicrin, a pesticide that had been used as a chemical weapon by both Germany and the Allies in World War I.

Twelve hours later there was an embarrassed retraction: a butcher had accidentally let off a pepper spray. It didn't help that at about that same time, Paris closed parts of its Metro after Washington had tipped off the French about an imminent Madrid-like bomb attack. It didn't happen—not then, at any rate.

We have unfortunately not seen the last time that those opposed to Western values will attempt to damage those societies which don't share their belief in the *Qur'an.* It is worth noting that, like Madrid, had any of these devices gone off as originally planned—the airport bombs in particular—non-military and security personnel would have been a tiny percentage of those targeted. Those responsible for the planning clearly had women and children in their crosshairs.

Neither Britain nor America is waiting for history to repeat itself. There are many active programs in place to cope with just such disasters

One news report, headed "Censored Study on Bioterror Doubts U.S. Preparedness" appeared in the *New York Times* on March 29, 2004.[5] It stated, "The Pentagon has released parts of (an) unclassified document which concludes that the nation is woefully ill-prepared to detect and respond to a bioterrorist attack." Judith Miller's conclusions as to whether America could withstand a chemical or biological warfare attack would unquestionably also have raised a few eyebrows abroad, particularly in the Middle East.

Which brings to mind a comment made a generation ago by Dr. James A.F. Compton that "Chemical (and biological) weapons work." As he stated in 1987, "They are undergoing revolutionary developments which make them practical and very lethal participants in those human affairs which are ultimately resolved with blood and iron. Be ignorant and be damned, and condemn your children as well."

In my last book, *The Iraqi War Debrief,* I also mentioned that at about the time Dr. Compton wrote that well-considered introduction to his primer, "Military Chemical and Biological Agents," another American, Dr. Jane Orient, published something on the subject in *The Journal of the American Medical Association.*[6] It was titled "Chemical and Biological Warfare: Should Defenses be Researched and Deployed?"

I quote: "Dr. Orient made observations that were strident at a time when such matters were regarded by the medical world as arcane; especially where they concerned Third World nations and their relationships to the West."

She pointed out that, against civilian populations, chemical and biological weapons were extremely attractive because of simple economics. Casualties, she wrote, might cost $2,000 per square mile with conventional weapons, $800 with nerve gas and a single dollar per square mile with biological weapons. This was a groundbreaking prognosis and acknowledged accordingly by her peers.

Iran's mullahs and scientists would also have taken note of all these observations and, as the Federation of American Scientists told us, they now have chemical and biological warfare programs of their own.[7]

Judith Miller's article underscored this threat. She said that the report identified weaknesses in "almost every aspect of U.S. biopreparedness and response." A good deal of it was focused on an ongoing battle to determine who was responsible for the October 2001 anthrax letter attacks that killed five people. Issues were compounded by the fact that the Defense Threat Reduction Agency, the Pentagon unit that originally commissioned the $150,000 study, initially refused to release the document. Though parts were finally made public, some were not. The reason: the study could "circumvent" Pentagon "rules and practices" established to prevent the spread of information associated with WMD, referring top nuclear, biological, chemical and other WMD.

Probably the most notable issue touched on by Ms. Miller was a paragraph in the core of her article. While parts of the original report had been censored by the U.S. military, the excised parts were read to her. In one version of the redacted version the summary states, "The Fall 2001 anthrax attacks may turn out to be . . . to confront." The deleted passage reads: "the easiest of bioterrorist attacks."

Now we all know it, and, it should be mentioned, so does Tehran.

Another category of weapons that is of major concern to the nuclear pundits involves radiological explosives. While low-key compared to something fissionable, detonating a radiological device within the confined space of, for instance, downtown Manhattan or adjacent to Liverpool Street Station in London's central city area, would cause serious dislocation rather than huge numbers of immediate casualties. Paula deSutter tells us that Iran is known to be working on such a weapon.

As she explains, radiological weapons, or radiological dispersal devices (RDD), are defined as "any explosive device that is intended to spread radioactive material in detonation. An improvised nuclear device can also be an RDD if the explosion does not cause a nuclear yield, but 'fizzles,' spreading radioactive materials." Iran, we know, possesses enough uranium to proceed with this kind of work and a CIA assessment that Tehran has pursued RDD is supported by the frequent training of Iran's Shim-Mim-Re, its chemical, biological, and radiological units.

It is Ms. deSutter's view that the Iranians may see such weapons as offering what is termed in the domain of terrorist capability "area denial applicability." Radiological weapons, she says, could be used as a means to deny the United States access to key ports or air bases in somewhat the same manner as biological weapons, but probably with less loss of life. It would however, wreak havoc among civilian populations, but then only if there was highly radioactive fissile material involved.

"There are limitations on the effectiveness of radiological weapons that would almost certainly make them less attractive to the Iranians than biological weapons or even chemical weapons, to include that their use could, with limited military utility, be perceived as 'nuclear' and entail an escalation in conflict. While the radiation effects could likely be cleaned up rather expeditiously, the requirement to do so is cost-associated with operating in a radiological environment. Clean-up operations could be further hindered with subsequent attacks."

That declared, the U.S. has been unusually active in working out a variety of systems to counter such threats. Of late, Washington has initiated a series of nationwide programs that have involved almost all of the hundred and twenty largest American cities on the basis of "training first responders in the event of a chemical or nerve agent attack on the civilian population."

One of the first exercises, named "Measured Response—San Francisco" was held at the turn of the millennium and involved a "nerve gas attack" on that city's subway system. Details of the proceedings were kept secret, but in a confidential aside, a participant told me that the planners were motivated by the successful Aum Shinrikyo terrorist attack on a Tokyo subway some years before. In that attack a dozen people were killed and there were thousands injured after sarin nerve gas was released at five different points underground. The Bush and the Blair administrations feared then—and still do—that something similar might eventually happen in the West.

In the U.S., one consequence that subsequently emerged was that various city, state and federal agencies were involved in countering a fictional anti-governmental group named "Sui Juris."

In the San Francisco exercise, though the exact procedures to be followed during a real attack remain under wraps, the program established by the U.S. Army Chemical and Biological Defense Command (CBDCOM) triggered a reaction by the city's Hazardous Materials (Hazmat) team in conjunction with officials from the Bay Area Rapid Transit (BART) system. The FBI and the San Francisco Police Department were also involved.

As medical teams were alerted, bomb disposal units were brought in to scour other potential target areas. A tactical unit (with gas masks) was mustered for perimeter crowd control. Other, unspecified elements were also deployed. Following a medical red alert, paramedics triaged the victims as red, yellow or green, depending on the severity of their symptoms. Concurrently, San Francisco alerted its Metropolitical Medical Strike Team, a group of medics who had been taught how to respond to a chemical attack of this nature.

Following a declaration of an emergency by the President, the FBI (as the lead federal agency for domestic terrorism) created a Joint Operations Center (JOC) and brought in agents with special protective suits to process evidence from the crime scene which, by now, was categorized a "Hot Zone." Under FBI coordination, the Federal Emergency Management Agency, the Public Health Service and the Environmental Protection Agency also provided support to city and state agencies.

While most of the lessons learned from the exercise remain classified, several points are noteworthy:

- The first is that public information in the event of such a serious emergency needs to be broadcast in several languages, especially in multi-lingual California.
- Most lives are saved or lost during what is referred to as the "golden hour" after a chemical attack.
- Some of those providing assistance might themselves become vulnerable to contamination unless they are properly equipped.
- There will be a need to house and feed disaster workers brought in from other areas; these would certainly run into hundreds, possibly thousands.
- While some transport systems will be affected, it would be essential to keep other forms of public transport going.

Since then, the U.S. government has conducted further field exercises nationwide, including measures to counter the possible use of biological weapons by terrorist groups. This scenario, it is accepted by all of those involved in these measures, will be even more complex because biological weapons are more difficult to detect than chemical agents. Also, the effects of pathogens such as anthrax, smallpox or botulinum toxin might take several days or longer to take effect, by which time it might be too late.

A major reason for concern in the West about chemical and biological weapons proliferation has been the flurry of activity in many Third World countries to expand their own programs. The Israelis tell us that even progressive Egypt under President Hosni Mubarak has chemical and biological warfare programs, in spite of his having for decades now accepted $3 billion a year in aid handouts from the United States.

Disturbing revelations regarding the proliferation of South African chemical and biological weapons have also emerged in the United States. Some of these activities date from the Apartheid era. Other developments include Pretoria's contacts with Libya and Iran in the mid-1990s after President Nelson Mandela had taken over.

The furor has focused on how a South African scientist named Daan Goosen approached the FBI with a genetically altered strain of the pathogen that causes gas gangrene. He said that he had many other germ warfare products besides, and offered to lead U.S. authorities to the trove.

His price: $5 million and entry to America for himself and key participants together with their families, about twenty people in all. The FBI rejected the offer. Instead, Washington tipped off South African law enforcement agents who investigated Goosen several times but never charged him.

Among Apartheid-era authorities most often quoted with regard to South African biological weapons is Dr. Wouter Basson, former commander of South Africa's notorious 7th Medical Battalion. Dubbed "Doctor Death" by the media, he has always spoken candidly about his shopping sprees abroad for pathogens and related equipment, and is forthright that his original intention was to use this material "to destroy South Africa's enemies."

Of significance here is that former Apartheid-era President F.W. de Klerk scheduled all South African weapons of mass destruction—nuclear, chemical and biological—for destruction prior to the handover of government. While South Africa's six low-yield atom bombs were dismantled in conjunction with U.S. scientists and Vienna's International Atomic Energy Agency, it seems that chemical and biological weapons controls were less stringent.

This emerged during a two-and-a-half-year trial in Pretoria of Basson and other top scientists on charges of murder and fraud. Though the case ended with acquittal for all, Basson revealed that during the time that he was head of the clandestine biological and chemical weapons program, that we now know as "Project Coast," his group of scientists developed pathogens for several new diseases. Some were genetically engineered so that they would be difficult to treat.

Obviously, the Americans have serious concerns about all of these developments, including the fact that Basson and his associates tested a new kind of "stealth" anthrax that the experts say "could fool tests to detect the disease." Worse, South African scientists formerly involved with Project Coast are now either unable or unwilling to disclose who actually controls an arsenal that includes microbes, as well as bacteria that cause plague, cholera, hemorrhagic fever and a host of other diseases.

Some unsubstantiated reports maintain that this group worked on both the Ebola and Marburg fevers, two of the deadliest killers in this arsenal. What also does not help is Pretoria's close ties with Tehran.

Of interest here—in light of the offer made by Goosen to the United States—is the fact that both Basson and South Africa's new black government assured the international community that after the old political order had been displaced, all these deadly germ cocktails were destroyed. Some had been dumped at sea and still more were incinerated, Basson stated at an official inquiry.

South African officials are also having difficulty explaining why Basson—with the rank of Brigadier General—remained a serving officer in the new South African National Defence Force for some years after the white government had been ousted. Nor why he was allowed free rein—under this same government's auspices—to visit scientists involved in similar projects in Libya as well as several other countries labeled "rogue" by the U.S. State Department.

Basson is not prepared to comment what he did during several lengthy stays in Libya as a guest of Muammar Gadhaffi. Prior to that maverick country "coming in from the cold" and forswearing weapons of mass destruction in early 2004, Israel accused Libya of having established several advanced chembio warfare research installations. The Israeli report specifically mentioned the construction of an underground CW factory at Tarhunah.

More recently, Basson disclosed in a South African Broadcasting Corporation interview (prior to the U.S. invasion of Iraq) that he had visited Baghdad several times *in the mid-1990s*. He surprised listeners by telling them that he was allowed access to some of Saddam's biological warfare plants which, he admitted, were advanced.

The extent of South Africa's chembio industries during both the Apartheid and Mandela eras was recently heralded in two articles in *The Washington Post*: the first by Joby Warrick on April 20 2003, and another by Warrick and John Mintz the next day. Warrick made the point that Project Coast's legacy continues to haunt the international community.

"There are so many questions unanswered," he declared, adding that issues such as the nature and kinds of weapons made, how they were used and finally, what happened to them are all conveniently fudged. "Bacterial strains that supposedly were destroyed continue to turn up in private hands," Warrick reported.

Tehran's weapons industries have come a long way since the first days of its war with Iraq, when the Iranian Army was barely able to equip its troops with conventional weapons. Right now, a vast range of weapons are being either produced or acquired on international arms markets by the Iranian government.

The list is impressive. Iran produces the full range of infantry weapons that it needs. Its factories are pushing out a variety of wheeled and tracked armed vehicles, as well as a range of medium and long-range artillery, rocket-propelled grenades, machine guns, mortars, landmines and automatic squad weapons such as the Kalashnikov.

Among more recent hybrids is a sophisticated self-propelled anti-tank weapons system. Mounted on the Boragh armored personnel vehicle—produced by Iran's DIO or Defense Industries Organization's Shahid Kolahdooz Industrial Complex—it is a crib of the Russian tracked BMP infantry fighting vehicle. Mounted on top is a one-person turret that is able to launch Toophan long-range anti-tank guided weapons.

These ATGWs have proved most effective. One version has an eight-pound warhead that can be fired more than two miles and will penetrate a foot-and-a-half of conventional steel armor. The business end of an even larger version weighs nine pounds and will penetrate twenty-four inches of steel.

What has surprised Western weapons specialists is the excellent quality of some (but not all) Iranian war matériel: Iranian ATGWs are advanced for the normal range of weapons produced by the majority of Third World countries. Significantly, the Toophan design has similar characteristics to an anti-tank missile produced by the American company Raytheon Systems, colloquially referred to as a TOW missile. Clearly, the Iranians have become adept at reverse engineering, especially with the kind of hardware they need most. But that's not the end of it.

Some developments have involved the Iranian Navy. Tehran's defense specialists have fired a modified version of an advanced Chinese anti-ship missile dubbed the Nour. Some were launched during naval exercises that involved all three Kilo Class submarines that Iran recently acquired from Moscow.

The eight-day exercise was remarkable for its size and complexity: it involved some hundred and thirty vessels together with almost sixty aircraft. The West took a keen interest, if only because the maneuvers stretched all the way down the coast of the Gulf from the northwest border with Iraq to Bushehr in the southwest where Russia is building Iran's 1,000-megawatt nuclear reactor.

Although details of the Nour C-802 missiles are sketchy, Vice Admiral Ali Shamkhani, the Iranian defense minister and armed forces logistics minister at the time, disclosed that his country would soon begin full scale production. *Jane's Defence Weekly* reported shortly afterward that Iran had between seventy and eighty of these maritime missiles.

Interestingly, also mobilized in the largest naval exercises ever held in Iranian waters were Tehran's new miniature submarines. Known as Al Sabiha-15s, they were built and launched at the country's strategic Bandar Abbas naval base. Numbers are classified, but the tiny submersibles are a potent factor in what was, until fairly recently, a moribund Iranian Navy. With the three Russian diesel submarines, one American naval authority told *The Middle East* that Iran's maritime and strategic threat capability has "almost overnight been quadrupled."

Soon after that news became public, Washington protested to Moscow about the release of a new range of "smart" torpedoes having been sold to Iran. Capable of striking targets stealthily at enhanced distances, the Americans regard the new combination of submarines and torpedoes a challenge to U.S. hegemony in Gulf waters.

Possibly the most important recent Iranian weapons development was the unveiling of its own "manportable" ground-to-air missile. Called the Misagh-1, it looks identical to the American shoulder-fired Stinger that Washington supplied in quantity to anti-Soviet Mujahadeen fighters in Afghanistan. Many are believed to have been smuggled abroad and, it would seem, Iran—inadvertently or otherwise—ended up with some of them. By one intelligence account they were reverse engineered for domestic production.

The Iranian "Stinger" is advanced for its origins. Not only does it incorporate a "fire and forget" configuration, but Tehran claims that it has the capability to engage fixed-wing as well as helicopter targets from all angles, at altitudes of between one hundred and twelve thousand feet and at ranges of from about half a mile to three miles. The Misagh-1 has since been offered by Iran for sale on the international arms market.

For its army, Iran, with technical assistance from North Korea, has also developed a series of Fadjr unguided surface-to-surface weapons systems.

First revealed in the mid-1990s, the Fadjr—an advanced version of the Russian Katyusha—were first supplied to Hizbollah for what was termed, "Field testing against the Israeli occupation forces in South Lebanon." The Party of God is known to have had some successes with it against the IDF in Lebanon, where the weapon came mounted on a Japanese 6x6 Isuzu chassis. Among other Iranian weapons systems, the Fadjr has also been seen in quantity in Sudan's ongoing war against that country's recalcitrant black southern communities.

The latest version of the Fadjr-3, with twelve 240mm rocket tubes in two banks of six, is more advanced, mounted on a Mercedes Benz truck. The rockets have a maximum range of twenty-five miles. The larger Fadjr-5, in contrast, consists of four ten-foot tubes with, it is said, a forty-five-mile range. Providing awesome firepower, the rockets can be launched singly or in ripples, after which the tubes have to be reloaded by crane. Mobile units can be moved across country at speeds of about forty miles per hour.

Before the Israelis pulled out of southern Lebanon, Hizbollah militants were using sophisticated night vision goggles (NVGs) against IDF units. These originated in South Africa and have apparently found a widespread application among Iranian front-line units.

One question that has been raised often enough is how much involvement South Africa has had in some of these weapons development programs. Ten years ago Pretoria tried to sell tank laser sighting systems to Syria and was only stopped by threats of U.S. sanctions. Since then, very little is allowed to emerge about who sells what to who. It is perhaps pertinent that one Cape Town observer suggested that there were a few curious similarities with what was coming out of South African arms factories to what was now being produced by the mullahs.

There have been a few other developments that have caught the public eye.

Washington's Institute for Science and International Security (ISIS) recently detailed how materials found in radioactive nuclear waste can be used to make nuclear weapons.

Iraq, said ISIS, acquired a small amount of one of these materials in separated form some years before the 1991 Gulf War. Fortunately Iraqi scientists did not understand that this stuff could be used in nuclear weapons, otherwise Baghdad may have obtained enough for a nuclear explosive, especially given the weak international controls on these materials at that time.

David Albright, head of ISIS, has stated that there are two man-made elements of particular concern, neptunium 237 and americium 241—both of which are by-products of nuclear power stations. Neptunium 237 might already have been used in nuclear weapons.

"There is a strong feeling within the nuclear establishment that both America and France have actually conducted nuclear explosive experiments with neptunium 237, thus proving the suitability of this material for use in nuclear explosives," he said.

Because the separation of neptunium 237 and americium 241 was being evaluated by several countries starting in the early 1990s, Washington had no choice but to state openly that these materials could be used in nuclear weapons and that they required more domestic and international controls against misuse. Not long afterward (in response to requests from Albright and others), the U.S. Department of Energy declassified information that nuclear explosives can be made from these materials.

Neptunium and americium—produced when nuclear fuel is irradiated—are discussed in detail in a report written by Albright and ISIS staff scientist Lauren Barbour and included in a new ISIS book titled *Challenges of Fissile Material Control*. The authors maintain that the two elements have received little or no attention for half a century because only small quantities have been separated from spent power reactor fuel.

"Yet right now," say Albright and Barbour, "the world inventory of neptunium and americium is estimated to exceed eighty metric tonnes, or enough for more than two-thousand nuclear warheads." They told *Jane's Defence Weekly* that the amount is growing by about ten tons a year.

"A principal concern is that a civilian reprocessing facility or a waste processing facility anywhere in the world—and in full compliance with its safeguards obligations—could extract these two elements and they would not be subject to any sort of international inspection." In essence, Albright added, a non-weapon state such as Iran—which is known to have a covert nuclear weapons program—could accumulate significant quantities of these separated nuclear explosive materials beyond the scope of IAEA verification.

At present only plutonium, uranium-235 or material enriched in uranium 235 or 233 is required by the IAEA to be safeguarded.

To include these new categories as "special fissionable materials" by the IAEA is likely to take time. Nonetheless, the IAEA plans to increase its monitoring capacity in non-nuclear states that are party to the Nuclear Nonproliferation Treaty.

Separated neptunium is used as a target in producing plutonium 238, while tiny amounts of americium are used in smoke detectors, neutron generators and research activities. Although the information is incomplete, admits Albright, non-nuclear weapons states are believed to possess little separated neptunium or americium.

This could change, he maintains. Since the early 1990s, several key countries, including several non-nuclear weapons states, have stepped up research into the removal of these and other actinides (categories of elements that are highly radioactive) from nuclear waste. "They believe that they can make high-level waste significantly easier to dispose of if they separate actinides from fission products. They also hope to use them later as fuel in reactors. This path is an example of a process known as partitioning and transmutation of nuclear waste. Currently Japan, India, Belgium, Britain, China, France, Germany, Russia, Switzerland and the U.S. are researching these options.

"Then there is a commercial application, which could foster international trade in these materials," he said.

The Iraqi connection stems from Britain having sold Iraq two hundred milligrams of neptunium oxide in the 1980s. About a quarter of it was irradiated to produce plutonium-238, which Iraq evaluated as a material for a neutron initiator for nuclear weapons. The rest was used in reprocessing research and developing activities at the Tuwaitha Nuclear Research Center south of Baghdad.

Albright makes the point that over the years Saddam Hussein pursued many available avenues to build an atomic bomb, even taking some fanciful paths. If his scientists had known the true potential of neptunium, they might have sought out this material more aggressively. He adds that Iraq may even have succeeded in obtaining enough for a weapon while the IAEA and most suppliers were ignorant of the true dangers.

"This time we were lucky," Albright concluded, "but depending upon ignorance is too risky a strategy."

12

PASDARAN: THE ISLAMIC REPUBLICAN GUARDS CORPS

"Chemical and biological weapons are the poor man's atomic bombs and can easily be produced. We should at least consider them for our defense. Although the use of such weapons is inhuman, the war taught us that international laws are only scraps of paper."

Speaker Ali Akbar Hashemi Rafsanjani, addressing the Iranian Majlis in Tehran, 1988

There is a lethal inscrutability that surrounds the role of the Pasdaran, or as it is more commonly known in Western circles, the Islamic Republican Guards Corps (IRGC). The activities of this top-level intelligence gathering and secret service body in Iran are equated by those living in fear of persecution as equivalent to that of the old Soviet NKVD.

Those Iranian political dissidents arrested by them face a frightening set of dangers: nobody can be certain of their fate. Indeed, to be hauled in by the Pasdaran usually predicates the worst, if only because the majority of murders, assassinations, tortures, beatings, and arrests that occur in the country can be laid at the threshold of this organization. In short, its members use unbridled terror and coercion to achieve their aims.

Another distinction is that unlike the rest of Tehran's security establishment, IRGC members are answerable only to the country's Supreme Spiritual Guide, Ayatollah Ali Hoseini Khamene'i.

I got a glimpse of the way this force operated while covering Lebanon in the early 1990s. That was some years after the Israeli Defense Force had pulled back from Beirut following its invasion in 1982. I'd gone in to do something for Jane's *International Defense Review* on a Scandinavian United Nations Interim Force in Lebanon (UNIFIL) detachment ensconced in a small town perched on the slopes of Mount Hermon.

My host, the UN representative at Naqoura at the time, was a tough, no-nonsense two-packs-a-day Turkish Army veteran by the name of Timur Goskell. He delegated one of his aides to take me into the interior and we made our way along a remote mountain road leading northeast, past Nabitiye and the sprawlingly untidy Christian-dominated Marj'ayoun. We were headed in the direction of Kfair ez-Zait.

It wasn't a tough trip, except that we were in an open vehicle and it snowed. From time to time we would be stopped at a roadblock, first UN and then several that were termed "non-United Nations roadblocks." These were manned by irregular forces of what my escort referred to as Pasdaran. It was the first time I'd heard the name.

Asked to explain, he couldn't say much except that he called them "a nasty bunch . . . bastards fight like they're possessed when they have to." Apparently the Israelis weren't too pleased with them either, he intimated. As he commented later, "Nobody screwed with the Pasdaran."

So it transpired that Hizbollah, a Pasdaran offshoot, was eventually responsible for forcing the Israeli Army to vacate its much-vaunted southern Lebanese security cordon. The IDF had held on to that stretch of real estate, at most about ten miles deep, for almost two decades, and Hizbollah was thus the first Arab guerrilla force to have inflicted a defeat on the Israeli Army.

It was a significant, unheard-of achievement at the time because the insurgents had no match for the kind of air cover provided by the Israeli Air Force. It was also Jerusalem's first real military reversal. The event continues to be hailed throughout the Islamic world, and today, almost a decade later, Hizbollah leaders are accorded what amounts to almost head-of-state status whenever they visit other Arab capitals.

What soon became clear during my UNIFIL visit was that most Pasdaran militants were Iranian nationals. Also, their presence was more commonplace in this much-disputed part of the country than those Hizbollah cadres that eventually replaced them. In Lebanon, it eventually became the job of the Pasdaran to create an irregular army of ethnic Shi'ite fighters who, like the much-feared Hezbollahi back home, ended up calling themselves Hizbollah or, literally translated, The Party of God.

For this reason the Hizbollah military wing (as opposed to the legitimate Hizbollah political party that is represented in Parliament in Beirut in 2004) is regarded by those who have examined their origins, loyalties, methodology and even the weapons that they use, as a clone of their Iranian cousins.

It was interesting that for all the mystery that surrounded their activities, among those members of this Iranian guerrilla group that were active in Lebanon when I was there, not one of them minded being referred to as Pasdaran. It was only afterward, once they had "vanished into the wadis" and allowed Hizbollah to get on with the job of creating a revolutionary Islamic force, that they retreated from public view. Question one of the local insurgents today about Pasdaran and he's likely to give you a look reserved for the village idiot. He knows very well of course, but then duplicity is what it's all about in the vagaries of Arab politics.

Truth is, the Pasdaran is still out there and remains extremely active throughout most parts of Lebanon. Its headquarters is to be found in the Beqá Valley, at Baalbek, and in hideouts adjacent to the Cheba'a Farms where the IDF, notwithstanding being regularly pounded by Katyushas, has stayed put.

But you won't find anybody in Lebanon acknowledging it. It is also ironic that some of Lebanon's best wine growing areas are to be found around Baalbek where local Imams absolutely prohibit the use of alcohol.

As for present and future roles of the IRGC, Paula deSutter gets close to the nub of the long-term implications in her thesis for Washington's National Defense University.[1] She informs us that the Islamic Revolutionary Guard Corps—created in the early days of Tehran's revolution—has the lead in Iran for the production and employment of weapons of mass destruction as well as their means of delivery.

The United States, she suggests, "would certainly want to understand the Guard from an operational perspective in order to deter NBC use, but the organization is far more critical at the strategic level than any other entity." If Washington were able to deter the Guard, she argues, it would be far better able to deter Iran.

As deSutter points out, Iran's position on chemical and other weapons of mass destruction weapons (in the early post-revolutionary period) was that they were essentially contrary to the tenets of Islam. During the eight-year with Iraq however, as Iraqi chemical weapons use became more frequent and the international community failed to respond, Tehran reversed this rationale. At one stage the Iranian army even used chemical artillery rounds captured from Iraq.

As the war continued, she tells us, Iran started producing its own chemical weapons and it wasn't long before it had embarked on the production of biological weapons. By then, too, as the Iranian government admitted in late 2003, it had begun the pursuit of a nuclear weapon.

The ideological breakthrough seemed to come in September 1987, when the then Majlis Speaker Rafsanjani spoke to a group of "Personnel of the Chemical, Biological, and Radioactive Warfare Units of the Islamic Revolutionary Guards Corps." He stated that "Moslems should equip themselves with a deterrent weapon to counter the arsenal used by world blasphemy against them," and vowed, "We declare that if we are invaded in any way, we will counter them the same way as ordered by the Koran."

A year later Rafsanjani made his historic speech when he told the Majlis that "Chemical and biological weapons are the poor man's atomic bombs and can easily be produced."

He went on: "We should at least consider them for our defense. Although the use of such weapons is inhuman, the war taught us that international laws are only scraps of paper." After becoming president, Rafsanjani went even further: "We should fully equip ourselves in the defensive and offensive use of chemical, bacteriological and radiological weapons." It was not by chance that the IRGC was earmarked to be the instrument.

According to deSutter: "Significantly, this relative openness, if not outright pride regarding NBC programs, changed abruptly in the aftermath of Desert Storm." Until UNSCOM dismantlement operations in Iraq began to produce results and showed the mullahs that the possession of such weapons could have burdensome international consequences, Tehran made public references to its pursuit of NBC capabilities. "After that, its statements, particularly those in English rather than Farsi, generally asserted that Iran abhorred such weapons and, instead, embraced arms control."

In 1994, for example, she elucidates, an English language newspaper published an interview with IRGC Commander Rezai in which he scoffed at reports that Iran was pursuing nuclear weapons, arguing on military grounds that Iran did not want nuclear weapons: "Political logic, morality, our own culture and above all the situation in today's world does not allow us to have such deadly weapons. Of course, we are for traditional weapons and that too just for self-defense," he concluded.

For all that, suggests deSutter, the decision to develop WMD came reluctantly. In 1993, for example, Ayatollah Khamene'i told a ceremony for the air, land, and sea units of the IRGC, "The use of science in the service of force and deception is a bitter truth."

Then, on October 4, 1996, the First Deputy Speaker of the Assembly of Experts was quoted as saying: "How many times have I said this to you, that any weapon that kills human beings is banned by Islam, mass destruction weapons in particular. Initially it has banned them. However, if someone has embarked on this banned activity and produced weapons, it is incumbent upon you to make more superior ones."

A lot of this might be regarded as bluster, but a good deal was based on strict Shi'ite precepts. As Paula deSutter maintains, "Iran is a religious state whose political leadership is guided by religious leaders who emphasize the most violent aspects of its religious tradition."

She goes on: "The Iranian Shi'ite interpretations of Islam appear to enable a declaration of religious war, or *jihad*. The religious fervor of the leadership and the majority of the population raises the specter of 'true believers' who would die for the cause and gain paradise and its virgins. The political, religious, and military leadership has consequently fostered a cult of martyrdom and death that could be used to strengthen its ability to conduct war and to accept casualties. While it appears that there is a growing gap between the population and the leadership, and while their emphasis on martyrdom may not succeed, Iran's leadership may be prepared to take risks and to accept casualties at levels other modern states would deem unacceptable."[2]

There was good reason for Tehran's leaders to establish the Iranian Revolutionary Guard Corps (IRGC), or, in Farsi, the *Pasdaran-e Inqilab*. (Some prefer the movement's original title: Qods Force—*Qods* or more phonetically Quds, being Jerusalem in Arabic and a word that can be spotted on just about every Palestinian poster in the Middle East.)

While the revolutionary constitution of Iran originally entrusted the traditional military with guarding Iran's territorial integrity and political independence, it was Ayatollah Khomeini who entrusted the Pasdaran with the responsibility of guarding the Revolution itself. Established under a decree issued by the Supreme Spiritual Guide in May 1979, the Pasdaran was intended to guard the Revolution and, as it was phrased, "To assist the ruling clerics in the day-to-day enforcement of the government's Islamic codes and morality."

It was Khomeini's view that his revolution needed to rely on a force of his own making rather than borrow the previous regime's tainted units. By 1986 the Pasdaran consisted of three hundred and fifty thousand personnel organized into battalion-size units that operated either independently or with units of the regular armed forces. By then it had acquired small naval and air elements. A decade later the IRGC's ground and naval forces were reported to number one hundred thousand and twenty thousand respectively.

The Federation of American Scientists[3] puts out a very comprehensive study on the Pasdaran and its origins. It states that in bringing such an organization to fruition, the primacy of state interest over revolutionary ideology was reflected in the Khomeini regime's treatment of the military.

"Reports to the contrary notwithstanding, Khomeini never went so far as to totally eliminate imperial Iran's regular armed forces that served under the Shah. Certainly, key military personnel identified with the deposed leader were arrested, tried, and executed, many of them summarily. But the purges were limited to high-profile military and political figures rather than the mass of foot soldiers, and had a clear purpose: to eliminate Pahlavi loyalists." As a means of countering the threat posed either by leftist guerrillas or officers suspected of continued loyalty to the Shah, Khomeini created his "Guardians of the Revolution" and thus, the IRGC.

Apart from enforcing Islamic codes and morality of Tehran's new government, there were other more important, reasons for establishing the Pasdaran. The revolution needed to rely on a force of its own rather than borrowing the previous regime's units, many of which remained suspect for some years. As one of the first revolutionary institutions, the Corps helped legitimize the revolution. It gave the new regime an armed basis of support.

Moreover, the establishment of the Pasdaran served notice to both the population and the regular armed forces that Ayatollah Khomeini's regime was quickly developing its own enforcement body. The IRGC—along with its political counterpart, the Crusade for Reconstruction—thus brought a new order to Iran. In time, as the Federation of American Scientists report states, the Pasdaran would rival the police and the judiciary in terms of its functions. It would even challenge the performance of the regular armed forces on the battlefield, as it did during the eight-year war with Iraq.

The report makes the important point that since 1979, the Pasdaran has undergone fundamental changes in mission and function. Some of these demands are reflected in the government's exclusive reliance on the Pasdaran to carry out sensitive missions. Others indicate personal ambitions of certain Pasdaran leaders. It was not surprising therefore that the IRGC, with its own separate ministry, evolved into one of the most powerful organizations in the entire Middle East.

"Not only did it function as an intelligence organization, both within and outside the country, but it also exerted considerable influence on government policies. In addition to its inherent political strength, the Pasdaran during the course of several years became a formidable military instrument for defending the Revolution and Islamic Iran." More recently, the Pasdaran has turned to subterfuge and its activities have taken it abroad on a variety of missions.

The Israeli DEBKA-Net-weekly regularly highlights the movement's activities, such as the raid on May 21, 2003 when Israeli naval commandos intercepted an Egyptian boat that had made its way from Alexandria to Lebanese waters, collected Hizbollah passengers and lethal cargo and was heading for Gaza. Quoting Israeli military and political sources, the ship, its cargo and crew had been brought together by the Pasdaran. The haul included Lebanese Hizbollah elements as well as close advisers of Yasser Arafat who had originally set out for Iran from his Ramallah headquarters.

DEBKA: "This wasn't a repeat of the *Karine-A* arms smuggling venture (where the IRGC had earlier been caught shipping a load of weapons to the Palestinian Authority in January 2001) but some of the features were similar.

"Rather, its purpose this time was to upgrade the terrorist capabilities of Arafat's combined force of Fatah together with its suicide arm, the al-Aqsa Martyrs Brigades, Hamas and Jihad Islami. Found onboard the captured weapons was a potent new explosive.

"Also on the ship was Hizbollah's chief bomb expert, Hamad Amara, on loan from the Party of God with samples of the tank-busting super-powerful explosive that he had developed, together with a course of instruction in its application among Arafat's partisans and allies in the Gaza Strip. His capture was significant for Israel after a string of Palestinian suicide attacks had claimed a dozen lives. DEBKA informs us that it was also a painful setback for the Lebanese terror group."

This was only one of the occasions when the IRGC operated abroad. An even more devastating terrorism charge could be laid on Iran's doorstep if intelligence reports linking Iran to al-Qaeda are confirmed. A report by Kenneth Timmerman, senior writer at the U.S. publication *Insight*, writes of new links between top Iranian intelligence officials and the al-Qaeda leadership. These suggest direct Iranian government involvement in the destruction of the Twin Towers and other airborne attacks on the U.S. mainland. Documents and information provided by an Iranian defector, if confirmed as authentic, could ultimately open a new front in the war on terror. Certainly, Washington has carefully examined the evidence. Until now, nothing has been released.

The defector, Hamid Reza Zakeri, said that he worked in the intelligence office of Supreme Leader Ali Khamene'i, and personally handled security at two meetings in Iran between top al-Qaeda operatives and Iranian officials only months before September 11. Zakeri spoke to *Insight* from an unidentified location about these links, probably a CIA safe house in the Washington area. His information dovetailed with an earlier report on Tehran's ties with al-Qaeda, produced by Washington's Defense Intelligence Agency that the magazine first revealed in November 2001 under the heading "Iran Cosponsors al-Qaeda Terrorism."

Zakeri was able to support his account of the meetings between al-Qaeda and Iran with a document signed by Hojjatoleslam Ali Akbar Nateq-Nouri, of the country's Ministry of Information and Security (MOIS) and, again, answerable directly to Khamene'i.

Dated May 14, 2001, the letter carried instructions from Khamene'i to MOIS regarding relations with al-Qaeda. In it, Nateq-Nouri quoted the Supreme Leader as ordering the ministry to "strike at [America's] economic structure, its reputation—and its internal peace and security." Above all, said the Guide, "We should be very careful and very clever, so as not to leave behind any evidence that could negatively impact our future standing or policies."

In closing, Nateq-Nouri instructed his counterpart at MOIS, Hojjatoleslam Mustafa Pourghanad, to work to "improve our plans, especially in coordination with fighters of al-Qaeda and Hizbollah to find one objective that is beneficial to both sides." Significantly he added, "The Leader mentioned that we should limit our relations with al-Qaeda to just two people, as before—Imad Mugniyah and Ayman al-Zawahiri—and deal only with them."

The letter from Nateq-Nouri was written days after the second of two top-level meetings between an al-Qaeda delegation and the Iranian leadership, Zakeri told *Insight*. The first meeting took place in January 2001, when top Osama bin Laden deputy al-Zawahiri traveled to Iran from Afghanistan for a four-day get-together, accompanied by almost thirty other al-Qaeda leaders.

"Zawahiri informed my boss, Mustafa Hadadian, that they were planning a 'major operation' against the United States and Israel," Zakeri told the magazine. That meeting was held at a special mountain guest house near the town of Varamin outside Tehran. Zakeri claimed that he handled security for the meeting.

According to Zakeri, he did not speak with the Arabs who attended, but based his account on what he was told by his boss and his colleagues in Iranian intelligence.

"After the event, twelve of those involved stayed on in Iran," he told Timmerman. They were talking about their "plans for the future," and that they had the "same enemy" as the Iranians. They declared that they were trying to build up one movement to cooperate together, and were asking Iran for operational support, equipment and money-laundering help in Dubai, as well as assistance with travel documents to help them travel from Iran to Europe.

Ayman al-Zawahiri told his boss that al-Qaeda was "very soon" going to launch a major operation against the United States. Zakeri said that Nateq-Nouri, a former speaker of the Iranian parliament and top aide to Khamene'i, led the Iranian delegation and was assisted by Ali Akbar Parvaresh, the former education minister cited in the AIMA bombing case.

Parvaresh was apparently a member of Section 43, the ultra-secret planning unit of the Iranian intelligence ministry, Zakeri explained. It was Timmerman's view that U.S. intelligence officials who regularly tracked events in Iran, confirmed the role of Parvaresh and of Section 43 in planning terrorist operations.

Talks with al-Zawahiri apparently went so well that bin Laden dispatched his eldest son, Saad bin Laden, on a return trip to Tehran exactly four months and seven days before September 11, according to Zakeri. The younger bin Laden was flown from the Tayebat border crossing with Afghanistan to the Damavand air base outside Tehran.

"He came with three other people," Zakeri said. "They were not introduced to me and they spoke Arabic amongst themselves. But Saad spoke good English." Zakeri says he stayed in Iran for three weeks but held just one official meeting, which took place at three in the morning at the late Ayatollah Khomeini's former meeting house in Jamaran, on the slopes of the Elburz Mountains in Tehran's northern suburbs.

Present were all five members of the Iranian Leadership Council, Zakeri stated: Khamene'i himself, former president Hashemi Rafsanjani, and the Ayatollahs Mohammad Yazdi, Mahdavi Kani and Ali Meshkini.

It was at that assembly on May 4, 2001, according to Zakeri, that final plans for the attack on the U.S. mainland were made.

Shortly afterward, he recalled seeing a striking exhibit in the entry hall to the main headquarters of the MOIS in Tehran. "It was a model of the World Trade Center, the White House, the Pentagon and Camp David," he told the Americans. "From the ceiling, a missile was suspended, as if to strike the buildings. 'Death to America' was written on its side in Arabic, not Farsi."

Zakeri maintained that the intelligence ministry frequently displayed photographs of Iranian dissidents that it planned to assassinate in the same entry hall. It also was used as a prayer room and amphitheater. "Everyone saw it. And after 9/11, everybody understood what it meant," he said.

Timmerman goes on: As a trusted security official, Zakeri held a diplomatic passport with permanent visas, allowing him to move in and out of the country at will. He also told *Insight* that he traveled to Baku, Azerbaijan, where he met with officials at the U.S. Embassy on July 26, 2001, including the CIA station chief. "I warned them that something big was going to happen on Sept. 10. I didn't know what it was, we argued and I left. The CIA said they didn't want to work with me," Zakeri said.

Since then, an American intelligence official has categorically denied that Zakeri delivered such a warning. "We have no record that he made such a claim. He is a fabricator of monumental proportion," he told Timmerman, but did not deny that the meeting had actually taken place.

A spokesman for the State Department's Office of Counterterrorism, Joe Reap, referred *Insight*'s inquiries about Zakeri's July 26 warning to the Joint Intelligence Committee in Congress investigating the World Trade Center attacks. "You're asking me to reveal intelligence information," Reap said testily. "I'm not going to do that."

There is good reason for the IRGC to involve itself abroad, as Paula deSutter spells out in her thesis. The Iranian revolution was portrayed by Ayatollah Khomeini as being only the first step "in a wider Islamic revolution," she declares.

The 1979 Iranian Constitution included a preambular passage stating that the Iranian army "will be responsible not only for safe-guarding the borders, but also for accomplishing an ideological mission, that is, the Jihad for the sake of God, as well as for struggling to open the way for the sovereignty of the Word of God throughout the world." This, she states, is the mission adopted by the IRGC.

Thus, one of the IRGC's primary missions remains that of exporting the Islamic revolution outside Iran: "Foremost among the responsibilities stemming from its self-proclaimed status as pathfinder and model is solidarity with oppressed Muslims everywhere. This is a core value of the revolution rather than a vital security interest, but it is an important part of Islamic Iran's sense of legitimacy and one of the few areas in which the regime can claim to be principled and unique."

It must be concluded then that this same objective has been the basis for support of terrorist groups outside Iran, including Hizbollah in southern Lebanon. It is also the thinking behind Iranian intrusions into the internal politics of other states, very much as is going on right now in Iraq. Such actions could assist Iran in instituting opposition groups or even successor leadership groups in neighboring states that would draw their own legitimacy from the Iranian revolution.

The foreign operations by the IRGC, which also encompass the activities of Islamic Jihad, are usually carried out through what Ms. deSutter refers to as the Committee on Foreign Intelligence Abroad. Then there is the Committee on Implementation of Actions Abroad. Ideally then, with conditions in Iraq having gone sour, nothing would delight Tehran more than having as its surrogate a majority Shi'ite government in Baghdad. In one stroke, that would remove an ancient and traditional enemy, and in its place install a malleable, pro-Iranian government.

As with agents of Iran's Ministry of Intelligence, Pasdaran personnel operate through front companies and non-governmental organizations, employees or officials of trading companies, banks, cultural centers, or as representatives of welfare organizations such as the Foundation of the Oppressed and Dispossessed (*Bonyade-e- Mostafazan*), or the Martyrs Foundation.

It is the *Qods* (Jerusalem) Force of the Guard Corps that is responsible for a multiplicity of extraterritorial operations, including terrorist operations. A primary focus for this element is the training of Islamic fundamentalist terrorist groups. Currently, it conducts such work throughout Iran, in Lebanon (Beqá) and in the Sudan.

The Qods Force is also responsible for gathering information required for targeting and attack planning, and has contacts with underground movements throughout the Gulf region. As has already been noted, Pasdaran members are assigned to Iranian diplomatic missions, where, in the course of routine intelligence activities they are known to monitor dissidents. This influence has been particularly visible in Kuwait, Bahrain, and the United Arab Emirates.

The deSutter thesis highlights the fact that the largest branch of Pasdaran foreign operations consists of approximately twelve thousand Arabic speaking Iranians, Afghans, Iraqis, and Lebanese Shi'ites, as well as North Africans who trained in Iran or received training in Afghanistan during the years of hostilities.

The second largest foreign operations linked to the Pasdaran relate to the Kurds (and, in particular, Iraqi Kurds), while the third largest relates to the Kashmiris, the Balouchis and the Afghans. Apart from Lebanon, the Pasdaran has also supported the establishment of Hizballah branches in Iraqi Kurdistan, Jordan and Palestine as well as the Islamic Jihad in a number of other Moslem countries including Egypt, Turkey and Chechnya as well as in Caucasia.

It is not only basic terror in which these offshoots are involved. Lebanon's Hizbollah, for instance, has been implicated in the counterfeiting of U.S. dollars and European currencies, both to finance its operations and to disrupt Western economies by impairing international trade and tourism.

For some time it ran the biggest car smuggling operation in the Northern Hemisphere, something about which I have personal experience. While with UNIFIL at Naqoura, it was sometimes worth my while to visit the Biblical port city of Tyre, about thirty miles up the coast. There, most evenings, you could spot smuggling gangs on the waterfront offering up-to-date versions of the most modern German, French and Italian cars for sale. I was once tempted to take an almost new Mercedes 500 with Swiss plates, going for about US$10,000 with no questions asked.

Curiously, while the "Great Satan" is vociferously drubbed by Hizbollah's Imams—especially at mosque on Fridays—the currency of choice throughout the region in such matters (as with the drug trade out of the Beqá Valley) is invariably the American greenback, though the Euro is gradually becoming popular.

Within Iran's military establishment, it is the Iranian Navy that is the branch of service most closely tied to the IRGC. By all accounts, says deSutter, it is the military force seen by Iran as spearheading Iran's war with the United States:

As the situation in the Gulf continues to deteriorate, Iran is strengthening its naval defenses in the region. In addition to the regular Navy, the newly formed naval units of the Revolutionary Guards have been active. She recalls the words of Mohsen Rezai, a senior commander of the Revolutionary Guards, who operated out of Bandar Abbas, saying that his people were not only capable of attacking U.S. warships, but could also capture some of them.

"While the Pasdaran has its own naval forces, these have increasingly merged with the regular navy." It was the IRGC navy that "in contradiction to the wishes of the political leaders in Tehran, may have been responsible for mining the Gulf shipping lanes during the Iran–Iraq War of the 1980s."

It is deSutter's view—backed by recent intelligence disclosures in Washington—that the IRGC is the primary advocate within Iran for the funding of terrorist groups. The organization places tremendous emphasis on ideological correctness. Its approach during the Iran–Iraq war, she explains, quoting a Tehran cleric, was that a *"maktab* (ideologically pure) army is better than a victorious one."

Thus, "Ideological correctness and commitment to the revolution led in earlier years to its undertaking numerous high-risk military operations 'rich in ideological content but militarily ill advised and potentially detrimental to the Guards' own military posture and prestige.'

"This connection to the Islamic revolution defines and orients the IRGC and could lead it to take risks that more traditional and conservative military institutions would not." The IRGC retains ideological loyalty to Ayatollah Khomeini, who defined the purposes of the revolution and the IRGC with these words: "Our war is one of ideology and does not recognize borders or geography. We must ensure the vast mobilization of the soldiers of Islam around the world in our ideological war."

"God willing, the great Iranian nation, through its material and moral support for the revolution, will compensate for the hardships of war with the sweetness of the defeat of God's enemies in the world. What is sweeter than the fact that the great Iranian nation has struck the United States on the head like lightening?"

The IRGC's self-defined role as defender of the revolution also appears to require it to oppose any hint of liberalization within Iran.

IRGC leader General Mohsen Rezai said in April 1996, while urging voters to vote conservatively, "The fate of the Islamic Revolution would be dependent on the results of the cultural and political war of Hizbollah with liberals in Iran."

He is on record as having pointed out that liberalism was "a cancerous tumor that was growing up in parts of the country without having ever been seriously grappled with by the authorities." Linking the problem to the continued need to fight the West, he added, "The *velayat-e-faqih* (supreme religious Jurisprudent) and the *ulema* (the religious faithful) were the number one target of Washington in its fight with the Islamic revolution."

Other issues to emerge here include the fact that the IRGC leadership also believes that Islam, and in particular its faith in the value of martyrdom, actually empowers Iran in its fight against America. IRGC Commander Rezai said it clearly in June 1996: "The U.S. is unable to grasp the faith and spiritual power of the forces of Islam and is quite helpless against the martyrdom-seeking spirit of the Islamic combatants."

Michael Eisenstadt makes an interesting observation about the Pasdaran in his report, *Iranian Military Power*.[4] By establishing another military entity in parallel with the Iranian Army, or as Eisenstadt puts it, "The division of the armed forces into two competing entities—the regular military and the IRGC, and the involvement of the latter in internal security and exporting Iran's Islamic revolution—have been major obstacles to creating a modern and effective military."

While recent developments have overtaken events, and observers now regard the Iranian defense structure as a good deal more effective than previously believed, Eisenstadt suggested that this organizational division initially reflected divergent approaches to modern warfare. This could still be the case, if only from an ideological point of view.

According to Eisenstadt, "The regular military tended to embrace a more conventional approach to war, with a balanced emphasis on hardware, technology and the human component. By contrast, the IRGC elevated the human factor above all others in the belief that faith, ideological commitment and morale would be sufficient to bring victory." As he points out, the latter approach ultimately came to dominate Iranian thinking during the Iran-Iraq and Gulf Wars.

Then in August 1995, the Supreme Guide Khamene'i—who is also the country's commander-in-chief of the armed forces—ordered the IRGC to be reduced in size and reorganized as a "rapid deployment force" to defend the country's politically-threatened frontiers. Its internal security function was transferred to the Basij, who until then were a poorly trained civilian militia whose capabilities, equipment and training have since been substantially improved.

What it comes down to, looking at the broader canvas, is that the IRGC is a versatile, committed and relatively efficient mobile force. In Western terminology, and on a larger scale, the IRGC can be compared to a "fire force" that numbers several hundred thousand well-trained operators, with, incidentally, quite a few women within its ranks. Moreover, all or some of its constituent parts can be mustered anywhere, at any time.

The Pasdaran also tends to be more virulently anti-U.S. than the rest of the leadership. It might also be willing and able to act independently of the political or even religious leadership of Iran.

There are other indicators that the Pasdaran is more virulently anti-Western than the rest of the Iranian leadership.

In May 1995, the then-Iranian President Rafsanjani responded to the U.S. embargo on Iran with assertions of its ineffectiveness: "In a world which has pressing need for energy resources, Iran cannot be shut out of world markets."

The head of the IRGC, General Rezai, however, called upon his forces to prepare for conflict: "A military confrontation with the U.S. is inevitable and Iranian forces must be ready for war." Iran then held military maneuvers that Rezai said were in preparation for war.

In response to a question of whether Rezai's words and the exercise meant that the next armed conflict in the Gulf would take place between Iranian and American troops, Iranian Foreign Minister Ali Akbar Velayati said: "There is absolutely no reason for concern, no matter what Rezai has said." Consequently, the political Iranian approach was far different from that of the IRGC. In fact, the Foreign

Ministry actually sought to downplay Rezai's statements, contradicting him in public. No change in the IRGC maneuvers or military acquisitions was evident after this exchange.

Other evidence of IRGC intransigence and ideological zeal exist, and Kenneth Katzman in his dissertations, noted that the Corps, while not openly defying civilian authority or acting to formulate major military, internal security, or external revolutionary policies in contravention of the wishes of the civilian leadership, had taken a lead role.

"It can be argued that the IRGC was able to drive most aspects of war strategy throughout the conflict, and that, without necessarily countermanding specific orders, it undertook hard-line actions and operations that sometimes conflicted with the goals of its civilian superiors," he stated.

We have already seen that by the end of the Iran–Iraq war, the IRGC was directing thirty-seven secret weapons development projects. It was also working closely with another revolutionary entity that acted as its corps of engineers—the "Construction Jihad" or "Crusade for Reconstruction."

In addition to setting up defensive emplacements and other infrastructure for tactical operations, it was also charged with developing Iran's indigenous military production capabilities to circumvent that country's international arms embargo, including the production of material for its NBC and missile programs.

As long ago as April 1986, the IRGC Minister announced that the armament industries of the Pasdaran had made notable progress in the missile, aircraft, biological, chemical and nuclear fields, as well as in construction of engineering equipment, such as a variety of portable bridges, mortar launchers, and rocket-propelled grenades.

In addition, the IRGC role is reflected in the fact that the Pasdaran Commander Rezai led the Iranian side in 1994 talks with North Korea on arms cooperation. The North Korean delegation, headed by Air Force Commander General Cho Myong-nok, consisted of twenty-eight "scientists, technicians, and officers." These talks were reportedly extended to include efforts for the development of new weapons systems, including missiles such as the No Dong.

DOMESTIC OPERATIONS

The Pasdaran has established its own intelligence branch to monitor the regime's domestic adversaries and to participate in their arrests and trials. Khomeini originally implied Pasdaran involvement in intelligence when he congratulated the IRGC on the arrest of several Iranian Tudeh (Communist) leaders. In 1988 almost a million Basij, under direct Pasdaran command, were mobilized.

Some Basij perform the role of "morals police" and monitor the activities of citizens. Typically, they harass or arrest women whose clothing does not adequately cover their hair and all open skin surfaces of the body except hands and face. Taliban-style, they also go after women who wear makeup. During the year ending in June 1995, they reportedly "notified more than nine hundred thousand people verbally and issued three hundred and seventy thousand written notices against 'social corruption' and arrested almost one hundred thousand people." In taking action against what are termed criminal elements, the Basij broke up more than five hundred "corrupt gangs," arresting their twenty-five hundred members as well as seizing eighty-six thousand "indecent" videocassettes and photographs.

An ancillary force is the Ashura Brigades, reportedly created in 1993 after anti-government riots erupted in various Iranian cities. It consists of seventeen thousand Islamic militia men and women. The Ashura Brigades are reportedly composed of elements of the Revolutionary Guards and the Basij volunteer militia.

It is worth remembering, though, that even in Iran not everything goes according to plan. In August 1994, some Pasdaran units that were rushed to quell riots in the city of Ghazvin west of Tehran refused orders from the Interior Minister to intervene in clashes that left more than thirty people dead. There were another four hundred wounded and over a thousand people arrested. Subsequently, senior officers in the army, air force and the usually loyal IRGC declared that they would no longer order their troops into battle to quell civil disorder.

A Pasdaran commander was among four senior army officers who are said to have sent a letter to the country's political leadership, warning the clerical rulers against "using the armed forces to crush civilian unrest and internal conflicts." A communiqué sent to Ayatollah Ali Khamene'i stated, "The role of the country's armed forces is to defend its borders and to repel foreign enemies from its soil, not to control the internal situation or to strengthen one political faction above another." They are said to have then recommended the use of Basij volunteers for this purpose.

In a move believed to indicate a shift in the trust of the ruling clerics from the Pasdaran to the Basij volunteer force, on April 17, 1995, Supreme Guide Khamene'i reportedly promoted a civilian, veterinary surgeon Hassan Firuzabadi, to the rank of full general, placing him above both Brigadier General Mohsen Rezai, commander-in-chief of the Pasdaran, and Brigadier General Ali Shahbazi of the regular armed forces. According to Eisenstadt, General Firuzabadi had no military training but was someone who had been close to Khamene'i in the past.

13
WHAT'S NEXT?

"Caught publicly in lie after lie by the International Atomic Energy Agency, Iran continues to react to exposure by dragging its feet, reneging on commitments made to the IAEA and European governments last autumn, and temporarily obstructing the work of IAEA inspectors."
Assistant Secretary of State Paula deSutter, at the Preparatory Committee meeting for the 2005 Nuclear Nonproliferation Treaty Review Conference: April 30, 2004

"The United States is least authoritative to talk about others' compliance with the NPT provisions."
Iran's Deputy Foreign Minister for Legal and International Affairs, Gholam Ali Khoshroo, at the NPT PrepCom, April 27, 2004

Almost overnight, it would seem, Iran's nuclear aspirations have become an issue that is not only of immediate concern to the people of many countries both east and west of Suez, but is also hugely controversial. Barely a day goes by without an update appearing in print about Tehran's weapons of mass destruction programs. What is clear to all is that Iran and its people stand at the crossroads of their ultimate destiny: the outcome, if not properly handled, could prove to be cataclysmic.

That the Persian religious hierarchy is pursuing a robust nuclear weapons option is no longer in doubt. What remains obscure is what the mullahs propose to do with the bomb once they've got it.

The imponderables are multitudinous, if only because Iran has manifestly demonstrated extremist tendencies, not only in its hard-line domestic policies but also in its efforts to influence other nations.

Teheran's support for such subversives as al-Qaeda, Hamas, Islamic Jihad and even Hizbollah, despite its dozen or so perfectly legal seats in the Lebanese Parliament, is just shy of blatant. It is sparing no effort to set up terrorist and subversive networks among Iraq's Shi'ites. Even as I write, the Iraqi dissident Moqtada al-Sadr takes his orders from Iranian agents who have infiltrated increasingly across the Euphrates. He could never have achieved what he has against preponderant Coalition forces had he not been clandestinely supported by Tehran. There is adequate evidence that almost all of this succor has come from Iran's Pasdaran.

In such matters, Iran is certainly not another India, a responsible and compliant nation with regard to most of the obligations and disciplines linked to the handling and control of nuclear weapons. Nor is it a Pakistani clone, a state that we're told is now acting more responsibly in safeguarding those selfsame secrets. At least Islamabad has stopped selling them, or so the phlegmatic Pakistani President General Pervez Musharraf would like us to believe.

A nuclear Iran—a multi-layered theocracy equipped with atom bombs—would be a very different kind of creature. It is a society where, to many of the spiritually committed, pain, whether physical, spiritual or intellectual, is a solvent, almost a decoration. Strategically, to quote one knowledgeable wag, Iran with the bomb would probably be akin to a tenth-level sphincter crisis. Certainly, should that happen, Tehran's new nuclear order will forever alter the dynamics of a region almost as large as Western Europe. And it is not only America that is worried.

Almost a decade-a-half ago, the Israeli publication Kol Yisrael told us in an interview with the then Israeli Air Force Major General Herzl Bodinger that a nuclear-equipped Iran could only result in war. He warned that if his country was to receive a report that "any country in the region is getting close to achieving a nuclear capability" and if efforts to prevent that eventuality by political means fail, then it may "consider an attack" on the facilities. There was no doubt about the country in his sights on June 15, 1992. Looking at the broader picture, very little has changed.

Things haven't altered very much inside Iran either. With a protracted history of international terrorism that goes back decades, and demonstrably holding very little regard for international legal or diplomatic norms, the result is that there are others who view what is going on along the eastern fringes of the Gulf with trepidation. This group includes the entire Arab community, including Kuwait, the new Iraqi political dispensation, Bahrain, Jordan, Egypt, Oman—and especially the Saudis.

Remember too that the Persians are very different from their neighbors. Though Islamic, they have always regarded their Arab cousins as inferior and, as they like to say, without the proud tradition of great cultures (even though Pharonic influences along the Nile pre-date Persopolis and its Achaemenid culture by several thousand years).

Iranians differ in other respects as well. In the modern period it was Tehran's zealots that sent to their deaths tens of thousands of combatants—many of them still in their early teens—in desperate bids to clear paths through Iraqi minefields. They used these human waves with total disregard for the consequences, even though it soon became evident that the results were disastrous. Since then, those debacles did not deter Iran's leaders from warning that the same thing could happen should their country again come under attack. And it probably will, should America try to invade Iran, as some members of the Pentagon neoconservative cabal have suggested it should.

It is curious that in discussions with foreigners, the leaders of the Islamic Republic like to refer to their present-day machinations as "fair and just before the all-seeing eyes of Allah." Across the political spectrum the Iranians have always argued that the purpose of their pursuit is justified on the basis that they needed nuclear weapons to counter Israel's arsenal.

These fears were further heightened in August 2004 when Iran's foreign minister, Kamal Kharazi, declared that his country had "a legitimate right" to enrich uranium, the most sensitive part of the nuclear fuel cycle that Tehran is now under strong pressure from both the East and the West to abandon. He went on, according to the Islamic Republic News Agency: "We will never allow the enemy to trample upon our legitimate rights enshrined in the international conventions."

There is nothing subtle, much less lucidly polished here—neither in politics nor in terms of any kind of linking ethics.

In spite of a bitter and bloody eight-year war with Iraq that left up to a million combatants dead, coupled to retrogressive social, political and economic policies instituted by the all-beloved Sayyid Ayatollah Ruhollah Khomeini on his return from exile, the Iranians have come far from the heady days of toppling Shah Reza Pavlavi. On the academic side, much was explained in a recent report titled "Schooling Iran's Atom Squad" in an edition of the *Bulletin of the Atomic Scientists*.[1]

The authors, Jack Boureston and Charles D. Ferguson, made the point that Tehran had "taken care to build its nuclear program around indigenous capabilities, including new universities where a new generation of science students is training." During the renewal of the Iranian nuclear program in the mid-1980s, they pointed out, Iran sent between fifteen and eighteen thousand students abroad for nuclear-related training. "Also, at this time, the Sharif University of Technology was established for the indigenous education of physical scientists and engineers. Much of its curriculum today is applicable to nuclear power or weapons programs," they maintained.

By then Iran was also posting advertisements in foreign editions of the *Kayhan*, the Iranian newspaper, inviting expatriate Iranian nuclear scientists to participate in a March, 1986 technical conference. Thirty months later, President Ali Akbar Rafsanjani appealed for Iranian scientists living in exile to return home. U.S. intelligence sources noted that several prominent Iranian nuclear physicists heeded the call, including Feredun Fesharaki, the man suspected of having directed the Shah's secret nuclear weapons program.

Concurrently, Rafsanjani established a special task force, the name of which might be translated as "Absorbing the Brightest." Meanwhile, a number of Iranian students have trained and may almost certainly have learned about centrifuge technology at the Khan Research Laboratories in Pakistan. Back home, meanwhile, Boureston and Ferguson told us that Khatami's Iran has stayed the course. The number of state universities has increased from twenty-two in 1978 to more than a hundred today.

One consequence of this activity was that by September 2003, almost two million students were receiving a tertiary education throughout the country with some twenty-three thousand faculty members and thirteen thousand part-time instructors active in almost seven hundred fields of study. In this regard Iran is now streets ahead of any comparable Islamic society, Pakistan's included.

It is ironic that Putin's Russia remains a viable component of the Iranian equation. Moscow's soft Islamic underbelly in places like Grozny, Tashkent and elsewhere, where sporadic insurgencies are still part of the way of life, have underscored a distinct vulnerability to the kind of international terrorism to which the Islamic Republican Guards Corps is partial. Things are also not helped by the fact that rebel Chechnyan leaders have, on occasion, sought both refuge and support in Tehran.

The Wall Street Journal got it right when it said in an editorial on June 14, 2004 that if Iran were to go nuclear within the next year or two, "We shouldn't blame the International Atomic Energy Agency."

In a piece subtitled "The World Shrugs as Iran Builds it Bomb," the paper warned that "when Mohamed ElBaradei's UN team issued another damaging report on the mullahs, describing a pattern of deception and non-cooperation that all but screams 'bomb program,' the international community, with the apparent acquiescence of the Bush Administration, is treating it all as a matter of indifference.

"Remember," said the august paper that is read by just about every leader in the civilized world, "Iran is a petroleum-rich country that doesn't need nuclear power and whose former president (Rafsanjani) declared that the 'world of Islam' should acquire the bomb so that it can threaten the existence of Israel and thwart American 'colonialism' in the Middle East."

Even more resonant, only two days before that editorial appeared, the Associated Press quoted Iran's foreign minister as declaring that "Iran has to be recognized by the international community as a member of the nuclear club." Cryptically he added: "This is an irreversible path."

All this, the *Journal* said, "has finally provoked even the U.S. State Department to declare that Iran's nuclear activities are in no way peaceful." It added that the entire program was "specifically designed to create weapons," and went on: "We've heard a disturbing number of quiet remarks in Washington and other Western capitals recently to the effect that the world will just have to 'get used to' the idea of the Iranians having nukes.

"Have these people thought through the consequences of such a resignation? With the presumed American security umbrella suddenly jeopardized by the mullahs' bomb, the political calculations of every Mideast government would change. Many countries may conclude that they themselves have no choice but to go nuclear and the world could be off to another nuclear arms race."

History, it declared in closing, "would not look kindly on the leaders who let Iran get the bomb on their watch." And that presumably includes the heads of all the countries that might, had they put their minds to it, have been able to do something about it. That tally includes George W. Bush, Tony Blair, Jacques Chirac, Gerhard Shroeder and, most specifically, Vladimir Putin, who continues not only to build nuclear assets in Iran itself, but also to educate Iranian nuclear scientists at some of his country's best universities.

Nor is the problem restricted to the Islamic Republic. There are other players, like South Africa, North Korea, Malaysia and Thailand, together with a handful more on the periphery of what may yet become a dreadful scenario. While we've already examined South Africa's role (Chapters 7 and 8), those of Malaysia and Thailand are less obtrusive. They, too, have been exceedingly successful in getting into the nuclear proliferation act. Take Libya, a nation not renowned for any kind of expertise: when Gadaffi was forced to come clean about his WMD programs, UN nuclear inspectors proclaimed themselves to have been shocked at the scope of Libya's nuclear weapons program.

"The ease with which the complex bomb-making equipment was acquired stunned experienced international inspectors," one source claimed. He added that it soon became clear that the scale and the sophistication of the networks supplying so-called rogue states seeking nuclear weapons were then (and still are) considerably more extensive than previously believed.

American Assistant Secretary of State John S. Wolf said it all when he discussed problems associated with illegal nuclear proliferation in an interview with Washington's *Arms Control Today*.[2] The business of trading in dangerous weapons and technologies was widespread, he stated for the record. Further, the task of improving export controls and enforcing measures to prevent this sort of thing happening was proving difficult.

"There's a whole universe of state-state, state-nonstate, nonstate-nonstate, nonstate-state [transactions] and all of those need to be covered." More to the point, he added, "We're not any safer if it's state proliferation to another state. We're certainly not safer if it's North Korea shipping weapons technology to Iran or if Iran is acquiring weapons technologies through state purchasing agencies."

Much worse is the reality that nobody knows what exactly is going on in Iran today. I was present when John Pike, a commentator of note and founder of the Washington think-tank GlobalSecurity.org, conducted an hour-long conference call with a Kuwaiti journalist. The subject, inevitably, was Iran.

While there were some solid leads about what is going on in Iran today, Pike declared in his usual pared-down, succinct style—most often with unerring perception—that much of what was coming out of Tehran was speculation.

"There have been some solid leads from dissident groups, but for the rest, nobody really has the complete picture—or anything approaching what is going on. in present-day Iran," he told the other party. He added that "since much of what is coming out of that country is based on intelligence, inaccuracies are unavoidable."

Discussing this afterward, Pike was of three minds as to what Iran's religious leaders the mullahs were actually trying to achieve. He suggested that in allowing the IAEA access to heavy and light water sites at Isfahan and Arak and enrichment facilities at Natanz—ostensibly after a series of intelligence leaks—Tehran might conceivably be very astutely manipulating those arms inspectors already in the country into believing that they had uncovered most of it. In fact, he suggested, the converse was more likely to be true.

Alternatively, he said, Iran might already have the bomb. There are many more sites than those mentioned above, including those in Fase, Nekka and Karaj, together with a score or more that have not yet been made public. There was also the reality, he said, that these people mullahs had worked closely for some years with the group of maverick Pakistani scientists that are now referred to by pundits as the A.Q. Khan clique. "Who was to know how far they had gone?" Pike asked. It was common knowledge, he added, that a lot of money had changed hands, and that would not have happened had Tehran been unhappy with the progress, never mind that there were an unspecified number of foreign nuclear physicists also involved in these and other WMD programs.

Then, in cooperating with Vienna, said Pike, Tehran could conceivably be buying time needed to prepare for the ultimate objective: a full-blown nuclear weapons test. "That done, an Iran with the bomb would be a reality that the rest of the world would simply have to accept. More important, it would effectively make Iran a member of the ultra-exclusive nuclear club, which has been Tehran's objective all along."

Last, he said, Iran could be on the cusp of achieving nuclear parity and, while cooperating one day and obfuscating the next, that country's leaders might—very much like Saddam in his heyday—have found another way of extending the time frame needed to finish the job. Again he stressed, much of what is known about Iran right now lies in the domain of military intelligence, which, as the word implies, "is really not much more than activity devoted to uncovering that which is hidden."

"And let's face it," he stated, "if it were not secreted, it would be fact and that is a luxury that we just don't have at the present time."

Pike's analysis underscores a comment made by the British historian Sir John Keegan in his recent book *Intelligence In War*. In the conflict against fundamentalist Islamic terrorists (Shi'ite extremists are as much a part of that lumpen proletariat as al-Qaeda) there is no visible opponent as in conventional warfare. Keegan stated: "To win, we may be driven back to the world of John Buchan and Kipling, infiltrating the enemy by agents with the linguistic skills and knowledge of the opponent's culture that will enable them to go native. Such men are in short supply."

That said, what just about everything else in the region boils down to is the political reality of militant Islam, whether it be Sunni or, in Iran's case, the more dominant, passionate and often reckless Shi'a persuasion. With Iran, it goes much further. Almost unnoticed, Tehran's activism has spread far beyond its own frontiers into the Persian Gulf, the Caucasus and beyond, plus, as we have seen, into Iraq.

In an article published by Washington's Institute for National Strategic Studies titled "Islamic Radicalism," the point was made that in examining all these issues, the basis of Islamic religion is a vital element in traditional Iranian culture. But in addition, it stressed, "Islam is the embodiment of the alternative to Western culture in every possible sphere of life. By focusing on Islam as the center of the conflict with Westernism, Iranians can see the conflict not as a matter of narrow national pride but as a clash of civilizations, each of which claims to be universal."

Add to that conundrum the reality that the Iranian regime (and its very disparate leaders) is a difficult political entity to comprehend: "There is a gap between its rhetoric and its actions; between its sense of grievance and its inflammatory behavior; and between its ideological and national interests.

"Nor are its actions consistent. However, it remains hostile to the United States and its allies and unreconciled to the current international order.

"It has not renounced its revolutionary aims and it continues to support international terrorism. Its ideology remains a potent motive force, and it seeks to exploit weakness where it can, locally in the Persian Gulf, regionally in the wider Middle East, as well as farther afield."

So what to do about the Islamic Republic of the new millennium? At the time of going to press, Tehran has stirred passions, some to the Left and more to the Right. To some, the regime of the mullahs is regarded as a two-headed political hydra. Mark Corcoran, just returned from Tehran after completing a "Foreign Correspondent" program for the Australian Broadcasting Corporation (ABC-TV) told me that he was appalled by the actions of groups of political goons in stifling political opposition.[3]

"What struck me most about the current political climate in Iran," he said, "was the sense of confidence, bordering on arrogance, of the conservatives—they believe they've finally won a seven year struggle with the reformists—and they may be right. In February 2004, they rigged a Parliamentary election, ensuring that most moderate candidates could not stand. The result—not surprisingly—was a landslide victory, with the reformists wiped out politically.

"This sense of arrogance by the hard-liners worked to our advantage in producing our report, titled 'Iran Cyber Dissidents.' They didn't seem too worried about whom we talked to, a marked change compared to my last trip to Iran in November 2000 when, ironically, the reformist movement was at it's peak. Government security agencies then made our lives extremely difficult.

"Our report 'Iran's Cyber Dissidents' focused on the new wave of reformists, mainly young students/graduates, many of whom have already been in jail. They believe that the reformist-minded President Khatami has failed to deliver, as did many of the 'moderates' who sat in the last Majlis.

"Surprisingly those Iranian issues that dominate news in the West—Iran's nuclear weapons research program, and the U.S.-led occupation of neighboring Iraq—do not dominate the agenda of many of the more liberal young Iranians. They prefer to focus on what they regard as the 'basics': rebuilding a shattered reformist movement, human rights, and establishing a working democracy—all viewed as greater priorities. As for protest over Iraq, they feel that the issue—or rather the expression of opposition to the presence of the U.S.-led coalition—has been hijacked by the hard-liners. A tailor-made 'Death to America' issue . . . for a regime that adopted the slogan 'Death to America' as an unofficial national anthem."

The global view is even more disturbing. Iran is increasingly viewed as a tormented nation harboring belligerent intent in an extremely unsettled corner of the globe. Others maintain that with its massive oil and gas resources, it has the potential to become one of the richest nations on earth.

Among the vocal proponents of the latter are Germany and France—both make no secret of their intentions to angle for a tidy slice of the concessional oil-production cake. True to form they oppose just about everything said and done by Washington and, as one observer commented wryly, the French in today's Quai d'Orsay appear to enjoy behaving like small-time Tallyrands.

In stark contrast, the consequences of Iran achieving its nuclear objectives is not yet an issue among the majority of the world's leaders. Why should they believe a tub-thumping America when the CIA and just about every other Western intelligence agency were perceived to have lied about similar developments in Iraq?

The truth is that the likelihood of Tehran going nuclear is very much a reality. With vast uranium enrichment facilities and a variety of other bomb-related resources in various centers in Iran, even the IAEA is prepared to testify to as much. For this reason alone, it is essential to clearly understand what it will mean to the world—and the Middle East in particular—to have Iran onboard with the bomb.

The first question that needs to be asked is why Tehran is as fixated as it is on acquiring nuclear weapons? Second, why has it expended almost limitless financial and material resources over almost twenty years in getting there? The third question must be why Iran would be prepared to disregard the demands of the international community and face the strictures of United Nations-imposed sanctions?

Granted, in getting this far, one has to acknowledge that the country's level of commitment can only be regarded as exceptional. Its weapons of mass destruction programs are immense and reflect the kind of dedication that is nothing short of remarkable for a country that can be regarded as neither developed nor industrialized. But still, one needs to ask, to what purpose? Should Tehran have displayed the financial or technological acumen of a Korea, or even of a Malaysia, then things might begin to gel. But it has not. In Iran's case, a nuclear objective has about as much to do with the fundamental tenets of Islam as pork belly prices on the Chicago commodity exchange.

Iran's quest for the bomb, to date, must have swallowed a sizable chunk of the country's budget. And at the end of it all, the entire program has absolutely nothing to show for it but the kind of tactical weapon that most nations shun. It hardly makes sense, unless of course, there is a motive. That much is to be seen in the almost daily, often inflammatory, anti-Israel and Western pronouncements to which Tehran's leaders are prone.

In some respects, the Iranian issue—and a variety of ancillary issues like guided missiles, Iraq, Hizbollah's role in Lebanon, the procurement of illegal fissile material from former Soviet Union states and a lot else besides—is driven by an intensity not seen anywhere else in the region.

Ilan Berman, vice president for policy at the American Foreign Policy Council in Washington, has his own views on "How to Tame Iran." In an article published by the *Middle East Quarterly* in the Spring of 2004, he underscored the need for the West to come to grips with "a nuclear Iran." It is his view that there is a very distinct vision and method behind Iran's policies, comprising a structure of its own.

In the words of Moheen Reza'i, secretary of Iran's Expediency Council, Iran believes that it is destined to become the "center of international power politics in the post-Saddam Middle East." He points to this new confrontational strategic doctrine as having been labeled "deterrent defense," a new phrase, and one that has an immediacy about it.

According to the country's foreign minister, "This national security concept is designed to confront a broad spectrum of threats to Iran's national security, among them foreign aggression, war, border incidents, espionage, sabotage, regional crises derived from the proliferation of weapons of mass destruction, state terrorism and discrimination in manufacturing and storing WMD."

In line with a significant transformation in Iranian foreign policy, Berman informs us of several new developments. For a start, the Islamic Republic codified an unprecedented military and defense accord with Syria, a country with which it has shared an uneasy relationship over the past quarter century. This one, he says, formally enshrines an Iranian commitment to Syria's defense in the event of a U.S. or Israeli offensive. It has since also been extended to include Lebanon and Hizbollah, Iran's most potent regional proxy.

And if that weren't enough, Iranian foreign minister Kharrazi embarked on a diplomatic tour of the region in a bid to drum up support for what was euphemistically termed "a common regional security framework." While the objective was clear, the intention intrinsically to bolster anti-American sentiment, the results were not. Responses in Georgia, Armenia, Azerbaijan and Russia were cool, prompting—in a clear show of force—a series of military maneuvers along the Iranian-Azeri border and a corresponding naval build-up in the Caspian Sea.

On diplomatic efforts to deflect Iran's newest drive for regional hegemony, Berman remains skeptical. He points to a "critical dialogue" conducted by the EU with Iran from 1991 to 1997 that achieved nothing. Indeed, he states, it had the opposite effect, "infusing Iran with much needed foreign currency while failing to alter Tehran's support for terrorism, its pursuit of WMD and its violations of human rights." It was a debacle and played straight into the hands of Tehran.

If anything, matters got worse, with a stepped-up campaign of domestic repression that has resulted in the arrests of many thousands of political dissidents and untold numbers of people missing, many of them presumed killed.

Much of the blame for what is going on in Iran today (and Iraq yesterday) can only be laid squarely at the doors of major Western intelligence agencies. Cumulatively, it was they that failed us all in their bid to determine the extent of these and other critical Middle Eastern developments, never mind any amount of backsliding or obfuscation on the part of Tehran's leaders. Simply put, it would appear that they did not grasp history's cuticle of lies.

That this happened in the Middle East has made them all the more culpable, especially in an environment where the unwritten laws of spies—often with rules as formal as the structure of a sonnet—went out of fashion long before the KGB settled Kim Philby into his comfortable apartment in Moscow. Efraim Halevy is more adroit in dealing with the matter in an article that he wrote "By Invitation" for Britain's *Economist*. As head of Mossad, Israel's intelligence service from 1998 to 2002, there are few people anywhere who have as complete a grasp of the Iranian nettle than this erstwhile spy chief.

"There are no 'legal' rules and regulations in the dense field of intelligence, espionage and collection," he writes,[4] adding that it seems only logical that the more you know, the safer you are and the greater the chance that you will get things right. That should have been the case with Britain's SIS and Langley but it wasn't.

"It is not by chance that the international statute book has neither a chapter nor a verse on espionage, although this has been a vital tool of war from time immemorial," he goes on, adding that "we are in the throes of a world war, which is distinct and different from all the wars the world has hitherto experienced. There are no lines of combat; the enemy is often elusive and escapes identification."

But let us be fair. It is more than safe to presume that while the scoreboard reflects unfavorably, there have been many intelligence successes, which, of necessity, we will never hear about. George Tenet made exactly that point prior to his resignation as the head of the CIA in June 2004, and he had no reason to blow his own horn, At the end, the Director of Intelligence was out in open water, all guns firing.

Halevy has his say about George Tenet, someone who he obviously got to know well during the course of his duties and whose example he believes was instructive:

"Mr. Tenet was in office for seven years and his many successes cannot be publicly revealed. But there is one achievement of which one can speak: the rare knack of pulling together a genuine international effort in this third world war against Islamic terror and the proliferation of WMD. American leadership in these sensitive issues cannot be taken for granted. Mr. Tenet inspired the confidence of his subordinates and peers in all four corners of the earth, and this was a vital ingredient in the war effort. It still is."

The assessment is flattering but hardly unctuous. It places in solid perspective what others thought of the leadership of the Director of Central Intelligence which is a good deal more than he got from a grandstanding Congress eager to score points with the media. More important still, it was leveled at American leadership at a time when the entire U.S. security apparatus was coming under unprecedented— and Halevy believes, unwarranted—criticism. It might perhaps have been more than apposite to have reminded those involved in these proceedings of the old Nazi slogan, *Der Feind Hort mit*—the enemy is listening!

Read the piece for yourself; it is one of the most inspired and informative comments on the subject to have appeared in print on any continent. That a British paper should have invited Halevy to add his two bits worth at this critical time is all the more commendable.

For another view, one needs to quote Michael O'Hanlon, senior fellow at the Brookings Institution and someone who has been a valuable contact source from time to time while I was doing work for Jane's.

The Senate report about which Halevy wrote, says O'Hanlon with an irony so thick you could choke on it, spared the politicians by scapegoating spies. It is his uncluttered view that we must also accept that it would have taken an overwhelming body of evidence for any reasonable person in 2002 to think that Saddam Hussein did not possess stockpiles of chemical and biological agents.

"Intelligence is a difficult craft and getting things wrong is an occupational hazard, not necessarily a sign of negligence or incompetence," he suggested in an Op-Ed piece for the *New York Times*.[5]

Nor is this anything new. The Romans had a word, *discrimen*, for a choice hanging in the balance that might bring either triumph or catastrophe. It could as easily have included foggy intelligence as victory in battle.

The basic problem—in Iraq then, and in Iran today—is that the only people to possess such information are "friendly sources" inside the target country which itself is in a state of almost total siege. And since one has no other recourse but to rely on the word of people whose trust you and others may have cultivated over a period of years, who could really tell whether they were lying or not? None of us was aware of their duplicity until it was too late. More to the point, they were serving their own ends and the Americans—as always—were willing paymasters.

On a lighter note, could a possibility remain that the issue is all a part, if not of Arab culture, then of the Bedouin tradition that has had a saying since the beginning of time that "sinning is the best part of repentance"?

History has a most unusual way of repeating itself. One has only to look at current newspaper editorials and network editorializing when dealing with Iran to appreciate the complexity of the issue. Substitute the word Iraq for Iran in most of these reports, go back two or so years, and it looks like the same kind of looming confrontation that we faced when Saddam still ruled.

An article headlined "U.S. Steps Up Efforts to Stop Iran's Nuclear Program" by Warren P. Strobel, carried by Knight Ridder Newspapers in mid-August 2004[6] follows this trend.

"Get ready for another crisis over weapons of mass destruction," screams Strobel in his introduction. He goes on to list efforts by the Bush Administration to draw attention to what is going on in Tehran, stating that Washington now faces "a fundamental dilemma similar to the one it faced two years ago in Iraq." He then asks whether the United States should continue to work with its allies who favor negotiation or should take pre-emptive, unilateral action to stop Iran.

While Strobel is more objective than most and does bring important facts into play, his thrust is clear: Bush is leading America into another conflict. Parts of his article might have been a statement from the 2004 Democratic electoral platform, which, coincidentally it is. Yet were the American president to do nothing—in the face of some of the most compelling evidence yet to emerge from this embattled nation—he would almost certainly get the chop.

Damned if he does and damned if he doesn't, was one of the cartoons on the wires that got big play earlier that same week.

And if that weren't bad enough, Strobel's piece was followed the next day with an op-ed in the *New York Times*, this time from Dilip Hiro, someone who makes no secret of his admiration for those in Tehran who are intent on jeopardizing the security of America.[7] In a lengthy diatribe he argues that America "must win the hearts and minds of Iranians," but he doesn't tell us how to go about it except that we should accept that country's peaceful intentions.

The submission hardly warrants comment, never mind being given prominence in one of the world's leading dailies. What is important to remember is that there is nothing abstract about the implications of Iran acquiring or being likely to acquire nuclear weapons. A huge number of lives could be at stake. Cities could be destroyed. And at the end, about the only people that might be pleased by Western appeasement is Iran's supreme spiritual leader Ayatollah Ali Khamene'i and his bloody-minded clique. Like the "useful tools" of an earlier epoch, Hiro, wittingly or otherwise, has played right into their hands.

He ends his piece with a classic touch that, almost appropriately, goes some distance toward reflecting events in Munich sixty-five years ago. I quote: "One way Washington might turn Iranian minds more toward America is to stop constantly threatening Tehran and start engaging in meaningful dialogue." What does he really think America and the rest of the developed world have been doing in recent years?

At the end of the day, certain critical issues must be carefully examined afresh, for the problem with Iran is simply not going to go away. It is the view of some authorities on the subject that Tehran might explode its first test bomb within a year, perhaps two. Thus, the situation at the head of the Persian Gulf begs several immediate questions.

Tehran's reply in late September 2004 to the one hundred and thirty-seven nation International Atomic Energy Agency to desist from enriching uranium was blunt. It was also unequivocal. Iran would continue to defy the United Nations and go along the path of turning raw uranium into the gas needed for enrichment, a process that can be used to make nuclear weapons. It would do so even if it meant a rupture with the watchdog agency and a suspension of all inspections, which, Western intelligence bodies maintain, was what Iran was aiming for all along. President Khatami, meantime, gave his usual limp-wrist excuse for doing so: "We've made our choice: yes to peaceful nuclear technology, no to atomic weapons," he declared at a military parade in the capital in the Fall of 2004.

While Iran has said it all before, the scale of the current project—involving about forty tons of raw uranium at the Isfahan nuclear establishment—is worrying because it goes far beyond the kind of basic laboratory testing in which the country maintains it was previously involved. According to David Albright, this could theoretically result in a couple of hundred pounds or more of weapons-grade, highly-enriched uranium.

Speaking hypothetically, Albright declared, "It's roughly enough for about five crude nuclear weapons of the type Iran could conceivably build."

Clearly, it took some doing for Tehran to get this far. Iran has built more than a dozen major nuclear-related establishments that the West knows about, and only Allah knows how many more that we don't. This has led one European pundit to declare that some Iranian security establishments—Pasdaran, in particular—have lately begun to share many of the Machiavellian qualities reflected by organizations like al-Qaeda and, to a lesser extent, Hizbollah and Hamas, both of which are tied to Tehran's apron strings.

Take al-Qaeda's greatest asset: its ability to wage covert operations on a global scale. Pasdaran follows similar dogmas, all of them secretive and known only to a select few at the highest level of government. Though not yet fully internationalized, Pasdaran's machinations involve it in activities on other continents. We are aware that its operators successfully assassinated at least one "enemy of the state" in the United States (see Chapters 10 and 12). The terror group has also issued death threats on American soil.

At the same time, the goal is not mindless or random violence. The idea, at base, is to recreate the ancient precept of Muslim empire, the Caliphate. In this regard Tehran's leaders (now, with Saddam Hussein taken care of) see themselves at the vanguard of a rejuvenated Islamic Empire that stretches from Indonesia and the Philippines in the east all the way through—Department of Homeland Security or not—the heart of Western civilization. Not for nothing do some writers now talk about us facing World War IV.

The Islamic world is receptive to all this, in large part because it views Europe and America as a spent force. NATO (and specifically Ankara) proved as much when the majority of members could not agree on basic policy at the start of Gulf War II.

Worse, the Arabs and Persians have good reason for this kind of mindset. There is simply no arguing that countries like America, Germany, Britain, France and many others must be viewed as greedy and materialistic by communities who earn in a year what the majority of Western folk take home in a month.

They also point out, correctly, that many of these states are fractious. Washington, doggedly sometimes, is in the face of many of its former allies, often not too discreetly either. France and Germany continue to take the lead in the anti-U.S., or perhaps more accurately, the anti-Bush lobby.

Couple to this a perception that has gathered immense strength in recent years. Right or wrong, our Arabic and Islamic friends firmly believe that the West, like Rome almost two millennia ago, has, as the saying goes, had its day. Speak to the man on the street in Amman, Cairo, Mombassa and Khartoum, or Muslims in other parts of the world, and they will tell you that America is weak and emasculated. A British-educated Islamic scholar in Durban used the phrase "gone flabby, a bit broad around the beam."

When you listen to some of the tapes emanating from Middle Eastern centers (they are freely available in English) that same concept is constantly repeated. From the pulpits of tens of thousands of mosques around the world, the word goes out: There is no longer any real or lasting cohesion or political unity between Western countries. "Islam's Great New Day" has arrived, say these Islamic holy men. Worse, they really believe it. And of course for people who have little, these are the noises of hope. Certainly, judging by what they see on television (they watch many of the same programs as you and I), the spoils look rather alluring.

Exactly the same situation holds for America at war. Muslims everywhere took heart each time John Kerry suggested before a camera that the United States was wrong in sending its soldiers to fight in

Iraq. There would be whoops of delight in cafés across the Middle East when the translator echoed his words that the war was a massive, incontrovertible mistake. Here was an American leader powerfully propagating their "inalienable cause" for them.

Think about it. They probably couldn't have paid money to achieve better publicity for what they believed in, implicitly and passionately enough for some of them to strap bombs to their bodies and give their lives for the cause. In a sense it was the Vietnam syndrome all over again—a nation divided between two staggeringly divergent causes.

"This is all Allah's work," are the words of Muslim holy men that reverberate around the mosques each Friday in all four corners of the globe—in Iran, Baghdad's Sadr City, Lebanon's Shi'ite enclaves, among Britain's more militant Muslims, South Africa's Qibla (the military wing of PAGAD), along the Indian Ocean shores of Kenya and Tanzania and so on. Naturally, all of it suits the purposes of al-Qaeda. It pleases Pasdaran too. Both movements have gathered, in tandem, a strident militant momentum of their own.

Unquestionably, Saudi's al-Qaeda dominated Wahhabists and Iran's Shi'ite command structure—though in theory, at opposite religious poles (the one Suni and the other Shi'ite), share a remarkable common purpose. In part, they put to work those same Western shortcomings that I've mentioned.

The activities of both groups are so intertwined that there is no Western authority willing to go on record to categorically declare that acts like the bombing of the USS *Cole*, the attacks on two American embassies in Africa, the December 2002 bombing of a hotel in Mombassa—and similar episodes before that in Bali, Tunisia, Turkey, Morocco and elsewhere—while regarded by many authorities to be the work of al-Qaeda, sometimes reveal surprising evidence that the Hizbollah connection is also manifest. The latter organization is not al-Qaeda at all, but rather, Pasdaran.

Others are not so sure. Hizbollah, the Pasdaran's Lebanese handmaiden (and thus a servant of Tehran) is so active in the U.S. that California law authorities recently published a restricted manual on the activities of this terror organization. I was able to peruse a copy in the offices of the Intelligence Unit in the Boston Police Department and the contents are sobering. This is not the kind of document that should remain in the hands of the few: the American public needs to be told about the activities of radical Islamic groups living in their midst.

Nor is Europe immune. The trend continues elsewhere and was graphically displayed not long ago in Madrid's rail bombings. And in countries like Turkey, Morocco, Tunis, Egypt and wherever else Muslim militants have been militarily active. Nor is that the end of it.

As Amin Tarzi, an analyst at Radio Free Europe/Radio Liberty (RFE/RL) declared in a recent paper for the *Middle East Review of International Affairs*,[8] unlike the United States, the European Union has never totally withdrawn its presence from Iran. Even during times of political tension, trade between EU member states and Iran continued. Indeed, Yuval Steinitz, chairman of the Knesset's foreign and defense committee, maintains that it is not only Israel that is threatened by Iran's developing intercontinental missile program but also Europe and NATO.

It is Tarzi's conclusion that in maintaining, and even fostering closer ties between Europe and Tehran, the EU has achieved almost nothing. In fact, the reverse might be the case, with Tehran cleverly manipulating real or imagined European friends to get what it did not have before. Here, it might be added, political points are as significant as material things, especially when Washington is at the receiving end of such duplicity.

At the forefront of all this, as we have already seen, stands Israel, the one country that Tehran's mullahs have vowed to destroy.

Following the American trend, not a day goes by without the Israeli media highlighting Iran's nuclear threat. That was compounded a hundredfold after Natanz and Arak were exposed by a dissident Iranian political group, the more so since these disclosures did not come at the behest of the CIA or the Mossad.

In truth, Jerusalem has been hard at work for decades, if not in trying to penetrate Tehran's heavily-foliated security mantles, then in a bid trying to understand the transition of Iran from a relatively obscure, undeveloped nation to one that now stands on the cusp of its own nuclear era. In a word, Israel is threatened. Its leaders are prepared to say as much, some of them maintaining that the country will do what it has to, threatening to do what needs to be done, unilaterally if need be.

Gerald M. Steinberg of Bar-Ilan University told Steven Erlanger[9] that should Iran develop nuclear weapons, there will be a new Middle East. "It would lead to a lot more brinkmanship and higher stakes for Israel's survival, and pressure on other countries like Egypt, Saudi

Arabia and Syria to develop nuclear weapons of their own."

Professor Paul Bracken of Yale University who recently visited the Jewish state was of a similar mind. He spelt out "The Threat of Nuclear Terror" in graphic terms to Israeli writer Ze'ev Schiff of *Ha'aretz*.[10] He subscribes to the same view that has been dealt with earlier (Chapters 4 and 5) that the danger is increasing because of the wild proliferation of nuclear materials and know-how to states like Iran by people like Abdul Qadeer Khan, the so-called father of the Pakistani atomic bomb.

This affair, in which a country that is considered a friend of the United States becomes the largest single disseminator of nuclear expertise, is also extensively dealt with by a former senior Pentagon official, Professor Graham Allison of Harvard University.[11] Allison holds the view that if preventative measures are not taken against atomic terror, then an "American Hiroshima," as some call it, is inevitable.

So what to do about the other countries that have recently been shown to be involved, if only on the periphery, in disseminating weapons of mass destruction? Reams of documents were provided to Western weapons inspectors by Libya's President Gadaffi after his nuclear weapons program was exposed. Some of the disclosures that followed were nothing short of astonishing.

We've already talked about Malaysian involvement as a conduit of some of these goods. And Thailand as a manufacturer of parts and a dissemination point. More recently, there were unsubstantiated reports from Brazil, claiming that that government had bought sensitive nuclear technology from Pakistan. The matter is further clouded by a seemingly impenetrable veil of secrecy now draped over that country's nuclear program. Vienna's IAEA is not even prepared to comment on the matter.

What cannot be ignored is that states will continue to do this kind of clandestine business. Already in the 1990s, a former British security chief, Stella Rimmington, told a closed gathering that there were more than thirty countries set on acquiring nuclear weapons, and in this regard South Africa, despite having abandoned its own atom bomb program, is increasingly in the news. On the one hand, in 2004, we had a maverick Israeli former army officer shipping nuclear triggers from the U.S. through Cape Town, while shortly afterward, a South African businessman was arrested by the police following an IAEA tip-off.

Johan Meyer, 53, who owns an engineering plant south of Johannesburg, denied everything. His lawyer, Heinrich Badenhorst told the press that Meyer "was arrested on charges that he was building a nuclear weapon." The charges followed a lengthy police investigation, which involved the IAEA.

According to official police documents, he was accused of offenses between 2000 and 2001 relating to the import and export of regulated goods "which could contribute to the design, development, manufacture and deployment" of weapons of mass destruction. He was also accused of "unlawfully and willfully possessing . . . nuclear-related equipment and material." Then quietly and inexplicably, Meyer was released from jail.

There are many such incidents, some of them involving Arabs traveling on false South African passports, quite a few of them bought "under the table" from a passport official at the Embassy in Jordan. In July 2004, U.S. agents arrested a South African woman who had recently arrived in the country while trying to board a flight to New York. Whatever the reason, newspaper reports at the time indicated that she may have played a role in Washington's decision a day later to raise the threat level and announce specific buildings as potential terror targets in three American cities.

What is taking place in South Africa today has bearing on developments in the Islamic world, particularly in Iran. This is a nation that under the acclaimed Nelson Mandela relinquished its hated race policies and joined the international community with the kind of fanfare that the event deserved. One needs to know its future course, because this young country exemplifies the plight in which dozens of others with large Muslim communities now find themselves. Many of them also have close ties to Tehran.

At the southern tip of a great continent—despite progression to a full and equitable democracy—South Africa remains politically controversial. Apartheid as a national creed has been dead for more than a decade, but there are other influences that have become manifest, underscoring the old homily that power corrupts.

One of these is close ties to a number of rogue states that are involved in producing WMD, Iran and Syria among them (and, until recently, Libya). Another is almost a million-strong Muslim community in Cape Town and Durban that has become increasingly radical and, in some quarters, belligerently anti-Western. The largest Islamic printing works outside Cairo—in the past, a benefactor of Osama bin Laden's largesse—is there for all to see in downtown Durban.

Similarly, in all South African Muslim centers there are pictorial homages to Arab suicide bombers, whether they be in Israel or Iraq. There have been reports—in and out of Parliament—of six South African training camps for Hizbollah militants in the KwaZulu/Natal interior. Then we have PAGAD, a militant Islamic group with a military offshoot named Qibla, which has recently seen a resurgence of activity (surprising, since we all thought it had gone underground). Significantly, both movements have strong ties to Tehran. Moreover, of the more than two hundred bombs that have gone off in public places in South Africa in recent years (with deaths as a consequence) just about all were shown to have been laid by Islamic dissidents, many of them linked to PAGAD, since declared a terror organization by the U.S. State Department.

The bottom line is that there is a real fear in both Washington and London that South Africa, with its remarkable array of natural resources and industries, could become what some people like to term "a terrorist breeding ground." Some say it already is one. Exactly the same premise applies to countries like Kenya, Tanzania, Zimbabwe, Namibia, Nigeria, the Ivory Coast and dozens of others.

Pretoria makes no secret of a vigorous and extremely outspoken anti-American stance. There is also a groundswell of support among the populace for people like Osama bin Laden and Saddam Hussein. Wherever you go in predominantly African townships like Soweto and Guguletu, you can hardly ignore a plethora of t-shirts bearing their visages with slogans like "Long Live Bin-Laden" and "Saddam Hussein: Innocent Until Proven Guilty."

During my last swing through southern Africa while doing research for this book in the summer of 2004, I spent almost a month in an apartment in Cape Town. Not a day went by without groups of people, quite often entire families, doing the rounds of our garbage bins. They were in search of food. It is said (though the Mbeki government denies it), that almost half the country is out of work. That is not only a catastrophe for a nation of more than forty million; it could, in the long term, become dangerous. In one sense, this is a revolution in the making.

Meanwhile, the fat cats who inherited power from their former white overlords are now positively bloated. One of them, a close associate of Nelson Mandela and former African National Congress regional head, "Tokyo" Sexwale, has made enough money since his party came to power to buy a platinum mine. In adjacent plots, people starve. Obviously, this sort of environment quickly becomes a recruiting ground for disenchanted elements who might possibly be linked to international terrorism. Worse, in South Africa's case, it has already happened.

There were many young South Africans recruited to fight with the Mujahadeen in Afghanistan, and by accounts that I heard from friends in the city of Port Elizabeth, they acquitted themselves pretty well against the Russians. Local people are also known to have been linked to Palestinian dissidents in Gaza and the West Bank. More recently, the Pakistanis killed a bunch of South Africans fighting with the rebels in mountains adjacent to Afghanistan and captured more, a handful of whom are still held in custody in Islamabad. There are also South African Islamics active against American forces in the Iraqi Sunni Triangle, though in typical al-Qaeda fashion, the identities of those KIA against "The Satanic Invader" are never made public.

Then we have South African arms factories selling sensitive military equipment to countries like Iran, Syria and elsewhere. Before Gadaffi came clean, some of it went to Libya, as did former South African Special Forces to train first a Libyan strike force and then commando elements within the Sudanese Army. Now, with Libya's books open to inspection by the West, it is only a matter of time before we discover the full extent of South African involvement in Gadaffi's chemical and biological factories. And, who knows, possibly his nuclear installations as well. There has already been speculation about this kind of involvement.

What is certain is that none of it—including restricted arms being sold to Iran—could be happening without some kind of involvement by Mbeki's government. With the highest murder rate in the world, weapons in the wrong hands are a serious and persistent issue in present day South Africa, so none of it can happen without the right authority from "on high."

So too, one would have thought, would be the recruitment of young men to fight in strange lands. There is an Act of Parliament that specifically prohibits such activity, and while there have been some white South Africans persecuted for having involved themselves in foreign conflicts, the possibility of Muslims fighting abroad is an issue that is not allowed to be raised.

The answer for much of what is going on in present-day South

Africa must rest with the fundamental Islamic cartel which both Presidents Mandela and Mbeki have embraced. Some of these men served time with Mandela on Robben Island and the reward of a cabinet or advisory post is totally justified. Others, like President Thabo Mbeki, studied abroad, and these people eventually became part of the "Inner Sanctum" of the ANC in Exile.

To America and the West, it is what they do with their new power that matters.

For all this, hope still remains. Interestingly, there have been a few Islamic commentators proclaiming as much in Western publications. One of these was Amir Taheri, an authority on Iranian affairs who offered a distinctly minority view in one of several op-ed pieces written for the *London Times*.

One of these, headed "Will the Arab World Catch the Democracy Bug?" makes important distinctions between the perceived results of America's actions and the long-term effect of this "war of liberation" as it was described by another, less sanguine observer. Referring to the Greater Middle East Plan launched by President Bush in the summer of 2003, the aim, he said, was essentially to bring democracy to the Arab heartland. And though the debate was focused on the Arab world, it did include Iran. Taheri was of a mind that though it might take a while longer, it could very well happen.

"Some will claim that the exercise is merely a photo opportunity for Bush's reelection campaign," he stated. "But the plan has already had one positive effect—reinvigorating the region's tired political lexicon. Such terms as *islah* (reform), *taaduhiyah* (pluralism) and *hawar* (dialogue) now dominate debate, even if many speakers may not mean the words they use. There is no disputing the fact that the successful elections in Afghanistan in the Fall of 2004 went some way toward vindicating this argument.

Something else struck a chord with some of those who regarded developments in the Middle East as a hopeless muddle, he said. "This is not idealistic waffle; it is realpolitik. The process that led to the Helsinki accords between the West and the Soviet bloc in the 1970s could serve as a precedent. Then the West did not insist that the Soviet bloc nations change their systems, which none of their ruling elites would have accepted. Instead, the emphasis was put on a slow but steady change of course with the support of domestic forces, including some within the communist regimes.

"In the case of Iraq, progress had to come through war. Elsewhere in the region, a combination of politics, military threat and economic and diplomatic inducements could help to drain the swamp that breeds terror." Democracy, he concluded, was the prize in the Middle East—"and it could be won."

As for Iran, this is a nation that regards itself in a state of war, not only with the United States, but with any country with whom it has serious differences, and that includes half the Arab world. Israel, of course, stands at the top of the list.

With hostilities continuing in Iraq, Tehran has had a prominent ringside seat to what has been going on along its western borders, and the fact that Washington is fighting a media war, very much as it did during the Vietnamese epoch, has not been lost on the mullahs. Every one of them have taken note of the efficacy of the kind of unconventional warfare being waged by insurgents in places like Fallujah and Baghdad's Sadr City.

They are also asking each other how this system of unconventional warfare evolved and how it could be applied by their own forces, should the need ever arise.

Abu Ubeid al-Quarashi, an Islamic writer, provides us with part of the answer and it is a proud one:[12] Since the late 1980s, "The Islamic nation has chalked up the most victories, in a short time, in a way [the world] has not known since the rise of the Ottoman Empire. These victories were achieved . . . against the best armed, best trained, and most experienced armies in the world (the USSR in Afghanistan, the United States in Somalia, Russia in Chechnya, and the Zionist entity in southern Lebanon)."

According to al-Quarashi, the mujahideen proved their superiority in what he terms "Fourth Generation Warfare," using only light weaponry: "They are part of the people, and hide amongst the multitudes." These victories established "precedents for world powers and large countries being defeated by [small] units of mujahideen . . . despite the great difference between the two sides."

The ultimate example, he underscored, was on September 11, 2001, when al-Qaeda "dealt Americans the most severe blow ever to their morale." The key lesson learned was that "the time has come for the Islamic movements facing a general crusader offensive to internalize the rules of fourth-generation warfare. They must consolidate appropriate strategic thought, and make appropriate military preparations."[13]

Iran must have had similar thoughts when it embarked on its very substantial nuclear weapons and missile programs twenty years ago. With weapons of mass destruction at their disposal, as the argument probably went in Tehran's bazaars and byways, the Shi'ite empire would be invincible.

APPENDICES

Appendix A
THE RUSSIA-IRAN NUCLEAR CONNECTION AND U.S. POLICY OPTIONS

By Dr. Victor Mizin
Courtesy of MERIA, *Middle East Review of International Affairs Journal,* Vol. 8, No. 1 (March 2004)

Dr. Victor Mizin, is a former Russian diplomat specializing in arms control, nonproliferation and global security problems. At the time of writing, Dr. Mizin was Diplomat-in-Residence and Senior Research Associate with the Center for Nonproliferation Studies of the Monterey Institute for Nonproliferation Studies in Monterey, California.

Russian involvement in Iran's nuclear program has long been one of the most controversial aspects of Moscow's Middle East policy. Dr. Mizin evaluates the nature of this cooperation, especially in regard to its effect on U.S.-Russian relations, and options for having an effective non-proliferation strategy on this front.

On October 21, 2003, as part of a deal brokered by Britain, France, and Germany, Iran finally yielded to intense international pressure and agreed to sign the Additional Protocol to the Non-Proliferation Treaty (NPT), which will allow the International Atomic Energy Agency (IAEA) short-notice access to its nuclear facilities. Tehran also consented to provide an account of all its nuclear-related activities and to suspend its highly controversial uranium enrichment program.

However, it remains to be seen whether this accord, finally signed after intense diplomatic pressure in December 2003, will actually result in Iran foregoing its drive for a nuclear fuel cycle program. To prevent the appearance of another nuclear weapon state, it is critically important that the international community seal the external channels that provide nuclear technologies which enhance Iran's capability to acquire nuclear weapons. This requires effective U.S. policies toward Tehran's most active suppliers. In dealing with the most prominent of these, Russia, the dialogue over this issue has so far been almost a total fiasco for American nonproliferation strategy.

The dramatic outcome of the 2003 Gulf War, despite the ongoing pandemonium of the post-war restoration period, has been changing approaches to key foreign policy issues, such as traditional arms control and nonproliferation. The immediate consequences will also influence the Middle Eastern political landscape and in particular Iran. There remains a major unanswered question of what will happen with the two other members of the "axis of evil?" Are Iran and North Korea now "off the hook" due to the embarrassing turmoil in Iraq, which revealed the hazards of regime change?

Will the nuclear programs of these states continue and will there be major international consequences for them? And how will these issues affect Russia, whose nuclear assets and expertise might be available to such countries?

At the same time, U.S.-Russian bilateral relations have progressed remarkably well in the wake of September 11. While Moscow has been written off as a substantial military threat to the United States, the concerns about the potential spillover of critical WMD technologies from Russia are still bedeviling the minds of Western strategic planners and nonproliferation experts. These American anxieties are intensified by the tumultuous and still unstable character of bilateral U.S.-Russian relations that continue to be challenged by Moscow's periodic efforts to demonstrate its independence and global clout, as the developments around the Iraqi operation demonstrated. Domestically, the much-hyped Moscow's "campaign against unruly oligarchs" on a par with the general Soviet-style "stabilization" alignment of the Russian society has led many Western observers to question the democratic nature and core values of the emerging regime.[1]

Though generally inclined to promoting good relations with the West—which is vital for its economic well being and development—Russia still has yet to shirk off its Soviet-era policy of external arms and technology transfers and aid to rogue states and countries of proliferation concern. This policy continues despite the fact that these traditional clients are declared enemies of the United States, a purported strategic partner.

Russia's inability to secure larger investments from the West is influenced by the country's internal problems—rampant corruption, bureaucratic mismanagement, and crumbling socio-economic infrastructure—which lie behind the facade of steady growth. The economic shortfall here then provides an additional incentive for Russians to argue that they need to sell sophisticated weaponry and dual-use items to states like China, India, Syria, and Iran as legitimate trade operations. There should be no problem in doing this, Russia claims, as it pledges strict observance of nonproliferation and export control treaties. In any case, these weapons systems and technology find few eager or legal customers in the West or Western-aligned countries.

The rationale for these connections is not solely economic. Moscow s promoting its own network of alliances, ostensibly to offset current U.S. unilateralism and strengthen its position as the leading global player. Indeed, Russia has regained much ground, even if it still falls short of the international role it enjoyed during the existence of the USSR.

In this pattern, Iran is emerging as the exemplar for Russia's global positioning in the 21st century as well as in the US-Russian bilateral dialogue. This is especially true regarding the nuclear issue there, an area where Moscow has historically tried to appear as the leading protagonist,[2] though it has often bent existing international norms.[3]

HARD CHOICES FOR WASHINGTON

Of course, Moscow must take into account possible U.S. countermoves on the Iranian and other issues. There are several different options for U.S. policies regarding the Iranian nuclear question:

Desperate for a practical solution, the United States might ultimately turn to the idea of a limited Osiraq-type strike or larger-scale military operation to knock out the major Iranian nuclear facilities. This seems to be, at least for the time being, an improbable scenario.

It is obvious that such an operation would produce great opposition in Europe and the Middle East, as well as unforeseeable consequences in terms of Iran's response. Iran has also scattered its facilities in an attempt to avoid such a development. Given the deep involvement in Iraq, the United States also lacks the resources to take such an extreme action. Moreover, the immediate threat does not seem so great as to foster such a desperate response.

Another option would be to continue the current sanctions against the regime while helping Iranian indigenous opposition forces. This is an easy strategy and might yield long-run benefits but would not produce an immediate dramatic change regarding Iran's nuclear capacity.[4] There could also be efforts to increase the isolation of Tehran's rulers through economic and political sanctions on an international level. Considering previous experience—for instance, Cuba and Iraq—such efforts need to be all-encompassing to be meaningful. They would have to affect the interaction between Iran and countries like Russia, North Korea, Pakistan and China.

This regime's attrition might be impossible, even for the current American administration.[5]

Finally, there is the more conventional diplomatic track of rallying the international community through channels of multilateral diplomacy, the

International Atomic Energy Agency, and perhaps the United Nations. While many arms control experts and academics hope that the difficulties the U.S. is experiencing in Iraq will push Washington to better coordinate its future arms control efforts, this route might also let Tehran maneuver in a way that allows it to continue its nuclear weapons development at no political or economic cost.

WHITHER TRADITIONAL NONPROLIFERATION?

As many experts concur, the current international arrangements demonstrate their glaring inefficacy to halt attempts of the most dangerous, destabilizing and proliferation-prone regimes to obtain nuclear technologies, assets and know-how. The major drawback of the Non-Proliferation Treaty (NPT), a product of the Cold War era, is that it basically permits any state to accomplish its nuclear weapons program short of finally assembling a nuclear explosive device itself. The NPT does not observe any distinction between well-behaved members of the international community such as say Denmark and aggressive or failed quasi-states like war-ridden Liberia, totalitarian North Korea or Saddam-era Iraq.[6] Moreover, these are the type of regimes that frequently dominate various UN-run agendas.

The basic question is do dangerous states merit nuclear technology handouts, as stipulated in the NPT's Article IV support for peaceful use of nuclear energy? Such efforts could instead augment nuclear expertise potentially aiding research on nuclear weapons. The challenge is in reconciling the legitimate right of any Third World country's access to nuclear energy for "peaceful purposes," the ideological cornerstone of the NPT, with the recognition of the danger that such transfers could create the material and intellectual prerequisites for potential proliferators determined to produce an indigenous nuclear weapon capability. The current, even enhanced, outreach of NPT inspections prove to be incapable of exposing such furtive programs.

The nonproliferation regimes in their present forms are an important pillar of the international legal system of arms control and a valuable way to track the spillover of critical technologies. But they have also failed to block the transgressions of rogue states such as Saddam's Iraq, North Korea or Iran.

Implied, however, is the question of whether those legal regimes are in truth binding only for respectable, law-abiding members of the world community, meaning that they serve as cover for unrestrained proliferators from the Third World who use the enforcement effort as a pretext to extort more aid and concessions from donors. If so, they are irrelevant or even harmful to nonproliferation efforts.

The presumption of innocence given by NPT membership to the potential seekers of nuclear weapons status, in the opinion of the leading Russian security experts, should not lead to the scrapping of this important document. Rather, it should be drastically adapted to the changed realities of the post-September 11 era, where meaningless diplomatic formalities would make way for effective nonproliferation efforts.[7]

THE RUSSIAN NONPROLIFERATION GAMBLE

Unfortunately, for the time being the United States and Russia differ on which countries qualify as rogue states that must be contained or confronted. Like North Korea or China, Russia—the soothing or indignant pronouncements of its leaders notwithstanding—according to many experts and officials in the area, remains the world's leading source of WMD-related items and expertise proliferation.[8]

Despite assertions that the two states share a common basic approach toward nonproliferation issues, the United States and Russia basically stick to opposite views on all major entanglements in the current nonproliferation debates.[9]

With that in mind, the manner in which this Iranian nuclear conundrum unfolds will shape the future of nonproliferation. So far, Russian-Iranian connections, especially in the area of nuclear and missile arms sales, continue to be a major irritant in U.S.-Russian relations, specifically with regard to bilateral deliberations over nonproliferation issues. The current status of this dialogue at any given moment can be viewed as a good indicator of the situation in U.S.-Russian affairs.[10]

While recognizing that Iran is an important geopolitical ally, Russian politicians tend to weigh carefully the costs of any moves regarding ties with Tehran.[11] Moscow's nuclear cooperation with Iran, which Russian officials pledge is exclusively confined to civilian nuclear plant construction, has emerged as the most conspicuous issue in which the Russian leadership attempts to establish its own foreign and strategic policy.[12] During a 2002 visit to Iran, Russian First Deputy Foreign Minister Vyacheslav Trubnikov said, "Russia does not accept President George W. Bush's view that Iran is part of an axis of evil."[13]

There are several key reasons for this approach. First, Russia, despite the statements of its experts and politicians, has never been seriously concerned with the military threat emanating from WMD development in the Third World, aside from China. Therefore, politically correct declarations from Moscow's dignitaries should be seen more as a tribute to the international consensus on promoting nonproliferation regimes than an expression of actual strategic awareness or sincere concern.

The Russian military, though wary of any nascent nuclear/missile potential in contiguous countries, has realized that these build-ups are oriented against regional rivals and the U.S. military presence. This is partly explained by the fact that, similar to other client states of the former USSR—like North Korea, Libya, Syria and Iraq—Tehran has been pragmatically regarded in Moscow as an important regional counterpart, if not potential ally, and a vast market for Russian military-related technologies.[14]

Especially due to the worldwide decline in demand on the world armaments' markets and the ongoing decline of the Russian military-industrial complex, Moscow feels compelled to develop relations with such current or prospective buyers of cost-effective Russian weapons as Iran, China, India, or Syria. In other words, while Russia has become the largest exporter of conventional arms since 2001 (responsible for 36 percent of all global arms transfers in 2002),[15] most of the armaments exported are, technologically speaking, relatively unsophisticated. Thus while other countries can compete well on the open market, Russia's strategy has been to sell lower quality weapons at considerably lower prices, and to do so means selling to poorer client states, some of whom are inevitably going to be rogue regimes. Thus, the overall proliferation-prone forays of the Russian defense and high-tech enterprises are ultimately the result of the poor state of the Russian manufacturing industry, which still lags far behind the country's booming oil and gas-pumping sector on which the national economy basically survives.

Finally, from a diplomatic perspective, Iran is still viewed in Moscow as the major eventual supporter of Russia's role in the region. Iran's importance as the prospective recipient of the newest Russian arms and dual-use technologies will only grow with vigorous U.S. military-political activity in the Middle East and Persian Gulf.

RUSSIA'S IRANIAN CONNECTION

Still, Russia's relations with Iran are inconsistent and characterized by discord within Moscow's political and military circles. There is a compact pro-Western group, who think that cooperation with the major industrial states, primarily the United States, could benefit Russia much more than murky dealings with questionable partners like China, Iran, Iraq, or Libya. The recent friction with Iran regarding regional problems in the Caspian Sea basin strengthened this position.

There is also another powerful group consisting of the representatives of the floundering Russian Defense Industrial Complex (OPK) and the special services. This group promotes a different course of developing traditional strategic and economic ties with China and India or such former Moscow clients as Iran, Syria, and North Korea, while maintaining only conditional token cooperation with Washington in the global arena. It attempts to lobby its position through a "class-friendly" faction of KGB veterans in Putin`s entourage. It seems that the members of this faction are driven not only by the desire to ensure purely economic benefits for the survival and expansion of the ailing Russian defense enterprises (and for their personal enrichment), but they are also driven by an inbred animosity toward America.

This group sees the United States as Russia's main adversary from the Cold War era and an alleged impediment to Russia's great power revival. The defense industry, secret services, and the disgruntled military's mistrust of the goals of current U.S. foreign and military policy—perceived as being ultimately anti-Russian—leads them to predictably conclude that Washington is attempting to impose arbitrary restraints on Russian exports of high technologies in order to stymie their country as a competitor for influence in the CIS.

Third, there is the usual midway faction represented mostly by OPK officials and managers who change their positions depending on the context. Today, by winning an occasional large-scale contract, say, from Lockheed Martin, they can actively lobby for the expansion of Russian-American cooperation in space, but tomorrow—as money peters out—they would turn to buyers from rogue regimes or other suspicious clients. Thus, the particular instability of the Russian economy seems to provide the basic reason for the duality and inconsistency of Russian policy concerning the dangers of WMD-related technology transfers, specifically to Iran.[16]

Proponents of special ties with preferred clients in the Third World have actively pushed for a continuation of arms deals with Iran. They were particularly resolute in their advocating for the annulment of the Chernomyrdin commitment—a deal made in June 1995 between U.S. Vice President Al Gore and former Russian Premier Viktor Chernomyrdin to stop military cooperation with Iran in 2000 after the completion of previous contracts. This faction finally prevailed in 2000 after the disclosure of the secret deal by *The New York Times* on October 13, 2000, which accordion to *The Washington Times*, Gore had agreed not to make the public to any third parties, including the US Congress.[17]

At the same time, persistent calls by Washington to terminate Russian exports to Iran were portrayed by these circles in Moscow as being motivated by the desire of American corporations to save future opportunities in the Iranian market for themselves. To prove this, they cited the recent writings of such foreign policy gurus as Henry Kissinger, Zbigniew Brzezinski, and Brent Scowcroft that advocated closer ties with the putatively reformist Iranian political elite.[18]

Russian cooperation with Iran in developing its nuclear technology, as well as its suspected aid in developing Iranian missiles, led to one of the rare difficult moments during the Moscow-St. Petersburg summit in May 2002.

Russia resolutely denied any wrongdoing and pledged that its cooperation with Iran was strictly within the limits of its international obligations and in compliance with international nonproliferation regimes. President Putin remarked that Western companies, not Russian entities, had furnished Iran with missile and nuclear technology. As Putin pointed out wryly, "The United States has taken on the obligation of building a nuclear power station identical to the one in Bushehr in North Korea."[19] At the same time, he has suggested pressuring Iran to allow further and more extensive international inspections of the Russian-built nuclear reactor there.[20]

The issue of enticing Iran into accepting further IAEA inspection commitments to their nuclear facilities was reiterated at the St. Petersburg 2003 festivities, and more recently in June and July when Iranian nuclear officials visited Moscow to discuss their cooperation on nuclear power.[21]

Moscow continues to deny vehemently all direct U.S. accusations of government-sponsored nuclear and missile technology transfers to Iran that would be in violation of its international nonproliferation obligations. These assurances by Russia have, however, been repeatedly questioned.

Further arguments appeared when reports surfaced in early 1998 that the Russian FSB was in fact coordinating clandestine missile technology transfers to the Iranians--allegations denied by Russian officials.[22] The vigorously developed missile industry of Iran is supposed—along with Russian-supplied aircraft—to provide reliable carriers for potential nuclear warheads. Furthermore, the mere existence of the Shihab-3 missile program, with its relatively poor accuracy (Circle of Error Probable 1–3 kms over distance), implies that it is most likely meant to carry a strictly WMD payload.[23] Moscow has always declared that no infringements of the MTCR have been committed, but did admit the existence of "individual contacts" between Iranian and Russian entities. Through it all, the Russians refuse to be shut out of the lucrative market of missile technologies.[24]

Regarding Russia's nuclear cooperation with Iran, Putin is, perhaps, quite correct when he underscores that "as far as energy is concerned, it focuses exclusively on economic issues."[25] Russia expects to reap up to $10 billion from its Bushehr deal and arms sales to Iran, even if it is currently building the reactor on credit to be paid by Iran only after the completion of the project. Sanctions and admonitions will not change Russia's relationship with one of the most demonized states in America's "axis of evil" if no sound substitute is provided by the United States.

One can only agree with Richard Perle, an influential conservative member of the Defense Policy Board, who considers that this problem can be solved in a "business-like manner," and suggests, "If you want to get this solved, don't send a diplomat. Send a banker to discuss it."[26]

A U.S.-Russia working group was formed before the 2003 summit to resolve the problem. It is difficult, however, to imagine what Washington could actually propose to the cash-strapped enterprises in the Russian military industrial complex as an offset to the lucrative Iranian deals, short of buying out the most thriving of them. The most that could be achieved is to place as many stringent controls and checks on the Iranian nuclear cooperation with Russia as possible.[27]

IS THERE SUFFICIENT U.S. LEVERAGE TO BUDGE MOSCOW ON IRAN?

There is, however, much more than just comprehensible commercial reasons for Moscow's clinging to its Iranian connection. Similar to the Russian opposition to American policy regarding Iraq in 2002 and 2003, this Iranian imbroglio demonstrates that the Russian regime is anxious to show it is nobody's pawn and must be seriously reckoned with as a major international player, if not a re-emerging superpower.

Even in the first major U.S.-Russian discussion of the Iran connection following the September 11, 2001 attacks, American diplomats acknowledged Moscow's special relationship with Tehran. However, the United States also argued "there are other fields for Russia to make economic gains than transferring weapons and nuclear technologies to Iran."[28] The United States has allegedly offered Russia different possible compensations in return for 'reconsidering' its Iran link. At the same time, it was pointed out that Iran was not a side issue. U.S.-Russian relations "cannot move forward while Russia is still closely involved with Iran and Iran is supporting terrorism and aspiring to nuclear weapons," a U.S. diplomat stressed.[29]

However, U.S. emissaries did not make much progress on the Russia-Iran issue. According to a high-ranking U.S. diplomat directly involved in these talks, the Pentagon was ready to purchase a number of Russian-made armaments (specifically helicopters for use in Afghanistan by the Northern Alliance), but only after Moscow severed its ties with Tehran. As a powerful incentive, the United States contemplated agreeing to the Russian import of nuclear waste (processed NPP fuel) from Taiwan, South Korea or Japan. Washington was reportedly prepared, moreover, to order NASA to procure more services from the Russian aviation and space agency and to pay for some additional work on the International Space Station. The Iranian link, however, was the only obstacle to this.

Evidently, influential circles in Moscow considered American advances not enticing enough to sever the established relationship with Tehran. Arms sales and nuclear transfers are, by and large, completely opaque, especially if notorious rogue regimes are the recipients. This is what differentiates these kinds of deals from the proposed contracts with the Pentagon or NASA that were supposed to remain under the oversight of Congress and relevant US agencies, thus making any kind of payoffs to Russian officials or entities almost impossible.

Therefore, Iranian dealings with the Russian defense and nuclear lobbies continue, as the United States is unable to offset them with any meaningful policy or wide-range financial bailout of the Russian entities. In the words of a Russian diplomat, the United States 'never understood that unless Minatom is offered an alternative way to make money' it would not stop doing business with Iran.[30] However, probably taking Putin's regime too much for granted, the United States did not seriously pursue the avenue of buying out Moscow from its "Iranian connection," instead limiting its efforts only to the habitual tug-of-war of bilateral diplomatic squabbles and verbal admonition.

HISTORY OF RUSSIAN INTRANSIGENCE

In defiance of U.S. pressure, Russia declared in July 2002 that it will finish construction of the $840 million nuclear reactor in Bushehr, and that it plans to build five more reactors over the next decade (another in Bushehr and four in Ahvaz, 40 miles from Tehran), for an additional $10 billion.[31]

U.S. concerns focus not on the mishandling of nuclear material from the 1,000-megawatt Bushehr light-water reactor—Russia promises to import it as waste fuel—but on the possibility that Russian know-how and expertise will create a core cadre of Iranian nuclear experts who could then apply their acquired knowledge to a weapons program. Moscow has in the past denied such an eventuality. It underscores the fact that it declined Iranian demands in 1990 to build a more powerful heavy-water reactor and turned down Tehran's request for gas centrifuges (though Moscow was under serious pressure from Washington).[32]

Additionally, the Yeltsin government also reportedly rejected a proposal to help the Iranians with their uranium mining project. Similarly, the plans to sell Russian laser-based isotope separation enrichment technology were scuttled under U.S. pressure in 2000.[33]

However, one can not fully exclude some intangible exchanges between leading Russian laser technology research centers and the Laser Research Center (RCLA) in Tehran that continuously works for the AEOI (Iran's Atomic Energy Organization) on both the molecular laser isotope separation (MLIS) and atomic laser isotope separation (AVLIS).

Some Russian experts predict, though clearly without any plausible basis, that if no compromise over Bushehr is found in the coming months, the United States may use its new strategy of preemptive counterproliferation and bomb the Russian-built reactor even if Russian technicians are still there.[34] In addition to the possibility of American action, some Israeli cabinet figures have mentioned that they are contemplating taking preemptive action (similar to the 1981 bombing of the Iraqi Osiraq reactor) in order to remove the growing nuclear threat to its own survival.[35] The Russians seem to be running out of time to demonstrate a concerted effort to halt nuclear cooperation with Iran hoping, similar to the case in Iraq, that the international community would prevent the United States from radical actions.

RADICAL STRATEGIES TO HEAD OFF IRAN'S NUCLEAR STRIVE

U.S. officials are concerned that Iran could evade the IAEA safeguards it pledged to heed, citing Iraq's ability to conceal an extensive nuclear weapons program that international experts were unable to uncover. CIA experts estimate that Iran is now only two years away from having a nuclear bomb.[36] In any case, now that IAEA safeguards have been strengthened based on the Iraqi experience, Iranian power plants and nuclear activities must remain under stringent oversight by the agency. Russian authorities persist in assuring the 'business-as-usual' nature of Moscow's nuclear cooperation with Tehran, hinting the entire affair is artificially inflated by the United States.[37]

Naturally, even if Tehran finally caved in to U.S. pressure for IAEA inspections along the lines of the Agency's Additional Protocol (as recent events indicate), nothing prevents the regime, if bent on nuclear weapons status, from stringing along the international overseers while continuing the clandestine research at undisclosed and dispersed facilities. Nothing in the internationally imposed arrangements, even possible UN Security Council sanctions, could stop a country from deceiving the world community, as the North Korean and Iraqi examples demonstrated.[38]

Recent revelations of extensive Iranian nuclear program facilities point to Tehran's strong efforts toward the appropriation of a full-fledged nuclear cycle program that could allow the indigenous manufacturing of nuclear weapons, in contravention of Russian allegations to the contrary.

According to the U.S. position, these enrichment facilities and the full-cycle are unjustified for Iranian needs. Additionally, the known resources of indigenous uranium in Iran are limited and cannot provide enough fuel for the projected NPP program.[39] While Iran and Russia claim to be following international agreements on their nuclear activities, much of Iran's current revelations are even in contravention with its original agreement with Moscow on the handling of spent fuel.[40]

Constant U.S. tracking and diplomatic pressure have thwarted such potentially dangerous transfers of Russian technology as laser enrichment from Yefremov Scientific Research Institute (NIIEFA).[41] Iran's initial deal with Russia in 1995 included a centrifuge plant that would have provided Iran with fissile material. The plant deal was then canceled (as was the laser deal and a uranium mining project) under American insistence.

At the same time, recent U.S.-Russian bilateral contacts over the matter as well as Tehran's ostensibly new openness on its nuclear program toward the IAEA could indicate that Moscow will finally secure this important Iranian deal.

ENTER PUTIN

Similar to its position on Iraq, Russia is playing a complex game regarding its cooperation with Iran. Putin's stunning gesture at the Evian G-8 meeting allegedly promising to forego the Iranian nuclear deal was correctly regarded by the Western commentators as another KGB-style trick in attempt to demonstrate Russia's good will and new spirit of cooperation in the aftermath of the Iraq fiasco.[42] It arguably intended to create a certain confusion in the West on real Russian intentions and even prompted Russian assurances to Iran that all those mixed signals did not mean Moscow is practicing double standards with regards to its nuclear ties with Iran.[43]

Russian officials later scurried to explained that Putin actually meant the precondition of making Iran sign the bilateral protocol on the return of the processed nuclear fuel from Bushehr to Russia, and not the IAEA Additional protocols on the enhanced inspections of Tehran's nuclear Facilities.[44]

However, the mighty Minatom, the Russian Leviathan of nuclear energy ministry, soon overruled the president himself.[45] Minatom made it clear, after some vague pronouncements of Russian mid-level officials, that Moscow will continue its nuclear dealings with Tehran. Russia is contemplating a proposal to increase Iran's nuclear capacity by 6000 megawatts by 2020.[46]

The Russian Ministry of Foreign Affairs has confirmed that Moscow will supply Iran with fuel for the Bushehr reactor even if it does not sign the IAEA Additional protocols.[47] While President Putin has assured the world that Iran is bound to demonstrate full NPT compliance before the Russian nuclear transfers occur, the Russian Foreign Ministry has stated that the IAEA's failure to condemn Iran has opened the door for Russia to help build future reactors in that country.[48] The real question will be whether Russia will supply any fuel to Iran if it appears that Tehran will not return it and how Tehran's possible machinations with it can be controlled.

ANY SOLUTIONS IN SIGHT?

U.S.-Russian sparring over Iran could hardly be easily resolved. However, both sides are aware of the need for a compromise and are seemingly interested in smoothing over remaining contradictions on this issue. Some vague hints on possible Russian flexibility on the issue were aired, but so far Russia has given no official commitment to abandon nuclear assistance to Iran.[49]

By the same token, the U.S. administration has not, perhaps, used all of the tools of persuasion in its arsenal.[50] An innovative approach in American diplomacy regarding Iran is needed for any possible breakthrough to occur.

It is clear that the United States is not able to provide enough sources of revenue to equal Moscow's profits from its dealings with Iran in nuclear and arms sales, which Russia considers to be absolutely legitimate, while compensating for the political loss of face.[51]

The most that could realistically be achieved here is making Russia adhere to its commitments that it would provide only defensive weapons to Tehran, also pressing Moscow to restrict the volume of such shipments.[52] The arms dealers in Moscow, however, are ready to turn Iran into Russia's third most important client after China and India.[53] The United States could start discussing with Russia the possibility of launching a new initiative, building on the 1991 Arms Control and Regional Security (ACRS) in the Middle East.

Russia could also be made to continue proceeding with utmost care in its further nuclear cooperation with Iran, doing everything possible to provide for verification of transactions, which would exclude any military spin-offs, even though they have begun to air concerns (agreeing with the United States) that Iran is becoming a nuclear threat.[54] Ideally, Russia could be cajoled into building just one reactor at Bushehr.

Further, the United States could award Moscow with commercial contracts and politically support its accession to the WTO, which could completely compensate for the loss of nuclear cooperation with Iran. However, it is possible that Russia would balk at this deal, because for Moscow to relinquish its stance could be seen as a softening its image as an unbendable, independent player in international relations.[55]

Despite diplomatic overtures, there are no signs of Moscow's actual desire to close the deal, thus signaling a kind of diplomatic victory for Moscow's relations with Washington. On the contrary, all indications point to the Kremlin's desire to upgrade its nuclear connection, if not to persuade Washington of the benign and legitimate nature of Tehran's nuclear aspirations, in an attempt to portray itself as a sort of honest broker in the region.[56]

Tehran has declared its theoretical readiness to sign an additional IAEA protocol if relevant clarifications are given and other countries would in return assist Iran in developing a broader peaceful nuclear power program.[57] However, it is difficult to determine if this is a sincere overture by the Iranians to put a halt to their nuclear ambitions or only a tactical move designed to assuage the immediate pressure of the international community while gaining additional time to create the infrastructure for its nuclear weapons programs. Of course, in the end, much will depend on the domestic Iranian struggle between moderates and conservatives, the resolution of which could have significant repercussions the country's ties with Moscow and Washington.

Thus far, the U.S.-Russian exchange regarding the Iranian conundrum could be termed as a dialogue of the deaf. Perhaps, Washington should start negotiations directly with Minatom and other nuclear enterprises that prosper from the nuclear contracts with Iran rather than with the Kremlin, which appears to have little say in the matter.[58] Moscow and Washington should definitely address ways to further patch the gaps in the current NPT enforcement. In this particular case, it could lead to a kind of ad hoc agreement to prevent Iran from uranium enrichment and plutonium manufacturing in return to certain concessions from Washington like a non-aggression pledge or the resumption of diplomatic relations. Even President Nixon, at the height of the war in Vietnam, sent Henry Kissinger to work out deals with Chinese, Vietnamese and Laotian adversaries. The nuclear conundrum provides a possible pretext for establishing, at a minimum, a representation office in Tehran, if the United States does not want to completely relegate the solution of this issue to its European allies.

Washington policy planners might wish to assess the entire Iranian tangle in a broader scope of the regional security issues while contemplating the motives behind Tehran's quest for nuclear status (the inferiority complex stemming from its confrontation with Iraq, the obsession with Israeli strategic plans, or the suspicion of U.S. power projection in the Middle East). A shrewd move would be the initiation of a regional security conference under U.S.-Russian-French (EU) co-sponsorship. This not only would heal the wounded relationship with both Paris and Moscow, but also bridge the restoration of some kind of relation with the putatively 'democratizing' regime in Tehran to assure American presence in the area.

CONCLUSIONS

While the U.S. and Iran's positions are clear, it is Russia who appears to have room for potential flexibility in the situation by once again serving as a useful middleman, if not an ally, of the United States.[59] Many of the recent revelations have begun to make some Russian experts worry about Iran's facilities and end goal.[60] According to some sources, Russian diplomacy has been tirelessly engaged in persuading Tehran to accede to the IAEA demands demonstrating its good will and full compliance with the NPT. Nevertheless, this seems to be only a tribute to political correctness regarding nonproliferation as Minatom is pushing forward with the signature of the approved draft of the protocol on the return of the spent fuel to open the way to the deliveries of new fuel to the Iranian reactor.

The Iranian nuclear connection to Moscow's ruling elite stands out as a telling symbol of a new Russian external policy. It would require a lot of inventiveness, vision and audacity from Washington to drastically change the course of events in what might become a symbolic shift of the two countries' dialogue and interaction on a global level while simultaneously benefiting stability in the Middle East.

Appendix B
IAEA IMPLEMENTATION OF THE NPT SAFEGUARDS AGREEMENT IN THE ISLAMIC REPUBLIC OF IRAN

Report by the Director General,
International Atomic Energy Agency (IAEA)[1]

A. INTRODUCTION

1 At the meeting of the Board of Governors on 17 March 2003, the Director General reported on discussions taking place with the Islamic Republic of Iran (hereinafter referred to as Iran) on a number of safeguards issues that needed to be clarified and actions that needed to be taken with regard to the implementation of the Agreement between Iran and the IAEA for the Application of Safeguards in connection with the Treaty on the Non-Proliferation of Nuclear Weapons (the Safeguards Agreement).[2] This report provides further information on the nature of the safeguards issues involved and the actions that need to be taken, and describes developments in this regard since March. More general reporting of safeguards implementation in Iran is not addressed in this document, but in the Safeguards Implementation Reports.

B. RECENT DEVELOPMENTS

2 At the September 2002 regular session of the IAEA General Conference, Vice President of the Islamic Republic of Iran and President of the Atomic Energy Organization of Iran (AEOI), H.E. Mr. R. Aghazadeh, stated that Iran was "embarking on a long-term plan to construct nuclear power plants with a total capacity of 6000 MW within two decades." He also stated that such a sizeable project entailed "an all out planning, well in advance, in various field of nuclear technology such as fuel cycle, safety and waste management."

3 During the General Conference, the Director General met with the Vice President, and asked that Iran confirm whether it was building a large underground nuclear related facility at Natanz and a heavy water production plant at Arak, as reported in the media in August 2002. The Vice President provided some information on Iran's intentions to

develop further its nuclear fuel cycle, and agreed on a visit to the two
sites later in 2002 by the Director General, accompanied by safeguards
experts, and to a discussion with Iranian authorities during that meeting on Iran's nuclear development plans.

4   The visit to Iran was originally scheduled for October 2002, but finally took place from 21 to 22 February 2003. The Director General was
accompanied by the Deputy Director General for Safeguards (DDG-
SG) and the Director of the Division of Safeguards Operations.

5   During his visit, the Director General was informed by Iran of its uranium enrichment program, which was described as including two new
facilities located at Natanz, namely a pilot fuel enrichment plant
(PFEP) nearing completion of construction, and a large commercial-
scale fuel enrichment plant (FEP) also under construction. These two
facilities were declared to the Agency for the first time during that
visit, at which time the Director General was able to visit both of them.
Iran also confirmed that the heavy water production plant, referred to
in paragraph 3 above, was under construction in Arak.

6   During the visit, the Director General was informed that Iran would
accept modifications to its Subsidiary Arrangements, as requested by
the Board of Governors in 1992, which would henceforth require the
early provision of design information on new facilities and on modifications to existing facilities, as well as the early provision of information on new locations outside of facilities where nuclear material is
customarily used (LOFs). This was confirmed to the Agency in a letter
dated 26 February 2003.

7   In addition, in response to the Agency's enquiry about certain transfers of nuclear material to Iran, only recently confirmed by the supplier State in response to repeated Agency enquiries, Iran acknowledged
the receipt in 1991 of natural uranium, which had not been reported
previously to the Agency, in the form of UF_6 (1000 kg), UF_4 (400 kg)
and UO_2 (400 kg), which was now being stored at the previously
undeclared Jabr Ibn Hayan Multipurpose Laboratories (JHL) located
at the Tehran Nuclear Research Centre (TNRC). Iran also informed
the Agency that it had converted most of the UF_4 into uranium metal
in 2000 at JHL. This information was subsequently confirmed by Iran
in a separate letter to the Agency dated 26 February 2003.

8   During the discussions in Iran in February between DDG-SG and the
Iranian authorities, reference was made by the Agency to information
in open sources on the possible conduct of enrichment activities at the
workshop of the Kalaye Electric Company in Tehran. The Iranian
authorities acknowledged that the workshop had been used for the
production of centrifuge components, but stated that there had been

no operations in connection with its centrifuge enrichment development program involving the use of nuclear material, either at the
Kalaye Electric Company or at any other location in Iran. According
to the Iranian authorities, all testing had been carried out using simulation studies. While a centrifuge component production facility is not
a nuclear facility required to be declared to the Agency under Iran's
NPT Safeguards Agreement, Iran was requested, in light of its stated
policy of transparency, to permit the Agency to visit the workshop and
to take environmental samples there to assist the Agency in verifying
Iran's declaration and confirming the absence of undeclared nuclear
material and activities. The request was initially declined. The Iranian
authorities told the Agency that Iran considered such visits, and the
requested environmental sampling, as being obligatory only when an
Additional Protocol was in force. However, they subsequently agreed
to permit access to the workshop (to limited parts of the location in
March, and to the entire workshop in May), and have recently indicated that they would consider permitting the taking of environmental
samples during the visit of the Agency's enrichment experts to Iran
scheduled to take place between 7 and 11 June 2003 (see paragraph
11 below).

9 On 26 February 2003, a list of additional questions and requests
   for clarification was submitted to Iran regarding its centrifuge and
   laser enrichment programs and its heavy water program, and a written reply requested. A written response was received from Iran on 4
   June 2003, and its contents will be followed up with the Iranian
   authorities.

10 In a letter dated 5 May 2003, Iran informed the Agency for the first
   time of its intention to construct a heavy water research reactor at
   Arak (the 40 MW(th) Iran Nuclear Research Reactor IR- 40). Iran also
   informed the Agency of its plan to commence construction in 2003 of
   a fuel manufacturing plant at Esfahan (FMP).

11 During a meeting between the Vice President and the Director General
   on 5 May 2003, the Director General reiterated the Agency's earlier
   request for permission to send Agency inspectors to the workshop of
   the Kalaye Electric Company in Tehran, and to take environmental
   samples. The Director General also referred to an earlier proposal the
   Agency had made in April for a group of Agency experts to visit Iran
   to discuss the centrifuge research and development program to seek to
   assess how the current status of the project could have been achieved
   without using any nuclear material during tests. Iran agreed to consider the proposal for an expert mission, and subsequently agreed that
   the mission could take place from 7 to 11 June 2003.

C. IMPLEMENTATION OF SAFEGUARDS

12 Article 8 of Iran's Safeguards Agreement requires Iran to provide the Agency with information "concerning nuclear material subject to safeguards under the Agreement and the features of facilities relevant to safeguarding such material."

13 As provided for in Article 34(c) of the Safeguards Agreement, nuclear material of a composition and purity suitable for fuel fabrication or for being isotopically enriched, and any nuclear material produced at a later stage in the nuclear fuel cycle, is subject to all of the safeguards procedures specified in the Agreement. These procedures include, inter alia, requirements for Iran to report to the Agency changes in the inventory of nuclear material through the submission of inventory change reports (ICRs). Certain inventory changes entail additional reporting requirements. These include the import of nuclear material in quantities in excess of one effective kilogram, which, in accordance with Article 95 of the Safeguards Agreement, requires reporting to the Agency in advance of the import.

14 To enable the Agency to verify the inventory and flow of nuclear material, Iran is also required to provide design information on facilities (as defined in Article 98.I of Iran's Safeguards Agreement), and information on LOFs. Pursuant to Article 42 of Iran's Safeguards Agreement, the time limit for the provision of design information on new nuclear facilities is to be specified in the Subsidiary Arrangements, but in any event it is to be provided "as early as possible before nuclear material is introduced into a new facility." Article 49 requires that information on LOFs be provided "on a timely basis."

15 The Subsidiary Arrangements General Part in force with Iran from 1976 to 26 February 2003 included what was, until 1992, standard text which called for provision to the Agency of design information on a new facility no later than 180 days before the introduction of nuclear material into the facility, and the provision of information on a new LOF together with the report relating to the receipt of nuclear material at the LOF. With the acceptance by Iran on 26 February 2003 of the modifications to the Subsidiary Arrangements proposed by the Agency, the Subsidiary Arrangements General Part now requires Iran to inform the Agency of new nuclear facilities and modifications to existing facilities through the provision of preliminary design information as soon as the decision to construct, to authorize construction or to modify has been taken, and to provide the Agency with further design information as it is developed. Information is to be provided early in the project definition, preliminary design, construction and commissioning phases.

C.1. IMPORTED NUCLEAR MATERIAL

16 The UF_6, UF_4 and UO_2 imported by Iran in 1991 are materials that, as provided for in Article 34(c)of Iran's Safeguards Agreement, are subject to all of the safeguards procedures specified in the Agreement, including, in particular, the requirement to report inventory changes. Therefore, Iran was obliged to have reported the import of the material in question at the time of import. Equally, Iran was obliged to have reported design information as soon as possible before nuclear material was introduced to the receiving facility, and a Facility Attachment concluded for that facility.

17 In its letter of 26 February 2003 confirming its receipt of the material in question, Iran stated that its interpretation of Articles 34(c) and 95 of the Safeguards Agreement had been that no reporting to the Agency was required since the total amount of uranium did not exceed one effective kilogram. However, as indicated in paragraph 13 above, all material referred to in Article 34(c) of the Safeguards Agreement must be reported to the Agency. Article 95 simply imposes an additional requirement, that of advance notification, with respect to imports of material in excess of one effective kilogram.

18 Iran submitted on 15 April 2003 an ICR with regard to the import of the nuclear material, and, on 5 May 2003, preliminary design information for JHL, where most of the material is currently being stored.

C.1.1. PROCESSING OF UF_6

19 The Iranian authorities have stated that the imported UF_6 has not been processed, and specifically that it has not been used in any enrichment, centrifuge or other tests. The one large and two small UF_6 cylinders declared as containing the imported UF_6 were shown to the Agency in February. The cylinders were made available for Agency verification at JHL in March, at which time, after the Agency inspectors noted that one of the small cylinders was lighter than declared, the State authorities explained that a small amount of the UF_6 (1.9 kg) was missing due to leaking valves on the two small cylinders. It was explained during the subsequent inspection in April that the leaks had only been noticed a year before. Final evaluation will be completed when destructive samples have been taken,environmental samples have been analysed, and supporting documentation provided by the operator has been examined.

C.1.2. PROCESSING OF UF$_4$

20 Iran has informed the Agency that most of the imported UF$_4$ was converted to uranium metal at JHL. While the equipment for the conversion process has been dismantled and stored in a container (shown to the Agency during the February visit), Iran is now refurbishing that part of the facility as a uranium metal processing laboratory. The uranium metal, together with the remaining UF4 and the related waste, has been presented for Agency verification. Final evaluation will be done when the results of destructive analysis become available, and supporting documentation provided by the facility operator has been examined. The role of uranium metal in Iran's declared nuclear fuel cycle still needs to be fully understood, since neither its light water reactors nor its planned heavy water reactors require uranium metal for fuel.

C.1.3. PROCESSING OF UO$_2$

21 During the February 2003 discussions, the Agency was informed by Iran that some of the imported UO$_2$ had been used at JHL for the testing of uranium purification and conversion processes. The experiments involved the dissolution of UO$_2$ with nitric acid, and the use of the resulting uranyl nitrate for testing a pulse column and ammonium uranyl carbonate (AUC) production processes envisioned for the Uranium Conversion Facility (UCF), a facility declared to the Agency in 2000 and currently under construction at Esfahan. In April, in response to Agency enquiries, the Iranian authorities informed the Agency that some of the UO$_2$ had also been used for isotope production experiments, including the undeclared irradiation of small amounts of the UO$_2$, at the Tehran Research Reactor (TRR). In addition, they informed the Agency that another small amount of UO$_2$ had been used in pellets to test the chemical processes of the Molybdenum, Iodine and Xenon Radioisotope Production Facility (MIX Facility). The unused UO$_2$ has been presented for Agency verification at JHL.

22 Most of the UO$_2$ used in the UCF-related experiments has been presented for Agency verification as liquid waste at Esfahan; the remaining waste has been disposed of at a location near Qom and cannot be verified. The whereabouts of the AUC produced during the UCF-related experiments is being discussed. Final evaluation of the accountancy will be completed when the results of destructive analysis become available, and the supporting documentation provided by the facility operator has been examined.

23 With respect to the isotope production experiments, Iran has stated

that small amounts of the imported UO_2 were prepared for targets at JHL, irradiated at TRR, and sent to a laboratory belonging to the MIX Facility in Tehran for separation of I-131 in a lead-shielded cell. Iran has informed the Agency that the remaining nuclear waste was solidified and eventually transferred to a waste disposal site at Anarak. The operators at TRR and the MIX Facility have provided supporting documentation, which is being examined. The Agency is still awaiting relevant updated design information for the MIX Facility and TRR. Plans are in place to visit the waste site at Anarak in June of that year.

24 With respect to the UO_2 to test the chemical processes of the MIX Facility, the material, including the resulting waste, has been presented for Agency verification at JHL. Final evaluation will be completed when the results of the destructive analysis become available, and supporting documentation provided by the facility operator has been examined.

C.2. URANIUM ENRICHMENT PROGRAM

25 During the visit of the Director General in February 2003, the Vice President informed the Agency that over 100 of the approximately one-thousand planned centrifuge casings had already been installed at the pilot plant and that the remaining centrifuges would be installed by the end of the year. In addition, he informed the Agency that the commercial scale enrichment facility, which is planned to contain over fifty thousand centrifuges, was not scheduled to receive nuclear material in the near future.

26 The Agency has been informed that the pilot enrichment plant is scheduled to start operating in June 2003, initially with single machine tests, and later with increasing numbers of centrifuges. The Iranian authorities have also informed the Agency that the commercial enrichment plant is planned to start accepting centrifuges in early 2005, after the design is confirmed by the tests to be conducted in the pilot enrichment plant. Iran has also stated that the design and research and development work, which had been started about five years ago, were based on extensive modelling and simulation,including tests of centrifuge rotors both with and without inert gas, and that the tests of the rotors, carried out on the premises of the Amir Khabir University and the AEOI in Tehran, were conducted without nuclear material.

27 In May 2003, Iran provided preliminary design information on the enrichment facilities under construction in Natanz, which are being examined by the Agency. Since March 2003, Agency inspectors have visited facilities at Natanz three times to conduct design information verification and to take environmental samples at the pilot enrichment

plant. A first series of environmental and destructive analysis samples has been taken at a number of locations. Additional samples are expected to be taken in the near future. Iran has cooperated with the Agency in this regard. The Agency has presented to the Iranian authorities a safeguards approach for the pilot enrichment plant.

28 As indicated above, on 26 February 2003, the Agency forwarded a number of questions regarding Iran's research and development on centrifuges, including the chronology of its enrichment program, with a view to assessing, inter alia, Iran's declaration that it had been developed without the centrifuges having been tested with UF_6 process gas. Similar questions and concerns have been raised by the Agency in relation to the UO_2, UF_4 and UF_6 production at the large scale conversion facility UCF, which is stated to have been constructed without any testing, even on a small scale, of key processes.

29 The Agency is also pursuing enquiries into Iran's laser program. Iran has acknowledged the existence of a substantial program on lasers, and Agency inspectors have visited some locations said to have been involved in that program. However, Iran has stated that no enrichment related laser activities have taken place.

C.3. HEAVY WATER PROGRAM

30 According to information provided by the Iranian authorities (see Section B above), the Iranian heavy water reactor program consists of the heavy water production plant currently under construction at Arak; the 40 MW(th) IR-40, construction of which is planned to start at Arak in 2004; and the FMP at Esfahan, construction of which is planned for 2003, commissioning for 2006 and commencement of operation for 2007.

31 The stated purposes of the IR-40, which will use natural UO_2 fuel and heavy water (both as a coolant and as a moderator), are reactor research and development, radioisotope production and training. The stated purpose of the FMP is fabrication of fuel assemblies for the IR-40 and for the Bushehr Nuclear Power Plant (BNPP).

D. FINDINGS AND INITIAL ASSESSMENT

32 Iran has failed to meet its obligations under its Safeguards Agreement with respect to the reporting of nuclear material, the subsequent processing and use of that material and the declaration of facilities where the material was stored and processed. These failures, and the actions taken thus far to correct them, can be summarized as follows:

(a) Failure to declare the import of natural uranium in 1991, and its subsequent transfer for further processing. On 15 April 2003, Iran submitted ICRs on the import of the UO_2, UF_4 and UF_6. Iran has still to submit ICRs on the transfer of the material for further processing and use.

(b) Failure to declare the activities involving the subsequent processing and use of the imported natural uranium, including the production and loss of nuclear material, where appropriate, and the production and transfer of waste resulting therefrom. Iran has acknowledged the production of uranium metal, uranyl nitrate, ammonium uranyl carbonate, UO_2 pellets and uranium wastes. Iran must still submit ICRs on these inventory changes.

(c) Failure to declare the facilities where such material (including the waste) was received, stored and processed. On 5 May 2003, Iran provided preliminary design information for the facility JHL. Iran has informed the Agency of the locations where the undeclared processing of the imported natural uranium was conducted (TRR and the Esfahan Nuclear Technology Centre), and provided access to those locations. It has provided the Agency access to the waste storage facility at Esfahan, and has indicated that access would be provided to Anarak, as well as the waste disposal site at Qom.

(d) Failure to provide in a timely manner updated design information for the MIX Facility and for TRR. Iran has agreed to submit updated design information for the two facilities.

(e) Failure to provide in a timely manner information on the waste storage at Esfahan and at Anarak. Iran has informed the Agency of the locations where the waste has been stored or discarded. It has provided the Agency access to the waste storage facility at Esfahan,and has indicated that access will be provided to Anarak.

33 Although the quantities of nuclear material involved have not been large, and the material would need further processing before being suitable for use as the fissile material component of a nuclear explosive device, the number of failures by Iran to report the material, facilities and activities in question in a timely manner as it is obliged to do pursuant to its Safeguards Agreement is a matter of concern. While these failures are in the process of being rectified by Iran, the process of verifying the correctness and completeness of the Iranian declarations is still ongoing.

34 The Agency is continuing to pursue the open questions, including through:

(a) The completion of a more thorough expert analysis of the research and development carried out by Iran in the establishment of its enrichment capabilities. This will require the submission by Iran of a complete chronology of its centrifuge and laser enrichment efforts, including, in particular, a description of all research and development activities carried out prior to the construction of the Natanz facilities. As agreed to by Iran, this process will also involve discussions in Iran between Iranian authorities and Agency enrichment experts on Iran's enrichment program, and visits by the Agency experts to the facilities under construction at Natanz and other relevant locations.

(b) Further follow-up on information regarding allegations about undeclared enrichment of nuclear material, including, in particular, at the Kalaye Electric Company. This will require permission for the Agency to carry out environmental sampling at the workshop located there.

(c) Further enquiries about the role of uranium metal in Iran's nuclear fuel cycles.

(d) Further enquiries about Iran's program related to the use of heavy water, including heavy water production and heavy water reactor design and construction.

34 The Director General has repeatedly encouraged Iran to conclude an Additional Protocol. Without such protocols in force, the Agency's ability to provide credible assurances regarding the absence of undeclared nuclear activities is limited. This is particularly the case for States, like Iran, with extensive nuclear activities and advanced fuel cycle technologies. In the view of the Director General, the adherence by Iran to an Additional Protocol would therefore constitute a significant step forward. The Director General will continue to keep the Board informed of developments.

Appendix C
IRAN'S ECONOMY AND
OIL AND GAS RESOURCES[1]

Iran is OPEC's second largest oil producer and holds seven percent of the world's proven oil reserves. It also has the world's second largest natural gas reserves.

GENERAL BACKGROUND

Iran's economy, which relies heavily on oil export revenues (around 80 percent of total export earnings, 40–50 per cent of the government budget, and 10–20 percent of GDP), was hit hard by the plunge in oil prices during 1998 and early 1999, but with the rebound in oil prices since then, has recovered to a great degree.

For 2002, Iran's real GDP grew by around 5.9 percent; for 2003 and 2004 it is expected to grow at slightly slower, but still healthy, 4.5 percent and 4.4 percent rates, respectively. Relatively high oil export revenues the past year or two have allowed Iran to set up an oil stabilization fund. For 2003, Iran's budget anticipated a price of around $18.50 per barrel, well below current levels.

Despite relatively high oil export revenues, Iran continues to face budgetary pressures, a rapidly growing, young population with limited job prospects and high levels of unemployment; heavy dependence on oil revenues; significant external debt (including a high proportion of short-term debt); high levels of poverty; expensive state subsidies (billions of dollars per year) on many basic goods; a large, inefficient public sector and state monopolies (bonyads, which control at least a quarter of the economy and constitutionally are answerable only to supreme leader Ayatollah Ali Khamenei); international isolation and sanctions.

Iran is attempting to diversify by investing some of its oil revenues in other areas, including petrochemicals. Iran also is hoping to attract billions of dollars worth of foreign investment to the country by creating a more favorable investment climate (i.e., reduced restrictions and duties on imports, creation of free-trade zones).

In May 2002, the country's Expediency Council approved the "Law on the Attraction and Protection of Foreign Investment," which aims at encouraging foreign investment by streamlining procedures, guaranteeing profit repatriation, and more.

This law, which was sent to the government for implementation in January 2003, represents the first foreign investment act passed by Iran's legislature since the 1978/79 revolution. The legislation was delayed for several years due to disagreements between reformers and conservatives. In June 2001, the Council of Guardians had rejected the bill as passed by the Majlis (parliament) the previous month.

In November 2001, the Majlis had passed a second, heavily amended, version of the bill. Although this version was far weaker than the first bill, the Council of Guardians again rejected it (in December 2001).

Sanctions

In March 2003, President Bush extended sanctions originally imposed in 1995 by President Clinton for another year, citing Iran's "support for international terrorism, efforts to undermine the Middle East peace process, and acquisition of weapons of mass destruction."

The 1995 executive orders prohibit U.S. companies and their foreign subsidiaries from conducting business with Iran, while banning any "contract for the financing of the development of petroleum resources located in Iran."

In addition, the U.S. Iran-Libya Sanctions Act (ILSA) of 1996 (renewed for 5 more years in July 2001) imposes mandatory and discretionary sanctions on non-U.S. companies investing more than $20 million annually in the Iranian oil and natural gas sectors. In May 2002, the United States announced that it would review an $80 million contract by Canada's Sheer Energy (see below) to develop an Iranian oilfield to determine whether or not it violates ILSA.

OIL

Iran holds around 90 billion barrels of proven oil reserves, roughly 7 percent of the world's total, and claims another 30 billion barrels. The vast majority of Iran's crude oil reserves are located in giant onshore fields in the southwestern Khuzestan region near the Iraqi border and the Persian Gulf. Iran has 32 producing oil fields, of which 25 are onshore and 7 offshore.

Major onshore fields include the following: Ahwaz-Asmari (700,000 bbl/d); Bangestan (around 245,000 bbl/d current production, with plans to increase to 550,000 bbl/d), Marun (520,000 bbl/d), Gachsaran (560,000 bbl/d), Agha Jari (200,000 bbl/d), Karanj-Parsi (200,000 bbl/d); Rag-e-Safid (180,000 bbl/d); Bibi Hakimeh (130,000 bbl/d), and Pazanan (70,000 bbl/d). Major offshore fields include: Dorood (130,000 bbl/d); Salman (130,000 bbl/d); Abuzar (125,000 bbl/d); Sirri A&E (95,000 bbl/d); and Soroush/Nowruz (60,000 bbl/d).

Iran's crude oil is generally low in sulfur, with gravities mainly in the 28°–35° API range.

During the first eight months of 2003, Iran produced 3.9 million bbl/d of oil (of which 3.7 million bbl/d was crude oil), up from 3.5 million bbl/d in 2002. Iran's current sustainable crude oil production capacity is estimated at around 3.75 million bbl/d, which is around 0.15 million bbl/d above Iran's latest (November 1, 2003) OPEC production quota of 3.597 million bbl/d. Some analysts believe that Iran's capacity is lower, perhaps 3.6 million bbl/d, and that it could fall even further until new oilfield developments (Azadegan, Bangestan—see below) come online in a few years.

Iran has net exports of around 2.6 million bbl/d Major customers for Iranian oil include Japan, China, South Korea, Taiwan, and Europe. Iran's main export blends include Iranian Light (34.6° API, 1.4 percent sulphur); Iranian Heavy (31° API, 1.7 percent sulphur); Lavan Blend (34°-35° API, 1.8 percent-2 percent sulphur); and Foroozan Blend/Sirri (29-31° API). Iran is also the largest heavy fuel oil exporter in the Middle East. Iranian oil is traded on the spot market by NIOC's London division.

Iran's domestic oil consumption, 1.3 million bbl/d in 2003, is increasing rapidly (about 7 percent per year) as the economy and population grow. Iran subsidizes the price of oil products heavily, to the tune of $3 billion or so per year, resulting in a large amount of waste and inefficiency in oil consumption.

Iran also is forced to spend around $1 billion per year to import oil products (mainly gasoline) which it cannot produce locally. In early April 2003, as part of an effort to curtail the rise in gasoline subsidy expenditures, gasoline consumption and imports (both of which are growing rapidly), Iran raised gasoline prices by 30–35 percent, to around 31–44 cents per gallon. In November 2003, Iran announced that it might even be forced to start rationing gasoline.

It is possible that, with sufficient investment, Iran could increase its oil production capacity significantly. Iran produced 6 million bbl/d in 1974, but has not surpassed 3.8 million bbl/d on an annual basis since the 1978/79 Iranian revolution.

During the 1980s, it is believed that Iran may have maintained production levels at some older fields only by using methods which have permanently damaged the fields. Also, Iran's oilfields are— according to Oil Minister Zanganeh—experiencing a depletion rate of 200,000–300,000 bbl/d per year, and are in need of upgrading and modernization. Despite these problems, Iran has ambitious plans to double national oil production to more than 7 million bbl/d by 2015 or so.

The country is counting on foreign investment to accomplish this, possibly as high as $5 billion per year.

NIOC's onshore field development work is concentrated mainly on sustaining output levels from large, aging fields. Consequently, enhanced oil recovery (EOR) programs, including natural gas injection, are underway at a number of fields, including Marun, Karanj, and the presently inactive Parsi fields. EOR programs will require sizeable amounts of natural gas, infrastructure development, and financing. Overall, Iran's oil sector is considered old and inefficient, needing thorough revamping, advanced technology, and foreign investment.

In October 1999, Iran announced that it had made its biggest oil discovery in thirty years, a giant onshore field called Azadegan located in the southwestern province of Khuzestan, a few miles east of the border with Iraq.

Reportedly, the Azadegan field contains in-place oil reserves of 26–70 billion barrels, with potential production of 300,000–400,000 bbl/d (and possibly higher) over a 20-year period.

On November 1, 2000, agreement was reached between Japan and Iran for Japanese firms (Japex, Indonesia Petroleum, and Tomen) to receive priority negotiating rights in developing Azadegan. In exchange, Japan was to loan Iran $3 billion. In January 2001, the Majlis approved development of Azadegan by foreign investors using the so-called "buyback" model (see below). In early March 2003, however, the Iranian official in charge of developing Azadegan said that Iran and Japan had not yet reached a final agreement on the $2.5 billion project.

Meanwhile, Japan has come under pressure from the United States to hold off on signing a deal with Iraq on Azadegan until Iran allows international inspectors greater access to its nuclear facilities (see below).

In September 2003, Iran's oil minister said that Japan had lost its exclusive rights on Azadegan, and that Iran would negotiate with other companies, but President Khatami said in late October 2003 that Japan still had "priority" on the field. Reportedly, the Japanese are pushing for a long-term presence at Azadegan, possibly 20 years, while the Iranians are offering less than 10 years. In early November 2003, Iran disclosed that it was in advanced negotiations with Total and Statoil on Azadegan development. It is possible that Statoil would be at a disadvantage vis-a-vis Total due to a kickback and corruption scandal involving Statoil and various Iranian officials, including Mehdi Hashemi Rafsanjani, son of the country's former President and Chairman of an NIOC subsidiary.

Since 1995, NIOC has made several sizable oil discoveries, including the 3–5-billion-barrel Darkhovin onshore oilfield, located near Abadan and containing low sulfur, 39° API crude oil. In late June 2001, Italy's ENI signed a nearly $1 billion, 5-1/2-year buyback deal to develop Darkhovin, with the added incentive of a limited risk/reward element (payment is to be linked to production capacity). ENI has a 60 percent stake in the project, with NIOC holding the remaining 40 percent. Ultimately, production at Darkhovin is expected to reach 160,000 bbl/d.

Foreign Investment/Buybacks

The Iranian constitution prohibits the granting of petroleum rights on a concessionary basis or direct equity stake. However, the 1987 Petroleum Law permits the establishment of contracts between the Ministry of Petroleum, state companies and "local and foreign national persons and legal entities." "Buyback" contracts, for instance, are arrangements in which the contractor funds all investments, receives remuneration from NIOC in the form of an allocated production share, then transfers operation of the field to NIOC after the contract is completed.

This system has drawbacks for both sides: by offering a fixed rate of return (usually around 15 to 17 percent), NIOC bears all the risk of low oil prices.

If prices drop, NIOC has to sell more oil or natural gas to meet the compensation figure. At the same time, companies have no guarantee that they will be permitted to develop their discoveries, let alone operate them. Finally, companies do not like the short terms of buyback contracts.

The first major project under the buyback investment scheme became operational in October 1998, when the offshore Sirri A oil field (operated by Total and Malaysia's Petronas) began production at 7,000 bbl/d (Sirri A currently is producing around 20,000 bbl/d). The neighboring Sirri E field began production in February 1999, with production at the two fields expected to reach 120,000 bbl/d.

In March 1999, France's Elf Aquitaine and Italy's Eni/Agip were awarded a $1 billion contract for a secondary recovery program at the offshore, 1.5-billion-barrel Doroud oil and natural gas field located near Kharg Island. The program is intended to boost production from around 136,000 bbl/d to as high as 205,000 bbl/d by 2004. TotalFinaElf is operator of the project, with a 55 percent share, while Eni holds the other 45 percent.

In April 1999, Iran awarded TotalFinaElf (46.75 percent share), along with Canada's Bow Valley Energy (15 percent share), a buyback contract to develop the offshore Balal field. The field, which contains some 80 million barrels of reserves, started producing at a 20,000-bbl/d rate in early 2003, reportedly reached 40,000 bbl/d in October 2003. In February 2001, ENI-Agip acquired a 38.25 percent share in Balal.

In November 2000, Norway's Statoil signed a series of agreements with NIOC to explore for oil in the Strait of Hormuz area. The two companies also will cooperate on developing a natural gas-to-liquids processing plant for four southern onshore fields, and possibly will develop the Salman offshore field at a cost of $850 million, with eventual production of 130,000 bbl/d. Iran appears to be accelerating its plans to boost production of natural gas liquids (NGL), as well as liquefied petroleum gas (LPG). NGL expansion plans, including a $500 million plan to build two NGL plans on the south coast of Iran, are aimed mainly at making ethane feedstock available for Iran's growing petrochemical industry.

A much-sought-after deal to develop the giant Bangestan field has been delayed several times after an expected award in 2001. Bangestan includes three oilfields (Anwaz, Mansuri, Ab-Teymour) which currently produce about 250,000 bbl/d of oil. In April 2003, Shell stated that it was frustrated with the slow pace of negotiations on Bangestan, including numerous changes to terms of the project.

In May 2002, Iran's Oil Ministry signed a $585 million buyback contract with local company PetroIran to develop the Foroozan and Esfandiar offshore oilfields. PetroIran is expected to increase production at the fields from around 40,000 bbl/d at present to 109,000 bbl/d within 3 years. The two oilfields straddle the border with Saudi Arabia's Lulu and Marjan fields.

In other news related to "buyback" deals, the Cheshmeh-Khosh field, which had been awarded to Spain's Cepsa for $300 million, is likely to be re-awarded to a consortium of Cepsa and OMV. The two companies are to raise crude production at the field from 30,000 bbl/d to 80,000 bbl/d within four years.

Recently, Iran appears to have had some second thoughts about buybacks (including charges of corruption, insufficient benefits to Iran, and also worries that buybacks are attracting too little investment), and reportedly is considering substantial changes in the system. In late May 2002, Canada's Sheer Energy became the first foreign company since ENI's Darkhovin deal to reach agreement ($80 million to develop the Masjed-I-Suleyman, or MIS, field) under the ENI terms. Sheer aims to boost MIS production from 4,500 bbl/d to 20,000 bbl/d.

In general, however, the addition of a limited risk/reward element has not attracted the flood of foreign energy investment which Iran both needs and wants. As a result, Iran reportedly is considering a further modification to its 'buy-back' model, possibly extending the length of such contracts from the current 5–7 years.

In early November 2003, NIOC announced the launch of a new tender for 16 oil blocks. The contracts reportedly are to be based on the buyback model, but for the first time will cover exploration, appraisal, and development.

In September 2003, Russia's Lukoil said it had been granted approval by NIOC to explore for oil in the Anaran block along the border with Iraq. Norsk Hydro is currently in charge of the project.

Offshore Developments

The Doroud 1&2, Salman, Abuzar, Foroozan, and Sirri fields comprise the bulk of Iran's offshore oil output. Iran plans extensive development of existing offshore fields and hopes to raise its offshore production capacity to 1.1 million bbl/d (from around 675,000 bbl/d currently). It is estimated that development of new offshore Persian Gulf and Caspian Sea oil fields will require investment of $8–$10 billion.

In October 2003, Iran relaunched a tender for eight exploration blocks in the Persian Gulf after receiving little interest from a January 2003 announcement.

One area considered to have potential is located near the Strait of Hormuz. Another interesting area is offshore near Bushehr, where Iran claimed in July 2003 to have discovered three fields with potentially huge (38 billion barrels) oil reserves.

In late 2001 and early 2002, Shell brought part of the $1.1 billion Soroush-Nowrooz development online, with production of around 60,000 bbl/d. The two fields are located offshore, about 50 miles west of Kharg Island, and contain estimated recoverable reserves of around 1 billion barrels of mainly heavy oil. Although Soroush was shut down briefly in March 2003 at the outset of war with Iraq, output from the field is still expected to reach 190,000 bbl/d by the end of 2003 (the first of four new oil platforms at Soroush was launched in October 2003). In early 2003, a consortium of three Japanese companies bought a 20 percent share in the Soroush/Nowrooz development project.

Caspian Sea Region

Aside from acting as a transit center for other countries' oil and natural gas exports from the Caspian Sea, Iran has potentially significant Caspian reserves of its own, including up to 15 billion barrels of oil and 11 trillion cubic feet of natural gas. It is important to note, however, that almost none of this is 'proven' to be recoverable (although preliminary seismic surveys conducted by Lasmo and Shell indicated 2.5 billion barrels of oil).

Currently, Iran has no oil or natural gas production in the Caspian region, although in March 2001, NIOC signed a $226 million deal with Sweden's GVA Consultants and Iran's Sadra to build an oil rig in the Caspian Sea off Mazandaran province. This marks Iran's first exploration attempt in the Caspian Sea, whose legal status among regional states remains in dispute.

At the present time, Iran maintains the most isolated position among the Caspian Sea's littoral states on the division of the Sea. Iran insists that regional treaties signed in 1921 and 1940 between Iran and the former Soviet Union, which call for joint sharing of the Caspian's resources between the two countries, remain valid. Iran has rejected as invalid all unilateral and bilateral agreements on the utilization of the Sea. As such, Iran is insisting that either the Sea should be used in common, or its floor and water basin should be divided into equal (20 percent) shares.

Under this plan, the so-called "condominium" approach, the development of the Caspian Sea would be undertaken jointly by all of the littoral states. However, using the equidistant method of dividing the seabed on which Kazakhstan, Azerbaijan, and Russia have agreed, Iran would only receive about 12 to 13 percent of the Sea.

In March 2002, Iran's Oil Minister Zanganeh asserted that Iran would begin exploiting its fifth of the Sea within a short time, and would not permit "any other party to engage in oil exploration" in this area. In January 2003, Iranian Foreign Minister Kamal Kharrazi reiterated the country's claim to a 20percent share of the Caspian, and in early April 2003, Oil Minister Zanganeh said that Iran would start Caspian drilling within a year or two.

As of April 2003, no agreement has been reached among Caspian Sea region states on this matter. In March 2003, Iran and Turkmenistan noted "the need to achieve a consensus between the five [littoral] countries," while the two countries reportedly moved ahead in charting their common border in the Sea.

In late April 2002, a meeting between the five Caspian littoral states ended without agreement on a new treaty. On May 20, 2002, Iran and Azerbaijan also failed to reach agreement on a Caspian Sea division. On July 23, 2001, tensions flared in the Caspian Sea region when an Iranian gunboat intercepted two BP oil exploration vessels off Azerbaijan's coast. Following the incident, BP suspended exploration in the disputed block (which Iran calls Alborz).

Crude Swaps

In order to get around restrictions in dealing with Iran, several firms have proposed oil "swaps" involving the delivery of Caspian (Azeri, Kazakh, Turkmen) oil to refineries in northern Iran, while an equivalent amount of Iranian oil is exported through Persian Gulf terminals. According to Iranian Oil Minister Bijan Namdar-Zangeneh, Iran is planning to retool its oil infrastructure to accommodate such swaps, including construction of a $400 million, 240-mile pipeline from the Caspian area via Iran's Caspian port of Neka to refineries in northern Iran and to Tehran. Eventually, this could lead to the transport of 370,000 bbl/d of Caspian crude.

Iran also plans to boost capacity at its northern refineries at Arak, Tabriz, and Tehran to about 800,000 bbl/d in order to process this oil (in August 2003, a $500 million tender was issued to upgrade the Tehran and Tabriz refineries).

As of the summer of 2003, about 50,000 bbl/d of Turkmen oil were being shipped to Neka, and then on to Tehran by the existing Neka-Tehran pipeline. Iran is aiming to increase this volume to 150,000 bbl/d in the near term and as much as 500,000 bbl/d in the long term, with a new pipeline carrying crude from Neka to the Tehran refinery.

Meanwhile, in November 2002, Russia's Lukoil began sending around 25,000 bbl/d of Russian Siberian Light crude from the Caspian port of Astrakhan to Neka, and Kazakhstan reportedly is shipping around 20,000 bbl/d to Iran. Finally, Iran reportedly has proposed that its refinery at Abadan be used to process up to 350,000 bbl/d of Iraqi crude oil in yet another swap arrangement.

Refining and Transportation
As of January 2003, Iran had nine operational refineries with a combined capacity of 1.47 million bbl/d. Major refineries include: Abadan (400,000-bbl/d capacity); Isfahan (265,000 bbl/d); Bandar Abbas (232,000 bbl/d); Tehran (225,000 bbl/d); Arak (150,000 bbl/d); and Tabriz (112,000 bbl/d). There reportedly are plans to increase capacity at Abadan to 540,000 bbl/d and at Bandar Abbas to around 320,000 bbl/d.

In order to meet burgeoning domestic demand for middle and light distillates, Iran has imported refined products since 1982, and is attempting to boost its refining capacity to 2 million bbl/d. Two planned grass-roots refineries include a 225,000-bbl/d plant at Shah Bahar and a 120,000-bbl/d unit on Qeshm Island.

The $3 billion Shah Bahar refinery project was approved by the government in late 1994 and would be built by private investors. Under Iranian law, foreign companies are permitted to won no more than 49percent of Iranian oil refining assets.

Iran exports crude oil via four main terminals—Kharg Island (by far the largest), Lavan Island, Sirri Island (reopened on April 13, 2003 for the first time since 1988, when it was damaged by an Iraqi air raid), and Ras Bahregan. Refined products are exported via the Abadan and Bandar Mahshahr terminals. Many Iranian oil export terminals were damaged during the Iran-Iraq War, but all have been rebuilt.

NATURAL GAS

Iran contains an estimated 812 trillion cubic feet (Tcf) in proven natural gas reserves—the world's second largest and surpassed only by those found in Russia. Around 62 percent of Iranian natural gas reserves are located in non-associated fields, and have not been developed, meaning that Iran has huge potential for gas development.

Major non-associated gas fields include: South Pars (280-500 Tcf of gas reserves), North Pars (50 Tcf), Kangan (29 Tcf), Nar (13 Tcf), Khangiran (11 Tcf), and several others.

Despite the fact that domestic natural gas demand is growing rapidly, Iran has the potential to be a large natural gas exporter due to its enormous reserves. In 2001, Iran produced about 2.2 Tcf of natural gas. Of this, around 10 percent is flared, and approximately 30 percent is reinjected—in part for enhanced oil recovery efforts. Natural gas treatment and processing plants include Kangan-Nar, Aghar-Dalan, Ahwaz, Marun-4, Bid Boland, and Asaluyeh.

Currently, natural gas accounts for nearly half of Iran's total energy consumption, and the government plans billions of dollars worth of further investment in coming years to increase this share. The price of natural gas to consumers is state-controlled. In March 2003, Russia's Gazprom said that it might form a joint company with Iran to develop Iranian gas resources.

South Pars
Iran's largest non-associated natural gas field is South Pars, geologically an extension of Qatar's 380-Tcf North Field, most likely the largest non-associated gas field in the world.

South Pars was first identified in 1988 and originally appraised at 128 Tcf in the early 1990s. Current estimates are that South Pars contains 280 Tcf or more (some estimates go as high as 500 Tcf) of natural gas, of which a large fraction will be recoverable, and over 17 billion barrels of liquids. Development of South Pars is Iran's largest energy project, and already has attracted billions of dollars in investment.

In early March 2003, the chairman of Petropars stated that another $8 billion would be spent on South Pars development during the Iranian year starting March 21, 2003. South Pars development is proceeding, but has been delayed by various problems—technical (i.e., high levels of mercaptans - foul-smelling sulfur compounds—in the South Pars gas), contractual (i.e., controversy over 'buy-back' arrangements), etc.

Phase 1, for instance, which is being handled by Petropars (owned 60 percent by NIOC), has been delayed several times and now is scheduled for completion in mid-2004 (around 3 years behind schedule), involves production of 900 million cubic feet per day (Mmcf/d) of natural gas and 40,000 bbl/d of condensate.

Natural gas from South Pars largely is slated to be shipped north via the planned 56-inch, 300-mile, $500 million, IGAT-3 pipeline (a section of which is now being built by Russian and local contractors), as well as possible IGAT-4 and IGAT-5 lines. Gas also will be reinjected to boost oil output at the mature Agha Jari field (output peaked at 1 million bbl/d in 1974, but has since fallen to 200,000 bbl/d), and possibly the Ahwaz and

Mansouri fields (which make up part of the huge Bangestan reservoir in the southwest Khuzestan region).

South Pars natural gas also is intended for export, by pipeline and also possibly by liquefied natural gas (LNG) tanker. Sales from South Pars could earn Iran as much as $11 billion per year over 30 years, according to Iran's Oil Ministry.

However, Iran likely will face stiff competition for LNG customers, particularly given the fact that many other LNG suppliers (Oman, Qatar, the UAE) are already in the market, having locked up much of the Far East market. U.S. sanctions also mean that Iran is limited to non-U.S. liquefaction technology. For now, Iran appears intent on moving ahead with two LNG trains, each of which will likely have a capacity of around 4.8 million tons per year.

On September 29, 1997, Total signed a $2 billion "buy back" deal (along with Russia's Gazprom and Malaysia's Petronas) to explore South Pars and to help develop the field during Phases 2 and 3 of its development. Total has a 40 percent share of the project, with the other two companies each having 30 percent shares. NIOC estimates that South Pars has a natural gas production potential of up to 8 billion cubic feet per day (Bcf/d) from four individual reservoirs.

In February 2003, Oil Minister Zanganeh officially inaugurated Phases 2 and 3 of South Pars development, which began to come onstream in September 2002. Already, Phases 2 and 3 reportedly are producing around 2 Bcf per day of natural gas, and 85,000 bbl/d of condensates.

Twin undersea pipelines will carry gas from South Pars to onshore facilities at Asaluyeh. In March 2002, Hyundai signed another contract, this one for $1 billion, to build four natural gas processing trains. The Asaluyeh facility comprises four natural gas processing trains, sulphur recovery units, condensate stabilization and storage units, and export compressors.

Phases 4 and 5, estimated to cost $1.9 billion each, are being handled by ENI and Petropars, and involve construction (by Agip and Petropars) of onshore treatment facilities at the port of Bandar Asaluyeh.

These two phases are expected to come online by late 2004 or early 2005 at around 2 Bcf per day, plus 1 million tons per year of liquefied petroleum gas (LPG).

Phases 6–8, which are to produce a combined 3 Bcf/d of natural gas and 120,000 bbl/d of condensate at a cost of $2.6 billion, are being handled by Petropars and Norway's Statoil, which signed an agreement in October 2002.

First stages of the project are scheduled to come online in late 2004, with gas being transported via the planned $235 million IGAT-5 pipeline to the Agha Jari oilfield for injection as part of enhanced oil recovery efforts. NIOC is to take over as operator when development is finished. In May 2003, Iran signed a $1.2 billion deal with a Japanese-led consortium for construction of an onshore natural gas and condensate processing facility for Phases 6–8.

Phases 9 and 10, being developed by South Korea's LG Engineering and Construction Corp., are expected to supply 2 Bcf per day to the domestic market, possibly by 2007. In September 2002, South Korea's LG signed a $1.6 billion deal with NIOC on phases 9 and 10. LG's share is 42 percent, and the deal reportedly uses international bank project financing rather than a "buy-back" model. Bids on Phase 11, which is slated for LNG export, were opened in March 2003. Possible consortia include Iran LNG (BP, Reliance of India, NIOC), Pars LNG (Total, Petronas, NIOC), Persian LNG (Shell, Repsol, NIOC), and NIOC LNG (BG, Eni, and NIOC).

Phase 12, which had been slated for LNG export and condensate production, possibly by 2008, reportedly is on hold for now. Meanwhile, Shell hopes to win Phase 13, which is slated for LNG production but may be left unused. Phase 14 is slated for gas-to-liquids (GTL) development, with Statoil and Shell reportedly interested. In May 2003, invitations were sent out for bids on Phases 15–16 of the South Pars project, which is to produce 1.8 Bcf/d of natural gas for domestic use, plus 80,000 bbl/d of condensate and 1 million tons per year of LPG for export.

Other Natural Gas Development
In addition to South Pars, Iran's long-term natural gas development plans may involve: the 48-Tcf North Pars field (a separate structure from South Pars); the 6.4-Tcf, non-associated Khuff (Dalan) reservoir of the Salman oil field (which straddles Iran's maritime border with Abu Dhabi, where it is known as the Abu Koosh field); the 800-Bcf Zireh field in Bushehr province; the 4-Tcf Homa field in southern Fars province; the 14-Tcf Tabnak natural gas field located in southern Iran; the onshore Nar-Kangan fields, the 13-Tcf Aghar and Dalan fields in Fars province, and the Sarkhoun and Mand fields.

In September 2003, President Khatami inaugurated the first phase of Tabnak development, along with a related gas processing plant and combined cycle power facility.

Natural Gas Trade
With almost unlimited natural gas production potential, Iran is looking to export large volumes of gas. Besides Turkey, potential customers for Iranian gas exports include: Ukraine (Kiev reportedly is interested in building an Iran-Armenia-Georgia-Crimea-Ukraine line), Europe, India,

Pakistan, Armenia, Azerbaijan, Taiwan, South Korea, and coastal China. Exports could be either via pipeline or by LNG tanker, with possible LNG export terminals at Asaluyeh or Kish Island.

In March 2003, BG and NIOC reportedly were in advanced talks on developing a $1.4 billion LNG plant at Bandar Tombak on the Persian Gulf coast.

The plant is to comprise two LNG trains, with capacity of 4.5–5 million tons per year each, with possible completion in 2007-2008.

In late January 2002, Iran and Turkey officially inaugurated a much-delayed natural gas pipeline link between the two countries. This follows several years of delays due to economic, political, and technical factors. In 1996, Iran and Turkey had signed a $20 billion agreement that called for Iran to supply Turkey with more than 8 Tcf of natural gas over a period of 22 years beginning in late 1999. Officials in Turkey and Iran variously blamed US sanctions, financing problems on the Turkish leg of the $1.9 billion pipeline, economic recession in Turkey, and delays by the Iranians in completing an important metering station for delaying the project.

Exports of Iranian natural gas to Turkey could reach 350 Bcf per year by 2007. There are questions, however, whether Turkish demand will grow rapidly enough to absorb this volume of gas from Iran, in addition to gas slated to be supplied by Russia, Algeria, and Nigeria.

In June 2002, for instance, Turkey halted Iranian gas imports, ostensibly due to 'quality problems' but more likely due to lack of demand in Turkey. In mid-November 2002, Turkey announced that it was resuming gas imports from Iran.

In October 2002, the International Atomic Energy Agency (IAEA) predicted that "Iran will be a major global natural gas supplier in the future," especially to Europe.

Iran is reportedly shooting for around 300 Bcf per year of natural gas exports to Europe via Turkey by 2007. Along these lines, Greece and Iran signed a $300 million agreement in March 2002 which calls for extending the natural gas pipeline from Iran to Turkey into northern Greece.

After that, gas could be transported to Europe via Bulgaria and possibly Romania (a memorandum of understanding—MOU—was signed on this possibility in January 2003, and a joint working group set up in October 2003), or via an undersea pipeline to Italy, where gas demand is expected to grow rapidly in coming years. A deep water option could be extremely expensive, however, making an overland route more likely.

In January 2003, Iran and Kuwait signed an MOU on Iranian gas exports of around 110 Bcf per year to Kuwait by 2005. The gas is to be used for power generation.

ELECTRIC POWER

As of 2001, Iran had installed power generation capacity of about around 31 gigawatts (GW), of which three-quarters or more was natural gas-fired, with the remainder either hydroelectric (7 percent) or oil-fired.

As a result of significant state investment in this area, a number of new power plants (mainly hydroelectric and combined cycle) have come online in recent years in Iran, including the 2,000-MW Shahid Rai thermal power station in Qazvin; a 1,290-MW combined-cycle plant in Rasht; a doubling of the Tabriz power plant's capacity to 1,500 MW; two, 200-MW, steam-powered units at the Martyr Montazeri plant; a 215-MW steam-powered unit at the Ramin Power Plant; a 107-MW combined cycle generator at Montazer Qa'em Power Plant, and three-fourths of the Shazand power plant near Arak in central Iran.

In September 2003, President Khatami inaugurated a 1,053-MW combined cycle power plant in Fars, and the country plans to reach total power generating capacity of 33.4 GW by March 2004.

With power demand growing rapidly (7–8 percent annually), Iran is building significant new generation capacity, both thermal and hydroelectric, with the goal of adding total generating capacity of 30 GW within 10 years (according to Iran's Energy Minister). Around 3 GW is expected to come online during the current Iranian year, which ends on March 19, 2004.

Currently, the largest hydropower projects are the 3,000-megawatt (MW) Karun 3 plant, the 2,000-MW Godar-e Landar facility, a 1,000-MW station in Upper Gorvand, and the 400-MW Karkheh dam (came online in late summer 2003). New thermal projects include two 1,040-MW combined cycle plants in the South, an 1,100-MW combined cycle plant at Arak, and a 1,000-MW facility in Bandar Abbas. In February 2003, 1,272-MW combined-cycle plant came online in Kerman.

In January 2003, plans were announced to build Iran's first geothermal plant, in the northwestern province of Ardebil. In early April 2002, the 1,000-MW, natural-gas-fired, combined-cycle Shahid Raja'i power plant came online in the northern Iranian province of Qazvin.

NUCLEAR

Currently, Iran has several small nuclear research reactors, in addition to a large-scale nuclear power plant under construction at the southern town of Bushehr.

Iran claims that its nuclear power is for peaceful purposes and that it will help free up oil and natural gas resources for export, thus generating additional hard-currency revenues. The country has stated its aim of having 7,000 MW of nuclear power online by 2020, accounting for 10 percent of the country's power generation capacity at that point.

In September 2003, the International Atomic Energy Agency (IAEA) gave Iran until October 31 to provide guarantees that its nuclear program was for peaceful purposes and to open the country to snap inspections by the IAEA.

On October 6, Iran's envoy to the IAEA, Ali Akbar Salehi, said that Iran would withdraw from the nuclear non-proliferation treaty if Western pressure continued.

On October 30, IAEA head Mohammed el-Baradei declared that Iran's report on its nuclear activities appeared to be "comprehensive," but that he would still have a lot of questions.

On November 6, U.S. Energy Secretary Spencer Abraham said, "If Iran carries out the obligations it has undertaken—especially if it abandons its enrichment and reprocessing activities—it will show what can be achieved when the international community sends the same firm message on the need to comply with nonproliferation requirements."

The IAEA Board of Governors met on November 20 to discuss Iran's nuclear program. Before than, on November 14, Iran's Foreign Minister, Kamal Kharazzi, said that his country was committed to "complete transparency," and added that the IAEA report made clear that Iran's nuclear program was for peaceful purposes.

In December 2002, Iran and Russia had already signed a protocol for peaceful cooperation in nuclear power. Russia has been assisting Iran on the Bushehr nuclear power facility, work on which first began in 1974 by West Germany, but was halted (80 percent complete) following the 1978/1979 revolution.

Significant amounts of money, possibly billions of dollars, had been spent on Bushehr to that point. Following the Iran-Iraq War (1980–1988), during which time Bushehr was bombed six times and seriously damaged, progress on the plant resumed when Russia signed an $800 million contract in 1995.

The contract with Russia called for completion of a 1,000-MW, pressurized-light-water reactor, as well as the possible supply of two modern VVER-440 units. Since then, work has proceeded slowly, although reports in early March 2003 indicated that Bushehr was 70 percent complete, and was expected to come online as early as March 2004.

Subsequently, the completion date for Bushehr-1 was pushed off by a year—supposedly due to technical difficulties—and is now scheduled to come online in 2005.

In early September 2003, a Russian Atomic Energy Ministry spokesman said that it would cost '$1.2–$1.3 billion to complete the construction' of Bushehr's first unit. In November 2003, Russia proposed that it build a "totally new" second nuclear unit at Bushehr, instead of completing the one started in the late 1970s.

Although Iran is a signatory to the Nuclear Non-Proliferation Treaty and insists that its nuclear program is for peaceful purposes (i.e., power generation), the United States strongly opposes the Bushehr project and has in the past provided Russia with information pointing to the existence of an Iranian nuclear weapons program.

In May 2002, U.S. Energy Secretary Spencer Abraham met with Alexander Rumyantsev, head of Russia's nuclear agency, and discussed this issue, with Rumyantsev stating the Russian position that Bushehr "is not a source of proliferation of nuclear material."

In late March 2003, U.S. Undersecretary of State for Arms Control, John Bolton, said, "In the aftermath of Iraq, dealing with the Iranian nuclear weapons program will be of equal importance as dealing with the North Korean nuclear weapons program."

In April 2003, Russia and Iran reached a deal on returning spent nuclear fuel rods from Bushehr back to Russia for reprocessing. Russia hopes to earn as much as $40 million per year supplying Iran with nuclear fuel and with shipping out spent fuel. The two countries also have discussed construction of additional nuclear power plants in Iran.

Appendix D

HOW SADDAM HUSSEIN ALMOST BUILT HIS BOMB

From *The Iraqi War Debrief: Why Saddam Hussein Was Toppled*
(Casemate Publishers, US, Verulam Publishing, UK, 2004)

After President Saddam Hussein stopped a United Nations strip-search of his country for real or imagined stocks of weapons of mass destruction, nobody really knew what he had been doing in the interim. For its part, Tehran was also alarmed at the lack of any kind of monitoring process in place. The story behind Baghdad's bid to build a nuclear weapon makes is a remarkable mix of deception, intrigue, political power play as well as downright greed on the part of some of those in both East and West who gave him a hand. This was to have been the first Arab bomb: Iraq's atom bomb.

What the aftermath of "Operation Desert Storm" did for those involved in the Middle East was to stir the recurrent nightmare of a major Israeli-Arab conflict involving nuclear weapons. This dreadful scenario continues to haunt strategists on both sides of the Atlantic. Looking back, there are quite a few arms specialists who concede that the prospect of Saddam getting a bomb of his own was a pretty close-run thing.

The boffins reckon that while Iraq had serious problems with some of the more arcane disciplines associated with building a nuclear weapon, Baghdad, using indigenous facilities, might have been as little as two or three years from producing the first Arab atom bomb. Others talk about six or eight months. And while it was Pakistan that built the first Islamic bomb, there was a brief window when Islamabad began to share some of its secrets associated with weapons of mass destruction with Baghdad.

Some specialists also maintain that had he taken the short cut (which is what his Iranian neighbors are suspected of doing right now, with plutonium and weapons' grade uranium bought on the former Soviet Union black market) that objective might have been achieved even sooner.

It is worth noting that it was Saddam Hussein's original intention, once it became clear that the invasion of Kuwait would be fiercely opposed, to use his safeguarded highly enriched uranium (HEU)—covered by the Nuclear Non-Proliferation Treaty (NPT)—for the construction of a single nuclear device. Had he succeeded, he might well have had his bomb within a year. And while he would still have lacked the means to deliver it to target, he was spending a lot of money and effort on working on that as well.

United States National Intelligence estimates said at the time, "Iraq (with a supply of HEU) could build such a device in six months to a year." At the same time, it concluded that the final product was fraught with problems and, in any event, it would have been "too big to deliver by missile."

Vienna's International Atomic Energy Agency (IAEA), and by inference, the major powers, were very much aware that when the Coalition forces launched Desert Storm, Iraq had in stock a total of more than thirty lbs of fresh Russian-supplied 80 percent-enriched uranium as well as twenty-six lbs. of lightly irradiated 93 percent uranium together with about a pound of 93 HEU, the last two bought from France.

All had been subject to IAEA scrutinies which, according to Dr. David Kay (chief inspector of the three early UN nuclear weapons inspection programs in post-Gulf War Iraq), had been cleverly manipulated by Baghdad. The point made here by several observers is the fact that Saddam was in possession of HEU and that gave him a certain amount of leverage.

During the course of subsequent weapons' searches, the Iraqis were obliged to admit to UN inspectors that after the IAEA made its routine inspection of this material in November 1990 (following the invasion of Kuwait, but before the Allies started bombing), they intended to divert all their HEU and further enrich a portion of it.[1] Indeed, they were planning to convert it to metal "buttons" for the final weaponization process, which should have taken place by April 1991. The intention was to present the world with a fait accompli: that Iraq had its bomb.

Israeli sources in Washington have suggested to this author that in order to do this, Saddam Hussein might have exercised one of two options:

- He could have test fired his bomb in the desert at a site to be built near the Saudi Arabian border. This would have demonstrated to the world that Iraq had nuclear capability (and thus, possibly, bring about a stalemate in the Kuwaiti issue with his forces still ensconced at the head of the Gulf). As it was, he was pre-empted by the invasion.

- Alternatively, there is a school of thought that believed he might have considered trying to transport such a bomb to Israel, possibly by boat, for detonation in the roadstead to Haifa harbor. This is a premise that made the rounds in Beirut during the mid-1990s and is thought to have originally been mooted by Iran's Pasdaran, or Revolutionary Guards (author's visit to Lebanon, August 1997).

Significantly, people involved in such things have maintained all along that it is not necessary to physically land a nuclear weapon on American soil in order to cause destruction. Such a device could be detonated while still onboard a ship in New York (or any other) harbor.

It is clear that the biggest shock of post-war IAEA inspections was the discovery that Iraq had a very substantial electromagnetic isotope separation (EMIS) program for the envisaged production of an A-bomb. It was vast. Numerous buildings were constructed at Al-Tuwaitha, about twenty miles south of Baghdad. These housed the research and development phases of both the EMIS and gaseous diffusion enrichment programs.

The diffusion program (which lasted from 1982 until mid-1987) occupied three large buildings. Interestingly, the EMIS project was located in other structures at Al Tuwaitha, which disconcerted a lot of the staff working there. They were only too aware of what had happened at Osiraq in June 1981 when the Israelis bombed that reactor. They knew, too, that Israel had already complained about the huge conglomeration of buildings at the complex. When Saddam added still more structures, it did little for morale.

In the meantime, though, his EMIS program had a home. EMIS is such a large and energy-intensive technology that intelligence agencies have always assumed that with modern electronic and satellite-surveillance techniques they would easily be able to detect such a development, even in its infancy.

More significant, neither Russia nor America believed that any nation would pursue "obsolete" calutron technology in a bomb program. It was outdated, World War II stuff, the pundits argued. In any event, the U.S. abandoned that route soon after Japan capitulated. Yet the detail is there, in print, among documentation that was declassified years ago. For decades it has been available for public inspection by anybody who knows where to look. (In the U.S., old timers recalled that the magnets were so strong that they could feel their shoes affected by the magnetic field, due to the customary tiny metal tacks in the soles.)

After Iraq lost the war and the first of the international inspectors arrived, they uncovered what was termed at the time "a remarkable clandestine nuclear materials production and weapons design of unexpected size and sophistication."[2] The total value of the program was initially estimated at about $5 billion. Later considerations put it at double that. Dr. David Kay, in his testimony before the U.S. Senate Foreign Relations

Committee in October 1991 reckoned that there were about seven thousand scientists and twenty thousand workers involved on the nuclear side alone, never mind all those still working on chemical and biological programs as well as missile delivery systems.

One of the most comprehensive reports on how the Iraqis managed to befuddle the West is contained in a report that Kay wrote for the Center for Strategic and International Studies at Boston's Massachusetts Institute of Technology. Another was authored by Dr. Khidir Hamza, at the time the most senior Iraqi nuclear physicist to defect to the West. He detailed the extent of his (and others') work in a report published in *The Bulletin of the Atomic Scientists*[3] and, subsequently, in his book, *Saddam's Bomb Maker*. Dr. Hamza now lives in the U.S. with his family, all of whom the CIA successfully smuggled out of Iraq.

Kay pointed out that in terms of Security Council Resolution 687, Iraq was required to give the UN precise details of the quantities and locations of all its nuclear, chemical, biological and ballistic missile stockpiles. These listings were designed to provide a touchstone for subsequent inspection activities and were to lead to the dismantling of Iraq's WMD.

"What really happened was that just about every detail that emanated from Baghdad thereafter was misleading," Dr Kay stated.

"On the nuclear front," declared Kay, "the scale of deception was even greater. Iraq's initial declaration on April 19, 1991 was that it had no proscribed nuclear materials This was amended eight days later to acknowledge that it had only what was reported to the IAEA before the war, as well as a peaceful research program centered on the Al-Tuwaitha Nuclear Research Center."

Subsequent inspections found something altogether different. It soon became clear that Iraq had been involved in a massive nuclear weapons program (certainly the largest in any Third World country) for some years. Kay writes: "At the time of the invasion of Kuwait, (Iraq) had begun the start-up for industrial-scale enrichment using calutrons and had acquired the material, designs and much of the equipment for perhaps as many as twenty-thousand modern centrifuges. Design, component testing and construction of manufacturing facilities for actual bomb production were well advanced."

UN inspectors reckoned about that time that the electromagnetic isotope separation program had put Iraq just eighteen to thirty months from having enough material for between one and three atom bombs. (It is worth noting that prior to going pro-Iraq in the early years of this millennium, former UNSCOM inspector Scott Ritter confirmed to this writer that there were three or four. Indeed, he was about to uncover them in September 1998, when the State Department halted his vigorous inspection program.

The UN Action Team also found a great deal of sophisticated European centrifuge technology. This seemed to indicate a leak of substantial—as yet unspecified—proportions from the triple-nation (Germany, the Netherlands and Britain) Uranium Enrichment Company better known as Urenco.

What quickly became apparent was that there were detailed plans for building an "implosion" nuclear device which can use either HEU or plutonium. This type of weapon contains a mass of nuclear material, in this case, HEU, at its core. Iraqi scientists envisioned building an implosion device with conventional explosives around the central mass detonating simultaneously: it has the effect of compressing fissile material into a supercritical mass. At that instant, neutrons are injected into the material to initiate a chain reaction and explosion. (China uses something similar in their warheads with HEU.)

The appropriately-named "Fat Man," an American atom bomb dropped on the city of Nagasaki that caused about twenty thousand immediate deaths (and another seventy thousand over the next twelve months or so) was such a weapon. It had a yield of less than 20 kT.

All this was no easy task. Vienna's IAEA discovered early on that the Iraqis appeared to be just starting to comprehend the extremely complex principles associated with spherical geography linked to this kind of weapons' research.

Another IAEA inspector told this writer that Iraqi scientists were planning a device with a solid core of about forty lbs. of weapons-grade uranium. It would have included a reflector of natural uranium metal about an inch thick and a tamper of hardened iron. An atom bomb of this type would weigh about a ton with an outer diameter of about thirty-six inches (just less than a meter), making it significantly smaller and lighter than the devices developed by Robert Oppenheimer and his Los Alamos club in the mid-1940s.

The circumference would still have precluded it from being fitted to Scuds, the only missile available to Baghdad.

Astonishment has always been expressed at the "true breadth of Saddam's nuclear weapons enterprise," as well as the amount of maneuvering—both adroit and malfeasant—that was needed to keep it hidden from prying eyes both on the ground and above it, says David Albright. He spent time with the IAEA Action Team in Iraq and is president of Washington's Institute of Science and International Security (ISIS). These discoveries shook the international nonproliferation regime and the tremors persist since there are now other nations getting into the act, North Korea and Iran included.

What was revealed were critical weaknesses in inspection routines, export controls and in intelligence gathering and the sharing of these assets. Albright reckons that the reality of those first disclosures, and the well-founded suspicion that more lay ahead, led to the initial assumption that Saddam was "on the brink" of putting his own atomic weapon on the international table.

Yet while the Iraqi nuclear program involved tens of thousands of people, no one in the West was even vaguely aware until long afterward of the numbers of Iraqi students that had been sent abroad to acquire the necessary expertise.

These youngsters—and some not-so-young academics—were rarely sent to the same universities or countries, which made it difficult for any single authority to appreciate the breadth of technical skills being acquired by Baghdad. It also presented problems for the world community to keep track of individual Iraqi scientists. The two exceptions, peculiarly, were France and Italy, who together hosted about four hundred Iraqis; yet none were officially approached about the subjects or courses that they were actually following. Dr. Hamza told me that nearly all the current leaders of the program were drawn from those batches of trainees.

Dr. Kay highlighted all this with a disturbing observation. While in Iraq, he said, he dealt for months with a senior Iraqi scientist whose entire university training—from undergraduate level all the way through to his doctorate—had been in America. His first real job was at a U.S. nuclear power plant. Yet, declared Kay, all basic data on or pictures of this key individual could not be found at any of the academic institutions where he had spent time. In retrospect, the issue has a something of Dr. Strangelove resonance about it.

It is interesting that the Iraqi experience (together with developments that followed September 11) has since led to a significant tightening up of IAEA inspection procedures which, essentially, is to prevent such things from happening again.

You only need to look at developments in Iran toward the close of the millennium and it would appear that history is repeating itself.[4]

There have been other anomalies. It is no longer a secret that prior to Desert Storm the Iraqis received generous amounts of tactical aid from the people who later became their chief antagonists, the Americans. During the Iran-Iraq War, while Washington was providing arms to Iran in the hope of getting their hostages in Lebanon freed, it was also rushing classified satellite intelligence to Baghdad almost as soon as it came in. This gave Baghdad a good idea what the Americans were able to see, and, by inference, how they could be fooled. With time, they would use this knowledge to good advantage.[5]

Before that, Baghdad managed to gain acceptance by Vienna's IAEA by placing Abdul-Wahid Al-Saji, a mild-mannered Iraqi physicist, in a position to serve his country as a bona fide IAEA inspector. Gradually, the Iraqis came to understand the machinations of the agency: this knowledge ultimately proved useful to Baghdad's weapons program in obtaining nuclear technology.

According to Dr. Hamza, the agency accepted Iraq's importation of HEU for its research reactor without ever evaluating the possibility that it might be diverted for military use. Most important, Iraqis were able to gain a complete understanding of IAEA inspection procedures. Iraqi officials were also alerted to the success of satellite remote sensing in uncovering clandestine and, especially, underground activities. For this reason, Saddam, with few exceptions, built almost no underground facilities.

Kay makes instructive comments about the way the Iraqis demonstrated their ability to understand the limitations of U.S. technical collection systems, and of how data gathered by such systems were interpreted by the experts. "The catalogue of these techniques is long. It includes the erection of buildings within buildings (Tuwaitha); deliberately constructing buildings designed to the same plans and for the same purposes to look different (Ash Sharqat and Tarmiya); hiding power and water feeds to mislead as to facility use (Tarmiya); disguising operational state (Al Atheer); diminishing the value of a facility by apparent low security and lack of defenses (Tarmiya); severely reducing off-site emissions (Tuwaitha and Tarmiya) moving critical pieces of equipment as well as dispersing and placing some facilities below ground level."

Hamza points out that even though Al-Tuwaitha had hundred-foot high berms (which from the start should have attracted suspicion that the plant was being used for other purposes) good effort went into carefully escorting IAEA inspectors each time they arrived. Customarily they were shunted along pre-designated paths that exposed none of the buildings where secret research was being conducted. Also, answers to possible difficult questions would be endlessly rehearsed for days beforehand.

It was only after the first invasion, Desert Storm, when Vienna received aerial photos of the site, that the IAEA learned about many other buildings that they had never been allowed to enter.

When the bombings were done, the Pentagon had to concede that while Iraq had suffered through the most sophisticated aerial bombardment in history, the country emerged, in the words of former U.S. Air Force Chief of Staff Merrill A. McPeak, with enough nascent nuclear capability to produce weapons early in the new millennium.

Now that there have been two invasions of Iraq, there is sentiment among some of the major powers at UN headquarters in New York that Iraq might have gone nuclear if UN sanctions had been prematurely lifted. Partly, the rationale was based on reports that reached the world outside through defectors (and from sources close to the IAEA) that Iraq remained on the nuclear path for many years following Operation Desert Storm. There was also a lot of other evidence.

For a start, the fundamental scientific and industrial infrastructure to build a nuclear weapon remained firmly in place. More pertinent, the staff responsible—there were hundreds of them—were on permanent standby. They and their families were supported by the state as if they were employed full-time. And while it is acknowledged that some of the material intended for use to construct such a bomb had been either uncovered or destroyed, there was good evidence that much still remained hidden.

There were also unsettling indications in late 1998 that some kind of "technical cooperation" between Iraq and its former blood enemy, Syria, was in place. Israeli intelligence sources indicated that this could have included a joint development program of WMD. Certainly, Damascus has been proved to be involved with both chemical and biowarfare agents and while it is too early to speculate about any kind of nuclear link, it could have been a feasible scenario for the next decade, especially if UN sanctions on Iraq remained rooted.

Remember too that Saddam was always keen to make use of his assets in what he termed "the interests of Islamic hegemony," especially if the ultimate target was to have been the Jewish homeland. We know too that after the first Gulf War, he managed to get some of his WMD assets to Libya. These were then forwarded overland to the Sudan.[6]

Meanwhile, in the decade that followed Operation Desert Storm, Syria continued to demonstrate an interest in acquiring WMD of its own. By early 1997, Israeli reports said that Damascus had tipped some of its Scud-C missiles deployed along the southern (Israeli) front with sarin and the even more deadly VX nerve gas. This prompted an IDF spokesman to declare that if such weapons were used against the Israeli state, it would automatically be followed by nuclear retaliation; harsh words in an already tough environment.

According to Paul Stokes, a former UNSCOM Action Team deputy leader, frequent inspections prevented Iraq from conducting nuclear weapons development work at declared sites after the end of the war. There was evidence—including a good deal from defectors who had come across to the West—that this did not prevent Saddam's people from going ahead elsewhere in clear violation of a variety of Security Council resolutions. Dr. Kay provided explicit evidence of such deceptions in his MIT report; it was often a nightmare of duplicity, he said. What became clear with time is that Iraq was devious throughout the inspection period. As one observer stated, "The Iraqis lied fluently from day one."

He told this correspondent that, among those who had originally worked with the UN in the region (before they were ignominiously kicked out) it was common knowledge that the Iraqis had stalled, obfuscated, covered up or confused wherever and whomever they could. They did everything possible to hide what had been going on.

For instance, he declared, one of the conclusions already reached in 1997 was that while the Iraqis claimed to have had little success with the centrifuge enrichment program, there was a mismatch between the sophistication of the materials that they admitted to having imported and those that were actually turned over to UN inspection.[7] This gap raised real concerns that a hidden centrifuge facility still remained to be found. There are other examples.

It took the defection of Saddam's son-in-law, General Hussein Kamel, former head of the Ministry of Industry and Military Industrialization (MIMI), to expose the full extent of what Iraq had achieved after Desert Storm. Once he was safely ensconced in Jordan, Iraq had no option but to hand over to the IAEA half a million pages of secreted documents (from the "chicken farm") as well as almost twenty tons of high-strength maraging steel and stocks of carbon fiber for more than a thousand gas centrifuges, all of which (and much more) Kamel had detailed in his debrief. Some of these items, according to Ritter on his return to the U.S., were directly linked to what was believed to be still hidden.

There was good reason for this supposition. Iraq is known to have since tried to acquire hydrofluoric acid—a chemical used in the production of uranium hexafluoride feedstock. Scientists use it in gas centrifuge and other enrichment processes and as a purging agent to remove industrial residues from centrifuges and calutron parts. According to Michael Eisenstadt, a Military Affairs Fellow at the Washington Institute for Near East Policy, it raised questions—notwithstanding the current IAEA monitoring process—about the status of the Iraqi nuclear program8.

In the simplest terms, the Iraqi nuclear program comprehensively covers the years from 1976 (when construction on the French-supplied Tammuz 1RR/PPR [Osiraq] reactor began) to about mid-1991, when all major nuclear work was halted by the Gulf War. In-between, the most significant highlights were:

1981: Destruction of the nearly completed Tammuz reactor at Osiraq by Israeli warplanes

1982: Research concerning various gas enrichment methods gets into full swing

1987: Lab-scale quantities of LEU produced by calutrons, now referred to as "Baghdadtrons"

1987/88?: Construction of the Sharqat calutron enrichment plant begins

1989: Construction begins at the al-Furat centrifuge production facility

1990: Initiation of crash program using diverted reactor fuel

1991: Work halted by war as the IAEA and UNSCOM weapons' strip-search began

1999: Abrupt ending of both UNSCOM and IAEA monitoring of Iraq's weapons and nuclear programs

The Israeli Air Force bombing of the facilities at the Osiraq reactor (and subsequent developments) highlighted at a very early stage the fact that Iraq was fostering a nuclear weapons interest.

Saddam Hussein had bought two nuclear reactors from France: a 40 megawatt thermal research reactor, which was destroyed, and a fuel manufacturing plant together with nuclear fuel-reprocessing facilities, all under cover of acquiring the expertise needed to eventually build and operate nuclear power plants and to recycle nuclear fuel.

What is amazing is that nobody in the West questioned the logic of these programs, coming, as they were, from Iraq, the country with the second largest oil reserves in the world (as is the case with Iran today, with equally formidable resources). These are the last two nations on earth that need to generate electricity by burning uranium.

These deals were followed by further purchases from Italy of a radio-chemistry laboratory in 1978, which included three "hot cells" used for the reprocessing of plutonium. Until destroyed in the Gulf War, they were operating at Al-Tuwaitha. Meanwhile, Iraq signed the Nuclear Non-proliferation Treaty. Iran is also an NPT signatory.

Dr. Jafer dhia Jafar, leader of Iraq's nuclear-weapons effort (even though his curriculum vitae includes the notation that he was jailed for twenty months by Saddam for "political crimes") claims it was the Israeli bombing of Osiraq that originally prompted his government to proceed with a secret enrichment program. Educated at the University of Manchester and Imperial College, London, he spent four years thereafter working at CERN, the European accelerator center in Switzerland.

Of note here is the fact that this man was among the first of Saddam's "most wanted" who cut a deal with the Americans to come in from the cold after Baghdad had fallen in April 2003. It was Jafar's view that the Israeli bombing of the Osiraq nuclear facility cost his country almost a billion dollars. Yet, he says, the world community never punished Israel for what was clearly an act of war. This was one of the factors, he maintains, that caused his nation to resort to subterfuge. As he stated later to UN inspectors, "Let Israel believe it destroyed our nuclear capacity. Accept the sympathy being offered for this aggression and then proceed in secret with the bomb program: which is what we did."

Already in 1982 the Iraqis had begun to explore electromagnetic isotope separation at Al-Tuwaitha, which eventually became the principal focus of nuclear research in the country. Baghdad was said to be confident that its scientific establishment had the necessary skills and technology to master this extremely difficult process. They also reached out in other directions: gas centrifuge, gaseous diffusion, chemical enrichment and laser isotope separation.

To begin with, time, money and effort went into gaseous diffusion. This route was abandoned when some technical problems proved insurmountable. Also, Saddam's agents were having trouble getting their hands on essential equipment on the open market, much of which had been embargoed by the West. Looking at the lists, they appear, nonetheless, to have been remarkably successful.

Starting in the late 1980s, Iraqi scientists began working on centrifuge enrichment as a possible alternative, or as a source of LEU or Low Enriched Uranium (containing more than 0.71 and less than 20 per cent ^{235}U) for EMIS. They had hoped to achieve a production output of about thirty lbs. of 93 per cent weapons-grade uranium a year at each of the EMIS production units they intended to build.

"Originally, the gaseous diffusion elements would have provided low-enriched uranium as a feedstock for the EMIS plants, dramatically increasing HEU production," Jafar explained during an interview.

The Tarmiya complex on the Tigris River (built by a Yugoslavian firm, Federal Directorate of Supply and Procurement) and its "twin" at Ash Sharqat (a few hundred miles to the north of Baghdad) were designated to support industrial-scale EMIS production. While there were numerous problems of a technical nature, both plants together, ultimately, could have produced between sixty and two hundred lbs. of weapons-grade HEU a year had they operated successfully. This would have given Iraq the capacity to build up to four atomic bombs a year.

A small plutonium separation program was started in the mid-1970s. Following contact with SNIA-Techint of Italy, a facility was established in Baghdad for research on fuel processing under IAEA safeguards. This laboratory was eventually able to separate small quantities of plutonium; again contrary to the NPT safeguards agreement.

Kay's observations about some of the deception techniques employed by Baghdad are interesting. Iraq, he maintains, was able to use the strong desire of Western providers of technology to make sales in order to effectively conceal the true purposes of its efforts. Thus, they were able to extract a considerable amount of proprietary information from these firms without compensation. He gives the classic example that lay at the heart of Iraq's efforts to obtain technology for the chemical enrichment (Chemex) of uranium:

At the time there were two suppliers in the world of chemical enrichment technology; one is Japanese, the other French. In the mid-1980s Iraq initiated preliminary discussions with both and indicated a desire to acquire this capability. In the end they concentrated on France.

Iraq engaged the European company in lengthy negotiations, which would soon take a familiar pattern. Each time Iraq would say that it needed "only a little more data" to make a decision. The French would reveal more. The cycle would begin again later and this went on for several years. Finally, after the suppliers had disclosed just about all the technology involved, Baghdad announced that it was too expensive and was abandoning all interest in pursuing it. Iraqi scientists were then able to begin the clandestine development of Chemex on their own.

Years later, Washington's ISIS chief, David Albright, stressed that in the evaluation of enrichment technologies, the Iraqis saw many advantages in EMIS technology, the first being that the procedure involves large and static pieces of equipment.[9]

Baghdad regarded this as preferable to gas centrifuge programs which required advanced engineering technology and was perhaps ill suited to a developing country with a limited industrial base, he told me. For example, the rotors on gas centrifuges move at seven or eight times the speed of sound and the slightest instability can, in an instant, cause bearings to fail and rotors to crash. It is common knowledge that Pakistan battled with this technique for years. An intelligence source has indicated to this writer that for all their success in exploding a bomb, the Pakistanis never fully mastered it until quite recently, and then with foreign help.

The advantages of following the antiquated EMIS route are important, especially since they might well apply to other developing countries intent on following this path:

These include: (a) EMIS is well-documented in the open literature; (b) the basic scientific and technical problems associated with the operation of EMIS separators are relatively straightforward to master; (c) the computational software and main equipment are often not on international export control lists, making procurement easy; (d) the design and manufacture of the main equipment for prototypes can be accomplished indigenously; (e) the feed material is relatively easy to produce and handle; (f) final enrichment can be handled in two stages in machines that act independently of each other (one or more separator failures do not affect the operation of other separators) and (g) a LEU feed can be used for a substantial increase in productivity.

Now, as recent disclosures have indicated, Iran appears to be heading the same way. Like Iraq, Tehran likes to keep its options open with regard to gas centrifuge technology, laser as well as chemical separation. This is not at all unusual, because British Intelligence sources inform us that there are more than twenty countries—all of them Third World—intent on acquiring this kind of expertise.[10]

In Iraq, meanwhile, atom bomb design (weaponization) was the responsibility of scientists and technicians at Al Atheer, which the minister said—when he opened the plant about thirty miles south of the capital—was to be "like Los Alamos."

By the time David Kay and his IAEA Action Team associates visited the site—which was bombed by the Allies during the first Gulf War—the Iraqis had managed to acquire a variety of advanced equipment, much of it on Western export control (and thus embargoed) lists. Included were such items as high-speed streak cameras (from Hamamatsu Photonics of Japan) and maraging steel (which was found elsewhere in Iraq) from European suppliers.

Al Atheer was also involved in sophisticated work in metallurgy, chemistry and detonation engineering. Here, the Swiss company Asea Brown Boveri provided a state-of-the-art, cold isostatic press which could be used to shape explosive charges. More Swiss firms that supplied equipment to Iraq included Acomel SA of Neuchatel (five high frequency inverters suitable for centrifuge cascades) and, among other shipments, seven hundred uranium hexafluoride-resistant bellows-valves from Balzer AG and VAT AG (together with the American company Nupro).

There is little doubt that in pursuing his objective to acquire a bomb, Saddam relied heavily on foreign technical resources. The bulk, curiously, came from not from his old allies, the Soviets or their cohorts, but from free Europe. David Albright and Mark Hibbs stated in their reports that Iraq's "Petrochemical Project Three"—the code name for the secret program (conducted under the auspices of MIMI)—received massive infusions of money and resources. Like America's redundant Manhattan project, Iraq sought a number of different technical avenues to the bomb.[11]

The Iraqi leader sent out a minor army of secret agents to establish an elaborate procurement network that had operatives throughout the developed world. Even Africa was covered; South Africa (through Armscor) had much potential. By then the Apartheid regime had supplied Iraq with the vaunted G-5 gun, a 155mm artillery piece which, until silenced by airpower, was used to good effect against Coalition Forces in Operation Desert Storm.

The entire program was subject to the most stringent secrecy. There wasn't an Iraqi legation abroad that was not involved. Curiously, Gerald

Bull, the Canadian maverick arms developer who was involved in Saddam's "Super Gun" when Israel's Mossad killed him in Belgium, also had a hand in developing the G-5. (He was assassinated outside his Belgian apartment, itself a remarkable story of intrigue and betrayal.)

Ostensibly, everything that was acquired for Saddam's nuclear program was intended for what his agents liked to term civil or peaceful use. Purchases were hidden behind such innocuous pursuits as dairy production, car and truck manufacture, as well as oil refining. But it did not take the major powers long to click: Iraq was covering up its real activities and, what was even more disconcerting, it was happening on a breathtaking scale and pace.

Many of the bulky calutron pole magnets used to enrich uranium were produced in Austria by a state-owned firm that shipped the finished products to Iraq—half by truck through Turkey and the rest through Hamburg. The Austrians never asked the purpose of this equipment while the Iraqis volunteered nothing. Much the same story applies to the high-quality copper that was used to wrap these magnets. It was produced in Finland to Iraqi specifications.[12]

Hundreds of tons of HMX high explosives—in the trade, regarded by specialist demolition experts as the "big brother" of the better-known RDX (some of which would be used in the A-bomb program)—was imported from Carlos Cardoen of Chile, well known to members of the old South African Apartheid regime. This man eventually built a plant in Iraq to manufacture cluster bombs. Cardoen came under investigation by the U.S. Justice Department immediately afterward.

Germany (both pre- and post-unification) featured prominently in almost every phase of the Iraqi nuclear program, so much so that it is impossible that Bonn could not have been aware of the extent of it.

German companies included international conglomerates like Siemens AG (a workshop for "tube processing"); H&H Metalform (flow-forming machines to make steel maraging steel rotor tubes for centrifuges); Neue Magdeburger Werkzeugmachinen GmbH (aluminum forgings and a CNC machine to machine casings); Rhein-Bayern Fahrzeugbau GmbH (almost a quarter-million magnetizable ferrite spacers for centrifuges); oxidation furnaces from Degussa AG and Leybold Heraeus (electron beam welder); centrifuge balancing machines from Reutlinger und Sohne KG; Arthur Pfeiffer Vakuum Tecknik GmbH (vacuum induction furnace) and a host of other companies and products. It has been suggested by Western intelligence agencies that some companies doing work of a similar nature might now have shifted their focus toward Iran.

H&H was contracted by Baghdad for centrifuge assistance and served, while doing so, as a conduit for advanced technical expertise, material and equipment for the Iraqi nuclear effort. Much of the financing for the project was handled by the scandal-ridden Bank of Credit and Commerce International (BCCI) before it folded. Subsequently, the Atlanta-based branch of an Italian bank, Banco Nationale da Lavore (BNL) was placed under investigation in the U.S.

British companies were involved too and some remained under a cloud of suspicion for years afterwards. These included Endshire Export Marketing, a company that met an order for ring magnets which had come from Inwako GmbH, a firm directed by the German arms dealer Simon Heiner. Britain's Special Intelligence Service (SIS), aware by now that the magnets were for a nuclear program, let the shipment proceed in order to try to establish what technical route the Iraqis were taking. London tends to work closely with Langley on such matters.

It transpired too that the Technology Development Group, a company co-directed by an Iraqi intelligence agent, Safa Al-Haboudi, was an associate of some of the German firms involved in the transactions. Al-Haboudi eventually implicated the British firm Matrix Churchill; he was on that company's senior management too. Matrix Churchill offered a lucrative, long-term contract for a tool shop (ostensibly for automobile parts manufacturing) to the Swiss metal-working combine Schmiede-meccanica SA.

The records show that some of these exports never got through. Once the West had been alerted, they came down hard. Swiss and German customs officials halted a shipment of special computer numerically-controlled (CNC) machines for making the endcaps and baffles of centrifuges. Earlier, Iraqi operators were caught trying to smuggle detonation capacitators from CSI Technologies of California. This material would have been incorporated in an implosion-type bomb.

For all the help that Baghdad received from abroad, there were some serious technological gaps. Iraqi electronics expertise, for instance, did not warrant close scrutiny. The Iraqis, it was discovered later, were having difficulty developing adequate capacitators and bridge wire detonators. Rolf Ekeus, the former head of UNSCOM, said that while the Iraqis had blueprints and considerable knowledge, they tended to lag a bit in the engineering aspect. Also, Baghdad had been noticeably slowed by their inability to obtain what they needed from overseas as Western government controls began to stymie deliveries.[13]

It is important to observe that during its subterfuge stage, Iraq was not alone in this sort of skullduggery. The newsletter *NuclearFuel* reported on June 20, 1994 that several shipments of preformed tubes for scoops in gas centrifuges from the German metalworking firm Team GmbH were shipped to Pakistan after being declared in customs documents as bodies for ball-point pens. There are other examples, quite a few of them still under wraps.

Looking at the broader canvas, it is clear that this targeted Arab nation was able to demonstrate an astonishing level of enterprise by getting as far as it did. It is also worrying that there are other nations that might wish to emulate Iraq's efforts.

Basic items—factories, electrical supply, power equipment—were easy to buy. However, as Albright explained, "The more specific the equipment Iraq sought, the more export controls began to bite. Crucial transfers of components were thus effectively blocked."

Orders were subdivided into sub-components that, on paper, looked innocuous. Or machines were bought to manufacture something back home. Middlemen and unethical companies in their hundreds were bribed to disguise final destinations or to falsify end-users certificates in much the same way as South Africa (under UN sanctions) stocked its arsenal with embargoed items of choice.

German technicians were secretly hired to work on the Arab enrichment project. Once the IAEA went to work and uncovered names, some of these people were charged with treason as, ultimately, will South African scientists who have been helping Tehran build WMD.

In Iraq's case, several were jailed. Among these individuals were Bruno Stemmler, Walter Busse and Karl-Heinz Schaab. It was Schaab and Stemmler who provided Saddam with classified centrifuge blueprints. The three men had worked on the centrifuge program at MAN Technologie AG of Munich and came to Iraq under the sponsorship of the German company H&H Metalform.

Together, they operated efficiently as a team and met many of Iraq's technical requirements. They also assisted in locating international suppliers. Some sources were companies with whom they had previously been associated.

In the end, says Albright, their assistance greatly accelerated Iraq's gas centrifuge-design process. "It sped the acquisition of necessary materials, know-how and equipment for manufacture." During an earlier period, some Iraqis had already spent time in Urenco training programs in order to familiarize themselves with complex centrifuge-related procedures.

It was David Kay who observed that "the failed efforts of both IAEA safeguards inspectors and national intelligence authorities to detect—prior to [the Gulf War]—a nuclear weapons program of the magnitude and advanced character of Iraq's, should stand as a monument to the fallibility of on-site inspection and national intelligence when faced by a determined opponent."[14] He maintained that those words should be cast in concrete and embedded into the floor of Washington's Capitol.

According to Kay, "The Iraqi military build-up, as well as the multiple failures of its timely detection is an experience rich in lessons that, if correctly understood, may help in detecting other covert weapons programs and, equally important, U.S. understanding of the limits of its ability to guarantee timely detection."[15]

This followed a statement by John Deutch, the erstwhile and since discredited U.S. Director of Intelligence, in *Foreign Affairs* in 1992: "The point is not how wrong the United States was about Iraq's timetable for acquiring a bomb, but rather how greatly the U.S. underestimated the magnitude of the Iraqi covert effort. As it stands, such a massive miscalculation of a nation's ability, high or low, can surely happen again."[16]

Appendix E

CLOSE-QUARTER OBSERVATIONS: THE SOUTH AFRICAN NUCLEAR WEAPONS PROGRAM

Derek Smith, a British citizen living in Greece is arrested in Athens and charged with illegally possessing twenty-six pounds of pure uranium, says that it is a sample from about a ton of uranium stored in a secret location in South Africa. The material was offered by a South African friend for $180,000/kg.

An incident typical of nuclear scams, reported by
Athens News, October 12, 1989: "Uranium Destined For Libya."

In a presentation given in Castiglioncello, Italy in 1995, at the conference "Fifty Years After Hiroshima," Dr. Waldo Stumpf, head of the Atomic Energy Corporation of South Africa until he retired in the late 1990s, presented a paper titled "South Africa's Nuclear Deterrent Strategy."[1] While never personally involved with nuclear weapons work, his comments and especially his conclusions are incisive. They provide the kind of overview which, until then, had been lacking. Some useful extracts from his paper follow:

"Though the Atomic Energy Board was established in 1948 by Act of Parliament and assumed general nuclear research and development activities at its Pelindaba site near Pretoria in 1961, all activities in the early years was based on the peaceful uses of nuclear technology, especially since South Africa was (and still is) a prominent producer of uranium. It was to be accepted that attention was given to uranium enrichment technology as a means to mineral beneficiation.

"After encouraging laboratory results were achieved in 1969 with an indigenous uranium enrichment process based on a stationary wall vortex tube, approval was given for the further development of the process on an industrial scale. At the same time the construction of a pilot plant to prove the process was started.

"This work was undertaken within the newly created (1970) Uranium Enrichment Corporation on the Valindaba site adjacent to Pelindaba. In 1982, the Uranium Enrichment Corporation was again

359

incorporated with the Atomic Energy Board into a single state corporation, the present Atomic Energy Corporation. Construction of the Pilot Enrichment Plant (the Y Plant) commenced in 1971 and the first stages at the lower end of the cascade commissioned by the end of 1974. Full cascade operation of the entire plant was initiated in March 1977.

"Due to the long equilibrium time of the plant (the time necessary to establish the full enrichment gradient) the first and relatively small quantity of high enriched UF_6 was withdrawn from the plant only in January 1978. During the whole of 1978 and most of 1979, further high enriched UF_6 was withdrawn from the plant and converted to HEU in the metal form. This material was still of relatively low enrichment (about 80 per cent ^{235}U).

"In August 1979, Y Plant operations came to an abrupt end due to a massive catalytic in-process gas reaction between the UF_6 and the carrier gas, hydrogen. The plant was out of operation until April 1980 when it resumed operation, although withdrawal of high enriched product commenced again in July 1981. In the period June to December 1986, the plant was also utilized to produce 3.25 per cent ^{235}U for the first four locally produced Lead Test Assemblies for the 1920 MW twin Koeberg Nuclear Power Station, of PWR design. Thereafter, the Y Plant resumed production of highly enriched UF_6 until it ceased operation in February 1990."

It is Stumpf's view that valuable lessons were learnt from South Africa's brief but productive nuclear experience:

- Although the technology of uranium enrichment and unsophisticated nuclear weapons is of a very high level, it is still within the bounds of a reasonably advanced industrialized country and therefore, is not in itself an insurmountable barrier. This is particularly so where the technical goals are relatively modest, as with South Africa's gun-type devices without neutron initiators.
- Although the vast Iraqi nuclear weapons program and the huge financial and human resources it required may leave the impression of a self-limiting constraint, the South African experience proved otherwise.
- Although international political isolation may be an instrument to contain individual cases of nuclear proliferation, a point in such an isolation campaign may be reached where it actually becomes counter-productive and really pushes the would-be proliferator towards full proliferation. In the case of South Africa, this point was probably reached at the cut-off by the U.S. of contractual supplies of fuel to both its Safari and Koeberg (Commercial) reactors, together with the punitive financial measures applied by the U.S. Admin-

istration at the time. What little leverage the U.S. had over the South African nuclear program, was consequently lost.

- Where proliferation occurred due to a real or perceived political threat, a reversal towards de-proliferation may occur upon removal or neutralization of the threat, whether real or perceived. This means that international pressure by a superpower from outside the region on a would-be proliferator can be helpful, but only up to a point. In the final instance, regional tensions must be resolved before the cause of non-proliferation can be fully realized. This was the case with South Africa and is probably so in the Middle East, South Asia and the Korean peninsula.

- The reversal from a position of nuclear proliferation to a truly and permanent status of non-proliferation within the NPT will probably not be achieved by technical or military/strategic decisions, but rather, requires a fundamental political decision by the leader(s) of the country. The "roll-back" option for a so-called threshold non-nuclear weapon state is not an easy path to follow, as the NPT and its instruments were not designed to deal with such an eventuality. The international community should therefore take care in its application of pressure on the process of normalization where a threshold state already has taken the fundamental decision to embark on this road. South Africa experienced a lot of unnecessary international pressure during the "completeness investigation" by the IAEA, which, under different circumstances, could even have derailed the process.

- For a "threshold state" that has taken the political decision to "roll-back" and then to achieve international credibility and acceptance within the NPT, is not an easy process. It can be eased considerably, however, by a sustained policy of full openness and transparency with the IAEA. Once more, this is a political decision that must be taken.

A United States Air Force veteran and intelligence specialist, Lt. Col. Roy E. Horton III, added the results of his own study of the South African nuclear saga in Occasional Paper #27, completed for the USAF Institute for National Security Studies in August 1999.

Horton feels that it is possible that South Africa leap-frogged the testing phases and concentrated weaponization and delivery of its nuclear explosive device. As he states, "Afrikaners are a contingency-minded people and, as such, probably would prefer to have a deliverable nuclear weapon rather than be forced to develop one hastily in the face of a worsening security situation."

Thus, he continues, the ebb and flow of the South African nuclear deterrent effort is all the more remarkable given the small number of personnel involved (one thousand total and no more than three hundred at any one period). Those actually responsible for key programmatic decisions were reportedly never numbered more than between six and twelve individuals.

"Decisions emerged from the synthesis of four basic groups—the scientists, the politicians, the military, and the technocrats—who shaped the focus and direction of the program. The scientific zeal and drive of the AEB's AJA "Ampie" Roux and WE (Wally) Grant—who headed UCOR, which, with the AEB was replaced by the AEC—to demonstrate that South Africa could make a nuclear device established the technical foundation for the program." Yet, as this officer observes, their work was not done in isolation from the political leadership, the support of the military on military-to-military cooperation matters, and the technocrats for actual weapons production.

"The strong leadership of the ruling National Party supported the AEC's research during the Fifties and Sixties, before molding it into a key element of national strategy in the 1970s. Prime Minister BJ Vorster presided over the decision to pursue "peaceful nuclear explosives" and the aborted Kalahari nuclear test.

"The military exerted strong influence within the State Security Council (SSC) but their role focused primarily on domestic security and conventional military operations. Two Defense Ministers oversaw the nuclear program: P.W. Botha and his hand-picked successor, General Magnus Malan. Under Botha, the Defense Minister's power was merged with that of the Prime Minister's in supporting the nuclear deterrent program. With Malan, it would appear that the military's direct influence over the course of the nuclear deterrent program was more limited, although they remained engaged at some level as the ultimate customer for the nuclear weapons.

"Finally, the technocrats—the engineers at Armscor—exerted heavy influence over the nuclear program, particularly during its critical middle stage. Armscor Managing Director Tielman de Waal headed a corporation that not only produced nuclear weapons but also established the capability to mate them with ballistic missiles.

"There are also indications that Armscor was involved in more than just producing munitions—it also worked in developing the nuclear strategy itself. Together, these four groups formed a partnership that conceived, produced, and then discarded South Africa's nuclear deterrent."

Yet, in the end, he states, the political leadership exerted the pivotal influence over the program's progress.

Colonel Horton's annotated chronology (abridged), combined with comments from Dr. Von Wielligh, makes for some interesting observations:

1989

South Africa possesses six devices in its nuclear arsenal each containing 55kg of highly enriched uranium (HEU), and enough HEU for a seventh device. The devices are stored unassembled with the front and rear portions of the weapons kept in separate vaults. In order to prevent premature detonation, the weapons are designed to arm only when they reach a certain altitude while onboard delivery aircraft.

According to Dr. von Wielligh, the figures mentioned by Horton are strictly guesswork since the quantities used are proliferation-sensitive and therefor never published. Furthermore, the IAEA is bound by a confidentiality clause (in terms of the Safeguards Agreement with every country) not to divulge quantities of materials subject to safeguards)

1989

SIPRI[2] researcher Signe Landgren concluded that South Africa was developing "long-range missiles capable of carrying nuclear warheads." The study stated that in November 1989, the CIA confirmed that a joint South African-Israeli test of the "Arniston" missile, which could carry a nuclear warhead over twelve-hundred miles, had taken place.

Late 1980s

Armscor prepares to upgrade the seven gun-type weapons. Quoting David Albright, Horton notes that Armscor plans to "replace the seven cannon-type devices with seven upgraded devices, when they reach the end of their estimated life by the year 2000."[3]

January 1989

Argentina's *Comisión Nacional de Energia Atomica* (CNEA) is reported to have shared design information on nuclear fuel cycle technology with South Africa.[4]

Von Wielligh: Nuclear fuel cycle technology is a very broad term, which could include completely harmless, peaceful topics such as mining, conversion, enrichment, fuel fabrication as well as waste-handling and disposal. I am not aware of this specific example of cooperation with Argentina and it definitely had nothing to do with the weapons program.

June 1989

The Washington Times reported that with assistance from Israel, South Africa planned to test-launch a new intermediate-range ballistic missile. In response, an Armscor spokesman confirmed that over the previous six years, the company had built a missile test range at Overberg in the de Hoop nature reserve and that missiles were being fired from there to test their performance. At the same time, U.S. Intelligence sources reported that South Africa was close to launching a modified version of the Israeli Jericho II Intermediate-range ballistic missile (IRBM).

Reconnaissance satellite images showed that the test launch was likely to be carried out from a facility near Cape Town (Overberg). The facility is reportedly identical to an Israeli launch site in the Negev Desert. Officials said that the new missile had been under development since at least 1987, and would also be used as a booster for launching photo-reconnaissance satellites. A CIA assessment reportedly also suggested that a second test of the more advanced Israeli Shavit (Comet) SLV (which might be converted to a two-thousand-mile-range missile) was also being prepared at the site.[5]

5 July 1989

Armscor announced that it had successfully tested a booster rocket from the Overberg test range outside Cape Town. Although South African sources described the launch as a booster rocket, outside analysts suggested that it may have been a test-flight of an IRBM. A U.S. Defense Intelligence Agency (DIA) Special Assessment called the missile a "probable SRBM." U.S. intelligence sources reported that the rocket plume of the missile bore a striking resemblance to that of Israel's Jericho missile. The DIA noted that if Israel and South Africa were collaborating, a high-level if not senior-level Israeli delegation was probably present for the test. The missile flew about a thousand miles southeast, toward Prince Edward Island.[6]

June 1989

South Africa and the IAEA resume talks on opening fuel cycle facilities to inspection.[7]

14 September 1989

F.W. de Klerk elected President of South Africa.

September 1989

At a meeting of his senior political aides and advisors, President de Klerk declares that in order to end South Africa's isolation from the international community, both the political system of apartheid and the nuclear weapons program had to be dismantled. He summoned AEC Executive Chairman Wynand de Villiers and Dr. Stumpf to inform them of his intention to terminate the nuclear weapons program and accede to the NPT. De Klerk asked them to draw up a schedule to implement his directive.[8]

12 October 1989

Derek Smith, a British citizen living in Greece, is arrested in Athens and charged with illegally possessing twenty-six pounds (12.1 kg) of pure uranium.[9] (See heading at the top of this chapter.) It was an incident typical of nuclear scams (including red mercury) that emerged in the late 1980s/early 1990s. South Africa's total HEU production was less than a ton. This "pure uranium" was possibly depleted uranium metal, a commodity in relative abundance and used as radiation shielding in containers for medical and industrial radioactive sources in place of lead.

25 October 1989

NBC News reported that Israel has "secretly given South Africa access" to the "nuclear club." Quoting anonymous intelligence sources, the network said that Israel was in a partnership with Pretoria to produce a missile with a nuclear warhead for South Africa, in exchange for enriched uranium and access to a long-range test site. The report identified Armscor as builder of the missile and Urdan, an Israeli firm located outside Tel Aviv, as the front company responsible for transferring missile technology. Israeli General Hagai Ravev, a former senior adviser to Defense Minister Yitzhak Rabin, allegedly oversaw the project from Jerusalem.

Von Wielligh: It should be evident that the IAEA came to the conclusion that all the HEU ever produced could be accounted for and was placed under safeguards. There can consequently be no truth in the allegation that South Africa supplied Israel with HEU in exchange for missile technology.

In a follow-up report, NBC claimed that Israel was also sharing aviation technology with Pretoria and that at least seventy five Israeli engineers had gone to South Africa to work on aviation projects. The report also alleged that South Africa was developing a site to construct a long-range missile with Israel, which the CIA designated as IRAH-3.[10]

26 October 1989

Israeli Prime Minister Yitzhak Shamir further denied reports that Israel provided missile technology to South Africa. Shamir tells Israel Radio that there is "no truth" to the NBC News report alleging a partnership between Israel and South Africa to develop nuclear missile capability.

28 October 1989

U.S. President George Bush warned that any cooperation on nuclear missiles between Israel and South Africa would complicate U.S.-Israeli relations. Israeli Prime Minister Shamir responded by saying those responsible for leaking information to NBC News sought to sabotage U.S.-Israeli relations.[11]

October 1989

The U.S. Senate investigates reports that South Africa had obtained information on detonators, explosives, and firing sets from the U.S. Department of Energy. The information is not classified, but may be used in making and testing nuclear weapons.[12]

November 1989

An "Experts Committee" formed by de Klerk and composed of senior AEC, Armscor, and South African Defense Force (SADF) officials formally recommended the dismantlement of South Africa's nuclear weapons, and outlined dismantlement procedures. De Klerk and the South African cabinet approved the plan. The Y-plant subsequently stopped producing HEU.[13]

15 November 1989

Two Americans and three South Africans charged with trying to export U.S.-origin missile technology illegally to South Africa, using the government-owned Israel Aircraft Industries (IAI) as the mediator, thereby violating such U.S. laws as the Comprehensive Anti-Apartheid Act and the Arms Export Control Act.[14]

15 December 1989

UN General Assembly Resolution 44/113 noted "with great concern" that "collaboration between Israel and South Africa had resulted in the development by South Africa of a nuclear-tipped missile." The resolution also requested the secretary-general to report to the General Assembly at its 45th session on the military assistance that South Africa was receiving from Israel, and any other sources in advanced missile technology, and supporting technical facilities.[15]

1990

The de Klerk government implemented its decision to terminate South Africa's nuclear weapons program. All nuclear devices were dismantled and destroyed. Nuclear materials in Armscor's possession were recast and returned to the AEC, where they are stored according to internationally accepted procedures. Armscor's facilities were decontaminated and dedicated to non-nuclear commercial purposes. A date was set for South Africa to accede to the NPT and submit all of its nuclear materials and facilities to international safeguards.[16]

February 1990

The de Klerk government lifts the ban on the African National Congress (ANC), and ANC leader Nelson Mandela is released from prison.

1 February 1990

The Y-plant officially ceases operations.[17] [Note: Reiss reported that the Y-plant, which had an annual output of 100 kg, stopped enriching uranium in 1989. Albright, Berkhout, and Walker state that the Y-plant stopped producing HEU in November 1989, but was officially closed on February 1,1990. The IAEA reports that HEU production at the Y-plant began in January 1978 and ended in November 1989.]

Von Wielligh: The plant was kept running until it was switched off on February 1, 1990, so that the enrichment gradient over the cascade could be destroyed and the UF_6 inventory returned to natural isotopic composition.

26 February 1990

President de Klerk issues written instructions directing all relevant agencies to begin dismantling the nuclear weapons program. According to

Stumpf, this "should stand as the official date of implementation of the termination of South Africa's weapons program."[18]

30 April 1990

A Norwegian newspaper reports that Norway exported approximately 450 tons of heavy water between the 1930s and 1988, when the Brundtland government banned further exports.[19] The newspaper reports that South Africa received 6–7kg of Norwegian heavy water "figured to be for research purposes."

Von Wielligh: This reference is totally irrelevant to the weapons program. During the early years of the AEB's existence (late 1950s to early 1960s) one of two major projects, the Pelinduna Project was to develop an indigenous reactor which would have used natural uranium with heavy water as a moderator. It was decided in 1967 to stop the Pelinduna Project and continue with uranium enrichment.

July 1990

The dismantlement study commissioned by de Klerk completed. De Klerk opted to order the dismantlement of one complete nuclear device at a time. An alternative, more rapid disarmament option would have been to destroy one-half of each device before destroying the second half. The slower option allowed South Africa to maintain a nuclear deterrent until the last weapon was dismantled. Furthermore, Wynand Mouton, a retired nuclear physicist and university professor whom de Klerk appointed as independent auditor of the dismantlement project, believed the slower option would "help acclimate the dismantlement team to the reality" of de Klerk's decision to eliminate South Africa's nuclear arsenal.[20]

September 1990

The South African Air Force (SAAF) planned to retire the six Buccaneer aircraft stationed at Waterkloof Air Force Base near Pretoria. SAAF had planned to upgrade the aircraft and extend their service life, but an overhaul of the first plane revealed that the program would be too expensive. The Buccaneers entered service in October 1965 and were "believed to have been the SAAF's nuclear weapons strike unit."

1991

The ANC urged the government to fully disclose the extent of South Africa's nuclear program. U.S. officials believed that the South African government was withholding information because it feared that the ANC would interfere with its efforts to sell off its inventory of weapon-grade uranium to the United States. Furthermore, according to a U.S. official, the ANC was bound to view the sale of the weapons-grade stock as a signal that the governments involved in the transactions did not trust a prospective black majority government.[21]

1991

According to a member of an IAEA inspection team, the IAEA discovered nuclear design documents and non-nuclear components of nuclear weapons that had not been destroyed.[22]

Von Wielligh: When the weapons program was stopped, it was deliberately decided to keep documents on the build histories and other relevant features as well as certain non-nuclear parts to enable the IAEA Completeness Investigating Team to be able to make informed and logical conclusions on the abandoned program. The rest of the documents and items regarded as "proliferation sensitive" were destroyed under the supervision of the external auditor. The "discovery" by the IAEA inspection team was consequently no accidental history.

1991

South Africa terminated all work on the AVLIS project.[23]

Von Wielligh: The AEC never worked on AVLIS (Atomic Vapor Laser Isotope Separation) enrichment technology, but on MLIS (Molecular Laser Isotope Separation).

June 1991

According to Stumpf, the dismantling of South Africa's nuclear weapons program was "essentially complete."[24]

July 1991

The AEC completed dismantling the six Armscor-built nuclear bombs. The de Klerk government shredded all blueprints and minutes of meetings at which the weapons program was discussed.[25]

Von Wielligh: The nuclear devices were not dismantled by the AEC but by Advena (an Armscor subsidiary company). The AEC only received and stored the melted-down HEU.

10 July 1991

South Africa acceded to the Treaty on the Non-Proliferation of Nuclear Weapons (NPT) as a non-nuclear-weapon state. The IAEA began inspections of South Africa's nuclear weapon manufacturing facilities to verify the scope and history of the program and its subsequent dismantlement. U.S. President Bush lifted sanctions imposed by the Comprehensive Anti-Apartheid Act of 1986, although an arms embargo and several other measures remained in effect, along with restraints by some state and local governments in the United States.[26]

August 1991

South Africa terminated its gas-centrifuge enrichment program due to financial reasons.[27]

Von Wielligh: The competing MLIS and centrifuge projects ran in parallel for a time. The latter was stopped in favor of the MLIS process, which carried on for a number of years.

August 1991

General Magnus Malan, South Africa's minister of defense, banned the "development, manufacture, marketing, import and export of nuclear weapons or explosives." In a notice in the *Government Gazette,* Malan said that any attempt to produce these devices would be illegal.

5–6 September 1991

The HEU from the last dismantled nuclear weapon returned to the AEC.[28]

16 September 1991

South Africa signed full-scope safeguards agreement with the IAEA, which was effective immediately. Under the terms of the agreement, South Africa was to compile an "inventory of all materials and facilities to be safeguarded," and allow inspections at all of its nuclear sites, including the enrichment facilities.[29]

Von Wielligh: The terms of the Safeguards Agreement were not unique to South Africa. All countries signing a comprehensive Safeguards Agreement are subject to the same conditions. What was unique was the so-called Completeness Investigation, a process that has subsequently become standard procedure for all new Safeguards Agreements in countries with substantial fuel cycle activities.

October 1991

AEC Chief Executive Dr. Waldo Stumpf declared that South Africa had "abandoned its nuclear weapons program and is seeking instead to become competitive on the world nuclear fuel market within a few years." Stumpf said that the new commercial orientation of the AEC was "absolutely the right direction to go in." Stumpf noted that a "strategic emphasis" had been the catalyst to develop nuclear technology, but that it had become "counterproductive" to South Africa's efforts to revitalize the country's slowed economy. Furthermore, Stumpf said that the "strategic emphasis" of South Africa's nuclear program was "possibly far too narrow for the new South Africa," referring to the country's future black-majority government.[30]

3 September 1992

The IAEA reported that the high-enriched separation units of the Y-plant had been dismantled and removed, and that the remainder of the plant had been decommissioned and partially dismantled. South Africa was preparing the facility for use as a demonstration module in the laser enrichment project to be put into full operation in 1993–94. Using accounting data provided by the AEC, the IAEA estimated the ^{235}U balance of the Y-plant. The calculations "showed an apparent discrepancy in this balance" that could be the result of the material accounting system. The IAEA's balance calculations for the Z-plant also revealed an apparent discrepancy, which may likewise have been due to the material accounting system.

According to the AEC, blending operations to convert a certain amount of HEU to LEU would begin in September 1992. The IAEA

reported that it visited facilities involved in South Africa's abandoned centrifuge enrichment program, including the site of a proposed 48-cen-
trifuge cascade, and reports that the centrifuge program had been halted
at all locations visited. The AEC supplied information to the IAEA
regarding an unspecified quantity of unsafeguarded LEU imported to fuel
the Koeberg reactors. South Africa also imported natural uranium as
feedstock for the Y-plant until 1979.[31]

Von Wielligh: The nuclear materials accounting system implemented
over more than a decade-and-a-half by UCOR, before the Safeguards
Agreement entered into force, was never designed and implemented with
a view of one day enabling the IAEA to draw conclusions according to its
own stringent standards. Moreover, due to boycotts, South Africa could
never obtain sophisticated non-destructive measuring equipment to measure plant hold-up or the uranium and isotopic content of waste products.
Any "discrepancy" must be seen in this light.

12 September 1992

The IAEA determined that South Africa's Y-plant likely produced
more than 400kg of weapons-grade uranium during the 1970s and
1980s.[32]

Von Wielligh: As previously explained, the IAEA is not allowed in
terms of its own confidentiality arrangements and the Safeguards Agreement to divulge data on quantities of nuclear materials in countries subject to safeguards. The quantity given here is consequently guesswork.

8 October 1992

IAEA inspectors discovered "evidence of critical assemblies, testing
gear, and equipment for metallurgical research and processing" at
Building 5000, an abandoned site southwest of the enrichment complex
at Pelindaba. Unnamed sources said that South African technicians used
the equipment to work on "the shape of spherical fissile cores for a [more
sophisticated] nuclear explosive device."[33]

Von Wielligh: This "discovery" must be seen against the background
that the IAEA started inspections at the end of 1991, including full access
to all recovered weapons grade material, but that the President (for his
own reasons) decided not to acknowledge the weapons program until
March 1993. On Building 5000, this structure was abandoned many
years ago and was used to store redundant equipment. It had originally
been used for certain criticality experiments but not for designing "more
sophisticated" nuclear explosive devices.

22 December 1992

The African National Congress (ANC) expressed concern regarding
reports emanating from Europe and the United States that disclosed South
Africa's nuclear activities and ambitions. The reports indicated that the
IAEA confirmed that South Africa produced several hundred kilograms of

highly enriched uranium, a quantity large enough to support an active nuclear program. The IAEA had corroborating evidence from visits to an abandoned facility near the Pelindaba uranium enrichment complex where it found equipment to develop nuclear explosive devices. The CIA revealed Atomic Energy Council (AEC) chairman de Villiers' involvement in designing nuclear weapons at the Pelindaba center up to 1979. The ANC asked that the de Klerk government and the AEC disseminate past and present nuclear program information to the South African people and the international community.[34]

Appendix F
IRAN'S MISSILES: DEVILS IN THE DETAIL

By Charles P. Vick,
Senior Fellow, Space Policy, GlobalSecurity.org
Source: The Federation of American Scientists & GlobalSecurity.org

> **"[Iran's] reformists and conservatives agree on at least one thing:**
> **weapons of mass destruction are a necessary component**
> **of defense and a high priority."**
> CIA Director George Tenet, before the
> Senate Armed Services Committee, February 2, 1999

Patrick E Tyler of the *New York Times* recently had an interesting story. It was about one of Russia's leading missile scientists, Yuri P. Savelyev, who was apparently fixated by Iran. He loved the place and its people.

Consequently, says Tyler, he was always more than willing to teach advanced rocket building to Iranian missile engineers. As Tyler noted, it didn't matter that some of these people might have been working on missiles that could reach most Middle Eastern capitals, and even Alaska.

"When Russian government officials tried to stop him because Moscow had signed an international agreement to control the spread of ballistic missile technology, Mr. Savelyev persisted," he states.

"As the rector of the famous Baltic State Technical University, he developed a program to teach students from a leading Iranian university courses in advanced physics, metallurgy and the behavior of gases and fluids under high pressure and temperature—all disciplines essential to building rockets." That was done, he told Tyler, with the full knowledge of the Russian Defense Ministry and the national intelligence agency, which we now know as the Federal Security Service (FSS) and of which Mr. Savelyev's deputy was a member.

Then, after complaints from the Clinton administration, Mr. Savelyev was ordered to shut down the program. He was summoned to Moscow by the Ministry of Education, where he was reprimanded and threatened with dismissal for concealing an educational program that was under way both in Russia and in Iran.

"I really have big problems," he said, seated near a display cabinet where he kept a portrait of Iran's late supreme leader, Ayatollah Ruhollah

Khomeini. "I now have as my antagonists the Russian government and the American government and I think that one way or the other, they will find a way to fire me from the post of rector."

Days later Mr. Savelyev greeted an Iranian delegation that included two rocket experts from Iran's Ministry of Defense as well as an Iranian intelligence officer. That event, Tyler disclosed, resulted in a handwritten agreement to train Iranian scientists in rocketry. "But when Mr. Savelyev forwarded the document to the Education Ministry in Moscow, the program was rejected because only a year before, Russia had signed the Missile Technology Control Regime, an agreement reached by more than two dozen nations to control the spread of missile technology."

The event, as recorded by Patrick Tyler, is notable because it underscores the central role that the Soviet Union once played in arming its friends against common enemies. It also underscores the difficulties facing Western nations in trying to dissuade Former Soviet Union (FSU) stalwarts from going on the way they did before. There is also the money aspect: it was good in the old days. Now that such activities are illegal, the consensus is that it is even better.

Head of the queue handling such things in Tehran would be Iran's Defense Ministry—or, more correctly, *Vezarat-e Defa*. This body keeps an eye on administrative matters for the regular armed forces. The chain of command according to the Federation of American Scientists, flows from senior unit commanders (division, wing, and fleet) to intermediate-echelon service commanders and from there, to service commanders-in-chief and their staffs.

Prior to 1989, a separate Ministry of the Pasdaran handled the administrative affairs of the Islamic Republican Guard Corps. That chain flowed from senior unit commanders (operational brigades in the case of combat units) to ministry staff officers. The Joint Staff of the armed forces, composed of officers assigned from the various services, the Pasdaran, the National Police, and the Gendarmerie, was responsible for all operational matters. The manufacture, or even the acquisition of things like rockets or missiles would fall under Tehran's Defense Industries Organization (DIO) or *Sasadjah* (*Sazemane Sanaye Defa*).

The Military Industries Organization (MIO) of the Ministry of War had under their control military plants that produced small arms ammunition, batteries, tires, copper products, explosives, and mortar rounds, fuses and the rest. They also manufactured rifles and machine guns under West German license. In addition, helicopters, jeeps, trucks, and trailers were assembled from imported kits. Iran was on its way to manufacturing rocket launchers, rockets, gun barrels, and grenades, when the Revolution halted all military activities. The MIO, plagued by the upheavals of the time, was unable to operate without foreign specialists and technicians and by 1981 it had lost much of its management ability and control over its industrial facilities.

The outbreak of hostilities with Iraq and the Western arms embargo served as catalysts for reorganizing, reinvigorating, and expanding defense industries. By late 1981, FAS tells us that the revolutionary government had brought together the country's military industrial units and placed them under the Defense Industries Organization (DIO), which supervised all production activities.

In 1987, a mixed civilian-military board of directors and a managing director responsible for the actual management and planning activities governed the DIO. Although its director was accountable to the deputy minister of defense for logistics, Iran's president, in his capacity as the chairman of the SDC, had ultimate responsibility for all DIO operations.

Prior to 1989 the ballistic missiles program was the responsibility of the missile unit *Wakhid-e-Mashachekh* of the Revolutionary Guards. In 1989, elements of the Ministry of Defense and the Guards merged to form the Ministry of the Armed Forces Logistics (MODAFL), and their production facilities were merged into the Defense Industry Organization.

SUBSIDIARY ENTITIES

The following entities are responsible for Iran's missile programs. Unless otherwise noted, they are apparently located at the Gostaresh Research Center. Precise nomenclature and reporting relationships are unclear. According to some analysts, the Sanam Industries Group headquartered in Lavizan, which reportedly directs the nation's solid-fuel rocketry program, is also known as Department 140 or the Missile Industries Group.

- Department 140—Department of Guided and Unguided Missiles
- 140/4 (?? at Parchin)
- 140/11—Ya Makhdi industrial complex
- 140/12[?]—Saman [Samak?] Industrial Group / Aerospace Industries Organization (AIO) - liquid propellant missiles (Lavizan)
- 140/13—Shahid [Shakhid] Khassan Bagheri industrial-factory program (SHBIFG)
- 140/14—Shahid Bagheri industrial group (SBIG)—solid propellant missiles
- 140/15—Shahid Hemat industrial group (SHIG)—liquid propellant missiles (Parchin)
- 140/16—Mojtame Santy Ajzae Dahgigh - Instrumentation Factories Plant (IFP)
- 140/17—Shah Shah Abidi research center (MTSS)
- 140/18—Shahid Shafizadem industrial complex

- 140/31—Missile Industrial Group (MSM) (Parchin)
- 140/114/7—Shahid Babaye industrial complex (SBIC)
- Department 142—Mechanical Systems Industrial Group (MIG)
- Department 148/3—Education and Research Institute (ERI) [ex Scientific Research Group]
- Department 149/d—University of Science and Defense Technologies (USDT)
- Department 158—Mechanical Systems Industrial Group (MIG)
- Department 154—Special Industrial Groups of the Ministry of Defense (MIDSPCIG)

Though there is a range of missiles, just about all of them locally produced or assembled variants of what is coming out of North Korea or bought outright from Russia or China, most Western attention to date has been focused on the ubiquitous Shahab-3, in Farsi, the *Zelzal-3*

TECHNICAL DETAILS

Range (km)	1,350–1,500
CEP (m)	190 (Previously thought to be several thousand meters)
Diam. (m)	1.32–1.35
Height (m)	15.852–16
Launch Weight Mass (kg)	15,852–16,250
Stage Mass (kg)	15,092
Dry Weight Mass (kg)	1,780–2,180
Thrust (Kg f)	Effective: 26,051 (-709)
Actual:	26,760–26,600
Burn time (sec.)	110
Isp. (sec.)	Effective: 226—SL due to vains
steering drag	loss of 45 sec.
Actual:	230
Vac.:	264
Thrust Chamb.	1
Fuel	TM-185 (20% Gasoline/80% Kerosene)
Oxidizer	AK-27I (27% N2O4/73% HNO3)
Propellant Mass (kg)	12,912
Warhead (kg)	760/987–1,158
Type	MRBM

Note: The Iranian Shahab-3 ballistic missile means Meteor-3 or Shooting Star-3 [alternatively designated *Zelzal* (Earthquake)] and derived from the 700-950-mile range North Korean No-Dong missile]. The Shahab-3 can reportedly carry a three-quarter-ton/one-ton warhead.

In a BBC report[1] from Tehran on August 20, 2003, Iran's supreme leader Ayatollah Ali Khamene'i was said to have attended a televised ceremony to hand over to the armed forces Iran's latest version of the Shahab-3 ballistic missile which was said to be "capable of hitting Israel."

Khamene'i was shown on Iranian television flanked by officers and other clerics, and three of the Shahab-3 rockets on what appeared to be mobile launchers. "This divine force has answered all threats," he was quoted as saying in front of about a thousand troops in ceremonial dress, adding that his country's missile program was "purely meant as a deterrent."

Iranian television also reported that the Revolutionary Guards—who have their own air force—were given some new but unidentified attack and transport helicopters as well as an undisclosed number of Russian-built Sukhoi-25 jets. Head of the IRGC, Yahya Rahim-Safavi, was quoted as saying in his speech during the ceremony that his force was now 'ready to defend Iran against any threat'. The Federation of American Scientists reports that the Shahab-3 is based largely on the North Korean No-Dong ballistic missile.

DESIGN HERITAGE

The No-Dong ballistic missile was developed by North Korea with Soviet Gorbachev-era technical participation along with Chinese contributions and Iranian financial assistance. The FSU technology transfer contribution is circumstantially strongly suspected as having come from the Academy V. P. Makeyev OKB Design Bureau, developers of the Soviet era Scud-B, and its follow on SLBM's.

What we are also aware of is that the 9D21/S-2. Isayev OKB Scud-B engine was already in the possession of Pyongyang. The Isayev OKB, S-2.713 rocket engine design used on the Soviet SS-N-4 SLBM & the SS-N-6m Isayev engine and one other unidentified engine is also thought to have been a part of this technology transfer. This was directly the result of strategic arms reduction treaties creating unemployment in a large cadre of technically qualified former Soviet Union personnel because no other form of employment was successfully offered to them.

It is also worth noting that while the highly-modified Isayev OKB, S-2.713M rocket engine design reflects its Scud-B design heritage, it represents an entirely new liquid propellant rocket engine far beyond the growth potential of the modified Scud-B and C class engines for application to the No-Dong. Similarly, it reflects modern Soviet rocket engine start up design technology, such as the solid charge starter to spin up the turbo-pump, instead of start up propellant tanks. The same with pyrotechnics used to open the propellant flow and cut it off. It also reflects, too, the typical on-off rocket engine design philosophy used by the Soviets. All Soviet-era SLBM's owe their design heritage to the Scud-A and Scud-B tactical ballistic missiles.

China's contribution to the No-Dong project came from a joint North Korean/Chinese project conducted between 1976-78, the canceled DF-61 missile (essentially a Scud-C capability ballistic missile with a range of 600 km. carrying a 1,000 kg warhead that also featured a strap-down guidance system). Iran decided to totally rework the North Korean No-Dong design to their liking with Russian and now Chinese help.

In passing, it should be recalled that Pakistan flew its direct copy No-Dong missile (Ghauri-II) on April 6, 1998, some three months before Iran's Shahab-3

IRAN'S SHAHAB-3D MISSILE

As GlobalSecurtity.org. observes, the Shahab-3D is not the Shahab-3 nor is it the Iranian Shahab-4, better known as the North Korean Taep'o-dong-1/NKSL-1 which has a range of 1,240 miles (1,995.16 km). What can not be ruled out is that this missile is one of several other possibilities, or possibly, a truly domestic hybrid on which foreign rocket scientists have been working over the years. The Iranian statement that the Shahab-3D was powered by both liquid and solid propellant suggest that this is a totally different missile design from the Shahab-3.

It is also known that the Shahab-3 single engine is started by a solid propellant cartage that is expended before lift off. However, this does not explain the introduction of solid propellant on this variant. The indication of the presence of solid propellant suggest the introduction of the Iranian "IRIS" so called satellite launch vehicle or at least its precursor for the Iranian space program 'IRIS' launch vehicle.

To date, the only imagery publicly released of Shahab-3/3D flight tests by Iran has all been shown from the same position on the same facility. This brings into question whether it is the same video from the same first test launch of Shahab-3 since it is known that none of the launches have come from the same facility.

The video does reveal that the Shahab-3 requires many additional support vehicles for propellant transport and loading and power besides its Transport Erector Launcher (TEL). A through review of existing publicly available video has revealed that Iran has only shown the same first flight of the Shahab-3 video repeatedly on its news programs. No TV video of the Shahab-3D launch has been identified as of this writing.

However (recent developments apart), it is known that the Shahab-3, North Korea's No-Dong is not capable of covering all of Israel, but modified perhaps with a lighter warhead and or an additional small solid motor could extend that range to accomplish that mission.

The source of the solid motor technology for the Shahab-4 and 5 is in all probability China through a 'Know How', technology transfer agreement requested by Iran.

IRIS—THE FIRST POSSIBLE APPEARANCE OF "IRIS"/IRSL-X-1 SPACE BOOSTER?

There is another possibility that may not have been considered for Shahab-3D. Iran is committed to the development of the space booster "IRIS." This launch vehicle apparently consists of the No Dong/Shahab-3 first stage with a bulbous front section ultimately designed to carry an additional second stage solid motor as well as a communications satellite or scientific payload.

What the West is aware of is that the IRIS launch vehicle is a space-related derivation of the Shahab-3 ballistic missile (see diagrams in Chapter 9). A launch vehicle of this configuration is ideal as a vertical probe sounding rocket for ballistic missile warhead re-entry vehicle development. It would almost certainly not be capable of launching a satellite of appreciable mass or capability unless it were intended to be a second and third stage of a larger launch vehicle.

By the same token, were the Shahab-3D launch to be an IRIS launch vehicle test, then it was the first flight test of the Taep'o-dong-2/Shahab-5 second and third stages, part of a space booster concept that Iran is said to be developing.

The IRIS launch vehicle concept was first seen on public displays in model form in an Iranian aerospace show. However, this flight test failure may have caused a serious delay in the development program for the Taep'o-dong-2/Shahab-5 launch vehicle program and only time will answer this open question. Presumably a ballistic missile version of this could also be developed which may explain the Shahab-3D variant.

The description of a Solid propellant upper stage on top of a No-Dong/Shahab-3 design certainly fits the IRIS displayed design. It is not unusual for a nation to flight test the upper stages of a new booster as a testing procedure that has been used in both the East and West to expedite the development of a future larger space booster before flying the entire stack.

The Shahab-3D does however very strongly resemble the North Korean Taep'o-dong-2 second and third stages. Could it be that the Shahab-3D is in-fact a modified variant of the IRIS space related booster undergoing its first flight test?

Another question asked is whether this, in-turn, might be Iran's contribution to North Korea's Taep'o-dong-2 space booster ballistic missile program and their own Shahab-5 space booster or ballistic missile? To a degree it could suggest that Iran is working on the second and third stages of the Taep'o-dong-2 launch vehicle with North Korea while they both have apparently made contributions to the larger new Taep'o-dong-2 first stage. Recently North Korea static test fired that same new first stage on the rebuilt Taep'o-dong-1 (now Taep'o-dong-2) launch pad, gantry umbilical tower facility, between June 26 and July 2, 2001.

It is known that the Shahab-3D failed shortly after launch. This was well before the first stage would have completed its hundred-and-ten second burn when the aerodynamic shroud would have been jettisoned and the solid motor second stage would have ignited regardless of its true design configuration and the actual payload flown.

At the time of going to press all that is unclear, based on the available public information released to date. In general IRIS is believed to be waiting for Shahab-5 to fulfill its real goal.

BUILD-UP AND FLIGHT TEST ANALYSIS

The week before September 8th 2000, Iran attempted to launch the new variant of the Shahab-3 ballistic missile, the Shahab-3D missile but apparently had some trouble during the attempted build up as noted in the *Washington Times* on September 8, 2000: "delayed from the previous week . . . test expected later this month."[2]

Three weeks later both the Associated Press and the *Washington Times* noted the following new information: "Iran has successfully test-fired its first solid-liquid fueled missile, which the Defense Minister said was part of a program for launching satellites.[3] The *Times* added that the Iranian had tested the Shahab-3 MRBM for a third time, but that "the rocket exploded shortly after liftoff, U.S. Intelligence officials said."

An Iranian spokesman went on to say that the missile was "solid and liquid fueled and will be used only for launching communications satellites and not warheads."[4]

At about the same time *Jane's Intelligence Review* also noted that the September 21, 2000 flight test was a failure, according to U.S. officials. It was flown from near the city of Semnan.[5]

The description of this Shahab-3D launch failure certainly suggest that the Iranians are having considerable development trouble with their domestically produced Shahab-3 liquid propellant engines and/or their related systems. This same kind of engine or engine related systems failure along with instrumentation and or guidance failure could also account for the first Shahab-3 launch failure. In almost all cases they give hints of serious quality control problems leading to in-flight launch failure during the first stage engine burn.

During September 2000 testimony before the U.S. Senate, a National Intelligence officer for Strategic and Nuclear Programs discussed the Shahab-3D first launch and said that "Iran's Defense minister announced the Shahab-4, originally calling it a more capable ballistic missile than the Shahab-3, but later categorizing it as a space launch vehicle with no military applications."

Tehran also mentioned plans for the Shahab-5, strongly suggesting that it intended to develop even longer-range systems in the near future.

Iran has already displayed a mock-up satellite and space launch vehicle (IRIS), suggesting that it has plans to develop a vehicle to orbit Iranian satellites. Most believe that Iran could develop and test a three-stage Taep'o-dong-2 type ICBM during this same time frame, possibly with North Korean assistance. ICBM booster capability and a Taep'o-dong-type system tested as a space launch vehicle would be the shortest path to that goal.

On this matter, U.S. Senator Cochran is on record as stating in Congress that "As we have said in open session before, Iran procured No-Dong and then sought Russian assistance to modify that into the Shahab-3, which is a little different approach than Pakistan used to get the Ghauri, which is also a No-Dong.

"They did not mind trying to change it. They just decided to change its name and buy them outright."[6]

Appendix G
PASDARAN'S PROTEGÉ: HIZBOLLAH

"One of the central reasons for creating Hizbollah
was to challenge the Zionist program in the region. . . . Hizbollah
still preserves this principle, and when an Egyptian journalist visited
me after the liberation and asked me if the destruction of Israel
and the liberation of Palestine and Jerusalem were Hizbollah's
goal, I replied: 'That is the main objective of Hizbollah.
It is no less sacred than our [ultimate] goal'."

Sayyid Hassan Nasrallah, Secretary General of Hizbollah

From among the hundred or so disaffected and largely disorganized revolutionary groups active in and around Beirut during Lebanon's civil war of the 1970s–80s, Hizbollah is one of the few to have survived; and the guerrilla group has come a very long way in the past quarter century.

The movement first came to prominence when one of its founding members, the notorious Imad Mugniyah (today a terrorist with a $25 million bounty on his head), pioneered the technique of suicide bombings that killed hundreds of Americans in Beirut in 1983 and 1984. Even then, as retired CIA operative Robert Baer told *Jane's Islamic Affairs Analyst*, Iranian support for its Shi'ite protégé was a manifest, everyday thing.[1]

American spy writer John Weisman echoed these comments: Hizbollah was a creation entirely of Iran's Pasdaran, whose leaders, including Sheikh Mosleh, "set up shop in the 1980s in the Beqá and created the first truly non-hierarchical, cell-based terror organization. Totally controlled by Iran, it first went by such names as the Islamic Jihad Organization (IJO), Islamic Amal, and then, finally, Hizbollah, which means Party of God. But the core and the missions, he explained, were Iranian controlled.[2]

'What is also interesting (added Bob Baer) is the fact that the Iranians were able to recruit Sunnis as a part of this terror network. Many of the early recruits also came from Palestinian organizations (Fatah's Force 17 for example) whose operatives included Imad Mugniyah.

As its website indicates, Hizbollah's most important moment arrived with the Israeli invasion of Lebanon in 1982, "when the movement was able to hone its activities to cause enough destruction of Israeli military elements that they were eventually forced to withdraw."

The price for this success has not been inordinately high, though according to Eyal Zisser, some critics of the movement say that Nasrallah now sees himself as a hero on a divine mission, due in no small part to his portrayal "as a Shi'ite mastermind in the Israeli and Western media."

Writing in the *Middle East Quarterly*, Zisser declared that recent events confirmed two important developments related to Israel, the first being that despite hefty protests from the Lebanese parliament, Hizbollah has complete control over its own "Hizbollahland" throughout much of southern Lebanon. "The territory serves both as a base for anti-Israeli military operations and for mobilizing support for the organization's political activities within Lebanon," he said.

The other is that Hizbollah—much to the chagrin of the authorities in Beirut—is now the pre-eminent anti-Israeli player in the region. Nor is it lost on an array of Arab watchers in Washington that Iran holds much more powerful sway with Hizbollah's leaders than Syrian leaders, with whom all three entities share common anti-Israeli sentiment. Iran and Syria have been supportive of the guerrilla movement from the start.

At the same time, one cannot ignore Hizbollah's powerful Syrian connections. Writing in *The Daily Star*, one of two English-language newspapers in Beirut, veteran Middle East correspondent Nicholas Blandford made issue of the fact that the alliance was not only strategic, it was strong. A source closely connected to Hizbollah's thinking told him that the "strategic alliance" between Hizbollah and Syria had improved considerably since the young Syrian President Bashar Assad assumed office in July 2000.

"Syria needs Hizbollah, Hizbollah needs Syria. Hizbollah is a credible force" for Syria, Blandford reported, quoting his source.

He then asked what would happen if Washington chose to use the military option against Syria. Would Hizbollah come to the aid of Damascus, perhaps by opening up the Lebanese-Israeli border?

The reply was emphatic: "'If America attacks Syria, only then will we say what we shall do,' said Hassan Ezzeddine, head of Hizbollah's media department, echoing the party's usual ambiguity over its use of force," he reported.

"Hamzeh said that in such an event, Hizbollah would take its lead from Ayatollah Ali Khamene'i, Iran's Supreme Spiritual Leader. 'Hizbollah and Iran are tied by the concept of the *wilayet al-faqih* (the guardianship of the governance of the jurisprudence),' said Ezzeddine. "So long as the Hizbollah majority subscribe to Khamene'i as the *wilayet al-faqih*, then Hizbollah will follow (his rulings). This is part of the ideology of Hizbollah itself: the conception of obedience. Khamene'i is the one who decides on general issues while the details are left to the party."

"In the meantime, 'Hizbollah is watching carefully and is prepared for the worst,'" the Hizbollah source told Blandford.

What is of most concern to the Americans about these recent developments, is that the last thing the West needs now is the emergence of a Hizbollah clone from among Iraq's persecuted Shi'ite community. With sixty per cent of a largely impoverished and, until now, persecuted Iraqi population from which to draw recruits, such a development would be a formidable counter to the U.S. maintaining the status quo in that embattled country. We saw some of those dynamics emerge in Iraq's minor anti-American Intifada in early April 2004 with considerable loss of life. Nor is that the end of it.

What is interesting here is that there is an almost incestuous link between some of these revolutionaries. For instance, Moqtada el-Sadr—the same dissident Shi'ite that has caused problems for America's military in Iraq—is a blood-relative of the Hizbollah leader Sayyid Hassan Nasrallah. Both men hail from one of the seven clans who have led Iraq's Shi'ite community for two centuries.

It says much that following Moqtada's attacks on U.S. and Coalition Forces, the Hizbollah leader was succinctly quoted: "We may be unable to drive the Americans out of Iraq, but we can certainly drive George W. Bush out of the White House."

For a purely domestic organization, Hizbollah has expended a lot of effort abroad in recent years. There is evidence that it has linked up with like-minded Islamic terror organizations, including several in Africa. In this regard, British military intelligence sources[3] disclosed that following terror attacks against Israeli interests in Mombasa, Kenya in December 2002, new evidence emerged of a link between Osama bin Laden's al-Qaeda organization and the fundamentalist Hizbollah.

American, Israeli and British investigators at the bombings of Mombasa's Paradise Hotel, in which sixteen people were killed and eighty wounded—together with an attempt to shoot down an Israeli-registered passenger aircraft with more than two-hundred-and-fifty people onboard—linked the terrorists responsible for both actions with Hassan Nasrallah's guerrillas.

They point to the modus operandi of the suicide bombers. SAM missile launchers used by the attackers were of the same type and vintage as those used against Israeli warplanes in South Lebanon by Hizbollah. Furthermore, reports out of Nairobi afterward stated that the manner in which the hotel was bombed was identical to similar attacks in Lebanon in the 1980s.

There was also evidence of the imprint of Imad Mugniyah in the attacks. This arch international terrorist with strong Hizbollah links has been responsible for numerous acts of terror over the past quarter century. He now lives in exile—either in Damascus or Tehran—and shares the distinction, with several other Arab terrorists, of being on the list of "America's Most Wanted." The charge: orchestrating scores of attacks that began with the suicide bombings against the U.S. and French Embassies as well as a U.S. Marine base in Beirut in 1983.

More recently Mugniyah was linked by the CIA to the destruction of the U.S. Embassies in Nairobi, Kenya, and Dar es Salaam, Tanzania, as well as the bombing of the American warship USS *Cole* in Aden harbor. Following these disclosures, "credible and specific" threats of more attacks forced the closure of the British High Commission in Nairobi several times.

One report out of Washington, DC put matters into a more immediate perspective. According to Neil MacFarquhar of the *New York Times*, senior American officials have singled out Lebanon's Hizbollah as the "A-Team of international terrorism." Similarly, Democratic Senator Bob Graham of Florida—until recently chairman of the Senate Intelligence Committee—stated that "right now, Hizbollah is more menacing that al-Qaeda." At the time—shortly before the 2003 invasion of Iraq—he actually suggested that the Lebanese group be dealt with before Baghdad, "because it is the most dangerous terrorist group on earth."

For all that, the U.S. government has not been inactive. It took a tough line on the predominantly Shi'ite political and guerrilla group when American Secretary of State Colin Powell met the Syrian President in May, 2003. According to BBC correspondent Lyse Doucet, who was there to cover the visit, "Mr. Powell made it clear that the U.S. expected Syria and Lebanon to comply with Washington's plans for the region."

Judging by press reactions in several Arab capitals afterward, the consensus was that Hizbollah's activities have absolutely nothing to do with Mr. Powell or anybody else abroad. Some measure of the success of the meeting, or lack of it, came afterward from *The Washington Times* (May 6, 2003) which disclosed that the U.S. Administration "is considering legislation which would impose economic sanctions on Syria." (Interestingly, this has since happened).

Powell is known to have raised several security issues with Assad, including the fact that Hizbollah was reported by U.S. intelligence agencies to have acquired a supply of Russia's most sophisticated SA-18 Manpad missiles. These shoulder-fired ground-to-air devices are similar to those used by al-Qaeda in the Mombasa attacks, except that the SA-18 has a greater range (15,000 ft) and altitude (10,000 ft) as well as a higher speed, enabling it to hit faster targets. Washington leaked reports that Syria had bought a number of these missiles "with the intention of transferring them to Hizbollah."

Following visits to Moscow by Israeli national security advisor Ephraim Halevy (as well as a state visit by Prime Minister Sharon not long afterward) Israel was told by President Vladimir Putin that the sale had been canceled. However, the United Arab Emirates daily *Al-Bayan* had already disclosed a month earlier that Hizbollah received "a first installment of the rockets earlier in the year."

What is clear, according to one British strategist, is that Hizbollah appears to be concentrating on enhancing its missile strike capacity. Another report out of Washington disclosed that in the four years since the IDF was forced to vacate southern Lebanon, Hizbollah's secretary-general indicated that he wanted a "leaner, tougher and more sophisticated military machine" with which to tackle Israeli defenses.

From reliable sources, the *Middle East Intelligence Bulletin* disclosed at the end of 2002 that Hizbollah had accumulated an arsenal of ten thousand short and long-range rockets, including hundreds capable of striking as far south as the industrial suburbs of Haifa. While some of this may be hype, it did note that Israeli officials had been complaining about "massive Iranian weapons airlifts to Hizbollah since March 2001." Washington confirmed that among this hardware—airfreighted from Iran to Syria and then moved by road convoy into Lebanon—were long-range Iranian manufactured Fajr-3 and Fajr-5 rockets.[4]

Nasrallah had his say about this development on the Hizbollah-run Al Manar television station afterward. In a recorded Friday sermon from his favorite mosque in Beirut's Dahiya, he declared that his "missiles can now reach all the population centers in Israel. Then where can they flee?"

American strategists conclude that Hizbollah's offensive capabilities, while enhanced, remain modest compared to what Israel is able to field. But they have to concede that the movement's stock of war material is growing, both in numbers and in sophistication.

Most of its arsenal consists of antiquated equipment such as 105mm and 122mm Katyusha rockets with limited range. The arrival of Syrian 270mm rockets and several hundred 240mm Iranian Fajr-3 rockets that can strike at targets twenty-five miles away, and the even larger Fajr-5 (which carries a two-hundred-and-sixty-pound warhead almost as far and in addition, is mobile) has required some juggling of regional defenses by Israel. All towns, moshavim and kibutzims in northern Galilee now have their own underground bomb shelters.

At the same time, there appears to be some confusion as to whose fingers are actually on the triggers of these weapons: Iranian "military advisors" in Lebanon or the Syrians?

Both the Americans and the Israelis believe that, for now, Hizbollah's efforts are controlled by Syria to disallow the movement the ability to raise the anté without a say-so from either Damascus or Tehran. Even attacks on specific targets across the border are carefully scripted.

Amad Saad-Ghorayeb, a political science professor at the Lebanese-American University said that "The attacks in recent years had been largely symbolic . . . it is more psychological warfare than reality."

Still, they do damage and people are being killed and wounded.

At the start of the new millennium Hizbollah is both an extremely versatile and multifaceted political and military organization.

Just about everybody in Lebanon talks about its "two faces": the one public and the other notoriously secretive. On the one hand you have secretary-general Hassan Nasrallah who, most Lebanese accept, runs the most effective charitable social and public institution in the Arab world. His schedules include schools, more clinics than there have ever been, a hospital or two, agricultural outreach programs, and construction firms, as well as television and radio stations. On the political front, Hizbollah also has a healthy dozen members of his party ensconced in the Lebanese Parliament, which, despite its strictly Shi'ite coloring, makes it the fastest growing political force in the region. There is more.

Hizbollah's command structure maintains a vast clandestine military and security service, which, it has been suggested often enough, rivals that of the Lebanese government. Some of its activities are so hush-hush that their goings on are shielded from all but a select few, the majority having been "blood-tested in anti-Israeli operations." For its part, Tehran is directly involved through the Pasdaran, or the Iranian Revolutionary Guard Corps (IRGC).

All these aspects are likely to have been raised by Colin Powell in Damascus and Beirut. So too, might have been the fact that Washington was aware that while much had been made of the departure of about a hundred IRGC cadres from the Beqá Valley (following the September 11 attacks) the majority stayed on. What is not acknowledged is that some of those who were supposed to have left have since returned.

One report suggests that the scenario is part of a broader Iranian strategy ultimately geared "to strike against Israel." The head of Iran's missile development program almost said as much in an interview with the London-based Arabic daily *Al Hayat* in October 2003.

Also worrying is that Israel has since acknowledged that a significant proportion of Hizbollah's intelligence efforts within its borders are devoted to determining the precise locations of factories, fuel supplies, industrial sites, and power stations, as well as weapons and aircraft industries.

I was to experience a little of this myself during a visit to Lebanon in 1999. Ostensibly, the idea was do an article for Jane's IDR on the reconstruction of the Lebanese Army following the eight-year civil war that left the country in ruins. For this, I received valuable help from the former chief of the Lebanese Army, General Emile Lahoud, who became President of the country shortly after my visit. Part of my brief was to try to make contact with Hizbollah, and, if possible, ask to go on an operation with the guerrilla group along the Israeli border in the south of the country.

For a Westerner—and somebody who regularly visited Israel—to make contact with an organization as powerfully opposed to Western values as Hizbollah, the tasks were difficult but not impossible. There were a number of hurdles that needed to be traversed, including making that initial connection.

Still, it was hardly a tough assignment. Beirut had undergone a remarkable metamorphosis from the civil war period: these days you can walk about freely without the fear of being kidnapped and held for ransom. Hizbollah does not interfere with a society that has managed to pick up the pieces in the wake of one of the most horrific civil wars of the past century. In fact, it encourages tourism, as long as guests don't wander unescorted around any area adjacent to the Israeli border.

In the old days, prior to the conflict that affected millions and left hundreds of thousands dead, the city was special to millions, many of whom were neither Lebanese nor Arabic. Its opulence and sometimes brash, often elegant lifestyle made it the cherished venue of many thousands of Arabs from countries with more rigid political regimens. Quite a few people from throughout the Arab world maintain second homes (and sometimes, families) there.

There were, and still are, a lot of attractions in this former "Pearl of the Mediterranean" which has since retrieved much of its original luster. The glittering Casino du Liban, for instance, I found to be much more than the name implied. It epitomized the country's playground character. In those days Lebanon had a charm that was envied, often emulated but never matched.

With the war over, I discovered all these traits re-emerging from the rubble. One of the first to get in on the act was the old (and now, the new) St. George's. Like other hotels of the Minet al-Hosn, locals didn't even wait for them to finish renovations before they started packing the place on Sundays.

St. George's arriviste cousin, Hotel Phoenicia, has also been resurrected. Described in the 1972 New Horizons *World Guide* as "the best by far in Beirut," its contract has gone to the Intercontinental chain. So, too, with the Vendome, which boasts less than a hundred rooms, of which a third are suites. There is also an English pub and it's priced to match!

As before, the women are stunning, as much for their natural beauty as what they don't wear. Beirut is one of the very few places where you can observe Arab beauties from up close without impinging on family honor. But there is another, more fundamental side to Beirut.

While my time with the Lebanese Army and several of the country's Special Forces elements went off well—I was even able to visit the Southern Front—I tried from the start to make contact with Hizbollah headquarters in Beirut's southern suburbs, not far from the city's international airport. The most obvious way was possibly to speak to one of the bellhops at the hotel at which I was staying: being Muslim, he would know the ropes. Chances were good that he had somebody within the family circle close to the Party of God.

I wanted to meet with someone senior in Hizbollah, I told him. Two days later the man came back to me: it might be possible but I should wait for somebody to make contact with me, he said. It took another week for things to happen and by then I was thinking of getting back to London.

Finally, one Saturday afternoon, I was fetched from my hotel in a limousine and taken first to one office to explain my needs and then to several more. Two more days of delays followed. Meanwhile, I was asked to prepare a list of questions.

Finally, a few days before I was due to leave the country, another car came for me. I was to accompany him, the driver told me, but there were to be no cameras. Nor was there to be a blindfold and I wasn't searched for firearms. It was a pretty straightforward assignment.

Our destination was Harek Horeik, the impoverished, mainly Shi'ite quarter toward the south of the main city, but still within rifle shot of Beirut's fleshpots along the Corniche. What gave it away were as many ten-times-life-size posters of the Ayatollah Khomeini that could be squeezed onto a city block without obscuring the view of the residents. These replaced more explicit billboards of the latest Hollywood offerings, which became fewer the farther south we drove.

The meeting with Hizbollah secretary Ibrahim Moussawi on the first floor of a nondescript office block not far from one of Hizbollah's military encampments went off without incident. We'd passed the base on the way in, as well as what was obviously a well-guarded communications center. Then up two flights of stairs and a formal greeting at which tea was offered

In my initial approach to the group, I'd mentioned that I was intending to do an article for Jane's. Consequently I wasn't surprised when one of the first questions he asked was about something that I'd written a short while earlier after a visit to Israel: I'd been previously told that the organization keeps files of just about everything that anybody writes on the region and it fitted in with the image that this spokesman displayed, dressed as he was in a dark suit and collarless shirt, buttoned at the top. Moussawi's English was clipped, precise and Middle Eastern: always the pragmatist, this was no Ivy League or British public school-educated academic. A large *Qur'an* sat on his desk at his elbow.

I had my list of questions with me. These, he said, would need to be translated and then he needed a bit of time for them to be worked on. I'd have his answers, in Arabic, in a day or two. After some polite chitchat the meeting was almost over. Moussawi didn't mention my request about going to the front and I didn't raise it again. If it was going to happen it would have been one of the first things we would have talked about.

Curiously, nothing more was said about my having been in Israel a short while before, though he did let something pass about a second passport.

Since the chips were down, I told him that a month earlier I'd spent a short while at one of the IDF front-line positions to the west of Metullah, adjacent to what was once termed "The Good Fence." There was no point in being devious: his organization could just as easily have gleaned as much from one of several calls that I made to the office of the Military Attaché at the British Legation. I took it for granted that my phone at the hotel was tapped.

The last question Moussawi asked was pointed. Having been there on the other side, what did I think of the war in the south? Which way did I think this guerrilla conflict was heading?

I remained candid, replying that I believed Israel would pull back to behind its own lines within a year. This surprised him. He smiled, expressing what I suspected was more incredulity than humor.

Within an hour I was back at my hotel. Three days later I transited Cairo while heading for London, complete with my translated text which went into *Jane's Defence Weekly* a week later.

What did rankle, though, was that on my way back to the United States, perhaps a week after that, I was cleverly relieved of my briefcase on my way into Manhattan from JFK Airport.

The incident could not exactly have been construed as a mugging. Rather it was a clever bit of sleight of hand. One moment my baggage was there and in the next my briefcase was gone. What hurt was that with a lifetime of reporting behind me, I'm considerably more streetwise than most of my peers. Lost in the briefcase were all my notes covering the Moussawi meeting, a stack of operational photos from time spent with the Lebanese Army in various parts of the country including the southern front, as well as several sets of documents that I'd been working on that dealt with Saddam's efforts to acquire the bomb. Though I reported my loss to a local precinct, nothing was ever found.

As a modern-day revolutionary organization, I found Hizbollah to be perfectly at one within the environs in which it operated.

Uncompromisingly harsh and levying staunch discipline on its members, it was at the same time efficient and in tune with recent tactical and
technological developments. At the same time, it seemed that the movement, unlike its opposition, was amenable to change as it would have had
to be if it was at war with Israel.

But in the Lebanon of the late 1990s, there were also those who
regarded Hizbollah as having acquired "a schizoid" personality. That perception persists, largely because of the grandstand antics of its secretary
general Sheikh Hassan Nasrallah. There is also the Iranian connection,
which is no secret because on its website <www.hizbollah.org> the insurgency group stresses strong historical ties with Tehran.

Looking at the bigger picture, it might have been only natural for
Tehran's ideological Shi'ite doctrine in Iran to have taken root in
Lebanon. Hizbollah's website statement headed "Identity and Goals"
goes on to explain that this tie was very quickly translated on the ground
by direct support from Tehran "through its Revolutionary Guards,"
which is one of the few times that Hizbollah has admitted intimate ties
with Pasdaran publicly.

Another issue recently addressed in public by anonymous Hizbollah
spokespeople was a statement made by Nasrallah. He declared, with
some justification perhaps, that the most accomplished military minds (in
Israel) had failed to develop a means to counter suicide attacks.

"What will protect Jerusalem, its holy places and get it and Palestine
back [sic], is the path of the Palestine people through martyrdom seekers
who astonish the world each day and night," he said at an al-Qods day
parade. The Al Manar television station took a similar line, using filched
Israeli newsreel footage of suicide bombings across the border.
Meanwhile, a small team of interpreters who learnt Hebrew in Israeli
prisons provided commentary.

Speaking of Hizbollah's future, the secretary general disclosed that
one of the central reasons for creating Hizbollah in the first place was to
challenge Zionism, which he said had become entrenched in the neighboring region.

He went on: "Hizbollah still preserves this principle, and when an
Egyptian journalist visited me after the liberation [of the Israeli exclusion
zone in South Lebanon] and asked me if the destruction of Israel and the
liberation of Palestine and Jerusalem were Hizbollah's goal, I replied:
'That is the principal objective of Hizbollah, and it is no less sacred than
our [ultimate] goal.'

"The generation that lived through the creation of this entity is still
alive. This generation watches documentaries and reads documents that

show that the land conquered was called Palestine, not Israel.

"We face an entity that conquered the land of another people, drove them out of their land, and committed horrendous massacres. As we see, this is an illegal state; it is a cancerous entity and the root of all the crises and wars and cannot be a factor in bringing about a true and just peace in this region. Therefore, we cannot acknowledge the existence of a state called Israel, not even far in the future, as some people have tried to suggest. Time does not cancel the legitimacy of the Palestinian claim."

A new development in Lebanon is the trafficking in narcotics by Hizbollah in Europe and North America to fund its activities in the Middle East. According to the U.S. Drug Enforcement Agency (DEA) chief Asa Hutchinson, "A significant portion of some of these sales are returned to the Middle East to benefit terrorist organizations."

"Hizbollah not only used the poppy crop in Lebanon's Beqá Valley for funds, but also to buy support from Israeli Arabs ready to carry out operations," said another DEA source.

Similarly, according to Matthew Levitt, a Senior Fellow in Terrorism Studies at the Washington Institute for Near East Studies, smuggling, kidnapping and extortion are also well-established techniques employed by Hizbollah and other terrorist groups. For example, "In June 2002, two brothers, Mohammed and Chawki Hamud, involved in a Hizbollah support cell in Charlotte, North Carolina were found guilty of a variety of charges related to funding the organization's activities including a smuggling ring.

"In South America, Hizbollah operatives engage in a wide range of criminal enterprises to raise, transfer and launder funds in support of activities back home," he stated. Another authority points to the illicit diamond trade in Sierra Leone, Angola and the Congo where large expatriate Lebanese families have been active for years. Many of them are openly sympathetic to Hizbollah.

Levitt also makes the point that international terrorist groups do not operate in solitude. Expanding on this thesis in a paper titled "The Political Economy of Middle East Terrorism," he maintains "that contrary to the conventional wisdom—which pigeonholes al-Qaida in boxes of their own—militant Islamic groups interact and support one another in a matrix of international logistical, financial and sometimes operational terrorist activity."

Levitt was referring specifically to organizations such as Hizbollah, Hamas, Iran and Syria, all of them in boxes of their own militant Islamic groups.[5]

Gary C Gambill, editor of the *Middle East Intelligence Bulletin* (MEIB) and a Research Associate at Middle East Forum, is an outspoken authority on state-sponsored terror and authoritarianism in the Arab world. He has a lot to say about the activities of the Party of God.

In the January/February 2004 edition of MEIB he cited an incident involving Hizbollah leader Hassan Nasrallah that neatly encapsulated the adoration currently being accorded this man since his masterminding the eviction of Israeli forces from South Lebanon in 2000:[7]

"In late January, tens of thousands of people lined the road leading from Beirut International Airport into the capital to greet the return of twenty-three Lebanese militants released a short while before from Israeli prisons. Fireworks lit the sky . . . and street celebrations continued late into the night. Equally exuberant, if less flashy, festivities took place in the West Bank and Gaza as over four hundred Palestinian prisoners returned to their homes."

As he tells us, "The homecoming of so many people accused of planning or carrying out violence against Israelis did not result from a breakthrough in the peace process. It came just hours after the deadliest suicide bombing to hit Israel in months. In exchange for its mass repatriation of Arab combatants, the Jewish State obtained the release of a single Israeli citizen (and the remains of three others) held by Hizbollah." Gambill is prescient when he states that "Israel's strikingly asymmetrical concession consolidated secretary-general Hassan Nasrallah's status as one of the most widely revered public figures in the Islamic world today.

"Newspapers throughout the Middle East praised the forty-three-year-old Islamic fundamentalist leader as a paragon of courage and steadfastness. Iran's supreme leader, Ayatollah Ali Hoseini Khamene'i, hailed the prisoner exchange as proof that 'the evil Zionist regime can be defeated by the strong will and concrete faith of the fighters of Islam'."[8]

Ahmed Yassin, spiritual leader of the Palestinian terrorist group Hamas similarly pledged that his movement would follow in Hizbollah's footsteps by kidnapping more Israelis.

While there will always be militant Arab leaders inciting violence by preaching hatred, the staunch belief of many Palestinians today that violence can force Israel to make unilateral concessions is largely due to Nasrallah. Israel's May 2000 withdrawal from southern Lebanon—without even informal assurances of non-hostility from the enemy—is the organization's most resounding success story yet.

"It is no accident that, at Nasrallah's urging, Palestinian terrorist groups launched a holy war of unprecedented lethality against Israel four months later."

Drawing on open literature, Gambill tells us something about Hassan Nasrallah the man. He was born in 1960 in the Bourj Hammoud neighborhood of East Beirut, but his family was originally from Bassouriyeh, a village near the city of Tyre in south Lebanon. Although his family was not particularly religious by Lebanese standards, Nasrallah, the eldest of nine children, became obsessed with Islam. He began reading fundamentalist literature at an age when most of his friends were playing soccer.

In 1975, following the outbreak of civil war in Beirut, Nasrallah's family moved to south Lebanon. That brought him into contact with the Amal movement of Musa Sadr, a widely revered religious figure who campaigned against the feudalistic Shi'ite political elite. He soon became a member.

Having caught the attention of several Shi'ite religious leaders, the youngster was invited to attend the Shi'ite seminary (*hawza*) of Najaf. The following year, on finishing his secondary education and still barely sixteen years old, the youthful Nasrallah left for Najaf to begin his studies.

It was as the acknowledged leader of a group of expatriate Shi'ites that the much revered Muhammad Hussein Fadlallah, by now a *mujtahid* (authority in religious law), returned to Lebanon in 1966. Spurned by Sadr and the Lebanese Shi'ite clerical establishment, Fadlallah formed the Lebanese Islamic Da'wa Party and ran an independent network of clinics, schools, and charitable associations.

Saddam Hussein—always tough on the Iraqi Shi'ite community—had forced Nasrallah and his compatriots out of the country in 1978 after a clampdown. Their return to Lebanon coincided with the mysterious disappearance of Sadr during a visit to Libya. From what the authorities in Beirut have been able to piece together since, it would appear that Sadr the Elder was murdered by Gadhaffi in a bid to keep relations intact with the Levantine political hierarchy. Interestingly, it is his son, the volatile Moqtada el-Sadr, who rides his father's coattails in Iraq at the head of what he terms "a Mehdi (*Mahdi* in Arabic) Army" against "an illegal U.S. presence."

By now, as Gambil states, Nasrallah had accepted a teaching position at a religious institute in Baalbek. As he says, "His youth, charisma, and impassioned oratory appealed to many estranged young Shi'ites and he gained an impressive body of followers."

Then came June 1982 and the Israeli invasion of Lebanon. Iran quickly dispatched several hundred Islamic Revolutionary Guards into the Beqá Valley to organize a revolutionary movement aimed at waging *jihad* against the invaders and, ultimately, the establishment of an Islamic republic in Lebanon. At this point, Nasrallah, with many of his followers, set up a new organization that was to be the forerunner of Hizbollah, initially an umbrella group composed of militant pro-Iranian clerics and their followers.

Gambil says that some of the more spectacular suicide operations that followed against Israeli troops and Western peacekeeping forces from 1982 to 1984 were carried out under cover names, such as the "Revolutionary Justice Organization" and the "Organization of the Oppressed on Earth." Finally, in 1985, The Party of God officially told the world of its existence in an open letter to a Lebanese newspaper and vowed to wage holy war against Israel and its supporters.

It is notable that during this period of hostilities, Nasrallah distinguished himself as a military commander. In 1987 for instance, Hizbollah forces under his command succeeded in driving the Amal militia out of several positions in the southwestern suburbs of Beirut.

After Syria stepped in and used force to stop rival militias from fighting, Nasrallah went to Iran and resumed his studies in Ayatollah Khomeini's holy city of Qom. This was partly an act of protest against Syria's move into Beirut, but it stemmed too from his recognition that "proper" (Iranian) religious credentials were as important as military prowess in assuming a greater leadership role within Hizbollah.

Once fighting between Hizbollah and Amal reignited in 1989, Nasrallah returned to his homeland. Again he led Hizbollah forces in combat, this time in a successful drive against Amal in the Iqlim al-Toufah region of south Lebanon. It was here that he was lightly wounded in battle. By the end of the decade, he had become head of the group's Central Military Command and a member of its politburo. He took over as secretary-general of the movement not long afterward.

The first order of business for Hizbollah after Nasrallah's ascension was retribution for the assassination of Musawi, a Shi'ite cleric assassinated by the Israelis. On March 17, a car bomb hit the Israeli Embassy in Buenos Aires, killing twenty-nine people, in an attack that Argentine investigators later concluded was carried out by Hizbollah.[9] The embassy bombing was the first installment in a broader strategy of using terror attacks on Israeli and Jewish civilians at home and abroad to deter the IDF from forceful action in Lebanon. It worked.

Although Israeli intelligence planned and trained operatives for an assassination of Nasrallah, the order was never given. In the years that followed, the Hizbollah leader appeared regularly in public, often speaking before crowds numbering in the tens of thousands without fear of assassination.

According to Gambill, "Hizbollah operations became progressively more deadly after Nasrallah's ascension (twenty-six Israeli soldiers died in combat in south Lebanon in 1993, double the number for 1992). This was partly due to innate managerial skills and innovative tactics, but his actions also reflected the fact that the Iranians gave Nasrallah a much broader leadership mandate than his predecessors. He explains that

Nasrallah was allowed to appoint military commanders on the basis of competence, with less regard for their affiliations with this or that cleric. However, while major advances were made in Hizbollah's combat strength, its success on the battlefield remained integrally tied to its ability to strike Israeli and Jewish targets off the battlefield.

For example, Hizbollah's combat effectiveness against Israeli and South Lebanon Army (SLA) forces depended to a large extent on its use of villages near the security zone to shelter guerrillas. Hizbollah cadres typically retreated into civilian settlements after launching attacks. This tactic was viable only if Israel could be deterred from carrying out reprisals against attack squads when they fled into civilian areas. Although Hizbollah's Katyusha rocket attacks into northern Israel during the 1990s were commonly portrayed in the Israeli media as random acts of terror, they frequently came in response to Israeli reprisals in Lebanon.

During Israel's seven-day air and artillery offensive against Hizbollah in July 1993 (Operation Accountability), one hundred and forty-two Katyusha rockets hit Israel. Afterward, the Jewish state reached an informal understanding with Hizbollah: it would refrain from reprisals in civilian inhabited areas of Lebanon in exchange for the guerillas halting attacks on Israeli soil.

However, while Nasrallah cannot claim full credit for Hizbollah's performance on the battlefield, he was largely responsible for its sophisticated use of psychological warfare to prod Israeli public opinion, which, typically, had not been "softened" by casualties alone. The hardening of sentiments amid unprecedented civilian deaths during the current Palestinian Intifada is something of a testament to this.

Another feature of this bitter campaign is that Hizbollah propagandists learned Hebrew so as to keep abreast of the debate within Israel and identify "soft spots" in public support for the Israeli presence in Lebanon. Nasrallah was careful to maintain publicly that Hizbollah's war against Israel would end once the Israeli Army left South Lebanon. In 1996, Hizbollah's Al-Manar television station (and Al-Nur radio station) began Hebrew language broadcasts which centered largely on this message.

By the end of the decade, Israeli public opinion had shifted in favor of a pullout. In May 1999, Ehud Barak was elected prime minister on a platform calling for the evacuation of Israeli forces from the Security Zone, with or without a peace treaty with Syria or Lebanon. Although Barak honored his pledge and the IDF pulled back a year later, Hizbollah's war against Israel had really only just begun.

With Nasrallah's popularity at an all-time high, within both Lebanon and the larger Arab world, the Syrians allowed Hizbollah to increase the size of its parliamentary block from nine to twelve in the 2000 parliamentary elections. Nasrallah was received at the presidential palace by

Lebanese President Emile Lahoud—the first time a leader of Hizbollah had been so honored.

When UN secretary general Kofi Annan visited Beirut in the summer of 2000, Lebanese officials arranged a public meeting between Nasrallah and the visiting dignitary. That was another significant first.

Meantime, Hizbollah stepped up its support for Palestinian terrorism. The *Middle East Intelligence Bulletin* tells us[10] that according to Israeli officials, the paramilitary movement had expanded its network of Palestinian operatives. Although Hizbollah's recruitment of Palestinian operatives had mainly been restricted to the West Bank, its terror cells were also uncovered in the Gaza Strip and within the Israeli Arab community.

The *Bulletin* disclosed that Israel's Shin Bet security service had uncovered a major Hizbollah cell in the Khan Yunis refugee camp in Gaza. This group was apparently founded in 2000 by Shadi Abu al-Hasin, who decided to join Hizbollah after watching its television station, Al-Manar. Thereafter, two Israeli Arab brothers, Ghassan and Sirhan Atmallah, were indicted on charges of setting up a terrorist cell on behalf of Hizbollah. Its principal role was to carry out suicide bombings.

According to Israeli security officials, Ghassan was recruited during a late 2002 visit to Jordan by Ibrahim Ajwa, a Palestinian official of the Fatah Abu Moussa faction who coordinates Hizbollah's efforts to acquire Palestinian and Israeli Arab operatives. Ghassan and his younger brother were put in contact with Hizbollah agents in Turkey and set up a business to import goods from that country as cover.

Sirhan traveled to Turkey at least twice in 2003 and met with a Hizbollah agent known as Abu Waal to discuss the list of Israeli Arabs he planned to recruit. At the same time he made arrangements for Hizbollah to supply financing and equipment needed to carry out bombings. During this visit, he mailed a shipment of diapers back home in order to test Israeli mailing and security procedures.

In December 2003 he traveled to Lebanon via Turkey and underwent an intensive ten-day course of training in bomb-making and surveillance detection. Sirhan's visit to Lebanon caught the attention of Israeli intelligence and he and his brother were arrested after their return home. According to the indictment, the brothers were scheduled to receive a ready-made bomb for their first attack at about the time of their arrest and had recruited an unspecified number of other Israeli Arabs who remained at large.[11]

Which brings us to Hizbollah today: still powerfully motivated and as determined as ever to oust the Jews from the Holy Land. For this and a variety of other reasons, Hizbollah appears on every single U.S. (and most European and Eurasian) terror lists. It is therefore instructive to observe the way that the group goes about its work.

There can be no better insight to the revolutionary group than the role played in its day-to-day affairs by Al Manar, the Hizbollah television station founded by diehards and today run along surprisingly competitive Western lines. As one of its senior executives phrased it, "We need to compete with the best, Al Jazeera and the BBC included."

Israeli journalist Avi Jorisch gives us an insight to Al Manar (The Beacon), published in *Middle East Quarterly* in the Winter 2004 edition.[12] Hizbollah, says Jorisch, is unique in its operation of a full-fledged television station: it offers a rich menu of news, commentary, and entertainment, having beamed its first signal on June 3, 1991.

"Since then," he reckons, "Hizbollah has exploited its privileged position in Lebanon—a role fortified by its successful guerrilla war to end the Israeli occupation—and to create a mass media outlet with global reach. With access to continuous funding from Iran, the station has grown from a clandestine, two-bit makeshift operation to a most efficient and comprehensive Arab satellite station.

"This significance goes far beyond Lebanon. Calling itself the "station of resistance," or *qanat al-muqawama*, Al-Manar has become an integral part of Hizbollah's plan to reach the entire Islamic world. As a disseminator of radicalism throughout the region, the company has an impact second only to Al-Jazeera. It is also a potent instrument in what Hizbollah calls its 'psychological warfare against the Zionist enemy'."

Since Operation Iraq Freedom, Al-Manar has used the same methods to undermine the U.S. presence in Iraq. In a debate over Al-Jazeera, arguments on both sides were put forward as to whether its content informed or propagandized the Arab viewing public. Jorisch suggests that it does both.

"In the case of Al-Manar, there is no space for debate. Al-Manar is propaganda in its most undiluted form. Every aspect of its broadcast content—from news to filler—is fine-tuned to present a single point of view: that of a militantly Islamist sponsor. It consistently urges recourse to violence as the only legitimate response to Israel's existence as well as the American presence. Al-Manar consequently represents a darker side of the media revolution in the Middle East." Jorisch's view is also that it is one more example of how new technologies, born in the West, may be exploited to promote profoundly anti-Western agendas. "At the same time, it is the product of unique circumstances."

The Al-Manar broadcasting station is located in the poor, Shi'ite-populated neighborhood of Harat Hurayk in Beirut's southern suburbs. Unlike West Beirut, where clubs, alcohol, and Western culture abound, this is an extremely conservative area, strongly affiliated with every possible Hizbollah tenet.

Housed in a six-story building, Al Manar appears to the casual eye to be a conventional station with reporters, newsrooms, studios, state-of-the-art editing suites, and television screens with feeds from the world's leading media, including CNN, BBC, Al-Jazeera, and Israeli channels. However, comparisons end there.

"Armed Hizbollah security guards stand watch outside the station. Their job is to check visitors' papers and belongings. In a marble-floored lobby, two pictures of station cameramen killed in Israeli military operations in July 1993 are displayed." The station houses an extensive video library containing thousands of carefully labeled Al-Manar videotapes, all of it below ground in one of the basement floors for fear of Israeli or American attacks. Indeed, according to Bilal Zarur, the station's programming director, Al-Manar has "another base in case the station is bombed." While male employees are dressed in suits, woman are obliged to wear traditional robes which cover everything.

Describing the relationship between Hizbollah and Al-Manar, Nayef Krayem—its previous general manager and chairman of its board—maintains that "they breathe life into one another." Each provides the other with inspiration, he reckons. As he explains, "Hizbollah uses the TV company to express its stands and its views. Al-Manar, in turn, receives political support for its continuation." The station is run by Hizbollah members, reports to Hizbollah officials and takes its direction from the personal office of Hizbollah's secretary general.

Jorisch also provides some historical background about the founding of Al-Manar. It emerged, he says, at time when Lebanese political movements and militias ran television stations without licenses. In the years of civil war, the state exercised no effective authority over broadcasting, nor, it will be recalled by those of us who were there, anything else.

In the 1980s, he states, Hizbollah operated its own clandestine radio station and the move into television was the sequel to its earlier ventures in ideological television stations. It was Al-Manar's message, especially against Israel, that assured its continued freedom to broadcast, in spite of government efforts to close it down.

By 1994, the station was producing about half of its own material. Nine years later, that figure was almost seventy percent. Though run as a loss-making venture, Iranian money continues to keep it afloat. Jorisch records that when Al-Manar started operations, the station received seed money from Iran and had an operating budget of about $1 million. Its operating budget in 2004 was approximately $15 million, or about half of what it required to remain viable. Much of the rest comes from Iran, though Al-Manar officials deny this.

"Other sources of income include donations from overseas Shi'ite communities and other Arabs and Muslims who support both Hizbollah and Al-Manar. Reportedly, large donations have been received from Muslim communities in Europe, the United States, and Canada. Al-Manar makes appeals for donors during commercial breaks, urging viewers to make deposits directly into accounts in four Lebanese banks: Beirut Riyad Bank, the Banque Libanaise pour le Commerce SAL, the Byblos Bank SAL, and the Fransa Bank.

"Since the TV station's founding in 1991, it has had many commercial advertising requests, both from Lebanese and Western companies. It has been reported that since its establishment, the station has consistently turned down approximately ninety percent of potential clients for religious reasons The use in advertising of 'women as a possible source of temptation,' consequently, is out.

"In order to manage the station's commercial side, Al-Manar has set up its own advertising company, Media-Publi Management. Its backers say that the company works with over thirty-five advertising firms, including Britain's Saatchi and Saatchi. As of 2003, commercial advertisements were broadcast terrestrially only, and not on Al-Manar's satellite station. This suggests that the company might want to keep its commercial links away from the prying eyes of U.S.-based viewers.

"Al-Manar officials reported that as of July 2002, their biggest American commercial advertisers included Pepsi, Coke, Proctor and Gamble, and Western Union. Other corporate sponsors include the German chocolate Milka, the American washing powder Ariel, Nestle's Nido milk, German Maggie Cubes, Finnish Smeds cheese and butter, French Picon cheese, Austrian Red Bull, the French cigarette company Gauloises, and the German Henkel's Der general detergent. Following an op-ed that appeared in the *Los Angeles Times*, Pepsi, Coke, Proctor and Gamble, and Western Union ceased advertising on Al-Manar, but the other European companies continue to do so.

"The station employs about three hundred employees of Lebanese, Egyptian, Jordanian, Palestinian, Moroccan, and American nationality. While employees are not required to be Hizbollah members, 'We prefer it all the same,' explained Muhammad 'Afif Ahmad."

It has also been reported that most of the male reporters had previously been guerrilla fighters before joining Al-Manar. According to Zarur, most of the station's employees are in their twenties and thirties and learn their trade on the job. There are plans to open a link in Britain. The company has about a dozen individual correspondents abroad, filing reports from Belgium, France, Iraq, Kosovo, Kuwait, Morocco, Russia, Sweden, Syria, Turkey, and the United States.

ACRONYMS, TECHNICAL, ARABIC, AND PERSIAN WORDS AND PHRASES[1]

AEC—Atomic Energy Corporation (South Africa) successor to the Atomic Energy Board (AEB).

AEOI—Atomic Energy Organization of Iran

AI—Amnesty International

Atomic bomb—Nuclear device whose energy comes from the fission of uranium or plutonium.

ATTF—Anti-Terrorism Task Force

AVLIS—Atomic Vapor Laser Isotope Separation

Ayatollah—Literally, a reflection of Allah. In Iranian Shi'ite religious circles it signifies the most learned of teachers and there are an estimated five thousand ayatollahs in Iran alone. Thus Ayatollah Ozama, literally most exalted sign of God.

Baha'i—Member of the Baha'i religion, which evolved in the mid-19th century from a theological split in Twelver Shi'ism.

Ba'athist—Dominant, secularly-orientated political party in Syria (as well as Iraq under Saddam Hussein).

Barrels per day—Production of crude oil or petroleum products is frequently measured in barrels per day, often abbreviated bpd or bd. A barrel is a volume measure of forty-two United States gallons.

Basij—A sometimes poorly trained and equipped civilian militia under the same name and the direct command of the IRGC or Pasdaran.

Beryllium—A toxic metal possessing a low neutron absorption cross section and a high melting point, which can be used in nuclear reactors as a moderator or reflector.

BW—Biological Weapons

BWC—Biological Weapons Convention

Caliph—The one who comes after; successors to Mohammed the Prophet as leaders of the early Moslem nation—also signifies political and religious status. Thus: Caliphate.

CANDU—(Canadian deuterium-uranium reactor) the most widely used type of heavy water power reactor. The CANDU reactor employs natural uranium as a fuel and heavy water as a coolant.

Cascade—A connected series of enrichment machines, materials from one being passed to another for further enrichment.

Centrifuge—Used in a uranium-enrichment process that separates gaseous isotopes by rotating them rapidly in a spinning tube, thereby subjecting them to centrifugal force. Thousands of centrifuges can be linked in a cascade.

CEP—Circular Error Probable (in relation to missile strike accuracy)

Chador—A square of fabric, usually black, that covers Shi'ite women from head to toe.

Chemical enrichment—This method of uranium enrichment depends on a slight tendency of uranium-235 (^{235}U)and uranium-238 (^{238}U) to concentrate in different molecules when uranium compounds are continuously brought into contact.

CIA—Central Intelligence Agency

Core—The central portion of a nuclear reactor containing the fuel elements and usually the moderator.

CTBT—Comprehensive Nuclear Test Ban Treaty

Critical mass—The minimum mass required to sustain a chain reaction.

CW—Chemical Weapons

CWC—Chemical Weapons Convention

Depleted uranium—Uranium with a smaller percentage of uranium-235 than the 0.7 per cent found in natural uranium.

DIA—Defense Intelligence Agency

DIV—Design Information Verification

DoE—Department of Energy (United States) formerly Atomic Energy Commission

Elint—Electronic Intelligence (See Humint)

ENTC—Esfahan Nuclear Technology Center

EOR—Enhanced Oil Recovery Programs

Euratom—European Atomic Energy Commission

EW—Electronic Warfare

Faqih—An expert in religious jurisprudence or feqh, specifically a Shi'ite cleric whose mastery of the Qur'an, the traditions of the Prophet and the Twelve Imans, and the codices of Shi'ite Islamic law permit him to render binding interpretations of religious laws and regulations.

Farsi—Official language of Persian Iran

"Fat Man"—Atomic, implosion-type, fission bomb used by the Americans at Nagasaki on August 9, 1945. This is one of the nuclear concepts being assessed but not yet worked on by the Iranians (also see "Little Boy").

Fatwa—A formal legal opinion by a religious leader or mojtahed on a matter of legal law (as in the decree against the life of Salman Rushdie).

FBIS—Foreign Broadcast Information Service

FBR—Fast Breeder Reactor

Fertile material—Material composed of atoms, which readily absorb neutrons to produce fissionable materials. One such element is uranium-238, which becomes plotonium-239 (^{239}Pu) after it absorbs a neutron.

Fissile Material—Weapons-useable material such as Uranium 235 or Plutonium 239.

Fission—Fission weapons get their destructive power from the fission (splitting) of atomic nuclei.

Fissile material—Material composed of atoms which fission when irradiated by slow or 'thermal' neutrons. The most common examples of fissile materials are ^{235}U and ^{239}Pu.

FMC—Fuel Manufacturing Plant (intended for construction at Esfahan).

FSU—Former Soviet Union

FTO—Foreign Terrorist Organization

Fusion—Different type of nuclear reaction from the fission process. Involves the fusion together of the nuclei of isotopes of light atoms such as hydrogen: thus hydrogen bombs. Development of the H-bomb was impossible before the perfection of A-bombs, as this is the trigger of any thermonuclear device.

Gas-centrifuge process—See Centrifuge

Gaseous diffusion—A method of isotope separation based on the fact that gas atoms or molecules with different masses will diffuse through a porous barrier (or membrane) at different rates. This method is used to separate uranium-235 from uranium-238.

GW—Gigawatts

Hadith—A saying of the Prophet Mohammed, or a saying about him or his teachings by contemporaneous sources.

Hajj—Pilgrimage to the holy city of Mecca.

Halal—Religiously permitted, usually food or an animal slaughtered in the prescribed Moslem manner of slitting of the throat.

HANE—High-altitude nuclear explosion

Haram—Religiously forbidden: it is necessary to abstain from that which is Haram (pork, for instance).

Heavy water—Water that contains significantly more than the natural proportion (1 in 6500) of heavy hydrogen (deuterium) atoms to ordinary hydrogen atoms.

Heavy Water Reactor—A reactor that uses heavy water as its moderator and natural uranium as fuel. (See CANDU)

Hejab—Modesty in attire; defined by the Shi'ite clergy to mean that when in public, women and girls must cover all their hair and flesh except for hands and face. It is not necessary to wear a chador (a cloth serving as a cloak) to conform with hejab, though the two are often equated.

HEU—Highly enriched uranium or weapons-grade material in which the percentage of uranium-235 nuclei has been increased from the natural level of 0.7 percent to some level greater than 20 percent, usually around 90 percent.

Hezb— Political party (Iran)

Hezbollahi—Literally, a follower of the Iranian Party of God, transliterated from Hizballah (Arabic). Hezbollahis were originally followers of a particular religious figure who eventually came to constitute an unofficial political party.

Hizbollah—Lebanese "Party of God" that was founded in 1982 as a terror group. Originally responsible for bombing a US Marine base and two embassies in Beirut. Before becoming a legitimate political party, evolved into a highly motivated guerrilla force that eventually forced the IDF out of Lebanon.

Hojjatoleslam—Literally, "proof of Islam," a Shi'ite theological rank just below ayatollah that can be acquired with roughly a decade-and -a-half of study.

Houris—Mythical virgins or nymphs waiting for the zealous in Paradise. Purportedly a Hadith tradition: seventy Hauris await every martyr who gives up his life in the struggle. There is no equivalent for female martyrs.

Humint—Human intelligence gathered by field operatives or agents, as opposed to sigint (signal intelligence) or elint (electronic intelligence).

IAEA—International Atomic Energy Agency, a United Nations organization with over one hundred and seventy signatories: based in Vienna, Austria.

IAF—Israeli Air Force

IDF—Israeli Defense Force (usually applied to army units)

IDR—Jane's International Defense Review

Imam—Among "Twelver" Shi'ites, the principal meaning is a designation of one of the twelve legitimate successors of the Prophet Mohammed. Also used by both Shi'ites and Sunnis to designate a congregational prayer leader or cleric.

Iran Nuclear Research Reactor—A heavy water reactor planned for the Iranian nuclear facility at Arak.

IRGC—Islamic Revolutionary Guard Corps (see Pasdaran)

ISIS—Institute for Science and International Security (Washington)

Islamic clergy—The religious leaders of Shi'ite (or Shi'a) Islam, which group includes numerous mullahs who, in general, possess only rudimentary religious education; mujtahids, a relatively small body of religious scholars, the majority of whom are accorded the title of hojjatoleslam; and the most learned and pious of the mujtahids, who are most respectfully accorded the title of ayatollah.

ISTC—International Science and technology Center, a Russian body that caters for FSU scientists who had been involved in WMD pursuits to find other avenues of employment.

Jame'a—Society, university

JDW—Jane's Defence Weekly

JHL—Jabr Ibn Hayan Laboratories (an Iranian nuclear research center)

Jihad—The struggle to establish the law of God on earth, often interpreted to mean holy war. At the time of going to press, Tehran regards itself as having launched a Jihad at the United States, which it publicly refers to in all its pronouncements as "The Great Satan."

JIR—Jane's Intelligence Review

Kadkhuda—The village headman in rural Iran; also used as the title for some tribal clans.

Kiloton (kT)—The energy of a nuclear explosion that is equivalent to an explosion of 1,000 tons of TNT.

Laser enrichment—An experimental process of uranium enrichment in which lasers are used to separate uranium isotopes.

LEO—Low earth orbit (of satellites)

LEU—Low enriched uranium in which the percentage of uranium-235 nuclei has been enriched from the natural level of 0.7 percent to up to 20 percent.

"Little Boy"—Gun-type, fission bomb dropped over Hiroshima by the Americans on August 6, 1945. All six South African atom bombs were gun-type. Iran is following this path, among others (See also "Fat Man").

LNG—Liquefied natural gas

LPG—Liquefied petroleum gas

LRBM—Long Range Ballistic Missile

Madrassah—A religious college or seminary that trains men in Islamic jurisprudence.

Mahdi (also Mehdi)— Literally, "one who is guided (by God) along the right path" (Arabic/Persian). Among Shi'ites, the Mahdi is the long-awaited Twelfth Imam who, according to their belief, will emerge from occulation at the end of time and establish an Empire of Righteousness.

Majlis—The term is used in two senses: the legislative body of imperial Iran, which included both a senate—composed of members appointed by the shah and elected members—and an elected lower house of representatives; and, the lower house alone. The Senate provided for in the constitution did not come into existence until 1950; it was dissolved under the subsequently deposed Mossadeq but revived later. Khomeini's revolutionary Constitution of 1979 eliminated the Senate, leaving only the lower house, or Majlis, in existence.

Maktab—Primary school operated by Shi'ite clergy.

Manar or Al-Manar—Hizbollah television station headquartered in the mainly Shi'ite southern suburbs of Beirut.

MEIB—Middle East Intelligence Bulletin

MLIS—Molecular Laser Isotope Separation

Moderator—A component (usually water, heavy water or graphite) of some nuclear reactor types that slows neutrons, thereby increasing their chances of fissioning fertile material.

MOU—Memorandum of Understanding

MRBM—Medium Range Ballistic Missile

MTCR—Missile Technology Control Regime

Muezzin—Spiritual figure who sings or chants the call to prayer.

Mufti—Religious authority who is competent to issue a fatwa.

Mullah—Generic term for a member of the Islamic clergy; usually refers to a preacher or other low-ranking cleric who has not earned the right to interpret religious laws.

MW—Megawatt

MWth—Megawatt-thermal (usually reactor)

NCRI—National Council of Resistance of Iran (anti-Tehran insurgency group)

NGL— Natural gas liquids

NGO—Non Governmental Organization

NIA—National Intelligence Agency (of South Africa), currently headed by Ronnie Kasrils, a card-carrying member of the South African Communist Party.

NPT—Nuclear Nonproliferation Treaty (Treaty on the NonProliferation of Nuclear Weapons)

NSG—Nuclear Suppliers Group

Oguz—Israeli Special Forces group mostly involved against Hizbollah in South Lebanon in the past.

OPEC—Organization of Petroleum Exporting Countries responsible for coordinating oil policies of major producing countries.

Osiraq—French-built 40MWth nuclear materials test reactor destroyed in air strike by the Israeli Air Force in June, 1981.

P-1—An earlier, less-advanced centrifuge design of European origin.

P-2—A more advanced centrifuge design now being used by in the Pakistani nuclear program, examples of which have been found, without good reason, at Iranian nuclear establishments.

Pasdaran—*Pasdaran-e Enghelab-e Islami*, or Islamic Revolutionary Guard Corps (IRGC), an organization charged with safeguarding the Iranian Revolution. This group of ultra-secret activists is responsible solely to Iran's Supreme Spiritual Leader Sayyid Ali Hoseini Khamene'i.

Pars Trash—Where centrifuge equipment from the Kalaye Electric Company was stored and concealed from IAEA inspectors until October 2003, when it was presented for inspection to the agency at Natanz.

People's Libyan Arab Jamahiriya—Libya

PFEP—Pilot Fuel Enrichment Plant

Po-210 (Polonium-210)—An intensely radioactive alpha-emitting radioisotope that can be used not only for certain civilian applications (such as RTGs – in effect, nuclear batteries) but also, in conjunction with beryllium, for military purposes (specifically as a neutron initiator in some designs of nuclear weapons).

^{239}Pu—Plutonium: a fissile isotope generated artificially when uranium-238, through irradiation (as in a reactor) captures and extra neutron. It is one of the two fissile materials that have been almost extensively used for the core of nuclear weapons, the other being ^{235}U. (A small amount of nuclear explosives have been made with uranium-233.)

Radioactivity—The spontaneous disintegration of an unstable atomic nucleus resulting in the emission of sub-atomic particles.

RepU—Reprocessed uranium

Revcons—NPT Revue Conference

Rial—Iranian currency. The average official rate in the first half of 2004 was roughly 9 rials to US$1.

ROD—Radiological Dispersal Devices (radiological bombs involving radioactive matter)

RSB—Roadside bombs, initially developed by Hizbollah for use against Israeli vehicles and patrols and now commonplace in Iraqi theaters of military activity.

RTG—Radioisotope thermoelectric generator

Sayyid—Literally, "master" and of Persian extraction. This refers to clergy directly descended from Mohammed.

SDGT—Specially Designated Global Terrorists

Shariat—Sharia in Arabic: Islamic law

Shaykh or Sheikh—Leader or chief. Term is used by Iranian Arabs for tribal chiefs and by Lurs and Kurds for religious leaders.

Shi'ite or Shi'a—A member of the smaller of the two great divisions of Islam representing between ten and fifteen per cent of Muslims worldwide (the majority are Sunni). All Shi'ites support the claims of Ali and his line to presumptive right to the caliphate and leadership of the world Muslim community, and on this issue, more than a millennium ago, they hived off from the Sunnis in the first great schism of Islam. Later schisms have produced further divisions among these people.

Sigint—Signal intelligence (See entry for humint)

SRBM—Short Range Ballistic Missile

SST—State Sponsored Terrorism

Sunni—A member of the larger of the two great divisions of Islam. The Sunnis, who rejected the claim of Ali's line, believe that they are the true followers of the sunna, the guide to proper behavior composed of the Qur'an and the hadith.

RWSF—Radioactive Waste Storage Facility

SAM— Surface-to-air missile

SWU—Separative work unit, a measure of the effort required in an enrichment facility to separate uranium of a given ^{235}U content into two fractions, one with a higher percentage and one with a lower percentage.

Tails—Sometimes called tailings: The waste stream of an enrichment facility that contains depleted uranium.

tcf—Trillion cubic feet

Thermonuclear bomb—Hydrogen bomb

TNRC—Tehran Nuclear Research Center

Tritium—The heaviest hydrogen isotope customarily used to boost the explosive power of atom bombs. While Pakistan claims to have thermonuclear capability, the consensus is that it has only fission or atom bombs, which its scientists boost with tritium to allow for higher explosive yields.

TRR—Tehran Research Reactor

U—The scientific symbol for uranium: the radioactive element with 92 as its atomic number.

UCF—Uranium Conversion Facility (in Iran at Karaj)

UF_6—Uranium hexafluoride: A volatile compound of uranium and fluorine, which, while solid at atmospheric pressure and room temperature, can be transformed into a gas by heating. It is the feedstock in the uranium enrichment process.

Umma—The worldwide community of Islam.

UNIFIL—United Nations Interim Force in Lebanon

UNSCOM—United Nations Special Commission (on Iraq)

UO_2—Uranium Dioxide (purified uranium: the form of natural uranium used in heavy water reactors)

Urenco centrifuges—Urenco is a commercial consortium involving Britain, Germany and the Netherlands that has developed the gas centrifuge to make LEU for nuclear power reactors.

^{233}U—A fissile isotope bred in fertile thorium-232.

^{235}U—Also U-235: the only naturally occurring fissile isotope.

^{238}U—Also U-238: Natural uranium is comprised of about 99.3 per cent of this substance.

U_3O_8—Uranium oxide: the most common oxide of uranium found in typical ores.

Velayat-en faqih—The guardianship of the religious jurist (or rule by the jurisprudent). This concept was elaborated by Ayatollah Khomeini to justify political rule by the clergy.

Wahhabiya—An arch-purist orientated branch of the Sunni faith that can be traced back to the reformer Abd al-Wahhab (1701-98) and today dominant in Saudi Arabia and Yemen. The brutally repressive Wahhabist credo is espoused by followers of al-Qaeda and is responsible for funneling billions of Saudi dollars into revolutionary pursuits under the guise of charity.

Wajib—A religious obligatory act or commitment such as the giving of alms or daily prayer. Punishable in the hereafter if not observed.

Weapons-grade material—Nuclear material of the type most suitable for nuclear weapons.

Yellowcake—A concentrate produced during the milling process that contains about 80 per cent uranium oxide (U_3O_8). In preparation for uranium enrichment, the yellowcake is converted to uranium hexafluoride gas (UF_6).

Zirconium—A greyish-white lustrous material which is commonly used in an alloy (zircalloy) to encase fuel rods in nuclear reactors.

ACKNOWLEDGMENTS

As with my previous book, on Iraq,[1] this is hardly the work of one individual. I got help from all over. Had I not done so—even though I have been covering events west of the Euphrates Basin for Britain's Jane's Information Group and others for many years—we would not now have something in hand that engages such a vast range of topics,

A few notable individuals stand out. Among these is Dr. Nic von Wielligh, who guided me through the labyrinth of the South African nuclear program that ended with Pretoria building six atom bombs and enough fissile material for a seventh. He also gives us reason why South Africa felt it was sufficiently threatened by hostile forces "from outside" to resort to what some refer to as the "last ditch stand of the white man in Africa" should the existing "European" order there be threatened with oblivion.

As it happened, that country's white community eventually decided to take what Anglo American's Clem Sunter so often refers to as the "High Road" and share power with the country's more populous black population. His was a brilliant option, at a time when many South Africans believed the country to be heading in the same direction as the rest of the troubled continent. History will ultimately tell us whether this luminary pundit was right.

It is interesting that just before my meeting with Dr. von Wielligh, a modest but invaluable source on related topics was published in South Africa.[2] Titled *Armament and Disarmament: South Africa's Nuclear Weapons Experience*, its three authors offer us a vivid canvas of the beleaguered South Africa that successfully went ahead with a nuclear weapons program. Then, under the auspices of both the International Atomic Energy Agency and the United States, Pretoria dismantled the lot—coincidentally, the only nation in the world to have done so.

The three men are Dr. Richardt van der Walt, formerly Director, Reactor Development and Vice President of the Atomic Energy Board; Hannes Steyn, a kingpin at the Armaments Corporation (Armscor), a government weapons body responsible for putting the bombs together;

413

and finally, former Chief of the South African Air Force, Lt. General Jan van Loggerenberg. Had these weapons ever been deployed, it would have been aircraft under the general's command that would have had been tasked with delivery.

It is no longer a secret that among the targets circumspectly viewed by South Africa's military strategists at the time were three African capitals. Those in the firing line were Luanda (Angola), Lusaka (Zambia) and Dar es Salaam (Tanzania), all of which had populations well in excess of a million or more by the mid-1980s. Indeed, there were probably three or four million people living in Luanda by then. In one respect, I had something of personal a stake in this dreadful scenario. My son Johan, married into a Zambian family, could feasibly have been counted among the casualties should such an attack have taken place.

The three authors name no names apart from the obvious, which underscores the sensitivity that continues to surround the project, now defunct for more than a decade. But they do scotch a bundle of rumors, misconceptions, and occasionally deliberate pieces of misinformation, something that has beset the South African nuclear weapons program from the start. A lot of this was due to the extraordinary level of security under which the top secret program labored.

Interestingly, the CIA—for all its claims—never did manage to penetrate the security mantle around this Apartheid-era atom bomb project. Langley only found out afterward that it was at Advena—an Armscor facility in a West Pretoria suburb—where the six nuclear warheads were assembled and later stored. Included among the illustrations is a satellite photo of some of the South African nuclear assets.

While involved in the project in their professional spheres, the men admit to having sought no sanction to bring their account before the public eye, nor under the country's new constitution should they have been required to do so. A single quote from their introduction says it all: "The authors compiled this account to reduce the possibility of a skew reconstruction in an atmosphere of suspicion and speculation."

Further afield, David Albright, President of Washington's Institute for Science and International Security (ISIS), was of much help in my putting together this screed. As always, he was gracious to allow me to quote himself as well as his organization and to use some of the striking illustrations and satellite photographs on the ISIS website. The same with Cory Hinderstein, a senior associate at the ISIS Washington headquarters whom I visited shortly before going into print. Thanks to them as well as to Steve Schwartz of *The Bulletin of the Atomic Scientists* for letting me publish David and Corey's excellent assessments of the

Iranian centrifuge programs originally carried in two editions of Steve's *Bulletin*.

My good friend Eric Croddy—formerly with the Monterey Institute for Nonproliferation Studies and now with US Pacific Command in Hawaii—strode to the fore with comments about some of Iran's chemical and biological assets. He is the first to have acknowledged when we spoke in the summer of 2003, that Tehran—like Iraq, until fairly recently—has been remarkably astute in hiding its weapons of mass destruction facilities from "eyes that pry." Most times, he admits, anything to do with the conspiratorial collusions of the mullahs is guesswork. But then, sometimes people and things slip past. The occasional defector, as they say, is the name of the game. Sometimes it is an insurgent with an eye for the unusual (as when the cover of the Natanz and Arak nuclear establishments was blown by an anti-government group).

Now and again there are brave souls who make it to the West with things innocuously tucked into their belts or socks or, in extreme cases, secreted in an orifice. This is an old trick that drug smugglers have been using just about forever, in much the same way that Africans secrete miniature, elongated bars of gold when crossing frontiers such as between Ghana and Togo.

Those involved in identifying Iran's clandestine efforts can only be regarded as a dedicated, committed bunch of people. In their own way, I'd like to think that by staying behind and keeping us informed they are playing a significant role in helping to influence people, politics, trends, or possibly, long-term political events in this beleaguered land. With their Arak and Natanz disclosures, they actually changed history. Without this kind of participation—thoroughly intrusive and hugely embarrassing for Tehran—we would not now be aware that Iran has been hard at it for almost twenty years. Had I not believed that, I would long ago have reconciled myself to what some pessimists already refer to as Tehran's inevitable "Doomsday Scenario."

Let us not forget the many specialists in the West who day-by-day keep tabs on what is going on in the Middle East. At the forefront of latter-day research in this milieu is Michael Eisenstadt, Senior Fellow at the Washington Institute for Near East Policy. Our paths have crossed many times over the years but this was the first time that we made personal contact. Michael has often encapsulated (and sometimes expanded on) the intricacies of what is going on today in places like Iran, Syria, Libya and Iraq. One of his reports, titled "Delay, Deter and Contain, Roll-Back: Towards a Strategy for Dealing with Iran's Nuclear Program," was published by the Nixon Center in March 2004 in

Geoffrey Kemp's monologue titled *Iran's Bomb: American and Iranian Perspectives*.

Another authority that needs to be recognized is Charles P. Vick, probably the most knowledgeable authority on Iranian, Pakistani and North Korean missile systems outside any of the world's major intelligence organizations. His knowledge on the subject is so vast that it can only be regarded as encyclopedic. All the diagrams and cutaways of current or purported Iranian ballistic missiles come from his hand, as does much of the technical content about them in Chapter 9.

Charles had originally been on the staff of the Federation of American Scientists and then moved on to GlobalSecurity.org in Washington DC, joining John Pike, who also requires a nod. John and I have covered the same international events for years and I am indebted to him for his input.

In putting together this tome, what would I have done without the Federation of American Scientists? I am pleased that Henry Kelly, President of the FAS, granted me permission to quote liberally from his organization's resources. Indeed, it was he who put me in touch with another workhorse, Ivan Oelrich, director, Strategic Security Projects at the Federation. Ivan is another proliferation guru of international repute who briefly hosted me at his offices in downtown DC.

The same with Barry Rubin and Joy Pincus at Tel Aviv's Middle East Review of International Affairs. MERIA started modestly not that long ago and the organization has since become an indispensable tool for anybody contemplating research in what is arguably the most volatile region on the planet. Thanks to you both for letting me use former Russian diplomat Dr. Victor Mizin's insightful assessment of "The Russia-Iran Nuclear Connection and U.S. Policy Options" as Appendix A. Shortly before going to press, Dr. Mizin was Diplomat-in-Residence and Senior Research Associate at the Monterey Institute for Nonproliferation Studies in Monterey, California.

At the Department of Energy in Washington DC, the lead economist of the department's Contingency Analysis Team, Lowell S. Feld, gave me access to his compilation titled *Iranian Country Analysis Brief*, which details the extent of Tehran's oil and gas supplies (updated in August 2004). An educative source, it makes up Appendix C. So too with a paper titled *Iran's Programs to Produce Plutonium and Enriched Uranium*, a Carnegie Endowment for International Peace Fact Sheet by Marshal Breit. This document was specially updated by Marshall to tie in with Iran's latest disclosures about its illegal nuclear fuel activity and has been of great value to this endeavor. I thank you both.

Worthy of special mention is work done on the Islamic Republican Guards Corps (IRGC) by Paula deSutter while she was at the Center for Counterproliferation Research, National Defense University, Washington DC. Paula has since moved on to become Assistant Secretary of State for Verification and Compliance. Her original thesis, "Denial and Jeopardy: Deterring Iranian Use of NBC Weapons," was completed in the late-1990s and is one of the most comprehensive assessments of present-day conditions inside Iran that I've seen. With a few notable updates, it is as relevant today as it was then.

It is significant that her document underscores the contention that Iran is a closed society and that us Westerners have an inordinately difficult time making any sense of what is going on there. While I've never met Ms. deSutter in person, it was Dr. Seth Carus—then working at NDU while I was doing research for Jane's on Iraq—who introduced me to her work.

Additionally, I have included some observations made in reports by Michael Rubin that are both provocative and incisive, in particular excerpts from his Policy Paper, *Into the Shadows: Radical Vigilantes in Khatami's Iran.*[3] Apart from having spent five months on research inside Iran and winning Yale's prestigious John Addison Porter prize (for the top dissertation in any field) he has also produced several other works relating to developments within this most xenophobic of communities.

Important too, is an outstanding, not immodest monograph put together jointly by Henry Sokolski and Patrick Clawson titled *Checking Iran's Nuclear Ambitions*. Its seven chapters were completed under the auspices of the Strategic Studies Institute, U.S. Army War College,[4] and include another of Michael Eisenstadt's works, controversially titled "The Challenges of U.S. Preventive Military Action."

Thanks too to Gary C. Gambill for his input. A specialist in state-sponsored terrorism and editor of *The Middle East Intelligence Bulletin* (which I have been receiving for years) Gary has done seminal work on Hizbollah, the paramilitary Lebanese Shi'ite group that is tied to the apron strings of Iran's IRGC. I'd go so far as to say that to my mind, few "Near East Watchers" provide as valuable an insight to the way that Iran surreptitiously manipulates its militant surrogates as Gary.

Professor Mike Hough, Director of the Institute of Strategic Studies at Pretoria University, and an illustrious scholar in his own right, played a solid part helping me put heads together and make things happen, particularly with regard to that country's nuclear weapons program. Without his input, I would never have made contact with Dr. Nic von

Wielligh, together with several other specialists who continue to work with me in related projects and who, for fear of retribution, would rather not be named.

Going back a little, I am always grateful to Anne Joyce, editor of Washington's prestigious *Middle East Policy*, which her peers rate as among the fifty best publications in its particular category in the world. Anne nudged me through several articles after Iran had become an American embarrassment and sometimes faded from the headlines. That was also a time when, like now, Iran's Ayatollahs could never get past uttering America's name without referring to it as "The Great Satan." Not a lot has changed.

On illegal money issues—most often involving the Middle East and some countries in South America—Jeff Breinholt, Coordinator of the U.S. Department of Justice Terrorism Financing Task Force was the author of some of the fascinating information that make up the appendice labeled "Terror's Money Trail." The manner in which huge sums of cash are shifted about internationally is a cunning exercise in both subterfuge and guile. The subject is worth a book on its own.

Several of my colleagues at Britain's Jane's Information Group— both in Coulsdon, Surrey and London's West End—deserve thanks. As usual, Peter Felstead—editor of *Jane's Defence Weekly*—provided sterling support. So did Mark Daly, editor of Jane's *International Defense Review*. One of my very first reports on Iran's efforts to go nuclear was carried by IDR.

I need to single out Stephen Ulph, editor of several of Jane's publications that specialize in Islamic issues. Stephen was always around when things obtuse began to cloud my view, which provides part of the answer why this enterprising plurilingual scholar has become one of Britain's leading pundits on some of the more arcane aspects of Muslim culture, tradition and politics.

Stephen's strength is that he speaks, reads and writes both Arabic and Farsi—as he does Turkish, French, Italian and half a dozen other tongues—including the obscure language still in use today by Egypt's Copts. As he recounts, each time he goes to Cairo, he invariably finds himself in the middle of a crowd on Arab Street haranguing on about that day's most contentious issues, and in the vernacular.

In obtaining background material on Iran's bounteous array of history, culture, traditions and politics, I am particularly indebted to a series of works prepared by the Federal Research Division of the Library of Congress under the Country Studies/Area Handbook Program sponsored by the Department of the Army. In particular, I must acknowledge the work of all the writers of the 1978 edition of *Iran: A Country Study*, edited by Richard F. Nyrop. Other Federal Research Division staff included Thomas Collelo and editors Marilyn L. Majeska and Martha E. Hopkins. Houman Sadri wrote the section on the Iran-Iraq War (Chapter 2) with a contribution by Joseph A. Kechichian.

Richard Nyrop reviewed the transliteration of Persian words. For those that are of direct Arabic origin—such as Mohammed, or, if you prefer, Mohamed (the Prophet), Peace be unto Him, Moslem (Muslim), and Qur'an—I have followed, like those above, a modified version of the system for Arabic adopted by the United States Board on Geographic Names and the Permanent Committee on Geographic Names for British Official Use, known as the BGN/PCGN system. The modification, though not strictly applied, is a significant one, entailing the deletion of many diacritical marks and hyphens. For example, the reader will find Basra for the city rather than Al Basrah.

All satellite images included in this volume are with the permission of DigitalGlobe-ISIS and certainly, the book would have been a lot poorer without them. Most of the other pix—including those in Lebanon's Hizbollahland, the Eastern Mediterranean, Israel, Damascus and elsewhere—are mine. For the handful of Tehran, I have my Australian friend and colleague Mark Corcoran of ABC-Australia to thank. We missed each other by a day while covering the mercenary war in Sierra Leone. Here's to next time Mark!

Originally, I would have liked to send a photographer into Iran to provide us with a portfolio but I could find no takers. I spoke to several enthusiasts, but in the end they all gave it a miss. Perhaps the money wasn't good enough. Or it could have been the risk, for the authorities in Tehran don't have a kind word for foreigners with cameras.

It is worth mentioning here that there has already been at least one Western journalist who became a target of the mullahs' goons. That was fifty-four-year-old Zahra Kazemi, a Canadian national who, according the BBC, was "beaten into a coma" in June 2003 and later died in prison. The Iranian Government refused to release her body to her family for an independent autopsy after they had declared that her death was "due to natural causes."

My extraneous sources are abundant. I have tried to credit each of them in turn (unless security considerations preclude me from doing so) but in a work encompassing so vast a panoply, there must occasionally be a lapse. To those of you who did not get the recognition you deserve, I apologize: the fault is mine entirely.

One person needs special tribute: the man responsible for my completing this task in the first place, Master Sergeant Floyd Holcom, U.S. Army Special Forces, Operational Detachment "A" (ODA) 911. He had just returned from a year-long deployment in and around Iraq when he put the idea into my head. Just plain Floyd to his buddies, it is interesting that this former special forces operator typifies a thoroughly new generation of SF operative: he speaks, with equal facility, Arabic, Farsi and, of all things, Mandarin.

A veteran of Grenada, Haiti and several other operational deployments, Floyd had been following my scribblings for years, some of which went back decades. He recalled my having been trashed by the U.S. State Department's James Rubin after I had reported the visit to South Africa's nuclear establishment at Pelindaba in 1997 by Reza Amrollahi, Iranian deputy minister for atomic affairs. I had originally done the story for Jane's *International Defense Review* (see Chapter 8) before the *Mail & Guardian* ran it. It was Floyd's view—and this, mark you, before Tehran admitted that they had been trying for almost a generation to build the bomb—that somebody urgently needed to expose Iran's nuclear ambitions. "You owe it to society," were his words.

While it is nice to be told that somebody actually reads your stuff, he was also of the view that there was possibly nobody better suited for the task. I am sure there is, but having thrown down the challenge, I set to it, which wasn't all that difficult since I had accumulated reams of reports, garnered over half a lifetime of rather esoteric Middle East reportage.

At the same time, it wasn't all that easy simply to pull up sticks and begin work. In fact, having a short while earlier completed my Iraq book, the last thing I needed just then was the kind of doggedness a new task would entail. The research was another issue altogether.

Then the illustrious and equally industrious Sentgeorge family of Astoria, Oregon stepped in and provided for my immediate needs: I was embraced by Duane and Rebecca as well as Ryker and Katrina. (And who says that American kids aren't both focused and polite?)

In a sense, these good people became like an extended family. Without compunction, they provided everything that I needed for the commitment that followed. Granted, it was a regimen that ranged from ten to sixteen-hour stretches at the keyboard, but at the same time it was a close, comfortable environment in which I was able to do the necessary. How many authors have been that lucky?

At the same time, I would like to believe that my presence brought another kind of joy to the Sentgeorges. While staying there, Rebecca—

an artist of note—became one of two Oregon teachers to be granted a Fulbright Scholarship in Japan in 2004.

Everything to do with computers, the web and temperamental Windows systems I left to my old pal Martin Adams, also of Astoria. He always came up with the goods on those few critical occasions when it mattered.

My sometimes overambitious hiking buddy Joyce Otterson was there whenever I needed that one-or-two hour trek up the hills, right across the river behind Fort Columbia. This terrain overlooking the estuary of one of North America's great rivers holds some of the country's most beautiful forests. Even the names are resplendent of another era: God's Window and the Green Mile are only parts of it. Though these are tough walks, they never fail to awe. Yet, as Joyce and I have observed one year after the next, this section of the Pacific Northwest is hardly touched when compared to many of America's other natural attributes where you sometimes can't even find a place to park. Despite the vagaries of the weather, we managed to hike just about every day. Had we not done so, I'm not sure I could have finished the job. As my old pal Bogie Maglich once commented, "The mind comes into sharp focus once the body's in good shape."

Others along the banks of the Columbia River who offered time, expertise or advice were Chuck, Larry and the rest of the gang at The Compleat Photographer and my old pal, Astoria's police chief Rob Duepree. Let's not forget Ilwaco's Chuck McNeall for his constant egging-on.

Whenever in the American capital, I would put my bags down in the home of someone who used to visit me in Africa, former SEALS-team commander U.S. Navy Captain Larry Bailey and his wife Judy. Our trudges in the Spring of 2004, past George Washington's old farmhouse in Mount Vernon (only a crow's call from their own home) were a delight. Here's to repeating the process—and soon.

It was left to somebody else to pick up the pieces once I'd done the job and that was the role of one of my oldest friends, Richard Davis, a Michigan native who founded Second Chance Body Armor. This is the same person who invented the concept used today by untold numbers of men and women in uniform all over the world simply to stay alive while on their rounds. And yes, it is the same Richard Davis that we've all seen on television shooting himself in the stomach with a high-powered magnum handgun to prove that his vests really work. He's done that almost two hundred times and counting. Thus it was in Central Lake, Michigan that I afterward "came up for air." Thanks Richard.

Garth Choate and his sons Fred and Glen of Bald Knob, Arkansas were another milepost. Hospitality this side of the mosquito netting, alongside Arkansas' White River, was a treat.

After covering the South African nuclear side, I briefly hung up my boots at Johan Louw's pad in Pretoria before we all headed toward the Kalahari on safari. It was a long drive, but Johan, Pierre, Roy and Gerrit took my mind off more immediate issues. Oubaas Hattingh hosted us on his game farm within rifle shot of the Botswana border in one of the most beautiful corners of Africa. And there was biltong—springbok to boot. I came away from that trip believing that the Kalahari—primeval and mostly unblemished by man—should be compulsory viewing for anybody who believes that the globe is doomed.

I would like to extend my appreciation to historian Stephen Tanner of Long Island, who took an interest in this project from the beginning. He had just completed his own work on the conflicts in which the Bush family, *pater et filius,* had become embroiled during their respective tenures in office, and kindly lent his own illuminating perspective in the foreword. I am indebted to a man who is not only an outstanding wordsmith, but who has also in the interim, become a good friend.

It would be remiss of me not to credit the role of David Farnsworth who, within a relatively few years, has made Philadelphia's Casemate Publishers into one of the most significant military publishing houses in the country. David was unstinting when the book was first mooted; in fact, it was he that suggested that I get it done in time for the 2004 Frankfurt International Book Fair. Like me, David—who had been at Greenhill Books in London when Lionel Leventhal published *The Chopper Boys*—sensed an undefined urgency about the actions of Iran's leaders and I couldn't help feeling that this was perhaps a portent of things to come. Certainly both sides—Iran as well as the international nuclear lobby—are now playing some interesting, if exasperating games.

David and his lovely Sarah were my hosts during several visits to Philadelphia. Traveling through the United States, their hospitality and conviviality has become a beacon to me and other British expatriates passing through. Let it be known that the post-prandial delights of an evening or two at the Farnsworth table is an experience that needs to be savored. It is a literary and a cerebral occasion of consequence, inevitably with a vintage Cockburns to hand.

NOTES

INTRODUCTION
1. "Iran Hiding Its Nuclear Facilities," by Douglas Frantz and Sonni Efron, *Los Angeles Times,* March 27, 2004.
2. Check the website of the Washington Institute for Science and International Security for a more thorough examination of the subject, and, in particular, satellite photos of many of Pakistan's nuclear facilities at <www.isis-online.org>.
3. "Inspectors in Iran Examine Machines to Enrich Uranium," *New York Times,* February 23, 2003.
4. *The New Yorker,* March 8, 2004, pp32–37.
5. Personal Interview at UN Headquarters, Turtle Bay, New York.
6. Tel Aviv: *Yedi'ot Aharonot* in Hebrew: June 28, 2002, p. 7 (FBIS Translated Text).
7. URENCO is a commercial consortium involving Britain, Germany and the Netherlands that has developed the gas centrifuge to make low enriched uranium (LEU) for nuclear power reactors.
8. CIA's biannual "Unclassified Report to Congress on the Acquisition of Technology Relating to Weapons of Mass Destruction and Advanced Conventional Munitions," from January 1–June 30, 2003. Report released November 10, 2003.
9. "Nuclear Explosions in Orbit—The Spread of Nuclear Weapons and Ballistic Missiles Raises Fears of Atomic Attacks on the Global Satellite System," by Daniel G Dupont: *Scientific American,* June 2004 pp 68–75.
10. "'Dirty Bomb' Threat Growing," *Daily Telegraph,* London: June 3, 2004 (News Bulletin, p. 2).
11. "U.S. to Comb World for Nuclear Materials," *International Herald Tribune,* Paris: May 27, 2004.

Chapter 1—IRAN: ITS GOVERNMENT AND PEOPLE
1. Whit Mason: "Iran's Simmering Discontent," *World Policy Journal* (Volume XIX, No. 1: Spring 2002).
2. Molly Moore, "Women Say Yes to Khatami," *Washington Post,* June 8, 2001.
3. *Who Rules Iran—The Structure of Power in the Islamic Republic,* by Wilfried Buchta, a joint publication of The Washington Institute for Near East Policy and the *Konrad Adenhauer Stiftung,* Washington, 2000.
4. Ibid., Mason.
5. John Ward Anderson, "Islamic Democracy's Power Politics," *Washington Post,* May 26, 2001.

Chapter 2—THE IRAN-IRAQ WAR, 1980–1988
1. ASA Newsletter: Issue 81–3, #24, June 6, 1991, 12.

Chapter 3—IRAN'S SHI"ITES: PROVOCATIVE AND DRIVEN
1. "The History of Shia Muslims—Why the Aggravation?" *The Economist*, London, March 6, 2004.
2. Ibid., *The Economist*.
3. "Market Forces—How Hired Guns Succeeded Where the UN Failed," Jane's *International Defense Review*, London March 1, 1998.
4. *Fitna*, is an Arabic term that refers to civil strife, particularly the kind caused by religious schism such as that which exists between the Sunnis and the Shi'ites.
5. Library of Congress, Federal Research Division: Country Studies—Area Handbook Series—Iran.
6. 2001 U.S. State Department International Religious Freedom Report on Iran.
7. The Iraqi Shi'ite dissident Moqtada al-Sadr, at present active militarily against U.S. forces in Baghdad and other holy cities, claims that he is the Mahdi reincarnate. This is disputed by the majority of Iraq's religious leaders but they are powerless—Moqtada's claim is backed by military muscle.

Chapter 4—HOW CLOSE IS IRAN TO BUILDING AN A-BOMB?
1. "Analysis: Iran Postpones IAEA Inspection," UPI Report quoted in *The Washington Times*, March 13, 2004.
2. *IranMania* News, Tehran, March 18, 2004.
3. "Alarm Raised Over Quality of Uranium Found in Iran," Craig S Smith in *The New York Times*, March 11, 2004.
4. Congressional testimony of John R. Bolton, Under Secretary for Arms Control and International Security, U.S. Department of State: June 4, 2003.
5. See IAEA GOV/2003/75, paras 20–24.
6. Among those taken into custody were three scientists: former director general of the KRL, Mohammad Farooq, and two other close aides of Khan. Others were administrators and security personnel of the KRL, including two former military brigadiers and Khan's Personal Staff Officer.
7. Worse, Khan has been characterized as a "hard-core nationalist and a very ambitious person" by A.H. Nayyar, a physicist at Quaid-e-Azam University in Islamabad. "He's in for fame and money." Interestingly, the man is not a nuclear scientist per se, but a metallurgist. He did postgraduate work in Europe in the 1960s, and was then recruited to work at a uranium enrichment plant in Holland run by URENCO, a Dutch-British-German consortium (he is married to a Dutch woman). According to a report in *The Christian Science Monitor*, details of his return to Pakistan remain murky, except that Western intelligence agreed with Pakistani sources on one thing: Khan brought with him plans for URENCO enrichment technology. In 1983 a Dutch court convicted Khan in absentia for attempted espionage, but it was later overturned on a technicality. Khan himself denies that Pakistan's centrifuge design was purloined, despite its similarity to URENCO work.
8. A volatile compound of uranium and fluorine. UF_6 is a solid at atmospheric pressure and room temperature, but can be transformed into a gas by heating.
9. Iranfax quoting government sources.

10. *NuclearFuel*, August 27, 1997.
11. An enrichment method that separates gaseous isotopes by rotating them in a spinning tube, thereby subjecting them to a centrifugal force: *Plutonium and Highly Enriched Uranium 1996*, by David Albright, Frans Berkhout and William Walker: SIPRI: Stockholm International Peace Research Institute, 1997.
12. In a gesture of anti-Western solidarity, Iraq and Syria exchanged diplomats in March 2000, while ties between Syria and Iran, of late, have been good, to the extent that Tehran has paid off some of Assad's massive arms debts to Russia. Relations between Tehran and Baghdad continue to be testy. It might be recalled that Iran insisted that its war with Iraq was a full-blown *Jihad*, even though ninety-five percent of Iraqis are Islamic. It got around this prickly obstacle by drawing on the analogy with the war fought by Ali, the Prophet Mohammed's son-in-law with his Muslim opponents.
13. Fred Wehling, "Russian Nuclear and Missile Exports to Iran." *The Nonproliferation Review*, Monterey Institute of International Studies, Winter, 1999, Vol. 6, No. 2, pp. 134–143.
14. Ibid., Wehling.

Chapter 5—DOOMSDAY EQUATION

1. *The News International Pakistan*, Islamabad, June 2, 1998.
2. David Albright, in *The Bulletin of the Atomic Scientists*, Chicago, July/August, 1995.
3. Jim Hoagland, in *The Washington Post*, Washington May 17, 1995.
4. Jane's *International Defense Review*, London, Sept, 1997.
5. ISIS Issue Brief; "India's Nuclear Tests: Will They Open New Possibilities for Iraq to Exploit?" Washington DC, May 28, 1998.
6. Peter Baker, "Russia Unyielding on Iran Nuclear Project," *Washington Post*, August 16, 2002.
7. Scott Peterson, "Russian Nuclear Know-How Pours Into Iran," *Christian Science Monitor*, June 21, 2002.
8. Saddam Hussein had bought two nuclear reactors from France, one of which, a 40MWth research reactor which was nearing completion at Osiraq, not far from Baghdad. In a brilliantly planned and executed air strike, the Israeli Air Force totally destroyed the complex in June, 1981 because the Mossad believed (correctly, as it turns out) that Saddam Hussein would use it to provide plutonium for nuclear weapons. See *The Iraqi War Debrief*, Al J. Venter, Casemate Publishing, Philadelphia, 2004, pp. 27 and 109–110.
9. Scott Petterson, "Russian Nuclear Know-How Pours Into Iran," *Christian Science Monitor*, July 21, 2002, p. 1; Michael Eisenstadt, "Russian Arms and Technology Transfers to Iran: Policy Challenges for the United States," *Arms Control Today*, March 2001.
10. Zbigniew Brzezinski, Brent Scowcroft and Richard Murphy, "Differentiated Containment," *Foreign Affairs*, Vol. 76, No. 3 (May/June 1997); for a more recent opinion on this issue, see Brent Scowcroft, "An Opening to Iran," *Washington Post*, May 11, 2001.
11. Central Information Department, Jamaat-e-Islami, Lahore, Pakistan: e-mail <jipmedia@jamaat.org>: URL: <www.jamaat.org>.
12. At Birine, a facility in the remote Sahara, south of Algiers that for a while

Western intelligence believed might have had the capacity to produce plutonium. Though since disproved, it underscores another example of a Third
World country trying to acquire this kind of expertise.

13. Paula A. DeSutter, *Denial and Jeopardy: Deterring Iranian Use of NBC Weapons*, pp. 19 et al: Center for Counterproliferation Research, National Defense University, Washington DC, 1997.

14. See also Federation of American Scientists website <fas.org> under the heading "Shahab-4."

15. Barry Rubin's recent book, *Crises in the Contemporary Persian Gulf*, was published by Frank Cass in London and Portland, Oregon, 2002.

16. *The Nonproliferation Review* (1997), pp. 123–135.

17. *Middle East Intelligence Bulletin,* Vol. 4, No. 3, March/April 2002.

18. The ^{235}U content of natural uranium, as it occurs all over the world, is about 0.7 per cent. This is probably where the "about one percent" comes from and therefore has no special significance.

19. *Washington Post,* December 24, 2002. Also <http.msnbc.com.news/51280. asp>.

Chapter 6—IRAN'S MULTI-STEMMED CENTRIFUGE PROGRAM

1. This chapter by David Albright and Corey Hinderstein (originally metricated) is a composite of two articles that appeared in the U.S. publication *The Bulletin of the Atomic Scientists* in September/ October 2003 (Vol. 59, No. 5, pp. 52–58) and March/April 2004 (Vol. 60, No. 2, pp. 61–66). The author is grateful to the authors and to the *Bulletin* for authority to reproduce both pieces in a single, revised format.

Chapter 7— NUCLEAR LINK-UP: SOUTH AFRICA AND IRAN

1. South African Press Association (SAPA), September 11, 1997.

2. I mentioned the Amrollahi incident in my last book, *The Iraqi War Debrief*, p. 145. Though the book also has a South African edition, the government, once more, did not react. Nor did Dr. Stumpf.

3. *NuclearFuel,* Washington DC, January 12, 1998.

4. *Jane's Intelligence Review,* London, March, 1998.

Chapter 8—CASE STUDY: SOUTH AFRICA'S ATOM BOMB

1. A concept that is not as far-fetched as it sounds, since it was part of the Kremlin's strategic battleplan to eventually control all of southern Africa and its minerals, just as it wanted to dominate the Middle Eastern oil. With Soviet, Cuban, North Korean and other help, the military objective in Angola was to subjugate Unita forces in Eastern Angola and force South Africa to fight a "second war" in Caprivi (the first was already ongoing in Ovambo-land). Pretoria did not have the additional manpower and would have had to pull its forces back to the Orange River. Together with a popular uprising in South Africa's townships—which took place anyway—a Russian-backed invasion force could then have moved on to South African soil.

2. *The Risk Report,* Vol. 2, No. 1 (January–February 1996) pp 4–5 and 10.

3. David Albright, Frans Berhout and William Walker, *Plutonium and Highly Enriched Uranium 1996: World Inventories, Capabilities and Policies.* SIPRI, Stockholm, 1997.

4. An swu is a measure of the effort required to separate uranium of a given uranium-235 content into two fractions, one with a higher percentage and one with a lower percentage of uranium 235. The unit of separative work is the kilogram separative work unit (kg swu) or swu for short (Albright, Berkhout and Walker).
5. "Out of (South) Africa: Pretoria's Nuclear Weapon Experience," USAF Institute for National Security Studies Occasional Paper #27, August 1999, by Lt. Col. Roy E. Horton (with minor date changes and correct number of bombs built by Dr. Nic von Wielligh).

Chapter 9—BUILDING GUIDED MISSILES TO HIT ISRAEL
1. Somchem, the second most important company after Houwteq, had to destroy all the solid propellants and rocket casings it had made for the space launcher. This and other destructive activity was later verified by officials from the U.S. Embassy.
2. Johannesburg *Sunday Times*, March 27, 1994, pp. 1–2.
3. This was not strictly true because the next generation of missile, the RSA-4, blasted off in a southeasterly direction towards Marion island and touched down more than a thousand miles away.
4. Denel Aviation was also doing work on the SAAB Gripen fighter, for British Aerospace, Israeli Aircraft Industries as well as a selection of components for the Boeing 747.
5. *The Chopper Boys: Helicopter Warfare in Africa*. Stackpole Books (U.S.), Greenhill Books, London, 1994.
6. Congressional Review: Iran's Ballistic missile and Weapons of Mass Destruction Programs: (Document file S. Hrg. 106-800).
7. From the Federation of American Scientists website <www. fas.org>: *Iran Missile Brief* (updated March 25, 2004).
8. Islamic Revolutionary Guard Corps (IRGC, or Pasdaran) naval units tracked and targeted U.S. ships during their skirmishes with American forces in the Persian Gulf in 1987–88: Kenneth Katzman's *Report for Congress* (updated, January 2003).

Chapter 10—IRAN'S HISTORY OF TERROR
1. *Hezbollah: Born with a Vengeance*, by Hala Jaber. Columbia University Press, New York, 1997.
2. *Jerusalem Report*, March 25, 2002.
3. "Why Iran is Still a Menace," by Joshua Muravchik & Jeffrey Gedmin: *Commentary*, New York, Vol. 104, July 1997.
4. Jane's *Sentinel*: "The Gulf States," Jane's Information Group, London, 1995.
5. *God Has Ninety-Nine Names*, by Judith Miller. Touchstone, New York, 1996.
6. Jane's *International Defense Review*, London, June, 1997.
7. *Defense News*, Springfield, Virginia. July 7–13, 1997.
8. *Time*, December 2, 2002.

Chapter 11—IRAN'S UNCONVENTIONAL WEAPONS
1. Kenneth Katzman: Congressional Research Service, The Library of Congress, Order Code, RL30551.

2. Ibid., Katzman.
3. <www.globalsecurity.org/wmd/world/iran/cw/htm>
4. For more comprehensive details about Iraqi chemical and biological programs, see the author's *The Iraqi War Debrief* (Casemate Publishers, Philadelphia, 2004): Chapter 10, "New Era Threat: Iraq's Biological and Chemical Warfare Programs," pp. 146–165 as well as Chapter 11: "Some Fearsome Possible Newcomers to the Middle East Equation: Smallpox, Anthrax and Novichok," pp 166–185.
5. "Censored Study on Bioterror Doubts U.S. Preparedness," *New York Times*, March 29, 2004. See also "Iranians, Bioweapons in Mind, Lure Needy Ex-Soviet Scientists," by Judith Miller and William Broad: *New York Times* December 8, 1998.
6. Dr. Jane Orient in *The Journal of the American Medical Association*, August, 1987, pp. 644–648.
7. Federation of American Scientists website: www.fas.org.

Chapter 12—PASDARAN: THE ISLAMIC REVOLUTIONARY
GUARD CORPS
1. *Denial and Jeopardy: Deterring Iranian Use of NBC Weapons*, Paula deSutter, National Defense University Center for Counterproliferation Research, Washington DC, 1997.
2. Ibid., deSutter.
3. <fas.org> See Country Studies: Iran.
4. *Iranian Military Power—Capabilities and Intentions*, Michael Eisenstadt, The Washington Institute for Near East Policy, Paper #42, Washington, 1996.
5. Ibid., Eisenstadt.

Chapter 13—WHAT'S NEXT?
1. "Schooling Iran's Atom Squad," by Jack Boureston and Charles D, Ferguson. *Bulletin of the Atomic Scientists*, May/June, 2004.
2. Interview by Wade Boese and Miles A Pomper in *Arms Control Today*, Washington, June 2004.
3. "Foreign Correspondent" is the (Australian) ABC's weekly international affairs program, also seen on Asia Pacific, the ABC's satellite broadcaster in Asia. More than twenty-five other stations around the world including CBC Canada, Al Jazeera, CNN International, NHK Japan and others run these reports, many of them produced by veteran foreign correspondent Mark Corcoran.
4. *The Economist,* London, July 31, 2004, pp. 21–23
5. "Can the CIA Really be that Bad?" by Michael O'Hanlon, *New York Times*, July 13, 2004, p. 19.
6. The article appeared on Sunday, August 15, 2004.
7. "Fighting the Next War," by Dilip Hiro, *New York Times*, August 16, 2004.
8. MERIA Journal, Vol. 8, No. 3 (September 2004): "WMD in Iranian Security: Dangers to Europe," by Amin Tarzi.
9. "Israel Trades One Nightmare for Another," by Stephen Erlanger, *New York Times*, October 10, 2004.
10. *Ha'aretz* (English language version), September 28, 2004.

11. *Nuclear Terrorism: The Ultimate Preventable Catastrophe*, by Graham Allison, Times Books, New York, 2004.

12. For a translation, see "Bin Laden Lieutenant Admits to September 11 and Explains Al Qaeda's Combat Doctrine," The Middle East Media Research Institute (No. 344) at <www.memri.org/jihad.html>.

13. Ibid.

Appendix A—THE RUSSIA-IRAN NUCLEAR CONNECTION

1. "Vlad the Impaler," *Economist*, October 30, 2003; Ethan S. Burger and Evgenia Sorokina, "Vladimir Putin's 'Dictatorship of Law': Its Potential Implications for the Business and Legal Communities," November 19, 2003.

2. See for example the laudatory work of Vladimir Orlov, Roland Timerbaev, and Anton Khlopkov, "Nuclear Nonproliferation in U.S.-Russian Relations: Challenges and Opportunities," PIR CenterMoscow, 2002; Anton Khlopkov, "Iranian Nuclear Program in Russian-American Relations," (Russian) PIR Center Scientific Papers, No. 18, 2001.

3. Stephen Blank, "Russia: Proliferation Personified," *Asia Times*, April 17, 2003.

4. Chahram Chubin and Robert Litwak, "Debating Iran's Nuclear Aspirations," *Washington Quarterly*, Vol. 26, No. 43, p.111.

5. Glenn Kessler, "Powell Backs Iran Protests, But Says Talks Are Possible," *Washington Post*, June 18, 2003 <http://www.washingtonpost.com/wp-dyn/articles/A7148-2003Jun17.html>. For more on this, see Senator Biden's remarks as quoted in Charles Krauthammer, "A World Imagined," *The New Republic*, March 15, 1999 <http://216.247.220.66/archives/foreignpolicy/krauthammer3-10-99.htm>.

7. Evgeniy Antonov, "Russia: N. Korea Nuclear Program Demonstrates that Non-Proliferation Regime of 1968 is No Longer Effective," (Russian) *Politburo*, November 25, 2002. President Bush's recent initiative proposes interesting ways to clamp down on the WMD proliferation attempts of the few global rogues. "Remarks by the President on Weapons of Mass Destruction Proliferation," Fort Lesley J. McNair, National Defense University, Washington, D.C., February 11, 2004 <http://www.whitehouse.gov/news/releases/2004/02/20040211-4.html>.

8. Central Intelligence Agency, "Unclassified Report to Congress on the Acquisition of Technology Relating to Weapons of Mass Destruction and Advanced Conventional Munitions, 1 January through 30 June 2002." <http://www.cia.gov/cia/reports/721_reports/jan_jun2002. html#13>.

9. Ambassador G. Berdennikov, "Russian Priorities and Approaches to Nonproliferation: Preventing Mass Destruction Terrorism and Weapons Proliferation," A strategy session of the Monterey Nonproliferation Strategy Group; Robert J. Einhorn and Gary Samore, "Ending Russian Assistance to Iran's Nuclear Bomb," *Survival*, Vol. 44, No. 2 (Summer 2002), p. 60.

10. On various nuances of the Russian approach to the Iranian issue, see V. Orlov, "Russia, Iran, Iraq, and Export Controls: Facts and Conclusions," *The Monitor*, CITS, (Spring-Summer 1998); V. Moskvin, "The Russian-Iranian Conundrum and Proliferation Concerns," *The Monitor*, (Winter-Spring 1999); Y. Zvedre, "U.S. View of Russian-Iranian Relations: Instrumental Distortions," *The Monitor*, (Winter 2001); Gennady Khromov,

"Russian-Iranian Relations and Unilateral U.S. Sanctions," *The Monitor,* (Winter 2001); Alexander Pikayev, "Strategic Dimensions of the Russo-Iranian Partnership," *The Monitor,* (Winter 2001).

11. On Russian-Iranian geostrategic squabbles in the Caspian area, see Andrey Piontkovsky, "Russky Patriot kak Lobbist Irana," (Russian) Politcom.ru, June 14, 2002 <http://www.politcom.ru/print.php?fname>; "Burya nad Kaspiem," (Russian) <http://www.stringer-agency.ru/020Gazeta/85_16/012 Article/default.asp>.

12. A good factual piece on the initial phase of the bilateral cooperation is Ivan Safranchuk, "The Nuclear and Missile Programs of Iran and Russian Security," Scientific Papers, No. 8, PIR Center, May 1999.

13. "Russia, EU Oppose Inclusion of Iran on 'Axis of Evil' List," *Tehran Times,* July 21, 2002 <http://www.freerepublic.com/focus/f-news/719601/posts>; <http://www.iranvajahan.net/cgi-bin/news_en. pl?l=en&y=2002&m=7&d=21&a=13>.

14. Natalya Khmelik, "Torgovtzy Oruzhiem Potirayut Ruki," (Russian) <http://old.grani.ru/iran/articles/arms_laser/>

15. Bjorn Hagelin, Pieter D. Wezeman, Siemon T. Wezeman and Nicholas Chipperfield, "International arms transfers," SIPRI Yearbook 2003: *Armaments, Disarmament and International Security* (Oxford: Oxford University Press, 2003) <http://editors.sipri.se/pubs/yb03/ch13.html>.

16. Scott Petterson, " Russian Nuclear Know-How Pours Into Iran," Christian Science Monitor, July 21, 2002, p. 1; Michael Eisenstadt, "Russian Arms and Technology Transfers to Iran: Policy Challenges for the United States," *Arms Control Today,* March 2001.

17. John Broder, "Despite Secret '95 Pact by Gore, Russian Arms Sales to Iran Go On," *New York Times,* October 13, 2000; Steven Muffson, "Gore Hit on Russian Arms Deals," *New York Times,* October 14, 2000; *The Washington Times,* October 17, 2000; Jim Hoagland, "From Russia with Chutzpah," *Washington Post,* November 22, 2000; <http://www.csis.org/stratassessment/reports/iranarmstransf.pdf>.

18. Zbigniew Brzezinski, Brent Scowcroft and Richard Murphy, "Differentiated Containment," *Foreign Affairs,* Vol. 76, No. 3 (May/June 1997); for a more recent opinion on this issue, see Brent Scowcroft, "An Opening to Iran," *Washington Post,* May 11, 2001.

19. Ron Hutcheson, "Putin Offers Inspectors in Iran," *Philadelphia Inquirer,* May 27, 2002.

20. Hutcheson, "Putin Offers Inspectors in Iran."

21. Sabrina Tavernise, "Russia Presses Iran to Accept Scrutiny on Nuclear Sites," *New York Times,* June 30, 2003 <http://www.nytimes.com/2003/07/01/international/europe/01RUSS.html>.

22. "Russian-Iranian Cooperation Pursues Only Peaceful, Civilian Goals," Press Release No. 10, March 5, 1998 <http://www.fas.org/news/russia/1998/pr3_5.html>.

23. "Shahab-4," Federation of American Scientists, http://www.fas.org/nuke/guide/iran/missile/shahab-4.htm>.

24. Konstantin Makienko, "The Outlook for Russian-Iranian Arms Trade: Opportunities and Risks," <http://www.cast.ru/english/publish/2001/march-apr/makienko.html>.

25. Ron Hutcheson, "Putin Offers Inspectors in Iran," *Philadelphia Inquirer,* May 27, 2002; "Putin and Bush Sign N-Deal," CNN, May 24, 2002.
26. "US Sent Data to Russia on Iran," Middle East Newsline 4, May 29, 2002.
26. David Albright, "The Russian Iranian Reactor Deal," *Nonproliferation Review*, Vol. 2, No. 3 (Spring-Summer 1995), p. 51.
27. Pavel Felgenhauer, "Who Will Be Russia's Best Friend in the Future: The US or Iran and Other Undesirables?" *CDI Russia Weekly*, No. 224, September, 2002
28. <http://www.cdi.org/russia/224-4.cfm>.
29. Felgenhauer, "Who Will Be Russia's Best Friend in the Future"; and <http://www.bellona.no/en/international/russia/nuke_industry/waste_import s/28221.html>.
30. Mark Hibbs, Nuclear Fuel, September 30, 2002. A summary can be found at <http://www.nti.org/d_newswire/issues/2002/10/11/5s.html>.
31. Peter Baker, "Russia Unyielding on Iran Nuclear Project," *Washington Post*, August 16, 2002.
32. Scott Peterson, "Russian Nuclear Know-How Pours Into Iran," *Christian Science Monitor*, June 21, 2002 <http://www.csmonitor.com/2002/0621/ p01s03-woeu.html>.
33. Judith Miller, "U.S. Asks Putin Not to Sell Iran a Laser System," *New York Times*, September 19, 2000.
34. Pavel Felgengauer, "Dirty Bomb Threat Is Real," *Moscow Times*, June 20, 2002.
35. Anton La Guardia, "Rice warns of 'Made in America' solution to Iran's nuclear plans," *Daily Telegraph*, June 2003: <http://www.dailytelegraph.co. uk/news/main.jhtml?xml=/news/2003/06/27/wiran2   7.xml&sSheet=/news/ 2003/06/27/ixnewstop.html>.
36. Michael Ledeen, "The Nuclear Axis of Evil," *National Review* Online, May 12, 2003 <http://www.nationalreview.com/ledeen/ledeen051203.asp>. See also Michael Eisenstadt "Iranian Nuclear Weapons, Part I: The Challenges of US Preventive Action," *PolicyWatch*, No. 760, May 27, 2003 <http:// www. washingtoninstitute.org/watch/Policywatch/policywatch2003/760.htm>.
37. See, for example, the interview of former Deputy Foreign Minister Mamedov to Vremya Novostey, a Moscow-based pro-Kremlin newspaper, June 6, 2003, <http://www.ln.mid.ru/Bl.nsf/arh/2Do32A03>.
38. Additional Protocol (INFCIRC/540) should not be considered a panacea as only declared facilities related to Iran's nuclear program or those revealed by Tehran are open to inspection.
39. While it possesses nine percent of the world's proven oil reserves (and potentially even more if one counts the newly discovered Azadegan and Abadan sites), Iran's assured resources of uranium amount only to 491 tons, with recoverable potential of additional 876 tons at the cost of $130 per kg. Its goal program of 6,000 MW, however, needs around 900 tons of pure uranium annually – thus Iran is bound to be tied to Russian fuel supplies for the foreseeable future. "Survey of Energy Resources 2001," World Energy Council: <http://www.worldenergy.org/wecgeis/edc/countries/Iran.asp>.
40. Paul Kerr, "Iran Mining Uranium, Greatly Expanding Nuclear Facilities," *Arms Control Today*, March 2003 <http://www.armscontrol.org/act/ 2003_03/iran_mar03.asp?print>. The agreement, however, has yet to be

signed as of the publication of this article, as the proviso for the fuel to be shipped--though with Iran mining its own uranium now, Russia may be left out of its original profits from the return of the spent fuel.

41. Alex Wagner, "Moscow Puts Hold on Transfer of Laser Isotope Separator to Iran," *Arms Control Today,* October 2000 <http://www.armscontrol.org/act/2000_10/iranoct00.asp>.

42. Andrew Jack, "Putin's New Rules of Protocol," *Financial Times*, June 9, 2003; "Confusion on Russian Nuclear Deal with Iran," *Financial Times*, June 5, 2003.

43. "Russian Ambassador Discusses U.S. Stance Toward Iran, Nuclear Cooperation, Caspian," *Tehran Iran Daily* (Internet version), June 2, 2003.

44. Alexander Goltz, "Na Chistuyu Tyazhelyuyu Vodu," (Russian) *Ezhednevny Zhurnal,* June 25, 2003.

45. On Minatom's lobbying potential in Moscow's corridors of power, see Anna Badkhen, "Kremlin Can't Control Secretive Nuke Agency," *San Francisco Chronicle*, September 1, 2002.

46. "Russia Close to Delivering Nuclear Fuel to Iran, Minister Says," *The Russia Journal Daily*, July 3, 2003 <http://russiajournal.com/news/cnews-article.shtml?nd=39168>.

47. "Russia Insists it will Send Nuclear Fuel to Iran," *Gazeta*, June 6, 2003 <http://gazeta.ru/print/2003/06/06/Russiainsist.shtml>.

48. "Russia: Moscow says IAEA statement clears way for nuclear cooperation with Iran," Radio Free Europe/Radio Liberty, June 21, 2003.

49. Scott Petterson, "Russia Grows Wary of Iran Nukes," *Christian Science Monitor*, June 10, 2003; David Holley, "Iran Nuclear Threat Worries Russians," *Los Angeles Times*, February 27, 2003; "Russia Concerned at Possibility of WMD Development by Iran," *Interfax*, March 24,2003.

50. William Safire, "Testing Putin on Iran," *New York Times,* May 23, 2002; Robert J. Einhorn and Gary Samore, "Ending Russian Assistance to Iran's Nuclear Bomb."

51. For some suggestions for positive inducements regarding Moscow's approach to this issue, see Christina Chuen, "Russian Nuclear Exports to Iran: U.S. Policy Change Needed," Center for Nonproliferation Studies <http://cns.miis.edu/pubs/week/030327.htm>.

52. "Russian Defense Minister Defends Arms Sales to Iran, North Korea, Moscow," (Russian) *Agenstvo Voyennykh Novostey*, September 23, 2002.

53. Alexandr Plotnikov, "Raketnyi Komplex klassa 'Moskva-Tegeran' k startu-gotov," (Russian) February 25, 2003 <http://www.grani.ru/War/Arms/p.23979.html>.

54. Charles Digges, "Russia Agrees with U.S. That Iran Poses a Nuclear Threat," *Bellona*, May 20, <http://www.bellona.no/en/international/russia/nuke_industry/co-operation/29647.html>.

55. Simon Saradzhyan, "Russia Needs Iran Proof or Incentives," *Moscow Times*, June 03, 2003.

56. Viktor Sokolov, "Pochemu Tegeram ne podpisyvaet Dopolnitelnyi Protocol," (Russian) *Strana*, June 30, 2003 <http://strana.ru/print/185456.html>.

57. "Iran Will Agree to Tougher UN Inspections," IranMania.com, July 3, 2003.

58. Pavel Felgenhauer, "U.S. Talking to the Wrong Guy," *Moscow Times*, June 5, 2003.

59. Ariel Cohen, "Preventing A Crisis in U.S.-Russian Relations over Moscow's Nuclear Technology Exports," The Heritage Foundation Executive Memorandum, No. 863, March 2003.
60. David Holley, "Iran Nuclear Threat Worries Russians," *Los Angeles Times*, February 27, 2003; Rebecca Santana, "Iran Deal Makes Russia Uneasy," *The Atlanta Journal-Constitution*, June 15, 2003 <http://www.ajc.com/news/content/news/0603/15russiairan.html>.

Appendix B—IAEA IMPLEMENTATION OF THE
NPT SAFEGUARDS AGREEMENT
1. Source: The Federation of American Scientists & GlobalSecurity.org
2. The Safeguards Agreement, reproduced in document INFCIRC/214, entered into force on 15 May 1974.

Appendix C—IRAN'S ECONOMY AND OIL AND GAS RESOURCES
1. U.S. Department of Energy Brief: EIA Country Analysis on Iran—www.eia.doe.gov.

Appendix D—HOW SADDAM HUSSEIN ALMOST BUILT HIS BOMB
1. "Has Iraq Come Clean at Last?" by David Albright and Robert Kelley, *Bulletin of the Atomic Scientists*, Nov./Dec. 1995.
2. "Iraq's Secret Nuclear Weapons Program" by Jay C. Davis and David A. Kay, *Physics Today*, July, 1992.
3. September/October 1998.
4. Until Iranian opposition groups pinpointed several sites—among them, the one at Natanz, where they claimed Tehran was involved with nuclear work (small centrifuges were found for enriching uranium), the Iranians prevented IAEA staff from setting up environmental monitoring units in some areas where the Atomic Energy Organization of Iran was active. They were particularly restrictive at some newly established uranium processing plants. See "Inspectors in Iran Examine Machines to Enrich Uranium," *New York Times*, February 23, 2003.
5. *Critical Mass* by William Burrows & Robert Windrem, New York: Simon & Schuster, 1994; Ibid., Davis & Kay.
6. Ibid., Davis & Kay.
7. Pointer, supplement to *Jane's Intelligence Review*, London, March, 1998
8. *Like a Phoenix from the Ashes? The Future of Iraqi Military Power* by Michael Eisenstadt, The Washington Institute of Near East Policy, 1993.
9. *Plutonium and Highly Enriched Uranium 1996*, by David Albright, Frans Berkhout and William Walker, OUP, 1997.
10 *International Defense Review*, Jane's Information Group, London, Sept. 1997.
11. "Iraq's Shop-Till-You-Drop Nuclear Program," by David Albright and Mark Hibbs, *Bulletin of the Atomic Scientists,* April 1992.
12. "Denial and Deception Practices of WMD Proliferators: Iraq and Beyond," by Dr. David Kay, The Center for Strategic and International Studies & Massachusetts Institute of Technology, in *The Washington Quarterly*, Winter 1995.
13. Ibid., Albright and Hibbs.

14. Ibid., David Kay.
15. Note also Iraqi attempts to acquire krytons: In March, 1991, Iraq attempted to illegally import Krytons from CIS Technologies Inc. of the U.S. Several years earlier, Iraq had imported weapons-quality capacitors from other American concerns. IAEA investigators have also found about 230 metric tons of high-energy explosive HMX in Iraq that may have been purchased from Czechoslovakia: Monterey Institute, CNS, Iraqi Nuclear Abstracts, 1992 http://cns.miis.edu/research/iraq/iraqnu92.htm.
16. "The New Nuclear Threat," by John M. Deutch, *Foreign Affairs* 71, Fall 1992.

Appendix E—CLOSE-QUARTER OBSERVATIONS: THE SOUTH AFRICAN NUCLEAR WEAPONS PROGRAM
1. Organized by *Unione Scienziati per il Disarmo* (USPID).
2. SIPRI: Stockholm International Peace Research Institute.
3. David Albright, "South Africa's Secret Nuclear Weapons," ISIS Report, May 1994, p. 14, <http://www.isis-online.org/publications/southafrica/ir-594.html>.
4. Richard Kessler, "Menem Reported Ready to Name Castro Madero CNEA Boss Again," *Nucleonics Week*, January 12, 1989, pp. 4–5.
5. "South Africa to Test-launch IRBM," *Jane's Defence Weekly*, July 1, 1989, p. 1354; Martin Walker; "South Africa About to Test Medium-Range Missile," *The Guardian* (London), June 21, 1989, <http://web.lexis-nexis.com/universe>; Bill Gertz, "South Africa on the Brink of Ballistic Missile Test," *Washington Times*, June 24, 1989, pp. A1, A10.
6. "South African Missile Test," *Jane's Defence Weekly*, July 15, 1989, p. 59; Michael R. Gordon, "U.S. Sees Israeli Help in Pretoria's Missile Work," *New York Times*, October 27, 1989, <http://web.lexis-nexis.com/universe>; U.S. Defense Intelligence Agency, "Special Assessment, South Africa: Missile Activity," July 5, 1989, declassified and partially released, in *South Africa and the US: The Declassified History*, ed. Kenneth Mokoena (New York: New Press, 1993), pp. 167-168; William E. Burrows and Robert Windrem, *Critical Mass: The Dangerous for Superpowers in a Fragmented World*, New York: Simon & Schuster, 1994, pp. 446-448; John Pike, "Overberg Test Range OTB Arniston South Africa," Federation of Atomic Scientists, May 29, 2000, <http://www.fas.org/nuke/guide/rasa/facility/overberg.htm>.
7. "Republic of South Africa's Pressure to Sign NPT," *Nuclear Engineering International*, June 1989, p. 28.
8. Adrian Hadland, "SA's Nuclear Delusions Lie in Ruins, But They Still Cost a Fortune," *Independent Online*, January 26, 1998, <http://www.inc.co.za>; Waldo Stumpf, "South Africa's Limited Nuclear Deterrent Program and the Dismantling thereof Prior to South Africa's Accession to the Nuclear Non-Proliferation Treaty," press conference, Washington, DC, July 23, 1993.
9. *Athens News*, October 12, 1989, in "Uranium Destined For Libya," Nuclear Developments, October 26, 1989, p. 3.
10. Michael R. Gordon, "U.S. Sees Israeli Help in Pretoria's Missile Work," *New York Times*, October 27, 1989, <http://web.lexis-nexis.com/universe>; NBC Nightly News, October 25, 1989, transcript of broadcast, pp. 1-2.
11. Wolf Blitzer, David Makovsky, and Dan Petreanu, "It Would 'Complicate'

Jerusalem-Washington Ties. Bush Warns Israel on N-Deal with S. Africa," *Jerusalem Post*, October 29, 1989, <http://web.lexis-nexis.com/universe>.

12. U.S. General Accounting Office Report GAO/RCED-89-116, "Weapons Related Information and Technology Controls," June 1989; in "Developments of Concern for Horizontal Proliferation," PPNN Newsbrief, October 1989, p. 8.

13. Mitchell Reiss, "South Africa: Castles in the Air," in *Bridled Ambition: Why Countries Constrain Their Nuclear Capabilities,* Washington, DC: Woodrow Wilson Center, 1995, pp. 11, 17; David Albright, Frans Berkhout, and William Walker, *Plutonium and Highly Enriched Uranium 1996: World Inventories, Capabilities and Policies,* Oxford University Press, 1997, p. 380; International Atomic Energy Agency, Report on the Completeness of the Inventory of South Africa's Nuclear Installations and Material, attachment to Gov/2609, September 3, 1992, pp. 4-5.

14. U.S. Department of State, "Israel Aircraft Industries Indictment for Illegal Exports to South Africa," November 22, 1989, confidential cable declassified and released, Digital National Security Archive, <http://nsarchive.chadwyck.com/>.

15. UN General Assembly, "Implementation of the Declaration on the Denuclearization of Africa," A/RES/44/113, December 15, 1989, <http://www.un.org/documents/ga/res/44/a44r113.htm>.

16. "De Klerk Tells World South Africa Built and Dismantled Six Nuclear Weapons," *NuclearFuel*, March 29, 1993, p 7.

17. Waldo Stumpf, "South Africa's Nuclear Weapons Program: From Deterrence to Dismantlement," *Arms Control Today 25*, December 1995/January 1996, p. 6; Mitchell Reiss, "South Africa: Castles in the Air," in *Bridled Ambition,* Ibid., p. 11; David Albright, Frans Berkhout, and William Walker, *Plutonium and Highly Enriched Uranium 1996: World Inventories, Capabilities and Policies,* Ibid., p. 380; IAEA, Report on the Completeness of the Inventory of South Africa's Nuclear Installations and Material, Ibid., pp. 4-5.

18. Waldo Stumpf, "South Africa's Nuclear Weapons Program: From Deterrence to Dismantlement," Ibid., p. 6; David Albright, "South Africa's Secret Nuclear Weapons," ISIS Report, May 1994, p. 16, <htpp://www.isis-online.org/publications/southafrica/ir-594.html>.

19. "450 Tonnes Sold Abroad," *Stavanger Aftenblad*, April 30, 1990; in JPRS-TND-90-11, 28 June 1990, p. 39.

20. Ibid., Mitchell Reiss, "South Africa: Castles in the Air," p. 18.

21. David Albright and Mark Hibbs, "South Africa: The ANC and the Atom Bomb," *Bulletin of the Atomic Scientists,* April 1993, <http://www.bulatomsci.org/issues/1993/a93/a93AlbrightHibbs.html>, p. 1.

22. Ibid., Mitchell Reiss, "South Africa: Castles in the Air," p. 40.

23. Mark Gorwitz, "Section10; South Africa," Second-tier Nuclear Nations: Laser Isotope Separation Programs Technical Citations and Comments, unpublished paper, January 1996.

24. Waldo Stumpf, "South Africa's Nuclear Weapons Program: From Deterrence to Dismantlement," *Arms Control Today 25* (December 1995/January 1996)

25. "S. Africa Says It Has Destroyed Its Nuclear Bombs," Reuters, March 24, 1993; Waldo Stumpf, "South Africa's Limited Nuclear Deterrent Program and the Dismantling thereof Prior to South Africa's Accession to the Nuclear

Non-Proliferation Treaty," press conference, Washington, DC, July 23, 1993.

26. U.S. Arms Control and Disarmament Agency, "Signatories and Parties to the Treaty on the Non-Proliferation of Nuclear Weapons," December 3, 1998, <http://dosfan.lib.uic.edu/acda/treaties/npt3.htm>; Seth W. Carus, "Israeli Ballistic Missile Developments," Testimony before the Commission to Assess the Ballistic Missile Threat to the U.S., July 15, 1998, <http://www.fas.org/irp/threat/missile/rumfeld/pt2_carus2.htm>; Rita M. Byrnes ed., *South Africa: A Country Study*, Washington, DC: Federal Research Division, Library of Congress, 1997, 355; Ann Devroy and Helen Dewar, "Citing S. Africa's 'Transformation,' Bush Ends Most Sanctions," *Washington Post*, July 11, 1991, <http://web.lexis-nexis.com/universe>.

27. Ibid., David Albright, Frans Berkhout, and William Walker

28. Waldo Stumpf, "South Africa's Nuclear Weapons Program: From Deterrence to Dismantlement," *Arms Control Today*, 25 (December 1995/January 1996), p. 6.

29. Capital Radio (Umtata), September 16, 1991 in "Nuclear Sites Open to International Inspection," *NuclearFuel*, March 29, 1993, p. 8; *Proliferation Issues*, September 27, 1991, p. 1; "South Africa Has Signed a Safeguards Pact With the IAEA," *Nuclear News*, October 1991, p. 26; "De Klerk Tells World South Africa Built and Dismantled Six Nuclear Weapons," *NuclearFuel*, March 29, 1993, p. 8.

30. David B. Ottaway, "South Africa Said to Abandon Pursuit of Nuclear Weapons," *Washington Post*, October 18, 1991, pp. A23, A26; *The Guardian*, October 19, 1991 in "South Africa's Nuclear Arms Program," *Peace News Bulletin*, p. 15.

31. International Atomic Energy Agency, Report on the Completeness of the Inventory of South Africa's Nuclear Installations and Material, attachment to Gov/2609, September 3, 1992, pp. 4-7.

32. Mark Hibbs, "IAEA Believes South Africa Produced More Than 200 Kg of High-Enriched Uranium," *NuclearFuel*, September 28, 1992, p. 1.

33. Ibid., p. 2.

34. "ANC Deeply Concerned about Nuclear Program," South African Press Association, December 22, 1992, <http://www.aec. co.za>; in FBIS Document FBIS-AFR-92-246, December 23, 1992.

Appendix F—IRAN'S MISSILES: DEVILS IN THE DETAIL

1. http://news.bbc.co.uk/go/pr/fr/-/2/hi/middle_east/3081737.stm.

2. Bill Gertz, "Iran Set for Another Flight Test of Missile," *The Washington Times*, Sept. 8, 2000, p. 1.

3. "Iran test-fires missile," Associated Press, Sept. 22, 2000.

4. Bill Gertz, "Iran's Missile Test Fails After Takeoff," *The Washington Times*, Sept. 22, 2000, p. A5.

5. Andrew Koch, "Third Iranian Shahab Test a Fizzle," *Jane's Intelligence Review*, Nov. 2000, p. 5.

6. "Iran's Ballistic Missile and Weapons of Mass Destruction Programs," Hearing before the International Security, Proliferation, and Federal Services Subcommittee of the Committee on Governmental Affairs, United States Senate, September 21, 2000.

Appendix G—PASDARAN'S PROTEGÉ: HIZBOLLAH
1. *See No Evil*, Robert Baer, Crown Books, New York, 2002.
2. Personal communication, November, 2003.
3. Ian Coughlin in *The Weekly Telegraph*, December 7, 2002.
4. "The Political Economy of Middle East Terrorism," *Middle East Review of International Affairs* (MERIA), Journal Vol. 6, No. 4 (December 2002).
5. "Targeting Terror: U.S. Policy Towards Middle Eastern State Sponsors and Terrorist Organizations, Post-September 11," Washington Institute, 2002.
6. *The Washington Times*, May 6, 2003.
7. *Middle East Intelligence Bulletin*, Vol. 6, No. 2/3, February/ March 2004, Gary C Gambill.
8. "Iran, Arabs Sing Hizbollah's Praises Following Prisoner Swap," Agence France Presse, January 30, 2004.
9. In September 1999, Argentina issued an international arrest warrant for Imad Mughniyah, Hizbollah's head of overseas operations, in connection with the bombing.
10. Ibid., *Middle East Intelligence Bulletin*, February/March 2004.
11. "Balad men held for forming Hizbollah cell," *The Jerusalem Post*, February 9, 2004; *Ha'aretz*, February 8/9, 2004.
12. Avi Jorisch: *Middle East Quarterly*, Winter 2004: http:// www.meforum. org/article/583

ACRONYMS, TECHNICAL, ARABIC & PERSIAN WORDS AND PHRASES
1. With grateful thanks to various International Atomic Energy Agency publications as well as excerpts from the glossary of *Plutonium and Highly Enriched Uranium 1996,* by David Albright, Frans Berkhout and William Walker, Stockholm International Peace Research Institute (SIPRI) and Oxford University Press, 1997.

ACKNOWLEDGMENTS
1. *The Iraqi War Debrief: Why Saddam Hussein Was Toppled* (Casemate, Philadelphia, 2004 and Verulam Publishing, St. Albans, England) 2004.
2. *Armament and Disarmament: South Africa's Nuclear Weapons Experience,* by Hannes Steyn, Richardt van der Walt and Jan van Loggerenberg; Network Publishers, PO Box 36689, Menlo Park, Pretoria 0018, South Africa, 2003.
3. *Into The Shadows: Radical Vigilantes in Khatami's Iran*: Policy Paper #56 by Michael Rubin: The Washington Institute for Near East Policy, Washington DC, 2001.
4. All Strategic Studies Institute (SSI) monographs are available on the SSI homepage at HYPERLINK http://www/carlisle.army.mil/ ssi/.

INDEX

Abadan, Iran, 33, 50–51, 47–48
Abdulmalek, Molavi, 221
Abu Ghraib Prison, 230
Abuzar oil field, 59
Achaemenids, 28
Ad Dawah, 48
Additional Protocol to the Safeguards Agreement, 123
Advena nuclear facility, South Africa, 154, 165, 187–190, 197, 199
Afghanistan, 28, 216, 249, 261, 264
Africa Confidential, 173–174
African National Congress, 176, 292, 294
Aghazadeh, 134,
Aghazadeh, Gholam Reza, 132, 161
Ahl-e Haqq (Shi'ite sect), 78
Ahvaz, Iran, 33, 47–49, 113, 129
Ail Moradi, Abdul, 221
Ain Oussera, Algeria, 117
Al Amarah, 53
Al Aqsa Martyrs' Brigade, 223, 259
Al Faw, Iraq, 32, 50, 56–58, 61–64
Al Qurnah, Iraq, 55
Al Walid, Iraq, 51
al Zarqawi, Abu Musab, 68
al-Ali, Sheikh Hamed, 68
al-Aqsa Martyrs Brigade, 259
al-Fagih, Dr. Saad, 233
al-Qaeda, 68, 117, 119, 214–218, 220, 223, 232–233, 260–261, 271, 278, 286, 288, 293, 295
al-Quarashi, Abu Ubeid, 295
al-Sadr, Moqtada, 272
al-Sharistani, Hussein, 229–230
al-Zawahiri, Ayman, 216, 260–261
Albright, David, 91, 93, 102, 111, 122, 131, 165, 168, 188–189, 190, 250–252, 286

Albright, Madeline, 238
Algeria, 117, 177, 227
Algiers Agreement (1975), 47
Ali Rajai, Mohammad, 39
Ali, the First Imam, 70, 224, 225
Allison, Graham, 290
Amara, Hamad, 259
American Foreign Policy Council, 281
American Joint Distribution Committee, 81
americium 241, 250–252
Amir Khabir University, 135
Amirabad, Iran, 129
Amnesty International, 218, 220
Amrollahi, Reza, 97, 100–101, 157–158, 160–162
An Najaf, 46, 73, 77
Angola, 152, 169, 174–175, 177, 179, 181–192, 198, 202, 234
anthrax, 241
Apartheid regime (South Africa), 97, 151, 177, 182, 186, 202, 246–247, 291
Arab–Israeli War (1967), 47
Arabistan, Iran, 46–47
Arafat, Yasser, 215, 223, 259
Arak, Iran, 80, 91, 94, 127, 139, 277, 289
Argentina, 177
Armament and Disarmament, 197
Armaments Corporation of South Africa (Armscor), 127, 165, 171–172, 179, 181–182, 187–190, 192, 197–199
Armenia, 234, 281
Armenian Christians, 39, 80
Arms Control Today, 276
Armscor, (see Armaments Corporation of South Africa)

Asefi, Hamid Reze, 90
Asmal, Kadar, 166
Assembly of Experts, 35, 37, 65, 257
Assyrian Christians, 39, 80
Atlas Aircraft Corporation, 202,
Atomic Energy Agency, 275
Atomic Energy Corporation (South Africa), 97, 161, 164–165, 171, 181–182, 184, 189, 191
Atomic Energy Organization of Iran (AEOI), 87, 97, 129
atomic vapor laser isotope separation (AVLIS), 86
Australia, 177
Australian Broadcasting Corporation, 279
"Axis of Evil," 124
Azerbaijan, 281
Azim, Shah Abdol, 75
Aziz, Tariq, 48

Ba'ath Party, 46, 153
Badenhorst, Heinrich, 291
Baha'i community, 79–80
Bahrain, 62, 264, 272
Bakhtaran (Kermanshah) Iran, 47–49
Bakhtiari, Ahmed, 221
Bakr, President Ahmad Hassan, 47
Bali, 288
Baluchistan, 79
Bam, Iran, 27
Bandar Abbas (Iran) naval base, 101, 225, 210, 249, 265
Bandar-e Khomeini, 60
Bandar-e Langeh, Iran, 101
Bandar-e Mashur, 60
Bani Sadr, Abol Hassan, 39, 49, 51, 120–121, 222–224
Banias pipeline, 59
Baqr as Sadr, Ayatollah Sayyid Muhammad, 48
Bar-Ilan University, 289
Barbour, Lauren, 251
Basij (Popular Mobilization Army), 51–53, 55, 63, 269–270
Basra, Iraq, 49, 53, 56, 58, 63–64
Basson, Dr. Wouter, 172, 246–247
Bazargan, Prime Minister Mehdi, 31, 36, 47

Beal, Clifford, 159
Beirut, Lebanon, 216
Belfield, David, 214
Belgium, 252
Ben-Eliezer, Benjamin, 216
Berman, Ilan, 281–282
Besharati-Jahromi, Ali Mohammed, 223
bin Laden, Osama, 214, 216–217, 233, 261, 292
bin Laden, Saad, 261
biological weapons, 256
Bishkek, Iran, 93
Blair, Tony, 275
Blix, Hans, 118, 129
Bodinger, Herzl, 272
Bolton, John, 92
Bonab Atomic Energy Research Center, Iran, 129
Bosnia, 234
Botha, Pik, 97, 158, 160–162, 192
Boureston, Jack, 274
Bracken, Paul, 290
Brazil, 177
Bredasdorp, South Africa, 197
Breit, Marshall, 86, 88, 90, 102
Brzezinski, Zbigniew, 116
Buchan, John, 278
Buchta, Wilfried, 34
Bulgaria, 174, 241
The Bulletin of the Atomic Scientists, 110, 125, 165, 172, 188, 273
Bureau of Democracy, Human Rights and Labor, 220
Bush, George W., President, 89, 124, 223, 275, 285, 294
Bushehr (Iran) nuclear reactor, 60, 63, 89, 94–95, 102, 104, 113, 132–133, 141–142, 148, 164, 210, 225, 229, 248

Caliph Al Mamun, 71
Caliph Harun ar Rashid, 71
Carnegie Endowment for International Peace, 86, 124
Carter, Jimmy, 178
Center for Counterproliferation Research, National Defense University, 27, 119

Center for Nonproliferation Studies, 103, 113
Center for Theoretical Physics and Mathematics (Iran), 129
Central Aerohydrodynamic Institute (TsAGI) (Russia), 107
Central Intelligence Agency, 93, 125, 127, 185, 203, 207, 215, 217, 226, 234, 239, 243, 262, 280, 283, 289
Centre for the Study of Terrorism and Political Violence, 217
Challenges of Fissile Material Control, 251
Chechnyan conflict, 117
Chemical and Biological Warfare Elimination Act of 1991, 238
Chemical and Biological Weapons Non-proliferation Program, 161
Chemical Weapons Convention, 237, 239
chemical weapons, 56–57, 63, 65, 239, 247, 256
Cheong Lee Ltd., 238
Cheragh, Shah, 75
Chernomyrdin, Victor, 116
China National Nonferrous Industry Corporation, 168
China, 111, 114–115, 123, 126, 134, 164, 166–167, 170–171, 203, 208, 211, 239, 252
Chirac, Jacques, 275
The Chopper Boys: Helicopter Warfare in Africa, 201–202
Christopher, Warren, 112
Clinton, William J., 110, 155, 164, 238
USS *Cole,* 288
Committee for Special Operations, 219
Committee on Foreign Intelligence Abroad, 263
Committee on Implementation of Actions Abroad, 263
Commonwealth of Independent States, 100
Compton, Dr. James A.F., 241
Conference on Disarmament (1986), 57
Congo Airlines, 233
Constitution of the Islamic Republic, 35

"Construction Jihad," 268
Corcoran, Mark, 279
Costa Rica, 234
Council for Nonproliferation of Weapons of Mass Destruction, 168
Council of Guardians, 30–31, 36–38, 40, 42, 44
Crocker, Chester, 179
Crusade for Reconstruction, 258
Cuba, 116, 152, 155, 166, 175, 178–179, 181, 192, 200

Darabi, Kazem, 219
Darkhovin, Iran, 97, 129
de Gaulle, Charles, 37
de Klerk, F.W., 152–154, 176–177, 180, 187, 192, 196, 246
de Villiers, Dr. Wynand, 186
Defense Industries Organization (DIO), 97, 248
Defense Intelligence Agency (DIA), 260
Defense Nuclear Agency, 118
Defense Threat Reduction Agency, 241
Dehloran, Iran, 49
Delbani, Hassan, 68
Denel Aviation, 127, 152, 187, 190, 200–203
Department of Homeland Security, 287
deSutter, Paula, 27, 36, 119, 238, 243, 255–257, 263, 265, 271
Dezful, Iran, 33, 47–50
Dhahabi brotherhood, 78
Dhahran, 226
Divona, Iran, 129
Doroud oil field, 59
Doshen-Tappan, Iran, 48
Dover Air Force Base, Delaware, 99

Ebola virus, 246
Egypt, 28, 174, 177–178, 209, 226–227, 245, 264, 272, 289
Eighth Imam, 73–74
Eisenstadt, Michael, 93, 266, 270
ElBaradei, Mohamed, 85, 88–90, 124–125, 134, 136, 275
electromagnetic isotope separation machine, 111
enriched uranium, 141, 147, 286
Environmental Protection Agency, 244

Ereli, Adam, 90
Erlanger, Steven, 289
Esfahan Nuclear Technology Center (ENTC), Iran, 43, 74, 80–81, 94 127, 137, 139, 240
Euphrates River, 55
European Union, 133, 220, 228, 230, 282
Expediency Council at the University of Tehran, 128, 281

Fadayan (dissident group), 29
Fadjr, 249–250
Fallahian-Khuze, Ali, 219, 222–223
Fallujah, Iraq, 295
Faqih, (definition), 38, 41, 72
Fars, Iran, 80
Fase (Iran) site, 277
Federal Bureau of Investigation, 245
Federal Emergency Management Agency, 244
Federal Research Division, Library of Congress, 69
Federation of American Scientists, 128, 208, 258
Ferguson, Charles D., 274
Fesharaki, Feredun, 274
Firuzabadi, Hassan, 270
Fish Lake, 64
Forozan oil field, 59
Foundation of the Oppressed and Dispossessed, 263
Framatome, 97
France, 185, 252, 287
Freedom Movement, (Iran), 31
Freeh, Louis, 226
Frisch, Peter, 231
Fuchs International, 198

Gadhaffi, Moammer, 90, 109, 153, 172, 247, 276, 290, 293
Gandhi, Indira, 112
gas centrifuge uranium enrichment program, 134
gas centrifuge, 98, 138, 142–144, 184
gaseous diffusion, 184
Geneva Protocol (1925), 57
Germany, 122, 142, 144, 146, 185, 252, 287

Ghazvin, Iran, 269
GlobalSecurity.org, 208, 210, 239, 276
Goosen, Dan, 245–246
Gorbachev, Mikhail, 213
Gore, Albert, 116
Goskell, Timur, 254
Gottemoeller, Rose, 124
Great Britain, 29, 252, 287
Greater Middle Eest Plan, 294
Greece, 185
Grove, Frederick Christoffel, 174
Guerin, James, 198–199
Gulf War I, 65, 110, 118, 136, 149, 159, 228, 230, 250, 256, 267
Gulf War II, 93, 287

Hadadian, Mustafa, 261
Hajj pilgrimage, 228
Halabjah, Iraq, 57
Halevy, Efraim, 282–283
Hamadan, Iran, 48, 81, 224
Hamas, 223, 226, 228, 259, 271, 286
Hameed, Moinudden Ahmed, 233
Hamvand, Rahman Radjabi, 221
Hassan, Abu, 215
Hawizah Marshes, 55
Henry L. Stimson Center, 96
Highly enriched uranium, (HEU), 89, 91, 96, 98–100, 141, 165, 182, 184–189, 191–192, 286
Hibbs, Mark, 171–172
High Council of Justice (Iran), 40–41
Hinderstein, Corey, 131, 135
Hizbollah, 34, 119, 169–170, 215–218, 220, 223, 225–226, 231–232, 249–250, 254–255, 259–260, 263–264, 266, 271, 281, 286, 288, 292, 383–401
Horton III, Roy E., 175
Houw Hoek (South Africa) facility, 197
Houwteq (South Africa) facility, 197
Husayn, the Third Imam, 72
Hussein, Saddam, 33, 45–46, 48, 50, 52, 54, 57, 59, 87, 92, 111–112, 118, 153, 159, 166, 229–230, 240, 247, 277, 281, 284, 286, 292
Husseini, Pirooz, 88
hydrogen isotope, 183

Ilam Province, Iran, 49
India, 112, 114–115, 252, 272
Indonesia, 231, 287
Infrared Countermeasures Program, 235
Inkatha Freedom Party, 169
Inor Production Association, 107
Insight, 260–262
Institute for National Strategic Studies, 278
Institute for Nuclear Science and Technology (Pakistan), 95
Institute for Science and International Security (ISIS), 112, 131, 165, 250-1
Intelligence in War, 278
International Atomic Energy Agency (IAEA), 85–94, 96–97, 101–102, 104, 118, 122, 124, 126, 128–129, 131–142, 144–147, 149, 155, 158–159, 165, 176, 178, 183–188, 203, 246, 251–252, 264, 271, 277, 280, 286, 290–291
International Signal and Control, 198
iodine-131, 126
Iran Brief, 101, 214
Iran Defense Industries Organization, 248
Iran Nonproliferation Act of 2000, 239
Iran Republican Constitution; Article 5, 38; Article 62–90, 39; Article 69, 40; Article 88, 40; Article 89, 40; Article 107, 38; Article 108–112, 38; Article 113, 38; Article 132, 38, Article 156, 40; Article 157, 40; Article 158, 40; Article 160, 41; Article 161, 41; Article 162, 41; Article 170, 42
Iran (Islamic Republic of Iran), 30, 110, 125, 133, 136, 139–141, 149, 155–156, 164, 166, 177–178, 195, 198, 209, 211, 231, 245, 264, 277, 284, 293, 295; Achaemenids, 28; Assembly of Experts, 35, 37, 65, 257; Atomic Energy Organization of Iran, 87, 97, 129; ballistic missile inventory, 204; Bonab Atomic Energy Research Center, 129; Bushehr nuclear reactor, 60, 63, 89, 94–95, 102, 104, 113, 132–133, 141–142, 148, 164, 210, 225, 229, 248; capitalism and socialism, 33; Center for Theoretical Physics and Mathematics, 129; Committee on Foreign Intelligence Abroad, 263; Committee on Implementation of Actions Abroad, 263; "Construction Jihad," 268; Constitution of 1979, 263; Constitution of the Islamic Republic, 35; cooperation with South Africa, 155; Council of Guardians, 30–31, 36–38, 40, 42, 44; "Crusade for Reconstruction," 268; Defense Industries Organization, 97, 248; development, 27; enormous oil revenues, 29; Expediency Council, 128, 281; experienced high inflation, 29; Foundation of the Oppressed and Dispossessed, 263; Freedom Movement, 31; gas centrifuge facilities, 142–144; gas centrifuge uranium enrichment program, 134; High council of Justice, 40–41; infrastructure, 29; Islamic Consultative Assembly, (Mijlis), 29–31, 35–40, 44, 80, 81, 122, 222, 253, 256, 270; isolating by European Union, 133; Jabr Ibn Hayan Laboratory, 94, 126, 137; Kurdish Democratic Party of Iran, 221; Law of Qisas, 41; Leifeld machine, 143; Majlis (see Islamic Consultative Assembly); Ministry of Education, 81; Missile Designation: Cross Country Comparison chart, 205; missile development program, 210; National Council of Resistance, 123, 136; Navy, 265; Nonproliferation Act of 2000, 239; nuclear power program, 96, 274; Nuclear Research Center for Agriculture and Medicine, 129; procurement of material, 143, 145–146; Qajar monarchy, 28–29, 43; Radioactive Waste Storage Facility, 94; redistribution of land to peasants, 29; Safavids monarchy, 28; Sassanids, 28, 69; SAVAK, 28;

State Prosecutor General, 41; Supreme Defense Council, 36, 38; Tehran Nuclear Research Center, 94, 129; Tudeh Party, 29–30, 269; Umayyad Empire, 28; Uranium Conversion Laboratory, 94; Weapons; Al Sabiha-15 submarine, 249; Bell 214A helicopter, 52; F-4 Phantom, aircraft, 48, 52; F-5 aircraft, 52; F-14 aircraft, 52; Fadjr-3 rocket, 250; Fadjr-5 rocket, 250; Feteh-110, 204; Hudong fast attack craft, 208; Il-28 bomber, 51; Katyusha rocket, 249; Mi-24 helicopter, 68; Misagh-1 missile, 249; Nour C-802 missile, 248; Scud-B, 210; Scud-C, 210; Shahab missile, 205; Shahab-1, 204, 210; Shahab-2, 204; Shahab-3, 92, 127, 131, 204, 207, 209, 210; Shahab-4, 207, 210; Shahab-5, 210; Shahab-6, 207; Silkworm Missile, 61; SS-4 rocket, 105; Stinger missile, 249; T-22 bomber, 51; Tondor-68, 211; Tondar-69, 204; Toophan anti-tank guided missile, 248

Iran-Iraq War, 32–33, 45–66, 265, 267

Iranian Air Force, 47, 49–52

Iranian Atomic Energy Organization, 132, 135, 147

Iranian Jewish community, 81–82

Iranian Leadership Council, 262

Iranian Military Power, 266

Iranian National Army of Liberation, 31

Iranian People's Fedaian Organization, 221

Iranian Revolution 1978–1979, 59

Iranian Tudeh, 269

Iraq; 63, 114–115, 117, 122, 149, 177, 252, 263, 284, 292–293, 295; weapons: BM-21 Stalin Organ rocket launcher, 53; Mi-24 helicopter, 53; MiG-21, 48; MiG-23, 48; Mirage F-1 fighters, 54; SA-2 missile, 52, SA-3 missile, 52; SA-6 missile, 52; Scud missile, 209; T-55 tank, 53; T-62 tank, 53

Intermediate-range Ballistic Missile, 207

Irresolute Princes: Kremlin Decision Making in Middle East Crises, 103

Isenberg, David, 233–234

Isfahan (Iran) facility, 122, 128, 210, 277, 286

Islam, 28, 67

Islamabad, 110

Islamic Amal, 34

Islamic Consultative Assembly (Majlis), 29–31, 35–40, 44, 80, 81, 122, 222, 253, 256, 279

Islamic fundamentalist terrorist groups, 264

Islamic Iranian revolution of 1979, 35

Islamic Jihad, 215, 228, 263–264, 271

Islamic law, 42

Islamic Republic News Agency, 273

Islamic Republic of Iran, 27, 30, 34–35, 273, 276, 279, 281

Islamic Republican Party, 31

Islamic Revolution, 1979, 30, 47

Islamic Revolutionary Guard Corps, see "Pasdaran"

Islamic Salvation Front, 228

Islamic Ummah, 224

Israel, 121, 155, 169, 177, 179, 183, 186, 195, 197, 199, 247, 282, 292

Israeli Air Force, 95, 254, 272

Israel Defense Force, 65, 249, 253–255

Ivory Coast, 292

Ivy, Robert Clyde, 199

Jaber, Hala, 215, 227

Jabr Ibn Hayan Laboratory, 94, 126, 137

Jackson, Anthony, 191

Jafar, Dr. Jafer D., 229

Jafarzadeh, Alireza, 123–124

Jane's Defence Weekly, 187, 251, 248

Jane's Foreign Report, 216

Jane's International Defense Review, 159–160, 174, 253

Jane's Intelligence Review, 171, 232

Jane's Islamic Affairs Analyst, 110

Jane's Terrorism and Security Monitor, 93

Japan, 133–134, 252

Jasim, Latif Nayyif, 48

Jerusalem Report, 215, 217

Jiangsu Chemical Engineering and Technology Import/Export Corporation, 238
Jiangsu, 239
Jihad Islami, 223, 259
Jonker, Rob, 201, 203
Jordan, 33, 264, 272

Kahuta Research Laboratory, 96
Kalany, Mehrdad, 221
Kalaye Electric Company, 94, 136, 146–147
Kani, Ayatollah Mahdavi, 262
"Karachi Connection," 166
Karaj (Iran) site, 94, 129, 219, 277
Karbala, Iraq, 72–73, 75
Karine A (ship), 216–217, 259
Karun River, 47, 51
Kashan, Iran, 81
Kasrils, Ronnie, 172
Katzman, Kenneth, 204–205, 207–208, 237, 239, 268
Kay, Dr. David, 118
Kayhan, 274
Kazakhstan, 99
Keegan, Sir John, 278
Kempton Park, 127
Kentron (South Africa) facility, 197
Kenya, 288, 292
Kerry, John, 287
Kershner, Isabel, 215
Khamene'i, Hojjatoleslam Ali, 34, 36, 39–40, 42, 44, 65, 119, 166, 208, 213, 215, 218–219, 222–223, 227, 230, 253, 257, 260–261, 269– 270, 285
Khan Research Laboratories, 145, 274
Khan, Dr. Abdul-Quadeer, 89, 96, 109, 112, 144, 277, 290
Khan, Gohar Ayub, 110
Kharazi, Kamal, 88, 110, 132, 273, 281
Khardeh River, 47
Kharg Island, 56, 58–60
Kharksar brotherhood, 78
Khatami, President Mohammed, 30–31, 40, 119–120, 123, 128, 134, 213–214, 223, 227, 279, 286
Khobar Towers, 226

Khomeini, Ayatollah Sayyid Ruhollah Musavi, 27–28, 30–31, 33, 35–39, 42, 46-48, 51,54, 65, 72, 77, 85, 95, 119, 213, 221-222, 224, 226-229, 257-258, 262-263, 265, 269, 273
Khorasan, 79
Khorramshahr, Iran, 33, 49-52
Khorshidi, Mehdi Haeri, 213
Khoshroo, Gholam Ali, 271
Khuzestan (Arabistan), 46-49, 52
Kissinger, Henry, 116
Koch, Andrew, 128
Koeberg Nuclear Power Station, 89, 168, 178, 182
Kol Yisrael, 272
Kordestan, Iran, 78
Kosovo, 177
Krepon, Michael, 96
Kurchatov Institute (Russia), 105
Kurdish Democratic Party of Iran, 221
Kurdish region, 46, 79
Kuwait, 33, 61, 264, 272, 276
Kyrgyzstan, Iran, 93

Lakhani, Hemant, 233
Larak Island, 58
Large Aircraft Infrared Countermeasures, 234
laser-based enrichment, 184
Lashkar Ab'ad site, 94
Law of Qisas, 41
Lebanon, 34, 121, 169, 177, 216, 218, 253–255, 263–264, 271, 281
Leifeld machine, 143
Low enriched uranium, (LEU), 89, 99, 105, 141, 149, 182–183
Liberia, 114
Libya, 66, 96, 110, 115, 117, 141, 153, 155, 166, 172–173, 177, 200, 245, 247, 276, 290–291, 293
Lockheed Martin, 116
Lorestan, Iran, 78

Madagascar, 231
Madrid, Spain, 240
Maduna, Penuell, 161
Maglich, Dr. Bogdan, 183
Mahdi, 72

Majd-Abkahi, Abolghasem, 221
Majlis (Islamic Consultative Assembly), 29–31, 35–40, 44, 80, 81, 122, 222, 253, 256, 279
Majnun Island, 56, 64
Maktabs (school), 74
Malaysia, 276
Malek, Molavi Abdul, 221
Mandela, Nelson, former President, 151–153, 155, 157, 163, 165–166, 169, 172, 176, 179, 196, 200, 245, 247, 291–292, 294
Mandeleev University of Chemical Technology, 105
Manhattan Project, 190
Manpad, 232–234
Marais, Johan, 161
Marburg virus, 246
Marr, Phebe, 46
Marshes, Battle of the, 56
Marvdasht, 225
Mashhad, Iran, 43, 71, 74–75, 77, 225
Masluman, Reza, 221
Maslyukov, Yuriy, 106
Mason, Whit, 30–31, 40, 42
Mauritania, 234
Mawat, Iraq, 58
Mazandaran, Iran, 78, 80
Mbeki, Thabo, President. 152, 166, 173–174, 293–294
Mecca, 69–70
Medina, 69–70
Mehrabad, Iran, 48
Mehran, Iran, 49, 52, 57
Meshkinni, Ayatollah Ali, 262
Meyer, Johan, 291
Middle East Intelligence Bulletin, 128–129, 207
Middle East Quarterly , 281
The Middle East Review of International Affairs, 113, 128, 289
Mikhailov, Viktor, 105
Milhollin, Gary, 105
Miller, Judith, 229, 241
Mina al Bakr, Iraq, 50
Miniaturized Neutron Source Reactor, 128
Minister of Culture and Information, (Iraq), 48

Ministry of Atomic Energy (Minatom), Russia, 104, 122, 229
Ministry of Education, (Iran), 81
Ministry of Foreign Affairs (South Africa), 169
Ministry of Information and Security, (Iran), 260
Minty, Abdul, 166, 168, 171–172
Mintz, John, 247
Missile Designation: Cross Country Comparison chart, 205
Missile Technology Control Regime, 196, 208
Mizin, Dr. Victor, 113–116, 123
Moallam Kelaieh, 95
Mohajerani, Ayatollah, 128
Mojahedin organization, 29, 31, 295
Mojahedin-e-Khalq group, 95
molecular laser isotope separation (MLIS), 86
Mongol invasions, 28
Montazeri, Ayatollah, 224
Monterey Institute of International Studies, 103, 106, 113, 161, 172, 187
Moosa, M.V., 166
Morocco, 240, 288–289
Moscow Aviation Institute, 105
Mossad, 282, 289
Mossadeq, Mohammad, 29
Moussawi, Ibrahim, 170
Movement for Islamic Reform, 233
Mozambique, 231, 234
Mu'allimn Kalayeh, Iran, 129
Mubarak, Hosni, 226, 245
Mugabe, Robert, 231
Mugniyah, Imad, 215–218, 260
Muhammad, Ali, 217
Mujahadeen, 234, 249, 293
Murphy, Richard, 62
Musharraf, President Pervez, 96, 272
Myong-nok, Cho, 268

Najaf, Iraq, 35
Namibia, 152, 292
Nanjing Chemical Industries Group, 238
Naqshbandi brotherhood, 78
Nasrallah, Hassan, 218

Natanz (Iran) site, 91, 94, 123, 125, 130–131, 134–135, 139–141, 146, 148–149, 277, 289

Nateq-Nouri, Hojjatoleslam Ali Akbar, 260–261

National Council of Resistance of Iran, 123, 136

National Defence Force (South Africa), 247

National Defense University, 119, 255

National Defense Univ., Center for Counterproliferation Research, 27

National Intelligence Agency, 227

National Security Council, 185, 235

Nekka (Iran) site, 129, 277

neptunium 237, 250–252

Neuffer, Elizabeth, 132

News International Pakistan, 110

Nigeria, 292

Nonproliferation Act of 2000, 239

The Nonproliferation Revue, 103

Nonproliferation Center (CIA), 237

North Atlantic Treaty Organization, 207, 287, 289

North Korea, 66, 96, 114–115, 124, 127, 130, 141, 203, 207–209, 211, 225, 230, 249, 268, 276; weapons; No Dong missile, 114, 207, 209, 268, Taepo-dong missile, 209–210

Northrup Grumman Defensive Systems Division, 235

Novovoronezh Nuclear Power Plant (Russia), 105

Nuclear Energy Corporation of South Africa, 157

Nuclear Non-Proliferation Act, 178

Nuclear Non-Proliferation Treaty, 101, 110, 113–114, 116, 118, 131–132, 142, 158, 163, 181, 186, 192, 229, 251

Nuclear Nonproliferation Treaty Review Conference, 271

Nuclear Research Center for Agriculture and Medicine, 129

Nuclear Suppliers Group, 168, 184, 168–170

Nuclear Technology/Research Center, 128

NuclearFuel, 97, 167–171, 184, 189

Nur al-Din, Jawwad, 216

O'Hanlon, Michael, 283

Oak Ridge, Tennessee, 99

Office of Counterterrorism, 262

Official Secrets Act (South Africa), 162

Oman, 272

Omar, Dullah, 166

Operation Blessed Ramadan, 64

Operation Dawn V, 55

Operation Karbala Five, 52, 58

Operation Karbala Seven, 58

Operation Karbala Six, 52, 58

Operation Karbala Ten, 58

Operation Ramadan, 53

Operation Undeniable Victory, 52

Osiraq (Iraq) nuclear reactor, 63, 95, 113, 121

osmium tetroxide, 240

Overberg Test Range (South Africa), 179, 196

Paduna, Manuel, 158

Pahad, Aziz, 166

Pahad, Dr. Essop, 153, 166

Pahlavi, Mohammad Reza Shah, 27–31, 73, 78

Pahlavi, Reza Shah, 28–29, 31, 273

Pakistan, 85, 96, 110, 117, 141, 143–145, 177, 274

Palestinian Authority, 259

Palestinian Liberation Organization, 215

Parchin, Iran, 91, 240

Paris Conference on the Prohibition of Chemical Weapons, 57

Park, Manzarieh, 224

Parvaresh, Ali Akbar, 261

Pasdaran (Islamic Revolutionary Guard Corps), 32, 38, 46, 49–53, 55, 63, 119–121, 129, 170, 208, 215, 217, 223–225, 227–229, 231, 238, 253–260, 263–270, 272, 274, 286, 288

Pearl, Daniel, 219

Pelindaba (South Africa) nuclear site, 157–159, 164, 167–168, 170–171, 180, 182, 184–185, 188–189

People Against Gangsterism and Drugs (PAGAD), 228

Perez de Cuellar, Javier, 57

Persepolis, Iran, 28

Persia, 27
Persian Gulf, 32–33, 45, 56, 58, 79, 278, 285
Petrovsky, Vladimir, 62
Philby, Kim, 282
Philippines, 231, 287
Pike, John, 239–240, 276–278
Plasma Physics Laboratory, 147
plutonium, 138–139, 187, 252
Pohl, Reynaldo Galindo, 221
Pointer, 170
Polyrus Scientific Research Institute (Russia), 107
Port Sudan, Sudan, 119
Portugal, 179
Pourghanad, Hojjatoleslam Mustafa, 260
Program for Promoting Nuclear Non-proliferation, 164
Project of the Iranian Revolution, 224
Proliferation Research and Assessment Program (PRAP), 106
Prophet Mohammed, 30, 69–70
Public Health Service, 244
Putin, Vladimir, 104, 115, 133, 275

Qadiri brotherhood, 78
Qajar monarchy, 28–29, 43
Qasr-e Shirin, Iran, 48–49, 51
Qasvin, Iran, 129, 224, 240
Qinshin reactors, 129
Qods Force, 264
Qom, Iran, 71, 73–75, 77, 122

Radio Free Europe, 289
Radioactive Waste Storage Facility at Karaj, 94
radiological dispersal devices, 243
Rafsanjani, Ali Akbar Hashemi, 39, 66, 112, 128, 155, 219, 222–223, 253, 256, 262, 267, 274
Rajabi, Zahrah, 221
RAND Corporation, 234
Ranstorp, Magnus, 217–218
Raytheon Systems, 248
Reagan, Ronald, 178
Reap, Joe, 262
Red Sea, 232
Report for Congress: Iran-Arms and

Weapons of Mass Destruction, 204
Revolutionary Constitution of 1979, 80–81
Reyshari, 223
Reza'i, Moheen, 281
Reza, the Eighth Imam, 71, 74–75
Rezai, Mohsen, 223, 256, 265, 267–271
Rhodesia, 184
Rimmington, Stella, 290
Risk Report, 181, 183, 186–187
Rostam oil field, 62
Roux, Dr. Abraham Johannes Andries, 184
Rowhani, Hassan, 91
Rubin, Barry, 128
Rubin, James P., 162–164
Rushdie, Salman, 219
Russia, 113–114, 116, 133–134, 185, 208, 237, 252, 281
Russian Defense Industrial Complex (OPK), 115
Rykaart, Dukncan, 174

Sadr City, 288, 295
Safavid monarchy, 28, 69
Saghafinia, Dr. Amir, 57
Saghand, 100–101, 129
Salameh, Ali Hassan, 215
Samara State Scientific and Production Enterprise-NK Engines, 106
Sanandaj, Iran, 48
Sanders, Dr. Ben, 164
Sankoh, Foday, 68
Sassanid Empire, 28
The Satanic Verses, 219
Satari, Mansour, 229
Saudi Arabia, 31, 33–34, 61, 68, 223, 228, 233, 272, 289
SAVAK, 28
Sayyad, Molawi Ahamed, 221
Schiff, Ze'ev, 290
Scientific Research and Design Institute of Power Technology (Russia) (NIKIET), 105
Scowcroft, Brent, 116
Sea Isle City (ship), 61
Senate Armed Services Committee, 195
September 11, 226, 260, 262
Sergeyey, Igor, 106

Shafagh, General Sardar, 121, 229
Shahbazi, Ali, 270
Shahid Hemat Industrial group, 210
Shahid Kolahdooz Industrial Complex, 248
Shahroud facility, 210
Shalamjah, Iran, 64
Shamkhani, Ali, 91, 248
Sharif University of Technology, 274
Shatt al Arab waterway, 46, 49, 56, 48, 50, 58, 60
Sheikholeslam, Hossein, 226
Shi'ite clergy, 28, 30, 34, 37, 69, 78
Shi'ite Muslims, 29, 38, 42, 45, 48, 63, 67–68, 70, 72–73, 76, 79, 120, 122, 125, 151, 224, 229, 254, 257, 264, 272, 288, 296
Shinrikyo, Aum, 244
Shiraz, Iran, 43, 74, 81
Shroeder, Gerhard, 275
Sierra Leone, 68, 174
Sirjan facility, 210
Sirri Island, 58
Smith, Craig S., 91, 151
Sogget, Mungo, 97, 160–163
Somalia, 232, 234
Somchem (South Africa) facility, 197
Somerset West (South Africa) facility, 197
South Africa; 120, 127, 151, 154–156, 159, 161–162, 164–165, 173, 175, 178–180, 183, 185–187, 189, 195, 198, 201–203, 210, 227, 230–231, 247, 250, 276, 288, 290–293; 7th Medical Battalion, 246; abandons a successful nuclear weapons program, 176; *Africa Confidential*, 173–174; Air Force, 178, 200; Atomic Energy Corporation (AEC), 97, 161, 164–165, 171, 181–182, 184, 189, 191; chemical and biological weapons, 245; cooperation with Iran, 155; Defence Force, 175, 199; forces in Angola, 169; "Karachi Connection," 166; key events in nuclear weapons program, 191; Ministry of Foreign Affairs, 169; missile program, 196, 199; Missile Technology Control Regime, 196; National Defence Force, 247;

Nuclear Energy Corporation, 157; nuclear program, 153, 175–192; Official Secrets Act, 162; pilot enrichment facility, 190; Special Forces, 169, 174; Test Flight and Development Centre, 197; weapons; AH-2A Rooivalk, 200–201; Mi-24 helicopter, 178; RSA-2 rocket, 154; RSA-3 missile, 195, 197; Sukhoi strike aircraft, 178; Y-Plant, 190–192; zirconium plant, 167–168
South African Airways, 181
South African Atomic Energy Corporation (AEC), 97, 161, 164–165, 171, 181–182, 184, 189, 191,
South African Broadcasting Corporation, 247
South African Defence Force, 175, 178
South Korea, 177
Soviet NKVD, 253
Soviet Union, 29, 32–33, 181, 203, 281
Spain, 177
USS *Stark*, 61–62
Staudenmaeir, William O., 55
Steinberg, Gerald M., 289
Steinitz, Yuval, 289
Stellenbosch University, 197
Strait of Hormuz, 61–62
Strobel, Warren P., 284–285
Stumpf, Dr. Waldo, 97, 156–162, 164, 167–169, 171, 178, 182–183
Suakin, Sudan, 119
Sudan Airways, 233
Sudan, 119, 152, 166, 173, 217, 250
Suez Canal, 67, 232
Sufism, 77–78
Sunni caliphs, 71
Sunni Islam, 67–70, 78–79, 221, 278
Sunni Triangle, 293
Supreme Defense Council, 36, 38
Susangerd, Iran, 49, 52
Sweden, 177
Switzerland, 146, 252
Syria, 59, 115, 117, 152, 157, 166, 200, 281, 290–291, 293
Tabatabai, Ali, 214
Tabriz, Iran, 43, 48, 74, 80, 129
Taheri, Amir, 294
Taiwan, 177

Taliban, 269
Tamerlane, 28
Tammuz-1 (Iraq) reactor, 95
Tanzania, 292
Tarhunah, Israel, 247
Tarzi, Amin, 289
Tehran Nuclear Research Center (TNRC), 94, 129
Tehran Research Center, 126, 137
Tenet, George, 106, 195, 283
Test Flight and Development Centre (South Africa), 197
Thacker, Howard, 202–203
Thailand, 276
Thompson, Mark, 232
Tigris River, 55
Timmerman, Kenneth, 260–262
Tophoven, Rolf, 216–218
Torkan, Akbar, 128
Toward Freedom, 155
Transportation Security Administration, 235
tritium, 183
Tucker, Dr. Johathan B., 161, 172–173
Tudeh Party, 29–30, 62, 269
Tunisia, 227, 240, 288–289
Turkey, 207, 214, 228, 240, 264, 288–289
Turkomans, Kurds, 79
Tuwaitha Nuclear Research Center (Iraq), 147, 252
Twelfth Iman, 69, 71–72

U.S. Army, Chemical and Biological Defense Command, 244
Ublinsky Metallurgical Plant, 99–100
Uganda, 174, 227
Ulba, 100
Umayyad Empire, 28
United Arab Emirates, 62, 264
United Nations: 57, 65, 87, 91, 174, 177, 254, 286; Interim Force in Lebanon, 253–254; nuclear inspectors, 276; Oil-for-Food Program, 90; Security Council Resolution, 598, 62, 64; Security Council, 88, 93, 134; Special Commission for Iraq (UNSCOM), 110, 112, 118, 159, 237, 256

University of St. Andrews, 217
Uranium 235, 98
Uranium Conversion Laboratory (UCL), 94
uranium dioxide, 137
Uranium Enrichment Corporation (South Africa), 182, 184
Uranium hexafluoride, (UH6), 96–98, 111, 126, 137, 139, 142, 148, 182
uranium oxide, 129, 138
uranium tetrafluoride, 126, 137–138
Uranium-233, 125, 141, 147, 251, 286
Urmia, Iran, 48
Urumiyeh, Iran, 51

Vali, Sayyid Nimatollah, 75
Valindaba (South Africa) nuclear site, 165, 182
van Den Bergh, Nick, 174
van Niekerk, Phillip, 160
Vanunu, Mordechai, 185
vaqf, 76
Vastrap nuclear testing site (South Africa), 181, 188
Velayati, Ali Akbar, 57, 223, 267
Vesely, Milan, 155
Vesseghi, Ali, 225
Vick, Charles P., 195, 208–209
Vietnam, 178
von Wielligh, Dr. Nic, 93, 165, 180, 182–185, 187–188

Wahhabism, 68, 288
War Dog: Fighting Other People's Wars, 68
Warrick, Joby, 130, 247
The Washington Institute for Near East Policy, 93
Weapons of Mass Destruction, 93–95, 116, 118–119, 127, 129, 154, 162, 205, 224, 237, 241, 257, 276, 281–283, 291, 296
Weapons; AH-2A Rooivalk, 200–201; Al Sabiha-15 submarine, 249; anthrax, 241; Bell 214A helicopter, 52; biological, 256; BM-21 Stalin Organ rocket launcher, 53; chemical and biological, 56–57, 63, 65, 245, 256; Ebola, 246; F-4 Phantom air-

craft, 48, 52; F-5 aircraft, 52; F-14 aircraft, 52; Fadjr-3 rocket, 250; Fadjr-5 rocket, 250; Feteh-110, 204; Hudong fast attack craft, 208; Il-28 bomber, 51; Jericho-I, 179; Jericho II rocket, 154, 179, 195, 197, 199; Katyusha rocket, 249; Marburg fever, 246; M-1 missile, 211; M-9 missile, 211; Mi-24 helicopter, 53, 68, 178, 201–202; MiG-21, 48; MiG-23, 48, 60; Mirage F-1, 54, 60; Misagh-1 missile, 249; Missile Designation: Cross Country Comparison chart, 205; mustard gas, 57; nerve gas, 57; No-Dong missile, 127, 207, 209, 268; Nour C-802 missile, 248; nuclear, 256; radiological, 243; RSA-3, 195, 197; SA-2 missile, 52, 208; SA-3 missile, 52; SA-6 missile, 52; Scud missile, 63, 209–210; Shahab missile, 205; Shahab-1, missile, 204, 210; Shahab-2, missile, 204; Shahab-3 missile, 92, 127, 131, 204, 207, 209–210; Shahab-4 missile 207, 210; Shahab-5 missile, 207, 210; Shahab-6 missile, 207; Silkworm HY-2 missile, 32, 61, 211; SS-4 rocket engine, 105; Stinger missile, 249; Sukhoi strike aircraft, 178; Super Frelon helicopters, 60; T-22 bomber, 51; T-55 tank, 53; T-62 tank, 53; Taepo-dong missile, 209–210; Tondar, 204, 211; Toophan anti-tank guided missile, 248

Wehling, Dr. Fred, 103–105
Welch, Arnold, 235
West Azerbaijan, 79
West Germany, 184
Who Rules Iran, 34
Wolf, Jeanette, 128
Wolf, John S., 276
Woolsey, James, 226
World Trade Center (see September 11, 2001)

Y-Plant, 190–192
Yablokov, Aleksey, 104
Yair, General Yoram, 226
Yaz, Iran, 123
Yazd, Iran, 74
Yazdi, Ayatollah Mohammad, 262
yellowcake, 183
Yeltsin, Boris, 104, 110, 118
Yugloslavia, 177

Zahi, Jamshid, 221
Zaire, 184
Zakeri, Hamid Reza, 260–262
Zambia, 184
Zanjan, Iran, 74
Zarif, Mohammed Javad, 91
Zawahiri, Ayman, 217
Zendehdel, Hedayatollah, 221
Zimbabwe, 175, 231, 292
Zippe, Gernot, 140
Zirconium tube factory, 164, 166, 170
zirconium, 168
Zoroastrians, 82
Zubaydeh, Abu, 217